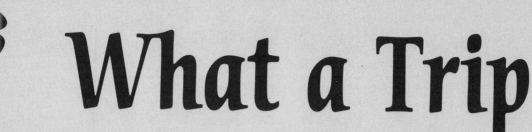

What a Trip

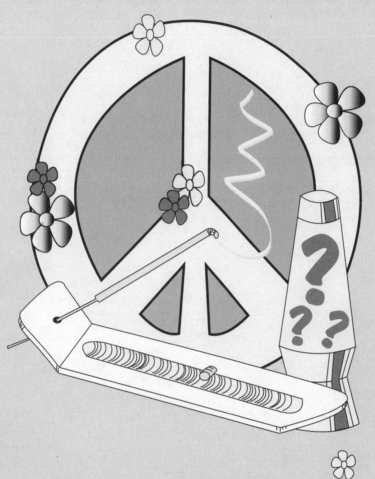

Jason McFaul

Eric MacDonald

W9-BNU-445

KENDALL/HUNT PUBLISHING COMPANY
4050 Westmark Drive   Dubuque, Iowa 52002

Cover art created by Jon St. Amant

Copyright © 2005 by Kendall/Hunt Publishing Company

ISBN 13: 978-0-7575-4014-1
ISBN 10: 0-7575-4014-7

Printed in the United States of America

10 9 8 7 6 5 4 3 2

Dedication

Jason McFaul
For Joel McFaul, a.k.a., my brother, my paisan.

Eric MacDonald
For my mother and father. Without their love, encouragement, and support, I would not be the man or teacher that I am today.

Contents

Section II   377

viii Contents

Foreword

by Dr. Jill Gold Wright

To the Students and Professors who are considering taking a trip:

Reading *What a Trip* is like being given a ticket around the world—all expenses paid—without having to apply for a passport, get your shots, or suffer jetlag. You don't have to secure a time machine or learn any foreign languages; here, the world of college reading and writing lies at your fingertips.

If you are a Freshman Composition student who has been assigned this text, congratulations! You're taking this class at just the right time. This book is far more exciting than others you could have been asked to buy. These pages hold great adventure and necessary resources for you; truly, you will rely on the information in this book throughout your college career. First, and most importantly, there is the literature. Whether or not you plan to pursue English as a major, you will be asked in both lower- and upper-division courses to read standard literary texts. Having this anthology on your bookshelf will be a great help. When your philosophy professor asks you to examine ancient Greek and Roman texts, they're right here. If your Nineteenth Century History teacher wants you to analyze an American essay, you've already got it in this book. You are only starting to realize how interdisciplinary your college education will be, and the readings in this text will assist you in ways that you can only begin to imagine.

Besides the wide range of literature, this book will be a great resource in other ways. It can teach (or remind) you about *how to write* a strong, argumentative paper. If you think that argumentative writing is only a classroom task, consider the personal statement you'll have to write when applying to a four-year university, to graduate school, or for a job. In that moment, you present yourself only in your words, and the selection committee will make a decision about your future based on how you write them! Won't it be helpful to feel confident about your argumentative writing before that time?

This book can teach you how to cite your papers according to MLA format, another necessary skill for this and every college course you will take. Later in future semesters, it will refresh your memory when documented essays will be assigned again. The writing section of this text can also give you the brush-up you may need in common grammatical errors and will offer your writing a boost by teaching you new and interesting possibilities in vocabulary. After traveling through the pages of this text, you will find yourself a better writer, reader, and thinker than you were before.

If you are an instructor considering this book for your course, you will find the combination of elements (writing instruction, MLA format, anthology, etc.) to be mag-

ical in the classroom. So often, professors find themselves bouncing between two books, a "rhetoric" and a "reader," quickly becoming dissatisfied with both. Not finding everything they want in those texts, they end up "supplementing" with their own readings or handouts, eager to teach what they know and like. The great benefit here is that you *will find* what you want in the pages of this text!

This book's writing component either can be a passing resource or a real step-by-step instructional guide to teach your students *how to write* analytical, argumentative essays. For example, you will certainly want to utilize the student papers and professional articles herein; you might build an entire day's lesson plan around them or, at least, present them as outside examples to the students who can benefit from extra focus and modeling.

In terms of the literature, you will be able to locate your own interests and expertise. Whether you're a Classicist, a Medievalist, a drama expert, an Americanist, or a generalist, you will find yourself comfortable within these pages because your training and course work are reflected here. Most of this reading will be new to your students, so you can design your course however you like. Because there is so much literature discussed here, you will probably find that you will not be able (or want) to get through the entire book in one semester. That is a great benefit; now you have the flexibility to design your course the way you choose. Since the literature in this book is categorized chronologically, you may romp through the centuries, picking out representative pieces. Instead, you may prefer to design your course thematically, avoiding chronological concerns altogether. There is a wide-enough scope here to conceive your course in any number of ways.

Further, this text will keep *you* interested. When you need a change of pace after a while, there will be no need to abandon all that you have come to rely on in this book. The variety here allows you to change the readings but stay with the writing and MLA instruction that will prove so helpful semester after semester. This book was written by professors who teach and who share your frustrations and concerns.

Whatever side of the podium you are on, you're in for a wild ride. As you and the hippy hitch rides through this text, you'll be amazed at the colorful and memorable characters you'll meet along the way. This time, you don't need a suitcase. No need to call a travel agent; just open the book. Begin, and enjoy.

Jill Gold Wright

Acknowledgments

Jason McFaul and Eric MacDonald would like to acknowledge the following:

We would like to thank Jon St. Amant for producing such wonderful art. We would like to thank Jill Gold Wright for composing the chapter on Renaissance Literature and for composing the foreword. We would also like to thank Matthew Judd for composing the afterword. Additionally, we would like to thank John Brantingham for allowing us to place his novella and short story on the Literature CD. Thanks to Jim Thomas for his essay, and thanks to Dominique Valencia, Monea Longoria, and Jordan Saiz for their essays. Thanks to Adam Truax and Rosemary Slack. Thanks to Dale Emery. Thanks to Ellen Kaune. And thanks to Henry.

Jason McFaul would like to acknowledge the following:

I would like to thank my parents, Jim and Janis. I would also like to thank Eric Mac-Donald for his hard work and dedication. Finally, I would like to raise a metaphorical glass to Emerson—the one that got away.

Eric MacDonald would like to acknowledge the following:

I would like to thank my entire family for all of their love and support, especially Douglas MacDonald and Frances and Alan Pearne. I am also forever indebted to Amy and her family (Jenny, Susan, Andrew, Katie, and Jim) for the compassion that they have always shown me. I have a number of close friends I would also like to thank. First, I want to thank my good friends: Gabriel Fernandez, Chris Gonzales, Jeff Piccinini, and "the Daiquiri King of room 4." This book would not have been written without their constant encouragement and support. To Mona Dobson, Dr. David Toise, and Dr. Amy Heckathorn, thank you so much for everything you taught me and for the patience you showed me while I was at California State University, Sacramento. Finally, I want to thank Jason McFaul for helping me get my first college teaching position and for his constant advice on teaching that I use in the classroom everyday.

To Instructors/Students

What a Trip is an attempt at taking readers on a literary journey, one that begins with Greek mythology and ends with 19th Century American literature. It is also an attempt at creating a textbook that can endure instructor and student mood swings and preferences. That is why *What a Trip* houses a literary cornucopia, one that includes *The Iliad* and *The Odyssey, The Canterbury Tales,* the complete works of William Shakespeare, *Gulliver's Travels,* and *The Adventures of Huckleberry Finn.* These are all found, in their entirety, on the Literature CD (found on the inside of this book's back cover). And while many will embrace the Literature CD, for those interested in a more traditionally-constructed textbook, they needn't look further, for all of the works in Chapter 7, "18th Century Irish and American Literature," are printed in this book. Further, all of the works in Chapter 8, "19th Century American Literature," are printed in this book. Thus, in counting the poems, short stories, and essays presented in Chapters 7 and 8, students and instructors have access to thirty-six works that have been printed in their entirety. These range from *A Modest Proposal* to *The Declaration of Independence, The Raven* to *Richard Cory, Bartleby the Scrivener* to *Young Goodman Brown, An Indian's Looking-Glass for the White Man* to *Life Without Principle.* It would be an extraordinary task to assign all thirty-six works to students in a traditional eighteen-week Freshman Composition class, and that is precisely why instructors *and* students have been presented with all of these options. However, couple these works with everything on the Literature CD, and *What a Trip* becomes a book that can span an instructor's career, a book that may whet the most insatiable student's appetite.

Little is required to use this textbook in a traditional manner, for Chapters 7 and 8 are constructed similarly to chapters in other textbooks that cater to Freshman Composition. And what follows is not intended to bemoan other textbooks; frankly, the primary reason for placing most of this book's literature onto a CD is to exert global consciousness. It's simple. The stereotypical 2000-page literature anthology is not as environmentally friendly as an anthology with fewer pages. Further, as we continue to enter an electronic age, more and more students are acquiring hand-held devices that help advance their education. Such devices enable students to access the Internet from a mobile phone or to copy text to their Palm Pilot. Soon, the laptop computer will be large and cumbersome. But the point is this: in an electronic age, it is not necessary to waste so much paper. Students can read the works from the Literature CD, and they can do so on their hand-held devices, or they can do so on their computer monitors. Some students will choose to print the works. And when discussing the works in class, instructors may simply request that students print certain pages that will be the subject of class discussion. Again, however, it seems probable that companies like Microsoft and Apple will ensure that within a decade, classrooms will be paperless, opting instead for wireless and digital capabilities.

In addition to the Literature CD, another CD is included with this book. *Money Words* is a vocabulary-building CD that has been designed to help students with word meanings and pronunciations. Unlike rote memorization from flashcards, *Money Words* attempts to target auditory learners. While the Literature CD consists only of text, *Money Words* is a spoken-word CD, and it preys on the phenomenon often witnessed when a person accidentally memorizes the lyrics to a song that he or she doesn't even like. It is this exposure to repetition that will help students retain word meanings and word pronunciations. Further, because many of the words are coupled with examples and mnemonic devices, students should have more success when attempting to use these words contextually. *Money Words* is an attempt at targeting auditory learners, and in doing so, it introduces students to 296 words. (Of course, since all of the words are listed in this book, the visual learners benefit as well.) In the end, the inclusion of *Money Words* may help curb the gross displays of vocabulary that seem rampant among recent college graduates. Ideally, *Money Words* will address this problem, planting verbal seeds that will germinate before diplomas are received and interviews are conducted. (Instructors can quiz students to observe their progress. Quizzes are found in the back of the book, and each page is perforated.)

While *What a Trip* may be used for a variety of academic courses, it was developed for courses in Freshman Composition. And, as is the case in many Freshman Composition classes, much writing is involved. This is where students and instructors should benefit, for after each work, a section titled "Research and Writing" is found. Here, potential prompts are offered, and instructors are invited to change the prompts to better represent their pedagogical agenda. Or, each prompt may be used as it appears. Essentially, the goal is to make instructors and students as effective as they can be. In this light, some prompts are specific in order to save instructors time and provide students with the specificity they require. However, other prompts are vague so that professors might sculpt the prompt in order to better meet the needs of the students in a particular class. Nonetheless, because Freshman Composition classes should house a research component, many of the potential prompts ask students to perform research in order to advance their arguments. And naturally, when students choose to implement the fruits of their research into their essays, they may benefit from the section in this book on research and MLA citations.

Instructors are invited to use this book to teach academic writing. The section on academic writing not only diagrams an academic paragraph but also offers examples of three student essays (written by real students). Following each student example is "Conversations with Writers," an interview with the student about his or her writing. "Play-by-play" follows in an attempt to examine the student essays, identifying strengths and weaknesses. After each "Play-by-play" are Pre-writing, Organization, and Development pages. These are perforated, and they are designed for students to use while attempting to develop their own essays.

Once the three student essays have been examined, students yearning to transcend the fundamentals of academic writing can read an essay written by a professional essayist. This essay integrates the fundamentals that are preached in the essays preceding it, but it does so with greater fluidity and latitude. Appropriately, this essay is accompanied by "Conversations with Writers" and "Play-by-play." Additionally, the Pre-writing, Organization, and Development pages are included, but the Organization page is without the direction found on the other Organization pages. Instead, it is blank—a canvas for the aspiring writer.

In the end, we have labored to compose a book that really does equip students with the skills to read and write across the curriculum. And unlike some textbook authors, we teach. We are in the trenches, attempting to enrich, inspire, amuse, and enthuse. And, yes, we face the same Brobdingnagian stacks of papers that, for whatever reason, never seem to endure much reduction in size. Sadly, while that may never change, at least there is the opportunity to use a textbook that enables instructors to grow with the book, allowing their curricula to do the same. In *What a Trip,* people can have theme-based classes—for instance, a semester on Greek Mythology, a semester on the Renaissance, a semester on American Literature, etc. *What a Trip* offers instructors so much that when they become bored with one method of presentation, they may simply embrace another.

Section I

Greek Mythology

Heroes, gods, and monsters surround us. And while the heroes of today might not trap great boars on Mount Erymanthus or retrieve three-headed dogs from the underworld, they do have many things in common. Among these is a desire to transcend the mundane. A firefighter might do this when rushing into a burning house while the less heroic stand outside. A father might do this when diving in front of a car to save his son from death's embrace. Yes, the heroes of old *do* share similarities with today's web-slinging, cape-wearing individuals. Naturally, so do the monsters. Of course, the monsters of today might not manufacture thunderbolts and see through only one eye. But today's monsters do seem to share the same myopic view of the world. Simply examine Andrew Jackson's approach to the Native Americans or Adolf Hitler's approach to the Jews. Examine the drug dealer, the suicide bomber, the Unibomber, the airplane hijacker. These people destroy. And arguably, these people are monsters. But isn't it reasonable to suggest that some people view these monsters as heroes?

See, if you agree that writing consists of pursuing meaning, of eventually getting people to see things through your eyes, then there should be some value in studying the derivation of meaning. Just as one might make the connection that all the planets are named after Greek and Roman gods, or that NASA's Atlas rocket boosters may have something to do with Atlas, the Titan who held up the sky, then you might make a connection between the first mythological heroes and the heroes of today. Further, you might make a connection between Greek mythology and your opinion of humanity's origins, the destination of the afterlife, the presence of supernatural beings, and the end of the world.

If we can share the assumption that one of the first places to truly develop the written language was Greece, then it shouldn't surprise us that literature throughout the ages has borrowed much from Greek mythology. Naturally, one could look to the box office for obvious examples like *O Brother Where Art Thou?*, starring George Clooney, or *Troy*, starring Brad Pitt. But if you look closely, there are less obvious examples. For instance, in Ovid's *Metamorphosis* (100 BCE), Zeus observes that humans are becoming far too evil, so he employs his brother, the sea god Poseidon, to create a storm that would flood the earth for nine days and nights. Of course, everyone drowns—except for Deucalion and his wife, Pyrrha. They are instructed by Prometheus to build a wooden chest, fill it with food, and get in the chest until the waters subside. Naturally, there seems to be a connection between this flood and the biblical flood. Which came first? Was one story influenced by the other?

A less controversial connection can be made between Ovid's *Metamorphosis* and William Shakespeare's *Romeo and Juliet*. Many suggest that 1500 years later, Shakespeare wrote a tale of woe based on the story of Pyramus and Thisbe in Ovid's *Metamorphosis*. But what does this mean? Does it suggest that history simply repeats itself? Does it suggest that everything comes from something? Or more startling, maybe it suggests that, as Mark Twain wrote, "There is no such thing as a new idea . . . We simply take a lot of old ideas and put them into a sort of mental kaleidoscope. We give them a turn and they make new and curious combinations. We keep on turning and making new combinations indefinitely, but they are the same old pieces of colored glass that have been in use through all the ages." If you can find value in studying the past in order to better understand the future, then studying Greek mythology should be valuable to you.

Homer (Dates of birth and death unknown)

Many historians place the author of *The Iliad* and *The Odyssey* in the fifth century BCE, possibly born in Ionia on the west coast of Asia Minor. Figuratively, his biography is considered a blank slate. Some depict him as a wandering, blind storyteller, who went from city to city, reciting poems that had been passed down to him through an oral tradition. If this is true, then it would have taken an incredible imagination—and memory—to retell some of the mythological tales with which many historians credit him. This belief also begs the question: Did Homer memorize his poems and add something new to them each time? While this question may go unanswered, this much is true: many consider him the father of the greatest epic poems of all time. *The Iliad* spotlights the Trojan war and its most famous warrior: Achilles. It is an epic poem that shows how one man's choice can turn the tide for an entire nation. *The Odyssey* begins where *The Iliad* ends, telling the story of Odysseus and his long journey home after the fall of Troy. Combined, these two epics represent the coming together of the Greeks, the legacy of Achilles, and the struggle of Odysseus to return to his wife and kingdom after the Trojan War.

The Iliad

1. Many believe that the poetry of Homer began as an oral tradition of songs that people performed publicly. Think about some of your favorite songs. How would they sound if you simply read the lyrics silently to yourself? Just as they may lack the requisite substance, some argue that *The Iliad* is compromised when read silently.
2. As you're identifying various myths, note how myths help define social customs and beliefs. Also, note the similarities between myths and rituals.
3. Consider one of Carl Jung's theories: Myths contain archetypes that reveal the collective unconscious of the human race.
4. Consider one of Claude Levi-Strauss' observations: Myths are a way for people to talk about things that cause anxiety.
5. Remember that whether or not you find these myths "believable," *The Iliad* is the first written record of Greece and, hence, Greek mythology begins with Homer. And if you believe that the myths we have now were simply built upon the foundation of Greek mythology, then you must recognize that we are Greek mythology's intellectual, artistic, and political descendants.

The Iliad

Homer

Book I

Sing, O goddess, the anger of Achilles son of Peleus, that brought countless ills upon the Achaeans. Many a brave soul did it send hurrying down to Hades, and many a hero did it yield a prey to dogs and vultures, for so were the counsels of Jove fulfilled from the day on which the son of Atreus, king of men, and great Achilles, first fell out with one another.

And which of the gods was it that set them on to quarrel? It was the son of Jove and Leto; for he was angry with the king and sent a pestilence upon the host to plague the people, because the son of Atreus had dishonoured Chryses his priest. Now Chryses had come to the ships of the Achaeans to free his daughter, and had brought with him a great ransom: moreover he bore in his hand the sceptre of Apollo wreathed with a suppliant's wreath and he besought the Achaeans, but most of all the two sons of Atreus, who were their chiefs.

"Sons of Atreus," he cried, "and all other Achaeans, may the gods who dwell in Olympus grant you to sack the city of Priam, and to reach your homes in safety; but free my daughter, and accept a ransom for her, in reverence to Apollo, son of Jove."

On this the rest of the Achaeans with one voice were for respecting the priest and taking the ransom that he offered; but not so Agamemnon, who spoke fiercely to him and sent him roughly away. "Old man," said he, "let me not find you tarrying about our ships, nor yet coming hereafter. Your sceptre of the god and your wreath shall profit you nothing. I will not free her. She shall grow old in my house at Argos far from her own home, busying herself with her loom and visiting my couch; so go, and do not provoke me or it shall be the worse for you."

The old man feared him and obeyed. Not a word he spoke, but went by the shore of the sounding sea and prayed apart to King Apollo whom lovely Leto had borne. "Hear me," he cried, "O god of the silver bow, that protectest Chryse and holy Cilla and rulest Tenedos with thy might, hear me oh thou of Sminthe. If I have ever decked your temple with garlands, or burned your thigh-bones in fat of bulls or goats, grant my prayer, and let your arrows avenge these my tears upon the Danaans."

Thus did he pray, and Apollo heard his prayer. He came down furious from the summits of Olympus, with his bow and his quiver upon his shoulder, and the arrows rattled on his back with the rage that trembled within him. He sat himself down away from the ships with a face as dark as night, and his silver bow rang death as he shot his arrow in the midst of them. First he smote their mules and their hounds, but presently he aimed his shafts at the people themselves, and all day long the pyres of the dead were burning.

For nine whole days he shot his arrows among the people, but upon the tenth day Achilles called them in assembly—moved thereto by Juno, who saw the Achaeans in their death-throes and had compassion upon them. Then, when they were got together, he rose and spoke among them.

"Son of Atreus," said he, "I deem that we should now turn roving home if we would escape destruc-

tion, for we are being cut down by war and pestilence at once. Let us ask some priest or prophet, or some reader of dreams (for dreams, too, are of Jove) who can tell us why Phoebus Apollo is so angry, and say whether it is for some vow that we have broken, or hecatomb that we have not offered, and whether he will accept the savour of lambs and goats without blemish, so as to take away the plague from us."

With these words he sat down, and Calchas son of Thestor, wisest of augurs, who knew things past, present, and to come, rose to speak. He it was who had guided the Achaeans with their fleet to Ilius, through the prophesyings with which Phoebus Apollo had inspired him. With all sincerity and goodwill he addressed them thus:—

"Achilles, loved of heaven, you bid me tell you about the anger of King Apollo, I will therefore do so; but consider first and swear that you will stand by me heartily in word and deed, for I know that I shall offend one who rules the Argives with might, to whom all the Achaeans are in subjection. A plain man cannot stand against the anger of a king, who if he swallow his displeasure now, will yet nurse revenge till he has wreaked it. Consider, therefore, whether or not you will protect me."

And Achilles answered, "Fear not, but speak as it is borne in upon you from heaven, for by Apollo, Calchas, to whom you pray, and whose oracles you reveal to us, not a Danaan at our ships shall lay his hand upon you, while I yet live to look upon the face of the earth—no, not though you name Agamemnon himself, who is by far the foremost of the Achaeans."

Thereon the seer spoke boldly. "The god," he said, "is angry neither about vow nor hecatomb, but for his priest's sake, whom Agamemnon has dishonoured, in that he would not free his daughter nor take a ransom for her; therefore has he sent these evils upon us, and will yet send others. He will not deliver the Danaans from this pestilence till Agamemnon has restored the girl without fee or ransom to her father, and has sent a holy hecatomb to Chryse. Thus we may perhaps appease him."

With these words he sat down, and Agamemnon rose in anger. His heart was black with rage, and his eyes flashed fire as he scowled on Calchas and said, "Seer of evil, you never yet prophesied smooth things concerning me, but have ever loved to foretell that which was evil. You have brought me neither comfort nor performance; and now you come seeing among Danaans, and saying that Apollo has plagued us because I would not take a ransom for this girl, the daughter of Chryses. I have set my heart on keeping her in my own house, for I love her better even than my own wife Clytemnestra, whose peer she is alike in form and feature, in understanding and accomplishments. Still I will give her up if I must, for I would have the people live, not die; but you must find me a prize instead, or I alone among the Argives shall be without one. This is not well; for you behold, all of you, that my prize is to go elsewhither."

And Achilles answered, "Most noble son of Atreus, covetous beyond all mankind, how shall the Achaeans find you another prize? We have no common store from which to take one. Those we took from the cities have been awarded; we cannot disallow the awards that have been made already. Give this girl, therefore, to the god, and if ever Jove grants us to sack the city of Troy we will requite you three and fourfold."

Then Agamemnon said, "Achilles, valiant though you be, you shall not thus outwit me. You shall not overreach and you shall not persuade me. Are you to keep your own prize, while I sit tamely under my loss and give up the girl at your bidding? Let the Achaeans find me a prize in fair exchange to my liking, or I will come and take your own, or that of Ajax or of Ulysses; and he to whomsoever I may come shall rue my coming. But of this we will take thought hereafter; for the present, let us draw a ship into the sea, and find a crew for her expressly; let us put a hecatomb on board, and let us send Chryseis also; further, let some chief man among us be in command, either Ajax, or Idomeneus, or yourself, son of Peleus, mighty warrior that you are, that we may offer sacrifice and appease the anger of the god."

Achilles scowled at him and answered, "You are steeped in insolence and lust of gain. With what heart can any of the Achaeans do your bidding, either on foray or in open fighting? I came not warring here for any ill the Trojans had done me. I have no quarrel with them. They have not raided my cattle nor my horses, nor cut down my harvests on the rich plains of Phthia; for between me and them there is a great space, both mountain and sounding sea. We have followed you, Sir Insolence! for your pleasure, not ours—to gain satisfaction from the Trojans for your shameless self and for Menelaus. You forget

this, and threaten to rob me of the prize for which I have toiled, and which the sons of the Achaeans have given me. Never when the Achaeans sack any rich city of the Trojans do I receive so good a prize as you do, though it is my hands that do the better part of the fighting. When the sharing comes, your share is far the largest, and I, forsooth, must go back to my ships, take what I can get and be thankful, when my labour of fighting is done. Now, therefore, I shall go back to Phthia; it will be much better for me to return home with my ships, for I will not stay here dishonoured to gather gold and substance for you." And Agamemnon answered, "Fly if you will, I shall make you no prayers to stay you. I have others here who will do me honour, and above all Jove, the lord of counsel. There is no king here so hateful to me as you are, for you are ever quarrelsome and ill affected. What though you be brave? Was it not heaven that made you so? Go home, then, with your ships and comrades to lord it over the Myrmidons. I care neither for you nor for your anger; and thus will I do: since Phoebus Apollo is taking Chryseis from me, I shall send her with my ship and my followers, but I shall come to your tent and take your own prize Briseis, that you may learn how much stronger I am than you are, and that another may fear to set himself up as equal or comparable with me."

The son of Peleus was furious, and his heart within his shaggy breast was divided whether to draw his sword, push the others aside, and kill the son of Atreus, or to restrain himself and check his anger. While he was thus in two minds, and was drawing his mighty sword from its scabbard, Minerva came down from heaven (for Juno had sent her in the love she bore to them both), and seized the son of Peleus by his yellow hair, visible to him alone, for of the others no man could see her. Achilles turned in amaze, and by the fire that flashed from her eyes at once knew that she was Minerva. "Why are you here," said he, "daughter of aegis-bearing Jove? To see the pride of Agamemnon, son of Atreus? Let me tell you—and it shall surely be—he shall pay for this insolence with his life."

And Minerva said, "I come from heaven, if you will hear me, to bid you stay your anger. Juno has sent me, who cares for both of you alike. Cease, then, this brawling, and do not draw your sword; rail at him if you will, and your railing will not be in vain, for I tell you—and it shall surely be—that you shall here-

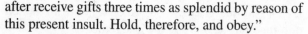

after receive gifts three times as splendid by reason of this present insult. Hold, therefore, and obey."

"Goddess," answered Achilles, "however angry a man may be, he must do as you two command him. This will be best, for the gods ever hear the prayers of him who has obeyed them."

He stayed his hand on the silver hilt of his sword, and thrust it back into the scabbard as Minerva bade him. Then she went back to Olympus among the other gods, and to the house of aegis-bearing Jove. But the son of Peleus again began railing at the son of Atreus, for he was still in a rage. "Wine-bibber," he cried, "with the face of a dog and the heart of a hind, you never dare to go out with the host in fight, nor yet with our chosen men in ambuscade. You shun this as you do death itself. You had rather go round and rob his prizes from any man who contradicts you. You devour your people, for you are king over a feeble folk; otherwise, son of Atreus, henceforward you would insult no man. Therefore I say, and swear it with a great oath—nay, by this my sceptre which shalt sprout neither leaf nor shoot, nor bud anew from the day on which it left its parent stem upon the mountains—for the axe stripped it of leaf and bark, and now the sons of the Achaeans bear it as judges and guardians of the decrees of heaven—so surely and solemnly do I swear that hereafter they shall look fondly for Achilles and shall not find him. In the day of your distress, when your men fall dying by the murderous hand of Hector, you shall not know how to help them, and shall rend your heart with rage for the hour when you offered insult to the bravest of the Achaeans."

With this the son of Peleus dashed his gold-bestudded sceptre on the ground and took his seat, while the son of Atreus was beginning fiercely from his place upon the other side. Then uprose smooth-tongued Nestor, the facile speaker of the Pylians, and the words fell from his lips sweeter than honey. Two generations of men born and bred in Pylos had passed away under his rule, and he was now reigning over the third. With all sincerity and goodwill, therefore, he addressed them thus:—

"Of a truth," he said, "a great sorrow has befallen the Achaean land. Surely Priam with his sons would rejoice, and the Trojans be glad at heart if they could hear this quarrel between you two, who are so excellent in fight and counsel. I am older than either of you; therefore be guided by me. Moreover I have been the familiar friend of men even greater than you

are, and they did not disregard my counsels. Never again can I behold such men as Pirithous and Dryas, shepherd of his people, or as Caeneus, Exadius, god-like Polyphemus, and Theseus son of Aegeus, peer of the immortals. These were the mightiest men ever born upon this earth: mightiest were they, and when they fought the fiercest tribes of mountain savages they utterly overthrew them. I came from distant Pylos, and went about among them, for they would have me come, and I fought as it was in me to do. Not a man now living could withstand them, but they heard my words, and were persuaded by them. So be it also with yourselves, for this is the more excellent way. Therefore, Agamemnon, though you be strong, take not this girl away, for the sons of the Achaeans have already given her to Achilles; and you, Achilles, strive not further with the king, for no man who by the grace of Jove wields a sceptre has like honour with Agamemnon. You are strong, and have a goddess for your mother; but Agamemnon is stronger than you, for he has more people under him. Son of Atreus, check your anger, I implore you; end this quarrel with Achilles, who in the day of battle is a tower of strength to the Achaeans."

And Agamemnon answered, "Sir, all that you have said is true, but this fellow must needs become our lord and master: he must be lord of all, king of all, and captain of all, and this shall hardly be. Granted that the gods have made him a great warrior, have they also given him the right to speak with railing?" Achilles interrupted him. "I should be a mean coward," he cried, "were I to give in to you in all things. Order other people about, not me, for I shall obey no longer. Furthermore I say—and lay my saying to your heart—I shall fight neither you nor any man about this girl, for those that take were those also that gave. But of all else that is at my ship you shall carry away nothing by force. Try, that others may see; if you do, my spear shall be reddened with your blood."

When they had quarrelled thus angrily, they rose, and broke up the assembly at the ships of the Achaeans. The son of Peleus went back to his tents and ships with the son of Menoetius and his company, while Agamemnon drew a vessel into the water and chose a crew of twenty oarsmen. He escorted Chryseis on board and sent moreover a hecatomb for the god. And Ulysses went as captain.

These, then, went on board and sailed their ways over the sea. But the son of Atreus bade the people purify themselves; so they purified themselves and cast their filth into the sea. Then they offered hecatombs of bulls and goats without blemish on the sea-shore, and the smoke with the savour of their sacrifice rose curling up towards heaven.

Thus did they busy themselves throughout the host. But Agamemnon did not forget the threat that he had made Achilles, and called his trusty messengers and squires Talthybius and Eurybates. "Go," said he, "to the tent of Achilles, son of Peleus; take Briseis by the hand and bring her hither; if he will not give her I shall come with others and take her—which will press him harder."

He charged them straightly further and dismissed them, whereon they went their way sorrowfully by the seaside, till they came to the tents and ships of the Myrmidons. They found Achilles sitting by his tent and his ships, and ill-pleased he was when he beheld them. They stood fearfully and reverently before him, and never a word did they speak, but he knew them and said, "Welcome, heralds, messengers of gods and men; draw near; my quarrel is not with you but with Agamemnon who has sent you for the girl Briseis. Therefore, Patroclus, bring her and give her to them, but let them be witnesses by the blessed gods, by mortal men, and by the fierceness of Agamemnon's anger, that if ever again there be need of me to save the people from ruin, they shall seek and they shall not find. Agamemnon is mad with rage and knows not how to look before and after that the Achaeans may fight by their ships in safety."

Patroclus did as his dear comrade had bidden him. He brought Briseis from the tent and gave her over to the heralds, who took her with them to the ships of the Achaeans—and the woman was loth to go. Then Achilles went all alone by the side of the hoar sea, weeping and looking out upon the boundless waste of waters. He raised his hands in prayer to his immortal mother. "Mother," he cried, "you bore me doomed to live but for a little season; surely Jove, who thunders from Olympus, might have made that little glorious. It is not so. Agamemnon, son of Atreus, has done me dishonour, and has robbed me of my prize by force."

As he spoke he wept aloud, and his mother heard him where she was sitting in the depths of the sea hard by the old man her father. Forthwith she rose as it were a grey mist out of the waves, sat down before him as he stood weeping, caressed him with her hand, and said, "My son, why are you weeping? What is it that grieves you? Keep it not from me, but tell me, that we may know it together."

Achilles drew a deep sigh and said, "You know it; why tell you what you know well already? We went to Thebe the strong city of Eetion, sacked it, and brought hither the spoil. The sons of the Achaeans shared it duly among themselves, and chose lovely Chryseis as the meed of Agamemnon; but Chryses, priest of Apollo, came to the ships of the Achaeans to free his daughter, and brought with him a great ransom: moreover he bore in his hand the sceptre of Apollo, wreathed with a suppliant's wreath, and he besought the Achaeans, but most of all the two sons of Atreus who were their chiefs.

"On this the rest of the Achaeans with one voice were for respecting the priest and taking the ransom that he offered; but not so Agamemnon, who spoke fiercely to him and sent him roughly away. So he went back in anger, and Apollo, who loved him dearly, heard his prayer. Then the god sent a deadly dart upon the Argives, and the people died thick on one another, for the arrows went everywhither among the wide host of the Achaeans. At last a seer in the fulness of his knowledge declared to us the oracles of Apollo, and I was myself first to say that we should appease him. Whereon the son of Atreus rose in anger, and threatened that which he has since done. The Achaeans are now taking the girl in a ship to Chryse, and sending gifts of sacrifice to the god; but the heralds have just taken from my tent the daughter of Briseus, whom the Achaeans had awarded to myself.

"Help your brave son, therefore, if you are able. Go to Olympus, and if you have ever done him service in word or deed, implore the aid of Jove. Ofttimes in my father's house have I heard you glory in that you alone of the immortals saved the son of Saturn from ruin, when the others, with Juno, Neptune, and Pallas Minerva would have put him in bonds. It was you, goddess, who delivered him by calling to Olympus the hundred-handed monster whom gods call Briareus, but men Aegaeon, for he is stronger even than his father; when therefore he took his seat all-glorious beside the son of Saturn, the other gods were afraid, and did not bind him. Go, then, to him, remind him of all this, clasp his knees, and bid him give succour to the Trojans. Let the Achaeans be hemmed in at the sterns of their ships, and perish on the sea-shore, that they may reap what joy they may of their king, and that Agamemnon may rue his blindness in offering insult to the foremost of the Achaeans."

Thetis wept and answered, "My son, woe is me that I should have borne or suckled you. Would indeed that you had lived your span free from all sorrow at your ships, for it is all too brief; alas, that you should be at once short of life and long of sorrow above your peers: woe, therefore, was the hour in which I bore you; nevertheless I will go to the snowy heights of Olympus, and tell this tale to Jove, if he will hear our prayer: meanwhile stay where you are with your ships, nurse your anger against the Achaeans, and hold aloof from fight. For Jove went yesterday to Oceanus, to a feast among the Ethiopians, and the other gods went with him. He will return to Olympus twelve days hence; I will then go to his mansion paved with bronze and will beseech him; nor do I doubt that I shall be able to persuade him."

On this she left him, still furious at the loss of her that had been taken from him. Meanwhile Ulysses reached Chryse with the hecatomb. When they had come inside the harbour they furled the sails and laid them in the ship's hold; they slackened the forestays, lowered the mast into its place, and rowed the ship to the place where they would have her lie; there they cast out their mooring-stones and made fast the hawsers. They then got out upon the sea-shore and landed the hecatomb for Apollo; Chryseis also left the ship, and Ulysses led her to the altar to deliver her into the hands of her father. "Chryses," said he, "King Agamemnon has sent me to bring you back your child, and to offer sacrifice to Apollo on behalf of the Danaans, that we may propitiate the god, who has now brought sorrow upon the Argives."

So saying he gave the girl over to her father, who received her gladly, and they ranged the holy hecatomb all orderly round the altar of the god. They washed their hands and took up the barley-meal to sprinkle over the victims, while Chryses lifted up his hands and prayed aloud on their behalf. "Hear me," he cried, "O god of the silver bow, that protectest Chryse and holy Cilla, and rulest Tenedos with thy might. Even as thou didst hear me aforetime when I prayed, and didst press hardly upon the Achaeans, so hear me yet again, and stay this fearful pestilence from the Danaans." Thus did he pray, and Apollo heard his prayer. When they had done praying and sprinkling the barley-meal, they drew back the heads of the victims and killed and flayed them. They cut out the thigh-bones,

wrapped them round in two layers of fat, set some pieces of raw meat on the top of them, and then Chryses laid them on the wood fire and poured wine over them, while the young men stood near him with five-pronged spits in their hands. When the thigh-bones were burned and they had tasted the inward meats, they cut the rest up small, put the pieces upon the spits, roasted them till they were done, and drew them off: then, when they had finished their work and the feast was ready, they ate it, and every man had his full share, so that all were satisfied. As soon as they had had enough to eat and drink, pages filled the mixing-bowl with wine and water and handed it round, after giving every man his drink-offering.

Thus all day long the young men worshipped the god with song, hymning him and chaunting the joyous paean, and the god took pleasure in their voices; but when the sun went down, and it came on dark, they laid themselves down to sleep by the stern cables of the ship, and when the child of morning, rosy-fingered Dawn, appeared they again set sail for the host of the Achaeans. Apollo sent them a fair wind, so they raised their mast and hoisted their white sails aloft. As the sail bellied with the wind the ship flew through the deep blue water, and the foam hissed against her bows as she sped onward. When they reached the wide-stretching host of the Achaeans, they drew the vessel ashore, high and dry upon the sands, set her strong props beneath her, and went their ways to their own tents and ships.

But Achilles abode at his ships and nursed his anger. He went not to the honourable assembly, and sallied not forth to fight, but gnawed at his own heart, pining for battle and the war-cry.

Now after twelve days the immortal gods came back in a body to Olympus, and Jove led the way. Thetis was not unmindful of the charge her son had laid upon her, so she rose from under the sea and went through great heaven with early morning to Olympus, where she found the mighty son of Saturn sitting all alone upon its topmost ridges. She sat herself down before him, and with her left hand seized his knees, while with her right she caught him under the chin, and besought him, saying—

"Father Jove, if I ever did you service in word or deed among the immortals, hear my prayer, and do honour to my son, whose life is to be cut short so early. King Agamemnon has dishonoured him by taking his prize and keeping her. Honour him then yourself, Olympian lord of counsel, and grant victory to the Trojans, till the Achaeans give my son his due and load him with riches in requital."

Jove sat for a while silent, and without a word, but Thetis still kept firm hold of his knees, and besought him a second time. "Incline your head," said she, "and promise me surely, or else deny me—for you have nothing to fear—that I may learn how greatly you disdain me."

At this Jove was much troubled and answered, "I shall have trouble if you set me quarrelling with Juno, for she will provoke me with her taunting speeches; even now she is always railing at me before the other gods and accusing me of giving aid to the Trojans. Go back now, lest she should find out. I will consider the matter, and will bring it about as you wish. See, I incline my head that you believe me. This is the most solemn vow that I can give to any god. I never recall my word, or deceive, or fail to do what I say, when I have nodded my head." As he spoke, the son of Saturn bowed his dark brows, and the ambrosial locks swayed on his immortal head, till vast Olympus reeled.

When the pair had thus laid their plans, they parted—Jove to his house, while the goddess quitted the splendour of Olympus, and plunged into the depths of the sea. The gods rose from their seats, before the coming of their sire. Not one of them dared to remain sitting, but all stood up as he came among them. There, then, he took his seat. But Juno, when she saw him, knew that he and the old merman's daughter, silver-footed Thetis, had been hatching mischief, so she at once began to upbraid him. "Trickster," she cried, "which of the gods have you been taking into your counsels now? You are always settling matters in secret behind my back, and have never yet told me, if you could help it, one word of your intentions."

"Juno," replied the sire of gods and men, "you must not expect to be informed of all my counsels. You are my wife, but you would find it hard to understand them. When it is proper for you to hear, there is no one, god or man, who will be told sooner, but when I mean to keep a matter to myself, you must not pry nor ask questions."

"Dread son of Saturn," answered Juno, "what are you talking about? I? Pry and ask questions? Never. I let you have your own way in everything. Still, I have a strong misgiving that the old merman's daughter Thetis has been talking you over, for she was with

you and had hold of your knees this self-same morning. I believe, therefore, that you have been promising her to give glory to Achilles, and to kill much people at the ships of the Achaeans."

"Wife," said Jove, "I can do nothing but you suspect me and find it out. You will take nothing by it, for I shall only dislike you the more, and it will go harder with you. Granted that it is as you say; I mean to have it so; sit down and hold your tongue as I bid you for if I once begin to lay my hands about you, though all heaven were on your side it would profit you nothing." On this Juno was frightened, so she curbed her stubborn will and sat down in silence. But the heavenly beings were disquieted throughout the house of Jove, till the cunning workman Vulcan began to try and pacify his mother Juno. "It will be intolerable," said he, "if you two fall to wrangling and setting heaven in an uproar about a pack of mortals. If such ill counsels are to prevail, we shall have no pleasure at our banquet. Let me then advise my mother—and she must herself know that it will be better—to make friends with my dear father Jove, lest he again scold her and disturb our feast. If the Olympian Thunderer wants to hurl us all from our seats, he can do so, for he is far the strongest, so give him fair words, and he will then soon be in a good humour with us."

As he spoke, he took a double cup of nectar, and placed it in his mother's hand. "Cheer up, my dear mother," said he, "and make the best of it. I love you dearly, and should be very sorry to see you get a thrashing; however grieved I might be, I could not help for there is no standing against Jove. Once before when I was trying to help you, he caught me by the foot and flung me from the heavenly threshold. All day long from morn till eve, was I falling, till at sunset I came to ground in the island of Lemnos, and there I lay, with very little life left in me, till the Sintians came and tended me."

Juno smiled at this, and as she smiled she took the cup from her son's hands. Then Vulcan drew sweet nectar from the mixing-bowl, and served it round among the gods, going from left to right; and the blessed gods laughed out a loud applause as they saw him bustling about the heavenly mansion. Thus through the livelong day to the going down of the sun they feasted, and everyone had his full share, so that all were satisfied. Apollo struck his lyre, and the Muses lifted up their sweet voices, calling and answering one another. But when the sun's glorious light had faded, they went home to bed, each in his own abode, which lame Vulcan with his consummate skill had fashioned for them. So Jove, the Olympian Lord of Thunder, hied him to the bed in which he always slept; and when he had got on to it he went to sleep, with Juno of the golden throne by his side.

For the entire epic poem, insert the Literature CD.

Questions

1. What were the causes of the Trojan War? Further, how do these causes help inform your view of the two nations' loyalty to king and country?
2. According to *The Iliad,* how long did the battle of Troy last? Why may it have taken so long to conclude?
3. What is the turning point of *The Iliad* or the moment that changes the direction of the war? Why is this significant?
4. Who is the protagonist of this epic poem and why? Is it likely that there might be more than one protagonist in this story?
5. What foreshadows Achilles' return to battle?
6. What is Helen's role in the poem? Some scholars believe that she is the genesis of the entire work. Is this a fair assessment?
7. Which of the gods plays the most significant role throughout *The Iliad?* Why?
8. What is Hector's greatest tactical error and why? Does this error signal the fall of Troy?
9. Does the atrocity that Paris commits lead to the fall of Troy, or is it something greater, perhaps battle-related?

1. There has always been a great deal of controversy surrounding the battle of Troy. Some historians argue that it might not have taken place, and some argue that it was a ten-year battle that changed the course of history. Determine whether or not you believe that *The Iliad* and other historical documents lend credence to the idea that this war actually took place.
2. There is something very heroic about *The Iliad,* something that reeks of pride and honor. However, there are particular characters from this work that use their pride in a destructive manner. Compose an essay that analyzes these characters and how their behavior affects the Trojan War.
3. Women play a vital role in *The Iliad.* Examine their characteristics, motivations, and actions, and then compare and contrast the women of this tale with the men.

Continued

4. What does Homer imply about the relationships between the humans and the gods? Construct an argument that examines these relationships, and support it by citing *The Iliad* and outside sources.
5. Is it possible for the reader to feel sympathy for any of the characters in *The Iliad?* If so, who are these characters, and what evidence is there to support your claim?

The Odyssey

1. While reading *The Odyssey*, pay special attention to the choices made by Odysseus, noting specifically how these choices affect his crew.
2. Notice that the first half of *The Odyssey* seems dedicated to questioning mortal life while the second half examines the value of an anonymous human life.
3. This poem is similar to *The Iliad*, for it examines heroism.

The Odyssey

Homer
Book I

Tell me, O muse, of that ingenious hero who travelled far and wide after he had sacked the famous town of Troy. Many cities did he visit, and many were the nations with whose manners and customs he was acquainted; moreover he suffered much by sea while trying to save his own life and bring his men safely home; but do what he might he could not save his men, for they perished through their own sheer folly in eating the cattle of the Sun-god Hyperion; so the god prevented them from ever reaching home. Tell me, too, about all these things, O daughter of Jove, from whatsoever source you may know them.

So now all who escaped death in battle or by shipwreck had got safely home except Ulysses, and he, though he was longing to return to his wife and country, was detained by the goddess Calypso, who had got him into a large cave and wanted to marry him. But as years went by, there came a time when the gods settled that he should go back to Ithaca; even then, however, when he was among his own people, his troubles were not yet over; nevertheless all the gods had now begun to pity him except Neptune, who still persecuted him without ceasing and would not let him get home.

Now Neptune had gone off to the Ethiopians, who are at the world's end, and lie in two halves, the one looking West and the other East. He had gone there to accept a hecatomb of sheep and oxen, and was enjoying himself at his festival; but the other gods met in the house of Olympian Jove, and the sire of gods and men spoke first. At that moment he was thinking of Aegisthus, who had been killed by Agamemnon's son Orestes; so he said to the other gods:

"See now, how men lay blame upon us gods for what is after all nothing but their own folly. Look at Aegisthus; he must needs make love to Agamemnon's wife unrighteously and then kill Agamemnon, though he knew it would be the death of him; for I sent Mercury to warn him not to do either of these things, inasmuch as Orestes would be sure to take his revenge when he grew up and wanted to return home. Mercury told him this in all good will but he would not listen, and now he has paid for everything in full."

Then Minerva said, "Father, son of Saturn, King of kings, it served Aegisthus right, and so it would any one else who does as he did; but Aegisthus is neither here nor there; it is for Ulysses that my heart bleeds, when I think of his sufferings in that lonely sea-girt island, far away, poor man, from all his friends. It is an island covered with forest, in the very middle of the sea, and a goddess lives there, daughter of the magician Atlas, who looks after the bottom of the ocean, and carries the great columns that keep heaven and earth asunder. This daughter of Atlas has got hold of poor unhappy Ulysses, and keeps trying by every kind of blandishment to make him forget his home, so that he is tired of life, and thinks of nothing but how he may once more see the smoke of his own chimneys. You, sir, take no heed of this, and yet when Ulysses was before Troy did he not propitiate you with many a burnt sacrifice? Why then should you keep on being so angry with him?"

And Jove said, "My child, what are you talking about? How can I forget Ulysses than whom there is no more capable man on earth, nor more liberal in his offerings to the immortal gods that live in heaven? Bear in mind, however, that Neptune is still furious with Ulysses for having blinded an eye of Polyphemus, king of the Cyclopes. Polyphemus is son to Neptune by the nymph Thoosa, daughter to the sea-king Phorcys; therefore though he will not kill Ulysses outright, he torments him by preventing him from getting home. Still, let us lay our heads together and see how we can help him to return; Neptune will then be pacified, for if we are all of a mind he can hardly stand out against us."

And Minerva said, "Father, son of Saturn, King of kings, if, then, the gods now mean that Ulysses should get home, we should first send Mercury to the Ogygian island to tell Calypso that we have made up our minds and that he is to return. In the meantime I will go to Ithaca, to put heart into Ulysses' son Telemachus; I will embolden him to call the Achaeans in assembly, and speak out to the suitors of his mother Penelope, who persist in eating up any number of his sheep and oxen; I will also conduct him to Sparta and to Pylos, to see if he can hear anything about the return of his dear father—for this will make people speak well of him."

So saying she bound on her glittering golden sandals, imperishable, with which she can fly like the wind over land or sea; she grasped the redoubtable bronze-shod spear, so stout and sturdy and strong, wherewith she quells the ranks of heroes who have displeased her, and down she darted from the topmost summits of Olympus, whereon forthwith she was in Ithaca, at the gateway of Ulysses' house, disguised as a visitor, Mentes, chief of the Taphians, and she held a bronze spear in her hand. There she found the lordly suitors seated on hides of the oxen which they had killed and eaten, and playing draughts in front of the house. Men-servants and pages were bustling about to wait upon them, some mixing wine with water in the mixing-bowls, some cleaning down the tables with wet sponges and laying them out again, and some cutting up great quantities of meat.

Telemachus saw her long before any one else did. He was sitting moodily among the suitors thinking about his brave father, and how he would send them flying out of the house, if he were to come to his own again and be honoured as in days gone by. Thus brooding as he sat among them, he caught sight of Minerva and went straight to the gate, for he was vexed that a stranger should be kept waiting for admittance. He took her right hand in his own, and bade her give him her spear. "Welcome," said he, "to our house, and when you have partaken of food you shall tell us what you have come for."

He led the way as he spoke, and Minerva followed him. When they were within he took her spear and set it in the spear-stand against a strong bearing-post along with the many other spears of his unhappy father, and he conducted her to a richly decorated seat under which he threw a cloth of damask. There was a footstool also for her feet, and he set another seat near her for himself, away from the suitors, that she might not be annoyed while eating by their noise and insolence, and that he might ask her more freely about his father.

A maid servant then brought them water in a beautiful golden ewer and poured it into a silver basin for them to wash their hands, and she drew a clean table beside them. An upper servant brought them bread, and offered them many good things of what there was in the house, the carver fetched them plates of all manner of meats and set cups of gold by their side, and a man-servant brought them wine and poured it out for them.

Then the suitors came in and took their places on the benches and seats. Forthwith men servants poured water over their hands, maids went round with the bread-baskets, pages filled the mixing-bowls with wine and water, and they laid their hands upon the good things that were before them. As soon as they had had enough to eat and drink they wanted music and dancing, which are the crowning embellishments of a banquet, so a servant brought a lyre to Phemius, whom they compelled perforce to sing to them. As soon as he touched his lyre and began to sing, Telemachus spoke low to Minerva, with his head close to hers that no man might hear.

"I hope, sir," said he, "that you will not be offended with what I am going to say. Singing comes cheap to those who do not pay for it, and all this is done at the cost of one whose bones lie rotting in some wilderness or grinding to powder in the surf. If these men were to see my father come back to Ithaca they would pray for longer legs rather than a longer purse, for money would not serve them; but he, alas, has fallen on an ill fate, and even when people do sometimes say that he is coming, we no longer heed them; we shall never see him again. And now, sir, tell me and tell me true, who you are and where you come from. Tell me of your town and parents, what manner of ship you came in, how your crew brought you to Ithaca, and of what nation they declared themselves to be—for you cannot have come by land. Tell me also truly, for I want to know, are you a stranger to this house, or have you been here in my father's time? In the old days we had many visitors for my father went about much himself." And Minerva answered, "I will tell you truly and particularly all about it. I am Mentes, son of Anchialus, and I am King of the Taphians. I have come here with my ship and crew, on a voyage to men of a foreign tongue being bound for Temesa with a cargo of iron, and I shall bring back copper. As for my ship, it lies over yonder off the open country away from the town, in the harbour Rheithron under the wooded mountain Neritum. Our fathers were friends before us, as old Laertes will tell you, if you will go and ask him. They say, however, that he never comes to town now, and lives by himself in the country, faring hardly, with an old woman to look after him and get his dinner for him, when he comes in tired from pottering about his vineyard. They told me your father was at home again, and that was why I came, but it seems the gods are still keeping him back, for he is not dead yet not on the mainland. It is more likely he is on some sea-girt island in mid-ocean, or a prisoner among savages who are detaining him against his will. I am no prophet, and know very little about omens, but I speak as it is borne in upon me from heaven, and assure you that he will not be away much longer; for he is a man of such resource that even though he were in chains of iron he would find some means of getting home again. But tell me, and tell me true, can Ulysses really have such a fine looking fellow for a son? You are indeed wonderfully like him about the head and eyes, for we were close friends before he set sail for Troy where the flower of all the Argives went also. Since that time we have never either of us seen the other."

"My mother," answered Telemachus, "tells me I am son to Ulysses, but it is a wise child that knows his own father. Would that I were son to one who had grown old upon his own estates, for, since you ask me, there is no more ill-starred man under heaven than he who they tell me is my father." And Minerva said, "There is no fear of your race dying out yet, while Penelope has such a fine son as you are. But tell me, and tell me true, what is the meaning of all this feasting, and who are these people? What is it all about? Have you some banquet, or is there a wedding in the family—for no one seems to be bringing any provisions of his own? And the guests—how atrociously they are behaving; what riot they make over the whole house; it is enough to disgust any respectable person who comes near them."

"Sir," said Telemachus, "as regards your question, so long as my father was here it was well with us and with the house, but the gods in their displeasure have willed it otherwise, and have hidden him away more closely than mortal man was ever yet hidden. I could have borne it better even though he were dead, if he had fallen with his men before Troy, or had died with friends around him when the days of his fighting were done; for then the Achaeans would have built a mound over his ashes, and I should myself have been heir to his renown; but now the storm-winds have spirited him away we know not wither; he is gone without leaving so much as a trace behind him, and I inherit nothing but dismay. Nor does the matter end simply with grief for the loss of my father; heaven has laid sorrows upon me of yet another kind; for the chiefs from all our islands, Dulichium, Same, and the woodland island of Zacynthus, as also all the principal men of Ithaca itself, are eating up my house under the pretext of paying their court to my mother, who will neither point blank say that she will not marry, nor yet bring matters to an end; so they are making havoc of my estate, and before long will do so also with myself."

"Is that so?" exclaimed Minerva, "then you do indeed want Ulysses home again. Give him his helmet, shield, and a couple lances, and if he is the man he was when I first knew him in our house, drinking and making merry, he would soon lay his hands about these rascally suitors, were he to stand once more upon his own threshold. He was then coming from Ephyra, where he had been to beg poison for his arrows from Ilus, son of Mermerus. Ilus feared the ever-living gods and would not give him any, but my father let him have some, for he was very fond of him. If Ulysses is the man he then was, these suitors will have a short shrift and a sorry wedding.

"But there! It rests with heaven to determine whether he is to return, and take his revenge in his own house or no; I would, however, urge you to set about trying to get rid of these suitors at once. Take my advice, call the Achaean heroes in assembly tomorrow—lay your case before them, and call heaven to bear you witness. Bid the suitors take themselves off, each to his own place, and if your mother's mind is set on marrying again, let her go back to her father, who will find her a husband and provide her with all the marriage gifts that so dear a daughter may expect. As for yourself, let me prevail upon you to take the best ship you can get, with a crew of twenty men, and go in quest of your father who has so long been missing. Someone may tell you something, or (and people often hear things in this way) some heaven-sent message may direct you. First go to Pylos and ask Nestor; thence go on to Sparta and visit Menelaus, for he got home last of all the Achaeans; if you hear that your father is alive and on his way home, you can put up with the waste these suitors will make for yet another twelve months. If on the other hand you hear of his death, come home at once, celebrate his funeral rites with all due pomp, build a barrow to his memory, and make your mother marry again. Then, having done all this, think it well over in your mind how, by fair means or foul, you may kill these suitors in your own house. You are too old to plead infancy any longer; have you not heard how people are singing Orestes' praises for having killed his father's murderer Aegisthus? You are a fine, smart looking fellow; show your mettle, then, and make yourself a name in history. Now, however, I must go back to my ship and to my crew, who will be impatient if I keep them waiting longer; think the matter over for yourself, and remember what I have said to you."

"Sir," answered Telemachus, "it has been very kind of you to talk to me in this way, as though I were your own son, and I will do all you tell me; I know you want to be getting on with your voyage, but stay a little longer till you have taken a bath and refreshed yourself. I will then give you a present, and you shall go on your way rejoicing; I will give you one of great beauty and value—a keepsake such as only dear friends give to one another."

Minerva answered, "Do not try to keep me, for I would be on my way at once. As for any present you may be disposed to make me, keep it till I come again, and I will take it home with me. You shall give me a very good one, and I will give you one of no less value in return."

With these words she flew away like a bird into the air, but she had given Telemachus courage, and had made him think more than ever about his father. He felt the change, wondered at it, and knew that the stranger had been a god, so he went straight to where the suitors were sitting.

Phemius was still singing, and his hearers sat rapt in silence as he told the sad tale of the return from Troy, and the ills Minerva had laid upon the Achaeans. Penelope, daughter of Icarius, heard his song from her room upstairs, and came down by the great staircase, not alone, but attended by two of her handmaids. When she reached the suitors she stood by one of the bearing posts that supported the roof of the cloisters with a staid maiden on either side of her. She held a veil, moreover, before her face, and was weeping bitterly.

"Phemius," she cried, "you know many another feat of gods and heroes, such as poets love to celebrate. Sing the suitors some one of these, and let them drink their wine in silence, but cease this sad tale, for it breaks my sorrowful heart, and reminds me of my lost husband whom I mourn ever without ceasing, and whose name was great over all Hellas and middle Argos."

"Mother," answered Telemachus, "let the bard sing what he has a mind to; bards do not make the ills they sing of; it is Jove, not they, who makes them, and who sends weal or woe upon mankind according to his own good pleasure. This fellow means no harm by singing the ill-fated return of the Danaans, for people always applaud the latest songs most warmly. Make up your mind to it and bear it; Ulysses is not the only man who never came back from Troy, but many another went down as well as he. Go, then, within the house and busy yourself with your daily duties, your loom, your distaff, and the ordering of your servants; for speech is man's matter, and mine above all others—for it is I who am master here."

She went wondering back into the house, and laid her son's saying in her heart. Then, going upstairs with her handmaids into her room, she mourned her dear husband till Minerva shed sweet sleep over her eyes. But the suitors were clamorous throughout the covered cloisters, and prayed each one that he might be her bed fellow. Then Telemachus spoke, "Shameless," he cried, "and insolent suitors, let us feast at our pleasure now, and let there be no brawling, for it is a rare thing to hear a man with such a divine voice as Phemius has; but in the morning meet me in full assembly that I may give you formal notice to depart, and feast at one another's houses, turn and turn about, at your own cost. If on the other hand you choose to persist in spunging upon one man, heaven help me, but Jove shall reckon with you in full, and when you fall in my father's house there shall be no man to avenge you."

The suitors bit their lips as they heard him, and marvelled at the boldness of his speech. Then, Antinous, son of Eupeithes, said, "The gods seem to have given you lessons in bluster and tall talking; may Jove never grant you to be chief in Ithaca as your father was before you."

Telemachus answered, "Antinous, do not chide with me, but, god willing, I will be chief too if I can. Is this the worst fate you can think of for me? It is no bad thing to be a chief, for it brings both riches and honour. Still, now that Ulysses is dead there are many great men in Ithaca both old and young, and some other may take the lead among them; nevertheless I will be chief in my own house, and will rule those whom Ulysses has won for me."

Then Eurymachus, son of Polybus, answered, "It rests with heaven to decide who shall be chief among us, but you shall be master in your own house and over your own possessions; no one while there is a man in Ithaca shall do you violence nor rob you. And now, my good fellow, I want to know about this stranger. What country does he come from? Of what family is he, and where is his estate? Has he brought you news about the return of your father, or was he on business of his own? He seemed a well-to-do man, but he hurried off so suddenly that he was gone in a moment before we could get to know him."

"My father is dead and gone," answered Telemachus, "and even if some rumour reaches me I put no more faith in it now. My mother does indeed sometimes send for a soothsayer and question him, but I give his prophecyings no heed. As for the stranger, he was Mentes, son of Anchialus, chief of the Taphians, an old friend of my father's." But in his heart he knew that it had been the goddess.

The suitors then returned to their singing and dancing until the evening; but when night fell upon their pleasuring they went home to bed each in his own abode. Telemachus's room was high up in a tower that looked on to the outer court; hither, then, he hied, brooding and full of thought. A good old woman, Euryclea, daughter of Ops, the son of Pisenor, went before him with a couple of blazing torches. Laertes had bought her with his own money when she was quite young; he gave the worth of twenty oxen for her, and shewed as much respect to her in his household as he did to his own wedded wife, but he did not take her to his bed for he feared his wife's resentment. She it was who now lighted Telemachus to his room, and she loved him better than any of the other women in the house did, for she had nursed him when he was a baby.

He opened the door of his bedroom and sat down upon the bed; as he took off his shirt he gave it to the good old woman, who folded it tidily up, and hung it for him over a peg by his bedside, after which she went out, pulled the door to by a silver catch, and drew the bolt home by means of the strap. But Telemachus as he lay covered with a woollen fleece kept thinking all night through of his intended voyage of the counsel that Minerva had given him.

For the entire epic poem, insert the Literature CD.

Questions

1. How is Odysseus tricked into being proven a liar about his sanity? Does this suggest he is gullible or trusting?
2. How long were Odysseus and his men gone from Ithaca? Does this length of time suggest something about his culture or his country?
3. How long was it supposed to take for Odysseus and his men to sail back to Ithaca from Troy? As time progresses, what starts to enter into his mind and why?
4. What happened to Odysseus and his men when they ventured into Polyphemus' cave? Thinking about this cave on a larger scale is interesting. What might this cave symbolize?
5. When Odysseus and his men are on the island of Laestrygones, what symbols can be identified?
6. What did Circe do to Odysseus' men, and why was he unable to perform this act on Odysseus?
7. What fateful event occurs to Odysseus as he is within sight of Ithaca? What does this suggest about the crew aboard Odysseus' ship?
8. In what way did Athena aid Odysseus in reclaiming his kingdom? Is it plausible to infer that without Athena's help, this would not have been possible?
9. What kind of kingdom does Odysseus come home to? What kind of rule is now being enforced on the people, and how has this affected them?
10. What does Penelope do in order to avoid choosing a suitor? Upon what action is this predicated, and how does it help advance the poem?

1. There are many father-son relationships in *The Odyssey*. Identify two of these relationships, and compose a comparison and contrast essay that examines how, specifically, these relationships help advance *The Odyssey*.

2. In both *The Odyssey* and *The Iliad*, the reader is given a portrayal of the humans' relationship with the gods. Differences, however, can be found when examining these portrayals. Using these two Homeric epics, compare and contrast the humans' relationship with the gods, noting not only how they are similar and different but also how they help advance each poem's argument.

3. Homer offers the reader an interesting glimpse of his views on hospitality. From how Odysseus and his men are treated, what might Homer be saying to the reader about the importance of Greek hospitality? It would be useful to think about how Odysseus and his men are treated as they go from one island to the next.

4. Homer refers to Odysseus as the "polytropos" or "man of many tricks." Take a stand on whether or not Odysseus is worthy of such a title?

5. In their own unique way, Achilles and Odysseus are both heroes. However, it seems that Homer has at least two definitions of heroism, for his definitions seem to differ when examining *The Odyssey* and *The Iliad*. Compare and contrast Homer's definition of heroism in *The Odyssey* and *The Iliad*.

2

Greek Theater

Taking a trip to a particular time period consists of more than just a brief description of the era itself. As a reader, you should want to know what the people were like and how their beliefs, interests, and motivations informed their civilization, for the era that brought us Sophocles and Euripides was what some might consider a renaissance, one that introduced the world to new, revolutionary ideas. For instance, the Greek theater's effect on this civilization was grand, and certain writers / playwrights contributed a great deal to the literary arts.

The Greeks were animated about their theater and would organize a festival once a year where playwrights would have their pieces performed and judged. This was called the Great Dionysia, and the winner of this theatrical festival would be crowned with praise for his work and would be glorified throughout the year as one of the great playwrights of Greece. The Dionysian festivals were a time for Greek playwrights to submit four plays to a panel of judges: three tragedies and one comedy. The judges would then assess the works of each playwright. Next, they would pick one of the plays from the four, and that play would be performed during the festival.

Theater-goers were fortunate, for few bad seats existed. All of the theaters were roofless and built in a semi-circular design. The seating was the equivalent of what one might call "stadium seating," similar to the seating in current football or baseball stadiums. As people looked out from their seats, they could see a stage, sometimes built of white stone, and rows of pillars that often served as a backdrop for theatrical buildings or palaces. Sitting in tiered seating, the audience would look down on the orchestra. This area was occupied by the chorus, a group of men who danced, chanted, and eventually served as the conscience of the Grecian people. The chorus was an integral part of Greek Theater because it served as a transitional device, advancing the play from one scene to the next.

The tragedies of the Greeks were divided into four parts. The first part was known as the *prologos*. Essentially, this was an introduction to the time period and characters; further, it offered a description of the setting. It gave the audience all of the information it needed in order to follow the play. The next part was known as the *parados*. At this point in the play, the chorus would offer its opinion on what was said during the *prologos*. The third part of the tragedy housed the main conflict, allowing the plot to emerge. This part was known as the *episodia*. Throughout the *episodia,* the chorus would interject and highlight particular parts that were vital to the meaning of the play. The idea was to make the members of the chorus seem like they were having a conversation with each other. First, the stroph would be read, and then the antistroph. These two parts would help give the audience various viewpoints on the characters and time period of the play. During the stroph, the chorus would move across the stage while singing, and then move in the opposite direction during the antistroph. These two parts were meant to be read as the conscience of one individual having a conversation with the conscience of another. The final part of the play was known as the *exodus*. This was the part of the play where the conflict was resolved and the actors left the stage.

Sophocles (495–405 BCE)

Like any playwright with a great imagination, Sophocles wrote in a way that affected people. He wanted his audiences to not only leave with a feeling of satisfaction but also a feeling of uneasiness in their stomachs. He had an uncanny ability to portray real-life events on the stage in a way that many of the playwrights of his time tried to mirror. He won first prize at the very first City Dionysis competition he entered, and he never failed to finish lower than second place. He even acted in some of his plays, but a weak voice eventually relegated him to simply writing. His life was replete with a passion for government affairs, including those revolving around the military, treasury, and ministry. With this mix of public service and public entertainment, Sophocles remains one of the most intriguing figures of his time and civilization.

Oedipus the King

1. As you read, it becomes increasingly clear that Oedipus has many character flaws. It's important that you focus on these flaws and investigate how they lead to his downfall.
2. Attempt to classify Oedipus based on how he acts and what he says.
3. Notice how the stroph and antistroph help advance the play.

Oedipus the King

Sophocles

DRAMATIS PERSONAE

OEDIPUS: king of Thebes
PRIEST: the high priest of Thebes
CREON: Oedipus' brother-in-law
CHORUS: of Theban elders
TEIRESIAS: an old blind prophet
BOY: attendant of Teiresias
JOCASTA: wife of Oedipus, sister of Creon
MESSENGER: an old man
SERVANT: an old shepherd
SECOND MESSENGER: a servant of Oedipus
ANTIGONE: daughter of Oedipus and Jocasta, a child
ISMENE: daughter of Oedipus and Jocasta, a child
SERVANTS AND ATTENDANTS: of Oedipus and Jocasta

[THE ACTION TAKES PLACE IN THEBES IN FRONT OF THE ROYAL PALACE. THE MAIN DOORS ARE DIRECTLY FACING THE AUDIENCE. THERE ARE ALTARS BESIDE THE DOORS. A CROWD OF CITIZENS CARRYING BRANCHES DECORATED WITH LAUREL GARLANDS AND WOOL AND LED BY THE PRIEST HAS GATHERED IN FRONT OF THE ALTARS, WITH SOME PEOPLE SITTING ON THE ALTAR STEPS. OEDIPUS ENTERS THROUGH THE PALACE DOORS]

OEDIPUS: My children, latest generation born from Cadmus, why are you sitting here with wreathed sticks in supplication to me, while the city fills with incense, chants, and cries of pain? Children, it would not be appropriate for me to learn of this from any other source, so I have come in person—I, Oedipus, whose fame all men acknowledge. But you there, old man, tell me—you seem to be the one who ought to speak for those assembled here. What feeling brings you to me—fear or desire? You can be confident that I will help. I shall assist you willingly in every way. I would be a hard-hearted man indeed, if I did not pity suppliants like these.

PRIEST: Oedipus, ruler of my native land, you see how people here of every age are crouching down around your altars, some fledglings barely strong enough to fly and others bent by age, with priests as well—for I'm priest of Zeus—and these ones here, the pick of all our youth. The other groups sit in the market place with suppliant sticks or else in front of Pallas' two shrines, or where Ismenus prophesies with fire. For our city, as you yourself can see, is badly shaken—she cannot raise her head above the depths of so much surging death. Disease infects fruit blossoms in our land, disease infects our herds of grazing cattle, makes women in labour lose their children. And deadly pestilence, that fiery god, swoops down to blast the city, emptying the House of Cadmus, and fills black Hades with groans and howls. These children and myself now sit here by your home, not because we think you're equal to the gods. No. We judge you the first of men in what happens in this life and in our interactions with the gods. For you came here, to our Cadmeian city, and freed us from the tribute we were paying to that cruel singer—and yet you knew no more than we did and had not been taught. In their stories, the people testify how, with gods' help, you gave us back our lives. So now, Oedipus, our king, most powerful in all men's eyes, we're here as suppliants, all begging you to find some help for us, either by listening to a heavenly voice, or learning from some other human being. For, in my view, men of experience provide advice which gives the best results. So now, you best of men, raise up our state. Act to consolidate your fame, for now, thanks to your eagerness in earlier days, the city celebrates you as its saviour. Don't let our memory of your ruling here declare that we were first set right again, and later fell. No. Restore our city, so that it stands secure. In those times past you brought us joy—and with good omens, too. Be that same man today. If you're to rule as you are doing now, it's better to be king in a land of men than in a desert. An empty ship or city wall is nothing if no men share your life together there.

OEDIPUS: My poor children, I know why you have come—I am not ignorant of what you yearn for. For I well know that you are ill, and yet, sick as you are, there is not one of you whose illness equals mine. Your agony comes to each one of you as his alone, a special pain for him and no one else. But the soul inside me sorrows for myself, and for the city, and for you—all together. You are not rousing me from a deep sleep. You must know I've been shedding many tears and, in my wandering thoughts, exploring many pathways. After a careful search I followed up the one thing I could find and acted on it. So I

have sent away my brother-in-law, son of Menoeceus, Creon, to Pythian Apollo's shrine, to learn from him what I might do or say to save our city. But when I count the days—the time he's been away—I now worry what he's doing. For he's been gone too long, well past the time he should have taken. But when he comes, I'll be a wicked man if I do not act on all the god reveals.

PRIEST: What you have said is most appropriate, for these men here have just informed me that Creon is approaching.

OEDIPUS: Lord Apollo, as he returns, may fine shining fortune, bright as his countenance, attend on him.

PRIEST: It seems the news he brings is good—if not, he would not wear that wreath around his head, a laurel thickly packed with berries.

OEDIPUS: We'll know soon enough—he's within earshot.

[ENTER CREON. OEDIPUS CALLS TO HIM AS HE APPROACHES]

My royal kinsman, child of Menoeceus, what message from the god do you bring us?

CREON: Good news. I tell you even troubles difficult to bear will all end happily if events lead to the right conclusion.

OEDIPUS: What is the oracle? So far your words inspire in me no confidence or fear.

CREON: If you wish to hear the news in public, I'm prepared to speak. Or we could step inside.

OEDIPUS: Speak out to everyone. The grief I feel for these citizens is even greater than any pain I feel for my own life.

CREON: Then let me report what I heard from the god. Lord Phoebus clearly orders us to drive away the polluting stain this land has harboured—which will not be healed if we keep nursing it.

OEDIPUS: What sort of cleansing? And this disaster—how did it happen?

CREON: By banishment—or atone for murder by shedding blood again. This blood brings on the storm which blasts our state.

OEDIPUS: And the one whose fate the god revealed—what sort of man is he?

CREON: Before you came, my lord, to steer our ship of state, Laius ruled this land.

OEDIPUS: I have heard that, but I never saw the man.

CREON: Laius was killed. And now the god is clear: those murderers, he tells us, must be punished, whoever they may be.

OEDIPUS: And where are they? In what country? Where am I to find a trace of this ancient crime? It will be hard to track.

CREON: Here in Thebes, so said the god. What is sought is found, but what is overlooked escapes.

OEDIPUS: When Laius fell in bloody death, where was he—at home, or in his fields, or in another land?

CREON: He was abroad, on his way to Delphi— that's what he told us. He began the trip, but did not return.

OEDIPUS: Was there no messenger—no companion who made the journey with him and witnessed what took place—a person who might provide some knowledge men could use?

CREON: They all died—except for one who was afraid and ran away. There was only one thing he could inform us of with confidence about the things he saw.

OEDIPUS: What was that? We might get somewhere if we had one fact—we could find many things, if we possessed some slender hope to get us going.

CREON: He told us it was robbers who attacked them—not just a single man, a gang of them— they came on with force and killed him.

OEDIPUS: How would a thief have dared to do this, unless he had financial help from Thebes?

CREON: That's what we guessed. But once Laius was dead we were in trouble, so no one sought revenge.

OEDIPUS: When the ruling king had fallen in this way, what bad trouble blocked your path, preventing you from looking into it?

CREON: It was the Sphinx—she sang her enigmatic song and thus forced us to put aside something we found obscure to look into the urgent problem we now faced.

OEDIPUS: Then I will start afresh, and once again shed light on darkness. It is most fitting that Apollo demonstrates his care for the dead man, and worthy of you, too. And so, as is right, you will see how I work with you, seeking vengeance for this land, as well as for the god. This polluting stain I will remove, not for some distant friend, but for myself. For whoever killed this man may soon enough desire to turn his hand in the same way against me, too, and kill me. Thus, in avenging Laius, I serve myself. But now, my children, as quickly as you can stand up from these altar steps and take your suppliant branches. Someone must call the Theban people to assemble here. I'll do everything I can. With the god's help this will all come to light successfully, or else it will prove our common ruin.

[OEDIPUS AND CREON GO INTO THE PALACE]

PRIEST: Let us get up, children. For this man has willingly declared just what we came for. And may Phoebus, who sent this oracle, come as our saviour and end our sickness.

 **For the entire play, insert the Literature CD.**

Questions

1. Many have argued that the second scene is the most important in the entire play. What makes this scene so important to the play and to Oedipus' character?
2. There are many events that lead to the end of Oedipus' reign as king. What are these events, and how and why do they lead to his fall from royalty?
3. Knowing that the Athenian audience already knew the story of Oedipus before watching the play, what is the dramatic irony in Sophocles' version?
4. Teiresias' role is to reveal the "horrible truth." What is the "horrible truth" he reveals to Oedipus, and what makes it horrible?
5. Oedipus' interaction with the Delphic Oracle is important for many reasons. Why is the message that he receives from the Oracle so important?
6. What is Oedipus' view of *chance* (sometimes referred to as "fortune" in the play)? How does this view affect the direction of the play and Oedipus' fate?
7. Whom does Oedipus blame for his sorrows, and why does this character seem fitting to shoulder the blame?

Research and Writing

1. Throughout the play, there is a particular focus on the relationship between Oedipus and the gods. Why are the gods tormenting Oedipus? Take a stand, and make sure to cite support from critical essays to bolster your stance.
2. *Oedipus the King* mirrors the downfalls suffered by many contemporary leaders. Identify two contemporary leaders, i.e. Kenneth Lay (former CEO of Enron) and William Jefferson Clinton (former President of the U.S.A.). First, detail what might be considered their "downfalls"; then, compare and contrast the two contemporary leaders with Oedipus.

Euripides (480–406 BC)

Euripides is often described as one of the greatest tragedians of his time. Not only did his plays have a Sophoclesian effect on audiences, but they helped showcase his ability to portray human feeling.

In *Medea,* one of his many masterpieces, Euripides displays his displeasure with what he believes is a very violent and sadistic Greek society. He does this by advancing the theme that jealousy, being a dominant human feature, always poisons any good that may exist in man. Euripides is able to capture the essence of human suffering, and he is able to do this while in the shadow of so many great playwrights. Although he did not dominate the Great Dionysia tournament like Sophocles, he did win first place six times.

Medea

1. It becomes quite clear that Medea has been wronged by Jason. As you read, notice how the play starts to slowly shift in favor of Medea.
2. Consider the argument that Euripides is trying to advance regarding human suffering.
3. Within drama, the reader can usually notice what is called "the rising action." This is an action that continues to build until it results in a climactic event. Pay close attention to the rising action in this play and Medea's role as part of this rising action.
4. In *Medea,* the protagonist is a female. This was not only a source of controversy but also a nuance that made Euripides revolutionary regarding the portrayal of women in Greek society.

Medea

Euripides

DRAMATIS PERSONAE

NURSE: a servant of Medea
TUTOR: a servant assigned to Jason's children
MEDEA: wife of Jason
CHORUS: a group of Corinthian women
CREON: king of Corinth
JASON: husband of Medea
AEGEUS: king of Athens
MESSENGER
CHILDREN: Medea's and Jason's two young sons
ATTENDANTS: of Creon and Jason

[OUTSIDE THE HOME OF JASON AND MEDEA
IN CORINTH. THE NURSE, A SLAVE WHO SERVES MEDEA,
IS STANDING BY HERSELF]

NURSE: Oh how I wish that ship the Argo had never sailed off to the land of Colchis, past the Symplegades, those dark dancing rocks which smash boats sailing through the Hellespont. I wish they'd never chopped the pine trees down in those mountain forests on Pelion, to make oars for the hands of those great men who set off, on Pelias' orders, to fetch the golden fleece. Then my mistress, Medea, never would've sailed away to the towers in the land of Iolcus, her heart passionately in love with Jason. She'd never have convinced those women, Pelias' daughters, to kill their father. She'd not have come to live in Corinth here, with her husband and her children—well loved in exile by those whose land she'd moved to. She gave all sorts of help to Jason. That's when life is most secure and safe, when woman and her husband stand as one. But that marriage changed. Now they're enemies. Their fine love's grown sick, diseased, for Jason, leaving his own children and my mistress, is lying on a royal wedding bed. He's married the daughter of king Creon, who rules this country. As for Medea, that poor lady, in her disgrace, cries out, repeating his oaths, recalling the great trust in that right hand with which he pledged his love. She calls out to the gods to witness how Jason is repaying her favours. She just lies there. She won't eat—her body she surrenders to the pain, wasting away, always in tears, ever since she discovered how her husband has dishonoured her. She's not lifted her eyes up from the ground, nor raised her head. She listens to advice, even from friends, as if she were a stone, or the ocean swell, except now and then she twists that white neck of hers and weeps, crying to herself for her dear father, her home, her own land, all those things she left behind, to come here with the man who now discards her. Her suffering has taught her the advantages of not being cut off from one's own homeland. Now she hates her children. When she sees them, there is no joy in her. And I'm afraid she may be up to some new mischief. Her mind thinks in extremes. I know her well. She'll not put up with being treated badly. I worry she may pick up a sharp sword and stab her stomach, or else she'll go into the house, in silence, to that bed, and kill the king and bridegroom Jason. Then she'll face an even worse disaster. She's a dangerous woman. It won't be easy for any man who picks a fight with her to think she's beaten and he's triumphed.

[ENTER MEDEA'S AND JASON'S CHILDREN WITH THEIR TUTOR]

Here come her children. They've finished playing. They've no idea of their mother's troubles. Young minds don't like to dwell on pain.

TUTOR: Old slave from my mistress' household, why are you here, standing by the gate, all alone, complaining to yourself about what's wrong? How come Medea is willing to stay inside without you?

NURSE: Old servant of Jason's children, when a master's lot falls out badly, that's bad for faithful servants, too—it touches their hearts also. My sorrow was so great, I wanted to come out here, to speak to earth and heaven, to tell them about the wrongs inflicted on my mistress.

TUTOR: Unhappy lady! Has she stopped weeping yet?

NURSE: Stopped crying? I envy your ignorance. Her suffering has only just begun—she's not even half way through it.

TUTOR: Poor fool—if I can speak that way about my masters—she knows nothing of her latest troubles.

NURSE: What's that, old man? Don't spare me the news.

TUTOR: Nothing. I'm sorry I said anything.

NURSE: Come on, don't hide it from a fellow slave. I can keep quiet if I have to.

TUTOR: Well, I was passing by those benches where the old men gamble by Peirene, at the holy spring, and I heard someone say (I was pretending I wasn't listening) that Creon, king of this country, intends to ship the children away from Corinth, with their mother, too. I've no idea if the story's true or not. I hope it's not.

NURSE: But surely Jason wouldn't let his children go into exile, even if he's squabbling with their mother?

TUTOR: Old devotions fade, pushed aside by some new relationship. Jason is no friend of people in this house.

NURSE: If we must add these brand-new troubles to our old ones, before we've dealt with them, then we're finished.

TUTOR: But listen—the time's not right to let your mistress know about these things. So keep quiet. Don't mention anything.

NURSE: Children, do you hear what sort of man your father is to you? My curse on him . . . No. He is my master—but a bad man to his own family. Of that he's guilty.

TUTOR: What mortal man is not? Don't you know yet all men love themselves more than their neighbours. And some are right to do that—while others just want some benefit. But this father, with his new wife, has no love for his children.

NURSE: Come on, children, get inside the house. Things will be fine. [TO THE TUTOR] You must keep them away—as far as possible—and don't bring them near their mother when she's in this state. I've seen her look at them with savage eyes, as if she means to do something hurtful. I know this anger of hers will not end, not before she vents it on someone. I hope it falls on enemies, not on friends!

MEDEA: [CRYING FROM INSIDE THE HOUSE] I can't stand this pain, this misery. What do I do? I wish I could die.

NURSE: My dear children, you hear your mother's cry. Her heart's upset. Her anger's growing, too. And quickly now, run inside the house. And stay out of sight. Don't try to go and see her. She's fierce, headstrong by nature. Take care. So go now—inside as quickly as you can.

[THE TUTOR AND CHILDREN ENTER THE HOUSE]

It's obvious the cloud of bitter grief rising inside her is only just the start. As her temper grows even more intense, it will soon catch fire. She's a passionate soul, hard to restrain. What will she do next, now her heart's been bitten by these injuries?

MEDEA: [FROM INSIDE THE HOUSE] The pain of this suffering—this intense pain. Am I not right to weep? Oh my children, cursed children of a hateful mother—may you die with your father and all his house, may it all perish, crash into ruins.

NURSE: Oh the sorrow of it all. Poor woman! Why link your children with the nasty things their father's done? Why do you hate them so? I'm terrified the children will be hurt. The pride of rulers is something to fear—they often give orders, but seldom obey. And when their tempers change it's hard to bear. It's better to get used to living life as an equal common person. Anyway, I don't want a grand life for myself—just to grow old with some security. They say a moderate life's the best of all, a far better choice for mortal men. Going for too much brings no benefits. And when gods get angry with some home, the richer it is, the more it is destroyed.

For the entire play, insert the Literature CD.

Questions

1. The nurse and the tutor play key roles in this play. Why are these characters' roles significant?
2. If a play is powerful and aesthetically moving, it must have a pivotal event that shifts the action. When does this happen in *Medea?* Cite lines from the play to advance your contention.
3. The reader can see that Medea's cunning nature is too much for Jason to comprehend. What does this reveal about Medea's motivation?
4. Labeling a single character of this play as the hero is a complicated task. While Jason may be a heroic figure, can it be argued that Medea is as well?
5. Jason's courting of "a real Greek" is significant for several reasons. Why does his new love deserve this term, and why is this important? Why is it significant that Medea's rival ("the real Greek") has no name?
6. Can Medea be compared to any other female literary figures?
7. At the end of the play, where is Medea, and why is this significant?

1. After researching Corinthian women, consider how they may have felt upon viewing *Medea*. Compare and contrast the effect this play might have had on Corinthian women with present-day females. In doing so, examine gender, gender roles, and gender expectations. Further, when researching present-day females and their respective roles and expectations, do not simply restrict your examination to North American females and how they might be affected when viewing *Medea*. Instead, examine females from various cultures and ethnic groups.

2. In one mythological tale, Medea is Achilles' wife. After researching ancient Greece and Achilles, examine this mythic marriage, focusing specifically on their home life, possible occupations, and societal status within the context of *Medea* and *The Iliad*.

3. Compare and contrast Medea's ethical concerns with either Jason's or Creon's.

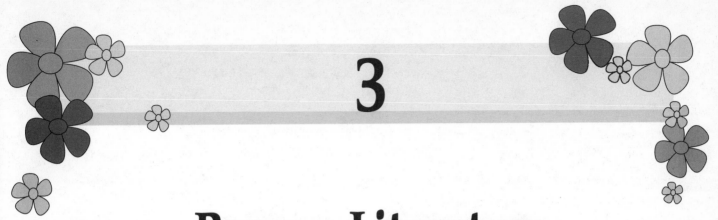

3

Roman Literature
of the "Golden and Silver Age"

JON ST. AMANT

Many of the Romans' ideas on government, philosophy, war, religion, and literature came from the Greeks. However, while many of the Greeks' conventions were spread through the arts and the written word, this was not the case with Roman ideology. As the Roman Empire spread across the western hemisphere, new ideas were born, and fascinating discoveries were made regarding the arts. Consequently, Rome was so self-absorbed with global conquest and the art of war that it did not encourage a great deal literarily. Many of the ideas from the Greeks were spread through their literary works, yet Rome embraced an imperialistic attitude and forced their culture upon the people they conquered. For many Romans, a chief concern was advancing the Roman way of life, and this meant expanding the empire and dedicating themselves to public service. This dedication did not leave much time for sitting down and writing poetic verse or taking in an evening at the theater. This is not to say, however, that Rome did not have an appreciation for the humanities. There are some authors who made an impression on Roman society, and it was their work that helped give the public something else to think about . . . besides who Rome was currently conquering.

Many historians consider the Roman Empire one of the most profound and productive of all time. At the height of its power in the first and second centuries CE, the Roman Empire consisted of approximately 2.5 million square miles. Sixty-million people (or as much as one-fifth of the world's population) claimed citizenship to Rome, and many of its citizens had no choice but to consider themselves Roman. It was widely believed that to claim citizenship to this empire was a great honor, and the government and the people of Rome could not see how someone would not want to be Roman. The paradox lies in the fact that many Romans actually never saw Rome, for it was such a vast empire. However, those who actually entered the gates saw the letters S.P.Q.R. etched into a stone archway that led the way to this hotbed of revolutionary ideas and futuristic thinking. These initials stand for *Senatus Populusque Pomanusqu,* or The Roman Senate and People Acting Together. This Roman motto was fitting for the Empire, for it promoted the idea that the government was, in fact, a representation of its people.

Virgil (70–19 BCE)

Virgil was born on October 15, 70 BCE, in Northern Italy. He was not born in Rome; therefore, he was not born a Roman. He was born in Gaul, but he later became a Roman in 49 BCE after studying mathematics, medicine, and rhetoric for about three years in the capital city. During the reign of Augustus, Virgil became a member of the court and was advanced by Maecenas, a patron of the arts and close friend of Horace. Before Virgil started on *The Aeneid,* he wrote a series of poems known as *Bucolic.* These lyrical works highlighted the beauty of Roman agriculture, and a careful reading will reveal descriptions of the Roman landscape that rival the great Romantic poetry of Blake and Wordsworth.

Composing *The Aeneid* was not one of Virgil's ideas. Some scholars believe that he had no choice but to write this epic poem. After a rise in power, Octavian took the title of Augustus in 27 BCE and wanted a work written that celebrated the glory of Rome. From 30 to 19 BCE, Virgil devoted his life to the writing of *The Aeneid,* and even though it was not finished by the time of his death, it is considered one of the most colorful depictions of the early Roman Empire. About *The Aeneid,* one contemporary poet from the Golden Age, Propertius, once said, "Make way, Greek and Roman writers! Something greater than 'The Iliad' is being born."

The Aeneid is not only a poem of one man's journey but of an entire civilization's search for a new homeland. It tells the story of Aeneas, a Trojan who has fled Troy after it has been sacked by the Greeks. Aeneas and his people find themselves in foreign lands and engage in various struggles until they arrive in Tiber. Here, a significant battle ensues, and the Trojans defeat King Latinus. From the spoils of war, Aeneus marries Latinus' daughter, Lavinia, and the seed of Rome is planted with the founding of Lavinium. Between the fall of Troy and the founding of Lavinium exists an epic tale of one man's struggle, experiences with Gods, and journey to the underworld that leads to the eventual birth of the Roman Empire.

The Aeneid

1. While reading *The Aeneid,* note the conflict between the power of the Gods and the supernatural forces, paying close attention to the roles they play and how they influence the poem.
2. Note the Roman belief in fate and piety, and note how these beliefs help shape Aeneas' character.
3. Obviously, the characters in *The Aeneid* are not aware of their fate; this makes them vulnerable to fear, desire, and surprise. Note how this vulnerability helps create a powerful world of mysticism and historical insight.

The Aeneid

Virgil

THE ARGUMENT.—The Trojans, after a seven years' voyage, set sail for Italy, but are overtaken by a dreadful storm, which Aeolus raises at Juno's request. The tempest sinks one, and scatters the rest. Neptune drives off the Winds, and calms the sea. Aeneas, with his own ship, and six more, arrives safe at an African port. Venus complains to Jupiter of her son's misfortunes. Jupiter comforts her, and sends Mercury to procure him a kind reception among the Carthaginians. Aeneas, going out to discover the country, meets his mother in the shape of an huntress, who conveys him in a cloud to Carthage, where he sees his friends whom he thought lost, and receives a kind entertainment from the queen. Dido, by a device of Venus, begins to have a passion for him, and, after some discourse with him, desires the history of his adventures since the siege of Troy, which is the subject of the two following books.

ARMS, and the man I sing, who, forc'd by fate,
And haughty Juno's unrelenting hate,
Expell'd and exil'd, left the Trojan shore.
Long labors, both by sea and land, he bore,
And in the doubtful war, before he won
The Latian realm, and built the destin'd town;
His banish'd gods restor'd to rites divine,
And settled sure succession in his line,
From whence the race of Alban fathers come,
And the long glories of majestic Rome.
O Muse! the causes and the crimes relate;
What goddess was provok'd, and whence her hate;
For what offense the Queen of Heav'n began
To persecute so brave, so just a man;

Involv'd his anxious life in endless cares,
Expos'd to wants, and hurried into wars!
Can heav'nly minds such high resentment show,
Or exercise their spite in human woe?
Against the Tiber's mouth, but far away,
An ancient town was seated on the sea;
A Tyrian colony; the people made
Stout for the war, and studious of their trade:
Carthage the name; belov'd by Juno more
Than her own Argos, or the Samian shore.
Here stood her chariot; here, if Heav'n were kind,
The seat of awful empire she design'd.
Yet she had heard an ancient rumor fly,
(Long cited by the people of the sky,)
That times to come should see the Trojan race
Her Carthage ruin, and her tow'rs deface;
Nor thus confin'd, the yoke of sov'reign sway
Should on the necks of all the nations lay.
She ponder'd this, and fear'd it was in fate;
Nor could forget the war she wag'd of late
For conqu'ring Greece against the Trojan state.
Besides, long causes working in her mind,
And secret seeds of envy, lay behind;
Deep graven in her heart the doom remain'd
Of partial Paris, and her form disdain'd;
The grace bestow'd on ravish'd Ganymed,
Electra's glories, and her injur'd bed.
Each was a cause alone; and all combin'd
To kindle vengeance in her haughty mind.
For this, far distant from the Latian coast
She drove the remnants of the Trojan host;
And sev'n long years th' unhappy wand'ring train
Were toss'd by storms, and scatter'd thro' the main.
Such time, such toil, requir'd the Roman name,
Such length of labor for so vast a frame.
Now scarce the Trojan fleet, with sails and oars,
Had left behind the fair Sicilian shores,
Ent'ring with cheerful shouts the wat'ry reign,
And plowing frothy furrows in the main;
When, lab'ring still with endless discontent,
The Queen of Heav'n did thus her fury vent:
"Then am I vanquish'd? must I yield?" said she,
"And must the Trojans reign in Italy?
So Fate will have it, and Jove adds his force;
Nor can my pow'r divert their happy course.
Could angry Pallas, with revengeful spleen,
The Grecian navy burn, and drown the men?
She, for the fault of one offending foe,

The bolts of Jove himself presum'd to throw:
With whirlwinds from beneath she toss'd the ship,
And bare expos'd the bosom of the deep;
Then, as an eagle gripes the trembling game,
The wretch, yet hissing with her father's flame,
She strongly seiz'd, and with a burning wound
Transfix'd, and naked, on a rock she bound.
But I, who walk in awful state above,
The majesty of heav'n, the sister wife of Jove,
For length of years my fruitless force employ
Against the thin remains of ruin'd Troy!
What nations now to Juno's pow'r will pray,
Or off'rings on my slighted altars lay?"
Thus rag'd the goddess; and, with fury fraught,
The restless regions of the storms she sought,
Where, in a spacious cave of living stone,
The tyrant Aeolus, from his airy throne,
With pow'r imperial curbs the struggling winds,
And sounding tempests in dark prisons binds.
This way and that th' impatient captives tend,
And, pressing for release, the mountains rend.
High in his hall th' undaunted monarch stands,
And shakes his scepter, and their rage commands;
Which did he not, their unresisted sway
Would sweep the world before them in their way;
Earth, air, and seas thro' empty space would roll,
And heav'n would fly before the driving soul.
In fear of this, the Father of the Gods
Confin'd their fury to those dark abodes,
And lock'd 'em safe within, oppress'd with
  mountain loads;
Impos'd a king, with arbitrary sway,
To loose their fetters, or their force allay.
To whom the suppliant queen her pray'rs address'd,
And thus the tenor of her suit express'd:
"O Aeolus! for to thee the King of Heav'n
The pow'r of tempests and of winds has giv'n;
Thy force alone their fury can restrain,
And smooth the waves, or swell the troubled
  main—
A race of wand'ring slaves, abhorr'd by me,
With prosp'rous passage cut the Tuscan sea;
To fruitful Italy their course they steer,
And for their vanquish'd gods design new temples
  there
Raise all thy winds; with night involve the skies;
Sink or disperse my fatal enemies.
Twice sev'n, the charming daughters of the main,

Around my person wait, and bear my train:
Succeed my wish, and second my design;
The fairest, Deiopeia, shall be thine,
And make thee father of a happy line."
To this the god: "'T is yours, O queen, to will
The work which duty binds me to fulfil.
These airy kingdoms, and this wide command,
Are all the presents of your bounteous hand:
Yours is my sov'reign's grace; and, as your guest,
I sit with gods at their celestial feast;
Raise tempests at your pleasure, or subdue;
Dispose of empire, which I hold from you."
He said, and hurl'd against the mountain side
His quiv'ring spear, and all the god applied.
The raging winds rush thro' the hollow wound,
And dance aloft in air, and skim along the ground;
Then, settling on the sea, the surges sweep,
Raise liquid mountains, and disclose the deep.
South, East, and West with mix'd confusion roar,
And roll the foaming billows to the shore.
The cables crack; the sailors' fearful cries
Ascend; and sable night involves the skies;
And heav'n itself is ravish'd from their eyes.
Loud peals of thunder from the poles ensue;
Then flashing fires the transient light renew;
The face of things a frightful image bears,
And present death in various forms appears.
Struck with unusual fright, the Trojan chief,
With lifted hands and eyes, invokes relief;
And, "Thrice and four times happy those," he cried,
"That under Ilian walls before their parents died!
Tydides, bravest of the Grecian train!
Why could not I by that strong arm be slain,
And lie by noble Hector on the plain,
Or great Sarpedon, in those bloody fields
Where Simois rolls the bodies and the shields
Of heroes, whose dismember'd hands yet bear
The dart aloft, and clench the pointed spear!"
Thus while the pious prince his fate bewails,
Fierce Boreas drove against his flying sails,
And rent the sheets; the raging billows rise,
And mount the tossing vessel to the skies:
Nor can the shiv'ring oars sustain the blow;
The galley gives her side, and turns her prow;
While those astern, descending down the steep,
Thro' gaping waves behold the boiling deep.
Three ships were hurried by the southern blast,
And on the secret shelves with fury cast.

Those hidden rocks th' Ausonian sailors knew:
They call'd them Altars, when they rose in view,
And show'd their spacious backs above the flood.
Three more fierce Eurus, in his angry mood,
Dash'd on the shallows of the moving sand,
And in mid ocean left them moor'd aland.
Orontes' bark, that bore the Lycian crew,
(A horrid sight!) ev'n in the hero's view,
From stem to stern by waves was overborne:
The trembling pilot, from his rudder torn,
Was headlong hurl'd; thrice round the ship was
        toss'd,
Then bulg'd at once, and in the deep was lost;
And here and there above the waves were seen
Arms, pictures, precious goods, and floating men.
The stoutest vessel to the storm gave way,
And suck'd thro' loosen'd planks the rushing sea.
Ilioneus was her chief: Alethes old,
Achates faithful, Abas young and bold,
Endur'd not less; their ships, with gaping seams,
Admit the deluge of the briny streams.
Meantime imperial Neptune heard the sound
Of raging billows breaking on the ground.
Displeas'd, and fearing for his wat'ry reign,
He rear'd his awful head above the main,
Serene in majesty; then roll'd his eyes
Around the space of earth, and seas, and skies.
He saw the Trojan fleet dispers'd, distress'd,
By stormy winds and wintry heav'n oppress'd.
Full well the god his sister's envy knew,
And what her aims and what her arts pursue.
He summon'd Eurus and the western blast,
And first an angry glance on both he cast;
Then thus rebuk'd: "Audacious winds! from whence
This bold attempt, this rebel insolence?
Is it for you to ravage seas and land,
Unauthoriz'd by my supreme command?
To raise such mountains on the troubled main?
Whom I—but first 't is fit the billows to restrain;
And then you shall be taught obedience to my reign.
Hence! to your lord my royal mandate bear—
The realms of ocean and the fields of air
Are mine, not his. By fatal lot to me
The liquid empire fell, and trident of the sea.
His pow'r to hollow caverns is confin'd:
There let him reign, the jailer of the wind,
With hoarse commands his breathing subjects call,
And boast and bluster in his empty hall."

He spoke; and, while he spoke, he smooth'd the sea,
Dispell'd the darkness, and restor'd the day.
Cymothoe, Triton, and the sea-green train
Of beauteous nymphs, the daughters of the main,
Clear from the rocks the vessels with their hands:
The god himself with ready trident stands,
And opes the deep, and spreads the moving sands;
Then heaves them off the shoals. Where'er he
   guides
His finny coursers and in triumph rides,
The waves unruffle and the sea subsides.
As, when in tumults rise th' ignoble crowd,
Mad are their motions, and their tongues are loud;
And stones and brands in rattling volleys fly,
And all the rustic arms that fury can supply:
If then some grave and pious man appear,
They hush their noise, and lend a list'ning ear;
He soothes with sober words their angry mood,
And quenches their innate desire of blood:
So, when the Father of the Flood appears,
And o'er the seas his sov'reign trident rears,
Their fury falls: he skims the liquid plains,
High on his chariot, and, with loosen'd reins,
Majestic moves along, and awful peace maintains.
The weary Trojans ply their shatter'd oars
To nearest land, and make the Libyan shores.
Within a long recess there lies a bay:
An island shades it from the rolling sea,
And forms a port secure for ships to ride;
Broke by the jutting land, on either side,
In double streams the briny waters glide.
Betwixt two rows of rocks a sylvan scene
Appears above, and groves for ever green:
A grot is form'd beneath, with mossy seats,
To rest the Nereids, and exclude the heats.
Down thro' the crannies of the living walls
The crystal streams descend in murm'ring falls:
No haulsers need to bind the vessels here,
Nor bearded anchors; for no storms they fear.
Sev'n ships within this happy harbor meet,
The thin remainders of the scatter'd fleet.
The Trojans, worn with toils, and spent with woes,
Leap on the welcome land, and seek their wish'd
   repose.
First, good Achates, with repeated strokes
Of clashing flints, their hidden fire provokes:
Short flame succeeds; a bed of wither'd leaves
The dying sparkles in their fall receives:

Caught into life, in fiery fumes they rise,
And, fed with stronger food, invade the skies.
The Trojans, dropping wet, or stand around
The cheerful blaze, or lie along the ground:
Some dry their corn, infected with the brine,
Then grind with marbles, and prepare to dine.
Aeneas climbs the mountain's airy brow,
And takes a prospect of the seas below,
If Capys thence, or Antheus he could spy,
Or see the streamers of Caicus fly.
No vessels were in view; but, on the plain,
Three beamy stags command a lordly train
Of branching heads: the more ignoble throng
Attend their stately steps, and slowly graze along.
He stood; and, while secure they fed below,
He took the quiver and the trusty bow
Achates us'd to bear: the leaders first
He laid along, and then the vulgar pierc'd;
Nor ceas'd his arrows, till the shady plain
Sev'n mighty bodies with their blood distain.
For the sev'n ships he made an equal share,
And to the port return'd, triumphant from the war.
The jars of gen'rous wine (Acestes' gift,
When his Trinacrian shores the navy left)
He set abroach, and for the feast prepar'd,
In equal portions with the ven'son shar'd.
Thus while he dealt it round, the pious chief
With cheerful words allay'd the common grief:
"Endure, and conquer! Jove will soon dispose
To future good our past and present woes.
With me, the rocks of Scylla you have tried;
Th' inhuman Cyclops and his den defied.
What greater ills hereafter can you bear?
Resume your courage and dismiss your care,
An hour will come, with pleasure to relate
Your sorrows past, as benefits of Fate.
Thro' various hazards and events, we move
To Latium and the realms foredoom'd by Jove.
Call'd to the seat (the promise of the skies)
Where Trojan kingdoms once again may rise,
Endure the hardships of your present state;
Live, and reserve yourselves for better fate."
These words he spoke, but spoke not from his heart;
His outward smiles conceal'd his inward smart.
The jolly crew, unmindful of the past,
The quarry share, their plenteous dinner haste.
Some strip the skin; some portion out the spoil;
The limbs, yet trembling, in the caldrons boil;

Some on the fire the reeking entrails broil.
Stretch'd on the grassy turf, at ease they dine,
Restore their strength with meat, and cheer their
    souls with wine.
Their hunger thus appeas'd, their care attends
The doubtful fortune of their absent friends:
Alternate hopes and fears their minds possess,
Whether to deem 'em dead, or in distress.
Above the rest, Aeneas mourns the fate
Of brave Orontes, and th' uncertain state
Of Gyas, Lycus, and of Amycus.
The day, but not their sorrows, ended thus.
When, from aloft, almighty Jove surveys
Earth, air, and shores, and navigable seas,
At length on Libyan realms he fix'd his eyes—
Whom, pond'ring thus on human miseries,
When Venus saw, she with a lowly look,
Not free from tears, her heav'nly sire bespoke:
"O King of Gods and Men! whose awful hand
Disperses thunder on the seas and land,
Disposing all with absolute command;
How could my pious son thy pow'r incense?
Or what, alas! is vanish'd Troy's offense?
Our hope of Italy not only lost,
On various seas by various tempests toss'd,
But shut from ev'ry shore, and barr'd from ev'ry
    coast.
You promis'd once, a progeny divine
Of Romans, rising from the Trojan line,
In after times should hold the world in awe,
And to the land and ocean give the law.
How is your doom revers'd, which eas'd my care
When Troy was ruin'd in that cruel war?
Then fates to fates I could oppose; but now,
When Fortune still pursues her former blow,
What can I hope? What worse can still succeed?
What end of labors has your will decreed?
Antenor, from the midst of Grecian hosts,
Could pass secure, and pierce th' Illyrian coasts,
Where, rolling down the steep, Timavus raves
And thro' nine channels disembogues his waves.
At length he founded Padua's happy seat,
And gave his Trojans a secure retreat;
There fix'd their arms, and there renew'd their
    name,
And there in quiet rules, and crown'd with fame.
But we, descended from your sacred line,
Entitled to your heav'n and rites divine,

Are banish'd earth; and, for the wrath of one,
Remov'd from Latium and the promis'd throne.
Are these our scepters? these our due rewards?
And is it thus that Jove his plighted faith regards?"
To whom the Father of th' immortal race,
Smiling with that serene indulgent face,
With which he drives the clouds and clears the
    skies,
First gave a holy kiss; then thus replies:
"Daughter, dismiss thy fears; to thy desire
The fates of thine are fix'd, and stand entire.
Thou shalt behold thy wish'd Lavinian walls;
And, ripe for heav'n, when fate Aeneas calls,
Then shalt thou bear him up, sublime, to me:
No councils have revers'd my firm decree.
And, lest new fears disturb thy happy state,
Know, I have search'd the mystic rolls of Fate:
Thy son (nor is th' appointed season far)
In Italy shall wage successful war,
Shall tame fierce nations in the bloody field,
And sov'reign laws impose, and cities build,
Till, after ev'ry foe subdued, the sun
Thrice thro' the signs his annual race shall run:
This is his time prefix'd. Ascanius then,
Now call'd Iulus, shall begin his reign.
He thirty rolling years the crown shall wear,
Then from Lavinium shall the seat transfer,
And, with hard labor, Alba Longa build.
The throne with his succession shall be fill'd
Three hundred circuits more: then shall be seen
Ilia the fair, a priestess and a queen,
Who, full of Mars, in time, with kindly throes,
Shall at a birth two goodly boys disclose.
The royal babes a tawny wolf shall drain:
Then Romulus his grandsire's throne shall gain,
Of martial tow'rs the founder shall become,
The people Romans call, the city Rome.
To them no bounds of empire I assign,
Nor term of years to their immortal line.
Ev'n haughty Juno, who, with endless broils,
Earth, seas, and heav'n, and Jove himself turmoils;
At length aton'd, her friendly pow'r shall join,
To cherish and advance the Trojan line.
The subject world shall Rome's dominion own,
And, prostrate, shall adore the nation of the gown.
An age is ripening in revolving fate
When Troy shall overturn the Grecian state,
And sweet revenge her conqu'ring sons shall call,

To crush the people that conspir'd her fall.
Then Caesar from the Julian stock shall rise,
Whose empire ocean, and whose fame the skies
Alone shall bound; whom, fraught with eastern
    spoils,
Our heav'n, the just reward of human toils,
Securely shall repay with rites divine;
And incense shall ascend before his sacred shrine.
Then dire debate and impious war shall cease,
And the stern age be soften'd into peace:
Then banish'd Faith shall once again return,
And Vestal fires in hallow'd temples burn;
And Remus with Quirinus shall sustain
The righteous laws, and fraud and force restrain.
Janus himself before his fane shall wait,
And keep the dreadful issues of his gate,
With bolts and iron bars: within remains
Imprison'd Fury, bound in brazen chains;
High on a trophy rais'd, of useless arms,
He sits, and threats the world with vain alarms."
He said, and sent Cyllenius with command
To free the ports, and ope the Punic land
To Trojan guests; lest, ignorant of fate,
The queen might force them from her town and
    state.
Down from the steep of heav'n Cyllenius flies,
And cleaves with all his wings the yielding skies.
Soon on the Libyan shore descends the god,
Performs his message, and displays his rod:
The surly murmurs of the people cease;
And, as the fates requir'd, they give the peace:
The queen herself suspends the rigid laws,
The Trojans pities, and protects their cause.
Meantime, in shades of night Aeneas lies:
Care seiz'd his soul, and sleep forsook his eyes.
But, when the sun restor'd the cheerful day,
He rose, the coast and country to survey,
Anxious and eager to discover more.
It look'd a wild uncultivated shore;
But, whether humankind, or beasts alone
Possess'd the new-found region, was unknown.
Beneath a ledge of rocks his fleet he hides:
Tall trees surround the mountain's shady sides;
The bending brow above a safe retreat provides.
Arm'd with two pointed darts, he leaves his friends,
And true Achates on his steps attends.
Lo! in the deep recesses of the wood,
Before his eyes his goddess mother stood:

A huntress in her habit and her mien;
Her dress a maid, her air confess'd a queen.
Bare were her knees, and knots her garments bind;
Loose was her hair, and wanton'd in the wind;
Her hand sustain'd a bow; her quiver hung behind.
She seem'd a virgin of the Spartan blood:
With such array Harpalyce bestrode
Her Thracian courser and outstripp'd the rapid
    flood.
"Ho, strangers! have you lately seen," she said,
"One of my sisters, like myself array'd,
Who cross'd the lawn, or in the forest stray'd?
A painted quiver at her back she bore;
Varied with spots, a lynx's hide she wore;
And at full cry pursued the tusky boar."
Thus Venus: thus her son replied again:
"None of your sisters have we heard or seen,
O virgin! or what other name you bear
Above that style—O more than mortal fair!
Your voice and mien celestial birth betray!
If, as you seem, the sister of the day,
Or one at least of chaste Diana's train,
Let not an humble suppliant sue in vain;
But tell a stranger, long in tempests toss'd,
What earth we tread, and who commands the coast?
Then on your name shall wretched mortals call,
And offer'd victims at your altars fall."
"I dare not," she replied, "assume the name
Of goddess, or celestial honors claim:
For Tyrian virgins bows and quivers bear,
And purple buskins o'er their ankles wear.
Know, gentle youth, in Libyan lands you are—
A people rude in peace, and rough in war.
The rising city, which from far you see,
Is Carthage, and a Tyrian colony.
Phoenician Dido rules the growing state,
Who fled from Tyre, to shun her brother's hate.
Great were her wrongs, her story full of fate;
Which I will sum in short. Sichaeus, known
For wealth, and brother to the Punic throne,
Possess'd fair Dido's bed; and either heart
At once was wounded with an equal dart.
Her father gave her, yet a spotless maid;
Pygmalion then the Tyrian scepter sway'd:
One who contemn'd divine and human laws.
Then strife ensued, and cursed gold the cause.
The monarch, blinded with desire of wealth,
With steel invades his brother's life by stealth;

Before the sacred altar made him bleed,
And long from her conceal'd the cruel deed.
Some tale, some new pretense, he daily coin'd,
To soothe his sister, and delude her mind.
At length, in dead of night, the ghost appears
Of her unhappy lord: the specter stares,
And, with erected eyes, his bloody bosom bares.
The cruel altars and his fate he tells,
And the dire secret of his house reveals,
Then warns the widow, with her household gods,
To seek a refuge in remote abodes.
Last, to support her in so long a way,
He shows her where his hidden treasure lay.
Admonish'd thus, and seiz'd with mortal fright,
The queen provides companions of her flight:
They meet, and all combine to leave the state,
Who hate the tyrant, or who fear his hate.
They seize a fleet, which ready rigg'd they find;
Nor is Pygmalion's treasure left behind.
The vessels, heavy laden, put to sea
With prosp'rous winds; a woman leads the way.
I know not, if by stress of weather driv'n,
Or was their fatal course dispos'd by Heav'n;
At last they landed, where from far your eyes
May view the turrets of new Carthage rise;
There bought a space of ground, which (Byrsa
   call'd,
From the bull's hide) they first inclos'd, and wall'd.
But whence are you? what country claims your
   birth?
What seek you, strangers, on our Libyan earth?"
To whom, with sorrow streaming from his eyes,
And deeply sighing, thus her son replies:
"Could you with patience hear, or I relate,
O nymph, the tedious annals of our fate!
Thro' such a train of woes if I should run,
The day would sooner than the tale be done!
From ancient Troy, by force expell'd, we came—
If you by chance have heard the Trojan name.
On various seas by various tempests toss'd,
At length we landed on your Libyan coast.
The good Aeneas am I call'd—a name,
While Fortune favor'd, not unknown to fame.
My household gods, companions of my woes,
With pious care I rescued from our foes.
To fruitful Italy my course was bent;
And from the King of Heav'n is my descent.
With twice ten sail I cross'd the Phrygian sea;

Fate and my mother goddess led my way.
Scarce sev'n, the thin remainders of my fleet,
From storms preserv'd, within your harbor meet.
Myself distress'd, an exile, and unknown,
Debarr'd from Europe, and from Asia thrown,
In Libyan deserts wander thus alone."
His tender parent could no longer bear;
But, interposing, sought to soothe his care.
"Whoe'er you are—not unbelov'd by Heav'n,
Since on our friendly shore your ships are driv'n—
Have courage: to the gods permit the rest,
And to the queen expose your just request.
Now take this earnest of success, for more:
Your scatter'd fleet is join'd upon the shore;
The winds are chang'd, your friends from danger
   free;
Or I renounce my skill in augury.
Twelve swans behold in beauteous order move,
And stoop with closing pinions from above;
Whom late the bird of Jove had driv'n along,
And thro' the clouds pursued the scatt'ring throng:
Now, all united in a goodly team,
They skim the ground, and seek the quiet stream.
As they, with joy returning, clap their wings,
And ride the circuit of the skies in rings;
Not otherwise your ships, and ev'ry friend,
Already hold the port, or with swift sails descend.
No more advice is needful; but pursue
The path before you, and the town in view."
Thus having said, she turn'd, and made appear
Her neck refulgent, and dishevel'd hair,
Which, flowing from her shoulders, reach'd the
   ground.
And widely spread ambrosial scents around:
In length of train descends her sweeping gown;
And, by her graceful walk, the Queen of Love is
   known.
The prince pursued the parting deity
With words like these: "Ah! whither do you fly?
Unkind and cruel! to deceive your son
In borrow'd shapes, and his embrace to shun;
Never to bless my sight, but thus unknown;
And still to speak in accents not your own."
Against the goddess these complaints he made,
But took the path, and her commands obey'd.
They march, obscure; for Venus kindly shrouds
With mists their persons, and involves in clouds,
That, thus unseen, their passage none might stay,

Or force to tell the causes of their way.
This part perform'd, the goddess flies sublime
To visit Paphos and her native clime;
Where garlands, ever green and ever fair,
With vows are offer'd, and with solemn pray'r:
A hundred altars in her temple smoke;
A thousand bleeding hearts her pow'r invoke.
They climb the next ascent, and, looking down,
Now at a nearer distance view the town.
The prince with wonder sees the stately tow'rs,
Which late were huts and shepherds' homely
    bow'rs,
The gates and streets; and hears, from ev'ry part,
The noise and busy concourse of the mart.
The toiling Tyrians on each other call
To ply their labor: some extend the wall;
Some build the citadel; the brawny throng
Or dig, or push unwieldly stones along.
Some for their dwellings choose a spot of ground,
Which, first design'd, with ditches they surround.
Some laws ordain; and some attend the choice
Of holy senates, and elect by voice.
Here some design a mole, while others there
Lay deep foundations for a theater;
From marble quarries mighty columns hew,
For ornaments of scenes, and future view.
Such is their toil, and such their busy pains,
As exercise the bees in flow'ry plains,
When winter past, and summer scarce begun,
Invites them forth to labor in the sun;
Some lead their youth abroad, while some condense
Their liquid store, and some in cells dispense;
Some at the gate stand ready to receive
The golden burthen, and their friends relieve;
All with united force, combine to drive
The lazy drones from the laborious hive:
With envy stung, they view each other's deeds;
The fragrant work with diligence proceeds.
"Thrice happy you, whose walls already rise!"
Aeneas said, and view'd, with lifted eyes,
Their lofty tow'rs; then, ent'ring at the gate,
Conceal'd in clouds (prodigious to relate)
He mix'd, unmark'd, among the busy throng,
Borne by the tide, and pass'd unseen along.
Full in the center of the town there stood,
Thick set with trees, a venerable wood.
The Tyrians, landing near this holy ground,
And digging here, a prosp'rous omen found:

From under earth a courser's head they drew,
Their growth and future fortune to foreshew.
This fated sign their foundress Juno gave,
Of a soil fruitful, and a people brave.
Sidonian Dido here with solemn state
Did Juno's temple build, and consecrate,
Enrich'd with gifts, and with a golden shrine;
But more the goddess made the place divine.
On brazen steps the marble threshold rose,
And brazen plates the cedar beams inclose:
The rafters are with brazen cov'rings crown'd;
The lofty doors on brazen hinges sound.
What first Aeneas in this place beheld,
Reviv'd his courage, and his fear expell'd.
For while, expecting there the queen, he rais'd
His wond'ring eyes, and round the temple gaz'd,
Admir'd the fortune of the rising town,
The striving artists, and their arts' renown;
He saw, in order painted on the wall,
Whatever did unhappy Troy befall:
The wars that fame around the world had blown,
All to the life, and ev'ry leader known.
There Agamemnon, Priam here, he spies,
And fierce Achilles, who both kings defies.
He stopp'd, and weeping said: "O friend! ev'n here
The monuments of Trojan woes appear!
Our known disasters fill ev'n foreign lands:
See there, where old unhappy Priam stands!
Ev'n the mute walls relate the warrior's fame,
And Trojan griefs the Tyrians' pity claim."
He said (his tears a ready passage find),
Devouring what he saw so well design'd,
And with an empty picture fed his mind:
For there he saw the fainting Grecians yield,
And here the trembling Trojans quit the field,
Pursued by fierce Achilles thro' the plain,
On his high chariot driving o'er the slain.
The tents of Rhesus next his grief renew,
By their white sails betray'd to nightly view;
And wakeful Diomede, whose cruel sword
The sentries slew, nor spar'd their slumb'ring lord,
Then took the fiery steeds, ere yet the food
Of Troy they taste, or drink the Xanthian flood.
Elsewhere he saw where Troilus defied
Achilles, and unequal combat tried;
Then, where the boy disarm'd, with loosen'd reins,
Was by his horses hurried o'er the plains,
Hung by the neck and hair, and dragg'd around:

The hostile spear, yet sticking in his wound,
With tracks of blood inscrib'd the dusty ground.
Meantime the Trojan dames, oppress'd with woe,
To Pallas' fane in long procession go,
In hopes to reconcile their heav'nly foe.
They weep, they beat their breasts, they rend their
	hair,
And rich embroider'd vests for presents bear;
But the stern goddess stands unmov'd with pray'r.
Thrice round the Trojan walls Achilles drew
The corpse of Hector, whom in fight he slew.
Here Priam sues; and there, for sums of gold,
The lifeless body of his son is sold.
So sad an object, and so well express'd,
Drew sighs and groans from the griev'd hero's
	breast,
To see the figure of his lifeless friend,
And his old sire his helpless hand extend.
Himself he saw amidst the Grecian train,
Mix'd in the bloody battle on the plain;
And swarthy Memnon in his arms he knew,
His pompous ensigns, and his Indian crew.
Penthisilea there, with haughty grace,
Leads to the wars an Amazonian race.
In their right hands a pointed dart they wield;
The left, forward, sustains the lunar shield.
Athwart her breast a golden belt she throws,
Amidst the press alone provokes a thousand foes,
And dares her maiden arms to manly force oppose.
Thus while the Trojan prince employs his eyes,
Fix'd on the walls with wonder and surprise,
The beauteous Dido, with a num'rous train
And pomp of guards, ascends the sacred fane.
Such on Eurotas' banks, or Cynthus' height,
Diana seems; and so she charms the sight,
When in the dance the graceful goddess leads
The choir of nymphs, and overtops their heads:
Known by her quiver, and her lofty mien,
She walks majestic, and she looks their queen;
Latona sees her shine above the rest,
And feeds with secret joy her silent breast.
Such Dido was; with such becoming state,
Amidst the crowd, she walks serenely great.
Their labor to her future sway she speeds,
And passing with a gracious glance proceeds;
Then mounts the throne, high plac'd before the
	shrine:
In crowds around, the swarming people join.

She takes petitions, and dispenses laws,
Hears and determines ev'ry private cause;
Their tasks in equal portions she divides,
And, where unequal, there by lots decides.
Another way by chance Æneas bends
His eyes, and unexpected sees his friends,
Antheus, Sergestus grave, Cloanthus strong,
And at their backs a mighty Trojan throng,
Whom late the tempest on the billows toss'd,
And widely scatter'd on another coast.
The prince, unseen, surpris'd with wonder stands,
And longs, with joyful haste, to join their hands;
But, doubtful of the wish'd event, he stays,
And from the hollow cloud his friends surveys,
Impatient till they told their present state,
And where they left their ships, and what their fate,
And why they came, and what was their request;
For these were sent, commission'd by the rest,
To sue for leave to land their sickly men,
And gain admission to the gracious queen.
Ent'ring, with cries they fill'd the holy fane;
Then thus, with lowly voice, Ilioneus began:
"O queen! indulg'd by favor of the gods
To found an empire in these new abodes,
To build a town, with statutes to restrain
The wild inhabitants beneath thy reign,
We wretched Trojans, toss'd on ev'ry shore,
From sea to sea, thy clemency implore.
Forbid the fires our shipping to deface!
Receive th' unhappy fugitives to grace,
And spare the remnant of a pious race!
We come not with design of wasteful prey,
To drive the country, force the swains away:
Nor such our strength, nor such is our desire;
The vanquish'd dare not to such thoughts aspire.
A land there is, Hesperia nam'd of old;
The soil is fruitful, and the men are bold—
Th' Œnotrians held it once—by common fame
Now call'd Italia, from the leader's name.
To that sweet region was our voyage bent,
When winds and ev'ry warring element
Disturb'd our course, and, far from sight of land,
Cast our torn vessels on the moving sand:
The sea came on; the South, with mighty roar,
Dispers'd and dash'd the rest upon the rocky shore.
Those few you see escap'd the storm, and fear,
Unless you interpose, a shipwreck here.
What men, what monsters, what inhuman race,

What laws, what barb'rous customs of the place,
Shut up a desart shore to drowning men,
And drive us to the cruel seas again?
If our hard fortune no compassion draws,
Nor hospitable rights, nor human laws,
The gods are just, and will revenge our cause.
Æneas was our prince: a juster lord,
Or nobler warrior, never drew a sword;
Observant of the right, religious of his word.
If yet he lives, and draws this vital air,
Nor we, his friends, of safety shall despair;
Nor you, great queen, these offices repent,
Which he will equal, and perhaps augment.
We want not cities, nor Sicilian coasts,
Where King Acestes Trojan lineage boasts.
Permit our ships a shelter on your shores,
Refitted from your woods with planks and oars,
That, if our prince be safe, we may renew
Our destin'd course, and Italy pursue.
But if, O best of men, the Fates ordain
That thou art swallow'd in the Libyan main,
And if our young Iulus be no more,
Dismiss our navy from your friendly shore,
That we to good Acestes may return,
And with our friends our common losses mourn."
Thus spoke Ilioneus: the Trojan crew
With cries and clamors his request renew.
The modest queen a while, with downcast eyes,
Ponder'd the speech; then briefly thus replies:
"Trojans, dismiss your fears; my cruel fate,
And doubts attending an unsettled state,
Force me to guard my coast from foreign foes.
Who has not heard the story of your woes,
The name and fortune of your native place,
The fame and valor of the Phrygian race?
We Tyrians are not so devoid of sense,
Nor so remote from Phoebus' influence.
Whether to Latian shores your course is bent,
Or, driv'n by tempests from your first intent,
You seek the good Acestes' government,
Your men shall be receiv'd, your fleet repair'd,
And sail, with ships of convoy for your guard:
Or, would you stay, and join your friendly pow'rs
To raise and to defend the Tyrian tow'rs,
My wealth, my city, and myself are yours.
And would to Heav'n, the storm, you felt, would
    bring
On Carthaginian coasts your wand'ring king.

My people shall, by my command, explore
The ports and creeks of ev'ry winding shore,
And towns, and wilds, and shady woods, in quest
Of so renown'd and so desir'd a guest."
Rais'd in his mind the Trojan hero stood,
And long'd to break from out his ambient cloud:
Achates found it, and thus urg'd his way:
"From whence, O goddess-born, this long delay?
What more can you desire, your welcome sure,
Your fleet in safety, and your friends secure?
One only wants; and him we saw in vain
Oppose the storm, and swallow'd in the main.
Orontes in his fate our forfeit paid;
The rest agrees with what your mother said."
Scarce had be spoken, when the cloud gave way,
The mists flew upward and dissolv'd in day.
The Trojan chief appear'd in open sight,
August in visage, and serenely bright.
His mother goddess, with her hands divine,
Had form'd his curling locks, and made his temples
    shine,
And giv'n his rolling eyes a sparkling grace,
And breath'd a youthful vigor on his face;
Like polish'd iv'ry, beauteous to behold,
Or Parian marble, when enchas'd in gold:
Thus radiant from the circling cloud he broke,
And thus with manly modesty he spoke:
"He whom you seek am I; by tempests toss'd,
And sav'd from shipwreck on your Libyan coast;
Presenting, gracious queen, before your throne,
A prince that owes his life to you alone.
Fair majesty, the refuge and redress
Of those whom fate pursues, and wants oppress,
You, who your pious offices employ
To save the relics of abandon'd Troy;
Receive the shipwreck'd on your friendly shore,
With hospitable rites relieve the poor;
Associate in your town a wand'ring train,
And strangers in your palace entertain:
What thanks can wretched fugitives return,
Who, scatter'd thro' the world, in exile mourn?
The gods, if gods to goodness are inclin'd;
If acts of mercy touch their heav'nly mind,
And, more than all the gods, your gen'rous heart,
Conscious of worth, requite its own desert!
In you this age is happy, and this earth,
And parents more than mortal gave you birth.
While rolling rivers into seas shall run,

And round the space of heav'n the radiant sun;
While trees the mountain tops with shades supply,
Your honor, name, and praise shall never die.
Whate'er abode my fortune has assign'd,
Your image shall be present in my mind."
Thus having said, he turn'd with pious haste,
And joyful his expecting friends embrac'd:
With his right hand Ilioneus was grac'd,
Serestus with his left; then to his breast
Cloanthus and the noble Gyas press'd;
And so by turns descended to the rest.
The Tyrian queen stood fix'd upon his face,
Pleas'd with his motions, ravish'd with his grace;
Admir'd his fortunes, more admir'd the man;
Then recollected stood, and thus began:
"What fate, O goddess-born; what angry pow'rs
Have cast you shipwreck'd on our barren shores?
Are you the great Æneas, known to fame,
Who from celestial seed your lineage claim?
The same Æneas whom fair Venus bore
To fam'd Anchises on th' Idaean shore?
It calls into my mind, tho' then a child,
When Teucer came, from Salamis exil'd,
And sought my father's aid, to be restor'd:
My father Belus then with fire and sword
Invaded Cyprus, made the region bare,
And, conqu'ring, finish'd the successful war.
From him the Trojan siege I understood,
The Grecian chiefs, and your illustrious blood.
Your foe himself the Dardan valor prais'd,
And his own ancestry from Trojans rais'd.
Enter, my noble guest, and you shall find,
If not a costly welcome, yet a kind:
For I myself, like you, have been distress'd,
Till Heav'n afforded me this place of rest;
Like you, an alien in a land unknown,
I learn to pity woes so like my own."
She said, and to the palace led her guest;
Then offer'd incense, and proclaim'd a feast.
Nor yet less careful for her absent friends,
Twice ten fat oxen to the ships she sends;
Besides a hundred boars, a hundred lambs,
With bleating cries, attend their milky dams;
And jars of gen'rous wine and spacious bowls
She gives, to cheer the sailors' drooping souls.
Now purple hangings clothe the palace walls,
And sumptuous feasts are made in splendid halls:
On Tyrian carpets, richly wrought, they dine;
With loads of massy plate the sideboards shine,

And antique vases, all of gold emboss'd
(The gold itself inferior to the cost),
Of curious work, where on the sides were seen
The fights and figures of illustrious men,
From their first founder to the present queen.
The good Æneas, whose paternal care
Iulus' absence could no longer bear,
Dispatch'd Achates to the ships in haste,
To give a glad relation of the past,
And, fraught with precious gifts, to bring the boy,
Snatch'd from the ruins of unhappy Troy:
A robe of tissue, stiff with golden wire;
An upper vest, once Helen's rich attire,
From Argos by the fam'd adultress brought,
With golden flow'rs and winding foliage wrought,
Her mother Leda's present, when she came
To ruin Troy and set the world on flame;
The scepter Priam's eldest daughter bore,
Her orient necklace, and the crown she wore;
Of double texture, glorious to behold,
One order set with gems, and one with gold.
Instructed thus, the wise Achates goes,
And in his diligence his duty shows.
But Venus, anxious for her son's affairs,
New counsels tries, and new designs prepares:
That Cupid should assume the shape and face
Of sweet Ascanius, and the sprightly grace;
Should bring the presents, in her nephew's stead,
And in Eliza's veins the gentle poison shed:
For much she fear'd the Tyrians, double-tongued,
And knew the town to Juno's care belong'd.
These thoughts by night her golden slumbers broke,
And thus alarm'd, to winged Love she spoke:
"My son, my strength, whose mighty pow'r alone
Controls the Thund'rer on his awful throne,
To thee thy much-afflicted mother flies,
And on thy succor and thy faith relies.
Thou know'st, my son, how Jove's revengeful wife,
By force and fraud, attempts thy brother's life;
And often hast thou mourn'd with me his pains.
Him Dido now with blandishment detains;
But I suspect the town where Juno reigns.
For this 't is needful to prevent her art,
And fire with love the proud Phoenician's heart:
A love so violent, so strong, so sure,
As neither age can change, nor art can cure.
How this may be perform'd, now take my mind:
Ascanius by his father is design'd
To come, with presents laden, from the port,

To gratify the queen, and gain the court.
I mean to plunge the boy in pleasing sleep,
And, ravish'd, in Idalian bow'rs to keep,
Or high Cythera, that the sweet deceit
May pass unseen, and none prevent the cheat.
Take thou his form and shape. I beg the grace
But only for a night's revolving space:
Thyself a boy, assume a boy's dissembled face;
That when, amidst the fervor of the feast,
The Tyrian hugs and fonds thee on her breast,
And with sweet kisses in her arms constrains,
Thou may'st infuse thy venom in her veins."
The God of Love obeys, and sets aside
His bow and quiver, and his plumy pride;
He walks Iulus in his mother's sight,
And in the sweet resemblance takes delight.
The goddess then to young Ascanius flies,
And in a pleasing slumber seals his eyes:
Lull'd in her lap, amidst a train of Loves,
She gently bears him to her blissful groves,
Then with a wreath of myrtle crowns his head,
And softly lays him on a flow'ry bed.
Cupid meantime assum'd his form and face,
Foll'wing Achates with a shorter pace,
And brought the gifts. The queen already sate
Amidst the Trojan lords, in shining state,
High on a golden bed: her princely guest
Was next her side; in order sate the rest.
Then canisters with bread are heap'd on high;
Th' attendants water for their hands supply,
And, having wash'd, with silken towels dry.
Next fifty handmaids in long order bore
The censers, and with fumes the gods adore:
Then youths, and virgins twice as many, join
To place the dishes, and to serve the wine.
The Tyrian train, admitted to the feast,
Approach, and on the painted couches rest.
All on the Trojan gifts with wonder gaze,
But view the beauteous boy with more amaze,
His rosy-color'd cheeks, his radiant eyes,
His motions, voice, and shape, and all the god's
   disguise;
Nor pass unprais'd the vest and veil divine,
Which wand'ring foliage and rich flow'rs entwine.
But, far above the rest, the royal dame,
(Already doom'd to love's disastrous flame,)
With eyes insatiate, and tumultuous joy,
Beholds the presents, and admires the boy.
The guileful god about the hero long,

With children's play, and false embraces, hung;
Then sought the queen: she took him to her arms
With greedy pleasure, and devour'd his charms.
Unhappy Dido little thought what guest,
How dire a god, she drew so near her breast;
But he, not mindless of his mother's pray'r,
Works in the pliant bosom of the fair,
And molds her heart anew, and blots her former care.
The dead is to the living love resign'd;
And all Æneas enters in her mind.
Now, when the rage of hunger was appeas'd,
The meat remov'd, and ev'ry guest was pleas'd,
The golden bowls with sparkling wine are crown'd,
And thro' the palace cheerful cries resound.
From gilded roofs depending lamps display
Nocturnal beams, that emulate the day.
A golden bowl, that shone with gems divine,
The queen commanded to be crown'd with wine:
The bowl that Belus us'd, and all the Tyrian line.
Then, silence thro' the hall proclaim'd, she spoke:
"O hospitable Jove! we thus invoke,
With solemn rites, thy sacred name and pow'r;
Bless to both nations this auspicious hour!
So may the Trojan and the Tyrian line
In lasting concord from this day combine.
Thou, Bacchus, god of joys and friendly cheer,
And gracious Juno, both be present here!
And you, my lords of Tyre, your vows address
To Heav'n with mine, to ratify the peace."
The goblet then she took, with nectar crown'd
(Sprinkling the first libations on the ground,)
And rais'd it to her mouth with sober grace;
Then, sipping, offer'd to the next in place.
'T was Bitias whom she call'd, a thirsty soul;
He took the challenge, and embrac'd the bowl,
With pleasure swill'd the gold, nor ceas'd to draw,
Till he the bottom of the brimmer saw.
The goblet goes around: Iopas brought
His golden lyre, and sung what ancient Atlas taught:
The various labors of the wand'ring moon,
And whence proceed th' eclipses of the sun;
Th' original of men and beasts; and whence
The rains arise, and fires their warmth dispense,
And fix'd and erring stars dispose their influence;
What shakes the solid earth; what cause delays
The summer nights and shortens winter days.
With peals of shouts the Tyrians praise the song:
Those peals are echo'd by the Trojan throng.
Th' unhappy queen with talk prolong'd the night,

And drank large draughts of love with vast delight;
Of Priam much enquir'd, of Hector more;
Then ask'd what arms the swarthy Memnon wore,
What troops he landed on the Trojan shore;
The steeds of Diomede varied the discourse,
And fierce Achilles, with his matchless force;
At length, as fate and her ill stars requir'd,
To hear the series of the war desir'd.
"Relate at large, my godlike guest," she said,
"The Grecian stratagems, the town betray'd:
The fatal issue of so long a war,

Your flight, your wand'rings, and your woes, declare;
For, since on ev'ry sea, on ev'ry coast,
Your men have been distress'd, your navy toss'd,
Sev'n times the sun has either tropic view'd,
The winter banish'd, and the spring renew'd."

For the entire epic poem, insert the Literature CD.

Questions

1. Aeneas' relationship with Dido provides insight into his character. What does this relationship tell us about Aeneas?
2. How do dreams help develop the main ideas and themes in *The Aeneid?*
3. Is Aeneas' will strong enough to get to Italy, or does he need to be motivated by his people along the way? Why is this significant?
4. The chronological structure of *The Aeneid* is slightly confusing for some readers. Where does *The Aeneid* start, and what is Aeneas' role?
5. What are the most significant symbols in *The Aeneid.*
6. When Harpy issues a prophecy that changes the course of the poem, how does this prophecy affect the Trojan's fate?
7. Who sets fire to the Trojan fleet in Sicily, and why does this treasonous act take place?
8. Of the many Gods that the reader is introduced to, which one plays the most important role and why?

1. Since Virgil was, essentially, forced to write *The Aeneid,* it makes perfectly good sense that there are hints of political propaganda throughout. Find examples of this political propaganda in *The Aeneid,* and show how it may have advanced the Empire's cause. Further, find examples of contemporary political propaganda, and show how it may be used to advance or thwart a government's cause.
2. Aeneas is a dynamic character, for he is a character that changes and grows throughout the poem. In what ways does he grow, and where is there evidence in the poem of his development?
3. There are two characters who commit suicide in *The Aeneid.* How do their suicides reflect the civilizations they represent and the time period?

Ovid (43 BCE–18 CE)

The Roman poet Ovid was born in 43 BCE, and at an early age it was clear that he was destined for greatness. He experienced all of the luxuries that any child would who was part of a wealthy Roman family. Even though much of his upbringing and education revolved around a future in public service, he loved writing poetry. He dined with some of Rome's finest, including Horace and Augustus. As fruitful as his relationship was with the Augustus family, it led to his exile in 8 CE. For reasons that are still unclear, Ovid was banished from Rome at the age of fifty and sent to the city of Tomi (present day Romania) because of something he might have said or something he might have witnessed within the Augustus family circle.

Ovid's new environment was rife with barbarians and a severe climate. Tomi was a far different atmosphere than what Ovid had grown accustomed to in Rome. His poetry took a dramatic turn from aiming to beautify the Roman landscape to simply belaboring misery and a life of hopelessness.

Before he was exiled, however, Ovid wrote one of the most influential tales of his time. His *Metamorphosis* is considered one of the best classical sources of 250 myths that expound historical events from the dawn of time to the rule of Augustus.

Metamorphosis

1. While reading Ovid's *Metamorphosis,* think about some of the emotions that Virgil's *The Aeneid* evokes within the reader. Do these same emotions present themselves when reading *Metamorphosis?*
2. Ovid was fascinated with the ideology of what it means for something to go through a metamorphosis. Specifically, note his empirical and character allusions; note the changes that these empires and characters undergo.
3. In Virgil's *The Aeneid,* the reader can recognize celebratory themes of Roman citizenry and pageantry. Note how Ovid, unlike other writers of his time, does not seem to celebrate the greatness of Rome.

Metamorphosis

Ovid

The Creation of the World

Of bodies chang'd to various forms, I sing:
Ye Gods, from whom these miracles did spring,
Inspire my numbers with celestial heat;
'Till I my long laborious work compleat:
And add perpetual tenour to my rhimes,
Deduc'd from Nature's birth, to Caesar's times.
Before the seas, and this terrestrial ball,
And Heav'n's high canopy, that covers all,
One was the face of Nature; if a face:
Rather a rude and indigested mass:
A lifeless lump, unfashion'd, and unfram'd,
Of jarring seeds; and justly Chaos nam'd.

No sun was lighted up, the world to view;
No moon did yet her blunted horns renew:
Nor yet was Earth suspended in the sky,
Nor pois'd, did on her own foundations lye:
Nor seas about the shores their arms had thrown;
But earth, and air, and water, were in one.
Thus air was void of light, and earth unstable,
And water's dark abyss unnavigable.
No certain form on any was imprest;
All were confus'd, and each disturb'd the rest.
For hot and cold were in one body fixt;
And soft with hard, and light with heavy mixt.
But God, or Nature, while they thus contend,
To these intestine discords put an end:
Then earth from air, and seas from earth were driv'n,
And grosser air sunk from ætherial Heav'n.
Thus disembroil'd, they take their proper place;
The next of kin, contiguously embrace;
And foes are sunder'd, by a larger space.
The force of fire ascended first on high,
And took its dwelling in the vaulted sky:
Then air succeeds, in lightness next to fire;
Whose atoms from unactive earth retire.
Earth sinks beneath, and draws a num'rous throng
Of pondrous, thick, unwieldy seeds along.
About her coasts, unruly waters roar;
And rising, on a ridge, insult the shore.
Thus when the God, whatever God was he,
Had form'd the whole, and made the parts agree,
That no unequal portions might be found,
He moulded Earth into a spacious round:
Then with a breath, he gave the winds to blow;
And bad the congregated waters flow.
He adds the running springs, and standing lakes;
And bounding banks for winding rivers makes.
Some part, in Earth are swallow'd up, the most
In ample oceans, disembogu'd, are lost.
He shades the woods, the vallies he restrains
With rocky mountains, and extends the plains.
And as five zones th' ætherial regions bind,
Five, correspondents, are to Earth assign'd:
The sun with rays, directly darting down,
Fires all beneath, and fries the middle zone:
The two beneath the distant poles, complain
Of endless winter, and perpetual rain.
Betwixt th' extreams, two happier climates hold
The temper that partakes of hot, and cold.
The fields of liquid air, inclosing all,
Surround the compass of this earthly ball:

The lighter parts lie next the fires above;
The grosser near the watry surface move:
Thick clouds are spread, and storms engender there,
And thunder's voice, which wretched mortals fear,
And winds that on their wings cold winter bear.
Nor were those blustring brethren left at large,
On seas, and shores, their fury to discharge:
Bound as they are, and circumscrib'd in place,
They rend the world, resistless, where they pass;
And mighty marks of mischief leave behind;
Such is the rage of their tempestuous kind.
First Eurus to the rising morn is sent
(The regions of the balmy continent);
And Eastern realms, where early Persians run,
To greet the blest appearance of the sun.
Westward, the wanton Zephyr wings his flight;
Pleas'd with the remnants of departing light:
Fierce Boreas, with his off-spring, issues forth
T' invade the frozen waggon of the North.
While frowning Auster seeks the Southern sphere;
And rots, with endless rain, th' unwholsome year.

High o'er the clouds, and empty realms of wind,
The God a clearer space for Heav'n design'd;
Where fields of light, and liquid aether flow;
Purg'd from the pondrous dregs of Earth below.
Scarce had the Pow'r distinguish'd these, when
    streight
The stars, no longer overlaid with weight,
Exert their heads, from underneath the mass;
And upward shoot, and kindle as they pass,
And with diffusive light adorn their heav'nly place.
Then, every void of Nature to supply,
With forms of Gods he fills the vacant sky:
New herds of beasts he sends, the plains to share:
New colonies of birds, to people air:
And to their oozy beds, the finny fish repair.

A creature of a more exalted kind
Was wanting yet, and then was Man design'd:
Conscious of thought, of more capacious breast,
For empire form'd, and fit to rule the rest:
Whether with particles of heav'nly fire
The God of Nature did his soul inspire,
Or Earth, but new divided from the sky,
And, pliant, still retain'd th' ætherial energy:
Which wise Prometheus temper'd into paste,
And, mixt with living streams, the godlike image cast.
Thus, while the mute creation downward bend

Their sight, and to their earthly mother tend,
Man looks aloft; and with erected eyes
Beholds his own hereditary skies.
From such rude principles our form began;
And earth was metamorphos'd into Man.

The Golden Age

The golden age was first; when Man yet new,
No rule but uncorrupted reason knew:
And, with a native bent, did good pursue.
Unforc'd by punishment, un-aw'd by fear,
His words were simple, and his soul sincere;
Needless was written law, where none opprest:
The law of Man was written in his breast:
No suppliant crowds before the judge appear'd,
No court erected yet, nor cause was heard:
But all was safe, for conscience was their guard.
The mountain-trees in distant prospect please,
E're yet the pine descended to the seas:
E're sails were spread, new oceans to explore:
And happy mortals, unconcern'd for more,
Confin'd their wishes to their native shore.
No walls were yet; nor fence, nor mote, nor mound,
Nor drum was heard, nor trumpet's angry sound:
Nor swords were forg'd; but void of care and crime,
The soft creation slept away their time.
The teeming Earth, yet guiltless of the plough,
And unprovok'd, did fruitful stores allow:
Content with food, which Nature freely bred,
On wildings and on strawberries they fed;
Cornels and bramble-berries gave the rest,
And falling acorns furnish'd out a feast.
The flow'rs unsown, in fields and meadows reign'd:
And Western winds immortal spring maintain'd.
In following years, the bearded corn ensu'd
From Earth unask'd, nor was that Earth renew'd.
From veins of vallies, milk and nectar broke;
And honey sweating through the pores of oak.

The Silver Age

But when good Saturn, banish'd from above,
Was driv'n to Hell, the world was under Jove.
Succeeding times a silver age behold,
Excelling brass, but more excell'd by gold.
Then summer, autumn, winter did appear:
And spring was but a season of the year.
The sun his annual course obliquely made,
Good days contracted, and enlarg'd the bad.
Then air with sultry heats began to glow;
The wings of winds were clogg'd with ice and snow;
And shivering mortals, into houses driv'n,
Sought shelter from th' inclemency of Heav'n.
Those houses, then, were caves, or homely sheds;
With twining oziers fenc'd; and moss their beds.
Then ploughs, for seed, the fruitful furrows broke,
And oxen labour'd first beneath the yoke.

The Brazen Age

To this came next in course, the brazen age:
A warlike offspring, prompt to bloody rage,
Not impious yet . . .

The Iron Age

Hard steel succeeded then:
And stubborn as the metal, were the men.
Truth, modesty, and shame, the world forsook:
Fraud, avarice, and force, their places took.
Then sails were spread, to every wind that blew.
Raw were the sailors, and the depths were new:
Trees, rudely hollow'd, did the waves sustain;
E're ships in triumph plough'd the watry plain.

Then land-marks limited to each his right:
For all before was common as the light.
Nor was the ground alone requir'd to bear
Her annual income to the crooked share,
But greedy mortals, rummaging her store,
Digg'd from her entrails first the precious oar;
Which next to Hell, the prudent Gods had laid;
And that alluring ill, to sight display'd.
Thus cursed steel, and more accursed gold,
Gave mischief birth, and made that mischief bold:
And double death did wretched Man invade,
By steel assaulted, and by gold betray'd,
Now (brandish'd weapons glittering in their hands)
Mankind is broken loose from moral bands;
No rights of hospitality remain:
The guest, by him who harbour'd him, is slain,
The son-in-law pursues the father's life;
The wife her husband murders, he the wife.

The step-dame poyson for the son prepares;
The son inquires into his father's years.
Faith flies, and piety in exile mourns;
And justice, here opprest, to Heav'n returns.

The Giants' War

Nor were the Gods themselves more safe above;
Against beleaguer'd Heav'n the giants move.
Hills pil'd on hills, on mountains mountains lie,
To make their mad approaches to the skie.
'Till Jove, no longer patient, took his time
T' avenge with thunder their audacious crime:
Red light'ning plaid along the firmament,
And their demolish'd works to pieces rent.
Sing'd with the flames, and with the bolts transfixt,
With native Earth, their blood the monsters mixt;
The blood, indu'd with animating heat,
Did in th' impregnant Earth new sons beget:
They, like the seed from which they sprung, accurst,
Against the Gods immortal hatred nurst,
An impious, arrogant, and cruel brood;
Expressing their original from blood.
Which when the king of Gods beheld from high
(Withal revolving in his memory,
What he himself had found on Earth of late,
Lycaon's guilt, and his inhumane treat),
He sigh'd; nor longer with his pity strove;
But kindled to a wrath becoming Jove:

Then call'd a general council of the Gods;
Who summon'd, issue from their blest abodes,
And fill th' assembly with a shining train.
A way there is, in Heav'n's expanded plain,
Which, when the skies are clear, is seen below,
And mortals, by the name of Milky, know.
The ground-work is of stars; through which the road
Lyes open to the Thunderer's abode:
The Gods of greater nations dwell around,
And, on the right and left, the palace bound;
The commons where they can: the nobler sort
With winding-doors wide open, front the court.
This place, as far as Earth with Heav'n may vie,
I dare to call the Louvre of the skie.
When all were plac'd, in seats distinctly known,
And he, their father, had assum'd the throne,
Upon his iv'ry sceptre first he leant,
Then shook his head, that shook the firmament:

Air, Earth, and seas, obey'd th' almighty nod;
And, with a gen'ral fear, confess'd the God.
At length, with indignation, thus he broke
His awful silence, and the Pow'rs bespoke.

I was not more concern'd in that debate
Of empire, when our universal state
Was put to hazard, and the giant race
Our captive skies were ready to imbrace:
For tho' the foe was fierce, the seeds of all
Rebellion, sprung from one original;
Now, wheresoever ambient waters glide,
All are corrupt, and all must be destroy'd.
Let me this holy protestation make,
By Hell, and Hell's inviolable lake,
I try'd whatever in the godhead lay:
But gangren'd members must be lopt away,
Before the nobler parts are tainted to decay.
There dwells below, a race of demi-gods,
Of nymphs in waters, and of fawns in woods:
Who, tho' not worthy yet, in Heav'n to live,
Let 'em, at least, enjoy that Earth we give.
Can these be thought securely lodg'd below,
When I myself, who no superior know,
I, who have Heav'n and Earth at my command,
Have been attempted by Lycaon's hand?

At this a murmur through the synod went,
And with one voice they vote his punishment.
Thus, when conspiring traytors dar'd to doom
The fall of Caesar, and in him of Rome,
The nations trembled with a pious fear;
All anxious for their earthly Thunderer:
Nor was their care, o Caesar, less esteem'd
By thee, than that of Heav'n for Jove was deem'd:
Who with his hand, and voice, did first restrain
Their murmurs, then resum'd his speech again.
The Gods to silence were compos'd, and sate
With reverence, due to his superior state.
Cancel your pious cares; already he
Has paid his debt to justice, and to me.
Yet what his crimes, and what my judgments were,
Remains for me thus briefly to declare.
The clamours of this vile degenerate age,
The cries of orphans, and th' oppressor's rage,
Had reach'd the stars: I will descend, said I,
In hope to prove this loud complaint a lye.
Disguis'd in humane shape, I travell'd round
The world, and more than what I heard, I found.

O'er Maenalus I took my steepy way,
By caverns infamous for beasts of prey:
Then cross'd Cyllene, and the piny shade
More infamous, by curst Lycaon made:
Dark night had cover'd Heaven, and Earth, before
I enter'd his unhospitable door.
Just at my entrance, I display'd the sign
That somewhat was approaching of divine.
The prostrate people pray; the tyrant grins;
And, adding prophanation to his sins,
I'll try, said he, and if a God appear,
To prove his deity shall cost him dear.
'Twas late; the graceless wretch my death prepares,
When I shou'd soundly sleep, opprest with cares:
This dire experiment he chose, to prove
If I were mortal, or undoubted Jove:
But first he had resolv'd to taste my pow'r;
Not long before, but in a luckless hour,
Some legates, sent from the Molossian state,
Were on a peaceful errand come to treat:
Of these he murders one, he boils the flesh;
And lays the mangled morsels in a dish:
Some part he roasts; then serves it up, so drest,
And bids me welcome to this humane feast.
Mov'd with disdain, the table I o'er-turn'd;
And with avenging flames, the palace burn'd.
The tyrant in a fright, for shelter gains
The neighb'ring fields, and scours along the plains.
Howling he fled, and fain he wou'd have spoke;
But humane voice his brutal tongue forsook.
About his lips the gather'd foam he churns,
And, breathing slaughters, still with rage he burns,
But on the bleating flock his fury turns.
His mantle, now his hide, with rugged hairs
Cleaves to his back; a famish'd face he bears;
His arms descend, his shoulders sink away
To multiply his legs for chase of prey.
He grows a wolf, his hoariness remains,
And the same rage in other members reigns.
His eyes still sparkle in a narr'wer space:
His jaws retain the grin, and violence of his face
This was a single ruin, but not one
Deserves so just a punishment alone.
Mankind's a monster, and th' ungodly times
Confed'rate into guilt, are sworn to crimes.
All are alike involv'd in ill, and all
Must by the same relentless fury fall.
Thus ended he; the greater Gods assent;
By clamours urging his severe intent;

The less fill up the cry for punishment.
Yet still with pity they remember Man;
And mourn as much as heav'nly spirits can.
They ask, when those were lost of humane birth,
What he wou'd do with all this waste of Earth:
If his dispeopl'd world he would resign
To beasts, a mute, and more ignoble line;
Neglected altars must no longer smoke,
If none were left to worship, and invoke.
To whom the Father of the Gods reply'd,
Lay that unnecessary fear aside:
Mine be the care, new people to provide.
I will from wondrous principles ordain
A race unlike the first, and try my skill again.
Already had he toss'd the flaming brand;
And roll'd the thunder in his spacious hand;
Preparing to discharge on seas and land:
But stopt, for fear, thus violently driv'n,
The sparks should catch his axle-tree of Heav'n.
Remembring in the fates, a time when fire
Shou'd to the battlements of Heaven aspire,
And all his blazing worlds above shou'd burn;
And all th' inferior globe to cinders turn.
His dire artill'ry thus dismist, he bent
His thoughts to some securer punishment:
Concludes to pour a watry deluge down;
And what he durst not burn, resolves to drown.
The northern breath, that freezes floods, he binds;
With all the race of cloud-dispelling winds:
The south he loos'd, who night and horror brings;
And foggs are shaken from his flaggy wings.
From his divided beard two streams he pours,
His head, and rheumy eyes distill in show'rs,
With rain his robe, and heavy mantle flow:
And lazy mists are lowring on his brow;
Still as he swept along, with his clench'd fist
He squeez'd the clouds, th' imprison'd clouds resist:
The skies, from pole to pole, with peals resound;
And show'rs inlarg'd, come pouring on the ground.
Then, clad in colours of a various dye,
Junonian Iris breeds a new supply
To feed the clouds: impetuous rain descends;
The bearded corn beneath the burden bends:
Defrauded clowns deplore their perish'd grain;
And the long labours of the year are vain.
Nor from his patrimonial Heaven alone
Is Jove content to pour his vengeance down;
Aid from his brother of the seas he craves,
To help him with auxiliary waves.

The watry tyrant calls his brooks and floods,
Who rowl from mossie caves (their moist abodes);
And with perpetual urns his palace fill:
To whom in brief, he thus imparts his will.

Small exhortation needs; your pow'rs employ:
And this bad world, so Jove requires, destroy.
Let loose the reins to all your watry store:
Bear down the damms, and open ev'ry door.
The floods, by Nature enemies to land,
And proudly swelling with their new command,
Remove the living stones, that stopt their way,
And gushing from their source, augment the sea.
Then, with his mace, their monarch struck the ground;
With inward trembling Earth receiv'd the wound;
And rising streams a ready passage found.
Th' expanded waters gather on the plain:
They float the fields, and over-top the grain;
Then rushing onwards, with a sweepy sway,
Bear flocks, and folds, and lab'ring hinds away.
Nor safe their dwellings were, for, sap'd by floods,
Their houses fell upon their houshold Gods.
The solid piles, too strongly built to fall,
High o'er their heads, behold a watry wall:
Now seas and Earth were in confusion lost;
A world of waters, and without a coast.

One climbs a cliff; one in his boat is born:
And ploughs above, where late he sow'd his corn.
Others o'er chimney-tops and turrets row,
And drop their anchors on the meads below:
Or downward driv'n, they bruise the tender vine,
Or tost aloft, are knock'd against a pine.
And where of late the kids had cropt the grass,
The monsters of the deep now take their place.
Insulting Nereids on the cities ride,
And wond'ring dolphins o'er the palace glide.
On leaves, and masts of mighty oaks they brouze;
And their broad fins entangle in the boughs.
The frighted wolf now swims amongst the sheep;
The yellow lion wanders in the deep:
His rapid force no longer helps the boar:
The stag swims faster, than he ran before.
The fowls, long beating on their wings in vain,
Despair of land, and drop into the main.
Now hills, and vales no more distinction know;
And levell'd Nature lies oppress'd below.
The most of mortals perish in the flood:

The small remainder dies for want of food.

A mountain of stupendous height there stands
Betwixt th' Athenian and Boeotian lands,
The bound of fruitful fields, while fields they were,
But then a field of waters did appear:
Parnassus is its name; whose forky rise
Mounts thro' the clouds, and mates the lofty skies.
High on the summit of this dubious cliff,
Deucalion wafting, moor'd his little skiff.
He with his wife were only left behind
Of perish'd Man; they two were human kind.
The mountain nymphs, and Themis they adore,
And from her oracles relief implore.
The most upright of mortal men was he;
The most sincere, and holy woman, she.

When Jupiter, surveying Earth from high,
Beheld it in a lake of water lie,
That where so many millions lately liv'd,
But two, the best of either sex, surviv'd;
He loos'd the northern wind; fierce Boreas flies
To puff away the clouds, and purge the skies:
Serenely, while he blows, the vapours driv'n,
Discover Heav'n to Earth, and Earth to Heav'n.
The billows fall, while Neptune lays his mace
On the rough sea, and smooths its furrow'd face.
Already Triton, at his call, appears
Above the waves; a Tyrian robe he wears;
And in his hand a crooked trumpet bears.
The soveraign bids him peaceful sounds inspire,
And give the waves the signal to retire.
His writhen shell he takes; whose narrow vent
Grows by degrees into a large extent,
Then gives it breath; the blast with doubling sound,
Runs the wide circuit of the world around:
The sun first heard it, in his early east,
And met the rattling ecchos in the west.
The waters, list'ning to the trumpet's roar,
Obey the summons, and forsake the shore.
A thin circumference of land appears;
And Earth, but not at once, her visage rears,
And peeps upon the seas from upper grounds;
The streams, but just contain'd within their bounds,
By slow degrees into their channels crawl;
And Earth increases, as the waters fall.
In longer time the tops of trees appear,
Which mud on their dishonour'd branches bear.

At length the world was all restor'd to view;
But desolate, and of a sickly hue:
Nature beheld her self, and stood aghast,
A dismal desert, and a silent waste.

Which when Deucalion, with a piteous look
Beheld, he wept, and thus to Pyrrha spoke:
Oh wife, oh sister, oh of all thy kind
The best, and only creature left behind,
By kindred, love, and now by dangers joyn'd;
Of multitudes, who breath'd the common air,
We two remain; a species in a pair:
The rest the seas have swallow'd; nor have we
Ev'n of this wretched life a certainty.
The clouds are still above; and, while I speak,
A second deluge o'er our heads may break.
Shou'd I be snatcht from hence, and thou remain,
Without relief, or partner of thy pain,
How cou'dst thou such a wretched life sustain?
Shou'd I be left, and thou be lost, the sea
That bury'd her I lov'd, shou'd bury me.
Oh cou'd our father his old arts inspire,
And make me heir of his informing fire,
That so I might abolisht Man retrieve,
And perisht people in new souls might live.
But Heav'n is pleas'd, nor ought we to complain,
That we, th' examples of mankind, remain.
He said; the careful couple joyn their tears:
And then invoke the Gods, with pious prayers.
Thus, in devotion having eas'd their grief,
From sacred oracles they seek relief;
And to Cephysus' brook their way pursue:
The stream was troubled, but the ford they knew;
With living waters, in the fountain bred,
They sprinkle first their garments, and their head,
Then took the way, which to the temple led.
The roofs were all defil'd with moss, and mire,
The desert altars void of solemn fire.
Before the gradual, prostrate they ador'd;
The pavement kiss'd; and thus the saint implor'd.
O righteous Themis, if the Pow'rs above
By pray'rs are bent to pity, and to love;
If humane miseries can move their mind;
If yet they can forgive, and yet be kind;
Tell how we may restore, by second birth,
Mankind, and people desolated Earth.
Then thus the gracious Goddess, nodding, said;
Depart, and with your vestments veil your head:

And stooping lowly down, with losen'd zones,
Throw each behind your backs, your mighty
    mother's bones.
Amaz'd the pair, and mute with wonder stand,
'Till Pyrrha first refus'd the dire command.
Forbid it Heav'n, said she, that I shou'd tear
Those holy reliques from the sepulcher.
They ponder'd the mysterious words again,
For some new sense; and long they sought in vain:
At length Deucalion clear'd his cloudy brow,
And said, the dark Aenigma will allow
A meaning, which, if well I understand,
From sacrilege will free the God's command:
This Earth our mighty mother is, the stones
In her capacious body, are her bones:
These we must cast behind. With hope, and fear,
The woman did the new solution hear:
The man diffides in his own augury,
And doubts the Gods; yet both resolve to try.
Descending from the mount, they first unbind
Their vests, and veil'd, they cast the stones behind:
The stones (a miracle to mortal view,
But long tradition makes it pass for true)
Did first the rigour of their kind expel,
And suppled into softness, as they fell;
Then swell'd, and swelling, by degrees grew warm;
And took the rudiments of human form.
Imperfect shapes: in marble such are seen,
When the rude chizzel does the man begin;
While yet the roughness of the stone remains,
Without the rising muscles, and the veins.
The sappy parts, and next resembling juice,
Were turn'd to moisture, for the body's use:
Supplying humours, blood, and nourishment;
The rest, too solid to receive a bent,
Converts to bones; and what was once a vein,
Its former name and Nature did retain.
By help of pow'r divine, in little space,
What the man threw, assum'd a manly face;
And what the wife, renew'd the female race.
Hence we derive our nature; born to bear
Laborious life; and harden'd into care.

The rest of animals, from teeming Earth
Produc'd, in various forms receiv'd their birth.
The native moisture, in its close retreat,
Digested by the sun's aetherial heat,
As in a kindly womb, began to breed:

Then swell'd, and quicken'd by the vital seed.
And some in less, and some in longer space,
Were ripen'd into form, and took a sev'ral face.
Thus when the Nile from Pharian fields is fled,
And seeks, with ebbing tides, his ancient bed,
The fat manure with heav'nly fire is warm'd;
And crusted creatures, as in wombs, are form'd;
These, when they turn the glebe, the peasants find;
Some rude, and yet unfinish'd in their kind:
Short of their limbs, a lame imperfect birth:
One half alive; and one of lifeless earth.

For heat, and moisture, when in bodies join'd,
The temper that results from either kind
Conception makes; and fighting 'till they mix,
Their mingled atoms in each other fix.
Thus Nature's hand the genial bed prepares
With friendly discord, and with fruitful wars.
From hence the surface of the ground, with mud
And slime besmear'd (the faeces of the flood),
Receiv'd the rays of Heav'n: and sucking in
The seeds of heat, new creatures did begin:
Some were of sev'ral sorts produc'd before,
But of new monsters, Earth created more.
Unwillingly, but yet she brought to light

Thee, Python too, the wondring world to fright,
And the new nations, with so dire a sight:
So monstrous was his bulk, so large a space
Did his vast body, and long train embrace.
Whom Phœbus basking on a bank espy'd;
E're now the God his arrows had not try'd
But on the trembling deer, or mountain goat;
At this new quarry he prepares to shoot.
Though ev'ry shaft took place, he spent the store
Of his full quiver; and 'twas long before
Th' expiring serpent wallow'd in his gore.
Then, to preserve the fame of such a deed,
For Python slain, he Pythian games decre'd.
Where noble youths for mastership shou'd strive,
To quoit, to run, and steeds, and chariots drive.
The prize was fame: in witness of renown
An oaken garland did the victor crown.
The laurel was not yet for triumphs born;
But every green alike by Phœbus worn,
Did, with promiscuous grace, his flowing locks adorn.

 **For the entire epic poem, insert the Literature CD.**

Questions

1. After reading *Metamorphosis,* many are confused about the narrative style in which Ovid chooses to tell his mythological tales. What is confusing about this structure, and how does it add to the complexity of the poem?
2. If Ovid is glorifying anything at all, what is it, and where do you find evidence of this glorification?
3. Where does Ovid's poem begin, and where does it end?
4. Many scholars agree that Ovid's piece has had more influence on European literature than any other text. Do you agree with this idea, and why?
5. *Metamorphosis* seems pagan in nature. Discuss what exactly is so pagan about this poem and where one might find evidence for this claim.
6. From the many stories that Ovid tells, which ones have you already read, and who authored them?
7. In *Metamorphosis,* which characters experience the most suffering, and what is the result of their suffering?
8. Identify examples from the poem that might have angered Augustus and led to Ovid's exile.

1. Compare and contrast the flood in *Metamorphosis* with the flood in the *Bible*. In doing so, examine the intended purposes of the floods and the effects they had on the people of that time period.
2. If one were to further investigate *Metamorphosis'* historical context, it might become clear that a lesson can be learned from the poem. What is Ovid attempting to teach the reader about history, and how is this lesson significant to the Roman Empire?
3. Identify one theme in *Metamorphosis,* and show its prevalence throughout the poem by citing lines to support it.

Roman Literature: "Silver Age"

After the death of Augustus in 14 CE, Rome underwent a series of changes. Many believe that the period of 14–180 CE is when Rome went through some of its most defining changes, for the empire grew to parts of Northern Africa and Great Britain; further, the political structure grew rather unstable as successive emperors were overthrown or killed. This was complemented by the birth of what the Romans considered a mystical religion: Christianity.

The Roman institution of government was one of the first signs of a crumbling empire. Augustus had been elected by the senate, but after his death, the military began to play a more prominent role in the affairs of state. In 68 CE the last Julian emperor, Nero, was overthrown by the army, and in 69 CE Rome saw four emperors take—and be taken from—the throne by military might. These emperors, who were formerly generals, soon began to understand how violence, or the threat thereof, could affect the decisions that were made on the senate floor.

After the assassination of Domitian in 96 CE, the senate elected the senator Nerva, since Domitian had died without appointing a successor. This senate-elected emperor led to a series of five senate-elected emperors, thus helping stabilize the Roman idea of democracy, establishing the senate as the voice of the people.

There were many writers and philosophers from the "Silver Age" who documented the decline of Roman values and the politically-corrupt atmosphere that enveloped this empire. Among the most significant writers were Horace, Juvenal, and Seneca.

Horace (65 BCE–8 BCE)

Horace (Quintus Horatius Flaccus) was a friend of Virgil's, and it was said that, due to his education in Athens and Rome, he had the perfect blend of Greek and Roman influences in his writing. He served as a military tribune from 44 to 42 CE and was able to write his way out of the military by way of the poignant satires he produced with the help of Virgil.

Horace's writing focuses on the weaknesses of the Roman Empire. In this regard, he was unlike many of the writers from the "Golden Age," for he did not glorify Rome's global dominance, like many of his counterparts had before him. He felt comfortable identifying the cultural flaws of the hubristic Roman society of Augustus and Octavian. Still, even though his poetry lead to some civil unrest during Augustus' reign, it was not seen as undermining or rebellious.

Defense of Satire

1. Before reading *Defense of Satire,* make sure to define *satire* in order to further clarify what you are about to read.
2. This reading is unlike many produced in the "Silver Age," for it has a conversational tone to it. Note that the "I" in this work is Horace. This helps provide insight into who he really was.

Defense of Satire

Horace

The dramatists, Eupolis, Cratinus, Aristophanes and other authors of the Old Comedy, called by their frank names anyone who deserved to be represented as a rogue, a thief, an adulterer or a cut-throat, or as infamous in any other way. Upon these poets Lucilius is wholly dependent. He followed them in all but the metre—witty, penetrating, rough in the construction of his verse.

In this last respect he was at fault. Often, as a great feat, he would dictate without effort two hundred verses in an hour. Since he flowed muddily there was always something that you would like to take out. He was wordy and too lazy to endure the fatigue of writing. Of writing properly, I mean, for the amount of his poetry is beside the point.

Well, well! Here is Crispinus offering me heavy odds.

"Pick up your tablet. Pick it up, please. Have a place, a time, and proctors set over us and let's see who can write most! Thank God for making me an unproductive, unaspiring intellectual, speaking seldom and very little at that. You go ahead as you choose, act like the air shut in a goatskin bellows, puffing away until the fire softens the iron! How happy is Fannius! His works and his bust are offered for sale without his asking, while no one reads my writings. And I fear to read them in public because there are persons who dislike satire heartily. Most people deserve criticism. Pick out anyone from the crowd—he suffers from avarice or from some deplorable ambition. One man is crazy about married women, another over boys, a third about glittering silver or Albius about bronzes. Another man keeps busy trading, from the rising sun to that which warms the evening landscape, but he is hurried headlong through dangers like a column of dust in a whirlwind, in terror lest he lose some of his capital, or in order to add to his wealth. All these people have a horror poetry and hat poets. "Keep away from him," they say. "He has hay on his horns. If only he can raise a laugh for his own diversion he will spare no friend, and whatever he has once smeared on his paper he will rejoice to have all the boys and old women know as they return from the bake shop and the lake."

But let me say a few words on the other side of the question. To begin with, I except myself from the catalogue of these I concede to be poets. One must do more than make verses scan. And you can't call a man a poet if he writes, as I do, in language more appropriate to conversation. If a man has talent, inspired genius and a grand and lofty style, you may grant him the honor of the title. Accordingly some people have questioned whether or not comedy is poetry. Neither in the words nor in the subject matter is there any inspiration or force, and, except for the fact that it is written in fixed metre, it is mere prose.

"But an angry father rags because his spendthrift son, mad about a wanton mistress, refuses a wife with a large dower, and to his great shame parades drunk through the town with torches by daylight."

Well, would Pomponius, if his father were alive, hear any milder reproofs than that? So it is not enough to write verses in plain everyday language which, if you take it apart, any father would use just as the father on the stage. If from these verses that I now write, or from those that Lucilius used to write, you take away the fixed quantities and rhythms, and if you put the last word first and the first last, you won't pull the poet's limbs to pieces as you would if you took apart the poem, "When dreadful Discord broke the iron-sheathed doors and gates of war."

So much for that! At some other time I shall enquire whether it be true poetry or not. At present I shall consider only whether this kind of writing deserves your dislike. Keen Sulcius and Caprius walk about horribly hoarse and armed with writs, each one of them a great terror to robbers. But if a man lives honestly and with clean hands he can despise them both. However true it may be that you are like the bandits Caelius and Birrus, as long as I am not like Caprius or Sulcius, why are you afraid of me? No shop or bookstand displays my books for vulgar hands (and those of Hermogenes Tigellius) to soil with perspiration. I don't recite my works to anyone but my friends, and to them under compulsion and not everywhere and in the presence of everybody. There are many poets who read their writings in the middle of the Forum, and others during the bath, the enclosed place lending melody to the voice. This pleases the vanity of men who never ask whether they act thus in bad taste or at the wrong time.

"You love to give pain," says someone, "and you do it maliciously."

Where do you find this to throw at me? Is your authority any one of my friends? A man who backbites a friend in his absence, who does not defend him when another finds fault with him, who raises

unbridled laughter in company to gain the reputation of being a wit, who invents things he never says, who cannot keep secrets, that man is a black-hearted slanderer. Avoid him, Roman!

You may often see at dinner groups of four persons on three couches. One of these delights to bespatter in any way he can everybody except the host. Presently he bespatters him too, when he is drunk and when the truth-telling god Liber reveals the hidden secrets of the heart. This man seems to you courteous and polished and frank. If I have laughed because silly Rufillus smells of perfume and Gargonius like a he-goat, do I seem to you to be spiteful and snarling?

If in your presence some mention happened to be made of the thefts of Petillius Capitolinus, you would defend him as is or habit, in your usual way, "Capitolinus has been a comrade and friend of mine from boyhood, and at my request has done me many favors, and I am happy that he lives in the city unmolested. Nevertheless I do wonder how he managed to escape conviction." This is the essence of black malignity, pure rust. Such malice, I promise you as surely as I can promise anything, will be far removed from my pages, but first of all from my heart.

If I speak too freely, with too rough jest, you will indulgently grant me this privilege. The best of fathers taught me this habit, that by his branding them one by one by examples I might avoid all sorts of mistakes. When he wanted to urge me to live thriftily, frugally and content with what he had provided, he would say, "Don't you see how miserable is the life of Albius' son and how beggarly that of Baius? An urgent warning not to squander your patrimony!" When he wished to deter me from the vulgar love of a mistress, "Don't be like Scetanus!" he said. To keep me from running after faithless wives when I could enjoy a decent amour, he would remark, "The reputation of Trebonius who was caught in the act is not a pretty one. The philosopher may give you reasons as to what it is better to avoid and what to pursue. It is enough for me if I can preserve the custom handed down from my ancestors, so long as you need a guardian to preserve your life and reputation from harm. As soon as years have matured your body and your mind you will swim without cork." Thus by his precepts he moulded my boyhood, and whenever he told me to do something he would say, "Here is your authority for this," and point to the judge on the bench. Or again, if he forbade something, he would say, "Can you doubt that this is dishonorable or inexpedient when so-and-so stands in the blaze of ill repute?"

As a funeral in the neighborhood dispirits sick gluttons and compels them to spare themselves because of the fear of death, so others' disgraces often deter youthful minds from blunders. In accordance with this principle I am free from all vices that bring ruin, and am guilty only of lesser faults, such as you can excuse. It may be that even these may be materially reduced by a maturer age, an honest friend, and my own determination. For when I retire to my couch or go for a walk in the colonnade I do not neglect myself. "This is the truer course." "By doing so I shall live happier." "In this way I shall be a delight to my friends." "This was not very pretty. I hope that I shall not some day, in an unguarded moment, do the like." With my lips shut tight I ponder these things to myself.

When I have some leisure I amuse myself with my papers. This is one of those lesser faults of which I spoke. If you aren't tolerant toward it a great host of poets—for we are more than half the world—shall come to my rescuer and, like the Jews, we will compel you to join our crowd.

Questions

1. Who is Horace's intended audience, and how do you think his intended audience reacted to this piece?
2. Does *Defense of Satire* benefit from its conversational tone? Why?

1. In *Defense of Satire,* Horace writes: "'You love to give pain,' says someone, 'and you do it maliciously.'" Is Horace making a comparison between himself and other satirists of his time? Research the satires by Juvenal and Horace, and compare and contrast their motivations for employing what might be deemed "verbal abrasiveness."
2. In *Defense of Satire,* the reader is provided with insight into the conventions of Roman society. After researching some of these conventions, construct an argument that examines whether these same conventions still exist in today's society.
3. Based on the methods employed by Horace in his satire, how might he define *satire?* In constructing his definition, consider a satire's purpose and intended audience. Also, examine word choice and the role of slanted argumentation. Make sure to defend your claim with examples from this work and from other sources.
4. Re-read the last paragraph of Horace's *Defense of Satire.* What is Horace's message to his critics in this paragraph, and is there something threatening about it? After identifying his message, research Judaism's role during Horace's time, examining how it affected Roman society. Explain why these effects might promote fear and / or make people feel threatened.

The Golden Mean

1. Thinking of Horace as a teacher will be extremely helpful in understanding his argument.
2. Horace writes on particular Roman topics such as the decline of morals and values. Because of this, his writing is typically seen as some of the earliest satirical work in Rome's history.

The Golden Mean

Horace

How is it, Maecenas, that no one is satisfied with his lot in life, whether he chose it himself or whether it came to him by accident, but envies those whose lot is different?

"Happy are the traders!" exclaims the soldier, weighted down with his years, his body broken in arduous service. The trader, when the south wind tosses his vessel about, cries, "War is better than this! Why? When once the ranks attack you have in an instant either death or victory." The legal expert, when a client knocks at his door before cockcrow, calls the farmer lucky. But the latter, dragged from the country into the city to answer a summons, is positive that "only those are happy who live in town!" To cite the many other similar instances would wear out even talkative Fabius.

Without boring you, let me give you the conclusion. If some god should say, "See here! I will grant what you wish. You, soldier, shall be a trader; you, counselor, a farmer. Change your lots and go your way. . . . Hurry up! Why do you hesitate?" They wouldn't do it. And yet they could! Would not Jupiter be justified in snorting with anger and saying that hereafter he would not be so indulgent as to listen to petitions?

I must not, like a jester, laugh the subject off. And still why may not one speak the truth with a smile like those kindly teachers who give candy to their pupils to induce them to learn their letters? Joking aside, however, let us be serious.

That fellow over there who turns a heavy sod with the hard plowshare, that rascally innkeeper, the soldier, the sailors who so bravely breast every sea, all of them say that they endure hardship in order that when they are old and have made sufficient provision for themselves they may retire to safety and peace. In the same way the tiny ant, that busiest of all creatures, drags in her mouth whatever she can to add to the heap she piles up, for she is aware of the future and anxious about it. When winter comes she never stirs but prudently uses the stores which she has gathered up before.

But you, neither summer nor winter, fire, sea nor sword can stop you from making money just so long as your neighbor is wealthier than you. What pleasure can it give you to dig stealthily, in fear and trembling, a hole in the ground and bury therein a huge quantity of silver and gold?

"Because if I began to spend it, I should soon have none left."

But if you don't spend it, what attraction is there in the pile that you have heaped up? Suppose your threshing-floor yields a hundred thousand bushels of wheat. Your belly cannot, on that account, hold more than mine. If you were one of a line of slaves and carried on your shoulder a basket of bread, you couldn't eat more than the man who carried nothing. What difference, tell me, does it make to the man who lives a normal life whether he plows a hundred or a thousand acres?

"It is pleasant to spend from a great pile."

Well, do you think your granaries are better than our bins if we can take just as much out of our small hoard? It is just the same as if you needed only a glass or a pitcher of water and said, "I'd rather draw the same amount from a river than from this little spring." That's why men who want more than enough are swept away, together with the bank they stand on, by the swift Aufidus River, while those who ask for only so much as they need have neither to drink roiled water nor lose their lives in the stream.

Most men, led astray by greed, say, "There is no such thing as enough. A man is judged by the amount he has." What can you do to people like this but tell them to be wretched since that's what they want? They are like the Athenian, as greedy as he was rich, who is said to have turned aside criticism with the remark, "People hiss me, but I congratulate myself in private when I think of all the money in my chest." Tantalus, with his thirst, strains at the waters that elude his lips.

What are you smiling at? Change names and the story fits you! You doze on, gloating over your money-bags whose contents you have raked and scraped together. But, as if they were holy, you don't dare to touch them, or to enjoy them any more than if they were paintings. Don't you know the value of money and its purpose? You can buy bread with it, vegetables, a bottle of wine, and other necessities from the lack of which human nature suffers. Perhaps you enjoy watching day and night half dead with fear, on the alert for wicked thieves, fires, or slaves who may rob you and run. Is that what satisfies you? If that is good living I want to be one of the paupers! If

you go to your bed with malaria or some other sickness, is there someone who will sit by you, prepare your medicine, call in the doctor to set you again on your feet and restore you to your children and dear relatives? Neither your wife nor your son wants you to get well. All your neighbors and acquaintances, even the boys and girls, dislike you. Can you wonder, since you prefer money to everything else, that no one gives you the affection that you don't earn? If you think you can without effort keep the friends whom nature has given you, you're wasting your time, idiot! You might just as well break an ass to reins and race him in the Field of Mars.

So put limits to your money-grabbing. As your wealth grows, have less fear of poverty. Begin gradually to taper off your work as you acquire what you longed for. Don't be like that Ummidius who was so rich that he measured his money, so cheap that he never had better clothes than a slave. To the very end of his life he was afraid that he would die of hunger. Instead, his freedwoman most courageous of Tyndareus' daughters, cut him down with an axe!

"Well, then, what do you want me to do? Live like a Navius or a Nomentanus?"

You always compare things which are utterly different. When I tell you not to be a miser, that doesn't mean that I am telling you to be a fool and a spendthrift. There is some middle ground between Tanais and Visellius, his father-in-law. There is a mean in things, fixed limits on either side of which right living cannot get a foothold.

So I come back to where I began to ask how it is that like the miser, no one prefers his own lot in life, but praises those whose lot is different, pines because his neighbor's goat gives more milk, doesn't compare himself with the vast multitude of poor people, but merely strives to outdo this one and that. The man who is eager to be rich is always blocked by one who is richer, just as when in a race the barriers are raised and the chariots are flying behind the horses' hoofs, the charioteer makes for the horses that are outrunning his own, ignoring those that are left behind. And this is why we rarely find a man who can say that he had led a happy life and that, content with his paths, he retires like a satisfied guest from a banquet.

Enough for now! For fear you'll think I have rifled the portfolios of blear-eyed Crispinus I will say no more.

Questions

1. Horace says, "If that is good living I want to be one of the paupers!" Why might he say this?
2. Do you think Horace is trying to unnerve a particular societal class? If so, what class does he address?
3. How does Horace's description of Ummidus help advance the satire?
4. What is the tone of this satire, and why and how is tone important in any satire?
5. How does Horace use "mean"? Is it a loaded word, or is he using it in a simpler manner?

Research and Writing

1. Think about stockpiling goods, gathering more than what is needed to sustain a healthy lifestyle, and being wasteful. Does this exist in today's society? Do the ideas that Horace examines in his society also exist in today's society? Compare and contrast our civilization's wastefulness with Horace's.
2. Horace writes: "There is a mean in things, fixed limits on either side of which right living cannot get a foothold." Is this Horace's central argument? Is this sentence reminiscent of any moral message the reader also gets from the satires of Juvenal? Examine Juvenal's satires, and then compare and contrast the arguments that can be extracted from his works with those that can be extracted from Horace's, noting specifically the moral messages that are present in each.

Juvenal (60–140 CE)

Juvenal (60–140 CE) became famous by writing satires. Not one to shy away from pointing out the declining greatness of Rome's emperors, his work provided insight into the evolution of corruption within the Roman government. Although he is not considered one of Rome's greatest satirists, his satirical style can be likened to Jonathan Swift's and Mark Twain's, suggesting that his place in the Roman literary canon has been overlooked.

Although little is known about Juvenal's childhood, it is believed that he had a wealthy upbringing and was educated in Rome. Upon completing his education, he began a career as a teacher of rhetoric but later believed that the educational system was under too much governmental control. This experience as a teacher was the genesis of one satire titled *The Miserable Pay of Teachers*. In it, Juvenal addresses topics that still resonate with many educators today.

Satire VII: The Miserable Pay of Teachers

1. Note the questions asked by Juvenal at the beginning of this satire. Note how they help establish the satire's tone.
2. Juvenal seems to be laughing at something or someone; in doing so, notice how he employs what some may call "literary eloquence."
3. While you are reading this satire, think about what you know about the teachers of today and the issues that typically arise regarding their profession.

Satire VII: The Miserable Pay of Teachers

Juvenal

Do you teach declamation? Oh what a heart of steel must Vectius have, when his numerous class ills cruel tyrants! For all that the boy has just conned over at his seat, he will then stand up and spout—the same stale theme in the same sing-song. It is the reproduction of the cabbage that wears out the master's life. What is the plea to be urged: what is the character of the cause; where the main point of the case hinges; what shafts may issue from the opposing party;—this all are anxious to know; but not one is anxious to pay! "Pay do you ask for? Why, what do I know?" The blame, forsooth, is laid at the teacher's door, because there is not a spark of energy in the breast of this scion of Arcadia who dins his awful Hannibal into my ears regularly every sixth day. Whatever the theme be that is to be the subject of his deliberation; whether he shall march at once from Cannae to Rome; or whether, rendered circumspect after the storms and thunderbolts, he shall lead his cohorts, drenched with the tempest, by a circuitous route. Bargain for any sum you please, and I will at once place it in your hands, on condition that his father should hear him his lesson as often as I have to do it! But six or more sophists are all giving tongue at once; and, debating in good earnest, have abandoned all fictitious declamations about the ravisher. No more is heard of the poison infused or the

vile ungrateful husband, or the drugs than can restore the aged blind to youth. He therefore that quits the shadowy conflicts of rhetoric for the arena of real debate, will superannuate himself, if my advice has any weight with him, and enter on a different path of life; that he may not lose even the paltry sum that will purchase that miserable ticket for corn: since receives, or Pollio, for teaching the sons of these fine gentlemen, and going into all the details of Theodorus's treatise.

The baths will cost six hundred sestertia, and the colonnade still more, in which the great man rides whenever it rains. Is he to wait, forsooth, for fair weather? Or bespatter his horses with fresh mud? Nay, far better here! For here the mule's hoof shines unsullied. On the other side must rise a spacious dining-room, supported on stately columns of Numidian marble, and catch the cool sun. However much the house may have cost, he will have besides an artist who can arrange his table scientifically; another, who can season made-dishes. Yet amid all this lavish expenditure, two poor sestertia will be deemed an ample remuneration for Quintilian. Nothing will cost a father less than his son's education.

"Then where did Quintilian get the money to pay for so many estates?" Pass by the instances of good fortune that are but rare indeed. It is good luck that makes a man handsome and active; good luck that makes him wise, and noble, and well-bred, and attaches the crescent of the senator to his black shoe. Good luck too that makes him the best of orators and debaters, and, though he has a vile cold, sing well! For it makes all the difference what planets welcome you when you first begin to utter your infant cry, and are still red from your mother. If fortune so wills it, you will become consul instead of rhetorician; or, if she will, instead of rhetorician, consul! What was Nentidius or Tullius aught else than a lucky planet, and the strange potency of hidden fate? Fate, that gives kingdoms to slaves, and triumphs to captives. Yes! Quintilian was indeed lucky, but he is a greater rarity even than a white crow. But many a man has repented of this fruitless and barren employment, as the sad end of Thrasymachus proves, and that of Secundus Carrinas. And you, too, Athens were witness to the poverty of him on whom you had the heart to bestow nothing save the hemlock that chilled his life-blood.

. . . But do you, parents, impose severe exactions on him that is to teach your boys; that he be perfect in the rules of grammar for each word—read all histories—know all authors as well as his own finger-ends; that if questioned at hazard, while on his way to the Thermae or the baths of Phoebus, he should be able to tell the name of Anchises' nurse, and the name and native land of the stepmother of Anchemolus—tell off-hand how many years Acestes lived—how many flagons of wine the Sicilian king gave to the Phrygians? Require of him that he mould their youthful morals as one models a face in wax. Require of him that he be the reverend father of the company, and check every approach to immorality.

It is no light task to keep watch over so many boyish hands, so many little twinkling eyes. "This," says the father, "be the object of your care!"—and when the year comes round again, "Receive for your pay as much gold as the people demand for the victorious charioteer!"

Questions

1. Identify three arguments that Juvenal attempts to advance in his satire. After examining the support he employs, do you agree or disagree with his arguments?
2. What is the purpose of Quintilian's role in Juvenal's satire?

1. What do you think life was like for Roman educators? How much money did these individuals earn? After researching this topic, can a connection be made between the educators of Juvenal's Rome and the educators of today? Make these connections in a comparison-and-contrast essay.
2. Juvenal writes: "No more is heard of the poison infused, or the vile ungrateful husband [. . .]." From some of the major literary characters you have studied, to whom might Juvenal be referring, and where might you find the strongest evidence to support your claims?

Satire XIV: Moral Education by Example

1. In this satire, Juvenal is clearly attacking an aspect of Roman society. Note how his examples help advance his argument.
2. In the second paragraph of this satire, Juvenal presents a series of household chores that one typically completed before having a guest over. The presentation of this list is important to the work as a whole.
3. Throughout this satire, there is clearly a theme revolving around generational corruption. Juvenal is attempting to show that one cause of Rome's decline is the decline of good parenting.

Satire XIV: Moral Education by Example

Juvenal

The greatest reverence is due to a child! If you are contemplating a disgraceful act, despise not your child's tender years, but let your infant son act as a check upon your purpose if sinning. For if, at some future time, he shall have done anything to deserve the censor's wrath, and show himself like you, not in person only and in face, but also the true son of your morals, and one who, by following your footsteps, adds deeper guilt to your crimes—then, forsooth! You will reprove and chastise him with clamorous bitterness, and then set about altering your will. Yet how dare you assume the front severe, and license of a parent's speech; you, who yourself, though old, do worse than this; and the exhausted cupping-glass is long ago looking out for your brainless head?

If a friend is coming to pay you a visit, your whole household is in a bustle. "Sweep the floor, display the pillars in all their brilliancy, let the dry spider come down with all her web; let one clean the silver, another polish the embossed plate," the master's voice thunders out, as he stands over the work, and brandishes his whip.

You are alarmed then, wretched man, lest your entrance-hall, befouled by dogs, should offend the eye of your friend who is coming, or your corridor be spattered with mud; and yet one little slave could clean all this with half a bushel of saw-dust. And yet, will you not bestir yourself that your own son may see your house immaculate and free from foul spot or crime? It deserves our gratitude that you have presented a citizen to your country and people, if you take care that he prove useful to the state—of service to her lands; useful in transacting the affairs both of ware and peace. For it will be a matter of the highest moment in what pursuits and moral discipline you train him.

The stork feeds her young on snakes and lizards which she has discovered in the trackless fields. They too, when flogged, go in quest of the same animals. The vulture, quitting the cattle, dogs, and gibbets, hastens to her callow brood, and bears to them a portion of the carcass. Therefore this is the food of the vulture too when grown up, and able to feed itself and build a nest in a tree of its own.

Questions

1. There is a sense of hypocrisy in this satire. At whom is this hypocrisy primarily aimed? Why?
2. The third paragraph of this satire is comical. What is Juvenal communicating about the importance of having one's house clean in comparison with the importance of good parenting?
3. Juvenal's final story is about a stork and her baby. How does this relate to various arguments that can be identified in his satire?

1. Juvenal writes: "For if, at some future time, he shall have done anything to deserve the censor's wrath, and show himself like you, not in person only and in face, but also the true son of your morals [. . .]." Who is this censor? What do you think Juvenal is intending to portray with these lines? Research who Juvenal's intended audience might have been, and support your assertions by citing examples from credible sources.
2. The reader is given an anecdote at the end of this satire. What message is Juvenal attempting to send his readers? Construct an argument that shows how this anecdote relates to the average American family of today, and support your argument by citing examples from Juvenal's work and outside sources.
3. Since Rome was enduring a cultural decline when Juvenal wrote this satire, how might it have been viewed by the populace? Further, does Juvenal's satire serve as a warning of what is to come for Rome? Make sure to support your argument by citing examples from Juvenal's work and outside sources.

Lucius Annaeus Seneca (4 BCE–65 CE)

Lucius Annaeus Seneca was born around 4 BCE in Cordova, Spain and was raised in a wealthy household. He was educated in Rome and quickly became famous for his talent as an orator and philosopher. This talent was so profound that it lead to his exile by the Emperor, Caligula. It was believed that Seneca's talent as an orator presented a political threat to Caligula. It was also believed that Seneca was banished because he had cheated on his own wife and committed adultery with Julia Livilla, Caligula's daughter, but this reason did not have nearly as solid a foundation as Caligula's jealousy toward Seneca. After Caligula's death in 49 CE, Seneca was recalled to Rome by Agrippina, who placed him as a tutor to her son, Nero, the heir apparent.

Seneca's relationship with the young Nero was rather paradoxical. When Nero became Emperor in 54 CE, he retained Seneca as an advisor, and often the young Emperor would look to his friend for political guidance. It was widely believed throughout the Empire that for the first five years of Nero's reign as Emperor (54–59 CE), the power of Seneca was second only to Nero. In 62 CE, Seneca retired as Nero's advisor, and in 65 CE—again out of fear—Seneca suffered a political act of jealousy. Nero believed that his former advisor was conspiring against him, and he ordered Seneca to commit suicide. While suffering a long, drawn out death (Seneca chose to commit suicide by slitting his wrists), he dictated an article on morality to his slaves and, eventually, was drowned by Nero's guards as he lay in the bath.

Seneca was considered one of the most influential philosophers and dramatists of his time. His writings played a vital role in shaping Roman culture, and his tragic exile rivals Ovid's. Seneca was fascinated with the stoic principle that man should be accepting of his fate and play the role that had been assigned to him. Coincidentally, Seneca's fate preyed upon the causal relationship between political savvy and exile. In other words, his ability to puppet the political system was inextricably linked to his eventual ostracization.

Seneca wrote all of his plays while in exile. And while there is no proof that his dramas were actually ever performed on stage, he was one of the first playwrights to effectively integrate the soliloquy and the aside. Both of these conventions became commonplace in the works of many Renaissance playwrights.

In Seneca's *Agamemnon,* the reader is thrust into a familiar time and place. It is after the fall of Troy, and Agamemnon, King of Argos, has just returned from the monumental victory of Troy. It's a battle with which many historians are familiar, but in this play, Seneca gives the reader an imaginary tale of the aftermath of this great battle, similar to the tale that Virgil constructs in *The Aeneid.*

Agamemnon

1. Note the similarities and differences between Virgil's *The Aeneid* and Seneca's *Agamemnon,* noting specifically how these two Roman authors portray the battle of Troy.
2. Women play a prominent role in this play, and there are two women who see each other as rivals, an idea that is prevalent throughout Euripides' *Medea* as well.
3. Examine heroism in *Agamemnon,* and attempt to make the distinction between acts of heroism and acts of violence and betrayal, noting that acts of violence and betrayal may also be considered heroic.

Agamemnon

Seneca

CHARACTERS IN THE PLAY

GHOST OF THYESTES: father of Aegisthus

CHORUS: of Argive Women

CLYTEMNESTRA: wife of Agamemnon

NURSE: of Clytemnestra

AEGISTHUS: son of Thyestes and paramour of Clytemnestra

EURYBATES: messenger of Agamemnon

CHORUS: of Captive Trojan Women

CASSANDRA: daughter of Priam, captive of Agamemnon

AGAMEMNON: king of Argos, and leader of the Greeks against Troyh

ELECTRA: daughter of Agamemnon and Clytemnestra

STROPHIUS: king of Phocis

ORESTES: son of Agamemnon

PYLADES: son of Strophius

[SCENE:—BEFORE THE PALACE OF AGAMEMNON AT MYCENAE OR ARGOS.]

ACT ONE.
SCENE I

[THE GHOST OF THYESTES APPEARS.]

GHOST:
> Escaped from gloomy Pluto's murky realm
> And leaving Tartara's deep pit I come,
> All doubting which abode I hate the more;
> That world I flee, but this I put to flight.
> My soul shrinks back, my limbs do quake with fear.
> I see my father's house—my brother's too!
> Here is the ancient seat of Pelpps' race;
> In this proud hall it is Pelasgians' wont
> To crown their kings; here sit those overlords
> Whose hands the kingdom's haughty scepter wield;
> Here is their council chamber—here they feast!
> Let me go hence. Were it not better far

> To sit beside the dark, sad pools of Styx,
> And see the hell-hound's black and tossing mane?
> Where one, bound fast upon a whirling wheel,
> Back to himself is borne; where fruitless toil
> Is mocked forever by the rolling stone;
> Where living vitals glut the vulture's greed,
> Consumed but e'er renewed; and one old man,
> By mocking waves surrounded, seeks in vain
> To sate his burning thirst, dire punishment
> For that he strove to trick th' immortal gods.
> But, ranked with mine, how slight that old man's sin!
> Take count of all whose impious deeds on earth
> Make them to tremble at the bar of hell:
> By my dread crimes will outdo them all—
> But not my brother's crimes. Three sons of mine
> Lie buried in me, yea, mine own dear flesh
> Have I consumed. Nor this the only blot
> With which dire fortune's hand hath stained my soul;
> But, daring greater sin, she bade me seek
> (Oh, foul impiety!) my daughter's arms.
> Bold for revenge, I dared and did the deed,
> And so the fearful cycle was complete:
> As sons the sire, so sire the daughter filled.
> Then were the laws of nature backward turned:
> I mingled sire with grandsire, sons with grandsons;
> Yea, monstrous! Husband and father did I join,
> And drove the day back to the shades of night.
> But fate at last, though doubtful, long deferred,
> Hath had regard unto my evil plight,
> And brought the day of vengeance near; for lo,
> This king of kings, this leader of the Greeks,
> This Agamemnon comes, whose royal flag
> A thousand Grecian vessels following
> Once filled the Trojan waters with their sails.
> Now ten bright suns have run their course, and Troy
> Has been o'erthrown, and he is close at hand—
> To place his neck in Clytemnestra's power.

Now, now, this house shall flow again with
    blood,
But this of Atreus' stock! Swords, axes, darts
I see, and that proud head with murderous stroke
Asunder cleft; now impious crimes are near,
Now treachery, slaughter, blood; the feast is
    spread.
The cause, Aegisthus, of thy shameful birth,
Is come at last. But why hangs down thy head
In shame? Why hesitates thy faltering hand
And sinks inactive? Why dost counsel take
Within thy heart, and turn away, and ask
Whether this deed become thee? Do but think
Upon thy mother; then wilt thou confess
It doth become thee well. But what drags out
In long delay this summer night's brief span
To winter's hours of darkness? And what cause
Prevents the stars from sinking in the sky?
The sun shrinks from my face. I must away,
That so he may bring back the light of day.

[The Ghost vanishes.]

ACT ONE.
SCENE II

[Enter Chorus of argive women.]

Chorus:
  On fortune's headlong brink they stand
    Who hold the scepter in their hand;
    No safe assurance can they know
    Who on too lofty pathways go:
  But care on care pursues them to the last,
  Their souls assailed and vexed by every blast.

    As seas on Libya's sandy shore
    Their waves in ceaseless billows pour;
    As Euxine's swelling waters rise
    Beneath the lowering northern skies,
    Where bright Boötes wheels his team
    High o'er the ocean's darksome stream:
  With such assaults, by such wild tempests blown,
  Does fortune batter at a kingly throne!

    Who would be feared, in fear must live.
    No kindly night can refuge give;

Nor sleep, that comforts all the rest,
  Can bring care-freedom to his breast.
What throne so safe, on such foundation stands,
That may not be destroyed by impious hands?

    For justice, shame, the virtues all,
    E'en wifely faith, soon flee the hall
    Where courtiers dwell. Within, there stands
    Bellona dire with blood's hands;
    Erinys too, the dogging fate,
    Of them who hold too high estate,
  Which any hour from high to low may bring.
    Though arms be lacking, wiles be none,
    Still is the will of fortune done:
  By force of his own greatness falls the king.
    'Tis ever thus: the bellying sail
    Fears the o'erstrong though favouring gale;
    The tower feels rainy Auster's dread
    If to the clouds it rear its head;
    Huge oaks most feel the whirlwind's lash;
    High mountains most with thunder crash;
  And while the common herd in safety feeds,
  Their mighty leader, marked for slaughter, bleeds.

    Fate places us on high, that so
    To surer ruin we may go.
  The meanest things in longest fortune live.
    Then happy he whose modest soul
    In safety seeks a nearer goal;
    Fearing to leave the friendly shore,
    He rows with unambitious oar,
  Content in low security to thrive.

ACT TWO.
SCENE I

[Enter Clytemnestra and her Nurse.]

Clytemnestra:
  Why, sluggish soul, dost thou safe counsel seek?
  Why hesitates? Closed is the better way.
  Once thou couldst chastely guard thy widowed
    couch,
  And keep thy husband's realm with wifely faith;
  But now, long since has faith thy palace fled,
  The homely virtues, honour, piety,
  And chastity, which goes, but ne'er returns.

Loose be thy reins, swift speed thy wanton course;
The safest way through crime is by the path
Of greater crime. Consider in thy heart
All woman's wiles, what faithless wives have
    done,
Bereft of reason, blind and passion-driven;
What bloody deeds stepmother's hands have
    dared;
Or what she dared, ablaze with impious love,
Who left her father's realm for Thessaly:
Dare sword, dare poison; else in stealthy flight
Must thou go hence with him who shares thy
    guilt.
But who would talk of stealth, of exile, flight?
Such were thy sister's deeds: some greater crime,
Some mightier deed of evil suits thy hand.

NURSE:
O Grecian queen, illustrious Leda's child,
What say'st thou there in whispered mutterings?
Or what unbridled deeds within thy breast,
By reckless passion tossed, dost meditate?
Though thou be silent, yet thy face declares
Thy hidden pain in speech more eloquent.
Whate'er thy grief, take time and room for thought.
Time often cures what reason cannot heal.

CLYTEMNESTRA:
Too dire my grief to wait time's healing hand.
My very soul is scorched with flaming pains:
I feel the goads of fear and jealous rage,
The throbbing pulse of hate, the pangs of love,
Base love that presses hard his heavy yoke
Upon my heart, and holds me vanquished quite.
And always, 'mid those flames that vex my soul,
Though faint indeed, and downcast, all undone,
Shame struggles on. By shifting seas I'm tossed:
As when here wind, there tide impels the deep,
The waves stand halting 'twixt the warring powers.
And so I'll strive no more to guide my bark.
Where wrath, where grief, where hope shall bear
    me on,
There will I speed my course; my helmless ship
I've giv'n to be the sport of winds and floods.
Where reason fails 'tis best to follow chance.

NURSE:
Oh, rash and blind, who follows doubtful chance.

CLYTEMNESTRA:
Who fears a doubtful chance, if 'tis his last?

NURSE:
Thy fault may find safe hiding if thou wilt.

CLYTEMNESTRA:
Nay, faults of royal homes proclaim themselves.

NURSE:
Dost thou repent the old, ye plan the new?

CLYTEMNESTRA:
To stop midway in sin is foolishness.

NURSE:
His fears increase, who covers crime with crime.

CLYTEMNESTRA:
But iron and fire oft aid the healer's art.

NURSE:
Yet desperate measures no one first attempts.

CLYTEMNESTRA:
The path of sin is headlong from the first.

NURSE:
Still let thy wifely duty hold thee back.

CLYTEMNESTRA:
What long-deserted wife regards her lord?

NURSE:
Your common children—hast no thought of
    them?

CLYTEMNESTRA:
I do think on my daughter's wedding rites,
Highborn Achilles, and my husband's lies.

NURSE:
She freed our Grecian fleet from long delay,
And waked from their dull calm the sluggish seas.

CLYTEMNESTRA:
Oh, shameful though! That I, the heaven-born
    child
Of Tyndarus, should give my daughter up
To save the Grecian fleet! I see once more
In memory my daughter's wedding day,
Which he made worthy of base Pelops' house,
When, with his pious face, this father stood
Before the altar fires—Oh, monstrous rites!
E'en Calchas shuddered at his own dread words
And backward-shrinking fires. O bloody house,
That ever wades through crime to other crime!
With blood we soothe the winds, with blood
    we war.

NURSE:
Yet by that blood a thousand vessels sailed.

CLYTEMNESTRA:
But not with favouring omens did they sail;
The port of Aulis fairly drave them forth.
So launched in war, he still no better fared.
Smit with a captive's love, unmoved by prayer,
He held as spoil the child of Phoebus' priest,
E'en then, as now, a sacred maiden's thrall.
Nor could the stern Achilles bend his will,
Nor he whose eye alone can read the fates
(A faithful seer to us, to captives mild),
Nor his pest-smitten camp and gleaming pyres.
When baffled Greece stood tottering to her fall,
This man with passion pined, had time for love,
Thought ever on amours; and, lest his couch
Should be of any Phrygian maid bereft,
He lusted for Achilles' beauteous bride,
Nor blushed to tear her from her lover's arms.
Fit foe for Paris! Now new wounds he feels,
And burns, inflamed by mad Cassandra's love.
And, now that Troy is conquered, home he comes,
A captive's husband, Priam's son-in-law!
Arise, my soul; no easy task essay;
Be swift to act. What dost thou, sluggish, wait
Till Phrygian rivals wrest thy power away?
Or do thy virgin daughters stay thy hand,
Or yet Orestes, image of his sire?
Nay, 'tis for these thy children thou must act,
Lest greater ills befall them; for, behold,
A mad stepmother soon shall call them hers.
Through thine own heart, if so thou must, prepare
To drive the sword, and so slay two in one.

Let thy blood flow with his; in slaying, die.
For death is sweet if with a foeman shared.

NURSE:
My queen, restrain thyself, check thy wild wrath,
And think how great thy task. Atrides comes,
Wild Asia's conqueror and Europe's lord;
He leads Troy captive, Phrygia subdued.
'Gainst him wouldst thou with sly assault prevail,
Whom great Achilles slew not with his sword,
Though he with angry hand the weapon drew;
Nor Telamonian Ajax, crazed with rage;
Nor Hector, Troy's sole prop and war's delay;
Nor Paris' deadly darts; nor Memmon black;
Nor Xanthus, choked with corpses and with arms;
Nor Simois' waves, empurpled with the slain;
Nor Cynus, snowy offspring of the sea;
Nor warlike Rhesus with his Thracian band;
Nor that fierce maid who led the Amazons,
Armed with the deadly battle-axe and shield?
This hero, home returned, dost thou prepare
To slay, and stain thy hearth with impious blood?
Would Greece, all hot from conquest, suffer this?
Bethink thee of the countless steeds and arms,
The sea a-bristle with a thousand ships,
The plains of Ilium soaked with streams of blood,
Troy taken and in utter ruin laid:
Remember this, I say, and check thy wrath,
And bid thy thoughts in safer channels run.

For the entire play, insert the Literature CD.

Questions

1. In act two, scene one, Clytemnestra says: "To stop midway in sin is foolishness." How might this line be interpreted, and what does this foreshadow about the remainder of the play?

2. The will of Clytemnestra is tested in act two, scene two. Who helps her follow through with the murder of Agamemnon? How does this character restore Clytemnestra's faith in the murderous plan?

3. What is the role of children in this play? How do they affect the direction of the play? Without them, how would the outcome of this play be different?

1. In act three, scene two, the Chorus of Trojan Women mentions that "fatal gift." What is the Chorus referring to? After researching the battle of Troy, explore the genesis of this fatal gift and its significance to the fall of Troy.
2. Based on Seneca's biographical information, and based on the characters in *Agamemnon*, articulate Seneca's definition of human suffering. Further, show how Seneca's definition of human suffering helps advance one theme in *Agamemnon*.
3. A Greek author, Aeschylus, was actually the first to write this play, but Seneca chose to re-dramatize it, for he wanted to portray a deeper level of human suffering in his version. *Agamemnon,* however, is not the only play that Seneca has re-dramatized. Compare some of Seneca's re-dramatized works with the originals (i.e., *Oedipus, Agamemnon,* or *Medea*). Upon doing this, compare and contrast the levels of human suffering in two of Seneca's plays.

The Trojan Women

1. *The Trojan Women* is a play that focuses not only on the spoils of war but the cataclysmic destruction of an entire culture. Once again, a theme revolving around human suffering is prevalent in this play as Seneca depicts a time of great peril for the citizens of Troy.
2. Among the most powerful lines in the play are those uttered by Pyrrhus. In Act two, Scene two, he says: "My father conquered Troy; the lesser task / Of pillage and destruction is your own." It would be extremely helpful to look up some information on Pyrrhus' father (Achilles) and study this great warrior's effect on the Trojan War.

The Trojan Women

Seneca

CHARACTERS

HECUBA: widow of Priam, one of the Trojan captives
CHORUS: of Trojan Women
TALTHYBIUS: a Greek messenger
PYRRHUS: son of Achilles, one of the active Greek leaders

AGAMEMNON: commander-in-chief of the Greek forces
CALCHAS: a priest and prophet among the Greeks
ANDROMACHE: widow of Hector, and one of the Trojan captives
AN OLD MAN: faithful to Andromache

ULYSSES: king of Ithaca, the most crafty of the
Greek leaders
ASTYANAX: little son of Hector and Andromache
HELEN: wife of Menelaus, king of Sparta, and
afterward of Paris, a prince of Troy; the exciting
cause of the Trojan war
POLYXENA: daughter of Hecuba and Priam

*[SCENE:—THE SEASHORE, WITH THE SMOULDERING
RUINS OF TROY IN THE BACKGROUND.]*

*ACT ONE.
SCENE I*

*[ENTER HECUBA, ATTENDANT BY THE CHORUS
OF TROJAN WOMEN.]*

HECUBA:
Whoe'er in royal power has put his trust,
And proudly lords it in his princely halls;
Who fears no shifting of the winds of fate,
But fondly gives his soul to present joys:
Let him my lot and thine, O Troy, behold.
For of a truth did fortune never show
In plainer wise the frailty of the prop
That doth support a king; since by her hand
Brought low, behold, proud Asia's capitol,
The work of heavenly hands, lies desolate.
From many lands the warring princes came
To aid her cause: from where the Tanais
His frigid waves in sevenfold channel pours;
And that far land which greets the newborn day,
Where Tigris mingles with the ruddy sea
His tepid waves; and where the Amazon,
Within the view of wandering Scythia
Arrays her virgin ranks by Pontus' shores.
Yet here, o'erthrown, our ancient city lies
Herself upon herself in ruins laid;
Her once proud walls in smouldering heaps recline,
Mingling their ashes with our fallen homes.
The palace flames on high, while far and near
The stately city of Assaracus
Is wrapped in gloomy smoke. Yet e'en the
flames
Keep not the victor's greedy hands from spoil;
And Troy, though in the grasp of fiery death,
Is pillaged still. The face of heaven is hid

By that dense, wreathing smoke; the shining day,
As if o'erspread by some thick, lowering cloud,
Grows black and foul beneath the ashy storm.
The victor stands with still unsated wrath,
Eyeing that stubborn town of Ilium,
And scarce at last forgives those ten long years
Of bloody strife. Anon, as he beholds
That mighty city, though in ruins laid,
He starts with fear; and though he plainly sees
His foe o'ercome, he scarce can comprehend
That she could be o'ercome. The Dardan spoil
Is heaped on high, a booty vast, which Greece,
In all her thousand ships, can scarce bestow.
Now witness, ye divinities whose face
Was set against our state, my fatherland
In ashes laid; and thou, proud king of Troy,
Who in thy city's overthrow hast found
A fitting tomb; thou shade of mighty Hector,
In whose proud strength abiding, Ilium stood;
Likewise ye thronging ghosts, my children all,
But lesser shades: whatever ill has come
Whatever Phoebus' bride with frenzied speech,
Though all discredited, hath prophesied;
I, Hecuba, myself foresaw, what time,
With unborn child o'erweighed, I dreamed a
dream
That I had borne a flaming brand. And though,
Cassandra-like, I told my fears, my warnings,
Like our Cassandra's words in after time,
Were all in vain. 'Tis not the Ithacan,
Nor yet his trusty comrade of the night,
Nor that false traitor, Sinon, who has cast
The flaming brands that wrought our overthrow:
Mine is the fire—'tis by my brands ye burn.
But why dost thou bewail the city's fall,
With ancient gossip's prattle? Turn thy mind,
Unhappy one, to nearer woes than these.
Troy's fall, though sad, is ancient story now.
I saw the horrid slaughter of the king,
Defiling the holy altar with its stain,
When bold Aeacides, with savage hand
Entwined in helpless Prima's hoary locks,
Drew back his sacred head, and thrust the sword
Hilt-buried in his unresisting side.
And when he plucked the deep-driven weapon
back,
So weak and bloodless was our aged king,
The deadly blade came almost stainless forth.

Whose thirst for blood had not been satisfied
By that old man just slipping o'er the verge
Of life? Whom would not heavenly witnesses
Restrain from crime? Who would not stay his hand
Before the sacred altar, last resort
Of fallen thrones? Yet he, our noble Priam,
The king, and father of so many kings,
Lies like the merest peasant unentombed;
And, though all Troy's aflame, there's not a brand
To light his pyre and give him sepulture.
And still the heavenly powers are not appeased.
Behold the urn; and, subject to its lot,
The maids and matrons of our princely line,
Who wait their future lords. To whom shall I,
An aged and unprized allotment, fall?
One Grecian lord has fixed his longing eyes
On Hector's queen; another prays the lot
To grant to him the bride of Helenus;
Anenor's spouse is object of desire,
And e'en thy hand, Cassandra, hath its suitor"
My lot alone they deprecate and fear.
And can ye cease your plaints? O captive throng,
Come beat upon your breasts, and let the sound
Of your loud lamentations rise anew,
The while we celebrate in fitting wise
Troy's funeral; let fatal Ida, seat
Of that ill-omened judgment, straight resound
With echoes of our pitiful refrain.

ACT ONE.
SCENE II

CHORUS:

Not an untrained band, to tears unknown,
Thou callest to grief, for our tears have rained
In streams unending through the years,
Since the time when the Phrygian guest arrived
At the friendly court of Tyndarus,
Sailing the sea in his vessel framed
From the sacred pines of Cybele.
Ten winters have whitened Ida's slopes,
So often stripped for our funeral pyres;
Ten years have ripened the waving grain
Which the trembling reaper has garnered in
From wide Sigean harvest-fields:
But never a day was without its grief,

Never a night but renewed our woe.
Then on with the wailing and on with the blows;
And thou, poor fate-smitten queen, be our guide,
Our mistress in mourning; we'll obey thy
    commands,
Well trained in the wild liturgy of despair.

HECUBA:

Then, trusty comrades of our fate,
Unbind your tresses and let them flow
Over your shoulders bent with grief,
The while with Troy's slow-cooling dust
Ye sprinkle them. Lay bare your arms,
Strip from your breasts their covering;
Why veil your beauty? Shame itself
Is held in captive bonds. And now
Let your hands wave free to the quickening blows
That resound to your wailings. So, now are ye
    ready,
And thus it is well. I behold once more
My old-time Trojan band. Now stoop
And fill your hands; 'tis right to take
Her dust at least from fallen Troy.
Now let the long-pent grief leap forth,
And surpass your accustomed bounds of woe.
Oh, weep for Hector, wail and weep.

CHORUS:

Our hair, in many a funeral torn,
We loose; and o'er our streaming locks
Troy's glowing ashes lie bestrewn.
From our shoulders the veiling garments fall,
And our breasts invite the smiting hands.
Now, now, O grief, put forth thy strength.
Let the distant shores resound with our
    mourning,
And let Echo who dwells in the slopes of the
    mountains
Repeat all our wailings, not, after her wont,
With curt iteration returning the end.
Let earth hear and heed; let the sea and the sky
Record all our grief. Then smite, O ye hands,
With the strength of frenzy batter and bruise.
With crying and blows and the pain of the
    smiting—
Oh, weep for Hector, wail and weep.

HECUBA:

Our hero, for thee the blows are descending,
On arms and shoulders that stream with our
blood;
For thee our brows endure rough strokes,
And our breasts are mangled with pitiless hands.
Now flow the old wounds, reopened anew,
That bled at thy death, the chief cause of our
sorrow.
O prop of our country, delayer of fate,
Our Ilium's bulwark, our mighty defender,
Our strong tower wast thou; secure on thy
shoulders,
Our city stood leaning through ten weary years.
By thy power supported, with thee has she fallen,
Our country and Hector united in doom.
Now turn to another the tide of your mourning;
Let Priam receive his due meed of your tears

CHORUS:

Receive our lamentings, O Phrygia's ruler;
We weep for thy death, who wast twice
overcome.
Naught once did Troy suffer while thou didst rule
o'er her:
Twice fell her proud walls from the blows of the
Grecians,
And twice was she pierced by great Hercules'
darts.
Now all of our Hecuba's offspring have perished,
And the proud band of kings who came to our aid;
Thy death is the last—our father, our ruler—
Struck down as a victim to Jove the Almighty,
All helpless and lone, a mute corpse on the ground.

HECUBA:

Nay, give to another your tears and your
mourning,
And weep not the death of Priam our king.
But call ye him blessed the rather; for free,
To the deep world of shadows he travels, and
never
Upon his bowed neck the base yoke shall he bear.
No proud sons of Atreus shall call him their
captive,
No crafty Ulysses his eyes shall behold;
As boast of their triumphs he shall not bear
onward
In humble submission their prizes of war.
Those free, royal hands to the scepter
accustomed,
Shall never be bound at his back like a slave,
As he follows the car of the triumphing chieftain,
A king led in fetters, the gaze of the town.

CHORUS:

Hail! Priam the blessed we all do proclaim him;
For himself and his kingdom he rules yet below;
No through the still depths of Elysium's shadows
'Midst calm, happy spirits he seeks the great
Hector
Then hail, happy Priam! Hail all who in battle
Have lost life and country, but liberty gained.

**For the entire play,
insert the Literature CD.**

Questions

1. Throughout the play, the flames of Troy light the background. What do these flames symbolize?
2. In act four, scene one, Andromache says: "For the blood of Asia flowed; for thee / Did Europe's heroes bleed [. . .] ." Who is Andromache addressing, and why is this character significant?
3. From the conversation that takes place between Pyrrhus and Agamemnon in act two, scene two, what can the reader infer about the relationship between Agamemnon and Achilles?
4. What makes Astyanax such an important character?

Continued

5. What is the story of Helen's past? Why is she such a significant figure in this play and in Troy's history?
6. At the beginning of act five, what heinous act does the messenger describe? How does this advance Seneca's message about human suffering?
7. What signifies the conclusion of this "great war," and who describes this final event? What is the purpose of this character's role throughout the play?

1. It seems plausible to say that Andromache embodies a certain level of human suffering. Classify the level of her suffering with other characters from this play, and support your classifications with support from the play and from outside sources.
2. From the religious beliefs and rites of death that Seneca introduces in *The Trojan Women*, what can one infer about these people? After performing some research, construct an argument that examines these beliefs and rites, noting how they help advance two themes in *The Trojan Women*.
3. In *The Trojan Women*, children play a vital role. Examine the role of children in *The Trojan Women*, and compare it with the role of children in Seneca's *Agamemnon*.

4

Old-English Literature

After the fall of Rome in 476 CE, Europe entered a period known as the "Dark Ages." This era was marked by a noticeable decline in European national security and a rise in bloodshed. Raping and pillaging became the norm, and Europe was without prominent leadership. This was also a time when Christianity's roots were starting to take hold in many European social circles. Many church leaders clearly saw their role in this period: to fight off the evil that was spreading throughout Europe. This evil typically came in the form of bloodthirsty, Viking brigands. These seafaring heathens were considered heartless and sought to seize any piece of land whenever the opportunity arose. They preyed on the weak, and it is believed that their brutal behavior helped support the church's argument that Satan was present on Earth. And it is from the ashes of this period that arose some of the finest lyrical verse found in literary history.

Before reading works from this time period, it is important to know the origins of the Old-English writers. When the Roman military left Britain in the early fifth century, it was left ill-prepared to defend itself against the vicious Scots, Picts, and the aforementioned Viking invaders (the Scots and Picts came from what is now considered Scotland). The settlers who remained in Britain sought help from nearby Anglo-Saxon tribes. These tribes were made up of Angles, Saxons, and Jutes. These people originally came from what is now considered Northern Germany and Southern Scandinavia. This is one reason why the Anglo-Saxon people are often referred to as a Germanic race. While many make the mistake of thinking that all three of these tribes came from the same area, "Germanic" is actually associated with the various civilizations who occupied "Dark Age England." After these tribes helped defeat the Scots and the Picts, the tribal leaders decided to mobilize and turn on the British settlers they had aided. Their inhabitance of England during the fifth century gave England the label: "Dark Age England." The heathen nature of these people helped contribute to this morbid title. There is no doubt, in fact, that these people were barbaric in nature, and with constant attacks coming from various Viking tribes, the Anglo-Saxons had no choice but to be an aggressive civilization.

Much of the literature from this time period is known as Old-English literature because it was the Angles, Saxons, and Jutes whom eventually combined to form the Anglo-Saxon race and call themselves English. There is, however, a great deal of speculation about the authors of the works during this time period. For instance, the authors of *Beowulf* and "The Battle of Maldon" are not even known. It is believed that these authors were of Anglo-Saxon descent, and their poetry is often replete with heroism and religious zeal.

Many of the poems from this time period involve a Christian, God-like character who is called upon to perform a heroic act of bravery. Typically, this character is of royal descent, which helps lend credence to one of the Anglo-Saxon's beliefs: the Anglo-Saxon people believed that a noble was blessed by God and granted special powers when performing on the battlefield. After this heroic character attained his monumental victory, he would become ruler of the people or land that he had helped defend (this Old-English theme ties in nicely with what the Anglo-Saxons did to the inhabitants of Britain). During the time of "Dark Age England," many persecuted people were in need of such heroes, and the literary works from this time period gave people a place where they could find such acts of heroism.

Beowulf

1. This poem was written during a time when Britain was predominantly Christian, yet it presents examples of Pagan thought.
2. Throughout this epic poem, look for historical and legendary allusions that lend credence to the idea that it was written in a Christian Britain.
3. Note how familial bonds and alliances play a vital role in *Beowulf.*

Beowulf

Anonymous

LO, praise of the prowess of people-kings of spear-armed Danes, in days long sped, we have heard, and what honor the athelings won!

Oft Scyld the Scefing from squadroned foes, from many a tribe, the mead-bench tore, awing the earls.

Since erst he lay friendless, a foundling, fate repaid him: for he waxed under welkin, in wealth he throve, till before him the folk, both far and near, whose house by the whale-path, heard his mandate, gave him gifts: a good king he!

To him an heir was afterward born, a son in his halls, whom heaven sent to favor the folk, feeling their woe that erst they had lacked an earl for leader so long a while; the Lord endowed him, the Wielder of Wonder, with world's renown.

Famed was this Beowulf: far flew the boast of him, son of Scyld, in the Scandian lands.

So becomes it a youth to quit him well with his father's friends, by fee and gift, that to aid him, aged, in after days, come warriors willing, should war draw nigh, liegemen loyal: by lauded deeds shall an earl have honor in every clan.

Forth he fared at the fated moment, sturdy Scyld to the shelter of God.

Then they bore him over to ocean's billow, loving clansmen, as late he charged them, while wielded words the winsome Scyld, the leader beloved who long had ruled. . . .

In the roadstead rocked a ring-dight vessel, ice-flecked, outbound, atheling's barge: there laid they down their darling lord on the breast of the boat, the breaker-of-rings, by the mast the mighty one.

Many a treasure fetched from far was freighted with him.

No ship have I known so nobly dight with weapons of war and weeds of battle, with breastplate and blade: on his bosom lay a heaped hoard that hence should go far o'er the flood with him floating away.

No less these loaded the lordly gifts, thanes' huge treasure, than those had done who in former time forth had sent him sole on the seas, a suckling child.

High o'er his head they hoist the standard, a gold-wove banner; let billows take him, gave him to ocean.

Grave were their spirits, mournful their mood.
No man is able to say in sooth, no son of the halls,
   no hero 'neath heaven,—who harbored that
   freight!

Now Beowulf bode in the burg of the Scyldings,
   leader beloved, and long he ruled in fame with all
   folk, since his father had gone away from the
   world, till awoke an heir, haughty Healfdene,
   who held through life, sage and sturdy, the
   Scyldings glad.
Then, one after one, there woke to him, to the
   chieftain of clansmen, children four:

Heorogar, then Hrothgar, then Halga brave; and I
   heard that—was—'s queen, the Heathoscylfing's
   helpmate dear.
To Hrothgar was given such glory of war, such
   honor of combat, that all his kin obeyed him
   gladly till great grew his band of youthful
   comrades.
It came in his mind to bid his henchmen a hall
   uprear, in a master mead-house, mightier far than
   ever was seen by the sons of earth, and within it,
   then, to old and young he would all allot that the
   Lord had sent him, save only the land and the
   lives of his men.
Wide, I heard, was the work commanded, for many
   a tribe this mid-earth round, to fashion the
   folkstead.
It fell, as he ordered, in rapid achievement that
   ready it stood there, of halls the noblest: Heorot
   he named it whose message had might in many a
   land.
Not reckless of promise, the rings he dealt, treasure
   at banquet: there towered the hall, high, gabled
   wide, the hot surge waiting of furious flame.

Nor far was that day when father and son-in-law
   stood in feud for warfare and hatred that woke
   again.
With envy and anger an evil spirit endured the dole
   in his dark abode, that he heard each day the din
   of revel high in the hall: there harps rang out,
   clear song of the singer.
He sang who knew tales of the early time of man,
   how the Almighty made the earth, fairest fields
   enfolded by water, set, triumphant, sun and moon
   for a light to lighten the land-dwellers, and
   braided bright the breast of earth with limbs and
   leaves, made life for all of mortal beings that
   breathe and move.
So lived the clansmen in cheer and revel a winsome
   life, till one began to fashion evils, that field of
   hell.
Grendel this monster grim was called, march-riever
   mighty, in moorland living, in fen and fastness;
   fief of the giants the hapless wight a while had
   kept since the Creator his exile doomed.
On kin of Cain was the killing avenged by sovran
   God for slaughtered Abel.
Ill fared his feud, and far was he driven, for the
   slaughter's sake, from sight of men.
Of Cain awoke all that woful breed, Etins and elves
   and evil-spirits, as well as the giants that warred
   with God weary while: but their wage was paid
   them!

**For the entire poem,
insert the Literature CD.**

Questions

1. This poem begins with the funeral of a great king. Who is this figure, and what is significant
   about his past? Why is it important for the reader to learn about this once proud king?
2. What role do thanes play in this poem? In what way do they help protect the kingdom, and
   how are they cared for?

3. What aggravates Grendel to the point of murder? What is symbolic about this act that drives Grendel to kill?

4. What is Beowulf's motivation for sailing to Denmark and destroying Grendel? What does this suggest about the Anglo-Saxon belief in the importance of family?

5. Beowulf's "war shirt" is of special importance. What does this piece of clothing symbolize, and why is it important that this shirt be sent back to Hygelac if Beowulf should fall?

6. How does Grendel's mother seek revenge for the death of her son? What does this vengeful act suggest about the will of Grendel's mother?

7. Why is Beowulf's sword considered a "veneration" to his culture?

8. What warning does Hrothgar issue to Beowulf after Beowulf returns from slaying Grendel's mother? What does this warning foreshadow?

9. What is the specific gift that makes Beowulf a lord? How does he become King of the Geats? From what the reader learns about Beowulf, what inferences can be made about the kind of ruler he will be?

10. Besides the fatal blow, what action leads to the death of Beowulf? What is the motivation for this action?

Research and Writing

1. *Beowulf* reinforces the belief that warlike feuds beget warlike feuds. Does this belief exist in any other work of ancient literature; does it exist today? Construct an argument for or against the notion that conflict begets conflict. In doing so, consider various examples, including the Jewish / Palestinian conflict, the Catholic / Protestant conflict, and the Indian / Pakistani conflict.

2. If one were to analyze *Beowulf's* settings, it would become evident that some have biblical significance—for instance, the home of Grendel and his mother. Construct an argument that examines biblical significance in *Beowulf,* and support it by citing the poem and other texts.

3. How does fate play a role in *Beowulf?* After addressing this question, analyze the role of fate when the dragon enters the poem, noting specifically how this idea is contrary to the Christian belief regarding predestination and God's plan. Construct an argument that examines the importance of fate, noting whether or not fate is the driving force throughout *Beowulf.*

4. Construct an argument that examines whether or not Beowulf is the ideal ruler of the Geats. Make sure to identify the characteristics of an ideal king and support these characteristics by citing outside sources.

5. Compare and contrast the reign of Beowulf with another ruler from canonical literature. Some possible comparisons can be made to Agamemnon, Aeneas, or Oedipus.

Cynewulf (Dates of birth and death unknown)

Much of what is known about Cynewulf is based on theories and conjecture. It can be inferred that he wrote in the latter part of the eighth century and that he was deeply religious. Further, the poems that he is credited with are revolutionary. There are only four known poems that actually have Cynewulf's signature assigned to them, and even though other poems from this genre seem influenced by Cynewulf, there is no evidence that he wrote them.

Cynewulf's *Constantine's Vision of the Cross* is a poem that glorifies the Emperor Constantine's historical vision in 312 CE. During this year, there was a scramble for power, for the Emperor Diocletian had just retired from the throne. Before the historic battle near the Tiber River, Constantine, a general at the time, knelt to pray on the night before the battle. During his prayer, it is believed that he saw a vision of the cross. During this vision, it is also believed that he saw the words, "In hoc signo vinces" ("In this sign you will be victorious"). This enlightening experience, coupled with a major military victory in the days that followed, changed the history of Rome, for Constantine eventually became Emperor of Rome, was more accepting of the Christian faith, and was even baptized shortly before he died. It is safe to assume that Constantine's vision of the cross—and his victory—paved the way for Christianity to flourish throughout the Empire. The fear of persecution slowly started to diminish for the Christians, and they soon saw Constantine as the ruler who helped provide them with religious freedom.

Constantine's Vision of the Cross

1. Note this poem's tone, and note how Cynewulf does not just revere Constantine as the leader of an army but a leader of mankind.
2. While reading this poem, realize that Constantine may have been the most significant ruler in the history of Rome. This should be impressive, especially considering Rome's celebrated history of rulers.

Constantine's Vision of the Cross

Cynewulf

The year was the sixth of Constantine's sway
Since he was raised up in the Roman kingdom
To be battle-lord and leader in war.
He was eager for praise, defender of peoples,
Unto men merciful; his princely might
Increased under heaven. He was true king,
War-lord of peoples. God prospered him
In glory and might so that for many
Through all the earth he became a comfort,
Defending the folk, when against the foe
He took up weapons.
       He was threatened with war,
Tumult of battle. The Hunnish tribe
And the Hreth-Goths also assembled a host.
Fierce in strife marched the Franks and the Hugas;
Bold men were they and ready for battle.
War-spears glittered and woven mail;
With shout and shield they raised their standards.
The men of war were openly mustered,
The clan was gathered, the folk fared forth.
The wolf in the wood sang his song of war,
Hid not his hope of carnage to come.
The wet-winged eagle clamored and cried
As he followed the foe. Straight through the cities
The greatest of battle-hosts hasted to war
In hordes as many as the Hunnish king
Might anywhere muster of neighboring men,
Mail-clad warriors. The mightiest of armies
Went forth to battle in bands made strong
With mounted legions, till in foreign land
They boldly camped on the Danube's bank
Near the river's torrent with tumult of men.
Fain would they conquer the kingdom of Rome,
Plunder and waste it. The approach of the Huns
Was known through the cities. And Caesar bade
Against the fierce foe's flying arrows
Summon the warriors straightway to strife,
Bring men to battle under the sky.
Straightway the Romans, strong in might,
Were weaponed for battle though their war-band
    was less
Than rode round the ruthless king of the Huns.
      Then shields resounded and war-wood sang;

The king with his troops advanced to attack.
The raven clamored cruel and dark.
The host moved forward; horn-bearers leaped;
Heralds shouted; horses trod earth;
The army assembled, the stalwart to strife.
      Then the king was affrighted, shaken with fear,
When he beheld the foreign foe,
The army of Huns, the horde of the Hreth-Goths,
Who there at the Roman Empire's end
On the river's margin mustered their host,
A countless force. The Roman king
Endured heart-sorrow. No hope had he
Of winning the battle for want of strength.
He had too few warriors, trusted comrades,
Against that overnight of stalwart men.
There the army encamped, eorls round their prince,
Near to the river for the night-long time
After first they beheld the march of the foe.
      Then to great Caesar as he lay in slumber
Asleep with his train was a vision revealed.
To him appeared a beauteous Presence,
In man's shape made manifest,
Whiet and shining, more fair of form
Than arly or late he beheld under heaven.
He started from slumber, did on his boar-helm,
And straightway the herald, fair heavenly form,
Spoke unto Caesar, named him by name,
And the veil of darkness vanished away:
    "O Constantine, the King of angels,
Leader of nations and Lord of fate,
Proclaims a compact. Be not afraid
Though these foreign tribes threaten with terror,
With hard battle to heaven look up,
To the Prince of glory. There find support
And a token of triumph."
      Straightway the king
Opened his heart to the angel's bidding
And looked on high as the herald bade,
Fair weaver of concord. Clothed with treasure
O'er the roof of clouds he beheld the Cross
Adorned with gold; its jewels glittered.
The radiant Tree was written round
With gleaming letters of glowing light:

"With this sign thou shalt halt the hostile host,
And crush the foe in this perilous fray."
    Then the radiance faded faring on high,
And the angel with it, to the host of the holy.
The king was the blither, the captain of heroes,
And the freer from sorrow in his inmost soul
By virtue of that vision so wondrous fair.
    Then Constantine, the glorious king,
Protector of princes and Giver of gifts,
War-lord of armies, bade quickly work
And shape a symbol like the Cross of Christ
As he saw that sign revealed in the heavens.
He bade at dawn, at the break of day,
Rouse the warriors to the weapon-storm,
Lift high the standard, the Holy Tree,
In the thick of the foe bear the Cross before them.
    Loud o'er the legions the trumpets sang.
The raven rejoiced; the wet-winged eagle
Gazed on the struggle, the cruel strife;
The wolf, woodland comrade, lifted his wail.
Battle-terror was come. Then was crashing of shields,
Crush of heroes and hard hand-swing,
The slaughter of many, when first they met
The flying darts. Against the doomed
The stalwart fighters with strong hand
Sent storms of arrows, their battle-adders,

O'er the yellow shield on the savage foe.
Stout-hearted they stormed, fiercely attacking;
Broke through the shield-hedge; drove home the
    sword.
Before the legions the banner was lifted,
The war-song was sung. Helmets of gold
And spear-points flashed on the field of war.
The pagans perished; peaceless they fell.
    Then headlong fled the Hunnish folk
When the Roman war-lord waging the fight
Bade lift on high the Holy Tree.
Heroes were scattered; some war took;
Some barely survived in the bitter fight;
Some half-alive fled to a fastness,
Sheltered themselves in the stony cliffs,
Beside the Danube defended a stronghold;
And some at life's end drowned in the river-depths.
    Then the heroes exulted pursuing the heathen
Until evening came from the dawn of day;
Ash-spears flew, their battle-adders.
The host was cut down, the hated horde;
Of the Hunnish troops but few returned home.
So was it clear that the King Almighty
Awarded to Constantine in that day's work
Fortune in battle, glory and fame
And an earthly kingdom, through the Holy Cross.

❓ Questions

1. Constantine is described as "[. . .] the King of angels, Leader of nations and Lord of fate." Are there any other characters from this genre that can be given this title? Also, why might this title be threatening to the Christian belief of the real "[. . .] Leader of nations and Lord of fate"?

2. Who is Constantine's enemy in this poem, and where is this battle taking place? Does this battle have biblical significance?

3. At what point in this poem does the battle occur, and why might it take so long for the author to present this battle to the reader?

4. Is there a sense of predestination in this poem, and if so, where might one find evidence of this?

5. Who is given more credit for Constantine's victory: God or Constantine?

6. How might this poem have affected an individual who lived in "Dark Age England"? How much would it depend on whether or not this person was a believer in Christianity?

1. What was Constantine's role in the development of Christianity? After investigating this period and Constantine, construct an argument that identifies another significant event in Rome's celebrated history, and compare it with Constantine's historic vision of the cross.
2. Some question the motivation of Constantine's decision to embrace Christianity. Knowing that Rome was rife with religious conflict during the time of this vision, construct an argument that examines whether or not it was "convenient" for Constantine to see such a life-altering vision.
3. Constantine's apparent battle was against the Heathen enemy. Research Heathenism, and construct an argument that examines whether or not Constantine's victory over the Heathens was actually a victory of biblical proportions.
4. After researching Constantine, construct an argument that explores the theory that Constantine's mother played a prominent role in his career as general and Emperor of Rome.

The Last Judgment

1. This poem is visual, beginning with the trumpets of darkness and gloom, and ending with the glow of the cross shining over Earth.
2. It is important to know that this poem was written during a time of religious enlightenment.
3. This poem's tone is both celebratory and threatening. Notice the way Cynewulf strikes fear into the hearts of sinners and hope into the hearts of believers.

The Last Judgment

Cynewulf

Suddenly in the midnight on mortal men
The Great Day of the Lord God shall come with
   might,
Filling with fear the fair Creation,
Like a wily thief who walks in darkness,

A robber bold in the black night
Who suddenly assails men fast in slumber,
Lying in wait for the unwary and the unprepared.
     So on Mount Sion a might host
Shall gather together faithful to God,

Bright and blithe; they shall know bliss.
From the four regions of earth's realm,
From the uttermost corners of earth's kingdom,
All-shining angels in unison sounding
Shall blow their trumpets in a great blast.
The earth shall tremble, the mold under men.
Loud shall resound the strains of the trumpets
Swelling clear to the course of the stars
They shall peal and sing from south and north,
From east and west over all creation.
They shall wake from death the sons of warriors,
All mankind, from the ancient earth
To the terror of Judgment, telling them rise,
Start up straightway from their deep sleep. . . .
      Suddenly on Mount Sion from the south and
        east
Shall come from the Creator light like the sun
Shining more bright than men may imagine,
Gleaming in splendor, when the Son of God
Through the arching heavens hither appears.
Then comes the wondrous presence of Christ,
The glory of the Great King, from the eastern skies,
Cordial and kind to his own people,
Severe to the sinful, wondrously varying:
Unto the blessed and the forlorn unlike!
      To all the good He is gracious of aspect,
Winsome and blithe to that holy band,
Joyous and loving, a gentle Friend.
'Tis a pleasant sight and sweet His dear ones,
That shining beauty gentle in joy,
The Coming of the Saviour, the King of might,
To all who earlier here on earth
Pleased Him well by their words and works.
      But to transgressors, to guilty souls
Who come before Him destroyed by sin
He shall be fearful and frightful to see.
This may serve as a warning of woe for sinners
That a man of wisdom need feel no dismay,
No whit of dread in the Day of Doom.
In the face of that terror he shall not fear
When he sees the Shaper of all Creation
Moving to Judgment with wondrous might,
And round Him circling on every side
The angel multitude in shining muster,
Hosts of the holy throng upon throng.
      There is din through the deep Creation. Before
        God
The greatest of raging fires flames over earth

The hot blaze surges, the heavens shall fall;
The steadfast light of the stars shall fail.
The sun shall be blackened to the hue of blood
Which shone so brightly for the sons of men
Over the ancient earth. The moon herself
That by night illumined mankind with her light
Shall sink from her station; so also the stars
Swept by the whirlwind through the storm-beat air
Shall vanish from heaven.
      With His angel host
The Lord of kings shall come to the Judgment,
The glorious Ruler; His gladsome thanes,
The hosts of the holy, shall attend their Lord
When the Prince of men amid pangs of terror
Himself shall seek out the peoples of earth.
      Then loud shall be heard through the wide
        world
The sound of heaven's trumpet; on seven sides
The winds shall rage raving in uproar;
They shall wake and wither the world with storm;
They shall fill with fear the creatures of earth.
Then shall be heard the heaviest of crashes,
Mighty and deafening, a measureless blast,
The greatest of tumults, terrible to men.
      There the doomed hordes and hosts of
        mankind
Shall turn away to the towering flames
Where consuming fire shall sieze them alive,
Some above, some below, filled full of flame.
Then shall be clear how the kin of Adam
Full of sorrow weep in distress,
Nor for little cause, those hapless legions,
But for the greatest of all griefs
When the dark surge of fire, the dusky flame,
Seizes all three: the seas with their fish
The earth with her hills, and the high heavens
Bright with stars. The destroying fire
In fiercest fury shall burn all three
Grimly together. And all the earth
Shall moan in misery in that awful hour.
      So the greedy spirit, the despoiling brands,
Shall search through earth and her high-built halls;
The wide-known blaze burning and greedy
Shall fill the world with a terror of flame
Broken city-walls shall crumble and crash;
Mountains shall melt, and the high cliffs
Which in olden days shielded the earth
Stout and steadfast against the floods,

Barriers against the waters, the breaking waves.
       In that dread hour the death-fire shall clutch
Every creature of bird and beast.
The fire-dark flame shall fare through earth
A raging warrior. As waters of old,
The rushing floods, flowed over earth,
In that hour shall burn in a bath of fire
All the fishes cut off from the sea;
All beasts of the deep shall wretchedly die.
Water shall burn like wax. And then shall be
More of marvels than man can imagine:
How the thunder and storm and the wild wind
Shatter the wide Creation. . . .
       Straightway all of Adam's kin
Shall be clothed with flesh, shall come to an end
Of their rest in earth; each of mankind
Shall rise up living, put on body and limbs,
Made young again at the Coming of Christ.
Each shall have on him of evil or good
All his soul garnered in years gone by,
Shall have both together, body and soul.
Then the manner of his works, and the memory of
   his words,
The hidden musing of his inmost heart,
Shall come to light before heaven's King. . . .
       Then the trumpet's strain and the shining
          standard,
The fiery heat and the heavenly host,
The throng of angels and the throes of fear,
The Day of terror and the towering Cross
Upraised as a sign of the Ruler's might,
Shall summon mankind before the King,
Every soul that early or late
Was fashioned in flesh with limbs and body.
       Then the greater legions, living and young,
Shall go before the face of the Lord God.
By need and by desire known by their names
They shall bring to God's Son the hoard of the
   breast,
The jewels of life. The Father will learn
How safely his sons have guarded their souls
In the former land where they lived on earth.
       Those shall be bold who bring unto God
A shining beauty. Their strength and joy
Shall be greatly abundant to bless their souls,
To reward their works. Well is it with them
Who find favor with God in that grim hour!
       There sin-stained men in anguish of spirit

Shall see as their fate the most fearful of woes:
It shall bring them no grace that the brightest of
   beacons,
The Rood of our Saviour, red with His Blood,
Over-run with bright gore, upreared before men,
With radiant light shall illumine the wide Creation.
No shadows shall lurk where the light of the Cross
Streams on all nations. Yet shall it stand
As a woe and a menace for evil men,
Sinners who gave no thanks to God
That for man's transgressions He grievously hung
On the holy Tree, where with love our Lord
Bought life for men with his ransoming body
(Which had wrought no evil nor any wrong)
Whereby He redeemed us. For that He ordains
A stern requital when the red-stained Rood
Shall shine in splendor in the place of the sun. . . .
       Then chosen souls shall bring before Christ
Their bright treasures; their bliss shall live
In the Day of Doom. They shall joy with God
In the sweet life assigned to the saints
In the heavenly kingdom. That is the home
That knows no ending, but there forever
The pure have delight in praising the Lord,
Dear Warden of life, in light encompassed,
Swathed peace, shielded from sorrow,
Honored with grace, endeared into God.
Always forever the angel band
Bright with glory shall blissfully joy
In the worship of God. The Warden of all
Shall have and shall hold the hosts of the holy.
       There is song of angels and bliss of the
          saints,
The Saviour's dear presence shining more bright
On all His beloved than light of the sun.
There is love of dear ones; life without death;
Exultant multitudes; youth without age
The splendor of heaven's hosts; health without pain;
For the souls of the righteous rest without toil.
There is glory of the saints; day without darkness
Bright with blessing; bliss without sorrow;
Accord among friends without envy forever
For the happy in heaven; love without hate
In that holy throng. No hunger there nor thirst,
Nor sleep nor sickness nor burning sun,
Nor cold nor care. But the bands of the blessed,
Most shining of legions, shall delight for ever
In the grace of the King and glory with God.

Questions

1. What is the mood at the start of this poem? How does it help advance the poem?
2. Why might this ecclesiastic event be referred to as "[. . .] the terror of Judgment [. . .]"?
3. Is this poem a warning of what is to come for the Anglo-Saxons and the Vikings? How might this poem have been perceived by the Anglo-Saxons and the Vikings?
4. What happens to the sun and the stars in this poem? What is symbolic about these events?
5. What eventually happens to the planet in this poem? How is this similar or different from what happens in the *Bible?*
6. What is the "red-stained Rood," and what might it symbolize?
7. Identify examples of imagery in this poem, and show how this imagery helps advance the poem.
8. How might this poem have affected individuals who were skeptical toward the legitimacy of Christianity?

1. Lines 31 and 32 of the poem read: "Cordial and Kind to His own people, / Severe to the sinful, wondrously varying." One might see a hopeful and fearful tone in these two lines. Construct an argument that examines which groups from this period might have been labeled sinful and cast down into Hell.
2. After researching the cultural and religious issues that were prevalent during Cynewulf's time, construct an argument that examines who Cynewulf's intended audience might have been and why.
3. A clear division of sinners and non-sinners is present in this poem. Who are some literary characters from Old-English literature who would be left behind during this day of judgment, and which characters would be received through the gates of Heaven? Write a classification essay that examines this topic, and support your argument by referencing the actions of your chosen characters, outside sources, and *The Last Judgment.*
4. When Mark Twain entered what some deem his "dark period," he contemplated the promise of eternal life in Christ's Kingdom. Based on Cynewulf's *The Last Judgment,* Twain's *Letters from the Earth,* and additional sources, what is the likelihood that an Old-English warrior would be enthusiastic about spending all of eternity in Heaven?

The Battle of Maldon

1. This epic poem celebrates the bravery of the Anglo-Saxon race, and it carries a tone similar to the tone in *Beowulf*.
2. When reading this, note how the accumulation of arms and the exchange of words crescendo, lending credence to the idea that the author of this poem was a master at setting the stage for battle.

The Battle of Maldon

Anonymous

. . . would be broken.

Then he ordered a warrior each horse be let free, driven afar and advance onward, giving thought to deeds of arms and to steadfast courage.

Then it was that Offa's kinsman first perceived, that the Earl would not endure cowardice, for he let then from his hand flee his beloved falcon towards the woods and there to battle went forth.

By this a man might understand that this youth would not prove soft at the coming battle, when he takes up arms.

Further Eadric desired to serve his chief, his lord to fight with; and so he advanced forward his spear to battle.

He had a dauntless spirit as long as he with hands might be able to grasp shield and broad sword: the vow he would carry out that he had made before his lord saying he would fight.

Then Byrhtnoth marshalled his soldiers, riding and instructing, directing his warriors how they should stand and the positions they should keep, and ordering that their shields properly stand firm with steady hands and be not afraid.

Then when he beheld that people in suitable array, he dismounted amid his people, where he was most pleased to be, there amid his retainers knowing their devotion.

Then stood on the shore, stoutly calling out a Viking messenger, making speech, menacingly delivering the sea-pirate's message to this Earl on the opposite shore standing: "I send to you from the bold seamen, a command to tell that you must quickly send treasures to us, and it would be better to you if with tribute buy off this conflict of spears than with us bitter battle share.

No need to slaughter each other if you be generous with us; we would be willing for gold to bring a truce.

If you believe which of these is the noblest path, and that your people are desirous of assurance, then pay the sea-farers on their own terms money towards peace and receive peace from us, for we with this tribute will take to our ships, depart on the sea and keep peace with you."

Byrhtnoth spoke, his shield raised aloft, brandishing a slender ash-wood spear, speaking words, wrathful and resolute did he give his answer: "Hear now you, pirate, what this people say?

They desire to you a tribute of spears to pay,
poisoned spears and old swords, the war-gear
which you in battle will not profit from.
Sea-thieves messenger, deliver back in reply, tell
your people this spiteful message, that here
stands undaunted an Earl with his band of men
who will defend our homeland, Aethelred's
country, the lord of my people and land.
Fall shall you heathen in battle!
To us it would be shameful that you with our coin to
your ships should get away without a fight, now
you thus far into our homeland have come.
You shall not so easily carry off our treasure: with
us must spear and blade first decide the terms,
fierce conflict, is the tribute we will hand over."
He then ordered their shields taken up, his soldiers
advancing until on the river-bank they all stood.
Because of the river they were not able this band of
men to fight the other: there came flowing the
flood after the tide; joining in the tidal stream.
Too long it seemed to him until the time when they
together with spears join in battle.
There they on the Pante stream with pride lined the
banks, East Saxon spears and the sea-raider army;
nor might any harm the other unless through an
arrow's flight death receive.
Then the tide went out.
The seamen stood ready, many Vikings eager for
battle.
Then the heroes' protector ordered that the
causeway be held by a warrior stern—Wulfstan
was his name—valiant with his people: that was
Ceola's son, who the first man with his spear
slain was one who boldly on the causeway stood.
There fought with Wulfstan warriors fearless,
Aelfere and Maccus, two great in courage, who
would not at this fjord take to flight, but stoutly
against the enemy defended themselves while
with their weapons they might wield.
Then they understood and clearly saw, that this
guarding of the causeway was a fierce encounter,
and so began to use guile, the hateful strangers,
asked that passage to land they might have, to the
shore and pass the fjord would this force lead.

Then the Earl permitted in his great pride to allow
land many of these hateful people; and so then
shouted on the shore of the cold water Byrhtelm's
child—and the warriors listened: "Now the way
is open to you: come quickly to us you men to
battle.
God alone knows who on this field of honor may be
allowed to be the master of."
Then advanced the wolves of slaughter, for water
they cared not for, this band of Vikings; west over
the Pante's shining water shore they carried their
shields, these men of the fleet towards land
advanced their linden shields.
There against the enemy stood ready Byrhtnoth
with his soldiers.
He with his shield commanded to form the battle
ranks and that force of men to hold fast firmly
towards the enemy.
Then was the fight near, glory in battle.
The time was come that these doomed men would
fall in battle.
There came the loud clamor.
Ravens circled around, eagles eager for carrion.
On Earth was the battlecry.
They then sent forth from their hands shafts hard as
file, murderously sharpened spears flew.
Bows were busily at work, shields received spears.
Fierce was that onslaught.
Warriors fell in battle on either side, young men lay
slain.
Wounded was Wulfmaer, meeting death on the
battlefield, Byrhtnoth's kinsman: he with sword
was, his sister's son, cruelly hewn down.
There were the Vikings given requital: I hear that
Eadweard smote one fiercely with his sword,
withholding not in his blow, so that at his feet fell
a doomed warrior; for this he of his people gave
thanks for, this chamber-thane, when the
opportunity arose.
So stood firm of purpose these young men in battle,
eagerly giving thought to who there with spear-
points was first able of doomed men's life
destroy, warriors with weapons.
The slain in battle fell to Earth.
Steadfast and unyielding, Byrhtnoth exhorted them,
bidding that each young warrior's purpose to this
battle, against the Danes a desire to win glory
in war.

Advanced again to fierce battle, weapons raised up,
shields to defense, and towards these warriors
they stepped.

Resolute they approached Earl to the lowest
Yeoman: each of them intent on harm for the
enemy.

Sent then a sea-warrior a spear of southern make
that wounded the warrior lord.

He thrust then with his shield such that the spear
shaft burst, and that spear-head shattered as it
sprang in reply.

Enraged became that warrior: with anger he stabbed
that proud Viking who had given him that wound.

Experienced was that warrior; he thrust his spear
forward through the warrior's neck, his hand
guiding so that he this ravager's life would fatally
pierce.

Then he with another stab speedily pierced the
ravager so that the chainmail coat broke: this man
had a breast wound cut through the linked rings;
through his heart stuck a deadly spear.

The Earl was the better pleased: laughed then this
great man of spirit, thanking the Creator for the
day's work which the Lord had given him.

And so then another warrior a spear from the other
side flew out of hand, which deeply struck
through the noble Aethelred's retainer.

To him by his side stood a young man not fully
grown, a youth on the battlefield, who valiantly
pulled out of this warrior the bloody spear,
Wulfstan's child, Wulfmaer the younger; and so
with blinding speed came the shaft in reply.

The spear penetrated, for that who on the Earth now
lay among his people, the one who had sorely
pierced.

Went then armed a man to this Earl; he desirous of
this warrior's belongings to take off with, booty
and rings and an ornamental sword.

Then Byrhtnoth drew his sword from its sheath
broad and bright of blade, and then struck the
man's coat of mail.

But too soon he was prevented by a certain sea-
scavenger, and then the Earl's arm was wounded.

Fall then to the ground with his gold-hilted sword:
his grip unable to hold the heavy sword, or wield
the weapon.

Then still uttered those words of the grey-haired
warrior, encouraging the younger warriors,
bidding to advance stoutly together.

Not could he on his feet any longer stand firmly up,
and so he looked to heaven: "I thank you, Lord of
my people, all the joys which I on this world have
experienced.

"Now I ask, oh merciful Creator, the greatest hope
that to you my spirit shall be granted salvation
that my soul to thee be permitted to journey and
into your power, King of Angels, with peace I
depart.

I only beseech that the fiends of hell shall not be
permitted to harm me."

Then he was slain by the heathen warriors; and both
of those warriors which by him stood, Aelfnoth
and Wulmaer were each slain, close by their lord
did they give up their lives.

Then turned away from battle those that would not
stay: there went Odda's child first to flight,
Godric fled from the battle, and the noble
abandoned the one which had often given him
many a horse.

He leapt upon the mount of the steed which had
once been his lord's, on those trappings of which
he was not fit, he and with his brothers both
galloped away, Godwine and Godwig not caring
for battle, but turned away from this battlefield
and to the forest fled, seeking a place of safety
and to protect their lives, and many more men
than what is right were there, then if they had
acted deservingly and all remembered he, who
had to them, all benefits did make.

Thus had Offa on that day first said at the meeting
place, there at the council, that there would be
boldly many a boastful speech which at the time
of stress would not endure.

So now was laid low the Chief of this army,
Aethelred's Earl.

All saw those sharers of the hearth that their lord lay
slain.

But then there advanced onward those splendid
retainers, undaunted men hastening eagerly: they
desired all one of two things, to leave life or else
to avenge their dear lord.

And so exhorting them to advance was the child of
Aelfrices, a warrior young in winters whose
words spoke, Aelfwine then said, he in valiant
talk: "Remember the speeches which we had
often at mead spoken, that we on the bench had
loudly uttered vows, warriors in the hall,
concerning bitter strife: Now may we prove who
is truly valiant!

I am willing that my royal descent be made known to all men, that I was of Mercian blood greatly kindred; my grandfather was named Ealhelm, a wise alderman and very prosperous.

Not shall me these people's liegeman reproach that I of this army am willing to depart from, a homeland seek, now that my lord lies slain and hewn down in battle.

Mine is that sorrow greatest: he was both my kinsman and my lord."

Then he advanced onward, remembering with hostility, then he with spear-point pierced one pirate in their host, and to the ground lie slain killed with the weapon.

He began then to exhort his comrades, friends and compatriots, that they advance onward.

Offa spoke, shaking his ashen spear: "Lo, thou Aelfwine, have your words thus reminded us liegemen to our allegiance.

Now our people's protector lies slain, the Earl is on the Earth, and to us all is our need that one another encourage each other warriors to battle, while with weapons we are able to have and grasp, the hard blade, the spear and the good sword.

To us has Godric, that cowardly sun of Odda, all betrayed.

Many men believed, then when he rode on the horse, on that splendid steed, that it was our lord.

Because of that happening here on the battlefield the people scattered, the wall of shields breaking asunder.

Shame on that action, for because of him thus many a man was caused to flee!"

Leofsunu spoke and his linden shield was raised, the board to defense; this warrior replied: "I that swear, that from here I will not flee a foot's space, as my desire is to advance further, avenge in battle-strife my lord and friend.

I have no desire among Sturmere's unyielding heroes to reproach my word, now that my patron has perished, that I now lordless go on a homeward journey, having turned away from battle, but rather I shall be taken by weapons, either spear or iron."

Wrathfully he advanced, fighting resolutely, for he despised flight.

Dunnere then said, brandishing his spear, a simple yeoman calling out to the entire shore, exhorting that each warrior avenge Byrhtnoth: "One cannot retreat who intends vengeance for our lord of the host, if their lives they care not for."

So then they pressed forward, caring not about their lives.

Then began these retainers to fiercely fight, ferocious warriors armed with spears, and praying to God that they might avenge their lord and patron and on their enemy death make.

Thus the hostage himself willingly helped; he was a Northumbrian of a brave family, Ecglaf's child; he was named Aescferth.

He hesitated not at the play of battle, but shot forward many arrows; here striking a shield, there cutting down a warrior, at almost every moment giving out some wound, all the while with his weapon he would wield.

Yet still at the battle front stood Eadweard the tall ready and eager, speaking vaunting words that he would not flee a foot's ground, or turn away back to the bank, then leave his superior where he lay.

He broke through that wall of shields and among the warriors fought, until his bounteous lord upon those sea-men did worthily avenge, and he on the battlefield lie slain.

So did Aetheric, noble comrade, press forward and eager to advance fight resolutely, Sibyrht's brother and very many others; splitting the enemy's shields, valiantly they defended themselves.

Rang the shield rims, and sang the corselets of mail a certain terrible dirge.

Then at the battle's height Offa a sea-farer sent to the Earth dead, and there Gadd's kinsman was laid low to the ground: soon it was at battle that Offa was hewn down.

He had however accomplished that vow to his lord that he had uttered before to his giver of rings, that either they both ride to the fortified home unhurt or else perish fighting on the battlefield and die of their wounds.

He lay slain nobly near the lord of his people.

Then it happened that the shields broke through.

The sea-warriors advanced, to battle enraged.

Spear often pierced the doomed houses of life.

Onward then advanced Wistan,
Thurhstan's son, to these warriors fought.
He was among the throng and slew three, before
   Wigelm's child lay slain in battle.
There was severe combat.
Stood firm did these warriors in battle.
Warriors perished exhausted by their wounds.
The slain fell dead to the Earth.
Oswold and Eadwold all this time, both of these
   brothers encouraged the soldiers, their beloved
   kinsman they would exhort through words that
   they needed to endure without weakening and
   make use of their weapons.
Byrhtwold spoke, shield raised aloft—he was an old
   loyal retainer—and brandished his spear; he very
   boldly commanded the warriors: "Our hearts
   must grow resolute, our courage more valiant, our
   spirits must be greater, though our strength grows
   less.

Here lies our Lord all hewn down, goodly he lies in
   the dust.
A kinsman mourns that who now from this battle-
   play thinks to turn away.
I am advanced in years.
I do not desire to be taken away, but I by my liege
   Lord, by that favorite of men I intend to lie."
So then did Aethelgar's child enbolden them all,
   Godric to battle.
Often he sent forth spears, deadly shaft sped away
   onto the Vikings; thus he on this people went out
   in front of battle, cutting down and smiting, until
   he too on the battlefield perished.
This was not that Godric who from the battle had
   flown away . . .

Questions

1. How might the words, "[. . .] would be broken," apply to this poem?
2. What act must the inhabitants complete in order for the Viking invaders to leave peacefully? What is symbolic about this act, and what is the relevance of it?
3. What environmental occurrence must take place before the two sides can engage in hand-to-hand combat? What tactic is used before this occurrence takes place?
4. At what point does this battle turn in the Vikings' favor? Without this turning point, what might the outcome of this battle have been?
5. At what point in this poem can the reader almost feel the piercing pain of war?
6. Who is the first of Byrhtnoth's kin to be slain? Does this slain individual hold a special place in Byrhtnoth's heart? Why?
7. How is Byrhtnoth hurt during the battle, and what might this suggest about how heroes are typically injured or killed during battle?
8. Who are Byrhtnoth's final words directed toward, and who is beside him when he says these words? Do these final words encapsulate the battle between the Viking invaders? Why?
9. Who takes Byrhtnoth's place as the brave defender against the Vikings? Does this new leader bring any value to the battlefield?
10. What is the reaction of Byrhtnoth's men after his fall? Does this reaction foreshadow the remainder of the battle? Why?

Research and Writing

1. In *The Battle of Maldon*, Byrhtnoth is the hero of his people. From what little the reader learns about this war leader, what can be said of his heroic traits, and where in literature might a reader find similar heroic traits in warlike situations? Compare and contrast Byrhtnoth's heroic traits with the heroic traits of another literary hero.

2. Byrhthelm's son says, "Now way is made open, come quickly to us, / Warriors to the onset; God only knows / Who shall hold sway on the field of slaughter." These are telling lines, for this battle clearly attempts to pit Good vs. Evil (or Christians vs. Heathens). Thinking about this battle on a grander scale is intriguing, especially when noting the victor of this encounter. What message might the writer of this piece be suggesting to the audience about biblical relationships between Heaven and Hell? Construct an argument that examines this poem's message, and support it by citing historical events from the time period and various lines from the poem.

3. The death of Byrhtnoth is a catalyst for further bloodshed. This action is reminiscent of William Wallace's death in the movie *Braveheart*. Examine a literary character, and show how and why this character's death lead to an invigorating feeling of pride and intensity on the battlefield.

5

Middle-English Literature

When the powerful leader, Robert of Normandy, died in 1035, his son inherited his father's title. Several leading Norman nobles supported this new leader. After surviving numerous assassination attempts (some Normans were rather angered by the fact that an illegitimate child was the leader of the Normans), William of Normandy began to govern Normandy in 1045. William's power in Normandy was constantly under threat. In 1053, for instance, he suppressed a revolt led by William of Arques. Nonetheless, after thwarting two French rebellions, William of Normandy had complete control over his empire. In 1051, William visited Edward the Confessor, King of England, and after this visit, William claimed that Edward had promised him the throne of England after his death. This was a politically-motivated rumor that William started so he might have the throne of England betrothed to him. However, after Edward died on January 5th, 1066, Harold of Wessex became King of England. Harold was a close ally of William of Normandy, and it was whispered that Harold would help William become King of England. After it became apparent that Harold had no intention of handing the throne over, William decided to take it by force. On September 27th, 1066, William, the Duke of Normandy, lead an invasion (with 700 ships) onto the Anglo-Saxon-inhabited island of England. On September 28th, the Normans stormed the beaches of Pevensey Bay and sacked many parts of England. After months of fighting King Harold's forces, William was crowned king of England by Aldred, Archbishop of York, at Westminster Abbey. Still, it took this French invader ten years before he had full control over the land. This campaign is known as the Norman conquest of England (William of Normandy eventually became known as William the Conqueror), and its effect on present-day England is immeasurable.

William's victory lead to the eventual unification of England; and it also lead to Anglo-Saxon cultural decline, for the Normans quickly seized control of several Anglo-Saxon territories and had many Anglo-Saxon nobles killed in order to diminish the threat of any rebellion. The tribal way of life was replaced by a monarchical system. Taxes were enforced, public law was enacted, and a sense of national unification began to change the way many English lived. With the change of leadership came a linguistic shift. French was the language of choice, and this language was reserved for the noble class, showing cultural superiority over the Anglo-Saxon peasantry. Coincidentally, the language born from this period was English, the language that the Anglo-Saxon peasantry spoke. This combination of cultures lead to a mix of ethnic groups, religions, and convictions that would soon find themselves under one title: English.

During this period, there were also four religious crusades that took place. This bloody struggle to take back the holiest city, Jerusalem, was actually a series of conquests among Holy warriors, where hundreds of thousands eventually lost their lives. The first three crusades (1095–1099, 1147–1148, and 1189–1192) all ended with the conquering of Jerusalem. The fourth and final crusade was aimed at conquering Constantinople. Again, many lives were lost, but the Crusaders were successful.

Geoffrey Chaucer (1340–1400)

Geoffrey Chaucer was born in 1343, and he lived during the courts of Edward III, Richard II, and John of Gaunt, all prominent leaders of their time. He was an inquisitive youth, and as he grew older, his fascination with the Middle English culture continued to grow. He studied Latin, French, and Italian poetry, and as a young man, he held many jobs—jobs that gave him access to a cornucopia of people and environments. He was enthralled by the idea of traveling from town to town, meeting people from all walks of life, and turning these experiences into some of the finest tales ever told.

The *Canterbury Tales* depict Medieval Europe for what it was during Chaucer's time. These narrative tales were written in 1387, blending the Anglo-Saxon dialect with the ruling French tongue. In fact, Chaucer's chosen dialect was embraced as the standard in the century after his death.

To better appreciate *The Canterbury Tales,* note Canterbury's historical significance: Under the rule of Caesar in 54 BCE, the Romans came to Canterbury and found its inhabitants to be quite congenial. Rome's influence on this city was considerable; there were theaters, baths, temples, and grandiose, "Roman" homes. In 43 CE, a full-scale invasion was launched on the citizens of Canterbury (by the Angles, Saxons, and Jutes) after the Roman military left England. Canterbury was eventually abandoned and left for ruin. After a century of desolation, however, the Anglo-Saxons built many housing structures atop the overgrown Roman village. Then, in 597 CE, Christianity was brought to Canterbury by Saint Augustine. Saint Augustine was so successful in converting many people to Christianity that Canterbury became known, and is still known today, as the birthplace of British Christianity. Canterbury had to endure numerous Viking raids from 991–1016 CE, and it peacefully surrendered to William the Conqueror in 1066.

"The Prologue" of The Canterbury Tales

1. "The Prologue" of *The Canterbury Tales* is an introduction to these characters' personas and physical appearances.
2. "The Prologue" of these tales is comical in many ways. For example, Chaucer writes of priests that covet wealth and a wife who has had five husbands.
3. Before reading a character's tale, it would be useful to go back to "The Prologue" and read the narrator's description of that character.

The Canterbury Tales
Chaucer
"THE PROLOGUE"

Here begins the Book of the Tales of Canterbury.

When April with his showers sweet with fruit
The drought of March has pierced unto the root
And bathed each vein with liquor that has power
To generate therein and sire the flower;
When Zephyr also has, with his sweet breath,
Quickened again, in every holt and heath,
The tender shoots and buds, and the young sun
Into the Ram one half his course has run,
And many little birds make melody
That sleep through all the night with open eye
(So Nature pricks them on to ramp and rage)—
Then do folk long to go on pilgrimage,

And palmers to go seeking out strange strands,
To distant shrines well known in sundry lands.
And specially from every shire's end
Of England they to Canterbury wend,
The holy blessed martyr there to seek
Who helped them when they lay so ill and weak
Befell that, in that season, on a day
In Southwark, at the Tabard, as I lay
Ready to start upon my pilgrimage
To Canterbury, full of devout homage,
There came at nightfall to that hostelry
Some nine and twenty in a company
Of sundry persons who had chanced to fall
In fellowship, and pilgrims were they all
That toward Canterbury town would ride.
The rooms and stables spacious were and wide,
And well we there were eased, and of the best.
And briefly, when the sun had gone to rest,
So had I spoken with them, every one,
That I was of their fellowship anon,
And made agreement that we'd early rise
To take the road, as you I will apprise.
But nonetheless, whilst I have time and space,
Before yet farther in this tale I pace,
It seems to me accordant with reason
To inform you of the state of every one
Of all of these, as it appeared to me,
And who they were, and what was their degree,
And even how arrayed there at the inn;
And with a knight thus will I first begin.

A knight there was, and he a worthy man,
Who, from the moment that he first began
To ride about the world, loved chivalry,
Truth, honour, freedom and all courtesy.
Full worthy was he in his liege-lord's war,
And therein had he ridden (none more far)
As well in Christendom as heathenesse,
And honoured everywhere for worthiness.
At Alexandria, he, when it was won;
Full oft the table's roster he'd begun
Above all nations' knights in Prussia.
In Latvia raided he, and Russia,
No christened man so oft of his degree.
In far Granada at the siege was he
Of Algeciras, and in Belmarie.
At Ayas was he and at Satalye
When they were won; and on the Middle Sea

At many a noble meeting chanced to be.
Of mortal battles he had fought fifteen,
And he'd fought for our faith at Tramissene
Three times in lists, and each time slain his foe.
This self-same worthy knight had been also
At one time with the lord of Palatye
Against another heathen in Turkey:
And always won he sovereign fame for prize.
Though so illustrious, he was very wise
And bore himself as meekly as a maid.
He never yet had any vileness said,
In all his life, to whatsoever wight.
He was a truly perfect, gentle knight.
But now, to tell you all of his array,
His steeds were good, but yet he was not gay.
Of simple fustian wore he a jupon
Sadly discoloured by his habergeon;
For he had lately come from his voyage
And now was going on this pilgrimage.

With him there was his son, a youthful squire,
A lover and a lusty bachelor,
With locks well curled, as if they'd laid in press.
Some twenty years of age he was, I guess.
In stature he was of an average length,
Wondrously active, aye, and great of strength.
He'd ridden sometime with the cavalry
In Flanders, in Artois, and Picardy,
And borne him well within that little space
In hope to win thereby his lady's grace.
Prinked out he was, as if he were a mead,
All full of fresh-cut flowers white and red.
Singing he was, or fluting, all the day;
He was as fresh as is the month of May.
Short was his gown, with sleeves both long and wide.
Well could he sit on horse, and fairly ride.
He could make songs and words thereto indite,
Joust, and dance too, as well as sketch and write.
So hot he loved that, while night told her tale,
He slept no more than does a nightingale.
Courteous he, and humble, willing and able,
And carved before his father at the table.

A yeoman had he, nor more servants, no,
At that time, for he chose to travel so;
And he was clad in coat and hood of green.
A sheaf of peacock arrows bright and keen
Under his belt he bore right carefully

(Well could he keep his tackle yeomanly:
His arrows had no draggled feathers low),
And in his hand he bore a mighty bow.
A cropped head had he and a sun-browned face.
Of woodcraft knew he all the useful ways.
Upon his arm he bore a bracer gay,
And at one side a sword and buckler, yea,
And at the other side a dagger bright,
Well sheathed and sharp as spear point in the light;
On breast a Christopher of silver sheen.
He bore a horn in baldric all of green;
A forester he truly was, I guess.

There was also a nun, a prioress,
Who, in her smiling, modest was and coy;
Her greatest oath was but "By Saint Eloy!"
And she was known as Madam Eglantine.
Full well she sang the services divine,
Intoning through her nose, becomingly;
And fair she spoke her French, and fluently,
After the school of Stratford-at-the-Bow,
For French of Paris was not hers to know.
At table she had been well taught withal,
And never from her lips let morsels fall,
Nor dipped her fingers deep in sauce, but ate
With so much care the food upon her plate
That never driblet fell upon her breast.
In courtesy she had delight and zest.
Her upper lip was always wiped so clean
That in her cup was no iota seen
Of grease, when she had drunk her draught of wine.
Becomingly she reached for meat to dine.
And certainly delighting in good sport,
She was right pleasant, amiable—in short.
She was at pains to counterfeit the look
Of courtliness, and stately manners took,
And would be held worthy of reverence.
But, to say something of her moral sense,
She was so charitable and piteous
That she would weep if she but saw a mouse
Caught in a trap, though it were dead or bled.
She had some little dogs, too, that she fed
On roasted flesh, or milk and fine white bread.
But sore she'd weep if one of them were dead,
Or if men smote it with a rod to smart:
For pity ruled her, and her tender heart.
Right decorous her pleated wimple was;
Her nose was fine; her eyes were blue as glass;
Her mouth was small and therewith soft and red;

But certainly she had a fair forehead;
It was almost a full span broad, I own,
For, truth to tell, she was not undergrown.
Neat was her cloak, as I was well aware.
Of coral small about her arm she'd bear
A string of beads and gauded all with green;
And therefrom hung a brooch of golden sheen
Whereon there was first written a crowned "A,"
And under, Amor vincit omnia.
Another little nun with her had she,
Who was her chaplain; and of priests she'd three.
A monk there was, one made for mastery,
An outrider, who loved his venery;
A manly man, to be an abbot able.
Full many a blooded horse had he in stable:
And when he rode men might his bridle hear
A-jingling in the whistling wind as clear,
Aye, and as loud as does the chapel bell
Where this brave monk was of the cell.
The rule of Maurus or Saint Benedict,
By reason it was old and somewhat strict,
This said monk let such old things slowly pace
And followed new-world manners in their place.
He cared not for that text a clean-plucked hen
Which holds that hunters are not holy men;
Nor that a monk, when he is cloisterless,
Is like unto a fish that's waterless;
That is to say, a monk out of his cloister.
But this same text he held not worth an oyster;
And I said his opinion was right good.
What? Should he study as a madman would
Upon a book in cloister cell? Or yet
Go labour with his hands and swink and sweat,
As Austin bids? How shall the world be served?
Let Austin have his toil to him reserved.
Therefore he was a rider day and night;
Greyhounds he had, as swift as bird in flight.
Since riding and the hunting of the hare
Were all his love, for no cost would he spare.
I saw his sleeves were purfled at the hand
With fur of grey, the finest in the land;
Also, to fasten hood beneath his chin,
He had of good wrought gold a curious pin:
A love-knot in the larger end there was.
His head was bald and shone like any glass,
And smooth as one anointed was his face.
Fat was this lord, he stood in goodly case.
His bulging eyes he rolled about, and hot
They gleamed and red, like fire beneath a pot;

His boots were soft; his horse of great estate.
Now certainly he was a fine prelate:
He was not pale as some poor wasted ghost.
A fat swan loved he best of any roast.
His palfrey was as brown as is a berry.

A friar there was, a wanton and a merry,
A limiter, a very festive man.
In all the Orders Four is none that can
Equal his gossip and his fair language.
He had arranged full many a marriage
Of women young, and this at his own cost.
Unto his order he was a noble post.
Well liked by all and intimate was he
With franklins everywhere in his country,
And with the worthy women of the town:
For at confessing he'd more power in gown
(As he himself said) than it good curate,
For of his order he was licentiate.
He heard confession gently, it was said,
Gently absolved too, leaving naught of dread.
He was an easy man to give penance
When knowing he should gain a good pittance;
For to a begging friar, money given
Is sign that any man has been well shriven.
For if one gave (he dared to boast of this),
He took the man's repentance not amiss.
For many a man there is so hard of heart
He cannot weep however pains may smart.
Therefore, instead of weeping and of prayer,
Men should give silver to poor friars all bare.
His tippet was stuck always full of knives
And pins, to give to young and pleasing wives.
And certainly he kept a merry note:
Well could he sing and play upon the rote.
At balladry he bore the prize away.
His throat was white as lily of the May;
Yet strong he was as ever champion.
In towns he knew the taverns, every one,
And every good host and each barmaid too—
Better than begging lepers, these he knew.
For unto no such solid man as he
Accorded it, as far as he could see,
To have sick lepers for acquaintances.
There is no honest advantageousness
In dealing with such poverty-stricken curs;
It's with the rich and with big victuallers.
And so, wherever profit might arise,
Courteous he was and humble in men's eyes.

There was no other man so virtuous.
He was the finest beggar of his house;
A certain district being farmed to him,
None of his brethren dared approach its rim;
For though a widow had no shoes to show,
So pleasant was his *in principio,*
He always got a farthing ere he went.
He lived by pickings, it is evident.
And he could romp as well as any whelp.
On love days could he be of mickle help.
For there he was not like a cloisterer,
With threadbare cope as is the poor scholar,
But he was like a lord or like a pope.
Of double worsted was his semi-cope,
That rounded like a bell, as you may guess.
He lisped a little, out of wantonness,
To make his English soft upon his tongue;
And in his harping, after he had sung,
His two eyes twinkled in his head as bright
As do the stars within the frosty night.
This worthy limiter was named Hubert.

There was a merchant with forked beard, and girt
In motley gown, and high on horse he sat,
Upon his head a Flemish beaver hat;
His boots were fastened rather elegantly.
His spoke his notions out right pompously,
Stressing the times when he had won, not lost.
He would the sea were held at any cost
Across from Middleburgh to Orwell town.
At money-changing he could make a crown.
This worthy man kept all his wits well set;
There was no one could say he was in debt,
So well he governed all his trade affairs
With bargains and with borrowings and with shares.
Indeed, he was a worthy man withal,
But, sooth to say, his name I can't recall.
A clerk from Oxford was with us also,
Who'd turned to getting knowledge, long ago.
As meagre was his horse as is a rake,
Nor he himself too fat, I'll undertake,
But he looked hollow and went soberly.
Right threadbare was his overcoat; for he
Had got him yet no churchly benefice,
Nor was so worldly as to gain office.
For he would rather have at his bed's head
Some twenty books, all bound in black and red,
Of Aristotle and his philosophy
Than rich robes, fiddle, or gay psaltery.

Yet, and for all he was philosopher,
He had but little gold within his coffer;
But all that he might borrow from a friend
On books and learning he would swiftly spend,
And then he'd pray right busily for the souls
Of those who gave him wherewithal for schools.
Of study took he utmost care and heed.
Not one word spoke he more than was his need;
And that was said in fullest reverence
And short and quick and full of high good sense.
Pregnant of moral virtue was his speech;
And gladly would he learn and gladly teach.

A sergeant of the law, wary and wise,
Who'd often gone to Paul's walk to advise,
There was also, compact of excellence.
Discreet he was, and of great reverence;
At least he seemed so, his words were so wise.
Often he sat as justice in assize,
By patent or commission from the crown;
Because of learning and his high renown,
He took large fees and many robes could own.
So great a purchaser was never known.
All was fee simple to him, in effect,
Wherefore his claims could never be suspect.
Nowhere a man so busy of his class,
And yet he seemed much busier than he was.
All cases and all judgments could he cite
That from King William's time were apposite.
And he could draw a contract so explicit
Not any man could fault therefrom elicit;
And every statute he'd verbatim quote.
He rode but badly in a medley coat,
Belted in a silken sash, with little bars,
But of his dress no more particulars.

There was a franklin in his company;
White was his beard as is the white daisy.
Of sanguine temperament by every sign,
He loved right well his morning sop in wine.
Delightful living was the goal he'd won,
For he was Epicurus' very son,
That held opinion that a full delight
Was true felicity, perfect and right.
A householder, and that a great, was he;
Saint Julian he was in his own country.
His bread and ale were always right well done;
A man with better cellars there was none.
Baked meat was never wanting in his house,
Of fish and flesh, and that so plenteous
It seemed to snow therein both food and drink
Of every dainty that a man could think.
According to the season of the year
He changed his diet and his means of cheer.
Full many a fattened partridge did he mew,
And many a bream and pike in fish-pond too.
Woe to his cook, except the sauces were
Poignant and sharp, and ready all his gear.
His table, waiting in his hall alway,
Stood ready covered through the livelong day.
At county sessions was he lord and sire,
And often acted as a knight of shire.
A dagger and a trinket-bag of silk
Hung from his girdle, white as morning milk.
He had been sheriff and been auditor;
And nowhere was a worthier vavasor.

 **For the entire story,
insert the Literature CD.**

 # Questions

1. Who is the most amiable of all the characters and why?
2. Of all the priests, which one is described as the most miserly? What is the purpose of this description?
3. Why is it so important that Chaucer go through the vivid descriptions of the characters? Without these descriptions in "The Prologue," what would readers be left without as they read the tales?

4. What kind of person is the poor parish Priest described as? Is this description consistent with Chaucer's descriptions of other religious figures?

5. At the end of "The Prologue," Chaucer cleverly offers additional information about each character. Why might he do this?

6. What proposition does the innkeeper make to all of the travelers before they leave on their journey? How does this proposition help advance the tales?

1. While reading these tales, contemplate why Chaucer chose the characters he did. In what way are the characters from "The Prologue" similar and different from the characters in *Everyman?* Construct an argument that compares a character from "The Prologue" with a character from *Everyman.*

2. From what little the reader learns about these characters, whose tale might be the most interesting, least believable, and most religious? Construct an argument that addresses these questions, and support your argument with evidence from "The Prologue."

"The Knight's Tale"

1. While fortune finds itself in "The Knight's Tale," for two soldiers from Thebes it is one of severe misfortune.

2. Make sure to pay close attention to the roles of the gods in this tale, and note subtle connections between their roles and the roles of gods in Greek mythology.

"THE KNIGHT'S TALE"

Once on a time, as old tales tell to us,
There was a duke whose name was Theseus:
Of Athens he was lord and governor,
And in his time was such a conqueror
That greater was there not beneath the sun.
Full many a rich country had he won;
What with his wisdom and his chivalry
He gained the realm of Femininity,
That was of old time known as Scythia.
There wedded he the queen, Hippolyta,
And brought her home with him to his country.
In glory great and with great pageantry,
And, too, her younger sister, Emily.
And thus, in victory and with melody,
Let I this noble duke to Athens ride
With all his armed host marching at his side.
And truly, were it not too long to hear,
I would have told you fully how, that year,
Was gained the realm of Femininity
By Theseus and by his chivalry;
And all of the great battle that was wrought
Where Amazons and the Athenians fought;
And how was wooed and won Hippolyta,
That fair and hardy queen of Scythia;
And of the feast was made at their wedding,
And of the tempest at their home-coming;
But all of that I must for now forbear.
I have, God knows, a large field for my share,
And weak the oxen, and the soil is tough.
The remnant of the tale is long enough.
I will not hinder any, in my turn;
Let each man tell his tale, until we learn
Which of us all the most deserves to win;
So where I stopped, again I'll now begin.
This duke of whom I speak, of great renown,
When he had drawn almost unto the town,
In all well-being and in utmost pride,
He grew aware, casting his eyes aside,
That right upon the road, as suppliants do,
A company of ladies, two by two,
Knelt, all in black, before his cavalcade;
But such a clamorous cry of woe they made
That in the whole world living man had heard
No such a lamentation, on my word;
Nor would they cease lamenting till at last

They'd clutched his bridle reins and held them fast.
"What folk are you that at my home-coming
Disturb my triumph with this dolorous thing?"
Cried Theseus. "Do you so much envy
My honour that you thus complain and cry?
Or who has wronged you now, or who offended?
Come, tell me whether it may be amended;
And tell me, why are you clothed thus, in black?"
The eldest lady of them answered back,
After she'd swooned, with cheek so deathly drear
That it was pitiful to see and hear,
And said: "Lord, to whom Fortune has but given
Victory, and to conquer where you've striven,
Your glory and your honour grieve not us;
But we beseech your aid and pity thus.
Have mercy on our woe and our distress.
Some drop of pity, of your gentleness,
Upon us wretched women, oh, let fall!
For see, lord, there is no one of us all
That has not been a duchess or a queen;
Now we are captives, as may well be seen:
Thanks be to Fortune and her treacherous wheel,
There's none can rest assured of constant weal.
And truly, lord, expecting your return,
In Pity's temple, where the fires yet burn,
We have been waiting through a long fortnight;
Now help us, lord, since it is in your might.
"I, wretched woman, who am weeping thus,
Was once the wife of King Capaneus,
Who died at Thebes, oh, cursed be the day!
And all we that you see in this array,
And make this lamentation to be known,
All we have lost our husbands at that town
During the siege that round about it lay.
And now the old Creon, ah welaway!
The lord and governor of Thebes city,
Full of his wrath and all iniquity,
He, in despite and out of tyranny,
To do the dead a shame and villainy,
Of all our husbands, lying among the slain,
Has piled the bodies in a heap, amain,
And will not suffer them, nor give consent,
To buried be, or burned, nor will relent,
But sets his dogs to eat them, out of spite."
And on that word, at once, without respite,

They all fell prone and cried out piteously:
"Have on us wretched women some mercy,
And let our sorrows sink into your heart!"
This gentle duke down from his horse did start
With heart of pity, when he'd heard them speak.
It seemed to him his heart must surely break,
Seeing them there so miserable of state,
Who had been proud and happy but so late.
And in his arms he took them tenderly,
Giving them comfort understandingly:
And swore his oath, that as he was a true knight,
He would put forth so thoroughly his might
Against the tyrant Creon as to wreak
Vengeance so great that all of Greece should speak
And say how Creon was by Theseus served,
As one that had his death full well deserved.
This sworn and done, he no more there abode;
His banner he displayed and forth he rode
Toward Thebes, and all his host marched on beside;
Nor nearer Athens would he walk or ride,
Nor take his ease for even half a day,
But onward, and in camp that night he lay;
And thence he sent Hippolyta the queen
And her bright sister Emily, I ween,
Unto the town of Athens, there to dwell
While he went forth. There is no more to tell.
The image of red Mars, with spear and shield,
So shone upon his banner's snow-white field
It made a billowing glitter up and down;
And by the banner borne was his pennon,
On which in beaten gold was worked, complete,
The Minotaur, which he had slain in Crete.
Thus rode this duke, thus rode this conqueror,
And in his host of chivalry the flower,
Until he came to Thebes and did alight
Full in the field where he'd intent to fight.
But to be brief in telling of this thing,
With Creon, who was Thebes' dread lord and king,
He fought and slew him, manfully, like knight,
In open war, and put his host to flight;
And by assault he took the city then,
Levelling wall and rafter with his men;
And to the ladies he restored again
The bones of their poor husbands who were slain,
To do for them the last rites of that day.
But it were far too long a tale to say
The clamour of great grief and sorrowing
Those ladies raised above the bones burning

Upon the pyres, and of the great honour
That Theseus, the noble conqueror,
Paid to the ladies when from him they went;
To make the story short is my intent.
When, then, this worthy duke, this Theseus
Had slain Creon and won Thebes city thus,
Still on the field he took that night his rest,
And dealt with all the land as he thought best.
In searching through the heap of enemy dead,
Stripping them of their gear from heel to head,
The busy pillagers could pick and choose,
After the battle, what they best could use;
And so befell that in a heap they found,
Pierced through with many a grievous, bloody
    wound,
Two young knights lying together, side by side,
Bearing one crest, wrought richly, of their pride,
And of those two Arcita was the one,
The other knight was known as Palamon.
Not fully quick, nor fully dead they were,
But by their coats of arms and by their gear
The heralds readily could tell, withal,
That they were of the Theban blood royal,
And that they had been of two sisters born.
Out of the heap the spoilers had them torn
And carried gently over to the tent
Of Theseus; who shortly had them sent
To Athens, there in prison cell to lie
Forever, without ransom, till they die.
And when this worthy duke had all this done,
He gathered host and home he rode anon,
With laurel crowned again as conqueror;
There lived he in all joy and all honour
His term of life; what more need words express?
And in a tower, in anguish and distress,
Palamon and Arcita, day and night,
Dwelt whence no gold might help them to take
    flight.
Thus passed by year by year and day by day,
Till it fell out, upon a morn in May,
That Emily, far fairer to be seen
Than is the lily on its stalk of green,
And fresher than is May with flowers new
(For with the rose's colour strove her hue,
I know not which was fairer of the two),
Before the dawn, as was her wont to do,
She rose and dressed her body for delight;
For May will have no sluggards of the night.

That season rouses every gentle heart
And forces it from winter's sleep to start,
Saying: "Arise and show thy reverence."
So Emily remembered to go thence
In honour of the May, and so she rose.
Clothed, she was sweeter than any flower that
    blows;
Her yellow hair was braided in one tress
Behind her back, a full yard long, I guess.
And in the garden, as the sun up-rose,
She sauntered back and forth and through each
    close,
Gathering many a flower, white and red,
To weave a delicate garland for her head;
And like a heavenly angel's was her song.
The tower tall, which was so thick and strong,
And of the castle was the great donjon,
(Wherein the two knights languished in prison,
Of whom I told and shall yet tell, withal),
Was joined, at base, unto the garden wall
Whereunder Emily went dallying.
Bright was the sun and clear that morn in spring,
And Palamon, the woeful prisoner,
As was his wont, by leave of his gaoler,
Was up and pacing round that chamber high,
From which the noble city filled his eye,
And, too, the garden full of branches green,
Wherein bright Emily, fair and serene,
Went walking and went roving up and down.
This sorrowing prisoner, this Palamon,
Being in the chamber, pacing to and fro,
And to himself complaining of his woe,
Cursing his birth, he often cried "Alas!"
And so it was, by chance or other pass,
That through a window, closed by many a bar
Of iron, strong and square as any spar,
He cast his eyes upon Emilia,
And thereupon he blenched and cried out "Ah!"
As if he had been smitten to the heart.
And at that cry Arcita did up-start,
Asking: "My cousin, why what ails you now
That you've so deathly pallor on your brow?
Why did you cry out? Who's offended you?
For God's love, show some patience, as I do,
With prison, for it may not different be;
Fortune has given this adversity.
Some evil disposition or aspect

Of Saturn did our horoscopes affect
To bring us here, though differently 'twere sworn;
But so the stars stood when we two were born;
We must endure it; that, in brief, is plain."
This Palamon replied and said again:"
Cousin, indeed in this opinion now
Your fancy is but vanity, I trow.
It's not our prison that caused me to cry.
But I was wounded lately through the eye
Down to my heart, and that my bane will be.
The beauty of the lady that I see
There in that garden, pacing to and fro,
Is cause of all my crying and my woe.
I know not if she's woman or goddess;
But Venus she is verily, I guess."
And thereupon down on his knees he fell,
And said: "O Venus, if it be thy will
To be transfigured in this garden, thus
Before me, sorrowing wretch, oh now help us
Out of this prison to be soon escaped.
And if it be my destiny is shaped,
By fate, to die in durance, in bondage,
Have pity, then, upon our lineage
That has been brought so low by tyranny."
And on that word Arcita looked to see
This lady who went roving to and fro.
And in that look her beauty struck him so
That, if poor Palamon is wounded sore,
Arcita is as deeply hurt, and more.
And with a sigh he said then, piteously:
"The virgin beauty slays me suddenly
Of her that wanders yonder in that place;
And save I have her pity and her grace,
That I at least may see her day by day,
I am but dead; there is no more to say."
This Palamon, when these words he had heard,
Pitilessly he watched him, and answered:
"Do you say this in earnest or in play?"
"Nay," quoth Arcita, "earnest, now, I say!
God help me, I am in no mood for play!"
Palamon knit his brows and stood at bay."
It will not prove," he said, "to your honour
After so long a time to turn traitor
To me, who am your cousin and your brother,
Sworn as we are, and each unto the other,
That never, though for death in any pain,
Never, indeed, till death shall part us twain,

Either of us in love shall hinder other,
No, nor in any thing, O my dear brother;
But that, instead, you shall so further me
As I shall you. All this we did agree.
Such was your oath and such was mine also.
You dare not now deny it, well I know.
Thus you are of my party, beyond doubt.
And now you would all falsely go about
To love my lady, whom I love and serve,
And shall while life my heart's blood may preserve.
Nay, false Arcita, it shall not be so.
I loved her first, and told you all my woe,
As to a brother and to one that swore
To further me, as I have said before.
For which you are in duty bound, as knight,
To help me, if the thing lie in your might,
Or else you're false, I say, and downfallen."
Then this Arcita proudly spoke again:"
You shall," he said, "be rather false than I;
And that you're so, I tell you utterly;
For par amour I loved her first, you know.
What can you say? You know not, even now,
Whether she is a woman or goddess!
Yours is a worship as of holiness,
While mine is love, as of a mortal maid;
Wherefore I told you of it, unafraid,
As to my cousin and my brother sworn.
Let us assume you loved her first, this morn;
Know you not well the ancient writer's law
Of 'Who shall give a lover any law?'
Love is a greater law, aye by my pan,
Than man has ever given to earthly man.
And therefore statute law and such decrees
Are broken daily and in all degrees.
A man must needs have love, maugre his head.
He cannot flee it though he should be dead,
And be she maid, or widow, or a wife.
And yet it is not likely that, in life,
You'll stand within her graces; nor shall I;
For you are well aware, aye verily,
That you and I are doomed to prison drear
Perpetually; we gain no ransom here.
We strive but as those dogs did for the bone;
They fought all day, and yet their gain was none.
Till came a kite while they were still so wroth
And bore the bone away between them both.
And therefore, at the king's court, O my brother,

It's each man for himself and not for other.
Love if you like; for I love and aye shall;
And certainly, dear brother, that is all.
Here in this prison cell must we remain
And each endure whatever fate ordain."
Great was the strife, and long, betwixt the two,
If I had but the time to tell it you,
Save in effect. It happened on a day
(To tell the tale as briefly as I may),
A worthy duke men called Pirithous,
Who had been friend unto Duke Theseus
Since each had been a little child, a chit,
Was come to visit Athens and visit
His play-fellow, as he was wont to do,
For in this whole world he loved no man so;
And Theseus loved him as truly—nay,
So well each loved the other, old books say,
That when one died (it is but truth I tell),
The other went and sought him down in Hell;
But of that tale I have no wish to write.
Pirithous loved Arcita, too, that knight,
Having known him in Thebes full many a year;
And finally, at his request and prayer,
And that without a coin of ransom paid,
Duke Theseus released him out of shade,
Freely to go where'er he wished, and to
His own devices, as I'll now tell you.
The compact was, to set it plainly down,
As made between those two of great renown:
That if Arcita, any time, were found,
Ever in life, by day or night, on ground
Of any country of this Theseus,
And he were caught, it was concerted thus,
That by the sword he straight should lose his head.
He had no choice, so taking leave he sped
Homeward to Thebes, lest by the sword's sharp
    edge
He forfeit life. His neck was under pledge.
How great a sorrow is Arcita's now!
How through his heart he feels death's heavy blow,
He weeps, he wails, he cries out piteously;
He thinks to slay himself all privily.
Said he: "Alas, the day that I was born!
I'm in worse prison, now, and more forlorn;
Now am I doomed eternally to dwell
No more in Purgatory, but in Hell.
Alas, that I have known Pirithous!

For else had I remained with Theseus,
Fettered within that cell; but even so
Then had I been in bliss and not in woe.
Only the sight of her that I would serve,
Though I might never her dear grace deserve,
Would have sufficed, oh well enough for me!
O my dear cousin Palamon," said he,"
Yours is the victory, and that is sure,
For there, full happily, you may endure.
In prison? Never, but in Paradise!
Oh, well has Fortune turned for you the dice,
Who have the sight of her, I the absence.
For possible it is, in her presence,
You being a knight, a worthy and able,
That by some chance, since Fortune's changeable.
You may to your desire sometime attain.
But I, that am in exile and in pain,
Stripped of all hope and in so deep despair
That there's no earth nor water, fire nor air,
Nor any creature made of them there is
To help or give me comfort, now, in this—
Surely I'll die of sorrow and distress;
Farewell, my life, my love, my joyousness!
"Alas! Why is it men so much complain
Of what great God, or Fortune, may ordain,
When better is the gift, in any guise,
Than men may often for themselves devise?
One man desires only that great wealth
Which may but cause his death or long ill-health.
One who from prison gladly would be free,
At home by his own servants slain might be.
Infinite evils lie therein, 'tis clear;
We know not what it is we pray for here.
We fare as he that's drunken as a mouse;
A drunk man knows right well he has a house,
But he knows not the right way leading thither;
And a drunk man is sure to slip and slither.
And certainly, in this world so fare we;
We furiously pursue felicity,
Yet we go often wrong before we die.
This may we all admit, and specially I,
Who deemed and held, as I were under spell,
That if I might escape from prison cell,
Then would I find again what might heal,
Who now am only exiled from my weal.
For since I may not see you, Emily,
I am but dead; there is no remedy."

And on the other hand, this Palamon,
When that he found Arcita truly gone,
Such lamentation made he, that the tower
Resounded of his crying, hour by hour.
The very fetters on his legs were yet
Again with all his bitter salt tears wet.
"Alas!" said he, "Arcita, cousin mine,
With all our strife, God knows, you've won the
     wine.
You're walking, now, in Theban streets, at large,
And all my woe you may from mind discharge.
You may, too, since you've wisdom and manhood,
Assemble all the people of our blood
And wage a war so sharp on this city
That by some fortune, or by some treaty,
You shall yet have that lady to your wife
For whom I now must needs lay down my life.
For surely 'tis in possibility,
Since you are now at large, from prison free,
And are a lord, great is your advantage
Above my own, who die here in a cage.
For I must weep and wail, the while I live,
In all the grief that prison cell may give,
And now with pain that love gives me, also,
Which doubles all my torment and my woe."
Therewith the fires of jealousy up-start
Within his breast and burn him to the heart
So wildly that he seems one, to behold,
Like seared box tree, or ashes, dead and cold.
Then said he: "O you cruel Gods, that sway
This world in bondage of your laws, for aye,
And write upon the tablets adamant
Your counsels and the changeless words you grant,
What better view of mankind do you hold
Than of the sheep that huddle in the fold?
For man must die like any other beast,
Or rot in prison, under foul arrest,
And suffer sickness and misfortune sad,
And still be ofttimes guiltless, too, by gad!"
What management is in this prescience
That, guiltless, yet torments our innocence?
And this increases all my pain, as well,
That man is bound by law, nor may rebel,
For fear of God, but must repress his will,
Whereas a beast may all his lust fulfill.
And when a beast is dead, he feels no pain;
But, after death, man yet must weep amain,

Though in this world he had but care and woe:
There is no doubt that it is even so.
The answer leave I to divines to tell,
But well I know this present world is hell.
Alas! I see a serpent or a thief,
That has brought many a true man unto grief,
Going at large, and where he wills may turn,
But I must lie in gaol, because Saturn,
And Juno too, both envious and mad,
Have spilled out well-nigh all the blood we had
At Thebes, and desolated her wide walls.
And Venus slays me with the bitter galls
Of fear of Arcita, and jealousy."
Now will I leave this Palamon, for he
Is in his prison, where he still must dwell,
And of Arcita will I forthwith tell.
Summer being passed away and nights grown long,
Increased now doubly all the anguish strong
Both of the lover and the prisoner.
I know not which one was the woefuller.

For, to be brief about it, Palamon
Is doomed to lie forever in prison,
In chains and fetters till he shall be dead;
And exiled (on the forfeit of his head)
Arcita must remain abroad, nor see,
For evermore, the face of his lady.
You lovers, now I ask you this question:
Who has the worse, Arcita or Palamon?
The one may see his lady day by day,
But yet in prison must he dwell for aye.
The other, where he wishes, he may go,
But never see his lady more, ah no.
Now answer as you wish, all you that can.
For I will speak right on as I began.

**For the entire story,
insert the Literature CD.**

Questions

1. What kind of reception does Theseus receive when he returns home? What is contradictory about this?
2. How does Arcita get out of prison? Is there any evidence to suggest that Palamon could have also gotten out if he wanted to?
3. What choice does Palamon give Arcita when they meet in the forest? What might this choice represent?
4. What was Theseus' reaction when he found out that Arcita had been tricking him for so many years? At this point, does the tale adopt a vengeful tone?
5. What religious structures did Theseus erect around his coliseum, and why are these structures significant?
6. Regarding marriage, what does Emily desire? Why?
7. What important decision does Saturn make? Further, how does this decision change the direction of the tale?
8. Who does Theseus award Emily to, and what happens to this person? What does this foreshadow about the marriage of these two individuals?

1. Arcita and Palamon are not the first literary characters to be associated with a conflict that revolves around a woman. What is it that drives these two characters to hate one another, and in what other tales from Chaucer has a woman been the source of a conflict between two comrades? Construct an argument that examines women's roles in Chaucer's tales and the conflicts they cause.
2. Compare and contrast the prayers of Arcita and Palamon to Emily's. Examine their words and the temples where they voice these prayers, and in doing so, examine the significance of these prayers, specifying the role that each prayer plays in the tale.
3. "The Knight's Tale" reeks of chivalry and knighthood; such chivalry and knighthood can also be seen in *Sir Gawain and the Green Knight*. Choose one character from each of these tales, and compare and contrast their definitions of *knighthood*.

Sir Gawain and the Green Knight

1. The atmosphere at the beginning of the story is clearly celebratory. With the entrance of the Green Knight, notice the instantaneous mood shift.
2. Color and symbolism are essential to this tale; both entities are interwoven throughout.
3. Religion's role in this story is paradoxical. The knights are druid-like, but they are firm believers in God and Christ's sacrifice.

Sir Gawain and the Green Knight

Anonymous

After the siege and the assault of Troy, when that burg was destroyed and burnt to ashes, and the traitor tried for his treason, the noble Æneas and his kin sailed forth to become princes and patrons of well-nigh all the Western Isles. Thus Romulus built Rome (and gave to the city his own name, which it bears even to this day); and Ticius turned him to Tuscany; and Langobard raised him up dwellings in Lombardy; and Felix Brutus sailed far over the French flood, and founded the kingdom of Britain, wherein have been war and waste and wonder, and bliss and bale, ofttimes since.

And in that kingdom of Britain have been wrought more gallant deeds than in any other; but of all British kings Arthur was the most valiant, as I have heard tell, therefore will I set forth a wondrous adventure that fell out in his time. And if ye will listen to me, but for a little while, I will tell it even as it stands in story stiff and strong, fixed in the letter, as it hath long been known in the land.

* * * * *

King Arthur lay at Camelot upon a Christmas-tide, with many a gallant lord and lovely lady, and all the noble brotherhood of the Round Table. There they held rich revels with gay talk and jest; one while they would ride forth to joust and tourney, and again back to the court to make carols; for there was the feast holden fifteen days with all the mirth that men could devise, song and glee, glorious to hear, in the day-time, and dancing at night. Halls and chambers were crowded with noble guests, the bravest of knights and the loveliest of ladies, and Arthur himself was the comeliest king that ever held a court. For all this fair folk were in their youth, the fairest and most fortunate under heaven, and the king himself of such fame that it were hard now to name so valiant a hero. Now the New Year had but newly come in, and on that day a double portion was served on the high table to all the noble guests, and thither came the king with all his knights, when the service in the chapel had been sung to an end. And they greeted each other for the New Year, and gave rich gifts, the one to the other (and they that received them were not wroth, that may ye well believe!), and the maidens laughed and made mirth till it was time to get them to meat. Then they washed and sat them down to the feast in fitting rank and order, and Guinevere the queen, gaily clad, sat on the high daïs. Silken was her seat, with a fair canopy over her head, of rich tapestries of Tars, embroidered, and studded with costly gems; fair she was to look upon, with her shining grey eyes, a fairer woman might no man boast himself of having seen.

But Arthur would not eat till all were served, so full of joy and gladness was he, even as a child; he liked not either to lie long, or to sit long at meat, so worked upon him his young blood and his wild brain. And another custom he had also, that came of his nobility, that he would never eat upon an high day till he had been advised of some knightly deed, or some strange and marvellous tale, of his ancestors, or of arms, or of other ventures. Or till some stranger knight should seek of him leave to joust with one of the Round Table, that they might set their lives in jeopardy, one against another, as fortune might favour them. Such was the king's custom when he sat in hall at each high feast with his noble knights, therefore on that New Year tide, he abode, fair of face, on the throne, and made much mirth withal. Thus the king sat before the high tables, and spake of many things; and there good Sir Gawain was seated by Guinevere the queen, and on her other side sat Agravain, à la dure main; both were the king's sister's sons and full gallant knights. And at the end of the table was Bishop Bawdewyn, and Ywain, King Urien's son, sat at the other side alone. These were worthily served on the daïs, and at the lower tables sat many valiant knights. Then they bare the first course with the blast of trumpets and waving of banners, with the sound of drums and pipes, of song and lute, that many a heart was uplifted at the melody. Many were the dainties, and rare the meats, so great was the plenty they might scarce find room on the board to set on the dishes. Each helped himself as he liked best, and to each two were twelve dishes, with great plenty of beer and wine.

Now I will say no more of the service, but that ye may know there was no lack, for there drew near a venture that the folk might well have left their labour to gaze upon. As the sound of the music ceased, and the first course had been fitly served, there came in at the hall door one terrible to behold, of stature greater than any on earth; from neck to loin so strong and thickly made, and with limbs so long and so great that he seemed even as a giant. And yet he was but a man, only the mightiest that might mount a steed; broad of chest and shoulders and slender of waist, and all his features of like fashion; but men marvelled much at his colour, for he rode even as a knight, yet was green all over.

For he was clad all in green, with a straight coat, and a mantle above; all decked and lined with fur was the cloth and the hood that was thrown back from his locks and lay on his shoulders. Hose had he of the same green, and spurs of bright gold with silken fastenings richly worked; and all his vesture was verily green. Around his waist and his saddle were bands with fair stones set upon silken work, 'twere too long to tell of all the trifles that were embroidered thereon—birds and insects in gay gauds of green and gold. All the trappings of his steed were of metal of like enamel, even the stirrups that he stood in stained of the same, and stirrups and saddle-bow alike gleamed and shone with green stones. Even the steed on which he rode was of the same hue, a green horse, great and strong, and hard to hold, with broidered bridle, meet for the rider.

The knight was thus gaily dressed in green, his hair falling around his shoulders; on his breast hung a beard, as thick and green as a bush, and the beard and the hair of his head were clipped all round above his elbows. The lower part of his sleeves were fastened with clasps in the same wise as a king's mantle. The horse's mane was crisp and plaited with many a knot folded in with gold thread about the fair green, here a twist of the hair, here another of gold. The tail was twined in like manner, and both were bound about with a band of bright green set with many a precious stone; then they were tied aloft in a cunning knot, whereon rang many bells of burnished gold. Such a steed might no other ride, nor had such ever been looked upon in that hall ere that time; and all who saw that knight spake and said that a man might scarce abide his stroke.

The knight bore no helm nor hauberk, neither gorget nor breast-plate, neither shaft nor buckler to smite nor to shield, but in one hand he had a hollybough, that is greenest when the groves are bare, and in his other an axe, huge and uncomely, a cruel weapon in fashion, if one would picture it. The head was an ell-yard long, the metal all of green steel and gold, the blade burnished bright, with a broad edge, as well shapen to shear as a sharp razor. The steel was set into a strong staff, all bound round with iron, even to the end, and engraved with green in cunning work. A lace was twined about it, that looped at the head, and all adown the handle it was clasped with tassels on buttons of bright green richly broidered.

The knight rideth through the entrance of the hall, driving straight to the high daïs, and greeted no man, but looked ever upwards; and the first words he spake were, "Where is the ruler of this folk? I would gladly look upon that hero, and have speech with him." He cast his eyes on the knights, and mustered them up and down, striving ever to see who of them was of most renown. Then was there great gazing to behold that chief, for each man marvelled what it might mean that a knight and his steed should have even such a hue as the green grass; and that seemed even greener than green enamel on bright gold. All looked on him as he stood, and drew near unto him wondering greatly what he might be; for many marvels had they seen, but none such as this, and phantasm and farie did the folk deem it. Therefore were the gallant knights slow to answer, and gazed astounded, and sat stone still in a deep silence through that goodly hall, as if a slumber were fallen upon them. I deem it was not all for doubt, but some for courtesy that they might give ear unto his errand. Then Arthur beheld this adventurer before his high daïs, and knightly he greeted him, for fearful was he never. "Sir," he said, "thou art welcome to this place—lord of this hall am I, and men call me Arthur. Light thee down, and tarry awhile, and what thy will is, that shall we learn after." "Nay," quoth the stranger, "so help me He that sitteth on high, 'twas not mine errand to tarry any while in this dwelling; but the praise of this thy folk and thy city is lifted up on high, and thy warriors are holden for the best and the most valiant of those who ride mail-clad to the fight. The wisest and the worthiest of this world are they, and well proven in all knightly sports. And here, as I have heard tell, is fairest courtesy, therefore have I come hither as at this time. Ye may be sure by the branch that I bear here that I come in peace, seeking no strife. For had I willed to journey in warlike guise I have at home both hauberk and helm, shield and shining spear, and other weapons to mine hand, but since I seek no war my raiment is that of peace. But if thou be as bold as all men tell thou wilt freely grant me the boon I ask."

And Arthur answered, "Sir Knight, if thou cravest battle here thou shalt not fail for lack of a foe."

And the knight answered, "Nay, I ask no fight, in faith here on the benches are but beardless children, were I clad in armour on my steed there is no man here might match me. Therefore I ask in this court but a Christmas jest, for that it is Yule-tide, and New Year, and there are here many fain for sport. If anyone in this hall holds himself so hardy, so bold both of blood and brain, as to dare strike me one stroke for another, I will give him as a gift this axe, which is heavy enough, in sooth, to handle as he may list, and I will abide the first blow, unarmed as I sit. If any knight be so bold as to prove my words let him come swiftly to me here, and take this weapon, I quit claim to it, he may keep it as his own, and I will abide his stroke, firm on the floor. Then shalt thou give me the right to deal him another, the respite of a year and a day shall he have. Now haste, and let see whether any here dare say aught."

Now if the knights had been astounded at the first, yet stiller were they all, high and low, when they had heard his words. The knight on his steed straightened himself in the saddle, and rolled his eyes fiercely round the hall, red they gleamed under his green and bushy brows. He frowned and twisted his beard, waiting to see who should rise, and when none answered he cried aloud in mockery, "What, is this Arthur's hall, and these the knights whose renown hath run through many realms? Where are now your pride and your conquests, your wrath, and anger, and mighty words? Now are the praise and the renown of the Round Table overthrown by one man's speech, since all keep silence for dread ere ever they have seen a blow!"

With that he laughed so loudly that the blood rushed to the king's fair face for very shame; he waxed wroth, as did all his knights, and sprang to his feet, and drew near to the stranger and said, "Now by heaven foolish is thy asking, and thy folly shall find its fitting answer. I know no man aghast at thy great words. Give me here thine axe and I shall grant thee the boon thou hast asked." Lightly he sprang to him and caught at his hand, and the knight, fierce of aspect, lighted down from his charger.

Then Arthur took the axe and gripped the haft, and swung it round, ready to strike. And the knight stood before him, taller by the head than any in the hall; he stood, and stroked his beard, and drew down his coat, no more dismayed for the king's threats than if one had brought him a drink of wine. Then Gawain, who sat by the queen, leaned forward to the king and spake, "I beseech ye, my lord, let this venture be mine. Would ye but bid me rise from this seat, and stand by your side, so that my liege lady thought it not ill, then would I come to your counsel before this goodly court. For I think it not seemly when such challenges be made in your hall that ye yourself should undertake it, while there are many bold knights who sit beside ye, none are there, methinks, of readier will under heaven, or more valiant in open field. I am the weakest, I wot, and the feeblest of wit, and it will be the less loss of my life if ye seek sooth. For save that ye are mine uncle naught is there in me to praise, no virtue is there in my body save your blood, and since this challenge is such folly that it beseems ye not to take it, and I have asked it from ye first, let it fall to me, and if I bear myself ungallantly then let all this court blame me."

Then they all spake with one voice that the king should leave this venture and grant it to Gawain. Then Arthur commanded the knight to rise, and he rose up quickly and knelt down before the king, and caught hold of the weapon; and the king loosed his hold of it, and lifted up his hand, and gave him his blessing, and bade him be strong both of heart and hand. "Keep thee well, nephew," quoth Arthur, "that thou give him but the one blow, and if thou redest him rightly I trow thou shalt well abide the stroke he may give thee after." Gawain stepped to the stranger, axe in hand, and he, never fearing, awaited his coming. Then the Green Knight spake to Sir Gawain, "Make we our covenant ere we go further. First, I ask thee, knight, what is thy name? Tell me truly, that I may know thee."

"In faith," quoth the good knight, "Gawain am I, who give thee this buffet, let what may come of it; and at this time twelvemonth will I take another at thine hand with whatsoever weapon thou wilt, and none other."

Then the other answered again, "Sir Gawain, so may I thrive as I am fain to take this buffet at thine hand," and he quoth further, "Sir Gawain, it liketh me well that I shall take at thy fist that which I have asked here, and thou hast readily and truly rehearsed all the covenant that I asked of the king, save that thou shalt swear me, by thy troth, to seek me thyself wherever thou hopest that I may be found, and win thee such reward as thou dealest me to-day, before this folk."

"Where shall I seek thee?" quoth Gawain. "Where is thy place? By Him that made me, I wot never where thou dwellest, nor know I thee, knight, thy court, nor thy name. But teach me truly all that pertaineth thereto, and tell me thy name, and I shall use all my wit to win my way thither, and that I swear thee for sooth, and by my sure troth." "That is enough in the New Year, it needs no more," quoth the Green Knight to the gallant Gawain, "if I tell thee truly when I have taken the blow, and thou hast smitten me; then will I teach thee of my house and home, and mine own name, then mayest thou ask thy road and keep covenant. And if I waste no words then farest thou the better, for thou canst dwell in thy land, and seek no further. But take now thy toll, and let see how thy strikest."

"Gladly will I," quoth Gawain, handling his axe.

Then the Green Knight swiftly made him ready, he bowed down his head, and laid his long locks on the crown that his bare neck might be seen. Gawain gripped his axe and raised it on high, the left foot he set forward on the floor, and let the blow fall lightly on the bare neck. The sharp edge of the blade sundered the bones, smote through the neck, and clave it in two, so that the edge of the steel bit on the ground, and the fair head fell to the earth that many struck it with their feet as it rolled forth. The blood spurted forth, and glistened on the green raiment, but the knight neither faltered nor fell; he started forward with out-stretched hand, and caught the head, and lifted it up; then he turned to his steed, and took hold of the bridle, set his foot in the stirrup, and mounted. His head he held by the hair, in his hand. Then he seated himself in his saddle as if naught ailed him, and he were not headless. He turned his steed about, the grim corpse bleeding freely the while, and they who looked upon him doubted them much for the covenant.

For he held up the head in his hand, and turned the face towards them that sat on the high daïs, and it lifted up the eyelids and looked upon them and spake as ye shall hear. "Look, Gawain, that thou art ready to go as thou hast promised, and seek leally till thou find me, even as thou hast sworn in this hall in the hearing of these knights. Come thou, I charge thee, to the Green Chapel, such a stroke as thou hast dealt thou hast deserved, and it shall be promptly paid thee on New Year's morn. Many men know me as the knight of the Green Chapel, and if thou askest, thou shalt not fail to find me. Therefore it behoves thee to come, or to yield thee as recreant."

With that he turned his bridle, and galloped out at the hall door, his head in his hands, so that the sparks flew from beneath his horse's hoofs. Whither he went none knew, no more than they wist whence he had come; and the king and Gawain they gazed and laughed, for in sooth this had proved a greater marvel than any they had known aforetime.

Though Arthur the king was astonished at his heart, yet he let no sign of it be seen, but spake in courteous wise to the fair queen: "Dear lady, be not dismayed, such craft is well suited to Christmas-tide when we seek jesting, laughter and song, and fair carols of knights and ladies. But now I may well get me to meat, for I have seen a marvel I may not forget." Then he looked on Sir Gawain, and said gaily, "Now, fair nephew, hang up thine axe, since it has hewn enough," and they hung it on the dossal above the daïs, where all men might look on it for a marvel, and by its true token tell of the wonder. Then the twain sat them down together, the king and the good knight, and men served them with a double portion, as was the share of the noblest, with all manner of meat and of minstrelsy. And they spent that day in gladness, but Sir Gawain must well bethink him of the heavy venture to which he had set his hand.

* * * * *

This beginning of adventures had Arthur at the New Year; for he yearned to hear gallant tales, though his words were few when he sat at the feast. But now had they stern work on hand. Gawain was glad to begin the jest in the hall, but ye need have no marvel if the end be heavy. For though a man be merry in mind when he has well drunk, yet a year runs full swiftly, and the beginning but rarely matches the end.

For Yule was now over-past, and the year after, each season in its turn following the other. For after Christmas comes crabbed Lent, that will have fish for flesh and simpler cheer. But then the weather of the world chides with winter; the cold withdraws itself, the clouds uplift, and the rain falls in warm showers on the fair plains. Then the flowers come forth, meadows and grove are clad in green, the birds make ready to build, and sing sweetly for solace of the soft summer that follows thereafter. The blossoms bud and blow in the hedgerows rich and rank, and noble notes enough are heard in the fair woods.

After the season of summer, with the soft winds, when zephyr breathes lightly on seeds and herbs, joyous indeed is the growth that waxes thereout when the dew drips from the leaves beneath the blissful glance of the bright sun. But then comes harvest and hardens the grain, warning it to wax ripe ere the winter. The drought drives the dust on high, flying over the face of the land; the angry wind of the welkin wrestles with the sun; the leaves fall from the trees and light upon the ground, and all brown are the groves that but now were green, and ripe is the fruit that once was flower. So the year passes into many yesterdays, and winter comes again, as it needs no sage to tell us. When the Michaelmas moon was come in with warnings of winter, Sir Gawain bethought him full oft of his perilous journey. Yet till All Hallows Day he lingered with Arthur, and on that day they made a great feast for the hero's sake, with much revel and richness of the Round Table. Courteous knights and comely ladies, all were in sorrow for the love of that knight, and though they spake no word of it, many were joyless for his sake. And after meat, sadly Sir Gawain turned to his uncle, and spake of his journey, and said, "Liege lord of my life, leave from you I crave. Ye know well how the matter stands without more words, to-morrow am I bound to set forth in search of the Green Knight." Then came together all the noblest knights, Ywain and Erec, and many another. Sir Dodinel le Sauvage, the Duke of Clarence, Launcelot and Lionel, and Lucan the Good, Sir Bors and Sir Bedivere, valiant knights both, and many another hero, with Sir Mador de la Porte, and they all drew near, heavy at heart, to take counsel with Sir Gawain. Much sorrow and weeping was there in the hall to think that so worthy a knight as Gawain should wend his way to seek a deadly blow, and should no more wield his sword in fight. But the knight made ever good cheer, and said, "Nay, wherefore should I shrink? What may a man do but prove his fate?" He dwelt there all that day, and on the morn he arose and asked betimes for his armour; and they brought it unto him on this wise: first, a rich carpet was stretched on the floor (and brightly did the gold gear glitter upon it), then the knight stepped on to it, and handled the steel; clad he was in a doublet of silk, with a close hood, lined fairly throughout. Then they set the steel shoes upon his feet, and wrapped his legs with greaves, with polished kneecaps, fastened with knots of gold. Then they cased his thighs in cuisses closed with thongs, and brought him the byrny of bright steel rings sewn upon a fair

stuff. Well burnished braces they set on each arm with good elbow-pieces, and gloves of mail, and all the goodly gear that should shield him in his need. And they cast over all a rich surcoat, and set the golden spurs on his heels, and girt him with a trusty sword fastened with a silken bawdrick. When he was thus clad his harness was costly, for the least loop or latchet gleamed with gold. So armed as he was he hearkened Mass and made his offering at the high altar. Then he came to the king, and the knights of his court, and courteously took leave of lords and ladies, and they kissed him, and commended him to Christ.

With that was Gringalet ready, girt with a saddle that gleamed gaily with many golden fringes, enriched and decked anew for the venture. The bridle was all barred about with bright gold buttons, and all the covertures and trappings of the steed, the crupper and the rich skirts, accorded with the saddle; spread fair with the rich red gold that glittered and gleamed in the rays of the sun.

Then the knight called for his helmet, which was well lined throughout, and set it high on his head, and hasped it behind. He wore a light kerchief over the vintail, that was broidered and studded with fair gems on a broad silken ribbon, with birds of gay colour, and many a turtle and true-lover's knot interlaced thickly, even as many a maiden had wrought diligently for seven winter long. But the circlet which crowned his helmet was yet more precious, being adorned with a device in diamonds. Then they brought him his shield, which was of bright red, with the pentangle painted thereon in gleaming gold. And why that noble prince bare the pentangle I am minded to tell you, though my tale tarry thereby. It is a sign that Solomon set ere-while, as betokening truth; for it is a figure with five points and each line overlaps the other, and nowhere hath it beginning or end, so that in English it is called "the endless knot." And therefore was it well suiting to this knight and to his arms, since Gawain was faithful in five and five-fold, for pure was he as gold, void of all villainy and endowed with all virtues. Therefore he bare the pentangle on shield and surcoat as truest of heroes and gentlest of knights.

For first he was faultless in his five senses; and his five fingers never failed him; and all his trust upon earth was in the five wounds that Christ bare on the cross, as the Creed tells. And wherever this knight found himself in stress of battle he deemed well that he drew his strength from the five joys which the Queen of Heaven had of her Child. And for this cause did he bear an image of Our Lady on the one half of his shield, that whenever he looked upon it he might not lack for aid. And the fifth five that the hero used were frankness and fellowship above all, purity and courtesy that never failed him, and compassion that surpasses all; and in these five virtues was that hero wrapped and clothed. And all these, five-fold, were linked one in the other, so that they had no end, and were fixed on five points that never failed, neither at any side were they joined or sundered, nor could ye find beginning or end. And therefore on his shield was the knot shapen, red-gold upon red, which is the pure pentangle. Now was Sir Gawain ready, and he took his lance in hand, and bade them all *Farewell,* he deemed it had been for ever.

Then he smote the steed with his spurs, and sprang on his way, so that sparks flew from the stones after him. All that saw him were grieved at heart, and said one to the other, "By Christ, 'tis great pity that one of such noble life should be lost! I' faith, 'twere not easy to find his equal upon earth. The king had done better to have wrought more warily. Yonder knight should have been made a duke; a gallant leader of men is he, and such a fate had beseemed him better than to be hewn in pieces at the will of an elfish man, for mere pride. Who ever knew a king to take such counsel as to risk his knights on a Christmas jest?" Many were the tears that flowed from their eyes when that goodly knight rode from the hall. He made no delaying, but went his way swiftly, and rode many a wild road, as I heard say in the book. So rode Sir Gawain through the realm of Logres, on an errand that he held for no jest. Often he lay companionless at night, and must lack the fare that he liked. No comrade had he save his steed, and none save God with whom to take counsel. At length he drew nigh to North Wales, and left the isles of Anglesey on his left hand, crossing over the fords by the foreland over at Holyhead, till he came into the wilderness of Wirral, where but few dwell who love God and man of true heart. And ever he asked, as he fared, of all whom he met, if they had heard any tidings of a Green Knight in the country thereabout, or of a Green Chapel? And all answered him, Nay,

never in their lives had they seen any man of such a hue. And the knight wended his way by many a strange road and many a rugged path, and the fashion of his countenance changed full often ere he saw the Green Chapel. Many a cliff did he climb in that unknown land, where afar from his friends he rode as a stranger. Never did he come to a stream or a ford but he found a foe before him, and that one so marvellous, so foul and fell, that it behoved him to fight. So many wonders did that knight behold, that it were too long to tell the tenth part of them. Sometimes he fought with dragons and wolves; sometimes with wild men that dwelt in the rocks; another while with bulls, and bears, and wild boars, or with giants of the high moorland that drew near to him. Had he not been a doughty knight, enduring, and of well-proved valour, and a servant of God, doubtless he had been slain, for he was oft in danger of death. Yet he cared not so much for the strife, what he deemed worse was when the cold clear water was shed from the clouds, and froze ere it fell on the fallow ground. More nights than enough he slept in his harness on the bare rocks, near slain with the sleet, while the stream leapt bubbling from the crest of the hills, and hung in hard icicles over his head.

Thus in peril and pain, and many a hardship, the knight rode alone till Christmas Eve, and in that tide he made his prayer to the Blessed Virgin that she would guide his steps and lead him to some dwelling. On that morning he rode by a hill, and came into a thick forest, wild and drear; on each side were high hills, and thick woods below them of great hoar oaks, a hundred together, of hazel and hawthorn with their trailing boughs intertwined, and rough ragged moss spreading everywhere. On the bare twigs the birds chirped piteously, for pain of the cold. The knight upon Gringalet rode lonely beneath them, through marsh and mire, much troubled at heart lest he should fail to see the service of the Lord, who on that self-same night was born of a maiden for the cure of our grief; and therefore he said, sighing, "I beseech Thee, Lord, and Mary Thy gentle Mother, for some shelter where I may hear Mass, and Thy mattins at morn. This I ask meekly, and thereto I pray my Paternoster, Ave, and Credo." Thus he rode praying, and lamenting his misdeeds, and he crossed himself, and said, "May the Cross of Christ speed me."

Now that knight had crossed himself but thrice ere he was aware in the wood of a dwelling within a moat, above a lawn, on a mound surrounded by many mighty trees that stood round the moat. 'Twas the fairest castle that ever a knight owned; built in a meadow with a park all about it, and a spiked palisade, closely driven, that enclosed the trees for more than two miles. The knight was ware of the hold from the side, as it shone through the oaks. Then he lifted off his helmet, and thanked Christ and S. Julian that they had courteously granted his prayer, and hearkened to his cry. "Now," quoth the knight, "I beseech ye, grant me fair hostel." Then he pricked Gringalet with his golden spurs, and rode gaily towards the great gate, and came swiftly to the bridge end.

The bridge was drawn up and the gates close shut; the walls were strong and thick, so that they might fear no tempest. The knight on his charger abode on the bank of the deep double ditch that surrounded the castle. The walls were set deep in the water, and rose aloft to a wondrous height; they were of hard hewn stone up to the corbels, which were adorned beneath the battlements with fair carvings, and turrets set in between with many a loophole; a better barbican Sir Gawain had never looked upon. And within he beheld the high hall, with its tower and many windows with carven cornices, and chalk-white chimneys on the turreted roofs that shone fair in the sun. And everywhere, thickly scattered on the castle battlements, were pinnacles, so many that it seemed as if it were all wrought out of paper, so white was it.

The knight on his steed deemed it fair enough, if he might come to be sheltered within it to lodge there while that the Holy-day lasted. He called aloud, and soon there came a porter of kindly countenance, who stood on the wall and greeted this knight and asked his errand.

"Good sir," quoth Gawain, "wilt thou go mine errand to the high lord of the castle, and crave for me lodging?"

"Yea, by St. Peter," quoth the porter. "In sooth I trow that ye be welcome to dwell here so long as it may like ye."

Then he went, and came again swiftly, and many folk with him to receive the knight. They let down the great drawbridge, and came forth and knelt on their knees on the cold earth to give him worthy welcome. They held wide open the great gates, and courteously he bid them rise, and rode over the bridge. Then men came to him and held his stirrup while he dismounted, and took and stabled his steed. There came down knights and squires to bring the guest with joy to the hall. When he raised his helmet there were many to take it from his hand, fain to serve him, and they took from him sword and shield.

Sir Gawain gave good greeting to the noble and the mighty men who came to do him honour. Clad in his shining armour they led him to the hall, where a great fire burnt brightly on the floor; and the lord of the household came forth from his chamber to meet the hero fitly. He spake to the knight, and said: "Ye are welcome to do here as it likes ye. All that is here is your own to have at your will and disposal."

"Gramercy!" quote Gawain, "may Christ requite ye." As friends that were fain each embraced the other; and Gawain looked on the knight who greeted him so kindly, and thought 'twas a bold warrior that owned that burg.

Of mighty stature he was, and of high age; broad and flowing was his beard, and of a bright hue. He was stalwart of limb, and strong in his stride, his face fiery red, and his speech free: in sooth he seemed one well fitted to be a leader of valiant men. Then the lord led Sir Gawain to a chamber, and commanded folk to wait upon him, and at his bidding there came men enough who brought the guest to a fair bower. The bedding was noble, with curtains of pure silk wrought with gold, and wondrous coverings of fair cloth all embroidered. The curtains ran on ropes with rings of red gold, and the walls were hung with carpets of Orient, and the same spread on the floor. There with mirthful speeches they took from the guest his byrny and all his shining armour, and brought him rich robes of the choicest in its stead. They were long and flowing, and became him well, and when he was clad in them all who looked on the hero thought that surely God had never made a fairer knight: he seemed as if he might be a prince without peer in the field where men strive in battle.

Then before the hearth-place, whereon the fire burned, they made ready a chair for Gawain, hung about with cloth and fair cushions; and there they cast around him a mantle of brown samite, richly embroidered and furred within with costly skins of ermine, with a hood of the same, and he seated himself in that rich seat, and warmed himself at the fire, and was cheered at heart. And while he sat thus the serving men set up a table on trestles, and covered it with a fair white cloth, and set thereon salt-cellar, and napkin, and silver spoons; and the knight washed at his will, and set him down to meat.

The folk served him courteously with many dishes seasoned of the best, a double portion. All kinds of fish were there, some baked in bread, some broiled on the embers, some sodden, some stewed and savoured with spices, with all sorts of cunning devices to his taste. And often he called it a feast, when they spake gaily to him all together, and said, "Now take ye this penance, and it shall be for your amendment." Much mirth thereof did Sir Gawain make.

Then they questioned that prince courteously of whence he came; and he told them that he was of the court of Arthur, who is the rich royal King of the Round Table, and that it was Gawain himself who was within their walls, and would keep Christmas with them, as the chance had fallen out. And when the lord of the castle heard those tidings he laughed aloud for gladness, and all men in that keep were joyful that they should be in the company of him to whom belonged all fame, and valour, and courtesy, and whose honour was praised above that of all men on earth. Each said softly to his fellow, "Now shall we see courteous bearing, and the manner of speech befitting courts. What charm lieth in gentle speech shall we learn without asking, since here we have welcomed the fine father of courtesy. God has surely shewn us His grace since He sends us such a guest as Gawain! When men shall sit and sing, blithe for Christ's birth, this knight shall bring us to the knowledge of fair manners, and it may be that hearing him we may learn the cunning speech of love." By the time the knight had risen from dinner it was near nightfall. Then chaplains took their way to the chapel, and rang loudly, even as they should, for the solemn evensong of the high feast. Thither went the lord, and the lady also, and entered with her maidens into a comely closet, and thither also went Gawain. Then the lord took him by the sleeve and led him to a seat, and called him by his name, and told him he was of all men in the world the most welcome. And Sir Gawain thanked him truly, and each kissed the other, and they sat gravely together throughout the service.

Then was the lady fain to look upon that knight; and she came forth from her closet with many fair maidens. The fairest of ladies was she in face, and figure, and colouring, fairer even than Guinevere, so the knight thought. She came through the chancel to greet the hero, another lady held her by the left hand, older than she, and seemingly of high estate, with many nobles about her. But unlike to look upon were those ladies, for if the younger were fair, the elder was yellow. Rich red were the cheeks of the one, rough and wrinkled those of the other; the kerchiefs of the one were broidered with many glistening pearls, her throat and neck bare, and whiter than the snow that lies on the hills; the neck of the other was swathed in a gorget, with a white wimple over her black chin. Her forehead was wrapped in silk with many folds, worked with knots, so that naught of her was seen save her black brows, her eyes, her nose and her lips, and those were bleared, and ill to look upon. A worshipful lady in sooth one might call her! In figure was she short and broad, and thickly made—far fairer to behold was she whom she led by the hand.

When Gawain beheld that fair lady, who looked at him graciously, with leave of the lord he went towards them, and, bowing low, he greeted the elder, but the younger and fairer he took lightly in his arms, and kissed her courteously, and greeted her in knightly wise. Then she hailed him as friend, and he quickly prayed to be counted as her servant, if she so willed. Then they took him between them, and talking, led him to the chamber, to the hearth, and bade them bring spices, and they brought them in plenty with the good wine that was wont to be drunk at such seasons. Then the lord sprang to his feet and bade them make merry, and took off his hood, and hung it on a spear, and bade him win the worship thereof who should make most mirth that Christmas-tide. "And I shall try, by my faith, to fool it with the best, by the help of my friends, ere I lose my raiment." Thus with gay words the lord made trial to gladden Gawain with jests that night, till it was time to bid them light the tapers, and Sir Gawain took leave of them and gat him to rest.

In the morn when all men call to mind how Christ our Lord was born on earth to die for us, there is joy, for His sake, in all dwellings of the world; and so was there here on that day. For high feast was held, with many dainties and cunningly cooked messes. On the daïs sat gallant men, clad in their best. The ancient dame sat on the high seat, with the lord of the castle beside her. Gawain and the fair lady sat together, even in the midst of the board, when the feast was served; and so throughout all the hall each sat in his degree, and was served in order. There was meat, there was mirth, there was much joy, so that to tell thereof would take me too long, though peradventure I might strive to declare it. But Gawain and that fair lady had much joy of each other's company through her sweet words and courteous converse. And there was music made before each prince, trumpets and drums, and merry piping; each man hearkened his minstrel, and they too hearkened theirs.

So they held high feast that day and the next, and the third day thereafter, and the joy on St. John's Day was fair to hearken, for 'twas the last of the feast and the guests would depart in the grey of the morning. Therefore they awoke early, and drank wine, and danced fair carols, and at last, when it was late, each man took his leave to wend early on his way. Gawain would bid his host farewell, but the lord took him by the hand, and led him to his own chamber beside the hearth, and there he thanked him for the favour he had shown him in honouring his dwelling at that high season, and gladdening his castle with his fair countenance. "I wis, sir, that while I live I shall be held the worthier that Gawain has been my guest at God's own feast." "Gramercy, sir," quoth Gawain, "in good faith, all the honour is yours, may the High King give it you, and I am but at your will to work your behest, inasmuch as I am beholden to you in great and small by rights."

Then the lord did his best to persuade the knight to tarry with him, but Gawain answered that he might in no wise do so. Then the host asked him courteously what stern behest had driven him at the holy season from the king's court, to fare all alone, ere yet the feast was ended? "Forsooth," quoth the knight, "ye say but the truth: 'tis a high quest and a pressing that hath brought me afield, for I am summoned myself to a certain place, and I know not whither in the world I may wend to find it; so help me Christ, I would give all the kingdom of Logres and I might find it by New Year's morn. Therefore, sir, I make re-

quest of you that ye tell me truly if ye ever heard word of the Green Chapel, where it may be found, and the Green Knight that keeps it. For I am pledged by solemn compact sworn between us to meet that knight at the New Year if so I were on life; and of that same New Year it wants but little—I' faith, I would look on that hero more joyfully than on any other fair sight! Therefore, by your will, it behoves me to leave you, for I have but barely three days, and I would as fain fall dead as fail of mine errand." Then the lord quoth, laughing, "Now must ye needs stay, for I will show you your goal, the Green Chapel, ere your term be at an end, have ye no fear! But ye can take your ease, friend, in your bed, till the fourth day, and go forth on the first of the year and come to that place at mid-morn to do as ye will. Dwell here till New Year's Day, and then rise and set forth, and ye shall be set in the way; 'tis not two miles hence."

Then was Gawain glad, and he laughed gaily. "Now I thank you for this above all else. Now my quest is achieved I will dwell here at your will, and otherwise do as ye shall ask."

Then the lord took him, and set him beside him, and bade the ladies be fetched for their greater pleasure, tho' between themselves they had solace. The lord, for gladness, made merry jest, even as one who wist not what to do for joy; and he cried aloud to the knight, "Ye have promised to do the thing I bid ye: will ye hold to this behest, here, at once?" "Yea, forsooth," said that true knight, "while I abide in your burg I am bound by your behest."

"Ye have travelled from far," said the host, "and since then ye have waked with me, ye are not well refreshed by rest and sleep, as I know. Ye shall therefore abide in your chamber, and lie at your ease tomorrow at Mass-tide, and go to meat when ye will with my wife, who shall sit with you, and comfort you with her company till I return; and I shall rise early and go forth to the chase." And Gawain agreed to all this courteously.

"Sir knight," quoth the host, "we shall make a covenant. Whatsoever I win in the wood shall be yours, and whatever may fall to your share, that shall ye exchange for it. Let us swear, friend, to make this exchange, however our hap may be, for worse or for better."

"I grant ye your will," quoth Gawain the good; "if ye list so to do, it liketh me well."

"Bring hither the wine-cup, the bargain is made," so said the lord of that castle. They laughed each one, and drank of the wine, and made merry, these lords and ladies, as it pleased them. Then with gay talk and merry jest they arose, and stood, and spoke softly, and kissed courteously, and took leave of each other. With burning torches, and many a serving-man, was each led to his couch; yet ere they gat them to bed the old lord oft repeated their covenant, for he knew well how to make sport.

* * * * *

Full early, ere daylight, the folk rose up; the guests who would depart called their grooms, and they made them ready, and saddled the steeds, tightened up the girths, and trussed up their mails. The knights, all arrayed for riding, leapt up lightly, and took their bridles, and each rode his way as pleased him best.

The lord of the land was not the last. Ready for the chase, with many of his men, he ate a sop hastily when he had heard Mass, and then with blast of the bugle fared forth to the field. He and his nobles were to horse ere daylight glimmered upon the earth. Then the huntsmen coupled their hounds, unclosed the kennel door, and called them out. They blew three blasts gaily on the bugles, the hounds bayed fiercely, and they that would go a-hunting checked and chastised them. A hundred hunters there were of the best, so I have heard tell. Then the trackers gat them to the trysting-place and uncoupled the hounds, and forest rang again with their gay blasts.

At the first sound of the hunt the game quaked for fear, and fled, trembling, along the vale. They betook them to the heights, but the liers in wait turned them back with loud cries; the harts they let pass them, and the stags with their spreading antlers, for the lord had forbidden that they should be slain, but the hinds and the does they turned back, and drave down into the valleys. Then might ye see much shooting of arrows. As the deer fled under the boughs a broad whistling shaft smote and wounded each sorely, so that, wounded and bleeding, they fell dying on the banks. The hounds followed swiftly on their tracks, and hunters, blowing the horn, sped after them with ringing shouts as if the cliffs burst asunder. What game escaped those that shot was run down at the outer ring. Thus were they driven on the hills, and harassed at the waters, so well did the men know their work, and the greyhounds were so great and swift that they ran them down as fast as the hunters could slay them. Thus the lord passed the day in mirth and joyfulness, even to nightfall. So the lord roamed the woods, and Gawain, that good night, lay ever a-bed, curtained about, under the costly coverlet, while the daylight gleamed on the walls. And as he lay half slumbering, he heard a little sound at the door, and he raised his head, and caught back a corner of the curtain, and waited to see what it might be. It was the lovely lady, the lord's wife; she shut the door softly behind her, and turned towards the bed; and Gawain was shamed, laid him down softly and made as if he slept. And she came lightly to the bedside, within the curtain, and sat herself down beside him, to wait till he wakened. The knight lay there awhile, and marvelled within himself what her coming might betoken; and he said to himself, "'Twere more seemly if I asked her what hath brought her hither." Then he made feint to waken, and turned towards her, and opened his eyes as one astonished, and crossed himself; and she looked on him laughing, with her cheeks red and white, lovely to behold, and small smiling lips.

"Good morrow, Sir Gawain," said that fair lady; "ye are but a careless sleeper, since one can enter thus. Now are ye taken unawares, and lest ye escape me I shall bind you in your bed; of that be ye assured!" Laughing, she spake these words.

"Good morrow, fair lady," quoth Gawain blithely. "I will do your will, as it likes me well. For I yield me readily, and pray your grace, and that is best, by my faith, since I needs must do so." Thus he jested again, laughing. "But an ye would, fair lady, grant me this grace that ye pray your prisoner to rise. I would get me from bed, and array me better, then could I talk with ye in more comfort."

"Nay, forsooth, fair sir," quoth the lady, "ye shall not rise, I will rede ye better. I shall keep ye here, since ye can do no other, and talk with my knight whom I have captured. For I know well that ye are Sir Gawain, whom all the world worships, wheresoever ye may ride. Your honour and your courtesy are praised by lords and ladies, by all who live. Now ye are here and we are alone, my lord and his men are afield; the serving men in their beds, and my maidens also, and the door shut upon us. And since in this hour I have him that all men love, I shall use my time well with speech, while it lasts. Ye are welcome to my company, for it behoves me in sooth to be your servant." "In good faith," quoth Gawain, "I think me that I am not him of whom ye speak, for unworthy am I of such service as ye here proffer. In sooth, I were glad if I might set myself by word or service to your pleasure; a pure joy would it be to me!"

"In good faith, Sir Gawain," quoth the gay lady, "the praise and the prowess that pleases all ladies I lack them not, nor hold them light; yet are there ladies enough who would liever now have the knight in their hold, as I have ye here, to dally with your courteous words, to bring them comfort and to ease their cares, than much of the treasure and the gold that are theirs. And now, through the grace of Him who upholds the heavens, I have wholly in my power that which they all desire!"

Thus the lady, fair to look upon, made him great cheer, and Sir Gawain, with modest words, answered her again: "Madam," he quoth, "may Mary requite ye, for in good faith I have found in ye a noble frankness. Much courtesy have other folk shown me, but the honour they have done me is naught to the worship of yourself, who knoweth but good."

"By Mary," quoth the lady, "I think otherwise; for were I worth all the women alive, and had I the wealth of the world in my hand, and might choose me a lord to my liking, then, for all that I have seen in ye, Sir Knight, of beauty and courtesy and blithe semblance, and for all that I have hearkened and hold for true, there should be no knight on earth to be chosen before ye!" "Well I wot," quoth Sir Gawain, "that ye have chosen a better; but I am proud that ye should so prize me, and as your servant do I hold ye my sovereign, and your knight am I, and may Christ reward ye." So they talked of many matters till midmorn was past, and ever the lady made as though she loved him, and the knight turned her speech aside. For though she were the brightest of maidens, yet had he forborne to shew her love for the danger that awaited him, and the blow that must be given without delay.

Then the lady prayed her leave from him, and he granted it readily. And she gave [the text reads "have"] him good-day, with laughing glance, but he must needs marvel at her words: "Now he that speeds fair speech reward ye this disport; but that ye be Gawain my mind misdoubts me greatly."

"Wherefore?" quoth the knight quickly, fearing lest he had lacked in some courtesy.

And the lady spake: "So true a knight as Gawain is holden, and one so perfect in courtesy, would never have tarried so long with a lady but he would of his courtesy have craved a kiss at parting."

Then quoth Gawain, "I wot I will do even as it may please ye, and kiss at your commandment, as a true knight should who forbears to ask for fear of displeasure." At that she came near and bent down and kissed the knight, and each commended the other to Christ, and she went forth from the chamber softly. Then Sir Gawain arose and called his chamberlain and chose his garments, and when he was ready he gat him forth to Mass, and then went to meat, and made merry all day till the rising of the moon, and never had a knight fairer lodging than had he with those two noble ladies, the elder and the younger.

And even the lord of the land chased the hinds through holt and heath till eventide, and then with much blowing of bugles and baying of hounds they bore the game homeward; and by the time daylight was done all the folk had returned to that fair castle. And when the lord and Sir Gawain met together, then were they both well pleased. The lord commanded them all to assemble in the great hall, and the ladies to descend with their maidens, and there, before them all, he bade the men fetch in the spoil of the day's hunting, and he called unto Gawain, and counted the tale of the beasts, and showed them unto him, and said, "What think ye of this game, Sir Knight? Have I deserved of ye thanks for my woodcraft?" "Yea, I wis," quoth the other, "here is the fairest spoil I have seen this seven year in the winter season."

"And all this do I give ye, Gawain," quoth the host, "for by accord of covenant ye may claim it as your own." "That is sooth," quoth the other, "I grant you that same; and I have fairly won this within walls, and with as good will do I yield it to ye." With that he clasped his hands round the lord's neck and kissed him as courteously as he might. "Take ye here my spoils, no more have I won; ye should have it freely, though it were greater than this."

"'Tis good," said the host, "gramercy thereof. Yet were I fain to know where ye won this same favour, and if it were by your own wit?"

"Nay," answered Gawain, "that was not in the bond. Ask me no more: ye have taken what was yours by right, be content with that."

They laughed and jested together, and sat them down to supper, where they were served with many dainties; and after supper they sat by the hearth, and wine was served out to them; and oft in their jesting they promised to observe on the morrow the same covenant that they had made before, and whatever chance might betide to exchange their spoil, be it much or little, when they met at night. Thus they renewed their bargain before the whole court, and then the night-drink was served, and each courteously took leave of the other and gat him to bed.

By the time the cock had crowed thrice the lord of the castle had left his bed; Mass was sung and meat fitly served. The folk were forth to the wood ere the day broke, with hound and horn they rode over the plain, and uncoupled their dogs among the thorns. Soon they struck on the scent, and the hunt cheered on the hounds who were first to seize it, urging them with shouts. The others hastened to the cry, forty at once, and there rose such a clamour from the pack that the rocks rang again. The huntsmen spurred them on with shouting and blasts of the horn; and the hounds drew together to a thicket betwixt the water and a high crag in the cliff beneath the hillside. There where the rough rock fell ruggedly they, the huntsmen, fared to the finding, and cast about round the hill and the thicket behind them. The knights wist well what beast was within, and would drive him forth with the bloodhounds. And as they beat the bushes, suddenly over the beaters there rushed forth a wondrous great and fierce boar, long since had he left the herd to roam by himself. Grunting, he cast many to the ground, and fled forth at his best speed, without more mischief. The men hallooed loudly and cried, *"Hay! Hay!"* and blew the horns to urge on the hounds, and rode swiftly after the boar. Many a time did he turn to bay and tare the hounds, and they yelped, and howled shrilly. Then the men made ready their arrows and shot at him, but the points were turned on his thick hide, and the barbs would not bite upon him, for the shafts shivered in pieces, and the head but leapt again wherever it hit.

But when the boar felt the stroke of the arrows he waxed mad with rage, and turned on the hunters and tare many, so that, affrightened, they fled before him. But the lord on a swift steed pursued him, blowing his bugle; as a gallant knight he rode through the woodland chasing the boar till the sun grew low. So did the hunters this day, while Sir Gawain lay in his bed lapped in rich gear; and the lady forgat not to salute him, for early was she at his side, to cheer his mood.

She came to the bedside and looked on the knight, and Gawain gave her fit greeting, and she greeted him again with ready words, and sat her by his side and laughed, and with a sweet look she spoke to him:

"Sir, if ye be Gawain, I think it a wonder that ye be so stern and cold, and care not for the courtesies of friendship, but if one teach ye to know them ye cast the lesson out of your mind. Ye have soon forgotten what I taught ye yesterday, by all the truest tokens that I knew!"

"What is that?" quoth the knight. "I trow I know not. If it be sooth that ye say, then is the blame mine own." "But I taught ye of kissing," quoth the fair lady. "Wherever a fair countenance is shown him, it behoves a courteous knight quickly to claim a kiss."

"Nay, my dear," said Sir Gawain, "cease that speech; that durst I not do lest I were denied, for if I were forbidden I wot I were wrong did I further entreat." "I' faith," quoth the lady merrily, "ye may not be forbid, ye are strong enough to constrain by strength an ye will, were any so discourteous as to give ye denial." "Yea, by Heaven," said Gawain, "ye speak well; but threats profit little in the land where I dwell, and so with a gift that is given not of good will! I am at your commandment to kiss when ye like, to take or to leave as ye list." Then the lady bent her down and kissed him courteously. And as they spake together she said, "I would learn somewhat from ye, an ye would not be wroth, for young ye bare and fair, and so courteous and knightly as ye are known to be, the head of all chivalry, and versed in all wisdom of love and war—'tis ever told of true knights how they adventured their lives for their true love, and endured hardships for her favours, and avenged her with valour, and eased her sorrows, and brought joy to her bower; and ye are the fairest knight of your time, and your fame and your honour are everywhere, yet I have sat by ye here twice, and never a word have I heard of love! Ye who are so courteous and skilled in such love ought surely to teach one so young and unskilled some little craft of true love! Why are ye so unlearned who art otherwise so famous? Or is it that ye deemed me unworthy to hearken to your teaching? For shame, Sir Knight! I come hither alone and sit at your side to learn of ye some skill; teach me of your wit, while my lord is from home."

"In good faith," quoth Gawain, "great is my joy and my profit that so fair a lady as ye are should deign to come hither, and trouble ye with so poor a man, and make sport with your knight with kindly countenance, it pleaseth me much. But that I, in my turn, should take it upon me to tell of love and such like matters to ye who know more by half, or a hundred fold, of such craft than I do, or ever shall in all my lifetime, by my troth 'twere folly indeed! I will work your will to the best of my might as I am bounden, and evermore will I be your servant, so help me Christ!"

Then often with guile she questioned that knight that she might win him to woo her, but he defended himself so fairly that none might in any wise blame him, and naught but bliss and harmless jesting was there between them. They laughed and talked together till at last she kissed him, and craved her leave of him, and went her way.

Then the knight arose and went forth to Mass, and afterward dinner was served and he sat and spake with the ladies all day. But the lord of the castle rode ever over the land chasing the wild boar, that fled through the thickets, slaying the best of his hounds and breaking their backs in sunder; till at last he was so weary he might run no longer, but made for a hole in a mound by a rock. He got the mound at his back and faced the hounds, whetting his white tusks and foaming at the mouth. The huntsmen stood aloof, fearing to draw nigh him; so many of them had been already wounded that they were loth to be torn with his tusks, so fierce he was and mad with rage. At length the lord himself came up, and saw the beast at bay, and the men standing aloof. Then quickly he sprang to the ground and drew out a bright blade, and waded through the stream to the boar.

When the beast was aware of the knight with weapon in hand, he set up his bristles and snorted loudly, and many feared for their lord lest he should be slain. Then the boar leapt upon the knight so that beast and man were one atop of the other in the water; but the boar had the worst of it, for the man had marked, even as he sprang, and set the point of his brand to the beast's chest, and drove it up to the hilt, so that the heart was split in twain, and the boar fell snarling, and was swept down by the water to where a hundred hounds seized on him, and the men drew him to shore for the dogs to slay.

Then was there loud blowing of horns and baying of hounds, the huntsmen smote off the boar's head, and hung the carcase by the four feet to a stout pole, and so went on their way homewards. The head they bore before the lord himself, who had slain the beast at the ford by force of his strong hand.

It seemed him o'er long ere he saw Sir Gawain in the hall, and he called, and the guest came to take that which fell to his share. And when he saw Gawain the lord laughed aloud, and bade them call the ladies and the household together, and he showed them the game, and told them the tale, how they hunted the wild boar through the woods, and of his length and breadth and height; and Sir Gawain commended his deeds and praised him for his valour, well proven, for so mighty a beast had he never seen before.

Then they handled the huge head, and the lord said aloud, "Now, Gawain, this game is your own by sure covenant, as ye right well know."

"'Tis sooth," quoth the knight, "and as truly will I give ye all I have gained." He took the host round the neck, and kissed him courteously twice. "Now are we quits," he said, "this eventide, of all the covenants that we made since I came hither." And the lord answered, "By St. Giles, ye are the best I know; ye will be rich in a short space if ye drive such bargains!"

Then they set up the tables on trestles, and covered them with fair cloths, and lit waxen tapers on the walls. The knights sat and were served in the hall, and much game and glee was there round the hearth, with many songs, both at supper and after; song of Christmas, and new carols, with all the mirth one may think of. And ever that lovely lady sat by the knight, and with still stolen looks made such feint of pleasing him, that Gawain marvelled much, and was wroth with himself, but he could not for his courtesy return her fair glances, but dealt with her cunningly, however she might strive to wrest the thing. When they had tarried in the hall so long as it seemed them good, they turned to the inner chamber and the wide hearthplace, and there they drank wine, and the host proffered to renew the covenant for New Year's Eve; but the knight craved leave to depart on the morrow, for it was nigh to the term when he must fulfil his pledge. But the lord would withhold him from so doing, and prayed him to tarry, and said,

"As I am a true knight I swear my troth that ye shall come to the Green Chapel to achieve your task on New Year's morn, long before prime. Therefore abide ye in your bed, and I will hunt in this wood, and hold ye to the covenant to exchange with me against all the spoil I may bring hither. For twice have I tried ye, and found ye true, and the morrow shall be the third time and the best. Make we merry now while we may, and think on joy, for misfortune may take a man whensoever it wills."

Then Gawain granted his request, and they brought them drink, and they gat them with lights to bed. Sir Gawain lay and slept softly, but the lord, who was keen on woodcraft, was afoot early. After Mass he and his men ate a morsel, and he asked for his steed; all the knights who should ride with him were already mounted before the hall gates.

'Twas a fair frosty morning, for the sun rose red in ruddy vapour, and the welkin was clear of clouds. The hunters scattered them by a forest side, and the rocks rang again with the blast of their horns. Some came on the scent of a fox, and a hound gave tongue; the huntsmen shouted, and the pack followed in a crowd on the trail. The fox ran before them, and when they saw him they pursued him with noise and much shouting, and he wound and turned through many a thick grove, often cowering and hearkening in a hedge. At last by a little ditch he leapt out of a spinney, stole away slily by a copse path, and so out of the wood and away from the hounds. But he went, ere he wist, to a chosen tryst, and three started forth on him at once, so he must needs double back, and betake him to the wood again.

Then was it joyful to hearken to the hounds; when all the pack had met together and had sight of their game they made as loud a din as if all the lofty cliffs had fallen clattering together. The huntsmen shouted and threatened, and followed close upon him so that he might scarce escape, but Reynard was wily, and he turned and doubled upon them, and led the lord and his men over the hills, now on the slopes, now in the vales, while the knight at home slept through the cold morning beneath his costly curtains.

But the fair lady of the castle rose betimes, and clad herself in a rich mantle that reached even to the ground, left her throat and her fair neck bare, and was bordered and lined with costly furs. On her head she wore no golden circlet, but a network of precious stones, that gleamed and shone through her tresses in clusters of twenty together. Thus she came into the chamber, closed the door after her, and set open a window, and called to him gaily, "Sir Knight, how may ye sleep? The morning is so fair."

Sir Gawain was deep in slumber, and in his dream he vexed him much for the destiny that should befall him on the morrow, when he should meet the knight at the Green Chapel, and abide his blow; but when the lady spake he heard her, and came to himself, and roused from his dream and answered swiftly. The lady came laughing, and kissed him courteously, and he welcomed her fittingly with a cheerful countenance. He saw her so glorious and gaily dressed, so faultless of features and complexion, that it warmed his heart to look upon her.

They spake to each other smiling, and all was bliss and good cheer between them. They exchanged fair words, and much happiness was therein, yet was there a gulf between them, and she might win no more of her knight, for that gallant prince watched well his words—he would neither take her love, nor frankly refuse it. He cared for his courtesy, lest he be deemed churlish, and yet more for his honour lest he be traitor to his host. "God forbid," quoth he to himself, "that it should so befall." Thus with courteous words did he set aside all the special speeches that came from her lips.

Then spake the lady to the knight, "Ye deserve blame if ye hold not that lady who sits beside ye above all else in the world, if ye have not already a love whom ye hold dearer, and like better, and have sworn such firm faith to that lady that ye care not to lose it—and that am I now fain to believe. And now I pray ye straitly that ye tell me that in truth, and hide it not."

And the knight answered, "By St. John" (and he smiled as he spake) "no such love have I, nor do I think to have yet awhile."

"That is the worst word I may hear," quoth the lady, "but in sooth I have mine answer; kiss me now courteously, and I will go hence; I can but mourn as a maiden that loves much."

Sighing, she stooped down and kissed him, and then she rose up and spake as she stood, "Now, dear, at our parting do me this grace: give me some gift, if it were but thy glove, that I may bethink me of my knight, and lessen my mourning."

"Now, I wis," quoth the knight, "I would that I had here the most precious thing that I possess on earth that I might leave ye as love-token, great or small, for ye have deserved forsooth more reward than I might give ye. But it is not to your honour to have at this time a glove for reward as gift from Gawain, and I am here on a strange errand, and have no man with me, nor mails with goodly things—that mislikes me much, lady, at this time; but each man must fare as he is taken, if for sorrow and ill."

"Nay, knight highly honoured," quoth that love-some lady, "though I have naught of yours, yet shall ye have somewhat of mine." With that she reached him a ring of red gold with a sparkling stone therein, that shone even as the sun (wit ye well, it was worth many marks); but the knight refused it, and spake readily, "I will take no gift, lady, at this time. I have none to give, and none will I take."

She prayed him to take it, but he refused her prayer, and sware in sooth that he would not have it.

The lady was sorely vexed, and said, "If ye refuse my ring as too costly, that ye will not be so highly beholden to me, I will give you my girdle as a lesser gift." With that she loosened a lace that was fastened at her side, knit upon her kirtle under her mantle. It was wrought of green silk, and gold, only braided by the fingers, and that she offered to the knight, and besought him though it were of little worth that he would take it, and he said nay, he would touch neither gold nor gear ere God give him grace to achieve the adventure for which he had come hither. "And therefore, I pray ye, displease ye not, and ask me no longer, for I may not grant it. I am dearly beholden to ye for the favour ye have shown me, and ever, in heat and cold, will I be your true servant."

"Now," said the lady, "ye refuse this silk, for it is simple in itself, and so it seems, indeed; lo, it is small to look upon and less in cost, but whoso knew the virtue that is knit therein he would, peradventure, value it more highly. For whatever knight is girded with this green lace, while he bears it knotted about him there is no man under heaven can overcome him, for he may not be slain for any magic on earth."

Then Gawain bethought him, and it came into his heart that this were a jewel for the jeopardy that awaited him when he came to the Green Chapel to seek the return blow—could he so order it that he should escape unslain, 'twere a craft worth trying. Then he bare with her chiding, and let her say her say, and she pressed the girdle on him and prayed him to take it, and he granted her prayer, and she gave it him with good will, and besought him for her sake never to reveal it but to hide it loyally from her lord; and the knight agreed that never should any man know it, save they two alone. He thanked her often and heartily, and she kissed him for the third time.

Then she took her leave of him, and when she was gone Sir Gawain arose, and clad him in rich attire, and took the girdle, and knotted it round him, and hid it beneath his robes. Then he took his way to the chapel, and sought out a priest privily and prayed him to teach him better how his soul might be saved when he should go hence; and there he shrived him, and showed his misdeeds, both great and small, and besought mercy and craved absolution; and the priest assoiled him, and set him as clean as if Doomsday had been on the morrow. And afterwards Sir Gawain made him merry with the ladies, with carols, and all kinds of joy, as never he did but that one day, even to nightfall; and all the men marvelled at him, and said that never since he came thither had he been so merry. Meanwhile the lord of the castle was abroad chasing the fox; awhile he lost him, and as he rode through a spinny he heard the hounds near at hand, and Reynard came creeping through a thick grove, with all the pack at his heels. Then the lord drew out his shining brand, and cast it at the beast, and the fox swerved aside for the sharp edge, and would have doubled back, but a hound was on him ere he might turn, and right before the horse's feet they all fell on him, and worried him fiercely, snarling the while. Then the lord leapt from his saddle, and caught the fox from the jaws, and held it aloft over his head, and hallooed loudly, and many brave hounds bayed as they beheld it; and the hunters hied them thither, blowing their horns; all that bare bugles blew them at once, and all the others shouted. 'Twas the merriest meeting that ever men heard, the clamour that was raised at the death of the fox. They rewarded the hounds, stroking them and rubbing their heads, and took Reynard and stripped him of his coat; then blowing their horns, they turned them homewards, for it was nigh nightfall. The lord was gladsome at his return, and found a bright fire on the hearth, and the knight beside it, the good Sir Gawain, who was in joyous mood for the pleasure he had had with the ladies. He wore a robe of blue, that reached even to the ground, and a surcoat richly furred, that became him well. A hood like to the surcoat fell on his shoulders, and all alike were done about with fur. He met the host in the midst of the floor, and jesting, he greeted him, and said, "Now shall I be first to fulfil our covenant which we made together when there was no lack of wine." Then he embraced the knight, and kissed him thrice, as solemnly as he might. "Of a sooth," quoth the other, "ye have good luck in the matter of this covenant, if ye made a good exchange!"

"Yea, it matters naught of the exchange," quoth Gawain, "since what I owe is swiftly paid."

"Marry," said the other, "mine is behind, for I have hunted all this day, and naught have I got but this foul fox-skin, and that is but poor payment for three such kisses as ye have here given me." "Enough," quoth Sir Gawain, "I thank ye, by the Rood."

Then the lord told them of his hunting, and how the fox had been slain.

With mirth and minstrelsy, and dainties at their will, they made them as merry as a folk well might till 'twas time for them to sever, for at last they must needs betake them to their beds. Then the knight took his leave of the lord, and thanked him fairly.

"For the fair sojourn that I have had here at this high feast may the High King give ye honour. I give ye myself, as one of your servants, if ye so like; for I must needs, as you know, go hence with the morn, and ye will give me, as ye promised, a guide to show me the way to the Green Chapel, an God will suffer me on New Year's Day to deal the doom of my weird." "By my faith," quoth the host, "all that ever I promised, that shall I keep with good will." Then he gave him a servant to set him in the way, and lead him by the downs, that he should have no need to ford the stream, and should fare by the shortest road through the groves; and Gawain thanked the lord for the honour done him. Then he would take leave of the ladies, and courteously he kissed them, and spake, praying them to receive his thanks, and they made like reply; then with many sighs they commended him to Christ, and he departed courteously from that folk. Each man that he met he thanked him for his service and his solace, and the pains he had been at to do his will; and each found it as hard to part from the knight as if he had ever dwelt with him.

Then they led him with torches to his chamber, and brought him to his bed to rest. That he slept soundly I may not say, for the morrow gave him much to think on. Let him rest awhile, for he was near that which he sought, and if ye will but listen to me I will tell ye how it fared with him thereafter.

Questions

1. What is the astonishing event that stuns Arthur and his court? What makes this event so stunning, considering the legend of Arthur and his court?
2. What does the color of the mysterious knight suggest?
3. From the description given by the author, what is symbolic about Gawain's shield?
4. What is the feeling of the people who see Gawain leaving for the Green Knight's castle? What does this feeling foreshadow?
5. What is the purpose of the lady's forceful words toward Gawain? Does she intend to help him or hurt him?
6. What kind of interaction takes place between Sir Gawain and the castle lord's wife? What does the lord's wife help Gawain realize?
7. What gift is given to Sir Gawain that could possibly save his life? What might this gift represent?

1. Like Tom Cruise in *The Last Samurai* and Theoden in *Lord of The Rings, The Two Towers,* Gawain's preparation for the ensuing engagement is ceremonial. How is imagery evoked in these scenes, and what other knight-like characters resemble Gawain in their preparation for battle? Construct an argument that compares Gawain's preparation for battle with another heroic figure from literature or cinema.
2. Label the Green Knight as a servant of Heaven or Hell, and then construct an argument that explores his motivations for representing said domain.
3. Compare and contrast Arthur's court with the court of the Green Knight. Both of these courts believe in the importance of a knight's honor, but they have their different approaches to knighthood. Examine these approaches and the purposes for their differences.
4. After revisiting *The Aeneid,* construct an argument that compares and contrasts the acts of adultery in *The Aeneid* and *Sir Gawain and the Green Knight.*
5. *Sir Gawain and the Green Knight* is a tale that gives the reader a glimpse of the Arthurian world. Although the author of this piece is unknown, it is clear that he was familiar with certain codes of knighthood and King Arthur's court. Throughout the tale, many Arthurian ideas are revealed, such as the belief in Christianity, the importance of having honor, and the idea of having loyalty to one's king and country. Examine Sir Gawain and the transformation that he undergoes. In doing so, make sure to address codes of knighthood, chivalry, and the Arthurian world.

Everyman

1. Note how the generalization of the character names in *Everyman* help make this a play of universality.
2. This is known as a "morality play" because it attempts to speak to all human beings while identifying their morals or lack thereof.
3. There is no escaping the religious tone in this play. God's presence exists throughout the play, and this becomes a fearful object of Everyman's fate.

Everyman

Anonymous

CHARACTERS:

EVERYMAN	KNOWLEDGE
STRENGTH	COUSIN
GOD: ADONAI	CONFESSION
DISCRETION	KINDRED
DEATH	ANGEL
FIVE-WITS	GOODS
MESSENGER	DOCTOR
BEAUTY	GOOD-DEEDS
FELLOWSHIP	

HERE BEGINNETH A TREATISE HOW THE HIGH FATHER OF HEAVEN SENDETH DEATH TO SUMMON EVERY CREATURE TO COME AND GIVE ACCOUNT OF THEIR LIVES IN THIS WORLD AND IS IN MANNER OF A MORAL PLAY.

MESSENGER:

I pray you all give your audience,
And here this matter with reverence,
By figure a moral play—
The *Summoning of Everyman* called it is,
That of our lives and ending shows
How transitory we be all day.
This matter is wonderous precious,
But the intent of it is more gracious,
And sweet to bear away.
The story saith,—Man, in the beginning,
Look well, and take good heed to the ending,
Be you never so gay!
Ye think sin in the beginning full sweet,
Which in the end causeth thy soul to weep,
When the body lieth in clay.
Here shall you see how *Fellowship* and *Jollity*,
Both *Strength, Pleasure,* and *Beauty,*
Will fade from thee as flower in May.
For ye shall here, how our heavenly king
Calleth *Everyman* to a general reckoning:
Give audience, and here what he doth say.

GOD:

I perceive here in my majesty,
How that all the creatures be to me unkind,
Living without dread in worldly prosperity:
Of ghostly sight the people be so blind,
Drowned in sin, they know me not for their God;
In worldly riches is all their mind,
They fear not my rightwiseness, the sharp rod;
My law that I shewed, when I for them died,
They forget clean, and shedding of my blood red;
I hanged between two, it cannot be denied;
To get them life I suffered to be dead;
I healed their feet; with thorns hurt was my head:
I could do no more than I did truly,
And now I see the people do clean forsake me.
They use the seven deadly sins damnable;
As pride, covetise, wrath, and lechery,
Now in the world be made commendable;
And thus they leave of angels the heavenly
   company;
Everyman liveth so after his own pleasure,
And yet of their life they be nothing sure:
I see the more that I them forbear
The worse they be from year to year;
All that liveth appaireth fast, is impaired
Therefore I will in all the haste
Have a reckoning of Everyman's person
For and I leave the people thus alone
In their life and wicked tempests,
Verily they will become much worse than beasts;
For now one would by envy another up eat;
Charity they all do clean forget.
I hope well that Everyman
In my glory should make his mansion,
And thereto I had them all elect;
But now I see, like traitors deject,
They thank me not for the pleasure that I to them
   meant,
Nor yet for their being that I them have lent;
I proffered the people great multitude of mercy,
And few there be that asketh it heartily;
They be so cumbered with worldly riches,
That needs on them I must do justice,
On Everyman living without fear.
Where art thou, *Death,* thou mighty messenger?

DEATH:

Almighty God, I am here at your will,
Your commandment to fulfil.

GOD:

Go thou to *Everyman,*
And show him in my name
A pilgrimage he must on him take,
Which he in no wise may escape;
And that he bring with him a sure reckoning
Without delay or any tarrying.

DEATH:

Lord, I will in the world go run over all,
And cruelly outsearch both great and small;
Every man will I beset that liveth beastly
Out of God's laws, and dreadeth not folly;
He that loveth riches I will strike with my dart,
His sight to blind, and from heaven to depart,
Except that alms be his good friend,
In hell for to dwell, world without end.
Lo, yonder I see *Everyman* walking;
Full little he thinketh on my coming;
His mind is on fleshly lust and his treasure,
And great pain it shall cause him to endure
Before the Lord Heaven King.
Everyman, stand still; whither art thou going
Thus gaily? Hast thou thy Maker forget?

EVERYMAN:

Why askst thou?
Wouldest thou wete?

DEATH:

Yea, sir, I will show you;
In great haste I am sent to thee
From God out of his great majesty.

EVERYMAN:

What, sent to me?

DEATH:

Yea, certainly.
Though thou have forget him here,
He thinketh on thee in the heavenly sphere,
As, or we depart, thou shalt know.

EVERYMAN:

What desireth God of me?

DEATH:

That shall I show thee;
A reckoning he will needs have
Without any longer respite.

EVERYMAN:

To give a reckoning longer leisure I crave;
This blind matter troubleth my wit.

DEATH:

On thee thou must take a long journey:
Therefore thy book of count with thee thou bring;
For turn again thou can not by no way,
And look thou be sure of thy reckoning:
For before God thou shalt answer, and show
Thy many bad deeds and good but few;
How thou hast spent thy life, and in what wise,
Before the chief lord of paradise.
Have ado that we were in that way,
For, wete thou well, thou shalt make none
    attournay.

EVERYMAN:

Full unready I am such reckoning to give
I know thee not: what messenger art thou?

DEATH:

I am *Death,* that no man dreadeth.
For every man I rest and no man spareth;
For it is God's commandment
That all to me should be obedient.

EVERYMAN:

O *Death,* thou comest when I had thee least in
    mind;
In thy power it lieth me to save,
Yet of my good will I give thee, if ye will be kind,
Yea, a thousand pound shalt thou have,
And defer this matter till another day.

DEATH:

Everyman, it may not be by no way;
I set not by gold, silver, nor riches,
Ne by pope, emperor, king, duke, ne princes.
For and I would receive gifts great,
All the world I might get;
But my custom is clean contrary.
I give thee no respite: come hence, and not tarry.

EVERYMAN:

Alas, shall I have no longer respite?
I may say *Death* giveth no warning:
To think on thee, it maketh my heart sick,
For all unready is my book of reckoning.
But twelve year and I might have abiding,
My counting book I would make so clear,
That my reckoning I should not need to fear.

Wherefore, *Death,* I pray thee, for God's mercy,
Spare me till I provided of remedy.

DEATH:

Thee availeth not to cry, weep, and pray:
But haste thee lightly that you were gone the
    journey,
And prove thy friends if thou can.
For, wete thou well, the tide abideth no man,
And in the world each living creature
For *Adam's* sin must die of nature.

EVERYMAN:

Death, if I should this pilgrimage take,
And my reckoning surely make,
Show me, for saint *charity,*
Should I not come again shortly?

DEATH:

No, *Everyman;* and thou be once there,
Thou mayst never more come here,
Trust me verily.

EVERYMAN:

O gracious God, in the high seat celestial,
Have mercy on me in this most need;
Shall I have no company from this vale terrestrial
Of mine acquaintance that way to me lead?

DEATH:

Yea, if any be so hardy
That would go with thee and bear thee company.
Hie thee that you were gone to God's
    magnificence,
Thy reckoning to give before his presence.
What, weenest thou thy life is given thee,
And thy worldly goods also?

EVERYMAN:

I had went so verily.

DEATH:

Nay, nay; it was but lent thee;
For as soon as thou art go,
Another awhile shall have it, and then go therefor
Even as thou hast done.
Everyman, thou art mad; thou hast thou wits five,
And here on earth will not amend thy life,
For suddenly I do come.

EVERYMAN:

O wretched caitiff, whither shall I flee,
That I might scape this endless sorrow!
Now, gentle *Death,* spare me till to-morrow,
That I may amend me
With good advisement.

DEATH:

Nay, thereto I will not consent,
Nor no man will I respite,
But to the heart suddenly I shall smite
Without any advisement.
And now out of thy sight I will me hie;
See thou make thee ready shortly,
For thou mayst say this is the day
That no man living may escape away.

EVERYMAN:

Alas, I may well weep with sighs deep;
Now have I no manner of company
To help me in my journey, and me to keep;
And also my writing is full unready.
How shall I do now for to excuse me?
I would to God I had never be gete!
To my soul a great profit it had be;
For now I fear pains huge and great.
The time passeth; Lord, help that all wrought;
For though I mourn it availeth nought.
The day passeth, and is almost a-go;
I wot not well what for to do.
To whom were I best my complaint do make?
What, and I to *Fellowship* thereof spake,
And show him of this sudden chance?
For in him is all my affiance;
We have in the world so many a day
Be on good friends in sport and play.
I see him yonder, certainly;
I trust that he will bear me company;
Therefore to him will I speak to ease my sorrow.
Well met, good *Fellowship,* and good morrow!

**For the entire play,
insert the Literature CD.**

Questions

1. What is the role of the messenger at the beginning of this play? How does this character help set the stage for the reader?
2. The lines, "To get them life I suffered to be dead; / I healed their feet; with thorns hurt was my head." To whom might the author be referring?
3. When God first enters the play, his lines are indicative of what vocal tone? Does he seem, for instance, angry or loving? What agenda might the author be attempting to advance with such a tone?
4. What does Death think Everyman is thinking about, and what might Everyman's thoughts symbolize?
5. What "reckoning" is Death referring to when he first talks to Everyman?
6. Why are so many characters afraid to go on this journey with Everyman? What is the author conveying about the human race's belief in camaraderie?
7. The character, Goods, mentions that there is something problematic about the relationship he has had with Everyman. What is so problematic about this relationship?
8. What is symbolic about the character, Good Deeds, and her weak condition?
9. Who is the first character that actually helps Everyman in his plight? What does this suggest about the author's belief in humanity's willingness to help one another?
10. Who goes with Everyman to Heaven? Carefully examine the passages where these characters are revealed; who finally goes with him in the end, and why?
11. What is symbolic about the characters that end up going with Everyman?
12. When Good Deeds remains by Everyman's side, what is the author trying to communicate regarding humanity, and what really matters regarding one's day of reckoning?

Research and Writing

1. In *Everyman*, the reader learns of the life that the main character has lead. What other characters in Middle English literature are guilty of the same actions as this character? Construct an argument that compares Everyman with another Middle English literary figure.
2. Fellowship says to Everyman: "Now, in good faith, I will not that way. / But and thou wilt murder, or any man kill, / In that I will help thee with a good will!" This is a telling line, for it reveals much about Fellowship's character. Are there any other literary figures from Middle English literature who are also willing to kill in order to help someone? Construct an argument that examines one of these characters and what this might suggest about the Middle English culture.
3. Everyman says: "Of all my works I must show / How I have lived and my days spent; / Also of ill deeds, that I have used / In my time, sith life was me lent; / and of all virtues that I have refused." If Beowulf or Oedipus were visited by death with a journey similar to the one that Everyman

Continued

must take, what might their outcome be? Construct an argument that places one of these figures in Everyman's predicament, and examine how he / she would have dealt with a similar situation.

4. *Everyman* is indicative of many works from this time period. The generalization of Good Deeds is rather paradoxical because it would be helpful to know how many good deeds one must perform in order to be forgiven. Further, it would be helpful to know what these good deeds are. Think about some of the more prominent leaders in today's world, i.e., the President of the United States, a famous athlete, or a ruthless dictator. If one of these prominent individuals accompanied Good Deeds on this celestial journey, what might their good deeds be, and would their good deeds be enough to grant them passage through the gates of Heaven?

6

Renaissance Drama: Marlowe and Shakespeare

*This chapter was authored by Jill Gold Wright, Ph.D.

Imagine what your city would be like if every afternoon, ten percent of the population went to the theater . . . if one in ten people saw a play every single day. In William Shakespeare's time, theatre-going was at its highest point of attendance ever. No one in the city of London lived or worked more than two miles away from a theatre which would present a full-length play every day except for Sundays, or in times of war or plague. In no other era or place in history has such a wide variety of people attended theatre in such numbers and with such frequency.

The plays presented in Renaissance England sparked the interest of audiences at their debuts and have remained in the imaginations of playgoers and readers ever since. It is difficult to imagine our contemporary culture without its countless allusions to Shakespeare: to the indecisiveness of Hamlet, the bloodiness of Lady Macbeth or the monumental tragedy of King Lear. Shakespeare's characters have become part of our international consciousness. As his plays are performed worldwide, in a broad range of approaches from authentic to innovative, scholars and playgoers celebrate Shakespeare as being the greatest dramatist the world has ever known. Inevitably, readers who study his texts desire to learn more about the man and the society in which he lived. They find themselves continually asking: "What was it actually like to see theatre in Renaissance England?"

One major difference to note is that the theatres were built and designed in a totally different way from the theatres you might see today. If you are imagining rows and rows of crushed velvet seats, shrouded in darkness, all facing a proscenium stage lit by footlights, or a small, black-box theatre with folding chairs in clumps around the stage, your ideas about theatre are too modern for Elizabethan England. The Renaissance stages were closer to Roman amphitheatres. If you have seen the film *Shakespeare in Love,* which depicts the Globe Theatre where Shakespeare wrote and worked, you may have a better visual idea of what Renaissance theatres were like. The Globe, built in 1599, was open to the sky and to the British weather elements. In order to take advantage of maximum daylight, the plays were performed at 2:00 in the afternoon, much to the dismay of the city churches, whose afternoon services also began at 2:00. The stage was elevated about five feet off the ground and thrust into a large open area called the "yard." The audience members in the yard, London's servants and wage-earners, paid the cheapest ticket (one penny) for admission. They stood, crammed together in this large open space, feet aching and necks craning while watching the plot unfold. But the yard was not a quiet, reserved place to watch a play. Prostitutes, pimps, and pickpockets would work the crowd as the play went on. Audience members would eat and drink during the performance, and if they didn't like the plot, they would yell, hiss, stamp, or use their apples, pears, or nuts as projectiles to throw at the actors on stage.

The viewers in the yard, later termed "groundlings" (a name Shakespeare invented himself in *Hamlet*), were also a great benefit to the actors. In essence, they became active participants in the plays. Standing in a mass, they could be used as crowds of soldiers, courtiers, or townspeople. For example, in *Julius Caesar,* when Antony addresses the crowd, "Friends, Romans, countrymen, lend me your ears!", the actor could speak directly to the audience and suddenly, the Renaissance yard was transformed into a funeral gathering in ancient Rome.

The Globe had two seating galleries behind and above the standing yard. The middle gallery is often referred to as the "two-penny gallery," so called because of its ticket price. Patrons in this section were also commoners, generally craftsmen, artisans, and citizens, who were given an unpadded bench seat that was open to the elements. The third and highest tier was the most expensive and, therefore, was patronized by aristocracy, nobles, and gentlemen. These viewers had a bird's-eye view of the stage and of everyone (actors and lesser audience members) assembled beneath them. The aristocracy went to the theatre not just to see but to be seen; they literally could "look down" on the action and audience. Hence, though they were there to enjoy a play, they could do so in the comfort of knowing that the English social system was being literally and symbolically enforced by the architecture of the theatre in which they sat.

The four plays covered in this chapter represent the major genres of Renaissance drama. Renaissance drama evolved from an already strong tradition in Medieval Europe, when theatre was used not only as entertainment but also as a pedagogical tool by the Church and Monarchy, which were all but inextricable. Since very few people in the Middle Ages could read, the Church found it useful to employ the dramatic and visual arts to teach Bible stories and ethics. Episodes from the Bible were depicted in stained glass windows in the cathedrals and in plays performed on festival and holy days.

Approximately a hundred years later, between 1400 and 1550, a new kind of drama called the Morality Play developed. The Medieval Morality Play, like *Everyman* and *Mankind,* was intended to teach ethical principles to the viewers. In the usual plot, an everyday character, called "Everyman" or something similar and representative of anyone in the audience, dabbles in sin, enjoying being sacrilegious and a bit naughty. This is fun for "Everyman" and entertaining for the audience. As his story develops, he becomes acquainted with virtues and vices, which are personified by actors on stage. For example, actors would play characters named "Knowledge," "Confession," or "Death." Through his interactions with these personifications, "Everyman" soon sees the darker side of sin and the destiny of eternal punishment if he is not redeemed. Together, "Everyman" and the audience discover that though sin may be tempting, it is ultimately damning. Traditionally, the Morality Play has a happy ending: the character is saved, and the audience attains a renewed belief in its own way to gain salvation.

It is from this tradition that Christopher Marlowe wrote *Doctor Faustus* (1592), the earliest of the plays covered in this chapter. *Doctor Faustus* is included as an example of the transition from late-Medieval to Renaissance drama. At first glance, Marlowe's *Doctor Faustus* seems to be a standard Morality Play. His character Faustus vacillates between sin and salvation, meeting personifications of virtue and vice along the way. However, a closer look will reveal that Marlowe expands and complicates the form of the Morality Play. Marlowe layers the basic plot with finer poetic language, deeper character development, and a more complex dramatic structure than is usual in Morality Plays. Further, Marlowe twists his play by writing a non-triumphant, tragic ending, and most importantly, he writes a strong and serious criticism of the church itself. Indeed, while stemming from a traditional form, *Doctor Faustus* is revolutionary because of its forward-looking complexities which identify it as a more sophisticated Renaissance drama.

Further, when comparing these two texts, it is important to remember that while *Everyman* was written before the Reformation, *Doctor Faustus* is a post-Reformation drama. European Christianity was never the same after the momentous influences of Martin Luther and John Calvin. An extremely important element of Marlowe's play is to examine how he portrays Catholicism versus Protestantism, what agenda he seems to put forward, and how that message colors the entire meaning of the play for the audience.

The Shakespeare plays covered here, which all date to around the same year, 1599 to 1600, represent the three major genres of his drama: History, Comedy, and Tragedy. In brief overview, each of these genres has its own set of characteristics, though even these generalities need qualification. The History Play traditionally centers on a grandiose figure from the past, like Antony,

Cleopatra, Julius Caesar, Richard III, and Henry V. There are two sub-types of History Plays: the Ancient Histories, like *Julius Caesar* and *Antony and Cleopatra,* and the English histories. When any type of History Play was to be performed, a red flag would fly over the theatre to advertise to all of London that a historical epic was on the boards for that day.

Most of the English Histories often read like tragedies, in that the central figure begins in a heightened position but falls by the end of the play; however, the one included in this chapter is an exception. Both in history and on the page, Henry V was considered a gloriously successful king. Shakespeare might have wanted to pay a compliment to Elizabeth I, the reigning queen of England who was a dedicated patron of theatre, and may have written *Henry V* as a tribute to the Crown. That, however, is for the reader to determine.

The inclusion of *Twelfth Night* in this chapter represents the genre of Comedy, though even that is a complicated case. Despite what modern audiences may assume, a Shakespearean Comedy is not a "laugh-out-loud" piece like a comedy we might see today. The genre of Comedy for Shakespeare has other important hallmarks; mostly, the plays are about the triumph of love. Usually, there is at least one young couple who overcomes obstacles presented by family or society and ends in marriage. Some Comedies, like *Much Ado About Nothing,* conclude with two sets of marriages, and *A Midsummer Night's Dream* ends with three! The institution of marriage brings with it the happy promise of children, and the Comedy ends with an optimistic look into the future, suggesting that with the progeny of the characters, life in general will progress and flourish.

But Shakespeare would not be pigeon-holed by generic limitations, and he often complicates the cheerful genre of Comedy. In the sub-genre often termed the Problem Comedy, Shakespeare incorporates a darker force, one that cannot be ignored by the characters or audiences. One striking example of the Problem Comedy is *Measure for Measure.* It is true that this play has minor characters who may make an audience laugh, and it does fulfill the tradition of having marriages at the end. The problem is that the bride in the primary marriage, Isabella, does not want to be a bride at all; she aspires to be a nun, chaste and devoted to religious service, not to a man. She is all but forced into the marriage by family and by royal decree. For audiences, it's difficult to feel celebratory or optimistic at the end of the play.

Another of Shakespeare's Problem Comedies, *Twelfth Night,* is covered in this chapter. It is left to the reader to figure out why, but here's a clue: focus on the character Malvolio, whose name in Italian means "ill will." Remember that the spirit of Comedy is to restore a sense of community and wholeness by the end of the play. When Shakespeare includes one character who "holds out" against a happy resolution, that creates a Problem. And even though a pure white flag flew when a Comedy was to be performed, it could be darkened by the shadows that Shakespeare drew around it.

Perhaps Shakespeare's most renowned plays are his Tragedies; certainly, the names Hamlet, Macbeth, Othello, and King Lear will sound familiar to most. Generally, Tragedies are about the suffering and fall of a great figure; quite often, this character will have a "tragic flaw," like greed, extreme arrogance, or excessive ambition, which unchecked, hastens his demise. Unlike Comedies, which look toward the promise of a new tomorrow, Tragedies usually close with a stage littered with corpses, with no potential for marriage or children, and with an overall feeling of desolation and hopelessness. Tragedies often illustrate the profound insignificance of Man in the Universe and the pointlessness of a life that leads only to death. It will not surprise readers that when a Tragedy was to be played, a black flag would fly over the theatre walls. This was not a deterrent; like the dramatic movies of today, audiences found real value in viewing a Tragedy. Viewers are riveted by tales of human suffering, because they recognize it as their own. Further, we learn as we watch the characters tragically fall; we understand human failing, and we recognize the potential to be better people ourselves.

Christopher Marlowe (1564-1593)

Christopher Marlowe was born in Canterbury, England, in the same year as William Shakespeare. His father was a successful shoemaker who saw to it that Marlowe was educated at the King's School in Canterbury. From there, Marlowe earned a scholarship that allowed him to study at Cambridge University, where he earned his B.A. in 1584 and his M.A. in 1587. Though there is much speculation about the dates of his plays, most scholars place *Tamburlaine* (parts 1 & 2) in 1587, *Doctor Faustus* in 1588, *The Jew of Malta* in 1590, and *Edward II* in 1592.

Much mystery surrounds the underworld connections and interests of Marlowe. Some scholars argue that he traveled abroad on a clandestine political mission. Others claim that he worked as a secret agent for the British Crown. Late in his lifetime, he was found to be a blasphemer and was arrested for heresy in 1593 but was never brought to trial. No one has determined why. As of today, no research has been able to prove or fully understand Marlowe's political or social leanings, and we cannot conclusively determine who his associates were. We do know that in 1593, Marlowe was drinking in a pub when he was stabbed through the eye and killed by a member of government, Ingram Frizar. The reasons for his murder are still unclear.

Marlowe's seven plays are touted as masterful examples of blank verse in drama. He is credited with having a great influence on the works of playwrights William Shakespeare, Ben Jonson, and John Webster.

Doctor Faustus

1. This play derives from the Morality Play, a tradition in Medieval Drama. Because people were largely illiterate and therefore could not read the Bible for lessons in ethics, the Church used drama as a teaching tool. Watch for how the tradition of using drama as pedagogy plays out in *Doctor Faustus*.

2. Marlowe's *Doctor Faustus* is usually dated at 1588, though some scholars place it in 1592 with the first production seemingly in 1594. Since then, the legend of Faust has appeared again and again, including Johann Wolfgang von Goethe's play *Faust* (1808), Thomas Mann's novel *Doktor Faustus* (1947) and several operas, including Charles Gounod's *Faust* (1859) and Hector Berlioz's *La Damnation de Faust* (1893).

Doctor Faustus

Christopher Marlowe

DRAMATIS PERSONAE.

THE POPE.
THE EMPEROR OF GERMANY.
RAYMOND, KING OF HUNGARY.
DUKE OF SAXONY.
BRUNO.
DUKE OF VANHOLT.
MARTINO, FREDERICK, GENTLEMEN.
BENVOLIO, FAUSTUS.
VALDES, FRIENDS TO FAUSTUS.
CORNELIUS, WAGNER, SERVANT TO FAUSTUS.
CLOWN.
ROBIN.
DICK.
VINTNER.
HORSE-COURSER.
CARTER.
AN OLD MAN.
SCHOLARS, CARDINALS, ARCHBISHOP OF RHEIMS,
    BISHOPS, MONKS, FRIARS, SOLDIERS, AND
    ATTENDANTS.
DUCHESS OF VANHOLT.
HOSTESS.
LUCIFER.
BELZEBUB.
MEPHISTOPHILIS.
GOOD ANGEL.
EVIL ANGEL.
THE SEVEN DEADLY SINS.
DEVILS.
SPIRITS IN THE SHAPES OF ALEXANDER THE GREAT,
    OF HIS PARAMOUR, OF DARIUS, AND OF HELEN.
CHORUS.

[THE TRAGICAL HISTORY OF DOCTOR FAUSTUS
FROM THE QUARTO OF 1616.]

[ENTER CHORUS.]

CHORUS:
  Not marching in the fields of Thrasymene,
  Where Mars did mate the warlike Carthagens;
  Nor sporting in the dalliance of love,
  In courts of kings where state is overturn'd;
  Nor in the pomp of proud audacious deeds,
  Intends our Muse to vaunt her heavenly verse:
  Only this, gentles,—we must now perform
  The form of Faustus' fortunes, good or bad:
  And now to patient judgments we appeal,
  And speak for Faustus in his infancy.
  Now is he born of parents base of stock,
  In Germany, within a town call'd Rhodes:
  At riper years, to Wittenberg he went,
  Whereas his kinsmen chiefly brought him up.
  So much he profits in divinity,
  That shortly he was grac'd with doctor's name,
  Excelling all, and sweetly can dispute
  In th' heavenly matters of theology;
  Till swoln with cunning, of a self-conceit,
  His waxen wings did mount above his reach,
  And, melting, heavens conspir'd his overthrow;
  For, falling to a devilish exercise,
  And glutted now with learning's golden gifts,
  He surfeits upon cursed necromancy;
  Nothing so sweet as magic is to him,
  Which he prefers before his chiefest bliss:
  And this the man that in his study sits.

[EXIT.]

[FAUSTUS DISCOVERED IN HIS STUDY.]

FAUSTUS:
  Settle thy studies, Faustus, and begin
  To sound the depth of that thou wilt profess:
  Having commenc'd, be a divine in show,
  Yet level at the end of every art,
  And live and die in Aristotle's works.
  Sweet Analytics, 'tis thou hast ravish'd me!
  Is, to dispute well, logic's chiefest end?
  Affords this art no greater miracle?
  Then read no more; thou hast attain'd that end:
  A greater subject fitteth Faustus' wit:
  Bid Economy farewell, and Galen come:
  Be a physician, Faustus; heap up gold,
  And be eterniz'd for some wondrous cure:

Summum bonum medicinoe sanitas,
The end of physic is our body's health.
Why, Faustus, hast thou not attain'd that end?
Are not thy bills hung up as monuments,
Whereby whole cities have escap'd the plague,
And thousand desperate maladies been cur'd?
Yet art thou still but Faustus, and a man.
Couldst thou make men to live eternally,
Or, being dead, raise them to life again,
Then this profession were to be esteem'd.
Physic, farewell! Where is Justinian?

A petty case of paltry legacies!
Such is the subject of the institute,
And universal body of the law:
This study fits a mercenary drudge,
Who aims at nothing but external trash;
Too servile and illiberal for me.
When all is done, divinity is best:
Jerome's Bible, Faustus; view it well.

The reward of sin is death: that's hard.

If we say that we have no sin, we deceive
    ourselves, and there is no truth in us.
Why, then, belike we must sin, and so
    consequently die:
Ay, we must die an everlasting death.
What doctrine call you this, Che sera, sera,
What will be, shall be? Divinity, adieu!
These metaphysics of magicians,
And necromantic books are heavenly;
Lines, circles, scenes, letters, and characters;
Ay, these are those that Faustus most desires.
O, what a world of profit and delight,
Of power, of honour, and omnipotence,
Is promis'd to the studious artizan!
All things that move between the quiet poles
Shall be at my command: emperors and kings
Are but obeyed in their several provinces;
But his dominion that exceeds in this,
Stretcheth as far as doth the mind of man;
A sound magician is a demigod:
Here tire, my brains, to gain a deity.

[ENTER WAGNER.]

Wagner, commend me to my dearest friends,
The German Valdes and Cornelius;
Request them earnestly to visit me.

WAGNER:
I will, sir.

[EXIT.]

FAUSTUS:
Their conference will be a greater help to me
Than all my labours, plod I ne'er so fast.

[ENTER GOOD ANGEL AND EVIL ANGEL.]

GOOD ANGEL:
O, Faustus, lay that damned book aside,
And gaze not on it, lest it tempt thy soul,
And heap God's heavy wrath upon thy head!
Read, read the Scriptures:—that is blasphemy.

EVIL ANGEL:
Go forward, Faustus, in that famous art
Wherein all Nature's treasure is contain'd:
Be thou on earth as Jove is in the sky,
Lord and commander of these elements.

[EXEUNT ANGELS.]

FAUSTUS:
How am I glutted with conceit of this!
Shall I make spirits fetch me what I please,
Resolve me of all ambiguities,
Perform what desperate enterprise I will?
I'll have them fly to India for gold,
Ransack the ocean for orient pearl,
And search all corners of the new-found world
For pleasant fruits and princely delicates;
I'll have them read me strange philosophy,
And tell the secrets of all foreign kings;
I'll have them wall all Germany with brass,
And make swift Rhine circle fair Wertenberg;
I'll have them fill the public schools with silk,
Wherewith the students shall be bravely clad;
I'll levy soldiers with the coin they bring,
And chase the Prince of Parma from our land,
And reign sole king of all the provinces;

Yea, stranger engines for the brunt of war,
Than was the fiery keel at Antwerp-bridge,
I'll make my servile spirits to invent.

[ENTER VALDES AND CORNELIUS.]

Come, German Valdes, and Cornelius,
And make me blest with your sage conference.
Valdes, sweet Valdes, and Cornelius,
Know that your words have won me at the last
To practice magic and concealed arts.
Philosophy is odious and obscure;
Both law and physic are for petty wits:
'Tis magic, magic that hath ravish'd me.
Then, gentle friends, aid me in this attempt;
And I, that have with subtle syllogisms
Gravell'd the pastors of the German church,
And made the flowering pride of Wittenberg
Swarm to my problems, as th' infernal spirits
On sweet Musaeus when he came to hell,
Will be as cunning as Agrippa was,
Whose shadow made all Europe honour him.

VALDES:
Faustus, these books, thy wit, and our experience,
Shall make all nations to canonize us.
As Indian Moors obey their Spanish lords,
So shall the spirits of every element
Be always serviceable to us three;
Like lions shall they guard us when we please;
Like Almain rutters with their horsemen's staves,
Or Lapland giants, trotting by our sides;
Sometimes like women, or unwedded maids,
Shadowing more beauty in their airy brows
Than have the white breasts of the queen of love:
From Venice shall they drag huge argosies,
And from America the golden fleece
That yearly stuffs old Philip's treasury;
If learned Faustus will be resolute.

FAUSTUS:
Valdes, as resolute am I in this
As thou to live: therefore object it not.

CORNELIUS:
The miracles that magic will perform
Will make thee vow to study nothing else.
He that is grounded in astrology,
Enrich'd with tongues, well seen in minerals,

Hath all the principles magic doth require:
Then doubt not, Faustus, but to be renown'd,
And more frequented for this mystery
Than heretofore the Delphian oracle.
The spirits tell me they can dry the sea,
And fetch the treasure of all foreign wrecks,
Yea, all the wealth that our forefathers hid
Within the massy entrails of the earth:
Then tell me, Faustus, what shall we three want?

FAUSTUS:
Nothing, Cornelius. O, this cheers my soul!
Come, shew me some demonstrations magical,
That I may conjure in some bushy grove,
And have these joys in full possession.

VALDES:
Then haste thee to some solitary grove,
And bear wise Bacon's and Albertus' works,
The Hebrew Psalter, and New Testament;
And whatsoever else is requisite
We will inform thee ere our conference cease.

CORNELIUS:
Valdes, first let him know the words of art;
And then, all other ceremonies learn'd,
Faustus may try his cunning by himself.

VALDES:
First I'll instruct thee in the rudiments,
And then wilt thou be perfecter than I.

FAUSTUS:
Then come and dine with me, and, after meat,
We'll canvass every quiddity thereof;
For, ere I sleep, I'll try what I can do:
This night I'll conjure, though I die therefore.

[EXEUNT.]

[ENTER TWO SCHOLARS.]

FIRST SCHOLAR:
I wonder what's become of Faustus, that was
    wont to make our schools ring with sic probo.

SECOND SCHOLAR:
That shall we presently know; here comes his
    boy.

[ENTER WAGNER.]

FIRST SCHOLAR:
How now, sirrah! where's thy master?

WAGNER:
God in heaven knows.

SECOND SCHOLAR:
Why, dost not thou know, then?

WAGNER:
Yes, I know; but that follows not.

FIRST SCHOLAR:
Go to, sirrah! leave your jesting, and tell us where
he is.

WAGNER:
That follows not by force of argument, which
you, being licentiates, should stand upon:
therefore acknowledge your error, and be
attentive.

SECOND SCHOLAR:
Then you will not tell us?

WAGNER:
You are deceived, for I will tell you: yet, if you
were not dunces, you would never ask me such
a question; for is he not corpus naturale? and is
not that mobile? then wherefore should you
ask me such a question? But that I am by
nature phlegmatic, slow to wrath, and prone to
lechery (to love, I would say), it were not for
you to come within forty foot of the place of
execution, although I do not doubt but to see
you both hanged the next sessions. Thus
having triumphed over you, I will set my
countenance like a precisian, and begin to
speak thus:—Truly, my dear brethren, my
master is within at dinner, with Valdes and
Cornelius, as this wine, if it could speak,
would inform your worships: and so, the Lord
bless you, preserve you, and keep you, my dear
brethren!

[EXIT.]

FISRT SCHOLAR:
O Faustus!
Then I fear that which I have long suspected,
That thou art fall'n into that damned art
For which they two are infamous through the
world.

SECOND SCHOLAR:
Were he a stranger, not allied to me,
The danger of his soul would make me mourn.
But, come, let us go and inform the Rector:
It may be his grave counsel may reclaim him.

FISRT SCHOLAR:
I fear me nothing will reclaim him now.

SECOND SCHOLAR:
Yet let us see what we can do.

[EXEUNT.]

[ENTER FAUSTUS.]

FAUSTUS:
Now that the gloomy shadow of the night,
Longing to view Orion's drizzling look,
Leaps from th' antartic world unto the sky,
And dims the welkin with her pitchy breath,
Faustus, begin thine incantations,
And try if devils will obey thy hest,
Seeing thou hast pray'd and sacrific'd to them.
Within this circle is Jehovah's name,
Forward and backward anagrammatiz'd,
Th' abbreviated names of holy saints,
Figures of every adjunct to the heavens,
And characters of signs and erring stars,
By which the spirits are enforc'd to rise:
Then fear not, Faustus, to be resolute,
And try the utmost magic can perform.

[ENTER MEPHISTOPHILIS.]

I charge thee to return, and change thy shape;
Thou art too ugly to attend on me:
Go, and return an old Franciscan friar;
That holy shape becomes a devil best.

[EXIT MEPHISTOPHILIS.]

I see there's virtue in my heavenly words.
Who would not be proficient in this art?
How pliant is this Mephistophilis,
Full of obedience and humility!
Such is the force of magic and my spells.

[RE-ENTER MEPHISTOPHILIS LIKE A FRANCISCAN FRIAR.]

MEPHIST:
Now, Faustus, what wouldst thou have me do?

FAUSTUS:
I charge thee wait upon me whilst I live,
To do whatever Faustus shall command,
Be it to make the moon drop from her sphere,
Or the ocean to overwhelm the world.

MEPHIST:
I am a servant to great Lucifer,
And may not follow thee without his leave:
No more than he commands must we perform.

FAUSTUS:
Did not he charge thee to appear to me?

MEPHIST:
No, I came hither of mine own accord.

FAUSTUS:
Did not my conjuring speeches raise thee? speak!

MEPHIST:
That was the cause, but yet per accidens;
For, when we hear one rack the name of God,
Abjure the Scriptures and his Saviour Christ,
We fly, in hope to get his glorious soul;
Nor will we come, unless he use such means
Whereby he is in danger to be damn'd.
Therefore the shortest cut for conjuring
Is stoutly to abjure all godliness,
And pray devoutly to the prince of hell.

FAUSTUS:
So Faustus hath
Already done; and holds this principle,
There is no chief but only Belzebub;
To whom Faustus doth dedicate himself.
This word "damnation" terrifies not me,
For I confound hell in Elysium:

My ghost be with the old philosophers!
But, leaving these vain trifles of men's souls,
Tell me what is that Lucifer thy lord?

MEPHIST:
Arch-regent and commander of all spirits.

FAUSTUS:
Was not that Lucifer an angel once?

MEPHIST:
Yes, Faustus, and most dearly lov'd of God.

FAUSTUS:
How comes it, then, that he is prince of devils?

MEPHIST:
O, by aspiring pride and insolence;
For which God threw him from the face of
    heaven.

FAUSTUS:
And what are you that live with Lucifer?

MEPHIST:
Unhappy spirits that fell with Lucifer,
Conspir'd against our God with Lucifer,
And are forever damn'd with Lucifer.

FAUSTUS:
Where are you damn'd?

MEPHIST:
In hell.

FAUSTUS:
How comes it, then, that thou art out of hell?

MEPHIST:
Why, this is hell, nor am I out of it:
Think'st thou that I, that saw the face of God,
And tasted the eternal joys of heaven,
Am not tormented with ten thousand hells,
In being depriv'd of everlasting bliss?
O, Faustus, leave these frivolous demands,
Which strike a terror to my fainting soul!

FAUSTUS:
What, is great Mephistophilis so passionate
For being deprived of the joys of heaven?
Learn thou of Faustus manly fortitude,
And scorn those joys thou never shalt possess.
Go bear these tidings to great Lucifer:

Seeing Faustus hath incurr'd eternal death
By desperate thoughts against Jove's deity,
Say, he surrenders up to him his soul,
So he will spare him four and twenty years,
Letting him live in all voluptuousness;
Having thee ever to attend on me,
To give me whatsoever I shall ask,
To tell me whatsoever I demand,
To slay mine enemies, and to aid my friends,
And always be obedient to my will.
Go, and return to mighty Lucifer,
And meet me in my study at midnight,
And then resolve me of thy master's mind.

MEPHIST:

I will, Faustus.

[*EXIT.*]

FAUSTUS:

Had I as many souls as there be stars,
I'd give them all for Mephistophilis.

By him I'll be great emperor of the world,
And make a bridge through the moving air,
To pass the ocean with a band of men;
I'll join the hills that bind the Afric shore,
And make that country continent to Spain,
And both contributary to my crown:
The Emperor shall not live but by my leave,
Nor any potentate of Germany.
Now that I have obtain'd what I desir'd,
I'll live in speculation of this art,
Till Mephistophilis return again.

[*EXIT.*]

 **For the entire play, insert the Literature CD.**

 # Questions

1. What does the Chorus tell the audience about Doctor Faustus' life in the opening speech?
2. What two fields of study does Faustus vacillate between in Act I, scene i? How do the angels advise him?
3. What criticism or satire is revealed in Faust's lines to the devil in Act I, scene iii: "Go, and return an old Franciscan friar: That holy shape becomes a devil best"?
4. What surprising message does Mephistophilis bring to Faustus? How does Faustus respond?
5. When Faustus signs his name in blood to Lucifer, he comments, "Consummatum est" (it is finished). To what does Marlowe allude in this line?
6. Why is it important that this play is set in Wittenberg and in Rome? What is the significance of these cities?
7. Why don't Lucifer and Belzebub want Faustus to talk about God and Creation?
8. Does God appear in any form in this play? If so, where? If not, why does Marlowe leave Him out?
9. How is the Pope characterized in Act III, scene ii?
10. How is Bruno restored to power in Germany? How does this plot point fit in with the political and religious agendas of the play?

11. Why does Faustus continue to play tricks on the Horse-Courser and Carter? Why does Marlowe spend so much time on these scenes in Act IV? How do these "comic" characters fit into the overall plot of this play?

12. Look at all the places in the play where Faustus decides to repent. Why does he consider repentance in those specific points? Why does he never follow through with it?

13. How does Helen of Troy get introduced into the plot, and what does she symbolize within the story?

14. On the eve of his death, how does Faustus finally feel about his decision to sell his soul to the devil? What important elements does he reveal in the final speech before his death?

1. Think about the characters of Wagner, the Clown, Robin, and Rafe. In what ways do they differ from Faustus, the scholars, and the clerics? How do the conjuring wishes of Robin and Rafe differ from those of Faustus? How do they feel when they are turned into an ape and a dog? Do you see these characters and their portrayals as a commentary about social rank? Why or why not?

2. There are very few women characters in this play. Think, however, about where femininity does appear, for example, in the personification of Lechery, in the conjuring of Alexander's wife, and in the appearance of Helen of Troy. Why does Marlowe reserve femininity for these specific roles? What is the role of gender in this play? Should women figure more prominently? Does Marlowe all but ignore women because they are not in need of his morality lesson? Build an argument about gender in this play.

3. Perhaps the most prominent Morality Play in Medieval Drama is *Everyman.* After reading *Everyman* on your own, do a comparison between it and *Doctor Faustus.* How are they similar, and in what ways are they different? Do they ultimately teach the same lesson? Are they equally as effective? Which do you think would reach audiences more deeply today, and why? To further explore this question, add to your comparison a contemporary book or film that you see as a modern example of a Morality Play. How does it compare and contrast to *Everyman* and *Doctor Faustus?* Why do you think the form of the Morality Tale remains prevalent and interesting in modern society?

4. You may be aware that there is a question of authorship that surrounds the playwrights William Shakespeare and Christopher Marlowe. Some scholars argue that there was no William Shakespeare, and that his plays were written by Christopher Marlowe. After you have read at least one play by each playwright, research this argument, and make your own decision. Do you argue that Marlowe is both men, who published under two names? Do you argue against this claim? Do a close reading of numerous passages within one Shakespeare play and one Marlowe play, and create your own argument about authorship.

William Shakespeare (1564–1616)

William Shakespeare was born in Stratford-on-Avon to a glove maker who belonged to the class of craftsmen until he earned enough money to buy his own Coat-of-Arms, thus making him a gentleman. John Stratford became a leading member of his town, even serving as bailiff (mayor) of Stratford when his son, William, was an infant. Though William Shakespeare did not have a formal university education, his plays are evidence that he had a working knowledge of Latin and French, as well as of European history. In many subjects, Shakespeare seems to have been self-taught; his writings reveal that he had a strong understanding of law, seamanship, and literature. Author Henry Fielding later commented that of all fields, Shakespeare was "learned in human nature."

After marrying Anne Hathaway and having three children, Shakespeare left for London to become an actor and playwright. Though about seven years of his life are obscured, we do know that in London, Shakespeare became the playwright of and a shareholder in the Lord Chamberlain's Men, the troupe which came to dominate the Renaissance stage. In his active career, from about 1589 to 1613, Shakespeare wrote 38 plays, 154 sonnets, and 5 epic poems. After 1613, Shakespeare left London for good to return to Stratford, where he died in 1616. He was buried in Holy Trinity Church in Stratford-on-Avon, the same church where he was baptized fifty-two years earlier. Though he died at a comparatively young age, he was recognized even in his day as being immortal. His contemporary, playwright Ben Jonson, praised, "He was not of an age, but for all time!"

Henry V

1. Notice that there is a Chorus that speaks to the audience before every act in this play. The dramatic Chorus has its roots in Greek theatre and has a long history of providing the audiences with narrative information and commentary. Be sure to notice what the Chorus is telling the reader as the play develops.
2. There is a good chance that when this play was performed in Shakespeare's day, actor doubling took place. The same men quite probably played the French / British armies, the nobles and clergymen, and the friends in the flashbacks to Henry's pub days. Small costume changes probably signaled the audience that the actors were playing different roles as the play went on.
3. Henry V was a real king who ruled England from 1413–1422. This dramatic account was written approximately 175 years after the real Henry's death. Knowing that this famous character is actually based on a real man, think about how your understanding of the play changes.

Henry V

William Shakespeare

CHARACTERS IN HENRY V

EARL RICHARD
SALISBURY
LORD RAMBURES
MONTJOY
NYM
WESTMORELAND
LEWIS THE DAUPHIN
WARWICK
SIR THOMAS ERPINGHAM
SIR THOMAS GREY
MICHAEL WILLIAMS
KING CHARLES VI OF FRANCE
MISTRESS QUICKLY
CAPTAIN GOWER
CAPTAIN FLUELLEN
ALICE
BARDOLPH
PISTOL
ALEXANDER COURT
JOHN BATES
CAPTAIN JAMY
CAPTAIN MACMORRIS
KATHARINE
ISABEL
KING HENRY V OF ENGLAND
LORD HENRY SCROOP
LORD GRANDPRE

ACT I
PROLOGUE

[*ENTER CHORUS*]

CHORUS:
O for a Muse of fire, that would ascend
The brightest heaven of invention,
A kingdom for a stage, princes to act
And monarchs to behold the swelling scene!
Then should the warlike Harry, like himself,
Assume the port of Mars; and at his heels,
Leash'd in like hounds, should famine, sword and
   fire

Crouch for employment. But pardon, and gentles
   all,
The flat unraised spirits that have dared
On this unworthy scaffold to bring forth
So great an object: can this cockpit hold
The vasty fields of France? or may we cram
Within this wooden O the very casques
That did affright the air at Agincourt?
O, pardon! since a crooked figure may
Attest in little place a million;
And let us, ciphers to this great accompt,
On your imaginary forces work.
Suppose within the girdle of these walls
Are now confined two mighty monarchies,
Whose high upreared and abutting fronts
The perilous narrow ocean parts asunder:
Piece out our imperfections with your thoughts;
Into a thousand parts divide on man,
And make imaginary puissance;
Think when we talk of horses, that you see them
Printing their proud hoofs i' the receiving earth;
For 'tis your thoughts that now must deck our
   kings,
Carry them here and there; jumping o'er times,
Turning the accomplishment of many years
Into an hour-glass: for the which supply,
Admit me Chorus to this history;
Who prologue-like your humble patience pray,
Gently to hear, kindly to judge, our play.

[*EXIT*]

SCENE I.
LONDON. AN ANTE-CHAMBER IN THE KING'S PALACE.

[*ENTER THE ARCHBISHOP OF CANTERBURY,
AND THE BISHOP OF ELY*]

CANTERBURY:
My lord, I'll tell you; that self bill is urged,
Which in the eleventh year of the last king's reign
Was like, and had indeed against us pass'd,
But that the scambling and unquiet time
Did push it out of farther question.

ELY:

But how, my lord, shall we resist it now?

CANTERBURY:

It must be thought on. If it pass against us,
We lose the better half of our possession:
For all the temporal lands which men devout
By testament have given to the church
Would they strip from us; being valued thus:
As much as would maintain, to the king's honour,
Full fifteen earls and fifteen hundred knights,
Six thousand and two hundred good esquires;
And, to relief of lazars and weak age,
Of indigent faint souls past corporal toil.
A hundred almshouses right well supplied;
And to the coffers of the king beside,
A thousand pounds by the year: thus runs the bill.

ELY:

This would drink deep.

CANTERBURY:

'Twould drink the cup and all.

ELY:

But what prevention?

CANTERBURY:

The king is full of grace and fair regard.

ELY:

And a true lover of the holy church.

CANTERBURY:

The courses of his youth promised it not.
The breath no sooner left his father's body,
But that his wildness, mortified in him,
Seem'd to die too; yea, at that very moment
Consideration, like an angel, came
And whipp'd the offending Adam out of him,
Leaving his body as a paradise,
To envelop and contain celestial spirits.
Never was such a sudden scholar made;
Never came reformation in a flood,
With such a heady currance, scouring faults
Nor never Hydra-headed wilfulness
So soon did lose his seat and all at once
As in this king.

ELY:

We are blessed in the change.

CANTERBURY:

Hear him but reason in divinity,
And all-admiring with an inward wish
You would desire the king were made a prelate:
Hear him debate of commonwealth affairs,
You would say it hath been all in all his study:
List his discourse of war, and you shall hear
A fearful battle render'd you in music:
Turn him to any cause of policy,
The Gordian knot of it he will unloose,
Familiar as his garter: that, when he speaks,
The air, a charter'd libertine, is still,
And the mute wonder lurketh in men's ears,
To steal his sweet and honey'd sentences;
So that the art and practic part of life
Must be the mistress to this theoric:
Which is a wonder how his grace should glean it,
Since his addiction was to courses vain,
His companies unletter'd, rude and shallow,
His hours fill'd up with riots, banquets, sports,
And never noted in him any study,
Any retirement, any sequestration
From open haunts and popularity.

ELY:

The strawberry grows underneath the nettle
And wholesome berries thrive and ripen best
Neighbour'd by fruit of baser quality:
And so the prince obscured his contemplation
Under the veil of wildness; which, no doubt,
Grew like the summer grass, fastest by night,
Unseen, yet crescive in his faculty.

CANTERBURY:

It must be so; for miracles are ceased;
And therefore we must needs admit the means
How things are perfected.

ELY:

But, my good lord,
How now for mitigation of this bill
Urged by the commons? Doth his majesty
Incline to it, or no?

CANTERBURY:

He seems indifferent,
Or rather swaying more upon our part
Than cherishing the exhibiters against us;
For I have made an offer to his majesty,

Upon our spiritual convocation
And in regard of causes now in hand,
Which I have open'd to his grace at large,
As touching France, to give a greater sum
Than ever at one time the clergy yet
Did to his predecessors part withal.

ELY:
How did this offer seem received, my lord?

CANTERBURY:
With good acceptance of his majesty;
Save that there was not time enough to hear,
As I perceived his grace would fain have done,
The severals and unhidden passages
Of his true titles to some certain dukedoms
And generally to the crown and seat of France
Derived from Edward, his great-grandfather.

ELY:
What was the impediment that broke this off?

CANTERBURY:
The French ambassador upon that instant
Craved audience; and the hour, I think, is come
To give him hearing: is it four o'clock?

ELY:
It is.

CANTERBURY:
Then go we in, to know his embassy;
Which I could with a ready guess declare,
Before the Frenchman speak a word of it.

ELY:
I'll wait upon you, and I long to hear it.

[EXEUNT]

SCENE II.
THE SAME. THE PRESENCE CHAMBER.

*[ENTER KING HENRY V, GLOUCESTER, BEDFORD,
EXETER, WARWICK, WESTMORELAND, AND ATTENDANTS]*

KING HENRY V:
Where is my gracious Lord of Canterbury?

EXETER:
Not here in presence.

KING HENRY V:
Send for him, good uncle.

WESTMORELAND:
Shall we call in the ambassador, my liege?

KING HENRY V:
Not yet, my cousin: we would be resolved,
Before we hear him, of some things of weight
That task our thoughts, concerning us and France.

*[ENTER THE ARCHBISHOP OF CANTERBURY,
AND THE BISHOP OF ELY]*

CANTERBURY:
God and his angels guard your sacred throne
And make you long become it!

KING HENRY V:
Sure, we thank you.
My learned lord, we pray you to proceed
And justly and religiously unfold
Why the law Salique that they have in France
Or should, or should not, bar us in our claim:
And God forbid, my dear and faithful lord,
That you should fashion, wrest, or bow your
      reading,
Or nicely charge your understanding soul
With opening titles miscreate, whose right
Suits not in native colours with the truth;
For God doth know how many now in health
Shall drop their blood in approbation
Of what your reverence shall incite us to.
Therefore take heed how you impawn our person,
How you awake our sleeping sword of war:
We charge you, in the name of God, take heed;
For never two such kingdoms did contend
Without much fall of blood; whose guiltless drops
Are every one a woe, a sore complaint
'Gainst him whose wrong gives edge unto the
      swords
That make such waste in brief mortality.
Under this conjuration, speak, my lord;
For we will hear, note and believe in heart
That what you speak is in your conscience wash'd
As pure as sin with baptism.

CANTERBURY:

Then hear me, gracious sovereign, and you peers,
That owe yourselves, your lives and services
To this imperial throne. There is no bar
To make against your highness' claim to France
But this, which they produce from Pharamond,
'In terram Salicam mulieres ne succedant:'
'No woman shall succeed in Salique land:'
Which Salique land the French unjustly gloze
To be the realm of France, and Pharamond
The founder of this law and female bar.
Yet their own authors faithfully affirm
That the land Salique is in Germany,
Between the floods of Sala and of Elbe;
Where Charles the Great, having subdued the
   Saxons,
There left behind and settled certain French;
Who, holding in disdain the German women
For some dishonest manners of their life,
Establish'd then this law; to wit, no female
Should be inheritrix in Salique land:
Which Salique, as I said, 'twixt Elbe and Sala,
Is at this day in Germany call'd Meisen.
Then doth it well appear that Salique law
Was not devised for the realm of France:
Nor did the French possess the Salique land
Until four hundred one and twenty years
After defunction of King Pharamond,
Idly supposed the founder of this law;
Who died within the year of our redemption
Four hundred twenty-six; and Charles the Great
Subdued the Saxons, and did seat the French
Beyond the river Sala, in the year
Eight hundred five. Besides, their writers say,
King Pepin, which deposed Childeric,
Did, as heir general, being descended
Of Blithild, which was daughter to King Clothair,
Make claim and title to the crown of France.
Hugh Capet also, who usurped the crown
Of Charles the duke of Lorraine, sole heir male
Of the true line and stock of Charles the Great,
To find his title with some shows of truth,
'Through, in pure truth, it was corrupt and
   naught.
Convey'd himself as heir to the Lady Lingare,
Daughter to Charlemain, who was the son
To Lewis the emperor, and Lewis the son
Of Charles the Great. Also King Lewis the Tenth,

Who was sole heir to the usurper Capet,
Could not keep quiet in his conscience,
Wearing the crown of France, till satisfied
That fair Queen Isabel, his grandmother,
Was lineal of the Lady Ermengare,
Daughter to Charles the foresaid duke of Lorraine:
By the which marriage the line of Charles the Great
Was re-united to the crown of France.
So that, as clear as is the summer's sun.
King Pepin's title and Hugh Capet's claim,
King Lewis his satisfaction, all appear
To hold in right and title of the female:
So do the kings of France unto this day;
Howbeit they would hold up this Salique law
To bar your highness claiming from the female,
And rather choose to hide them in a net
Than amply to imbar their crooked titles
Usurp'd from you and your progenitors.

KING HENRY V:

May I with right and conscience make this claim?

CANTERBURY:

The sin upon my head, dread sovereign!
For in the book of Numbers is it writ,
When the man dies, let the inheritance
Descend unto the daughter. Gracious lord,
Stand for your own; unwind your bloody flag;
Look back into your mighty ancestors:
Go, my dread lord, to your great-grandsire's tomb,
From whom you claim; invoke his warlike spirit,
And your great-uncle's, Edward the Black Prince,
Who on the French ground play'd a tragedy,
Making defeat on the full power of France,
Whiles his most mighty father on a hill
Stood smiling to behold his lion's whelp
Forage in blood of French nobility.
O noble English that could entertain
With half their forces the full Pride of France
And let another half stand laughing by,
All out of work and cold for action!

ELY:

Awake remembrance of these valiant dead
And with your puissant arm renew their feats:
You are their heir; you sit upon their throne;
The blood and courage that renowned them

Runs in your veins; and my thrice-puissant liege
Is in the very May-morn of his youth,
Ripe for exploits and mighty enterprises.

EXETER:
Your brother kings and monarchs of the earth
Do all expect that you should rouse yourself,
As did the former lions of your blood.

WESTMORELAND:
They know your grace hath cause and means and
    might;
So hath your highness; never king of England
Had nobles richer and more loyal subjects,
Whose hearts have left their bodies here in
    England
And lie pavilion'd in the fields of France.

CANTERBURY:
O, let their bodies follow, my dear liege,
With blood and sword and fire to win your right;
In aid whereof we of the spiritualty
Will raise your highness such a mighty sum
As never did the clergy at one time
Bring in to any of your ancestors.

KING HENRY V:
We must not only arm to invade the French,
But lay down our proportions to defend
Against the Scot, who will make road upon us
With all advantages.

CANTERBURY:
They of those marches, gracious sovereign,
Shall be a wall sufficient to defend
Our inland from the pilfering borderers.

KING HENRY V:
We do not mean the coursing snatchers only,
But fear the main intendment of the Scot,
Who hath been still a giddy neighbour to us;
For you shall read that my great-grandfather
Never went with his forces into France
But that the Scot on his unfurnish'd kingdom
Came pouring, like the tide into a breach,
With ample and brim fulness of his force,
Galling the gleaned land with hot assays,
Girding with grievous siege castles and towns;
That England, being empty of defence,
Hath shook and trembled at the ill
    neighbourhood.

CANTERBURY:
She hath been then more fear'd than harm'd, my
    liege;
For hear her but exampled by herself:
When all her chivalry hath been in France
And she a mourning widow of her nobles,
She hath herself not only well defended
But taken and impounded as a stray
The King of Scots; whom she did send to France,
To fill King Edward's fame with prisoner kings
And make her chronicle as rich with praise
As is the ooze and bottom of the sea
With sunken wreck and sunless treasuries.

WESTMORELAND:
But there's a saying very old and true,
'If that you will France win,
Then with Scotland first begin:'
For once the eagle England being in prey,
To her unguarded nest the weasel Scot
Comes sneaking and so sucks her princely eggs,
Playing the mouse in absence of the cat,
To tear and havoc more than she can eat.

EXETER:
It follows then the cat must stay at home:
Yet that is but a crush'd necessity,
Since we have locks to safeguard necessaries,
And pretty traps to catch the petty thieves.
While that the armed hand doth fight abroad,
The advised head defends itself at home;
For government, though high and low and lower,
Put into parts, doth keep in one consent,
Congreeing in a full and natural close,
Like music.

CANTERBURY:
Therefore doth heaven divide
The state of man in divers functions,
Setting endeavour in continual motion;
To which is fixed, as an aim or butt,
Obedience: for so work the honey-bees,
Creatures that by a rule in nature teach
The act of order to a peopled kingdom.
They have a king and officers of sorts;
Where some, like magistrates, correct at home,
Others, like merchants, venture trade abroad,
Others, like soldiers, armed in their stings,
Make boot upon the summer's velvet buds,

Which pillage they with merry march bring home
To the tent-royal of their emperor;
Who, busied in his majesty, surveys
The singing masons building roofs of gold,
The civil citizens kneading up the honey,
The poor mechanic porters crowding in
Their heavy burdens at his narrow gate,
The sad-eyed justice, with his surly hum,
Delivering o'er to executors pale
The lazy yawning drone. I this infer,
That many things, having full reference
To one consent, may work contrariously:
As many arrows, loosed several ways,
Come to one mark; as many ways meet in one
    town;
As many fresh streams meet in one salt sea;
As many lines close in the dial's centre;
So may a thousand actions, once afoot.
End in one purpose, and be all well borne
Without defeat. Therefore to France, my liege.
Divide your happy England into four;
Whereof take you one quarter into France,
And you withal shall make all Gallia shake.
If we, with thrice such powers left at home,
Cannot defend our own doors from the dog,
Let us be worried and our nation lose
The name of hardiness and policy.

KING HENRY V:
Call in the messengers sent from the Dauphin.
Exeunt some Attendants
Now are we well resolved; and, by God's help,
And yours, the noble sinews of our power,
France being ours, we'll bend it to our awe,
Or break it all to pieces: or there we'll sit,
Ruling in large and ample empery
O'er France and all her almost kingly dukedoms,
Or lay these bones in an unworthy urn,
Tombless, with no remembrance over them:
Either our history shall with full mouth
Speak freely of our acts, or else our grave,
Like Turkish mute, shall have a tongueless mouth,
Not worshipp'd with a waxen epitaph.

[ENTER AMBASSADORS OF FRANCE]

Now are we well prepared to know the pleasure
Of our fair cousin Dauphin; for we hear
Your greeting is from him, not from the king.

FIRST AMBASSADOR:
May't please your majesty to give us leave
Freely to render what we have in charge;
Or shall we sparingly show you far off
The Dauphin's meaning and our embassy?

KING HENRY V:
We are no tyrant, but a Christian king;
Unto whose grace our passion is as subject
As are our wretches fetter'd in our prisons:
Therefore with frank and with uncurbed plainness
Tell us the Dauphin's mind.

FIRST AMBASSADOR:
Thus, then, in few.
Your highness, lately sending into France,
Did claim some certain dukedoms, in the right
Of your great predecessor, King Edward the
    Third.
In answer of which claim, the prince our master
Says that you savour too much of your youth,
And bids you be advised there's nought in France
That can be with a nimble galliard won;
You cannot revel into dukedoms there.
He therefore sends you, meeter for your spirit,
This tun of treasure; and, in lieu of this,
Desires you let the dukedoms that you claim
Hear no more of you. This the Dauphin speaks.

KING HENRY V:
What treasure, uncle?

EXETER:
Tennis-balls, my liege.

KING HENRY V:
We are glad the Dauphin is so pleasant with us;
His present and your pains we thank you for:
When we have march'd our rackets to these balls,
We will, in France, by God's grace, play a set
Shall strike his father's crown into the hazard.
Tell him he hath made a match with such a
    wrangler
That all the courts of France will be disturb'd
With chaces. And we understand him well,
How he comes o'er us with our wilder days,
Not measuring what use we made of them.
We never valued this poor seat of England;
And therefore, living hence, did give ourself
To barbarous licence; as 'tis ever common
That men are merriest when they are from home.

But tell the Dauphin I will keep my state,
Be like a king and show my sail of greatness
When I do rouse me in my throne of France:
For that I have laid by my majesty
And plodded like a man for working-days,
But I will rise there with so full a glory
That I will dazzle all the eyes of France,
Yea, strike the Dauphin blind to look on us.
And tell the pleasant prince this mock of his
Hath turn'd his balls to gun-stones; and his soul
Shall stand sore charged for the wasteful vengeance
That shall fly with them: for many a thousand widows
Shall this his mock mock out of their dear husbands;
Mock mothers from their sons, mock castles down;
And some are yet ungotten and unborn
That shall have cause to curse the Dauphin's scorn.
But this lies all within the will of God,
To whom I do appeal; and in whose name
Tell you the Dauphin I am coming on,
To venge me as I may and to put forth
My rightful hand in a well-hallow'd cause.
So get you hence in peace; and tell the Dauphin
His jest will savour but of shallow wit,
When thousands weep more than did laugh at it.
Convey them with safe conduct. Fare you well.

[Exeunt Ambassadors]

Exeter:
  This was a merry message.

King Henry V:
  We hope to make the sender blush at it.
  Therefore, my lords, omit no happy hour
  That may give furtherance to our expedition;
  For we have now no thought in us but France,
  Save those to God, that run before our business.
  Therefore let our proportions for these wars
  Be soon collected and all things thought upon
  That may with reasonable swiftness add
  More feathers to our wings; for, God before,
  We'll chide this Dauphin at his father's door.
  Therefore let every man now task his thought,
  That this fair action may on foot be brought.

[Exeunt. Flourish]

For the entire play, insert the Literature CD.

Questions

1. Think about the two Archbishops in Act I, scene i. Why are they there, and what does Shakespeare intend the audience to feel about the clergy in the context of this play?
2. When the Dauphin of France sends the crate of tennis balls to the English court, why does Henry respond so violently? Why is this gift so offensive to him, and why does it elicit such a passionate response? Is Henry justified in his response?
3. One difference between Henry V and Hamlet is that in Act I, Henry V does not have any soliloquies or asides that show the readers his inner thoughts. Think about why Shakespeare makes that decision. What do Hamlet's interior monologues tell readers about him that doesn't seem true of Henry?

4. In the specific character of the Dauphin, Shakespeare characterizes the French in general. What attributes does he assign to the French? How does this depiction align itself with the overall rhetoric of the play?

5. Act III begins with Henry's famous "Once more into the breach, dear friends . . ." speech. What does this speech tell us about Henry in his new role as King? Do the soldiers feel like they are in good hands with this ruler? Do the readers?

6. Who is Katherine, why does she appear where she does, and what is her dramatic purpose in the play? What is your impression of Henry and Katherine's final wooing scene? Do you find it romantic, forced, funny, or oppressive? Why?

7. Think about the soldiers in the play (Fluellen, Macmorris, Gower, Pistol, Jamy, etc.) Why does Shakespeare give us one Irishman, one Welshman, and one Scotsman? What are the differences and similarities between these characters? How do they relate to the King?

8. Many of the scenes in this play depict battle. How would these scenes have been performed in the Shakespearean theatre? What about in modern productions? How do these differences affect the audience's understanding and appreciation of the various types of productions?

9. In the end of the play, the Chorus speaks of upcoming problems between England and France, implying that peace is not permanent. Knowing what you know about European history since the Renaissance, is this a fair criticism? What does Shakespeare want audiences to think about international relations at the close of his play?

Research and Writing

1. In *Henry V*, Shakespeare is very interested in the use of language. Remember Henry's ability to speak in the royal court and his convincing rhetoric in speaking to the common soldiers. Look carefully at the linguistic struggles between Henry and Katherine. You should also look at the comic scene between Katherine and Alice, which also focuses on language. Why does Shakespeare spend so much time thinking and writing about language? What effect does this have on the audience / reader? How are the greater themes of theatre affected when the topic of language is broached?

2. Write a paper analyzing Henry's "St. Crispin's Day" speech in Act IV, scene iii; do a close reading of the rhetoric and diction he uses in this speech. Who are the "Cripin / Crispian" brothers to whom Henry alludes, and why would he choose them as a basis for his rhetoric? Why is this such a riveting speech to both the soldiers at Agincourt and to audiences? How do the themes in this speech reflect Henry's argument with the soldier Williams, and how does Shakespeare refocus the themes in the two scenes? The "St. Crispin's Day" speech is still used today in military training and preparation for battle. Do you believe that it is still a successful motivational tool? Why or why not?

3. Read the first two plays in the "Henriad," *Henry IV, Part 1* and *Part 2*. Trace the development of how the young Prince Hal becomes the indomitable King Henry V. What changes does he make along the way, and

why do these changes have to happen to create the adult character? Does he make any mistakes while growing up? What are they, and what dramatic purpose might they have? How might things have been different if Henry V had acted differently in his youth? You should certainly include an analysis of Hal's friendship with Falstaff in your argument.

4. In contemporary business and politics, King Henry V is often held up as an ideal of successful leadership. In fact, many companies encourage their employees to read Shakespeare's play in order to educate and inspire them to greatness. What parts of the play do you think would be especially effective in this project and why? Which of Henry's attributes do you find to be especially noble and which to be repugnant? Overall, argue for or against the benefits of creating a paragon out of this character; do you believe that there is anything to be gained by emulating him in modern society?

5. There have been two important film versions of *Henry V;* Sir Lawrence Olivier filmed the play in 1944, and Kenneth Branagh created a version in 1989. Do in-depth analyses of both films; to do so you will have to watch them numerous times. Compare the Olivier version to both Shakespeare's original text and Branagh's more recent film. Analyze where the film departs from the text, where it remains faithful, and why you think Olivier makes those choices. Do the same for Branagh's version. Then, expand your argument into a larger thesis: do you think it is a benefit or a detriment to film Shakespeare's plays? What are the positive and negative consequences of doing so? Ultimately, do you find it a tribute or an injury to the original plays and playwright?

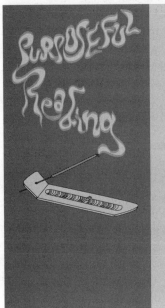

Twelfth Night

1. In contemporary scholarship, *Twelfth Night* is often categorized as a Problem Comedy. Unlike *A Midsummer Night's Dream* and other straightforward comedies, in which every character and situation resolves satisfactorily, this play ends with happiness for some but not all the characters. Watch for how and where these "problems" develop in the plot.

2. *Twelfth Night* is often categorized as a Romance, another sub-genre of Shakespeare's Comedies. This play has many of the staple characteristics of a Romance, including a shipwreck, the interlocking of love plots and one of Shakespeare's favorites: mistaken identities. Look for these "romantic" elements as you progress in your reading.

3. The very first line of the play, "If music be the food of love, play on [. . .]" sets up the theme of music that runs throughout the entire play. In fact, music figures very prominently in *Twelfth Night;* the play begins and ends with a song. Consider why music continues to infuse the play as you read it.

Twelfth Night

William Shakespeare

CHARACTERS IN TWELFTH NIGHT

DUKE ORSINO
OLIVIA
MARIA
SEBASTIAN
VIOLA
VALENTINE
SIR TOBY BELCH
CESARIO
ANTONIO
SIR ANDREW AGUECHEEK
CURIO
MALVOLIO
FESTE
FABIAN

ACT I

SCENE I.
DUKE ORSINO'S PALACE.

[ENTER DUKE ORSINO, CURIO, AND OTHER LORDS; MUSICIANS ATTENDING]

DUKE ORSINO:
If music be the food of love, play on;
Give me excess of it, that, surfeiting,
The appetite may sicken, and so die.
That strain again! it had a dying fall:
O, it came o'er my ear like the sweet sound,
That breathes upon a bank of violets,
Stealing and giving odour! Enough; no more:
'Tis not so sweet now as it was before.
O spirit of love! how quick and fresh art thou,
That, notwithstanding thy capacity
Receiveth as the sea, nought enters there,
Of what validity and pitch soe'er,
But falls into abatement and low price,
Even in a minute: so full of shapes is fancy
That it alone is high fantastical.

CURIO:
Will you go hunt, my lord?

DUKE ORSINO:
What, Curio?

CURIO:
The hart.

DUKE ORSINO:
Why, so I do, the noblest that I have:
O, when mine eyes did see Olivia first,
Methought she purged the air of pestilence!
That instant was I turn'd into a hart;
And my desires, like fell and cruel hounds,
E'er since pursue me.

[ENTER VALENTINE]

How now! what news from her?

VALENTINE:
So please my lord, I might not be admitted;
But from her handmaid do return this answer:
The element itself, till seven years' heat,
Shall not behold her face at ample view;
But, like a cloistress, she will veiled walk
And water once a day her chamber round
With eye-offending brine: all this to season
A brother's dead love, which she would keep fresh
And lasting in her sad remembrance.

DUKE ORSINO:
O, she that hath a heart of that fine frame
To pay this debt of love but to a brother,
How will she love, when the rich golden shaft
Hath kill'd the flock of all affections else
That live in her; when liver, brain and heart,
These sovereign thrones, are all supplied, and fill'd
Her sweet perfections with one self king!
Away before me to sweet beds of flowers:
Love-thoughts lie rich when canopied with bowers.

[EXEUNT]

SCENE II.
THE SEA-COAST.

[ENTER VIOLA, A CAPTAIN, AND SAILORS]

VIOLA:
What country, friends, is this?

CAPTAIN:
This is Illyria, lady.

VIOLA:
And what should I do in Illyria?
My brother he is in Elysium.
Perchance he is not drown'd: what think you,
    sailors?

CAPTAIN:
It is perchance that you yourself were saved.

VIOLA:
O my poor brother! and so perchance may he be.

CAPTAIN:
True, madam: and, to comfort you with chance,
Assure yourself, after our ship did split,
When you and those poor number saved with you
Hung on our driving boat, I saw your brother,
Most provident in peril, bind himself,
Courage and hope both teaching him the practise,
To a strong mast that lived upon the sea;
Where, like Arion on the dolphin's back,
I saw him hold acquaintance with the waves
So long as I could see.

VIOLA:
For saying so, there's gold:
Mine own escape unfoldeth to my hope,
Whereto thy speech serves for authority,
The like of him. Know'st thou this country?

CAPTAIN:
Ay, madam, well; for I was bred and born
Not three hours' travel from this very place.

VIOLA:
Who governs here?

CAPTAIN:
A noble duke, in nature as in name.

VIOLA:
What is the name?

CAPTAIN:
Orsino.

VIOLA:
Orsino! I have heard my father name him:
He was a bachelor then.

CAPTAIN:
And so is now, or was so very late;
For but a month ago I went from hence,
And then 'twas fresh in murmur,—as, you know,
What great ones do the less will prattle of,—
That he did seek the love of fair Olivia.

VIOLA:
What's she?

CAPTAIN:
A virtuous maid, the daughter of a count
That died some twelvemonth since, then leaving
    her
In the protection of his son, her brother,
Who shortly also died: for whose dear love,
They say, she hath abjured the company
And sight of men.

VIOLA:
O that I served that lady
And might not be delivered to the world,
Till I had made mine own occasion mellow,
What my estate is!

CAPTAIN:
That were hard to compass;
Because she will admit no kind of suit,
No, not the duke's.

VIOLA:
There is a fair behavior in thee, captain;
And though that nature with a beauteous wall
Doth oft close in pollution, yet of thee
I will believe thou hast a mind that suits
With this thy fair and outward character.
I prithee, and I'll pay thee bounteously,
Conceal me what I am, and be my aid
For such disguise as haply shall become
The form of my intent. I'll serve this duke:
Thou shall present me as an eunuch to him:
It may be worth thy pains; for I can sing
And speak to him in many sorts of music

That will allow me very worth his service.
What else may hap to time I will commit;
Only shape thou thy silence to my wit.

CAPTAIN:

Be you his eunuch, and your mute I'll be:
When my tongue blabs, then let mine eyes not
see.

VIOLA:

I thank thee: lead me on.

[EXEUNT]

SCENE III.
OLIVIA'S HOUSE.

[ENTER SIR TOBY BELCH AND MARIA]

SIR TOBY BELCH:

What a plague means my niece, to take the death
of her brother thus? I am sure care's an enemy
to life.

MARIA:

By my troth, Sir Toby, you must come in earlier
o'nights: your cousin, my lady, takes great
exceptions to your ill hours.

SIR TOBY BELCH:

Why, let her except, before excepted.

MARIA:

Ay, but you must confine yourself within the
modest limits of order.

SIR TOBY BELCH:

Confine! I'll confine myself no finer than I am:
these clothes are good enough to drink in; and
so be these boots too: an they be not, let them
hang themselves in their own straps.

MARIA:

That quaffing and drinking will undo you: I heard
my lady talk of it yesterday; and of a foolish
knight that you brought in one night here to be
her wooer.

SIR TOBY BELCH:

Who, Sir Andrew Aguecheek?

MARIA:

Ay, he.

SIR TOBY BELCH:

He's as tall a man as any's in Illyria.

MARIA:

What's that to the purpose?

SIR TOBY BELCH:

Why, he has three thousand ducats a year.

MARIA:

Ay, but he'll have but a year in all these ducats:
he's a very fool and a prodigal.

SIR TOBY BELCH:

Fie, that you'll say so! he plays o' the
viol-de-gamboys, and speaks three or four
languages word for word without book, and
hath all the good gifts of nature.

MARIA:

He hath indeed, almost natural: for besides that
he's a fool, he's a great quarreller: and but that
he hath the gift of a coward to allay the gust he
hath in quarrelling, 'tis thought among the
prudent he would quickly have the gift of a
grave.

SIR TOBY BELCH:

By this hand, they are scoundrels and subtractors
that say so of him. Who are they?

MARIA:

They that add, moreover, he's drunk nightly in
your company.

SIR TOBY BELCH:

With drinking healths to my niece: I'll drink to
her as long as there is a passage in my throat
and drink in Illyria: he's a coward and a
coystrill that will not drink to my niece till his
brains turn o' the toe like a parish-top. What,
wench! Castiliano vulgo! for here comes Sir
Andrew Agueface.

[ENTER SIR ANDREW]

SIR ANDREW:

Sir Toby Belch! how now, Sir Toby Belch!

SIR TOBY BELCH:
Sweet Sir Andrew!

SIR ANDREW:
Bless you, fair shrew.

MARIA:
And you too, sir.

SIR TOBY BELCH:
Accost, Sir Andrew, accost.

SIR ANDREW:
What's that?

SIR TOBY BELCH:
My niece's chambermaid.

SIR ANDREW:
Good Mistress Accost, I desire better acquaintance.

MARIA:
My name is Mary, sir.

SIR ANDREW:
Good Mistress Mary Accost,—

SIR TOBY BELCH:
You mistake, knight; 'accost' is front her, board her, woo her, assail her.

SIR ANDREW:
By my troth, I would not undertake her in this company. Is that the meaning of 'accost'?

MARIA:
Fare you well, gentlemen.

SIR TOBY BELCH:
An thou let part so, Sir Andrew, would thou mightst never draw sword again.

SIR ANDREW:
An you part so, mistress, I would I might never draw sword again. Fair lady, do you think you have fools in hand?

MARIA:
Sir, I have not you by the hand.

SIR ANDREW:
Marry, but you shall have; and here's my hand.

MARIA:
Now, sir, 'thought is free:' I pray you, bring your hand to the buttery-bar and let it drink.

SIR ANDREW:
Wherefore, sweet-heart? what's your metaphor?

MARIA:
It's dry, sir.

SIR ANDREW:
Why, I think so: I am not such an ass but I can keep my hand dry. But what's your jest?

MARIA:
A dry jest, sir.

SIR ANDREW:
Are you full of them?

MARIA:
Ay, sir, I have them at my fingers' ends: marry, now I let go your hand, I am barren.

[EXIT]

SIR TOBY BELCH:
O knight thou lackest a cup of canary: when did I see thee so put down?

SIR ANDREW:
Never in your life, I think; unless you see canary put me down. Methinks sometimes I have no more wit than a Christian or an ordinary man has: but I am a great eater of beef and I believe that does harm to my wit.

SIR TOBY BELCH:
No question.

SIR ANDREW:
An I thought that, I'd forswear it. I'll ride home to-morrow, Sir Toby.

SIR TOBY BELCH:
Pourquoi, my dear knight?

SIR ANDREW:
What is 'Pourquoi'? do or not do? I would I had bestowed that time in the tongues that I have in fencing, dancing and bear-baiting: O, had I but followed the arts!

SIR TOBY BELCH:
Then hadst thou had an excellent head of hair.

SIR ANDREW:
Why, would that have mended my hair?

SIR TOBY BELCH:

Past question; for thou seest it will not curl by nature.

SIR ANDREW:

But it becomes me well enough, does't not?

SIR TOBY BELCH:

Excellent; it hangs like flax on a distaff; and I hope to see a housewife take thee between her legs and spin it off.

SIR ANDREW:

Faith, I'll home to-morrow, Sir Toby: your niece will not be seen; or if she be, it's four to one she'll none of me: the count himself here hard by woos her.

SIR TOBY BELCH:

She'll none o' the count: she'll not match above her degree, neither in estate, years, nor wit; I have heard her swear't. Tut, there's life in't, man.

SIR ANDREW:

I'll stay a month longer. I am a fellow o' the strangest mind i' the world; I delight in masques and revels sometimes altogether.

SIR TOBY BELCH:

Art thou good at these kickshawses, knight?

SIR ANDREW:

As any man in Illyria, whatsoever he be, under the degree of my betters; and yet I will not compare with an old man.

SIR TOBY BELCH:

What is thy excellence in a galliard, knight?

SIR ANDREW:

Faith, I can cut a caper.

SIR TOBY BELCH:

And I can cut the mutton to't.

SIR ANDREW:

And I think I have the back-trick simply as strong as any man in Illyria.

SIR TOBY BELCH:

Wherefore are these things hid? wherefore have these gifts a curtain before 'em? are they like to take dust, like Mistress Mall's picture? why dost thou not go to church in a galliard and come home in a coranto? My very walk should be a jig; I would not so much as make water but in a sink-a-pace. What dost thou mean? Is it a world to hide virtues in? I did think, by the excellent constitution of thy leg, it was formed under the star of a galliard.

SIR ANDREW:

Ay, 'tis strong, and it does indifferent well in a flame-coloured stock. Shall we set about some revels?

SIR TOBY BELCH:

What shall we do else? were we not born under Taurus?

SIR ANDREW:

Taurus! That's sides and heart.

SIR TOBY BELCH:

No, sir; it is legs and thighs. Let me see the caper; ha! higher: ha, ha! excellent!

[EXEUNT]

SCENE IV.
DUKE ORSINO'S PALACE.

[ENTER VALENTINE AND VIOLA IN MAN'S ATTIRE]

VALENTINE:

If the duke continues these favours towards you, Cesario, you are like to be much advanced: he hath known you but three days, and already you are no stranger.

VIOLA:

You either fear his humour or my negligence, that you call in question the continuance of his love: is he inconstant, sir, in his favours?

VALENTINE:

No, believe me.

VIOLA:

I thank you. Here comes the count.

[ENTER DUKE ORSINO, CURIO, AND ATTENDANTS]

DUKE ORSINO:
Who saw Cesario, ho?

VIOLA:
On your attendance, my lord; here.

DUKE ORSINO:
Stand you a while aloof, Cesario,
Thou know'st no less but all; I have unclasp'd
To thee the book even of my secret soul:
Therefore, good youth, address thy gait unto her;
Be not denied access, stand at her doors,
And tell them, there thy fixed foot shall grow
Till thou have audience.

VIOLA:
Sure, my noble lord,
If she be so abandon'd to her sorrow
As it is spoke, she never will admit me.

DUKE ORSINO:
Be clamorous and leap all civil bounds
Rather than make unprofited return.

VIOLA:
Say I do speak with her, my lord, what then?

DUKE ORSINO:
O, then unfold the passion of my love,
Surprise her with discourse of my dear faith:
It shall become thee well to act my woes;
She will attend it better in thy youth
Than in a nuncio's of more grave aspect.

VIOLA:
I think not so, my lord.

DUKE ORSINO:
Dear lad, believe it;
For they shall yet belie thy happy years,
That say thou art a man: Diana's lip
Is not more smooth and rubious; thy small pipe
Is as the maiden's organ, shrill and sound,
And all is semblative a woman's part.
I know thy constellation is right apt
For this affair. Some four or five attend him;
All, if you will; for I myself am best
When least in company. Prosper well in this,
And thou shalt live as freely as thy lord,
To call his fortunes thine.

VIOLA:
I'll do my best
To woo your lady:

[ASIDE]

Yet, a barful strife!
Whoe'er I woo, myself would be his wife.

[EXEUNT]

SCENE V.
OLIVIA'S HOUSE.

[ENTER MARIA AND CLOWN]

MARIA:
Nay, either tell me where thou hast been, or I will
not open my lips so wide as a bristle may enter
in way of thy excuse: my lady will hang thee
for thy absence.

CLOWN:
Let her hang me: he that is well hanged in this
world needs to fear no colours.

MARIA:
Make that good.

CLOWN:
He shall see none to fear.

MARIA:
A good lenten answer: I can tell thee where that
saying was born, of 'I fear no colours.'

CLOWN:
Where, good Mistress Mary?

MARIA:
In the wars; and that may you be bold to say in
your foolery.

CLOWN:
Well, God give them wisdom that have it; and
those that are fools, let them use their talents.

MARIA:
Yet you will be hanged for being so long absent;
or, to be turned away, is not that as good as a
hanging to you?

CLOWN:

Many a good hanging prevents a bad marriage; and, for turning away, let summer bear it out.

MARIA:

You are resolute, then?

CLOWN:

Not so, neither; but I am resolved on two points.

MARIA:

That if one break, the other will hold; or, if both break, your gaskins fall.

CLOWN:

Apt, in good faith; very apt. Well, go thy way; if Sir Toby would leave drinking, thou wert as witty a piece of Eve's flesh as any in Illyria.

MARIA:

Peace, you rogue, no more o' that. Here comes my lady: make your excuse wisely, you were best.

[EXIT]

CLOWN:

Wit, an't be thy will, put me into good fooling! Those wits, that think they have thee, do very oft prove fools; and I, that am sure I lack thee, may pass for a wise man: for what says Quinapalus? 'Better a witty fool, than a foolish wit.'

[ENTER OLIVIA WITH MALVOLIO]

God bless thee, lady!

OLIVIA:

Take the fool away.

CLOWN:

Do you not hear, fellows? Take away the lady.

OLIVIA:

Go to, you're a dry fool; I'll no more of you: besides, you grow dishonest.

CLOWN:

Two faults, madonna, that drink and good counsel will amend: for give the dry fool drink, then is the fool not dry: bid the dishonest man mend himself; if he mend, he is no longer dishonest; if he cannot, let the botcher mend him. Any thing that's mended is but patched: virtue that transgresses is but patched with sin; and sin that amends is but patched with virtue. If that this simple syllogism will serve, so; if it will not, what remedy? As there is no true cuckold but calamity, so beauty's a flower. The lady bade take away the fool; therefore, I say again, take her away.

OLIVIA:

Sir, I bade them take away you.

CLOWN:

Misprision in the highest degree! Lady, *cucullus non facit monachum*; that's as much to say as I wear not motley in my brain. Good madonna, give me leave to prove you a fool.

OLIVIA:

Can you do it?

CLOWN:

Dexterously, good madonna.

OLIVIA:

Make your proof.

CLOWN:

I must catechise you for it, madonna: good my mouse of virtue, answer me.

OLIVIA:

Well, sir, for want of other idleness, I'll bide your proof.

CLOWN:

Good madonna, why mournest thou?

OLIVIA:

Good fool, for my brother's death.

CLOWN:

I think his soul is in hell, madonna.

OLIVIA:

I know his soul is in heaven, fool.

CLOWN:
The more fool, madonna, to mourn for your brother's soul being in heaven. Take away the fool, gentlemen.

OLIVIA:
What think you of this fool, Malvolio? doth he not mend?

MALVOLIO:
Yes, and shall do till the pangs of death shake him: infirmity, that decays the wise, doth ever make the better fool.

CLOWN:
God send you, sir, a speedy infirmity, for the better increasing your folly! Sir Toby will be sworn that I am no fox; but he will not pass his word for two pence that you are no fool.

OLIVIA:
How say you to that, Malvolio?

MALVOLIO:
I marvel your ladyship takes delight in such a barren rascal: I saw him put down the other day with an ordinary fool that has no more brain than a stone. Look you now, he's out of his guard already; unless you laugh and minister occasion to him, he is gagged. I protest, I take these wise men, that crow so at these set kind of fools, no better than the fools' zanies.

OLIVIA:
Oh, you are sick of self-love, Malvolio, and taste with a distempered appetite. To be generous, guiltless and of free disposition, is to take those things for bird-bolts that you deem cannon-bullets: there is no slander in an allowed fool, though he do nothing but rail; nor no railing in a known discreet man, though he do nothing but reprove.

CLOWN:
Now Mercury endue thee with leasing, for thou speakest well of fools!

[RE-ENTER MARIA]

MARIA:
Madam, there is at the gate a young gentleman much desires to speak with you.

OLIVIA:
From the Count Orsino, is it?

MARIA:
I know not, madam: 'tis a fair young man, and well attended.

OLIVIA:
Who of my people hold him in delay?

MARIA:
Sir Toby, madam, your kinsman.

OLIVIA:
Fetch him off, I pray you; he speaks nothing but madman: fie on him!

[EXIT MARIA]

Go you, Malvolio: if it be a suit from the count, I am sick, or not at home; what you will, to dismiss it.

[EXIT MALVOLIO]

Now you see, sir, how your fooling grows old, and people dislike it.

CLOWN:
Thou hast spoke for us, madonna, as if thy eldest son should be a fool; whose skull Jove cram with brains! for,—here he comes,—one of thy kin has a most weak pia mater.

[ENTER SIR TOBY BELCH]

OLIVIA:
By mine honour, half drunk. What is he at the gate, cousin?

SIR TOBY BELCH:
A gentleman.

OLIVIA:
A gentleman! what gentleman?

SIR TOBY BELCH:

'Tis a gentle man here—a plague o' these pickle-
herring! How now, sot!

CLOWN:

Good Sir Toby!

OLIVIA:

Cousin, cousin, how have you come so early by
this lethargy?

SIR TOBY BELCH:

Lechery! I defy lechery. There's one at the gate.

OLIVIA:

Ay, marry, what is he?

SIR TOBY BELCH:

Let him be the devil, an he will, I care not: give
me faith, say I. Well, it's all one.

[EXIT]

OLIVIA:

What's a drunken man like, fool?

CLOWN:

Like a drowned man, a fool and a mad man: one
draught above heat makes him a fool; the
second mads him; and a third drowns him.

OLIVIA:

Go thou and seek the crowner, and let him sit o'
my coz; for he's in the third degree of drink,
he's drowned: go, look after him.

CLOWN:

He is but mad yet, madonna; and the fool shall
look to the madman.

[EXIT]

[RE-ENTER MALVOLIO]

MALVOLIO:

Madam, yond young fellow swears he will speak
with you. I told him you were sick; he takes on
him to understand so much, and therefore
comes to speak with you. I told him you were
asleep; he seems to have a foreknowledge of
that too, and therefore comes to speak with
you. What is to be said to him, lady? he's
fortified against any denial.

OLIVIA:

Tell him he shall not speak with me.

MALVOLIO:

Has been told so; and he says, he'll stand at your
door like a sheriff's post, and be the supporter
to a bench, but he'll speak with you.

OLIVIA:

What kind o' man is he?

MALVOLIO:

Why, of mankind.

OLIVIA:

What manner of man?

MALVOLIO:

Of very ill manner; he'll speak with you, will you
or no.

OLIVIA:

Of what personage and years is he?

MALVOLIO:

Not yet old enough for a man, nor young enough
for a boy; as a squash is before 'tis a peascod,
or a cooling when 'tis almost an apple: 'tis
with him in standing water, between boy and
man. He is very well-favoured and he speaks
very shrewishly; one would think his mother's
milk were scarce out of him.

OLIVIA:

Let him approach: call in my gentlewoman.

MALVOLIO:

Gentlewoman, my lady calls.

[EXIT]

[RE-ENTER MARIA]

OLIVIA:

Give me my veil: come, throw it o'er my face.
We'll once more hear Orsino's embassy.

[ENTER VIOLA, AND ATTENDANTS]

VIOLA:

The honourable lady of the house, which is she?

OLIVIA:

Speak to me; I shall answer for her.
Your will?

VIOLA:

Most radiant, exquisite and unmatchable
beauty,—I pray you, tell me if this be the lady
of the house, for I never saw her: I would be
loath to cast away my speech, for besides that
it is excellently well penned, I have taken great
pains to con it. Good beauties, let me sustain
no scorn; I am very comptible, even to the least
sinister usage.

OLIVIA:

Whence came you, sir?

VIOLA:

I can say little more than I have studied, and that
question's out of my part. Good gentle one,
give me modest assurance if you be the lady of
the house, that I may proceed in my speech.

OLIVIA:

Are you a comedian?

VIOLA:

No, my profound heart: and yet, by the very fangs
of malice I swear, I am not that I play. Are you
the lady of the house?

OLIVIA:

If I do not usurp myself, I am.

VIOLA:

Most certain, if you are she, you do usurp
yourself; for what is yours to bestow is not
yours to reserve. But this is from my
commission: I will on with my speech in your
praise, and then show you the heart of my
message.

OLIVIA:

Come to what is important in't: I forgive you the
praise.

VIOLA:

Alas, I took great pains to study it, and 'tis
poetical.

OLIVIA:

It is the more like to be feigned: I pray you, keep
it in. I heard you were saucy at my gates, and
allowed your approach rather to wonder at you
than to hear you. If you be not mad, be gone; if
you have reason, be brief: 'tis not that time of
moon with me to make one in so skipping a
dialogue.

MARIA:

Will you hoist sail, sir? here lies your way.

VIOLA:

No, good swabber; I am to hull here a little
longer. Some mollification for your giant,
sweet lady. Tell me your mind: I am a
messenger.

OLIVIA:

Sure, you have some hideous matter to deliver,
when the courtesy of it is so fearful. Speak
your office.

VIOLA:

It alone concerns your ear. I bring no overture of
war, no taxation of homage: I hold the olive in
my hand; my words are as fun of peace as
matter.

OLIVIA:

Yet you began rudely. What are you? what would
you?

VIOLA:

The rudeness that hath appeared in me have I
learned from my entertainment. What I am,
and what I would, are as secret as maidenhead;
to your ears, divinity, to any other's,
profanation.

OLIVIA:

Give us the place alone: we will hear this divinity.

[EXEUNT MARIA AND ATTENDANTS]

Now, sir, what is your text?

VIOLA:

Most sweet lady,—

OLIVIA:

A comfortable doctrine, and much may be said of
it. Where lies your text?

VIOLA:

In Orsino's bosom.

OLIVIA:

In his bosom! In what chapter of his bosom?

VIOLA:

To answer by the method, in the first of his heart.

OLIVIA:

O, I have read it: it is heresy. Have you no more
to say?

VIOLA:

Good madam, let me see your face.

OLIVIA:

Have you any commission from your lord to
negotiate with my face? You are now out of
your text: but we will draw the curtain and
show you the picture. Look you, sir, such a one
I was this present: is't not well done?

[UNVEILING]

VIOLA:

Excellently done, if God did all.

OLIVIA:

'Tis in grain, sir; 'twill endure wind and weather.

VIOLA:

'Tis beauty truly blent, whose red and white
Nature's own sweet and cunning hand laid on:
Lady, you are the cruell'st she alive,
If you will lead these graces to the grave
And leave the world no copy.

OLIVIA:

O, sir, I will not be so hard-hearted; I will give
out divers schedules of my beauty: it shall be
inventoried, and every particle and utensil
labelled to my will: as, item, two lips,
indifferent red; item, two grey eyes, with lids
to them; item, one neck, one chin, and so forth.
Were you sent hither to praise me?

VIOLA:

I see you what you are, you are too proud;
But, if you were the devil, you are fair.
My lord and master loves you: O, such love
Could be but recompensed, though you were
crown'd
The nonpareil of beauty!

OLIVIA:

How does he love me?

VIOLA:

With adorations, fertile tears,
With groans that thunder love, with sighs of fire.

OLIVIA:

Your lord does know my mind; I cannot love him:
Yet I suppose him virtuous, know him noble,
Of great estate, of fresh and stainless youth;
In voices well divulged, free, learn'd and valiant;
And in dimension and the shape of nature
A gracious person: but yet I cannot love him;
He might have took his answer long ago.

VIOLA:

If I did love you in my master's flame,
With such a suffering, such a deadly life,
In your denial I would find no sense;
I would not understand it.

OLIVIA:

Why, what would you?

VIOLA:

Make me a willow cabin at your gate,
And call upon my soul within the house;
Write loyal cantons of contemned love
And sing them loud even in the dead of night;
Halloo your name to the reverberate hills
And make the babbling gossip of the air
Cry out 'Olivia!' O, You should not rest
Between the elements of air and earth,
But you should pity me!

OLIVIA:

You might do much.
What is your parentage?

VIOLA:

Above my fortunes, yet my state is well:
I am a gentleman.

OLIVIA:

Get you to your lord;
I cannot love him: let him send no more;
Unless, perchance, you come to me again,
To tell me how he takes it. Fare you well:
I thank you for your pains: spend this for me.

VIOLA:

I am no fee'd post, lady; keep your purse:
My master, not myself, lacks recompense.
Love make his heart of flint that you shall love;
And let your fervor, like my master's, be
Placed in contempt! Farewell, fair cruelty.

[EXIT]

OLIVIA:

'What is your parentage?'
'Above my fortunes, yet my state is well:
I am a gentleman.' I'll be sworn thou art;
Thy tongue, thy face, thy limbs, actions and
    spirit,
Do give thee five-fold blazon: not too fast:
    soft, soft!
Unless the master were the man. How now!
Even so quickly may one catch the plague?
Methinks I feel this youth's perfections
With an invisible and subtle stealth
To creep in at mine eyes. Well, let it be.
What ho, Malvolio!

[RE-ENTER MALVOLIO]

MALVOLIO:

Here, madam, at your service.

OLIVIA:

Run after that same peevish messenger,
The county's man: he left this ring behind him,
Would I or not: tell him I'll none of it.
Desire him not to flatter with his lord,
Nor hold him up with hopes; I am not for him:
If that the youth will come this way to-morrow,
I'll give him reasons for't: hie thee, Malvolio.

MALVOLIO:

Madam, I will.

[EXIT]

OLIVIA:

I do I know not what, and fear to find
Mine eye too great a flatterer for my mind.
Fate, show thy force: ourselves we do not owe;
What is decreed must be, and be this so.

[EXIT]

**For the entire play,
insert the Literature CD.**

Questions

1. What do Orsino's opening speech and scene reveal about his character? How does the audience expect him to behave based on what he says and does in the first scene?
2. What does Viola decide to do in Act I, scene ii, and what would lead her to make such an unorthodox decision?
3. Do a close reading of the wordplay and punning in Act I, scene iii between Maria, Sir Toby, and Sir Andrew Aguecheek. How is comedy created in these lines?
4. What is Andrew Aguecheek's thematic importance? What is the pun in his name? Why does Shakespeare create a comic portrayal of a fallen knight?
5. When Viola (as Cesario) is sent to woo Olivia on Orsino's behalf, how does she feel about her errand? Does she have a secret agenda of her own?

6. What does Feste "fool" about with Olivia in Act I, scene v? Why does he get away with such seemingly blasphemous and offensive jokes?

7. Why does Shakespeare introduce Feste and Malvolio in the same scene? What comparison is he asking the audience to make?

8. Why does Shakespeare include so much nautical language in the wooing scene in Act I, scene v? How does this language tie into a greater theme of the play?

9. If Olivia is so staunchly uninterested in Orsino's suit, why does she send after Cesario with a ring? How does she explain away this action to Malvolio and to herself?

10. What does Sir Toby mean when he snaps at Malvolio, "Dost thou think, because thou art virtuous, there shall be no more cakes and ale?" (II.iii). Why do Maria, Sir Toby, Sir Andrew, and Toby dislike Malvolio so much?

11. How does Malvolio interpret the letter's famous line, "Some are born great, some achieve greatness, and some have greatness thrust upon 'em?" (II.v). What does the letter seem to promise for him?

12. Who are Sebastian and Antonio, and why are they important to the plot?

13. Why does Feste impersonate Sir Topas the curate to further taunt Malvolio? What is the symbolism behind his disguise?

14. Think about the alternate title of this play: *What You Will.* What does that title mean to you? Which title is more significant, appropriate, or meaningful? Why?

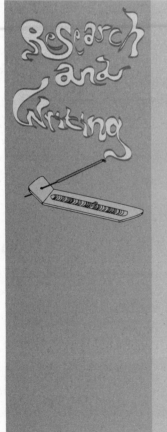

1. The cross-dressing of Viola to Cesario and the confusion between Viola and Sebastian create high comedy in the play. However, this device also points to a larger exploration of gender. What particular characteristics of masculinity and femininity does Shakespeare illuminate in the play? Who in the play is a "typical" man or woman and why? How does each gender exhibit and respond to overtures of love? Beyond comparing Viola and Cesario, you should also include an analysis of Orsino and Olivia. How do they define and explore issues of gender? Overall, how does the reader feel about love by the end of the play?

2. In what is often termed a Problem Comedy, Sir Toby, Sir Andrew and Maria play a trick on Malvolio that turns sour. By the end, even Feste is involved, and Malvolio is imprisoned against his will. When Olivia ultimately finds out the truth, she does not punish the culprits. Many readers find the ending of *Twelfth Night* unfair to Malvolio and feel uneasy at the end of the play. Why do you think Shakespeare allows the guilty characters to go unpunished? Why doesn't Malvolio get any justice? Is Shakespeare too good-natured in this play? Are the characters just innocently mischievous and nothing more? Regarding this issue, is the play's ending satisfactory to you, or does the text leave you uncomfortable?

3. Consider the character of Feste, the clown / fool in *Twelfth Night*. What is his function in the play? Is Feste a "good" fool and why? Analyze Feste's songs, and build them into your argument; what do they mean to the play at large? What do you make of his song at the play's end, "The rain it

raineth every day?" Why does Shakespeare give Feste the last word in *Twelfth Night?* For an additional challenge, compare Feste to the Fool in *King Lear.* How are the two fools alike, and how are they different? Why do they sing variations of the same song? Ultimately, who do you think is the "better" fool and why?

4. Twelfth Night, the holiday after which the play is named, is a festival that comes after Christmas, in which there is merriment, the playing of practical jokes, the performance of plays, and a general overturning of traditional social roles and behaviors. Research how this festival was observed in Renaissance England, and compare what you learn to what happens in Shakespeare's play. What similarities do you see? Where does Shakespeare follow tradition, and where does he veer from it? Does Illyria reflect Elizabethan England during the time of this festival? How and why?

5. In 1997, a musical play called *Play On!* debuted on Broadway. This musical is based on *Twelfth Night* and incorporates the music of Duke Ellington. Significant changes are made to the characters and plot; for example, the action takes place in Harlem instead of Illyria. Find a video or DVD version of *Play On!* and compare the two texts. Create an argumentative paper answering these or similar questions: Does the musical do justice to Shakespeare's play? Does Ellington's music replace Feste's effectively? Do you find the translation from one genre to the other clever or forced? For an additional challenge, compare another transition from a Shakespeare play to a musical, such as *The Taming of the Shrew* and *Kiss Me, Kate.* Overall, what is your opinion of the "musicalizing" of Shakespeare? What do you suspect Shakespeare himself would think of such projects?

Hamlet

1. A soliloquy is a monologue in which the sole character on stage speaks aloud his innermost thoughts for the benefit of the audience. Pay close attention to the soliloquies in this play—some of Shakespeare's most famous—to learn more about Hamlet's character.
2. Critics have called Hamlet "the first modern man." As you read the play, think about what attributes this character has which earn him this title.

Hamlet

William Shakespeare

CHARACTERS IN HAMLET

OSRIC
POLONIUS
MARCELLUS
OPHELIA
VOLTIMAND
YORICK
REYNALDO
ROSENCRANTZ
FORTINBRAS
FRANCISCO
CORNELIUS
BARNARDO
KING CLAUDIUS
QUEEN GERTRUDE
LAERTES
LUCIANUS
HORATIO
GUILDENSTERN
PRINCE HAMLET

ACT I

SCENE I.
ELSINORE. A PLATFORM BEFORE THE CASTLE.

[FRANCISCO AT HIS POST. ENTER TO HIM BERNARDO]

BERNARDO:
Who's there?

FRANCISCO:
Nay, answer me: stand, and unfold yourself.

BERNARDO:
Long live the king!

FRANCISCO:
Bernardo?

BERNARDO:
He.

FRANCISCO:
You come most carefully upon your hour.

BERNARDO:
'Tis now struck twelve; get thee to bed,
   Francisco.

FRANCISCO:
For this relief much thanks: 'tis bitter cold,
And I am sick at heart.

BERNARDO:
Have you had quiet guard?

FRANCISCO:
Not a mouse stirring.

BERNARDO:
Well, good night.
If you do meet Horatio and Marcellus,
The rivals of my watch, bid them make haste.

FRANCISCO:
I think I hear them. Stand, ho! Who's there?

[ENTER HORATIO AND MARCELLUS]

HORATIO:
Friends to this ground.

MARCELLUS:
And liegemen to the Dane.

FRANCISCO:
Give you good night.

MARCELLUS:
O, farewell, honest soldier:
Who hath relieved you?

FRANCISCO:
Bernardo has my place.
Give you good night.

[EXIT]

MARCELLUS:
Holla! Bernardo!

BERNARDO:
Say,
What, is Horatio there?

HORATIO:
A piece of him.

BERNARDO:
Welcome, Horatio: welcome, good Marcellus.

MARCELLUS:
What, has this thing appear'd again to-night?

BERNARDO:
I have seen nothing.

MARCELLUS:
Horatio says 'tis but our fantasy,
And will not let belief take hold of him
Touching this dreaded sight, twice seen of us:
Therefore I have entreated him along
With us to watch the minutes of this night;
That if again this apparition come,
He may approve our eyes and speak to it.

HORATIO:
Tush, tush, 'twill not appear.

BERNARDO:
Sit down awhile;
And let us once again assail your ears,
That are so fortified against our story
What we have two nights seen.

HORATIO:
Well, sit we down,
And let us hear Bernardo speak of this.

BERNARDO:
Last night of all,
When yond same star that's westward from the
   pole
Had made his course to illume that part of heaven
Where now it burns, Marcellus and myself,
The bell then beating one,—

[ENTER GHOST]

MARCELLUS:
Peace, break thee off; look, where it comes again!

BERNARDO:
In the same figure, like the king that's dead.

MARCELLUS:
Thou art a scholar; speak to it, Horatio.

BERNARDO:
Looks it not like the king? mark it, Horatio.

HORATIO:
Most like: it harrows me with fear and wonder.

BERNARDO:
It would be spoke to.

MARCELLUS:
Question it, Horatio.

HORATIO:
What art thou that usurp'st this time of night,
Together with that fair and warlike form
In which the majesty of buried Denmark
Did sometimes march? by heaven I charge thee,
   speak!

MARCELLUS:
It is offended.

BERNARDO:
See, it stalks away!

HORATIO:
Stay! speak, speak! I charge thee, speak!

[EXIT GHOST]

MARCELLUS:
'Tis gone, and will not answer.

BERNARDO:
How now, Horatio! you tremble and look pale:
Is not this something more than fantasy?
What think you on't?

HORATIO:
Before my God, I might not this believe
Without the sensible and true avouch
Of mine own eyes.

MARCELLUS:
Is it not like the king?

HORATIO:

As thou art to thyself:
Such was the very armour he had on
When he the ambitious Norway combated;
So frown'd he once, when, in an angry parle,
He smote the sledded Polacks on the ice.
'Tis strange.

MARCELLUS:

Thus twice before, and jump at this dead hour,
With martial stalk hath he gone by our watch.

HORATIO:

In what particular thought to work I know not;
But in the gross and scope of my opinion,
This bodes some strange eruption to our state.

MARCELLUS:

Good now, sit down, and tell me, he that knows,
Why this same strict and most observant watch
So nightly toils the subject of the land,
And why such daily cast of brazen cannon,
And foreign mart for implements of war;
Why such impress of shipwrights, whose sore task
Does not divide the Sunday from the week;
What might be toward, that this sweaty haste
Doth make the night joint-labourer with the day:
Who is't that can inform me?

HORATIO:

That can I;
At least, the whisper goes so. Our last king,
Whose image even but now appear'd to us,
Was, as you know, by Fortinbras of Norway,
Thereto prick'd on by a most emulate pride,
Dared to the combat; in which our valiant
    Hamlet—
For so this side of our known world esteem'd
    him—
Did slay this Fortinbras; who by a seal'd compact,
Well ratified by law and heraldry,
Did forfeit, with his life, all those his lands
Which he stood seized of, to the conqueror:
Against the which, a moiety competent
Was gaged by our king; which had return'd
To the inheritance of Fortinbras,
Had he been vanquisher; as, by the same covenant,
And carriage of the article design'd,
His fell to Hamlet. Now, sir, young Fortinbras,
Of unimproved mettle hot and full,

Hath in the skirts of Norway here and there
Shark'd up a list of lawless resolutes,
For food and diet, to some enterprise
That hath a stomach in't; which is no other—
As it doth well appear unto our state—
But to recover of us, by strong hand
And terms compulsatory, those foresaid lands
So by his father lost: and this, I take it,
Is the main motive of our preparations,
The source of this our watch and the chief head
Of this post-haste and romage in the land.

BERNARDO:

I think it be no other but e'en so:
Well may it sort that this portentous figure
Comes armed through our watch; so like the king
That was and is the question of these wars.

HORATIO:

A mote it is to trouble the mind's eye.
In the most high and palmy state of Rome,
A little ere the mightiest Julius fell,
The graves stood tenantless and the sheeted dead
Did squeak and gibber in the Roman streets:
As stars with trains of fire and dews of blood,
Disasters in the sun; and the moist star
Upon whose influence Neptune's empire stands
Was sick almost to doomsday with eclipse:
And even the like precurse of fierce events,
As harbingers preceding still the fates
And prologue to the omen coming on,
Have heaven and earth together demonstrated
Unto our climatures and countrymen.—
But soft, behold! lo, where it comes again!

[RE-ENTER GHOST]

I'll cross it, though it blast me. Stay, illusion!
If thou hast any sound, or use of voice,
Speak to me:
If there be any good thing to be done,
That may to thee do ease and grace to me,
Speak to me:

[COCK CROWS]

If thou art privy to thy country's fate,
Which, happily, foreknowing may avoid, O, speak!
Or if thou hast uphoarded in thy life

Extorted treasure in the womb of earth,
For which, they say, you spirits oft walk in death,
Speak of it: stay, and speak! Stop it, Marcellus.

MARCELLUS:
Shall I strike at it with my partisan?

HORATIO:
Do, if it will not stand.

BERNARDO:
'Tis here!

HORATIO:
'Tis here!

MARCELLUS:
'Tis gone!

[EXIT GHOST]

We do it wrong, being so majestical,
To offer it the show of violence;
For it is, as the air, invulnerable,
And our vain blows malicious mockery.

BERNARDO:
It was about to speak, when the cock crew.

HORATIO:
And then it started like a guilty thing
Upon a fearful summons. I have heard,
The cock, that is the trumpet to the morn,
Doth with his lofty and shrill-sounding throat
Awake the god of day; and, at his warning,
Whether in sea or fire, in earth or air,
The extravagant and erring spirit hies
To his confine: and of the truth herein
This present object made probation.

MARCELLUS:
It faded on the crowing of the cock.
Some say that ever 'gainst that season comes
Wherein our Saviour's birth is celebrated,
The bird of dawning singeth all night long:
And then, they say, no spirit dares stir abroad;
The nights are wholesome; then no planets strike,
No fairy takes, nor witch hath power to charm,
So hallow'd and so gracious is the time.

HORATIO:
So have I heard and do in part believe it.
But, look, the morn, in russet mantle clad,

Walks o'er the dew of yon high eastward hill:
Break we our watch up; and by my advice,
Let us impart what we have seen to-night
Unto young Hamlet; for, upon my life,
This spirit, dumb to us, will speak to him.
Do you consent we shall acquaint him with it,
As needful in our loves, fitting our duty?

MARCELLUS:
Let's do't, I pray; and I this morning know
Where we shall find him most conveniently.

[EXEUNT]

SCENE II.
A ROOM OF STATE IN THE CASTLE.

[ENTER KING CLAUDIUS, QUEEN GERTRUDE, HAMLET, POLONIUS, LAERTES, VOLTIMAND, CORNELIUS, LORDS, AND ATTENDANTS]

KING CLAUDIUS:
Though yet of Hamlet our dear brother's death
The memory be green, and that it us befitted
To bear our hearts in grief and our whole
      kingdom
To be contracted in one brow of woe,
Yet so far hath discretion fought with nature
That we with wisest sorrow think on him,
Together with remembrance of ourselves.
Therefore our sometime sister, now our queen,
The imperial jointress to this warlike state,
Have we, as 'twere with a defeated joy,—
With an auspicious and a dropping eye,
With mirth in funeral and with dirge in marriage,
In equal scale weighing delight and dole,—
Taken to wife: nor have we herein barr'd
Your better wisdoms, which have freely gone
With this affair along. For all, our thanks.
Now follows, that you know, young Fortinbras,
Holding a weak supposal of our worth,
Or thinking by our late dear brother's death
Our state to be disjoint and out of frame,
Colleagued with the dream of his advantage,
He hath not fail'd to pester us with message,
Importing the surrender of those lands
Lost by his father, with all bonds of law,

To our most valiant brother. So much for him.
Now for ourself and for this time of meeting:
Thus much the business is: we have here writ
To Norway, uncle of young Fortinbras,—
Who, impotent and bed-rid, scarcely hears
Of this his nephew's purpose,—to suppress
His further gait herein; in that the levies,
The lists and full proportions, are all made
Out of his subject: and we here dispatch
You, good Cornelius, and you, Voltimand,
For bearers of this greeting to old Norway;
Giving to you no further personal power
To business with the king, more than the scope
Of these delated articles allow.
Farewell, and let your haste commend your duty.

CORNELIUS VOLTIMAND:
In that and all things will we show our duty.

KING CLAUDIUS:
We doubt it nothing: heartily farewell.

[EXEUNT VOLTIMAND AND CORNELIUS]

And now, Laertes, what's the news with you?
You told us of some suit; what is't, Laertes?
You cannot speak of reason to the Dane,
And loose your voice: what wouldst thou beg,
    Laertes,
That shall not be my offer, not thy asking?
The head is not more native to the heart,
The hand more instrumental to the mouth,
Than is the throne of Denmark to thy father.
What wouldst thou have, Laertes?

LAERTES:
My dread lord,
Your leave and favour to return to France;
From whence though willingly I came to
    Denmark,
To show my duty in your coronation,
Yet now, I must confess, that duty done,
My thoughts and wishes bend again toward
    France
And bow them to your gracious leave and pardon.

KING CLAUDIUS:
Have you your father's leave? What says
    Polonius?

LORD POLONIUS:
He hath, my lord, wrung from me my slow leave
By laboursome petition, and at last
Upon his will I seal'd my hard consent:
I do beseech you, give him leave to go.

KING CLAUDIUS:
Take thy fair hour, Laertes; time be thine,
And thy best graces spend it at thy will!
But now, my cousin Hamlet, and my son,—

HAMLET:
[ASIDE] A little more than kin, and less than kind.

KING CLAUDIUS:
How is it that the clouds still hang on you?

HAMLET:
Not so, my lord; I am too much i' the sun.

QUEEN GERTRUDE:
Good Hamlet, cast thy nighted colour off,
And let thine eye look like a friend on Denmark.
Do not for ever with thy vailed lids
Seek for thy noble father in the dust:
Thou know'st 'tis common; all that lives must
    die,
Passing through nature to eternity.

HAMLET:
Ay, madam, it is common.

QUEEN GERTRUDE:
If it be,
Why seems it so particular with thee?

HAMLET:
Seems, madam! nay it is; I know not 'seems.'
'Tis not alone my inky cloak, good mother,
Nor customary suits of solemn black,
Nor windy suspiration of forced breath,
No, nor the fruitful river in the eye,
Nor the dejected 'havior of the visage,
Together with all forms, moods, shapes of grief,
That can denote me truly: these indeed seem,
For they are actions that a man might play:
But I have that within which passeth show;
These but the trappings and the suits of woe.

KING CLAUDIUS:
'Tis sweet and commendable in your nature,
    Hamlet,

To give these mourning duties to your father:
But, you must know, your father lost a father;
That father lost, lost his, and the survivor bound
In filial obligation for some term
To do obsequious sorrow: but to persevere
In obstinate condolement is a course
Of impious stubbornness; 'tis unmanly grief;
It shows a will most incorrect to heaven,
A heart unfortified, a mind impatient,
An understanding simple and unschool'd:
For what we know must be and is as common
As any the most vulgar thing to sense,
Why should we in our peevish opposition
Take it to heart? Fie! 'tis a fault to heaven,
A fault against the dead, a fault to nature,
To reason most absurd: whose common theme
Is death of fathers, and who still hath cried,
From the first corse till he that died to-day,
'This must be so.' We pray you, throw to earth
This unprevailing woe, and think of us
As of a father: for let the world take note,
You are the most immediate to our throne;
And with no less nobility of love
Than that which dearest father bears his son,
Do I impart toward you. For your intent
In going back to school in Wittenberg,
It is most retrograde to our desire:
And we beseech you, bend you to remain
Here, in the cheer and comfort of our eye,
Our chiefest courtier, cousin, and our son.

QUEEN GERTRUDE:

Let not thy mother lose her prayers, Hamlet:
I pray thee, stay with us; go not to Wittenberg.

HAMLET:

I shall in all my best obey you, madam.

KING CLAUDIUS:

Why, 'tis a loving and a fair reply:
Be as ourself in Denmark. Madam, come;
This gentle and unforced accord of Hamlet
Sits smiling to my heart: in grace whereof,
No jocund health that Denmark drinks to-day,
But the great cannon to the clouds shall tell,
And the king's rouse the heavens all bruit again,
Re-speaking earthly thunder. Come away.

[EXEUNT ALL BUT HAMLET]

HAMLET:

O, that this too too solid flesh would melt
Thaw and resolve itself into a dew!
Or that the Everlasting had not fix'd
His canon 'gainst self-slaughter! O God! God!
How weary, stale, flat and unprofitable,
Seem to me all the uses of this world!
Fie on't! ah fie! 'tis an unweeded garden,
That grows to seed; things rank and gross in
    nature
Possess it merely. That it should come to this!
But two months dead: nay, not so much, not two:
So excellent a king; that was, to this,
Hyperion to a satyr; so loving to my mother
That he might not beteem the winds of heaven
Visit her face too roughly. Heaven and earth!
Must I remember? why, she would hang on him,
As if increase of appetite had grown
By what it fed on: and yet, within a month—
Let me not think on't—Frailty, thy name is
    woman!—
A little month, or ere those shoes were old
With which she follow'd my poor father's body,
Like Niobe, all tears:—why she, even she—
O, God! a beast, that wants discourse of reason,
Would have mourn'd longer—married with my
    uncle,
My father's brother, but no more like my father
Than I to Hercules: within a month:
Ere yet the salt of most unrighteous tears
Had left the flushing in her galled eyes,
She married. O, most wicked speed, to post
With such dexterity to incestuous sheets!
It is not nor it cannot come to good:
But break, my heart; for I must hold my tongue.

[ENTER HORATIO, MARCELLUS, AND BERNARDO]

HORATIO:

Hail to your lordship!

HAMLET:

I am glad to see you well:
Horatio,—or I do forget myself.

HORATIO:

The same, my lord, and your poor servant ever.

HAMLET:

Sir, my good friend; I'll change that name with
you:

And what make you from Wittenberg, Horatio?
Marcellus?

MARCELLUS:

My good lord—

HAMLET:

I am very glad to see you. Good even, sir.
But what, in faith, make you from Wittenberg?

HORATIO:

A truant disposition, good my lord.

HAMLET:

I would not hear your enemy say so,
Nor shall you do mine ear that violence,
To make it truster of your own report
Against yourself: I know you are no truant.
But what is your affair in Elsinore?
We'll teach you to drink deep ere you depart.

HORATIO:

My lord, I came to see your father's funeral.

HAMLET:

I pray thee, do not mock me, fellow-student;
I think it was to see my mother's wedding.

HORATIO:

Indeed, my lord, it follow'd hard upon.

HAMLET:

Thrift, thrift, Horatio! the funeral baked meats
Did coldly furnish forth the marriage tables.
Would I had met my dearest foe in heaven
Or ever I had seen that day, Horatio!
My father!—methinks I see my father.

HORATIO:

Where, my lord?

HAMLET:

In my mind's eye, Horatio.

HORATIO:

I saw him once; he was a goodly king.

HAMLET:

He was a man, take him for all in all,
I shall not look upon his like again.

HORATIO:

My lord, I think I saw him yesternight.

HAMLET:

Saw? who?

HORATIO:

My lord, the king your father.

HAMLET:

The king my father!

HORATIO:

Season your admiration for awhile
With an attent ear, till I may deliver,
Upon the witness of these gentlemen,
This marvel to you.

HAMLET:

For God's love, let me hear.

HORATIO:

Two nights together had these gentlemen,
Marcellus and Bernardo, on their watch,
In the dead vast and middle of the night,
Been thus encounter'd. A figure like your father,
Armed at point exactly, cap-a-pe,
Appears before them, and with solemn march
Goes slow and stately by them: thrice he walk'd
By their oppress'd and fear-surprised eyes,
Within his truncheon's length; whilst they, distilled
Almost to jelly with the act of fear,
Stand dumb and speak not to him. This to me
In dreadful secrecy impart they did;
And I with them the third night kept the watch;
Where, as they had deliver'd, both in time,
Form of the thing, each word made true and good,
The apparition comes: I knew your father;
These hands are not more like.

HAMLET:

But where was this?

MARCELLUS:

My lord, upon the platform where we watch'd.

HAMLET:

Did you not speak to it?

HORATIO:

My lord, I did;
But answer made it none: yet once methought

It lifted up its head and did address
Itself to motion, like as it would speak;
But even then the morning cock crew loud,
And at the sound it shrunk in haste away,
And vanish'd from our sight.

HAMLET:
'Tis very strange.

HORATIO:
As I do live, my honour'd lord, 'tis true;
And we did think it writ down in our duty
To let you know of it.

HAMLET:
Indeed, indeed, sirs, but this troubles me.
Hold you the watch to-night?

MARCELLUS BERNARDO:
We do, my lord.

HAMLET:
Arm'd, say you?

MARCELLUS BERNARDO:
Arm'd, my lord.

HAMLET:
From top to toe?

MARCELLUS BERNARDO:
My lord, from head to foot.

HAMLET:
Then saw you not his face?

HORATIO:
O, yes, my lord; he wore his beaver up.

HAMLET:
What, look'd he frowningly?

HORATIO:
A countenance more in sorrow than in anger.

HAMLET:
Pale or red?

HORATIO:
Nay, very pale.

HAMLET:
And fix'd his eyes upon you?

HORATIO:
Most constantly.

HAMLET:
I would I had been there.

HORATIO:
It would have much amazed you.

HAMLET:
Very like, very like. Stay'd it long?

HORATIO:
While one with moderate haste might tell a
hundred.

MARCELLUS BERNARDO:
Longer, longer.

HORATIO:
Not when I saw't.

HAMLET:
His beard was grizzled—no?

HORATIO:
It was, as I have seen it in his life,
A sable silver'd.

HAMLET:
I will watch to-night;
Perchance 'twill walk again.

HORATIO:
I warrant it will.

HAMLET:
If it assume my noble father's person,
I'll speak to it, though hell itself should gape
And bid me hold my peace. I pray you all,
If you have hitherto conceal'd this sight,
Let it be tenable in your silence still;
And whatsoever else shall hap to-night,
Give it an understanding, but no tongue:
I will requite your loves. So, fare you well:
Upon the platform, 'twixt eleven and twelve,
I'll visit you.

ALL:
Our duty to your honour.

HAMLET:
Your loves, as mine to you: farewell.

[EXEUNT ALL BUT HAMLET]

My father's spirit in arms! all is not well;
I doubt some foul play: would the night were come!
Till then sit still, my soul: foul deeds will rise,
Though all the earth o'erwhelm them, to men's
    eyes.

[EXIT]

SCENE III.
A ROOM IN POLONIUS' HOUSE.

[ENTER LAERTES AND OPHELIA]

LAERTES:

My necessaries are embark'd: farewell:
And, sister, as the winds give benefit
And convoy is assistant, do not sleep,
But let me hear from you.

OPHELIA:

Do you doubt that?

LAERTES:

For Hamlet and the trifling of his favour,
Hold it a fashion and a toy in blood,
A violet in the youth of primy nature,
Forward, not permanent, sweet, not lasting,
The perfume and suppliance of a minute; No more.

OPHELIA:

No more but so?

LAERTES:

Think it no more;
For nature, crescent, does not grow alone
In thews and bulk, but, as this temple waxes,
The inward service of the mind and soul
Grows wide withal. Perhaps he loves you now,
And now no soil nor cautel doth besmirch
The virtue of his will: but you must fear,
His greatness weigh'd, his will is not his own;
For he himself is subject to his birth:
He may not, as unvalued persons do,
Carve for himself; for on his choice depends
The safety and health of this whole state;
And therefore must his choice be circumscribed
Unto the voice and yielding of that body
Whereof he is the head. Then if he says he loves
    you,
It fits your wisdom so far to believe it

As he in his particular act and place
May give his saying deed; which is no further
Than the main voice of Denmark goes withal.
Then weigh what loss your honour may sustain,
If with too credent ear you list his songs,
Or lose your heart, or your chaste treasure open
To his unmaster'd importunity.
Fear it, Ophelia, fear it, my dear sister,
And keep you in the rear of your affection,
Out of the shot and danger of desire.
The chariest maid is prodigal enough,
If she unmask her beauty to the moon:
Virtue itself 'scapes not calumnious strokes:
The canker galls the infants of the spring,
Too oft before their buttons be disclosed,
And in the morn and liquid dew of youth
Contagious blastments are most imminent.
Be wary then; best safety lies in fear:
Youth to itself rebels, though none else near.

OPHELIA:

I shall the effect of this good lesson keep,
As watchman to my heart. But, good my brother,
Do not, as some ungracious pastors do,
Show me the steep and thorny way to heaven;
Whiles, like a puff'd and reckless libertine,
Himself the primrose path of dalliance treads,
And recks not his own rede.

LAERTES:

O, fear me not.
I stay too long: but here my father comes.

[ENTER POLONIUS]

A double blessing is a double grace,
Occasion smiles upon a second leave.

LORD POLONIUS:

Yet here, Laertes! aboard, aboard, for shame!
The wind sits in the shoulder of your sail,
And you are stay'd for. There; my blessing with
    thee!
And these few precepts in thy memory
See thou character. Give thy thoughts no tongue,
Nor any unproportioned thought his act.
Be thou familiar, but by no means vulgar.
Those friends thou hast, and their adoption tried,
Grapple them to thy soul with hoops of steel;
But do not dull thy palm with entertainment

Of each new-hatch'd, unfledged comrade. Beware
Of entrance to a quarrel, but being in,
Bear't that the opposed may beware of thee.
Give every man thy ear, but few thy voice;
Take each man's censure, but reserve thy
    judgment.
Costly thy habit as thy purse can buy,
But not express'd in fancy; rich, not gaudy;
For the apparel oft proclaims the man,
And they in France of the best rank and station
Are of a most select and generous chief in that.
Neither a borrower nor a lender be;
For loan oft loses both itself and friend,
And borrowing dulls the edge of husbandry.
This above all: to thine ownself be true,
And it must follow, as the night the day,
Thou canst not then be false to any man.
Farewell: my blessing season this in thee!

LAERTES:
Most humbly do I take my leave, my lord.

LORD POLONIUS:
The time invites you; go; your servants tend.

LAERTES:
Farewell, Ophelia; and remember well
What I have said to you.

OPHELIA:
'Tis in my memory lock'd,
And you yourself shall keep the key of it.

LAERTES:
Farewell.

[EXIT]

LORD POLONIUS:
What is't, Ophelia, be hath said to you?

OPHELIA:
So please you, something touching the Lord
    Hamlet.

LORD POLONIUS:
Marry, well bethought:
'Tis told me, he hath very oft of late
Given private time to you; and you yourself
Have of your audience been most free and
    bounteous:

If it be so, as so 'tis put on me,
And that in way of caution, I must tell you,
You do not understand yourself so clearly
As it behoves my daughter and your honour.
What is between you? give me up the truth.

OPHELIA:
He hath, my lord, of late made many tenders
Of his affection to me.

LORD POLONIUS:
Affection! pooh! you speak like a green girl,
Unsifted in such perilous circumstance.
Do you believe his tenders, as you call them?

OPHELIA:
I do not know, my lord, what I should think.

LORD POLONIUS:
Marry, I'll teach you: think yourself a baby;
That you have ta'en these tenders for true pay,
Which are not sterling. Tender yourself more
    dearly;
Or—not to crack the wind of the poor phrase,
Running it thus—you'll tender me a fool.

OPHELIA:
My lord, he hath importuned me with love
In honourable fashion.

LORD POLONIUS:
Ay, fashion you may call it; go to, go to.

OPHELIA:
And hath given countenance to his speech, my
    lord,
With almost all the holy vows of heaven.

LORD POLONIUS:
Ay, springes to catch woodcocks. I do know,
When the blood burns, how prodigal the soul
Lends the tongue vows: these blazes, daughter,
Giving more light than heat, extinct in both,
Even in their promise, as it is a-making,
You must not take for fire. From this time
Be somewhat scanter of your maiden presence;
Set your entreatments at a higher rate
Than a command to parley. For Lord Hamlet,
Believe so much in him, that he is young
And with a larger tether may he walk
Than may be given you: in few, Ophelia,
Do not believe his vows; for they are brokers,

Not of that dye which their investments show,
But mere implorators of unholy suits,
Breathing like sanctified and pious bawds,
The better to beguile. This is for all:
I would not, in plain terms, from this time forth,
Have you so slander any moment leisure,
As to give words or talk with the Lord Hamlet.
Look to't, I charge you: come your ways.

OPHELIA:
I shall obey, my lord.

[EXEUNT]

SCENE IV.
THE PLATFORM.

[ENTER HAMLET, HORATIO, AND MARCELLUS]

HAMLET:
The air bites shrewdly; it is very cold.

HORATIO:
It is a nipping and an eager air.

HAMLET:
What hour now?

HORATIO:
I think it lacks of twelve.

HAMLET:
No, it is struck.

HORATIO:
Indeed? I heard it not: then it draws near the
    season
Wherein the spirit held his wont to walk.

*[A FLOURISH OF TRUMPETS, AND ORDNANCE SHOT OFF,
WITHIN]*

What does this mean, my lord?

HAMLET:
The king doth wake to-night and takes his rouse,
Keeps wassail, and the swaggering up-spring
    reels;
And, as he drains his draughts of Rhenish down,
The kettle-drum and trumpet thus bray out
The triumph of his pledge.

HORATIO:
Is it a custom?

HAMLET:
Ay, marry, is't:
But to my mind, though I am native here
And to the manner born, it is a custom
More honour'd in the breach than the observance.
This heavy-headed revel east and west
Makes us traduced and tax'd of other nations:
They clepe us drunkards, and with swinish phrase
Soil our addition; and indeed it takes
From our achievements, though perform'd at
    height,
The pith and marrow of our attribute.
So, oft it chances in particular men,
That for some vicious mole of nature in them,
As, in their birth—wherein they are not guilty,
Since nature cannot choose his origin—
By the o'ergrowth of some complexion,
Oft breaking down the pales and forts of reason,
Or by some habit that too much o'er-leavens
The form of plausive manners, that these men,
Carrying, I say, the stamp of one defect,
Being nature's livery, or fortune's star,—
Their virtues else—be they as pure as grace,
As infinite as man may undergo—
Shall in the general censure take corruption
From that particular fault: the dram of eale
Doth all the noble substance of a doubt
To his own scandal.

HORATIO:
Look, my lord, it comes!

[ENTER GHOST]

HAMLET:
Angels and ministers of grace defend us!
Be thou a spirit of health or goblin damn'd,
Bring with thee airs from heaven or blasts from
    hell,
Be thy intents wicked or charitable,
Thou comest in such a questionable shape
That I will speak to thee: I'll call thee Hamlet,
King, father, royal Dane: O, answer me!
Let me not burst in ignorance; but tell
Why thy canonized bones, hearsed in death,
Have burst their cerements; why the sepulchre,
Wherein we saw thee quietly inurn'd,

Hath oped his ponderous and marble jaws,
To cast thee up again. What may this mean,
That thou, dead corse, again in complete steel
Revisit'st thus the glimpses of the moon,
Making night hideous; and we fools of nature
So horridly to shake our disposition
With thoughts beyond the reaches of our souls?
Say, why is this? wherefore? what should we do?

[GHOST BECKONS HAMLET]

HORATIO:
It beckons you to go away with it,
As if it some impartment did desire
To you alone.

MARCELLUS:
Look, with what courteous action
It waves you to a more removed ground:
But do not go with it.

HORATIO:
No, by no means.

HAMLET:
It will not speak; then I will follow it.

HORATIO:
Do not, my lord.

HAMLET:
Why, what should be the fear?
I do not set my life in a pin's fee;
And for my soul, what can it do to that,
Being a thing immortal as itself?
It waves me forth again: I'll follow it.

HORATIO:
What if it tempt you toward the flood, my lord,
Or to the dreadful summit of the cliff
That beetles o'er his base into the sea,
And there assume some other horrible form,
Which might deprive your sovereignty of reason
And draw you into madness? think of it:
The very place puts toys of desperation,
Without more motive, into every brain
That looks so many fathoms to the sea
And hears it roar beneath.

HAMLET:
It waves me still.
Go on; I'll follow thee.

MARCELLUS:
You shall not go, my lord.

HAMLET:
Hold off your hands.

HORATIO:
Be ruled; you shall not go.

HAMLET:
My fate cries out,
And makes each petty artery in this body
As hardy as the Nemean lion's nerve.
Still am I call'd. Unhand me, gentlemen.
By heaven, I'll make a ghost of him that lets me!
I say, away! Go on; I'll follow thee.

[EXEUNT GHOST AND HAMLET]

HORATIO:
He waxes desperate with imagination.

MARCELLUS:
Let's follow; 'tis not fit thus to obey him.

HORATIO:
Have after. To what issue will this come?

MARCELLUS:
Something is rotten in the state of Denmark.

HORATIO:
Heaven will direct it.

MARCELLUS:
Nay, let's follow him.

[EXEUNT]

SCENE V.
ANOTHER PART OF THE PLATFORM.

[ENTER GHOST AND HAMLET]

HAMLET:
Where wilt thou lead me? speak; I'll go no
further.

GHOST:
Mark me.

HAMLET:
I will.

GHOST:
My hour is almost come,
When I to sulphurous and tormenting flames
Must render up myself.

HAMLET:
Alas, poor ghost!

GHOST:
Pity me not, but lend thy serious hearing
To what I shall unfold.

HAMLET:
Speak; I am bound to hear.

GHOST:
So art thou to revenge, when thou shalt hear.

HAMLET:
What?

GHOST:
I am thy father's spirit,
Doom'd for a certain term to walk the night,
And for the day confined to fast in fires,
Till the foul crimes done in my days of nature
Are burnt and purged away. But that I am forbid
To tell the secrets of my prison-house,
I could a tale unfold whose lightest word
Would harrow up thy soul, freeze thy young
    blood,
Make thy two eyes, like stars, start from their
    spheres,
Thy knotted and combined locks to part
And each particular hair to stand on end,
Like quills upon the fretful porpentine:
But this eternal blazon must not be
To ears of flesh and blood. List, list, O, list!
If thou didst ever thy dear father love—

HAMLET:
O God!

GHOST:
Revenge his foul and most unnatural murder.

HAMLET:
Murder!

GHOST:
Murder most foul, as in the best it is;
But this most foul, strange and unnatural.

HAMLET:
Haste me to know't, that I, with wings as swift
As meditation or the thoughts of love,
May sweep to my revenge.

GHOST:
I find thee apt;
And duller shouldst thou be than the fat weed
That roots itself in ease on Lethe wharf,
Wouldst thou not stir in this. Now, Hamlet, hear:
'Tis given out that, sleeping in my orchard,
A serpent stung me; so the whole ear of Denmark
Is by a forged process of my death
Rankly abused: but know, thou noble youth,
The serpent that did sting thy father's life
Now wears his crown.

HAMLET:
O my prophetic soul! My uncle!

GHOST:
Ay, that incestuous, that adulterate beast,
With witchcraft of his wit, with traitorous gifts,—
O wicked wit and gifts, that have the power
So to seduce!—won to his shameful lust
The will of my most seeming-virtuous queen:
O Hamlet, what a falling-off was there!
From me, whose love was of that dignity
That it went hand in hand even with the vow
I made to her in marriage, and to decline
Upon a wretch whose natural gifts were poor
To those of mine!
But virtue, as it never will be moved,
Though lewdness court it in a shape of heaven,
So lust, though to a radiant angel link'd,
Will sate itself in a celestial bed,
And prey on garbage.
But, soft! methinks I scent the morning air;
Brief let me be. Sleeping within my orchard,
My custom always of the afternoon,
Upon my secure hour thy uncle stole,
With juice of cursed hebenon in a vial,
And in the porches of my ears did pour
The leperous distilment; whose effect

Holds such an enmity with blood of man
That swift as quicksilver it courses through
The natural gates and alleys of the body,
And with a sudden vigour doth posset
And curd, like eager droppings into milk,
The thin and wholesome blood: so did it mine;
And a most instant tetter bark'd about,
Most lazar-like, with vile and loathsome crust,
All my smooth body.
Thus was I, sleeping, by a brother's hand
Of life, of crown, of queen, at once dispatch'd:
Cut off even in the blossoms of my sin,
Unhousel'd, disappointed, unanel'd,
No reckoning made, but sent to my account
With all my imperfections on my head:
O, horrible! O, horrible! most horrible!
If thou hast nature in thee, bear it not;
Let not the royal bed of Denmark be
A couch for luxury and damned incest.
But, howsoever thou pursuest this act,
Taint not thy mind, nor let thy soul contrive
Against thy mother aught: leave her to heaven
And to those thorns that in her bosom lodge,
To prick and sting her. Fare thee well at once!
The glow-worm shows the matin to be near,
And 'gins to pale his uneffectual fire:
Adieu, adieu! Hamlet, remember me.

[EXIT]

HAMLET:
O all you host of heaven! O earth! what else?
And shall I couple hell? O, fie! Hold, hold, my
   heart;
And you, my sinews, grow not instant old,
But bear me stiffly up. Remember thee!
Ay, thou poor ghost, while memory holds a seat
In this distracted globe. Remember thee!
Yea, from the table of my memory
I'll wipe away all trivial fond records,
All saws of books, all forms, all pressures past,
That youth and observation copied there;
And thy commandment all alone shall live
Within the book and volume of my brain,
Unmix'd with baser matter: yes, by heaven!
O most pernicious woman!
O villain, villain, smiling, damned villain!
My tables,—meet it is I set it down,

That one may smile, and smile, and be a villain;
At least I'm sure it may be so in Denmark:

[WRITING]

So, uncle, there you are. Now to my word;
It is 'Adieu, adieu! remember me.'
I have sworn 't.

MARCELLUS HORATIO:
[WITHIN] My lord, my lord,—

MARCELLUS:
[WITHIN] Lord Hamlet,—

HORATIO:
[WITHIN] Heaven secure him!

HAMLET:
So be it!

HORATIO:
[WITHIN] Hillo, ho, ho, my lord!

HAMLET:
Hillo, ho, ho, boy! come, bird, come.

[ENTER HORATIO AND MARCELLUS]

MARCELLUS:
How is't, my noble lord?

HORATIO:
What news, my lord?

HAMLET:
O, wonderful!

HORATIO:
Good my lord, tell it.

HAMLET:
No; you'll reveal it.

HORATIO:
Not I, my lord, by heaven.

MARCELLUS:
Nor I, my lord.

HAMLET:
How say you, then; would heart of man once
   think it?
But you'll be secret?

HORATIO MARCELLUS:
Ay, by heaven, my lord.

HAMLET:
There's ne'er a villain dwelling in all Denmark
But he's an arrant knave.

HORATIO:
There needs no ghost, my lord, come from the
grave
To tell us this.

HAMLET:
Why, right; you are i' the right;
And so, without more circumstance at all,
I hold it fit that we shake hands and part:
You, as your business and desire shall point you;
For every man has business and desire,
Such as it is; and for mine own poor part,
Look you, I'll go pray.

HORATIO:
These are but wild and whirling words, my lord.

HAMLET:
I'm sorry they offend you, heartily;
Yes, 'faith heartily.

HORATIO:
There's no offence, my lord.

HAMLET:
Yes, by Saint Patrick, but there is, Horatio,
And much offence too. Touching this vision here,
It is an honest ghost, that let me tell you:
For your desire to know what is between us,
O'ermaster 't as you may. And now, good friends,
As you are friends, scholars and soldiers,
Give me one poor request.

HORATIO:
What is't, my lord? we will.

HAMLET:
Never make known what you have seen to-night.

HORATIO MARCELLUS:
My lord, we will not.

HAMLET:
Nay, but swear't.

HORATIO:
In faith,
My lord, not I.

MARCELLUS:
Nor I, my lord, in faith.

HAMLET:
Upon my sword.

MARCELLUS:
We have sworn, my lord, already.

HAMLET:
Indeed, upon my sword, indeed.

GHOST:
[BENEATH] Swear.

HAMLET:
Ah, ha, boy! say'st thou so? art thou there,
truepenny?
Come on—you hear this fellow in the cellarage—
Consent to swear.

HORATIO:
Propose the oath, my lord.

HAMLET:
Never to speak of this that you have seen,
Swear by my sword.

GHOST:
[BENEATH] Swear.

HAMLET:
Hic et ubique? then we'll shift our ground.
Come hither, gentlemen,
And lay your hands again upon my sword:
Never to speak of this that you have heard,
Swear by my sword.

GHOST:
[BENEATH] Swear.

HAMLET:
Well said, old mole! canst work i' the earth so
fast?
A worthy pioner! Once more remove, good
friends.

HORATIO:
O day and night, but this is wondrous strange!

HAMLET:
And therefore as a stranger give it welcome.
There are more things in heaven and earth,
Horatio,

Than are dreamt of in your philosophy. But
  come;
Here, as before, never, so help you mercy,
How strange or odd soe'er I bear myself,
As I perchance hereafter shall think meet
To put an antic disposition on,
That you, at such times seeing me, never shall,
With arms encumber'd thus, or this headshake,
Or by pronouncing of some doubtful phrase,
As 'Well, well, we know,' or 'We could, an if we
  would,'
Or 'If we list to speak,' or 'There be, an if they
  might,'
Or such ambiguous giving out, to note
That you know aught of me: this not to do,
So grace and mercy at your most need help you,
  Swear.

GHOST:

[BENEATH] Swear.

HAMLET:

Rest, rest, perturbed spirit!

[THEY SWEAR]

So, gentlemen,
With all my love I do commend me to you:
And what so poor a man as Hamlet is
May do, to express his love and friending to you,
God willing, shall not lack. Let us go in together;
And still your fingers on your lips, I pray.
The time is out of joint: O cursed spite,
That ever I was born to set it right!
Nay, come, let's go together.

[EXEUNT]

**For the entire play,
insert the Literature CD.**

Questions

1. What important elements of setting, conflict, and character does Act I, scene i establish for the reader? What theatrical conventions does Shakespeare use to give this information to the reader or viewer?

2. In Act I, scene ii, we are introduced to almost all the protagonists of the play: Claudius, Gertrude, Hamlet, Laertes, Polonius and Ophelia. What can you tell about each of these characters from their opening lines? How does Shakespeare influence your feelings about these characters right away?

3. After his encounter with the Ghost, Hamlet solemnly swears to take revenge on Claudius. However, he loses his zeal quite quickly because of his uncertainty about the Ghost. What is his fear? What would be the repercussions of Hamlet's revenge if the Ghost is not honest?

4. The "To be, or not to be [. . .]" soliloquy is typical in that it portrays a character starting in a state of indecision, then weighing the sides of the argument and resolving the conflict at the end. What is the actual question of this speech? What does Hamlet fear most about death and suicide? What does he finally decide to do, and how do you know?

5. The "To be, or not to be [. . .]" speech is quite possibly the most famous soliloquy in all of Shakespeare, if not in all drama. What about this speech is so memorable and spellbinding to audiences, readers, and scholars? Why is it so often alluded to, discussed, and performed? What are the most intriguing images in the speech?

6. Why does Hamlet show so much interest in the Players who come to Elsinore? How does he figure he can use them to expedite his revenge? How does Hamlet direct their play, "The Murder of Gonzago?" What does he mean when he says, "The play's the thing / Wherein I'll catch the conscience of the King?"

7. Why doesn't Hamlet kill Claudius when he finds him praying? What do you learn about Claudius' prayers at the end of the scene?

8. In Act III, scene iv, why is it important that Hamlet can see the Ghost, but Gertrude cannot?

9. Pay close attention to the lyrics of Ophelia's songs in her mad scene. What do they tell the reader about her madness? Do they confirm any of the reader's suspicions about Ophelia's history or help to explain her descent into madness?

10. How is Laertes different from Hamlet in his perceived duty to revenge? Compare the two sons in terms of temperament and actions.

11. Why is Ophelia's funeral ceremony in question? What is your opinion about her drowning: accident or suicide?

12. After the carnage in the final scene, Shakespeare ends the play with the reemergence of Fortinbras. What is the significance of his name? What does his reappearance mean for the future of Denmark? Finally, what is the meaning of the last line, "Go bid the soldiers shoot"?

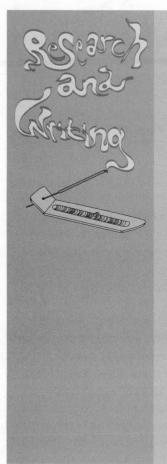

Research and Writing

1. Some readers argue that the reason Hamlet is overcome by inaction is because of his deep religious beliefs. In much of the play, fears and concerns stemming from Hamlet's piety seem to keep him from moving forward. Do a close reading of the key scenes in which this is true, and form an argument. When does Hamlet invoke God, and why? Do you believe Hamlet's religiousness, or do you argue that he uses it as a crutch or an excuse? Think about how religion affects the lives of the other characters, especially the Ghost, Claudius, and Ophelia. What overall argument about religion does Shakespeare make throughout the play?

2. Use the play-within-the-play, which Hamlet calls "The Mousetrap," to discuss the uses of theater and acting in *Hamlet* as a whole. Does Hamlet's mousetrap prove what Hamlet thinks it proves? Are there other mousetraps in the play? Why does Hamlet spend so much time discussing proper acting technique with the Players? Overall, what do you think Shakespeare wants the audience to think about the conventions and uses of theater?

3. What does *Hamlet* suggest about the connection between masculinity and violence? You might want to consider the character and actions of Old Hamlet, Claudius, Laertes, and Fortinbras as well as those of Hamlet himself. How do the female characters, Gertrude and Ophelia, tie into your argument about violence? Does the play endorse the idea of revenge? What does Shakespeare want the audience to decide about violence as a whole?

4. Much has been made about Hamlet's madness in the play, and many readers have explored whether this madness is real or feigned. What is your argument? In which scenes are you convinced, and what convinces you?

Create an argument by comparing Hamlet's "mad scenes" with Ophelia's. Whose madness seems more "true," and what makes it so? Are sanity and madness important themes in this play? Why?

5. To what extent is the comic dialogue between the two Gravediggers in Act V, scene i functional rather than just a means of providing an amusing relief in the midst of serious action? What does Hamlet learn from his conversation with the First Gravedigger? How does finding Yorick's skull affect Hamlet and why? Overall, what does Hamlet learn about death in the last two acts of the play, and why does Shakespeare include this as such an important theme?

6. In one of his stories, author Jorge Luis Borges creates a fictional conversation between William Shakespeare and God. Shakespeare says to God, "I who have been so many men in vain want to be one and myself." God's response is, "Neither am I anyone; I have dreamt your work, my Shakespeare, and among the forms in my dream are you, who like myself are many and no one." Now that you have read at least one (but probably more) of Shakespeare's plays, you have certainly pondered his enormous influence on all literature and society. Comment on Borges' imaginary dialogue between Shakespeare and God. What would prompt Borges to make this comparison? Do you agree with Borges' claim that both God and Shakespeare have universal influence? Create an argument about God's response, "Neither am I anyone," and Borges' description of both God and Shakespeare as "many and no one."

18th Century Irish and American Literature

JON ST.AMANT

Reading literature from 18th century America and Ireland means reading literature from a time of national strife and promise. For America, the 1700s is known as the time when America became a nation. After years of oppression from the English crown, the colonies chose to fight for what they believed in, to die for a nation of their own.

The literature from this period is especially fascinating, for it embodies the revolutionary mood of the era, reflecting the kind of idealistic thinking that was taking place at the time. Benjamin Franklin was a man who believed in human rights, and in his *Remarks Concerning the Savages of North America,* his contempt can be seen for the treatment of the Native Americans. It is also apparent that his message stretches far beyond the treatment of the Native Americans, for it seems applicable to many national conflicts. It is fascinating to see some of the same ideas in Jefferson's *The Declaration of Independence.* In this work, the reader is given a clear indication of, specifically, how wronged the colonists felt during the mid-to-late 1700s and how much conviction the founding fathers of this country had in attaining national independence.

Interestingly, on the other side of the Atlantic, England was also persecuting its Irish neighbor. An example of this persecution is evidenced by the astonishing number of landowners in Ireland who were not Irish. In 1750, 93 percent of the land was owned by non-Irish landowners, and by 1770 this number neared 100 percent. Greedy landowners increased their rental income by dividing and sub-dividing their land again and again until most families were attempting to subsist on less than an acre of land, paying rents that doubled the rent of their Anglo-Irish neighbors. Essentially, the country belonged to the so-called "Anglo Irish," people of English descent who lived in Ireland and, primarily, supported the established Protestant church. Jonathan Swift was an author who fit into this "Anglo Irish" category and who did not shy away from depicting Ireland's situation as one of dire starvation and stagnation. He saw England's rule over this island as cruel and unusual. In *A Modest Proposal,* Swift spotlights the ill treatment to which the Irish were subjected because of British rule, arguing that perhaps the ideal British plot is to have the poor Catholics of Ireland suffer as the ruling Protestants flourish. Swift saw this stranglehold as an atrocity of Brobdingnagian proportions, and he was determined to do anything he could, rhetorically, to help people see the plight of the Irish.

Jonathan Swift (1667–1745)

Jonathan Swift was born in Dublin, Ireland. The son of Protestant Anglo-Irish parents, Swift's father died three months before he was born, and Swift's mother left him shortly after his birth. In the care of relatives, Swift began his schooling, eventually graduating from Trinity College in Dublin, and later receiving a Master's Degree from Oxford University in England. After being diagnosed with Meniere's Disease (a disturbance of the inner ear which produces nausea and vertigo), however, Swift returned to Ireland where, five years later in 1695, he was ordained as a priest in the Church of Ireland. During this time, Swift authored various publications. Among the most well-known are his *Bickenstaff Papers* (consisting of satirical attacks upon an astrologer named John Partridge) and *Gulliver's Travels* (a humorous and sometimes abrasive examination of 18th century England and human beings in general). However, *A Modest Proposal,* an essay written in protest against the terrible poverty in which the Irish were forced to live while under British rule, is acknowledged by many critics as the most powerful example of irony in the English language.

A Modest Proposal

1. When Swift wrote this piece, Ireland was enduring one of its worst periods of famine and poverty. The Irish believed that England's power was the cause of these troubled times. In order to better understand this reading, it might be useful to research the relationship between these two countries and how it developed over the years.

A Modest Proposal

Jonathan Swift

It is a melancholy object to those who walk through this great town or travel in the country, when they see the streets, the roads, and cabin doors, crowded with beggars of the female sex, followed by three, four, or six children, all in rags and importuning every passenger for an alms. These mothers, instead of being able to work for their honest livelihood, are forced to employ all their time in strolling to beg sustenance for their helpless infants: who as they grow up either turn thieves for want of work, or leave their dear native country to fight for the Pretender in Spain, or sell themselves to the Barbadoes.

I think it is agreed by all parties that this prodigious number of children in the arms, or on the backs, or at the heels of their mothers, and frequently of their fathers, is in the present deplorable state of the kingdom a very great additional grievance; and, therefore, whoever could find out a fair, cheap, and easy method of making these children sound, useful members of the commonwealth, would deserve so well of the public as to have his statue set up for a preserver of the nation.

But my intention is very far from being confined to provide only for the children of professed beggars;

it is of a much greater extent, and shall take in the whole number of infants at a certain age who are born of parents in effect as little able to support them as those who demand our charity in the streets.

As to my own part, having turned my thoughts for many years upon this important subject, and maturely weighed the several schemes of other projectors, I have always found them grossly mistaken in the computation. It is true, a child just dropped from its dam may be supported by her milk for a solar year, with little other nourishment; at most not above the value of 2s, which the mother may certainly get, or the value in scraps, by her lawful occupation of begging; and it is exactly at one year old that I propose to provide for them in such a manner as instead of being a charge upon their parents or the parish, or wanting food and raiment for the rest of their lives, they shall on the contrary contribute to the feeding, and partly to the clothing, of many thousands.

There is likewise another great advantage in my scheme, that it will prevent those voluntary abortions, and that horrid practice of women murdering their bastard children, alas! too frequent among us! sacrificing the poor innocent babes I doubt more to avoid the expense than the shame, which would move tears and pity in the most savage and inhuman breast.

The number of souls in this kingdom being usually reckoned one million and a half, of these I calculate there may be about two hundred thousand couples whose wives are breeders; from which number I subtract thirty thousand couples who are able to maintain their own children, although I apprehend there cannot be so many, under the present distresses of the kingdom; but this being granted, there will remain an hundred and seventy thousand breeders. I again subtract fifty thousand for those women who miscarry, or whose children die by accident or disease within the year. There only remains one hundred and twenty thousand children of poor parents annually born. The question therefore is, how this number shall be reared and provided for, which, as I have already said, under the present situation of affairs, is utterly impossible by all the methods hitherto proposed. For we can neither employ them in handicraft or agriculture; we neither build houses (I mean in the country) nor cultivate land: they can very seldom pick up a livelihood by stealing, till they arrive at six years old, except where they are of towardly parts, although I confess they learn the rudiments much earlier, during which time, they can however be properly looked upon only as probationers, as I have been informed by a principal gentleman in the county of Cavan, who protested to me that he never knew above one or two instances under the age of six, even in a part of the kingdom so renowned for the quickest proficiency in that art.

I am assured by our merchants, that a boy or a girl before twelve years old is no salable commodity; and even when they come to this age they will not yield above three pounds, or three pounds and half-a-crown at most on the exchange; which cannot turn to account either to the parents or kingdom, the charge of nutriment and rags having been at least four times that value.

I shall now therefore humbly propose my own thoughts, which I hope will not be liable to the least objection.

I have been assured by a very knowing American of my acquaintance in London, that a young healthy child well nursed is at a year old a most delicious, nourishing, and wholesome food, whether stewed, roasted, baked, or boiled; and I make no doubt that it will equally serve in a fricassee or a ragout.

I do therefore humbly offer it to public consideration that of the hundred and twenty thousand children already computed, twenty thousand may be reserved for breed, whereof only one-fourth part to be males; which is more than we allow to sheep, black cattle or swine; and my reason is, that these children are seldom the fruits of marriage, a circumstance not much regarded by our savages, therefore one male will be sufficient to serve four females. That the remaining hundred thousand may, at a year old, be offered in the sale to the persons of quality and fortune through the kingdom; always advising the mother to let them suck plentifully in the last month, so as to render them plump and fat for a good table. A child will make two dishes at an entertainment for friends; and when the family dines alone, the fore or hind quarter will make a reasonable dish, and seasoned with a little pepper or salt will be very good boiled on the fourth day, especially in winter.

I have reckoned upon a medium that a child just born will weigh 12 pounds, and in a solar year, if tolerably nursed, increaseth to 28 pounds.

I grant this food will be somewhat dear, and therefore very proper for landlords, who, as they have already devoured most of the parents, seem to have the best title to the children.

Infant's flesh will be in season throughout the year, but more plentiful in March, and a little before and after; for we are told by a grave author, an eminent French physician, that fish being a prolific diet, there are more children born in Roman Catholic countries about nine months after Lent than at any other season; therefore, reckoning a year after Lent, the markets will be more glutted than usual, because the number of popish infants is at least three to one in this kingdom: and therefore it will have one other collateral advantage, by lessening the number of papists among us.

I have already computed the charge of nursing a beggar's child (in which list I reckon all cottagers, laborers, and four-fifths of the farmers) to be about two shillings per annum, rags included; and I believe no gentleman would repine to give ten shillings for the carcass of a good fat child, which, as I have said, will make four dishes of excellent nutritive meat, when he hath only some particular friend or his own family to dine with him. Thus the squire will learn to be a good landlord, and grow popular among his tenants; the mother will have eight shillings net profit, and be fit for work till she produces another child.

Those who are more thrifty (as I must confess the times require) may flay the carcass; the skin of which artificially dressed will make admirable gloves for ladies, and summer boots for fine gentlemen.

As to our city of Dublin, shambles may be appointed for this purpose in the most convenient parts of it, and butchers we may be assured will not be wanting; although I rather recommend buying the children alive, and dressing them hot from the knife, as we do roasting pigs.

A very worthy person, a true lover of his country, and whose virtues I highly esteem, was lately pleased in discoursing on this matter to offer a refinement upon my scheme. He said that many gentlemen of this kingdom, having of late destroyed their deer, he conceived that the want of venison might be well supplied by the bodies of young lads and maidens, not exceeding fourteen years of age nor under twelve; so great a number of both sexes in every country being now ready to starve for want of work and service; and these to be disposed of by their parents, if alive, or otherwise by their nearest relations. But with due deference to so excellent a friend and so deserving a patriot, I cannot be altogether in his sentiments; for as to the males, my American acquaintance assured me, from frequent experience, that their flesh was generally tough and lean, like that of our schoolboys by continual exercise, and their taste disagreeable; and to fatten them would not answer the charge. Then as to the females, it would, I think, with humble submission be a loss to the public, because they soon would become breeders themselves; and besides, it is not improbable that some scrupulous people might be apt to censure such a practice (although indeed very unjustly), as a little bordering upon cruelty; which, I confess, hath always been with me the strongest objection against any project, however so well intended.

But in order to justify my friend, he confessed that this expedient was put into his head by the famous Psalmanazar, a native of the island Formosa, who came from thence to London above twenty years ago, and in conversation told my friend, that in his country when any young person happened to be put to death, the executioner sold the carcass to persons of quality as a prime dainty; and that in his time the body of a plump girl of fifteen, who was crucified for an attempt to poison the emperor, was sold to his imperial majesty's prime minister of state, and other great mandarins of the court, in joints from the gibbet, at four hundred crowns. Neither indeed can I deny, that if the same use were made of several plump young girls in this town, who without one single groat to their fortunes cannot stir abroad without a chair, and appear at playhouse and assemblies in foreign fineries which they never will pay for, the kingdom would not be the worse.

Some persons of a desponding spirit are in great concern about that vast number of poor people, who are aged, diseased, or maimed, and I have been desired to employ my thoughts what course may be taken to ease the nation of so grievous an encumbrance. But I am not in the least pain upon that matter, because it is very well known that they are every day dying and rotting by cold and famine, and filth and vermin, as fast as can be reasonably expected. And as to the young laborers, they are now in as hopeful a condition; they cannot get work, and consequently pine away for want of nourishment, to a degree that if at any time they are accidentally hired to common labor, they have not strength to perform it; and thus the country and themselves are happily delivered from the evils to come.

I have too long digressed, and therefore shall return to my subject. I think the advantages by the proposal which I have made are obvious and many, as well as of the highest importance.

For first, as I have already observed, it would greatly lessen the number of papists, with whom we are yearly overrun, being the principal breeders of the nation as well as our most dangerous enemies; and who stay at home on purpose with a design to deliver the kingdom to the Pretender, hoping to take their advantage by the absence of so many good protestants, who have chosen rather to leave their country than stay at home and pay tithes against their conscience to an episcopal curate.

Secondly, the poorer tenants will have something valuable of their own, which by law may be made liable to distress and help to pay their land-lord's rent, their corn and cattle being already seized, and money a thing unknown.

Thirdly, Whereas the maintenance of an hundred thousand children, from two years old and upward, cannot be computed at less than ten shillings a-piece per annum, the nation's stock will be thereby increased fifty thousand pounds per annum, beside the profit of a new dish introduced to the tables of all gentlemen of fortune in the kingdom who have any refinement in taste. And the money will circulate among ourselves, the goods being entirely of our own growth and manufacture.

Fourthly, The constant breeders, beside the gain of eight shillings sterling per annum by the sale of their children, will be rid of the charge of maintaining them after the first year.

Fifthly, This food would likewise bring great custom to taverns; where the vintners will certainly be so prudent as to procure the best receipts for dressing it to perfection, and consequently have their houses frequented by all the fine gentlemen, who justly value themselves upon their knowledge in good eating: and a skilful cook, who understands how to oblige his guests, will contrive to make it as expensive as they please.

Sixthly, This would be a great inducement to marriage, which all wise nations have either encouraged by rewards or enforced by laws and penalties. It would increase the care and tenderness of mothers toward their children, when they were sure of a settlement for life to the poor babes, provided in some sort by the public, to their annual profit instead of expense. We should see an honest emulation among the married women, which of them could bring the fattest child to the market. Men would become as fond of their wives during the time of their pregnancy as they are now of their mares in foal, their cows in calf, their sows when they are ready to farrow; nor offer to beat or kick them (as is too frequent a practice) for fear of a miscarriage.

Many other advantages might be enumerated. For instance, the addition of some thousand carcasses in our exportation of barreled beef, the propagation of swine's flesh, and improvement in the art of making good bacon, so much wanted among us by the great destruction of pigs, too frequent at our tables; which are no way comparable in taste or magnificence to a well-grown, fat, yearling child, which roasted whole will make a considerable figure at a lord mayor's feast or any other public entertainment. But this and many others I omit, being studious of brevity.

After all, I am not so violently bent upon my own opinion as to reject any offer proposed by wise men, which shall be found equally innocent, cheap, easy, and effectual. But before something of that kind shall be advanced in contradiction to my scheme, and offering a better, I desire the author or authors will be pleased maturely to consider two points. First, as things now stand, how they will be able to find food and raiment for an hundred thousand useless mouths and backs. And secondly, there being a round million of creatures in human figure throughout this kingdom, whose whole subsistence put into a common stock would leave them in debt two millions of pounds sterling, adding those who are beggars by profession to the bulk of farmers, cottagers, and laborers, with their wives and children who are beggars in effect: I desire those politicians who dislike my overture, and may perhaps be so bold as to attempt an answer, that they will first ask the parents of these mortals, whether they would not at this day think it a great happiness to have been sold for food, at a year old in the manner I prescribe, and thereby have avoided such a perpetual scene of misfortunes as they have since gone through by the oppression of landlords, the impossibility of paying rent without money or trade, the want of common sustenance, with neither house nor clothes to cover them from the inclemencies of the weather, and the most inevitable prospect of entailing the like or greater miseries upon their breed forever.

I profess, in the sincerity of my heart, that I have not the least personal interest in endeavoring to promote this necessary work, having no other motive than the public good of my country, by advancing our trade, providing for infants, relieving the poor, and giving some pleasure to the rich. I have no children by which I can propose to get a single penny; the youngest being nine years old, and my wife past child-bearing.

Questions

1. Swift suggests that after a certain amount of time, a mother can give her child away to help support what cause? Why might Swift suggest this?
2. What role does religion play in this essay? Swift makes it clear that religion is an integral part of the problem. In what way does one's religion affect their place in society?
3. How are the Irish portrayed throughout this work, and why might it be important for Swift to portray them this way?
4. How might England have received this satire? What might make the satire a more provocative rhetorical mode in comparison to the traditionally-written argument?
5. What is the "one other collateral advantage" this proposal will have? What does this reveal to the reader about the Irish people's situation?
6. To whom does Swift talk about his proposal? What is the significance of these tavern-dwelling folk?
7. What could have been some of Swift's motivations for writing such a piece?
8. Is there something heroic about writing a piece of this nature? How might Swift be viewed by Irish historians?

1. Construct an argument that examines some of Swift's suggestions, and examine whether or not this work is so grotesque that it compromises the integrity of his argument.
2. Examine the satirical works of Juvenal and Horace. Then, juxtapose them with Swift's *A Modest Proposal*. After doing so, construct an argument that examines which writer is most effective at advancing his argument through the use of satire, and support your claim by citing the satires and outside sources.
3. The relationship between England and Ireland has been well documented. It is rarely considered amicable, and most historians consider England a long-time oppressor of Ireland. After studying the history of this cultural conflict, investigate its genesis and why these two countries have constantly been at odds with each other. Construct an argument that examines the relationship between these two countries and whether Swift's *A Modest Proposal* accurately addressed this relationship.

Benjamin Franklin (1706-1790)

When thinking of America and its earliest years as a nation, it is hard not to think of one of its greatest architects. Benjamin Franklin is considered one of the most influential figures in American history. He was born in Boston on January 17, 1706, and while his father (Josiah) had intended for him to enter the clergy, Benjamin was in love with the written word. He worked for his brother's newspaper, *The New England Courant,* when he was fifteen, but his brother (James) would not let him write for the paper, so Franklin would sneak letters underneath the door of the print shop at night under the following name: "Silence Dogood." After James was thrown in jail for his anti-clergy rhetoric, Franklin ran the paper. Unfortunately, James was ungrateful for Franklin's assistance, and this ungratefulness caused Franklin to run away from home.

Franklin found his way to the city of Philadelphia. In 1723, while in Philadelphia, Franklin worked as a printer's apprentice, and in 1724, he had earned enough money to leave for London to learn about the newest fonts and printing equipment in the newspaper business. When Franklin returned to the colonies in 1726, he went back to work as a printer's apprentice. He married Deborah Read in 1730, and after years of diligent work, he bought a newspaper called the *Pennsylvania Gazette.* This newspaper eventually became one of the most successful colonial publications of its time.

Until his retirement from the printing profession in 1748, Franklin dedicated his life to writing about the importance of public services. For example, in 1736, he founded the Philadelphia Union Fire Company, and it was this organization that insured individuals who had lost everything because of fire. By 1749, Franklin's interest had eagerly turned to science as he invented things such as the "Franklin Stove," swim fins, and bifocals. To solidify his reputation as a man *for the people,* he did not take out patents on any of these inventions. Among his inventions and experiments was one that brought Franklin international fame. In this experiment, he used a kite to harness electricity, which eventually contributed to the application of electricity to help power what is now a globally-electric infrastructure.

The final phase of Franklin's life was replete with political success and controversy. In 1757, he went to England as a delegate of the Pennsylvania Legislature. He was considered a loyal Englishman, but in 1765, he noticed how incensed America was with the Stamp Act, and in 1775, he was recalled to the colonies and named to the second Continental Congress. He signed *The Decleration of Independence* in 1776 and was on hand for the signing of the Treaty of Paris (the document that ended the Revolutionary War). Perhaps the crowning moment of Franklin's life was in 1787 when he and many of America's founders signed the Constitution of the United States of America. Franklin died on April 17, 1790, and over 20,000 people attended his funeral.

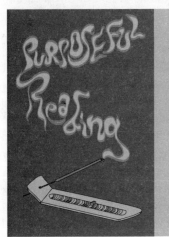

Remarks Concerning the Savages of North America

1. When this was written, Benjamin Franklin was dealing with an American government that considered Native Americans the equivalent of a modern-day terrorist organization.
2. Franklin was a firm believer in a human being's right to live life to its fullest. Note how this belief is advanced throughout his essay.

Remarks Concerning the Savages of North America

Benjamin Franklin

Savages we call them, because their manners differ from ours, which we think the perfection of civility; they think the same of theirs.

Perhaps, if we could examine the manners of different nations with impartiality, we should find no people so rude, as to be without any rules of politeness; nor any so polite, as not to have some remains of rudeness.

The Indian men, when young, are hunters and warriors; when old, counselors; for all their government is by counsel of the sages; there is no force, there are no prisons, no officers to compel obedience, or inflict punishment. Hence they generally study oratory, the best speaker having the most influence. The Indian women till the ground, dress the food, nurse and bring up the children, and preserve and hand down to posterity the memory of public transactions. These employments of men and women are accounted natural and honorable. Having few artificial wants, they have abundance of leisure for improvement by conversation. Our laborious manner of life, compared with theirs, they esteem slavish and base; and the learning, on which we value ourselves, they regard as frivolous and useless. An instance of this occurred at the Treaty of Lancaster, in Pennsylvania, anno 1744, between the government of Virginia and the Six Nations. After the principal business was settled, the commissioners from Virginia acquainted the Indians by a speech, that there was at Williamsburg a college, with a fund for educating Indian youth; and that, if the Six Nations would send down half dozen of their young lads to that college, the government would take care that they should be well provided for, and instructed in all the learning of the white people. It is one of the Indian rules of politeness not to answer a public proposition the same day that it is made; they think it would be treating it as a light matter, and that they show it respect by taking time to consider it, as of a matter important.

They therefore deferred their answer till the day following; when their speaker began, by expressing their deep sense of the kindness of the Virginia government, in making them that offer; "for we know," says he, "that you highly esteem the kind of learning taught in those Colleges, and that the maintenance of our young men, while with you, would be very expensive to you. We are convinced, therefore, that you mean to do us good by your proposal; and we thank you heartily. But who are wise, must know that different nations have different conceptions of things; and you will therefore not take it amiss, if our ideas of this kind of education happen not to be the same with yours. We have had some experience of it; several of our young people were formerly brought up at the colleges of the northern provinces; they were instructed in all your sciences; but, when they came back to us, they were bad runners, ignorant of every means of living in the woods, unable to bear either cold or hunger, knew neither how to build a cabin, take a deer, or kill an enemy, spoke our language imperfectly, were therefore neither fit for hunters, warriors, nor counselors; they were totally good for nothing. We are however not the less obliged by your kind offer, though we decline accepting it; and, to show our grateful sense of it, if the gentlemen of Virginia will send us a dozen of their sons, we will take great care of their education, instruct them in all we know, and make men of them."

Having frequent occasions to hold public councils, they have acquired great order and decency in conducting them. The old men sit in the foremost ranks, that warriors in the next, and the women and children in the hindmost. The business of the women is to take exact notice of what passes, imprint it in their memories (for they have no writing), and communicate it to their children. They are the records of the council, and they preserve traditions of the stipulations in treaties 100 years back; which, when we compare with our writings, we always find exact. He that would speak, rises. The rest observe a profound silence. When he has finished and sits down, they leave him 5 or 6 minutes to recollect, that, if he has omitted anything he intended to say, or has anything to add, he may rise again and deliver it. To interrupt another, even in common conversation, is reckoned highly indecent. How different this from the conduct of a polite British House of Commons, where scarce a day passes without some confusion, that makes the speaker hoarse in calling to order; and how different from the mode of conversation in many polite companies of Europe, where, if you do not deliver your sentence with great rapidity, you are cut off in the middle of it by the impatient loquacity of those you converse with, and never suffered to finish it.

The politeness of these savages in conversation is indeed carried to excess, since it does not permit them to contradict or deny the truth of what is asserted in their presence. By this means they indeed avoid disputes; but then it becomes difficult to know their minds, or what impression you make upon them. The missionaries who have attempted to convert them to Christianity all complain of this as one of the great difficulties of their mission. The Indians hear with patience the truths of the Gospel explained to them, and give their usual tokens of assent and approbation; you would think they were convinced. No such matter. It is mere civility.

A Swedish minister, having assembled the chiefs of the Susquehanah Indians, made a sermon to them, acquainting them with the principal historical facts on which our religion is founded; such as the fall of our first parents by eating an apple, the coming of Christ to repair the mischief, His miracles and suffering, etc. When he had finished, an Indian orator stood up to thank him. "What you have told us," he says, "is all very good. It is indeed bad to eat apples. It is better to make them all into cider. We are much obliged by your kindness in coming so far, to tell us these things which you have heard from your mothers. In return, I will tell you some of those we have heard from ours. In the beginning, our fathers had only the flesh of animals to subsist on; and if their hunting was unsuccessful, they were starving. Two of our young hunters, having killed a deer, made a fire in the woods to broil some part of it. When they were about to satisfy their hunger, they beheld a beautiful young woman descend from the clouds, seat herself on that hill, which you see yonder among the blue mountains. They said to each other, it is a spirit that has smelled our broiling venison and wishes to eat of it; let us offer some to her. They presented her with the tongue; she was pleased with the taste of it, and said 'Your kindness shall be rewarded; come to this place after thirteen moons, and you shall find something that will be of great benefit in nourishing you and your children to the latest generations.' They did so, and, to their sur-

prise, found plants they had never seen before; but which, from that ancient time, have constantly cultivated among us, to our great advantage. Where her right hand had touched the ground, they found maize; where her left hand had touched it, they found kidney-beans; and where her backside had sat on it, they found tobacco." The good missionary, disgusted with this idle tale, said, "What I delivered to you were sacred truths; but what you tell me is mere fable, fiction, and falsehood." The Indian, offended, replied "My brother, it seems your friends have not done you justice in your education; they have not well instructed you in the rules of common civility. You saw that we who understand and practice those rules, believed all your stories; you refuse to believe ours?"

When any of them come into our towns, our people are apt to crowd round them, gaze upon them, and incommode them, where they desire to be private; this they esteem great rudeness, and the effect of the want of instruction in the rules of civility and good manners. "We have," say they, "as much curiosity as you, and when you come into our towns, we wish for opportunities of looking at you, but for this purpose we hide ourselves behind bushes, where you are to pass, and never intrude ourselves into company."

Their manner of entering one another's village has likewise its rules. It is reckoned uncivil in traveling strangers to enter a village abruptly, without giving notice of their approach. Therefore, as soon as they arrive within hearing, they stop and hollow, remaining there till invited to enter. Two old men usually come out to them, and lead them in. There is in every village a vacant dwelling, called the stranger's house. Here they are placed, while the old men go round from hut to hut, acquainting the inhabitants, that strangers are arrived, who are probably hungry and weary; and every one sends them what he can spare of victuals, and skins to repose on. When the strangers are refreshed, pipes and tobacco are brought; and then, but not before, conversation begins, with inquiries who they are, whither bound, what news, etc.; and it usually ends with offers of service, if the strangers have occasion of guides, or any necessaries for continuing their journey; and nothing is exacted for the entertainment.

The same hospitality, esteemed among them as a principal virtue, is practiced by private persons; of which Conrad Weiser, our interpreter, gave the following instances. He had been naturalized among the Six Nations, and spoke well the Mohawk language. In going through the Indian country, to carry a meigage from our Governor to the Council at Onondaga, he called at the habitation of Canassatego, an old acquaintance, who embraced him, spread furs for him to sit on, placed before him some boiled beans and venison, and mixed some rum and water for his drink. When he was well refreshed, and had lit his pipe, Canassatego began to converse with him; asked how he had fared the many years since they had seen each other; whence he then came; what occasioned the journey, etc. Conrad answered all his questions; and when the discourse began to flag, the Indian, to continue it, said, "Conrad, you have lived long among the white people, and know something of their customs; I have been sometimes at Albany, and have observed, that once in seven days they shut up their shops, and assemble all in the great house; tell me what it is for? What do they do there?" "They meet there," says Conrad, "to hear and learn good things." "I do not doubt," says the Indian, "that they tell you so; they have told me the same; but I doubt the truth of what they say, and I will tell you my reasons. I went lately to Albany to sell my skins and buy blankets, knives, powder, rum, etc. You know I used generally to deal with Hans Hanson; but I was a little inclined this time to try some other merchant. However, I called first upon Hans, and asked him what he would give for beaver. He said he could not give any more than four shillings a pound; 'but,' says he , 'I cannot talk on business now; this is the day when we meet together to learn good things, and I am going to the meeting.' So I thought to myself, 'Since we cannot do any business today, I may as well go to the meeting too,' and I went with him. There stood up a man in black, and began to talk to the people very angrily. I did not understand what he said; but, perceiving that he looked much at me and at Hanson, I imagined he was angry at seeing me there; so I went out, sat down near the house, struck fire, and lit my pipe, waiting till the meeting should break up. I thought too, that the man had mentioned something of beaver, and I suspected it might be the subject of their meeting. So, when they came out, I accosted my merchant. 'Well, Hans,' says I, 'I hope you have agreed to give more than four shillings a pound.' 'No,' says he, 'I cannot give so much; I cannot give more than three shillings and sixpence.' I then spoke to several other dealers, but they all sung the same song,—three and sixpence,—three and sixpence. This made it clear to me, that my suspicion was right; and, that whatever they pretended of meeting to learn good things, the real purpose was to consult how to cheat Indians in the price of beaver. Consider but a little Conrad, and you must be of my opinion. If they met so often to learn good things, they would certainly have learned some before this time. But they are still ignorant. You know our practice. If a white man, in traveling through our country, enters one of our cabins, we all treat him as I treat you; we dry him if he is wet, we warm him if he is cold, we give him meat and drink, that he may allay his thirst and hunger; and we spread soft furs for him to rest and sleep on; we demand nothing in return. But; if I go into a white man's house at Albany and ask for victuals and drink, they say, 'Where is your money?' and if I have none they say, 'Get out, you Indian dog.' You see they have not yet learned those little good things, that we need no meetings to be instructed in, because our Mothers taught them to us when we were children; and therefore it is impossible their meetings should be, as they say, for any such purpose, or have any such effect; they are only to contrive the cheating of Indians in the price of beaver."

Questions

1. What is the treaty of Lancaster, and why is it relevant to this essay?
2. After experiencing the "white man college," what stories do the Native Americans come back to the tribe with? What do these stories suggest about the white man's attitude toward the Native American culture?
3. According to Franklin, in what way is the Native American governmental structure similar to the British Parliament? Why might Franklin make this connection?

Continued

4. Franklin mentions that the missionaries have a particular problem with the Native Americans. What is this problem, and what might this suggest about these missionaries?
5. What story do the Native Americans tell that rivals the biblical tale of Adam and Eve?
6. What does Franklin write about the treatment an individual receives upon entering a tribal area of the Native Americans? How does Franklin use this story to suggest something about the treatment a Native American receives when entering the land of a white man?
7. Why might Franklin re-tell the story of Conrad Weiser's visit to a nearby Native American tribe?
8. In the essay, what did the Native American think the Sunday meetings were for? What might this suggest about their culture?

Research and Writing

1. Franklin tells the story of a Swedish missionary explaining the story of Adam and Eve to a group of Native Americans. After the story, the Native Americans are accepting of the tale, and they decide to tell one of their own. The minister's reaction is a sign of the white man's arrogance and the Native Americans' sense of religious pluralism. Construct an argument that examines religious pluralism and arrogance within the context of the 18th century white man and Native American.
2. Throughout this work, Franklin has a central message. Construct an argument that examines this message, and support it with quotations from Franklin's essay and outside sources that are specific to 18th century U.S. history.
3. It is difficult to read any piece about the Native Americans and not think of Andrew Jackson. Investigate Jackson's role regarding this culture, and then construct an argument that examines whether these people deserved the treatment they received from the Jackson administration.

Thomas Jefferson (1743–1826)

Thomas Jefferson was born on April 13, 1743 in Albemarle County, VA. He was the son of Peter Jefferson, a well-to-do landowner. However, the Jefferson family was not wealthy but, instead, hard working and very proud to be from Virginia. Jefferson's childhood was filled with a constant emphasis on working hard and doing his share on the family's farm. After attending the College of William and Mary, where he studied law from 1760–1762, Jefferson established his reputation as a public servant and eventually was elected to the Virginia House of Burgesses in 1769. In 1772, he married Martha Walyles Skelton, and the two had six children (two of the children survived into adulthood). In 1774, Jefferson's reputation began to grow after he wrote a pamphlet that served as a stepping stone to America's independence. The thesis of the text was based on the idea that colonial allegiance to the King of England was voluntary. The ideology that God was the only being who had dominion over man was a key component to Jefferson's argument; this argument resonated with many of the colonies. Similarly controversial was his inheritance of 11,000 acres of land and 135 slaves from his father-in-law. This, in itself, was not controversial. The controversy lay in Jefferson speaking out against the ownership of slaves, even though he was a slave owner.

On June 11, 1776, Jefferson was appointed to head a committee of five that would prepare *The Declaration of Independence*. Although there are traces of Benjamin Franklin and John Adams in this historical document, Jefferson drafted much of the language himself, and a majority of the rhetoric is based on the central idea that humans are endowed with certain inalienable rights. *The Declaration of Independence* made Jefferson internationally famous and helped shape what would later be known as the United States of America.

During the Revolutionary War, Jefferson fought for the rights of Virginians, particularly the Planter class. He helped liberate the state from any national ties that might have crippled it economically or ideologically. Probably the most controversial topic that flung Jefferson into the mix of public opinion was his bill on religious liberty. It caused a great deal of turmoil in Virginia for eight years and introduced an idea that was unheard of during his time: complete religious liberty. The bill stated "that all men shall be free to profess, and by argument to maintain, their opinions on matters of religion, and that the same shall in no way diminish, enlarge, or affect their civil capacities." This language was seen as an attack on Christianity, and it was feared that this bill would open the door to religious pluralism, something the devout Christian groups did not condone. The bill did not pass until 1786, mainly through the perseverance of James Madison. After a truculent governership of Virginia in the years 1779–1781, Jefferson retired from public service and felt quite bitter about its rewards.

Jefferson lost his wife in 1782 but returned to public service in 1783 as a congressman of Virginia. While in congress, he submitted "Notes on the Establishment of a Money Unit and of a Coinage for the United States." This document lead to the conversion of the British pound to the U.S. dollar. And although Jefferson was a slave owner, he believed that slavery was evil, and in 1784, he proposed that it be banned in the newly acquired western territories.

From 1784–1789, Jefferson served as a commissioner in Paris; he went there to help negotiate trade agreements between the two countries. When he returned to the United States in 1789, Jefferson learned that he had been chosen to serve as Secretary of State during the first presidency of George Washington. During this time, Jefferson constantly warned of emerging Federalist Party ideas to implant monarchical ideals and institutions in the government. One of his greatest adversaries was Secretary of Treasury, Alexander Hamilton. Jefferson and Hamilton were constantly at odds over governmentally-related issues such as foreign affairs and the economic structure of the country. After a feeling of strong alienation within Washington's cabinet, Jefferson retired on December 31, 1793. Nevertheless, after devoting himself to his farm and his family for three years, Jefferson got back into politics in 1796 when he ran for President against Federalist candidate, John Adams. As the runner up, however, Jefferson became Vice President under the system in effect. His political partnership with Adams was tumultuous, and it was this relationship that drove Jefferson to run for president again.

In 1801, Jefferson ran for President, and after a tie in electoral votes, the election results shifted to the House of Representatives. The House saw Jefferson's opponent, Aaron Burr, as the lesser of two evils and voted to make Jefferson the next President of the country. As President, he reduced the national debt by one-third, and since the constitution made no provision for the acquisition of new land, he acquired the Louisiana Territory from Napoleon in 1803.

Much of Jefferson's second term was dedicated to keeping the country out of the Napoleonic wars and protecting the rights of American merchantmen. Jefferson's attempted solution to protect these merchantmen was an embargo upon American shipping. It was a plan that was unpopular and failed miserably. Jefferson retired from the presidency in 1809 and spent the last seventeen years of his life working to promote public education and tending to his many grandchildren. He founded the University of Virginia in 1819 and was a large contributor to its design, construction, and the hiring of its first faculty members. On July 4, 1826, the 50th anniversary of *The Declaration of Independence*, Jefferson died at Monticello (his home in Virginia).

The Declaration of Independence

1. Before reading this document, re-visit this time period and examine the volatile situation in which the United States found itself.
2. It would be wise to read this piece with a dictionary in hand, for Jefferson employs many polysyllabic words that some readers may find elusive.
3. Although Jefferson was not the sole author of *The Declaration of Independence,* he is considered one of the most significant architects of its rhetoric.

The Declaration of Independence

Thomas Jefferson

When in the Course of human events, it becomes necessary for one people to dissolve the political bands which have connected them with another, and to assume among the powers of the earth, the separate and equal station to which the Laws of Nature and of Nature's God entitle them, a decent respect to the opinions of mankind requires that they should declare the causes which impel them to the separation.

We hold these truths to be self-evident, that all men are created equal, that they are endowed by their Creator with certain unalienable Rights, that among these are Life, Liberty and the pursuit of Happiness.—That to secure these rights, Governments are instituted among Men, deriving their just powers from the consent of the governed,—That whenever any Form of Government becomes destructive of these ends, it is the Right of the People to alter or to abolish it, and to institute new Government, laying its foundation on such principles and organizing its powers in such form, as to them shall seem most likely to effect their Safety and Happiness. Prudence, indeed, will dictate that Governments long established should not be changed for light and transient causes; and accordingly all experience hath shown, that mankind are more disposed to suffer, while evils are sufferable, than to right themselves by abolishing the forms to which they are accustomed. But when a long train of abuses and usurpations, pursuing invariably the same Object evinces a design to reduce them under absolute Despotism, it is their right, it is their duty, to throw off such Government, and to provide new Guards for their future security.—Such has been the patient sufferance of these Colonies; and such is now the necessity which constrains them to alter their former Systems of Government. The history of the present King of Great Britain is a history of repeated injuries and usurpations, all having in direct object the establishment of an absolute Tyranny over these States. To prove this, let Facts be submitted to a candid world.

He has refused his Assent to Laws, the most wholesome and necessary for the public good.

He has forbidden his Governors to pass Laws of immediate and pressing importance, unless suspended in their operation till his Assent should be obtained; and when so suspended, he has utterly neglected to attend to them.

He has refused to pass other Laws for the accommodation of large districts of people, unless those people would relinquish the right of Representation in the Legislature, a right inestimable to them and formidable to tyrants only.

He has called together legislative bodies at places unusual, uncomfortable, and distant from the depository of their public Records, for the sole purpose of fatiguing them into compliance with his measures. He has dissolved Representative Houses repeatedly, for opposing with manly firmness his invasions on the rights of the people.

He has refused for a long time, after such dissolutions, to cause others to be elected; whereby the Legislative powers, incapable of Annihilation, have returned to the People at large for their exercise; the State remaining in the mean time exposed to all the dangers of invasion from without, and convulsions within.

He has endeavoured to prevent the population of these States; for that purpose obstructing the Laws for Naturalization of Foreigners; refusing to pass others to encourage their migrations hither, and raising the conditions of new Appropriations of Lands.

He has obstructed the Administration of Justice, by refusing his Assent to Laws for establishing Judiciary powers.

He has made Judges dependent on his Will alone, for the tenure of their offices, and the amount and payment of their salaries.

He has erected a multitude of New Offices, and sent hither swarms of Officers to harrass our people, and eat out their substance.

He has kept among us, in times of peace, Standing Armies without the Consent of our legislatures.

He has affected to render the Military independent of and superior to the Civil power.

He has combined with others to subject us to a jurisdiction foreign to our constitution, and unacknowledged by our laws; giving his Assent to their Acts of pretended Legislation:

For quartering large bodies of armed troops among us:

For protecting them, by a mock Trial, from punishment for any Murders which they should commit on the Inhabitants of these States:

For cutting off our Trade with all parts of the world:

For imposing Taxes on us without our Consent:

For depriving us in many cases, of the benefits of Trial by Jury:

For transporting us beyond Seas to be tried for pretended offences:

For abolishing the free System of English Laws in a neighbouring Province, establishing therein an Arbitrary government, and enlarging its Boundaries so as to render it at once an example and fit instrument for introducing the same absolute rule into these Colonies:

For taking away our Charters, abolishing our most valuable Laws, and altering fundamentally the Forms of our Governments:

For suspending our own Legislatures, and declaring themselves invested with power to legislate for us in all cases whatsoever.

He has abdicated Government here, by declaring us out of his Protection and waging War against us.

He has plundered our seas, ravaged our Coasts, burnt our towns, and destroyed the lives of our people.

He is at this time transporting large Armies of foreign Mercenaries to compleat the works of death, desolation and tyranny, already begun with circumstances of Cruelty & perfidy scarcely paralleled in the most barbarous ages, and totally unworthy the Head of a civilized nation.

He has constrained our fellow Citizens taken Captive on the high Seas to bear Arms against their Country, to become the executioners of their friends and Brethren, or to fall themselves by their Hands.

He has excited domestic insurrections amongst us, and has endeavoured to bring on the inhabitants of our frontiers, the merciless Indian Savages, whose known rule of warfare, is an undistinguished destruction of all ages, sexes and conditions.

In every stage of these Oppressions We have Petitioned for Redress in the most humble terms: Our repeated Petitions have been answered only by repeated injury. A Prince, whose character is thus marked by every act which may define a Tyrant, is unfit to be the ruler of a free people.

Nor have We been wanting in attentions to our British brethren. We have warned them from time to time of attempts by their legislature to extend an unwarrantable jurisdiction over us. We have reminded them of the circumstances of our emigration and settlement here. We have appealed to their native justice and magnanimity, and we have conjured them by the ties of our common kindred to disavow these usurpations, which, would inevitably interrupt our connections and correspondence. They too have been deaf to the voice of justice and of consanguinity. We must, therefore, acquiesce in the necessity, which denounces our Separation, and hold them, as we hold the rest of mankind, Enemies in War, in Peace Friends.

We, therefore, the Representatives of the united States of America, in General Congress, Assembled, appealing to the Supreme Judge of the world for the rectitude of our intentions, do, in the Name, and by Authority of the good People of these Colonies, solemnly publish and declare, That these United Colonies are, and of Right ought to be Free and Independent States; that they are Absolved from all Allegiance to the British Crown, and that all politi-cal connection between them and the State of Great Britain, is and ought to be totally dissolved; and that as Free and Independent States, they have full Power to levy War, conclude Peace, contract Alliances, establish Commerce, and to do all other Acts and Things which Independent States may of right do.

And for the support of this Declaration, with a firm reliance on the protection of divine Providence, we mutually pledge to each other our Lives, our Fortunes and our sacred Honor.

Questions

1. Who is the intended audience of this historical document, and why was it drafted?
2. What are the "Laws of Nature" that are referred to in this work?
3. What is the justification of this declaration?
4. Summarize the long list of atrocities that these authors identify. Do this in two or three sentences.
5. What are some of the war-like actions that the King and his army have exacted upon the colonies?
6. What is the mood of the colonies during this time, and is this mood justified?
7. What are the economic complaints made by the colonies? How might money play a role in the colonies' desire for independence?
8. What is the name of the governmental group or organization that drafted this document? From the diction in this document, what might one infer about this group's conviction for colonial independence? Why?
9. What are the authors willing to give in order to attain independence? Does this pledge make the document more or less powerful? Why?

1. *The Declaration of Independence* states: "We hold these truths to be self-evident, that all men are created equal, that they are endowed by their Creator with certain inalienable Rights, that among these are Life, Liberty, and the pursuit of Happiness." This idea seems to be contradictory with the way America treated slaves in the century that followed, especially when noting that the original language in *The Declaration of Independence* referred to "Life, Liberty, and the pursuit of Property." Construct an argument that examines how the colonies wanted to be treated within the context of how the African slaves were treated when they came to the new world.
2. In today's society, it is hard to turn on the news and not hear a reporter refer to terrorism. Research terrorism, and construct an argument that examines whether or not the founding fathers of America could be classified as terrorists. Draw examples from *The Declaration of Independence* and other documents from this period.

Continued

3. After carefully examining this document, identify the three greatest atrocities that England had committed against its colonial brethren. Construct an argument that examines each atrocity, and argue why these acts were considered heinous by the colonies. Further, take a stand that shows whether or not these acts were justified.
4. *The Declaration of Independence* states: "A Prince whose character is thus marked by every act which may define a Tyrant, is unfit to be the ruler of a free people." Research King George, and investigate whether his acts were, in fact, tyrannical. Construct an argument that examines England's King at the time this piece was written, and argue whether his actions really made him "unfit to be the ruler of a free people."

Jonathan Edwards (1703–1758)

Jonathan Edwards was born in East Windsor Connecticut, on October 5, 1703. His childhood involved an emphasis on strong Puritan values. He attended Yale University from 1716–1722. It was there that he studied some of the most diverse and revolutionary ideas that were coming out of Europe at the time. Issues such as British empiricism and Orthodox Calvinism were two of the subjects in which he immersed himself. He contemplated man's rightful place in the universe, and he challenged Aristotilianism. In 1726, Edwards became the pastor of Northampton, Massachusetts, a large influential church on the outskirts of Boston. As pastor, he published several works that gained him international acclaim. One of these works is titled, *A Faithful Narrative of the Surprising Work of God.* It was this piece, published in 1738, that led to a religious revival throughout the 1740s. Many historians, in fact, give Edwards a great deal of credit for the religious movement that took place during this time: The Great Awakening. The Great Awakening saw the spread of religion throughout the colonies, and many colonists were beginning to make a distinction between the sovereignty of God and the reality of Hell.

Edwards' career started to drift toward philosophy in the late 1740s with writings such as *A Treatise Concerning Religious Affections* and *The Life of David Brainerd.* In 1750, Edwards' church dismissed him from the Northampton congregation after he attempted to add more stringent guidelines for sacramental acceptance. His motivation was clear: he began to see the church accepting too many nonbelievers and hypocrites.

From Northampton, Edwards went to a small town on the western border of Massachusetts titled Stockbridge. He pastored a small English congregation and was a missionary to about one hundred Mohican and Mohawk families. Edwards died on March 22, 1758, following complications from a smallpox inoculation, and he is buried in the Princeton cemetery. Over the past two centuries, Edwards has emerged as a quintessential man, not in the usual sense, but because in some profound way he marked the culmination of one era, and he prefigured a subsequent one.

Sinners in the Hands of an Angry God

1. The four points that Edwards makes at the beginning of this essay are important because they provide the reader with historical context.
2. In this essay, Edwards uses fear to persuade his readers. Notice how, through the diction he employs, he attempts to make the reader feel the warmth of Hell's flames.
3. It is important to know that when Edwards wrote this work, he was going through a very troubling time in his life. His views on religion were radical, and especially in this essay, he expressed a great deal of anger and vengeance.

Sinners in the Hands of an Angry God

Jonathan Edwards

—Their foot shall slide in due time—Deut. 32:35

In this verse is threatened the vengeance of God on the wicked unbelieving Israelites, who were God's visible people, and who lived under the means of grace; but who, notwithstanding all God's wonderful works towards them, remained (as ver. 28.) void of counsel, having no understanding in them. Under all the cultivations of heaven, they brought forth bitter and poisonous fruit; as in the two verses next preceding the text. The expression I have chosen for my text, Their foot shall slide in due time, seems to imply the following doings, relating to the punishment and destruction to which these wicked Israelites were exposed.

1. That they were always exposed to *destruction;* as one that stands or walks in slippery places is always exposed to fall. This is implied in the manner of their destruction coming upon them, being represented by their foot sliding. The same is expressed, Psalm 73:18. "Surely thou didst set them in slippery places; thou castedst them down into destruction."
2. It implies, that they were always exposed to sudden unexpected destruction. As he that walks in slippery places is every moment liable to fall, he cannot foresee one moment whether he shall stand or fall the next; and when he does fall, he falls at once without warning: Which is also expressed in Psalm 73:18, 19. "Surely thou didst set them in slippery places; thou castedst them down into destruction: How are they brought into desolation as in a moment!"

3. Another thing implied is, that they are liable to fall *of themselves,* without being thrown down by the hand of another; as he that stands or walks on slippery ground needs nothing but his own weight to throw him down.

4. That the reason why they are not fallen already, and do not fall now, is only that God's appointed time is not come. For it is said, that when that due time, or appointed time comes, *their foot shall slide.* Then they shall be left to fall, as they are inclined by their own weight. God will not hold them up in these slippery places any longer, but will let them go; and then at that very instant, they shall fall into destruction; as he that stands on such slippery declining ground, on the edge of a pit, he cannot stand alone, when he is let go he immediately falls and is lost.

The observation from the words that I would now insist upon is this. "There is nothing that keeps wicked men at any one moment out of hell, but the mere pleasure of God." By the mere pleasure of God, I mean his sovereign pleasure, his arbitrary will, restrained by no obligation, hindered by no manner of difficulty, any more than if nothing else but God's mere will had in the least degree, or in any respect whatsoever, any hand in the preservation of wicked men one moment.

The truth of this observation may appear by the following considerations.

1. There is no want of *power* in God to cast wicked men into hell at any moment. Men's hands cannot be strong when God rises up. The strongest have no power to resist him, nor can any deliver out of his hands.—He is not only able to cast wicked men into hell, but he can most easily do it. Sometimes an earthly prince meets with a great deal of difficulty to subdue a rebel, who has found means to fortify himself, and has made himself strong by the numbers of his followers. But it is not so with God. There is no fortress that is any defense from the power of God. Though hand join in hand, and vast multitudes of God's enemies combine and associate themselves, they are easily broken in pieces. They are as great heaps of light chaff before the whirlwind; or large quantities of dry stubble before devouring flames. We find it easy to tread on and crush a worm that we see crawling on the earth; so it is easy for us to cut or singe a slender thread that any thing hangs by: thus easy is it for God, when he pleases, to cast his enemies down to hell. What are we, that we should think to stand before him, at whose rebuke the earth trembles, and before whom the rocks are thrown down?

2. They *deserve* to be cast into hell; so that divine justice never stands in the way, it makes no objection against God's using his power at any moment to destroy them. Yea, on the contrary, justice calls aloud for an infinite punishment of their sins. Divine justice says of the tree that brings forth such grapes of Sodom, "Cut it down, why cumbereth it the ground?" Luke xiii. 7. The sword of divine justice is every moment brandished over their heads, and it is nothing but the hand of arbitrary mercy, and God's mere will, that holds it back.

3. They are already under a sentence of *condemnation* to hell. They do not only justly deserve to be cast down thither, but the sentence of the law of God, that eternal and immutable rule of righteousness that God has fixed between him and mankind, is gone out against them, and stands against them; so that they are bound over already to hell. John iii. 18. "He that believeth not is condemned already." So that every unconverted man properly belongs to hell; that is his place; from thence he is, John viii. 23. "Ye are from beneath." And thither be is bound; it is the place that justice, and God's word, and the sentence of his unchangeable law assign to him.

4. They are now the objects of that very same anger and wrath of God, that is expressed in the torments of hell. And the reason why they do not go down to hell at each moment, is not because God, in whose power they are, is not then very angry with them; as he is with many miserable creatures now tormented in hell, who there feel and bear the fierceness of his wrath. Yea, God is a great deal more angry with great numbers that are now on earth: yea, doubtless, with many that are now in this congregation, who it may be are at ease, than he is with many of those who are now in the flames of hell.

So that it is not because God is unmindful of their wickedness, and does not resent it, that he does not let loose his hand and cut them off. God is not altogether such an one as themselves, though they may imagine him to be so. The wrath of God burns against them, their damnation does not slumber; the pit is prepared, the fire is made ready, the furnace is now hot, ready to receive them; the flames do now rage and glow. The glittering sword is whet, and held over them, and the pit hath opened its mouth under them.

5. The *devil* stands ready to fall upon them, and seize them as his own, at what moment God shall permit him. They belong to him; he has their souls in his possession, and under his dominion. The scripture represents them as his goods, Luke 11:12. The devils watch them; they are ever by them at their right hand; they stand waiting for

them, like greedy hungry lions that see their prey, and expect to have it, but are for the present kept back. If God should withdraw his hand, by which they are restrained, they would in one moment fly upon their poor souls. The old serpent is gaping for them; hell opens its mouth wide to receive them; and if God should permit it, they would be hastily swallowed up and lost.

6. There are in the souls of wicked men those hellish principles reigning, that would presently kindle and flame out into hell fire, if it were not for God's restraints. There is laid in the very nature of carnal men, a foundation for the torments of hell. There are those corrupt principles, in reigning power in them, and in full possession of them, that are seeds of hell fire. These principles are active and powerful, exceeding violent in their nature, and if it were not for the restraining hand of God upon them, they would soon break out, they would flame out after the same manner as the same corruptions, the same enmity does in the hearts of damned souls, and would beget the same torments as they do in them. The souls of the wicked are in scripture compared to the troubled sea, Isa. 57:20. For the present, God restrains their wickedness by his mighty power, as he does the raging waves of the troubled sea, saying, "Hitherto shalt thou come, but no further;" but if God should withdraw that restraining power, it would soon carry all before it. Sin is the ruin and misery of the soul; it is destructive in its nature; and if God should leave it without restraint, there would need nothing else to make the soul perfectly miserable. The corruption of the heart of man is immoderate and boundless in its fury; and while wicked men live here, it is like fire pent up by God's restraints, whereas if it were let loose, it would set on fire the course of nature; and as the heart is now a sink of sin, so if sin was not restrained, it would immediately turn the soul into a fiery oven, or a furnace of fire and brimstone.

7. It is no security to wicked men for one moment, that there are no visible means of death at hand. It is no security to a natural man, that he is now in health, and that he does not see which way he should now immediately go out of the world by any accident, and that there is no visible danger in any respect in his circumstances. The manifold and continual experience of the world in all ages, shows this is no evidence, that a man is not on the very brink of eternity, and that the next step will not be into another world. The unseen, unthought-of ways and means of persons going suddenly out of the world are innumerable and inconceivable. Unconverted men walk over the pit of hell on a rotten covering, and there are innumerable places in this covering so weak that they will not bear their weight, and these places are not seen. The arrows of death fly unseen at noon-day; the sharpest sight cannot discern them. God has so many different unsearchable ways of taking wicked men out of the world and sending them to hell, that there is nothing to make it appear, that God had need to be at the expense of a miracle, or go out of the ordinary course of his providence, to destroy any wicked man, at any moment. All the means that there are of sinners going out of the world, are so in God's hands, and so universally and absolutely subject to his power and determination, that it does not depend at all the less on the mere will of God, whether sinners shall at any moment go to hell, than if means were never made use of, or at all concerned in the case.

8. Natural men's prudence and care to preserve their own lives, or the care of others to preserve them, do not secure them a moment. To this, divine providence and universal experience do also bear testimony. There is this clear evidence that men's own wisdom is no security to them from death; that if it were otherwise we should see some difference between the wise and politic men of the world, and others, with regard to their liableness to early and unexpected death: but how is it in fact? Eccles. ii. 16. "How dieth the wise man? even as the fool."

9. All wicked men's pains and *contrivance* which they use to escape hell, while they continue to reject Christ, and so remain wicked men, do not secure them from hell one moment. Almost every natural man that hears of hell, flatters himself that he shall escape it; he depends upon himself for his own security; he flatters himself in what he has done, in what he is now doing, or what he intends to do. Every one lays out mat-

ters in his own mind how he shall avoid damnation, and flatters himself that he contrives well for himself, and that his schemes will not fail. They hear indeed that there are but few saved, and that the greater part of men that have died heretofore are gone to hell; but each one imagines that he lays out matters better for his own escape than others have done. He does not intend to come to that place of torment; he says within himself, that he intends to take effectual care, and to order matters so for himself as not to fail.

But the foolish children of men miserably delude themselves in their own schemes, and in confidence in their own strength and wisdom; they trust to nothing but a shadow. The greater part of those who heretofore have lived under the same means of grace, and are now dead, are undoubtedly gone to hell; and it was not because they were not as wise as those who are now alive: it was not because they did not lay out matters as well for themselves to secure their own escape. If we could speak with them, and inquire of them, one by one, whether they expected, when alive, and when they used to hear about hell ever to be the subjects of that misery: we doubtless, should hear one and another reply, "No, I never intended to come here: I had laid out matters otherwise in my mind; I thought I should contrive well for myself: I thought my scheme good. I intended to take effectual care; but it came upon me unexpected; I did not look for it at that time, and in that manner; it came as a thief: Death outwitted me: God's wrath was too quick for me. Oh, my cursed foolishness! I was flattering myself, and pleasing myself with vain dreams of what I would do hereafter; and when I was saying, Peace and safety, then suddenly destruction came upon me.

10. God has laid himself under *no obligation*, by any promise to keep any natural man out of hell one moment. God certainly has made no promises either of eternal life, or of any deliverance or preservation from eternal death, but what are contained in the covenant of grace, the promises that are given in Christ, in whom all the promises are yea and amen. But surely they have no interest in the promises of the covenant of grace who are not the children of the covenant, who do not believe in any of the promises, and have no interest in the Mediator of the covenant.

So that, whatever some have imagined and pretended about promises made to natural men's earnest seeking and knocking, it is plain and manifest, that whatever pains a natural man takes in religion, whatever prayers he makes, till he believes in Christ, God is under no manner of obligation to keep him a moment from eternal destruction.

So that, thus it is that natural men are held in the hand of God, over the pit of hell; they have deserved the fiery pit, and are already sentenced to it; and God is dreadfully provoked, his anger is as great towards them as to those that are actually suffering the executions of the fierceness of his wrath in hell, and they have done nothing in the least to appease or abate that anger, neither is God in the least bound by any promise to hold them up one moment; the devil is waiting for them, hell is gaping for them, the flames gather and flash about them, and would fain lay hold on them, and swallow them up; the fire pent up in their own hearts is struggling to break out: and they have no interest in any Mediator, there are no means within reach that can be any security to them. In short, they have no refuge, nothing to take hold of, all that preserves them every moment is the mere arbitrary will, and uncovenanted, unobliged forbearance of an incensed God.

Application

The use of this awful subject may be for awakening unconverted persons in this congregation. This that you have heard is the case of every one of you that are out of Christ.—That world of misery, that lake of burning brimstone, is extended abroad under you. There is the dreadful pit of the glowing flames of the wrath of God; there is hell's wide gaping mouth open; and you have nothing to stand upon, nor anything to take hold of, there is nothing between you and hell but the air; it is only the power and mere pleasure of God that holds you up.

You probably are not sensible of this; you find you are kept out of hell, but do not see the hand of God in it; but look at other things, as the good state of your bodily constitution, your care of your own life, and the means you use for your own preservation. But indeed these things are nothing; if God should withdraw his band, they would avail no more to keep you from falling, than the thin air to hold up a person that is suspended in it.

Your wickedness makes you as it were heavy as lead, and to tend downwards with great weight and pressure towards hell; and if God should let you go, you would immediately sink and swiftly descend and plunge into the bottomless gulf, and your healthy constitution, and your own care and prudence, and best contrivance, and all your righteousness, would have no more influence to uphold you and keep you out of hell, than a spider's web would have to stop a falling rock. Were it not for the sovereign pleasure of God, the earth would not bear you one moment; for you are a burden to it; the creation groans with you; the creature is made subject to the bondage of your corruption, not willingly; the sun does not willingly shine upon you to give you light to serve sin and Satan; the earth does not willingly yield her increase to satisfy your lusts; nor is it willingly a stage for your wickedness to be acted upon; the air does not willingly serve you for breath to maintain the flame of life in your vitals, while you spend your life in the service of God's enemies. God's creatures are good, and were made for men to serve God with, and do not willingly subserve to any other purpose, and groan when they are abused to purposes so directly contrary to their nature and end. And the world would spew you out, were it not for the sovereign hand of him who hath subjected it in hope. There are black clouds of God's wrath now hanging directly over your heads, full of the dreadful storm, and big with thunder; and were it not for the restraining hand of God, it would immediately burst forth upon you. The sovereign pleasure of God, for the present, stays his rough wind; otherwise it would come with fury, and your destruction would come like a whirlwind, and you would be like the chaff of the summer threshing floor.

The wrath of God is like great waters that are dammed for the present; they increase more and more, and rise higher and higher, till an outlet is given; and the longer the stream is stopped, the more rapid and mighty is its course, when once it is let loose. It is true, that judgment against your evil works has not been executed hitherto; the floods of God's vengeance have been withheld; but your guilt in the meantime is constantly increasing, and you are every day treasuring up more wrath; the waters are constantly rising, and waxing more and more mighty; and there is nothing but the mere pleasure of God, that holds the waters back, that are unwilling to be stopped, and press hard to go forward. If God should only withdraw his hand from the flood-gate, it would immediately fly open, and the fiery floods of the fierceness and wrath of God, would rush forth with inconceivable fury, and would come upon you with omnipotent power; and if your strength were ten thousand times greater than it is, yea, ten thousand times greater than the strength of the stoutest, sturdiest devil in hell, it would be nothing to withstand or endure it.

The bow of God's wrath is bent, and the arrow made ready on the string, and justice bends the arrow at your heart, and strains the bow, and it is nothing but the mere pleasure of God, and that of an angry God, without any promise or obligation at all, that keeps the arrow one moment from being made drunk with your blood. Thus all you that never passed under a great change of heart, by the mighty power of the Spirit of God upon your souls; all you that were never born again, and made new creatures, and raised from being dead in sin, to a state of new, and before altogether unexperienced light and life, are in the hands of an angry God. However you may have reformed your life in many things, and may have had religious affections, and may keep up a form of religion in your families and closets, and in the house of God, it is nothing but his mere pleasure that keeps you from being this moment swallowed up in everlasting destruction. However unconvinced you may now be of the truth of what you hear, by and by you will be fully convinced of it. Those that are gone from being in the like circumstances with you, see that it was so with them; for destruction came suddenly upon most of them; when they expected nothing of it, and while they were saying, Peace and safety: now they see, that those things on which they depended for peace and safety, were nothing but thin air and empty shadows.

The God that holds you over the pit of hell, much as one holds a spider, or some loathsome insect over the fire, abhors you, and is dreadfully provoked: his wrath towards you burns like fire; he looks upon you as worthy of nothing else, but to be cast into the fire; he is of purer eyes than to bear to have you in his sight; you are ten thousand times more abominable in his eyes, than the most hateful venomous serpent is in ours. You have offended him infinitely more than ever a stubborn rebel did his prince; and yet it is nothing but his hand that holds you from falling into the fire every moment. It is to be ascribed to nothing else, that you did not go to hell the last night; that you was suffered to awake again in this world, after you closed your eyes to sleep. And there is no other reason to be given, why you have not dropped into hell since you arose in the morning, but that God's hand has held you up. There is no other reason to be given why you have not gone to hell, since you have sat here in the house of God, provoking his pure eyes by your sinful wicked manner of attending his solemn worship. Yea, there is nothing else that is to be given as a reason why you do not this very moment drop down into hell.

O sinner! Consider the fearful danger you are in: it is a great furnace of wrath, a wide and bottomless pit, full of the fire of wrath, that you are held over in the hand of that God, whose wrath is provoked and incensed as much against you, as against many of the damned in hell. You hang by a slender thread, with the flames of divine wrath flashing about it, and ready every moment to singe it, and burn it asunder; and you have no interest in any Mediator, and nothing to lay hold of to save yourself, nothing to keep off the flames of wrath, nothing of your own, nothing that you ever have done, nothing that you can do, to induce God to spare you one moment. And consider here more particularly

1. *Whose* wrath it is: it is the wrath of the infinite God. If it were only the wrath of man, though it were of the most potent prince, it would be comparatively little to be regarded. The wrath of kings is very much dreaded, especially of absolute monarchs, who have the possessions and lives of their subjects wholly in their power, to be disposed of at their mere will. Prov. 20:2. "The fear of a king is as the roaring of a lion: Whoso provoketh him to anger, sinneth against his own soul." The subject that very much enrages an arbitrary prince, is liable to suffer the most extreme torments that human art can invent, or human power can inflict. But the greatest earthly potentates in their greatest majesty and strength, and when clothed in their greatest terrors, are but feeble, despicable worms of the dust, in comparison of the great and almighty Creator and King of heaven and earth. It is but little that they can do, when most enraged, and when they have exerted the utmost of their fury. All the kings of the earth, before God, are as grasshoppers; they are nothing, and less than nothing: both their love and their hatred is to be despised. The wrath of the great King of kings, is as much more terrible than theirs, as his majesty is greater. Luke 12:4, 5. "And I say unto you, my friends, Be not afraid of them that kill the body, and after that, have no more that they can do. But I will forewarn you whom you shall fear: fear him, which after he hath killed, hath power to cast into hell: yea, I say unto you, Fear him."

2. It is the *fierceness* of his wrath that you are exposed to. We often read of the fury of God; as in Isaiah lix. 18. "According to their deeds, accordingly he will repay fury to his adversaries." So Isaiah 66:15. "For behold, the Lord will come with fire, and with his chariots like a whirlwind, to render his anger with fury, and his rebuke with flames of fire." And in many other places. So, Rev. 19:15, we read of "the wine press of the fierceness and wrath of Almighty God." The words are exceeding terrible. If it had only been said, "the wrath of God," the words would have implied that which is infinitely dreadful: but it is "the fierceness and wrath of God." The fury of God! the fierceness of Jehovah! Oh, how dreadful must that be! Who can utter or conceive what such expressions carry in them! But it is also "the fierceness and wrath of *Almighty* God." As though there would be a very great manifestation of his almighty power in what the fierceness of his wrath should inflict, as though omnipotence should be as it were enraged, and exerted, as men are wont to exert their strength in the fierceness of their wrath. Oh! then, what will be the consequence! What will become of the poor worms that shall suffer it! Whose hands can be strong?

And whose heart can endure? To what a dreadful, inexpressible, inconceivable depth of misery must the poor creature be sunk who shall be the subject of this!

Consider this, you that are here present, that yet remain in an unregenerate state. That God will execute the fierceness of his anger, implies, that he will inflict wrath without any pity. When God beholds the ineffable extremity of your case, and sees your torment to be so vastly disproportioned to your strength, and sees how your poor soul is crushed, and sinks down, as it were, into an infinite gloom; he will have no compassion upon you, he will not forbear the executions of his wrath, or in the least lighten his hand; there shall be no moderation or mercy, nor will God then at all stay his rough wind; he will have no regard to your welfare, nor be at all careful lest you should suffer too much in any other sense, than only that you shall *not suffer beyond what strict justice requires*. Nothing shall be withheld, because it is so hard for you to bear. Ezek. viii. 18. "Therefore will I also deal in fury: mine eye shall not spare, neither will I have pity; and though they cry in mine ears with a loud voice, yet I will not hear them." Now God stands ready to pity you; this is a day of mercy; you may cry now with some encouragement of obtaining mercy. But when once the day of mercy is past, your most lamentable and dolorous cries and shrieks will be in vain; you will be wholly lost and thrown away of God, as to any regard to your welfare. God will have no other use to put you to, but to suffer misery; you shall be continued in being to no other end; for you will be a vessel of wrath fitted to destruction; and there will be no other use of this vessel, but to be filled full of wrath. God will be so far from pitying you when you cry to him, that it is said he will only "laugh and mock," Prov. 1:25, 26, &c.

How awful are those words, Isa. 63:3, which are the words of the great God. "I will tread them in mine anger, and will trample them in my fury, and their blood shall be sprinkled upon my garments, and I will stain all my raiment." It is perhaps impossible to conceive of words that carry in them greater manifestations of these three things, *vis.* contempt, and hatred, and fierceness of indignation. If you cry to God to pity you, he will be so far from pitying you in your doleful case, or showing you the least regard or favour, that instead of that, he will only tread you under foot. And though he will know that you cannot bear the weight of omnipotence treading upon you, yet he will not regard that, but he will crush you under his feet without mercy; he will crush out your blood, and make it fly, and it shall be sprinkled on his garments, so as to stain all his raiment. He will not only hate you, but he will have you, in the utmost contempt: no place shall be thought fit for you, but under his feet to be trodden down as the mire of the streets.

The misery you are exposed to is that which God will inflict to that end, that he might show what that wrath of Jehovah is. God hath had it on his heart to show to angels and men, both how excellent his love is, and also how terrible his wrath is. Sometimes earthly kings have a mind to show how terrible their wrath is, by the extreme punishments they would execute on those that would provoke them. Nebuchadnezzar, that mighty and haughty monarch of the Chaldean empire, was willing to show his wrath when enraged with Shadrach, Meshech, and Abednego; and accordingly gave orders that the burning fiery furnace should be heated seven times hotter than it was before; doubtless, it was raised to the utmost degree of fierceness that human art could raise it. But the great God is also willing to show his wrath, and magnify his awful majesty and mighty power in the extreme sufferings of his enemies. Rom. 9:22. "What if God, willing to show his wrath, and to make his power known, endure with much long-suffering the vessels of wrath fitted to destruction?" And seeing this is his design, and what he has determined, even to show how terrible the unrestrained wrath, the fury and fierceness of Jehovah is, he will do it to effect. There will be something accomplished and brought to pass that will be dreadful with a witness. When the great and angry God hath risen up and executed his awful vengeance on the poor sinner, and the wretch is actually suffering the infinite weight and power of his indignation, then will God call upon the whole universe to behold that awful majesty and mighty power that is to be seen in it. Isa. 33:12-14. "And the people shall be as the burnings of lime, as thorns cut up shall they be burnt in the fire. Hear ye that are far off, what I have done;

and ye that are near, acknowledge my might. The sinners in Zion are afraid; fearfulness hath surprised the hypocrites," &c.

Thus it will be with you that are in an unconverted state, if you continue in it; the infinite might, and majesty, and terribleness of the omnipotent God shall be magnified upon you, in the ineffable strength of your torments. You shall be tormented in the presence of the holy angels, and in the presence of the Lamb; and when you shall be in this state of suffering, the glorious inhabitants of heaven shall go forth and look on the awful spectacle, that they may see what the wrath and fierceness of the Almighty is; and when they have seen it, they will fall down and adore that great power and majesty. Isa. lxvi. 23, 24. "And it shall come to pass, that from one new moon to another, and from one sabbath to another, shall all flesh come to worship before me, saith the Lord. And they shall go forth and look upon the carcasses of the men that have transgressed against me; for their worm shall not die, neither shall their fire be quenched, and they shall be an abhorring unto all flesh."

4. It is *everlasting* wrath. It would be dreadful to suffer this fierceness and wrath of Almighty God one moment; but you must suffer it to all eternity. There will be no end to this exquisite horrible misery. When you look forward, you shall see a long forever, a boundless duration before you, which will swallow up your thoughts, and amaze your soul; and you will absolutely despair of ever having any deliverance, any end, any mitigation, any rest at all. You will know certainly that you must wear out long ages, millions of millions of ages, in wrestling and conflicting with this almighty merciless vengeance; and then when you have so done, when so many ages have actually been spent by you in this manner, you will know that all is but a point to what remains. So that your punishment will indeed be infinite. Oh, who can express what the state of a soul in such circumstances is! All that we can possibly say about it, gives but a very feeble, faint representation of it; it is inexpressible and inconceivable: For "who knows the power of God's anger?"

How dreadful is the state of those that are daily and hourly in the danger of this great wrath and infinite

misery! But this is the dismal case of every soul in this congregation that has not been born again, however moral and strict, sober and religious, they may otherwise be. Oh that you would consider it, whether you be young or old! There is reason to think, that there are many in this congregation now hearing this discourse, that will actually be the subjects of this very misery to all eternity. We know not who they are, or in what seats they sit, or what thoughts they now have. It may be they are now at ease, and hear all these things without much disturbance, and are now flattering themselves that they are not the persons, promising themselves that they shall escape. If we knew that there was one person, and but one, in the whole congregation, that was to be the subject of this misery, what an awful thing would it be to think of! If we knew who it was, what an awful sight would it be to see such a person! How might all the rest of the congregation lift up a lamentable and bitter cry over him! But, alas! instead of one, how many is it likely will remember this discourse in hell? And it would be a wonder, if some that are now present should not be in hell in a very short time, even before this year is out. And it would be no wonder if some persons, that now sit here, in some seats of this meeting-house, in health, quiet and secure, should be there before tomorrow morning. Those of you that finally continue in a natural condition, that shall keep out of hell longest will be there in a little time! Your damnation does not slumber; it will come swiftly, and, in all probability, very suddenly upon many of you. You have reason to wonder that you are not already in hell. It is doubtless the case of some whom you have seen and known, that never deserved hell more than you, and that heretofore appeared as likely to have been now alive as you. Their case is past all hope; they are crying in extreme misery and perfect despair; but here you are in the land of the living and in the house of God, and have an opportunity to obtain salvation. What would not those poor damned hopeless souls give for one day's opportunity such as you now enjoy!

And now you have an extraordinary opportunity, a day wherein Christ has thrown the door of mercy wide open, and stands in calling and crying with a loud voice to poor sinners; a day wherein many are flocking to him, and pressing into the kingdom of God. Many are daily coming from the east, west, north and south; many that were very lately in the same miserable condition that you are in, are now in a happy state, with their hearts filled with love to him who has loved them, and washed them from their sins in his own blood, and rejoicing in hope of the glory of God. How awful is it to be left behind at such a day! To see so many others feasting, while you are pining and perishing! To see so many rejoicing and singing for joy of heart, while you have cause to mourn for sorrow of heart, and howl for vexation of spirit! How can you rest one moment in such a condition? Are not your souls as precious as the souls of the people at Suffield, where they are flocking from day to day to Christ?

Are there not many here who have lived long in the world, and are not to this day born again? And so are aliens from the commonwealth of Israel, and have done nothing ever since they have lived, but treasure up wrath against the day of wrath? Oh, sirs, your case, in an especial manner, is extremely dangerous. Your guilt and hardness of heart is extremely great. Do you not see how generally persons of your years are passed over and left, in the present remarkable and wonderful dispensation of God's mercy? You had need to consider yourselves, and awake thoroughly out of sleep. You cannot bear the fierceness and wrath of the infinite God.—And you, young men, and young women, will you neglect this precious season which you now enjoy, when so many others of your age are renouncing all youthful vanities, and flocking to Christ? You especially have now an extraordinary opportunity; but if you neglect it, it will soon be with you as with those persons who spent all the precious days of youth in sin, and are now come to such a dreadful pass in blindness and hardness. And you, children, who are unconverted, do not you know that you are going down to hell, to bear the dreadful wrath of that God, who is now angry with you every day

and every night? Will you be content to be the children of the devil, when so many other children in the land are converted, and are become the holy and happy children of the King of kings?

And let every one that is yet out of Christ, and hanging over the pit of hell, whether they be old men and women, or middle aged, or young people, or little children, now harken to the loud calls of God's word and providence. This acceptable year of the Lord, a day of such great favours to some, will doubtless be a day of as remarkable vengeance to others. Men's hearts harden, and their guilt increases apace at such a day as this, if they neglect their souls; and never was there so great danger of such persons being given up to hardness of heart and blindness of mind. God seems now to be hastily gathering in his elect in all parts of the land; and probably the greater part of adult persons that ever shall be saved, will be brought in now in a little time, and that it will be as it was on the great out-pouring of the Spirit upon the Jews in the apostles' days; the election will obtain, and the rest will be blinded. If this should be the case with you, you will eternally curse this day, and will curse the day that ever you was born, to see such a season of the pouring out of God's Spirit, and will wish that you had died and gone to hell before you had seen it. Now undoubtedly it is, as it was in the days of John the Baptist, the axe is in an extraordinary manner laid at the root of the trees, that every tree which brings not forth good fruit, may be hewn down and cast into the fire.

Therefore, let every one that is out of Christ, now awake and fly from the wrath to come. The wrath of Almighty God is now undoubtedly hanging over a great part of this congregation: Let every one fly out of Sodom: "Haste and escape for your lives, look not behind you, escape to the mountain, lest you be consumed."

Questions

1. Do the four points that Edwards makes foreshadow the APPLICATIONS section?
2. On several occasions, Edwards speaks of "the wrath of God." What might be the justification of this wrath?
3. The God that Edwards describes is incongruent with the conventionally-perceived God. What are the adjectives one would use to describe Edwards' God?

4. After reading this text, what might one be able to infer about Edwards' view of his surroundings?

5. After thinking about the way Edwards describes God, decide whether this is an evil God or a merciful God.

6. In Edwards' opinion, does it matter if one has redirected his or her life's focus in order to avoid sauntering down the dark path to Hell? What might this say about his view of America and religion?

7. Why might Edwards occasionally quote from the *Bible?*

8. How might this have affected someone who was not a believer in God or Jesus Christ?

9. What is the message that Edwards is attempting to convey in his final passage?

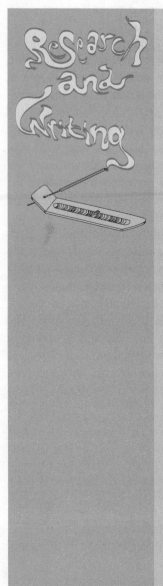

1. There is something very disconcerting about this piece. Edwards is obviously using religion in a manner that essentially scares someone into believing in God and Hell. Construct an argument that examines whether or not this is an effective manner of coercing an individual into accepting the faith, and support it with theological research and Edwards' *Sinners in the Hands of an Angry God.*

2. Although there is a strong sense of anger and hate in this work, Edwards probably did not intend to make it seem like every human being is destined for Hell. There is, however, no mention regarding how one gets into Heaven. Why might he have omitted the acceptance criteria for Heaven, and does this omission make his message more or less effective? Construct an argument that examines the strategy that Edwards employs throughout this work, focusing on the vivid descriptions of Hell and those who are destined to reside there.

3. According to Edwards, no one is exempt from the "wrath of God." Think about particular individuals today who have committed the most heinous crimes. From various perspectives, you might choose to examine Osama bin Laden, Adolf Hitler, Michael Moore, Kenneth Lay, or George W. Bush. What would be their reaction after reading a piece like this? Construct an argument that examines these individuals and what their reaction might be to such a document.

4. Edwards writes: "There is nothing that keeps wicked men at any one moment out of hell, but the mere pleasure of God." From these lines, what might one infer about Edwards' definition of God? Construct an argument that examines this definition, and support it by citing *Sinners in the Hands of an Angry God* and outside sources.

5. Compare and contrast the biblical God with Edwards' God. It might be helpful to first make a list of the adjectives used by the *Bible* to describe God, and then make a list of the adjectives that Edwards uses. Specifically, examine adjectival denotations and connotations, noting how using one word as opposed to another can more effectively advance the argument that "perception is reality."

8

19th Century American Literature

JON ST.AMANT

The 19th century was the time of frontier figures like Davy Crockett, a friend to the Indians. And it was the time of Andrew Jackson and his Indian Removal bill. It was a time that saw the paradox of progress. Land became available, and land lotteries were held. But America's progress came at a price: the original landowners had to be removed. In 1838, for instance, among the original landowners were the Cherokee Indians. And while one man's plea seemed to have little effect, Ralph Waldo Emerson still proffered his in a letter to President Van Buren: "You, sir will bring down that renowned chair in which you sit into infamy if your seal is set to this instrument of perfidy; and the name of this nation, hitherto the sweet omen of religion and liberty, will stink to the world." But this was 19th century America. And if the price of progress was genocide, then so be it. America was still in its infancy, and many were wondering if this idea called "America" would even work. Land speculators, however, continued to apply linear thinking, moving from Indian Removal to a "land swap" with Mexico. This was known as the Mexican-American War, though it seemed overwhelmingly motivated by land acquisition, specifically what we now recognize as Texas, New Mexico, Utah, Nevada, Arizona, California, and part of Colorado. Just as the land from Maine to Georgia once belonged to the Cherokee Indians, much of Mexico's land was acquired in the name of progress. And just as Emerson voiced his disapproval of Indian Removal, Henry David Thoreau denounced the Mexican-American War by not paying his poll tax and later, in "Civil Disobedience," writing: "Practically speaking, the opponents [. . .] are not a hundred thousand politicians at the South, but a hundred thousand merchants and farmers here, who are more interested in commerce and agriculture than they are in humanity, and are not prepared to do justice to the slave and to Mexico, *cost what it may.*" Thoreau's perspective was revolutionary, for he pointed his finger at the people instead of the politicians. Thoreau believed that the people did, in fact, have the power to affect change. And maybe that is the role of the writer: to invite people to see things from different perspectives. For instance, in 1847 an article in the *New York Herald* read: "The universal Yankee nation can regenerate and disenthrall the people of Mexico in a few years; and we believe it is a part of our destiny to civilize that beautiful country." On the other hand, a poet named James Russell Lowell tried to get people's attention by writing satirical poetry: "They jest want this Californy / So's to lug new slave-states in / To abuse ye, an' to scorn ye, / An' to plunder ye like sin." Lowell chose to bring attention not only to land acquisition but to its purpose: a place for new slave states.

It is important to realize that while people were battling for land in attempts to make America larger, many of the people working this land were slaves. And in the 19th century, slavery found itself more than simply a hotly-debated issue. Slaves were plotting escapes, uprisings, and rebellions. White abolitionists organized revolts. One white abolitionist, sixty-year-old John Brown, attempted to seize the federal arsenal at Harpers Ferry, Virginia, in hopes of leading slaves out of the South. When caught and hanged, Ralph Waldo Emerson said of Brown: "He will make the gallows holy as the cross." Emerson, who was once a minister, compares Brown's death to Christ's crucifixion. Interestingly, before Brown was hanged, he said: "I, John Brown, am quite certain that the crimes of this guilty land will never be purged away but with blood."

Enter Abraham Lincoln and the Civil War, a war that claimed 600,000 lives. Considered one of the bloodiest wars in human history, the Civil War seemed to originally be something spawned by the northern and southern elites. When faced with Lincoln's election, seven southern states seceded from the Union. Later, four more states seceded. This created the Confederacy. But amidst the battle between the Union and the Confederacy were the pushes to preserve or abolish slavery. There was the carefully-worded Emancipation Proclamation that helped make the Civil War look more like a war for the liberation of slaves. Racial tensions were high. Black soldiers entered the war. Poor whites were drafted. Rich white Northerners could avoid the draft by paying $300. Economic, racial, and geographical gaps abounded. And for America's poets, essayists, and short-story writers, there was no shortage of material.

I.
19th Century American Poetry

When the curtain rose to reveal the poets of 19th century American Literature, there was little room on the stage, for 19th century America was bristling with war, slavery, love, truth, dreams, and depression—all the makings for great poetry. And as expected, great poems were produced by many poets. Among these were Ralph Waldo Emerson, Edgar Allan Poe, Walt Whitman, Emily Dickinson, Edwin Arlington Robinson, and Paul Laurence Dunbar. Still, even if the 19th century did produce great poetry, why read it? What is the purpose? One contemporary film titled *Dead Poets Society* attempted an answer with the following: "We don't read and write poetry because it's cute. We read and write poetry because we are members of the human race." And so goes one purpose for poetry. We are humans. And if we humans are filled with passion, then perhaps poetry is where we keep it renewed. Perhaps this is where we go to be understood, where we go to tackle some of the big questions.

Try to imagine a world without beauty, a world without romance, a world without love. Poetry does not simply flirt with these things. Good poetry attempts to capture it. But make no mistake. Poetry is not simply a Hallmark card in a bottle. Poetry can provoke. It can outrage. It can make perceptions evolve. And in the end, after reading the poems and writing about them, what will you do next? Will you contribute to the evolution of the human species? To the evolution of truth, nature, peace, war, love? If everyone, in some small way, writes a poem to the world, what will yours read?

Ralph Waldo Emerson (1803–1882)

While not known for his poetry, Emerson was one of the first-born "poets" of the 19th century, living a life that spanned 1803 to 1882. Described by Robert D. Richardson as a "man on fire," Emerson did things that many would deem odd. For instance, when plagued by the vision of his dead wife, he visited her tomb and viewed her corpse (over one year after being entombed) in order to reach the realization that she was, indeed, dead. Though popularized by his essays, Emerson did write poetry that addressed issues representative of 19th century America: slavery, piety, nature, and love. Though once labeled by Herman Melville as a "big-nosed buffoon," Emerson wrote with a certain éclat, arguing passionately that "envy is ignorance" and "imitation is suicide."

Emerson's Poems

1. Realize that Emerson was among a long succession of ministers in his family. Perhaps his desire to become a minister, or lack thereof, is the problem about which he writes.
2. Note the power of metaphor. Specifically, note how metaphor affects you. Does it make one particular line more visual or visceral? For instance, when Emerson writes, "Like the volcano's tongue of flame," does such language advance his argument?
3. Notice similarities between the issues that Emerson grapples with in his poems and the issues that Emily Dickinson grapples with in her poetry.

The Problem

I like a church; I like a cowl;
I love a prophet of the soul;
And on my heart monastic aisles
Fall like sweet strains, or pensive smiles;
Yet not for all his faith can see
Would I that cowled churchman be.

Why should the vest on him allure,
Which I could not on me endure?

Not from a vain or shallow thought
His awful Jove young Phidias brought;
Never from lips of cunning fell
The thrilling Delphic oracle;
Out from the heart of nature rolled
The burdens of the Bible old;
The litanies of nations came,
Like the volcano's tongue of flame,
Up from the burning core below—
The canticles of love and woe:
The hand that rounded Peter's dome
And groined the aisles of Christian Rome
Wrought in a sad sincerity;
Himself from God he could not free;
He builded better than he knew;—
The conscious stone to beauty grew.

Know'st thou what wove yon woodbird's nest
Of leaves, and feathers from her breast?
Or how the fish outbuilt her shell
Painting with morn each annual cell?
Or how the sacred pine-tree adds
To her old leaves new myriads?
Such and so grew these holy piles,
Whilst love and terror laid the tiles.
Earth proudly wears the Parthenon,
As the best gem upon her zone,
And Morning opes with haste her lids

To gaze upon the Pyramids;
O'er England's abbeys bends the sky,
As on its friends, with kindred eye;
For out of Thought's interior sphere
These wonders rose to upper air;
And Nature gladly gave them place,
Adopted them into her race,
And granted them an equal date
With Andes and with Ararat.

These temples grew as grows the grass;
Art might obey, but not surpass.
The passive Master lent his hand
To the vast soul that o'er him planned;
And the same power that reared the shrine
Bestrode the tribes that knelt within.
Ever the fiery Pentecost
Girds with one flame the countless host,
Trances the heart through chanting choirs,
And through the priest the mind inspires.
The word unto the prophet spoken
Was writ on tables yet unbroken;
The word by seers of sibyls told,
In groves of oak, or fanes of gold,
Still floats upon the morning wind,
Still whispers to the willing mind.
One accent of the Holy Ghost
The heedless world hath never lost.
I know what say the fathers wise—
The book itself before me lies,
Old *Chrysostom*, best Augustine,
And he who blent both in his line,
The younger *Golden Lips* or mines,
Taylor, the Shakspeare of divines.
His words are music in my ear,
I see his cowled portrait dear;
And yet, for all his faith could see,
I would not the good bishop be.

Questions

1. What might Emerson mean by "sweet strains, or pensive smiles"?
2. Emerson writes: "These temples grew as grows the grass; / Art might obey, but not surpass." What does this mean? How can art "obey"? And why can it "obey" but not "surpass"? Further, what is it that "art" cannot "surpass"?
3. From the poem, it is not difficult to identify Emerson's "problem". However, what seems to be the source of this problem? In citing examples from the poem, explain why Emerson concludes: "And yet, for all his faith could see, / I would not the good bishop be."

Good-bye

Good-bye, proud world! I'm going home:
Thou art not my friend, and I'm not thine.
Long through thy weary crowds I roam;
A river-ark on the ocean brine,
Long I've been tossed like the driven foam;
But now, proud world! I'm going home.

Good-bye to Flattery's fawning face;
To Grandeur with his wise grimace;
To upstart Wealth's averted eye;
To supple Office, low and high;
To crowded halls, to court and street;
To frozen hearts and hasting feet;
To those who go, and those who come;
Good-bye, proud world! I'm going home.

I am going to my own hearth-stone,
Bosomed in yon green hills alone—
A secret nook in a pleasant land,
Whose groves the frolic fairies planned;
Where arches green, the livelong day,
Echo the blackbird's roundelay,
And vulgar feet have never trod
A spot that is sacred to thought and God.

O, when I am safe in my sylvan home,
I tread on the pride of Greece and Rome;
And when I am stretched beneath the pines,
Where the evening star so holy shines,
I laugh at the lore and the pride of man,
At the sophist schools and the learned clan;
For what are they all, in their high conceit,
When man in the bush with God may meet?

Questions

1. Emerson writes: "I tread on the pride of Greece and Rome." Within the context of his poem, what might this mean?
2. Emerson makes reference to a meeting with God when he writes: "For what are they all, in their high conceit, / When man in the bush with God may meet?" When he writes "they", to whom is he referring? And if one were to meet with God, why might it happen in "the bush"?

3. The poem suggests a farewell when Emerson writes: "Goodbye, proud world! I'm going home." First, where is this person going? Second, are we to assume this person to be Emerson? Or might it be representative of anyone interested in "going home"? Finally, could "going home" be a metaphor? For what might it be a metaphor?

Each and All

Little thinks, in the field, yon red-cloaked clown
Of thee from the hill-top looking down;
The heifer that lows in the upland farm,
Far-heard, lows not thine ear to charm;
The sexton, tolling his bell at noon,
Deems not that great Napolean
Stops his horse, and lists with delight,
Whilst his files sweep round yon Alpine height;
Nor knowest thou what argument
Thy life to thy neighbor's creed has lent.
All are needed by each one;
Nothing is fair or good alone.
I thought the sparrow's note from heaven,
Singing at dawn on the alder bough;
I brought him home, in his nest, at even;
He sings the song, but it cheers not now,
For I did not bring home the river and sky;
He sang to my ear—they sang to my eye.
The delicate shells lay on the shore;
The bubbles of the latest wave
Fresh pearls to their enamel gave,
And the bellowing of the savage sea
Greeted their safe escape to me.
I wiped away the weeds and foam,
I fetched my sea-born treasures home;
But the poor, unsightly, noisome things

Had left their beauty on the shore
With the sun and the sand and the wild uproar.
The lover watched his graceful maid,
As 'mid the virgin train she stayed,
Nor knew her beauty's best attire
Was woven still by the snow-white choir.
At last she came to his hermitage,
Like the bird from the woodlands to the cage;
The gay enchantment was undone,
A gentle wife, but fairy none.
Then I said, "I covet truth;
Beauty is unripe childhood's cheat;
I leave it behind with the games of youth":
As I spoke, beneath my feet
The ground-pine curled its pretty wreath.
Running over the club-moss burrs;
I inhaled the violet's breath;
Around me stood the oaks and firs;
Pine-cones and acorns lay on the ground;
Over me soared the eternal sky,
Full of light and of deity;
Again I saw, again I heard,
The rolling river, the morning bird;
Beauty through my senses stole;
I yielded myself to the perfect whole.

Questions

1. Who or what might the "red-cloaked clown" be?
2. What might Emerson mean when he writes, "I covet truth; / Beauty is unripe childhood's cheat"?
3. Emerson writes: "Beauty through my senses stole; / I yielded myself to the perfect whole." Why might he use "stole" to jell "beauty" and "senses"? Further, what is "the perfect whole"? And why might a person yield himself to it?

Poet

To clothe the fiery thought
In simple words succeeds,
For still the craft of genius is
To mask a king in weeds.

Questions

1. In your own words, explain what "the fiery thought" might be. And discuss why it might be valuable to clothe it in "simple words."
2. What might Emerson mean when he writes, "To mask a king in weeds"?
3. Is it coincidental that a "fiery thought" is being clothed and that a "king in weeds" is being masked? Juxtapose these two actions, and consider why they're being covered, hidden, or camouflaged.

Sacrifice

Though love repine, and reason chafe,
There came a voice without reply,—
"'Tis man's perdition to be safe,
When for the truth he ought to die."

Questions

1. Anthony Robbins, the motivational speaker, states: "People want to gain pleasure and avoid pain." Compare this to the last two lines of Emerson's poem.
2. Make a comparison between *Each and All* and *Sacrifice.* Note the following line in *Each and All:* "I covet truth." Then, compare it to the following line in *Sacrifice:* "[. . .] for the truth he ought to die." Compare and contrast these lines based on the context in which they are found.
3. Why is this poem titled *Sacrifice?* And when Emerson writes, "There came a voice without reply," whose voice might this be? And why is there no reply?

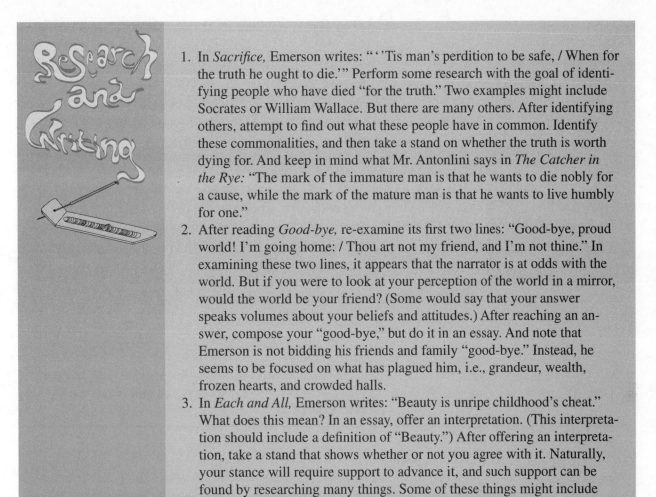

1. In *Sacrifice,* Emerson writes: " ' 'Tis man's perdition to be safe, / When for the truth he ought to die.' " Perform some research with the goal of identifying people who have died "for the truth." Two examples might include Socrates or William Wallace. But there are many others. After identifying others, attempt to find out what these people have in common. Identify these commonalities, and then take a stand on whether the truth is worth dying for. And keep in mind what Mr. Antonlini says in *The Catcher in the Rye:* "The mark of the immature man is that he wants to die nobly for a cause, while the mark of the mature man is that he wants to live humbly for one."

2. After reading *Good-bye,* re-examine its first two lines: "Good-bye, proud world! I'm going home: / Thou art not my friend, and I'm not thine." In examining these two lines, it appears that the narrator is at odds with the world. But if you were to look at your perception of the world in a mirror, would the world be your friend? (Some would say that your answer speaks volumes about your beliefs and attitudes.) After reaching an answer, compose your "good-bye," but do it in an essay. And note that Emerson is not bidding his friends and family "good-bye." Instead, he seems to be focused on what has plagued him, i.e., grandeur, wealth, frozen hearts, and crowded halls.

3. In *Each and All,* Emerson writes: "Beauty is unripe childhood's cheat." What does this mean? In an essay, offer an interpretation. (This interpretation should include a definition of "Beauty.") After offering an interpretation, take a stand that shows whether or not you agree with it. Naturally, your stance will require support to advance it, and such support can be found by researching many things. Some of these things might include people, wars, issues, problems, houses, or cars.

Edgar Allan Poe (1809–1849)

Sometimes likened to the Stephen King of the 19th century, Edgar Allan Poe is credited with starting the "dark tradition" in American Literature. Unfortunately, unlike King, Poe did not enjoy much fame and recognition for his contributions to the literary world. This may be what contributed to his depression, eventual alcoholism, and death, which occurred as he lay face down in the streets of Baltimore, Maryland. But as a former resident of Baltimore, it is no coincidence that Baltimore's football team, the Ravens, has the same name as one of Poe's most famous works.

The Raven

Once upon a midnight dreary, while I pondered, weak and weary,
Over many a quaint and curious volume of forgotten lore,
While I nodded, nearly napping, suddenly there came a tapping,
As of someone gently rapping, rapping at my chamber door.
"'Tis some visitor," I muttered, "tapping at my chamber door;
Only this, and nothing more."

Ah, distinctly I remember, it was in the bleak December,
And each separate dying ember wrought its ghost upon the floor.
Eagerly I wished the morrow; vainly I had sought to borrow
From my books surcease of sorrow, sorrow for the lost Lenore.
For the rare and radiant maiden whom the angels name Lenore,
Nameless here forevermore.

And the silken sad uncertain rustling of each purple curtain
Thrilled me—filled me with fantastic terrors never felt before;
So that now, to still the beating of my heart, I stood repeating,
"'Tis some visitor entreating entrance at my chamber door,
Some late visitor entreating entrance at my chamber door.
This it is, and nothing more."

Presently my soul grew stronger; hesitating then no longer,
"Sir," said I, "or madam, truly your forgiveness I implore;
But the fact is, I was napping, and so gently you came rapping,
And so faintly you came tapping, tapping at my chamber door,
That I scarce was sure I heard you." Here I opened wide the door;—
Darkness there, and nothing more.

Deep into the darkness peering, long I stood there, wondering, fearing
Doubting, dreaming dreams no mortals ever dared to dream before;
But the silence was unbroken, and the stillness gave no token,
And the only word there spoken was the whispered word, "Lenore!"
This I whispered, and an echo murmured back the word, "Lenore!"
Merely this, and nothing more.

Back into the chamber turning, all my soul within me burning,
Soon again I heard a tapping, something louder than before,
"Surely," said I, "surely, that is something at my window lattice.
Let me see, then, what thereat is, and this mystery explore.
Let my heart be still a moment, and this mystery explore.
"'Tis the wind, and nothing more."

Open here I flung the shutter, when, with many a flirt and flutter,
In there stepped a stately raven, of the saintly days of yore.
Not the least obeisance made he; not a minute stopped or stayed he;
But with mien of lord or lady, perched above my chamber door.
Perched upon a bust of Pallas, just above my chamber door,
Perched, and sat, and nothing more.

Then this ebony bird beguiling my sad fancy into smiling,
By the grave and stern decorum of the countenance it wore,
"Though thy crest be shorn and shaven thou," I said, "art sure no craven,
Ghastly, grim, and ancient raven, wandering from the nightly shore.
Tell me what thy lordly name is on the Night's Plutonian shore."
Quoth the raven, "Nevermore."

Much I marvelled this ungainly fowl to hear discourse so plainly,
Though its answer little meaning, little relevancy bore;
For we cannot help agreeing that no living human being
Ever yet was blessed with seeing bird above his chamber door,
Bird or beast upon the sculptured bust above his chamber door,
With such name as "Nevermore."

But the raven, sitting lonely on that placid bust, spoke only
That one word, as if his soul in that one word he did outpour.
Nothing further then he uttered; not a feather then he fluttered;
Till I scarcely more than muttered, "Other friends have flown before;
On the morrow he will leave me, as my hopes have flown before."
Then the bird said, "Nevermore."

Startled at the stillness broken by reply so aptly spoken,
"Doubtless," said I, "what it utters is its only stock and store,
Caught from some unhappy master, whom unmerciful disaster
Followed fast and followed faster, till his songs one burden bore,—
Till the dirges of his hope that melancholy burden bore
Of "Never—nevermore."

But the raven still beguiling all my sad soul into smiling,
Straight I wheeled a cushioned seat in front of bird, and bust and door;
Then, upon the velvet sinking, I betook myself to linking
Fancy unto fancy, thinking what this ominous bird of yore—
What this grim, ungainly, ghastly, gaunt and ominous bird of yore
Meant in croaking "Nevermore."

Thus I sat engaged in guessing, but no syllable
  expressing
To the fowl, whose fiery eyes now burned into my
  bosom's core;
This and more I sat divining, with my head at ease
  reclining
On the cushion's velvet lining that the lamplight
  gloated o'er,
But whose velvet violet lining with the lamplight
  gloating o'er
She shall press, ah, nevermore!

Then, methought, the air grew denser, perfumed
  from an unseen censer
Swung by seraphim whose footfalls tinkled on the
  tufted floor.
"Wretch," I cried, "thy God hath lent thee—by these
  angels he hath
Sent thee respite—respite and nepenthe from thy
  memories of Lenore!
Quaff, O quaff this kind nepenthe, and forget this
  lost Lenore!"
Quoth the raven, "Nevermore!"

"Prophet!" said I, "thing of evil!—prophet still, if
  bird or devil!
Whether tempter sent, or whether tempest tossed
  thee here ashore,
Desolate, yet all undaunted, on this desert land
  enchanted—
On this home by horror haunted—tell me truly, I
  implore:
Is there—is there balm in Gilead?—tell me—tell
  me I implore!"
Quoth the raven, "Nevermore."

"Prophet!" said I, "thing of evil—prophet still, if
  bird or devil!
By that heaven that bends above us—by that God
  we both adore—
Tell this soul with sorrow laden, if, within the
  distant Aidenn,
It shall clasp a sainted maiden, whom the angels
  name Lenore—
Clasp a rare and radiant maiden, whom the angels
  name Lenore?
Quoth the raven, "Nevermore."

"Be that word our sign of parting, bird or fiend!" I
  shrieked, upstarting—
"Get thee back into the tempest and the Night's
  Plutonian shore!
Leave no black plume as a token of that lie thy soul
  hath spoken!
Leave my loneliness unbroken!—quit the bust
  above my door!
Take thy beak from out my heart, and take thy form
  from off my door!"
Quoth the raven, "Nevermore."

And the raven, never flitting, still is sitting, still is
  sitting
On the pallid bust of Pallas just above my chamber
  door;
And his eyes have all the seeming of a demon's that
  is dreaming.
And the lamplight o'er him streaming throws his
  shadow on the floor;
And my soul from out that shadow that lies floating
  on the floor
Shall be lifted—nevermore!

Questions

1. Poe writes: "And each separate dying ember wrought its ghost upon the floor." Attempt to picture this. What does a dying ember's ghost look like? How does this image help advance the poem?

2. It has been said that the most frightening thing a movie audience can see is a closed door. On screen, when framed appropriately, a closed door is mysterious. And when captured on screen, audience members might find themselves saying, "No! Don't open the door." In Poe's poem, does something similar happen? When you first heard, "Some late visitor entreating

entrance at my chamber door. / This it is, and nothing more," what do you remember of your internal monologue? Were you pensive? Intrigued? Nervous? Why?

3. Identify various symbols in this poem. Some, for instance, might include the heart, the shutter, the wind, and the raven. But there are others. Identify these symbols, and explain what they may symbolize.

4. To have dialogue with any animal would be considered, by many, a little odd. Still, many people find themselves talking to their dogs or cats, their rabbits or birds. But when we think of talking to a bird, it's probably a parrot or a cockatoo. Poe, however, chooses a raven. Why? And if you were to write a poem similar to Poe's, what animal would you choose? And would the animal play a major role in dictating the poem's tone?

5. Describe this raven. Note its eyes, its posture, its aura. Make sure to support each description by citing lines from the poem.

6. Who is Lenore? What is Lenore's function in this poem?

7. In the narrator's search for meaning, what role does the raven play? In other words, what does the reader learn about the narrator when he is expressing his thoughts to the raven?

Annabel Lee

It was many and many a year ago,
    In a kingdom by the sea,
That a maiden there lived whom you may know
    By the name of ANNABEL LEE;
And this maiden she lived with no other thought
    Than to love and be loved by me.

I was a child and she was a child,
    In this kingdom by the sea;
But we loved with a love that was more than love—
    I and my Annabel Lee;
With a love that the winged seraphs of heaven
    Coveted her and me.

And this was the reason that, long ago,
    In this kingdom by the sea,
A wind blew out of a cloud, chilling
    My beautiful Annabel Lee;
So that her highborn kinsman came
    And bore her away from me,
To shut her up in a sepulchre
    In this kingdom by the sea.

The angels, not half so happy in heaven,
    Went envying her and me—
Yes!—that was the reason (as all men know,
    In this kingdom by the sea)
That the wind came out of the cloud by night,
    Chilling and killing my Annabel Lee.

But our love it was stronger by far than the love
    Of those who were older than we—
    Of many far wiser than we—
And neither the angels in heaven above,
    Nor the demons down under the sea,
Can ever dissever my soul from the soul
    Of the beautiful Annabel Lee.

For the moon never beams without bringing me
  dreams
    Of the beautiful Annabel Lee;
And the stars never rise but I feel the bright eyes
    Of the beautiful Annabel Lee;
And so, all the night-tide, I lie down by the side
Of my darling—my darling—my life and my bride,
    In the sepulchre there by the sea,
    In her tomb by the sounding sea.

Questions

1. In reading *Annabel Lee*, do you get the impression that Poe is remembering something that did, in fact, happen in his life? Or does he employ specific language that suggests something fantastic or fictitious?
2. Poe writes: "That the wind came out of the cloud by night, / Chilling and killing my Annabel Lee." Is Poe employing symbols? Might the wind symbolize something in particular? Further, how might this wind have been "killing" her?
3. Clearly, Poe believes that the narrator and Annabel Lee are souls intertwined. Yet, is there information suggesting that while she has died, the narrator remains alive?
4. The ending of this poem seems to parallel the ending of *Romeo and Juliet*. However, in *Annabel Lee*, is the narrator's purpose clear? Is he in her tomb to die next to her? Or is he in her tomb merely to lie next to her?

The Bells

I

Hear the sledges with the bells—
    Silver bells!
What a world of merriment their melody foretells!
   How they tinkle, tinkle, tinkle,
    In the icy air of night!
   While the stars that oversprinkle
   All the heavens, seem to twinkle
    With a crystalline delight;
     Keeping time, time, time,
    In a sort of Runic rhyme,
To the tintinnabulation that so musically wells
   From the bells, bells, bells, bells,
     Bells, bells, bells—
From the jingling and the tinkling of the bells.

II

Hear the mellow wedding bells,
    Golden bells!
What a world of happiness their harmony foretells!
   Through the balmy air of night
   How they ring out their delight!
    From the molten-golden notes,
     And an in tune,
   What a liquid ditty floats

To the turtle-dove that listens, while she gloats
    On the moon!
   Oh, from out the sounding cells,
What a gush of euphony voluminously wells!
    How it swells!
    How it dwells
   On the Future! How it tells
   Of the rapture that impels
To the swinging and the ringing
   Of the bells, bells, bells,
  Of the bells, bells, bells, bells,
    Bells, bells, bells—
To the rhyming and the chiming of the bells!

III

   Hear the loud alarum bells—
    Brazen bells!
What a tale of terror, now, their turbulency tells!
   In the startled ear of night
  How they scream out their affright!
    Too much horrified to speak,
    They can only shriek, shriek,
     Out of tune,

In a clamorous appealing to the mercy of the fire,
In a mad expostulation with the deaf and frantic fire,
  Leaping higher, higher, higher,
    With a desperate desire,
  And a resolute endeavor,
  Now—now to sit or never,
By the side of the pale-faced moon.
  Oh, the bells, bells, bells!
  What a tale their terror tells
    Of Despair!
  How they clang, and clash, and roar!
  What a horror they outpour
On the bosom of the palpitating air!
  Yet the ear it fully knows,
    By the twanging,
    And the clanging,
  How the danger ebbs and flows:
  Yet the ear distinctly tells,
    In the jangling,
    And the wrangling,
  How the danger sinks and swells,
By the sinking or the swelling in the anger of the
  bells—
    Of the bells—
  Of the bells, bells, bells, bells,
    Bells, bells, bells—
In the clamor and the clangor of the bells!

IV

  Hear the tolling of the bells—
    Iron Bells!
What a world of solemn thought their monody
  compels!
  In the silence of the night,
  How we shiver with affright
At the melancholy menace of their tone!
  For every sound that floats

From the rust within their throats
    Is a groan.
And the people—ah, the people—
They that dwell up in the steeple,
    All Alone
And who, tolling, tolling, tolling,
  In that muffled monotone,
Feel a glory in so rolling
  On the human heart a stone—
They are neither man nor woman—
They are neither brute nor human—
    They are Ghouls:
And their king it is who tolls;
And he rolls, rolls, rolls,
    Rolls
  A paean from the bells!
And his merry bosom swells
  With the paean of the bells!
And he dances, and he yells;
Keeping time, time, time,
In a sort of Runic rhyme,
  To the paean of the bells—
    Of the bells:
Keeping time, time, time,
In a sort of Runic rhyme,
  To the throbbing of the bells—
Of the bells, bells, bells—
  To the sobbing of the bells;
Keeping time, time, time,
  As he knells, knells, knells,
In a happy Runic rhyme,
  To the rolling of the bells—
Of the bells, bells, bells:
  To the tolling of the bells,
Of the bells, bells, bells, bells—
  Bells, bells, bells—
To the moaning and the groaning of the bells.

Questions

1. In Poe's *The Bells,* what might the "silver bells" represent?
2. Poe writes: "Now—now to sit or never." What might he be alluding to? Why is this such a big decision?
3. Trace Poe's third stanza as if you were creating a chalk outline for a symphony. Note when his third stanza begins to build. And then note when it further builds. And then note when it crescendos. During the crescendo, what sounds do you hear? Are cymbals crashing? Are brass instruments blaring? Are strings screeching? What do you hear behind the words?
4. In the fourth stanza, the bells are "sobbing" and "moaning and [. . .] groaning." Juxtapose the first stanza and the fourth stanza. What is different about the bells? Have they evolved? Devolved?

1. Identify an argument in one of Poe's poems, and cite various lines that help support that argument. Then, after doing some research, take a stand on whether or not you agree with the argument. Use what you unearthed during your research to help advance your contention.
2. After reading *The Raven,* watch Alfred Hitchcock's film *The Birds.* Then, compare and contrast the two.
3. Though you may not have much interest in ornithology, research the role of birds in literature, history, and pop culture. After gathering support, construct an argument that revolves around birds, and make sure to reference *The Raven.*
4. Choose one of Poe's poems, and identify its main argument. Then, choose one of Poe's short stories, and identify its main argument. After doing so, compare and contrast each text's argument.

Walt Whitman (1819–1892)

Born in Long Island, Walt Whitman attended grammar school in Brooklyn and was employed as a printer in New York City. However, prior to publishing *Leaves of Grass,* he was a reporter, writer, carpenter, farmer, seashore observer, teacher, and editor. Then, in Spring 1855, Whitman self-published *Leaves of Grass.* And even though many were bewildered by Whitman's use of free verse, Ralph Waldo Emerson, who had already established himself in American literary circles, hailed it. Among the twelve poems in *Leaves of Grass*' first edition was *Song of Myself.*

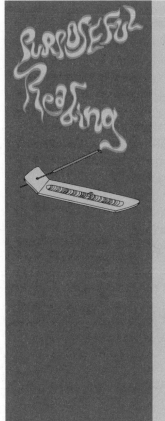

Walt Whitman's Poems

1. When reading Whitman, note his passion for life or, in *O Captain! My Captain!*, the absence thereof.
2. Notice how in *Song of Myself* Whitman celebrates life and provides the reader with some advice. Notice how in *O Captain! My Captain!* Whitman celebrates death (any advice is implicit). And notice how the styles he employs are different, possibly due to the messages he is attempting to convey.
3. Abraham Lincoln had much to do with the end of the Civil War and the victory of the North over the South. Many saw him as a hero, some as a paternal figure, others as simply a great leader. But like John F. Kennedy or Julius Caesar, Lincoln did not die of what many would deem "natural" causes. According to the *New York Herald,* he was shot at 9:30 p.m. on Friday, April 14, 1865 while seated in a box at Ford's Theater. It's important to realize that *O Captain! My Captain!* is a response to Lincoln's death.
4. In *Dead Poets Society,* John Keating says: "'Oh Captain, My Captain.' Who knows where that comes from? [. . .] Not a clue? It's from a poem by Walt Whitman about Mr. Abraham Lincoln. Now, in this class you can call me Mr. Keating. Or, if you're slightly more daring, Oh Captain, My Captain." While this poem was originally a reference to Lincoln, many have chosen to read this poem to pay homage to friends and loved ones.

from *Song of Myself*

1

I celebrate myself, and sing myself,
And what I assume you shall assume,
For every atom belonging to me as good belongs
   to you.

I loafe and invite my soul,
I lean and loafe at my ease observing a spear of
   summer grass.
My tongue, every atom of my blood, form'd from
   this soil, this air,
Born here of parents born here from parents the
   same, and their parents the same,
I, now thirty-seven years old in perfect health begin,
Hoping to cease not till death.

Creeds and schools in abeyance,
Retiring back a while sufficed at what they are, but
   never forgotten,
I harbor for good or bad, I permit to speak at every
   hazard,
Nature without check with original energy.

2

Houses and rooms are full of perfumes, the shelves
   are crowded with perfumes,
I breathe the fragrance myself and know it and like it,
The distillation would intoxicate me also, but I shall
   not let it.

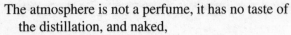

The atmosphere is not a perfume, it has no taste of
the distillation, and naked,
I am mad for it to be in contact with me.

The smoke of my own breath,
Echoes, ripples, buzz'd whispers, love-root, silk-
thread, crotch and vine,
My respiration and inspiration, the beating of my
heart, the passing of blood and air through my
lungs,
The sniff of green leaves and dry leaves, and of the
shore and dark-color'd sea rocks, and of hay in
the barn,
The sound of the belch'd words of my voice loos'd
to the eddies of the wind,
A few light kisses, a few embraces, a reaching
around of arms,
The play of shine and shade on the trees as the
supple boughs wag,
The delight alone or in the rush of the streets, or
along the fields and hill-sides,

The feeling of health, the full-noon trill, the song of
me rising from bed and meeting the sun.

Have you reckon'd a thousand acres much? have
you reckon'd the earth much?
Have you practis'd so long to learn to read?
Have you felt so proud to get at the meaning of
poems?

Stop this day and night with me and you shall
possess the origin of all poems,
You shall possess the good of the earth and sun,
(there are millions of suns left),
You shall no longer take things at second or third
hand, nor look through the eyes of the dead, nor
feed on the spectres in books,
You shall not look through my eyes either, nor take
things from me,
You shall listen to all sides and filter them from
your self.

Questions

1. Whitman writes: "I celebrate myself, and sing myself." What does this mean? If you were to
   spend an entire day celebrating yourself and "singing yourself," what might that involve?
2. Whitman writes: "And what I assume you shall assume." If we are not dealing in the world of
   fallacies and shared assumptions, how can a person expect that what "[he] assume[s] you
   shall assume"? How is this reasonable?
3. Whitman writes: "For every atom belonging to me as good belongs to you." This is interesting, for the ideas of good and bad tend to vary from person to person. In fact, Ralph Waldo
   Emerson, in his essay *Self-reliance,* writes of good and bad when he states: "Good and bad
   are but names, readily transferable to that or this. The only right is what is after my constitution; the only wrong, what is against it." Are Emerson and Whitman both attempting to communicate something similar? What is it, in fact, that they are attempting to communicate?
4. When Whitman writes, "Nature without check with original energy," what do you think he
   means? What is "Nature without check"?
5. In the last nine lines of Whitman's poem, the lines ending with "You shall listen to all sides
   and filter them from your self," what is he encouraging his readers to do? What is he suggesting about the power that each of us possesses as individuals? Further, do you agree with
   Whitman? Why?

O Captain! My Captain!

1

O CAPTAIN! my Captain! our fearful trip is done;
The ship has weather'd every rack, the prize we
    sought is won;
The port is near, the bells I hear, the people all
    exulting,
While follow eyes the steady keel, the vessel grim
    and daring:
    But O heart! heart! heart!
        O the bleeding drops of red,
            Where on the deck my Captain lies,
                Fallen cold and dead.

2

O Captain! my Captain! rise up and hear the bells;
Rise up—for you the flag is flung—for you the
    bugle trills;
For you bouquets and ribbon'd wreaths—for you
    the shores a-crowding;
For you they call, the swaying mass, their eager
    faces turning;
    Here Captain! dear father!
        This arm beneath your head;
            It is some dream that on the deck,
                You've fallen cold and dead.

3

My Captain does not answer, his lips are pale and still;
My father does not feel my arm, he has no pulse nor
    will;
The ship is anchor'd safe and sound, its voyage
    closed and done;
From fearful trip, the victor ship, comes in with
    object won;
    Exult, O shores, and ring, O bells!
        But I with mournful tread,
            Walk the deck my Captain lies,
                Fallen cold and dead.

Questions

1. Whitman writes: "O CAPTAIN! my Captain! our fearful trip is done." Describe this "fearful trip," and explain why Whitman employs the word "our."
2. In the second line of Whitman's poem, he refers to "the prize." What is this prize?
3. When you read aloud, "But O heart! heart! heart!", what do you hear? What do you see?
4. Whitman writes: "This arm beneath your head; / It is some dream that on the deck, / You've fallen cold and dead." What is he trying to communicate? Why might he be trying to communicate this?
5. What is "voyage closed" a reference to?
6. Whitman makes constant reference to a "deck." As we know, however, Lincoln was shot and killed in a theater. What, then, is the purpose of the maritime reference?

1. In Whitman's *Song of Myself,* he writes: "I celebrate myself, and sing myself." In Ralph Waldo Emerson's essay *Self-reliance,* Emerson writes: "Trust thyself." And later, he writes: "Know thyself." Are there similarities between what Whitman is attempting to communicate and what Emerson is attempting to communicate? In a comparison and contrast essay, compare and contrast *Song of Myself* and *Self-reliance.* Find a connection between the two, and then examine the differences within that connection.*

2. In *Song of Myself,* Whitman writes: "Stop this day and night with me and you shall possess the origin / of all poems." Clearly, it seems difficult (if not impossible) to write about possessing the "origin of all poems." Still, it does seem reasonable to suggest that one could argue for the origin of, say, ten poems. Thus, do this: examine ten poems of your choosing. In doing so, identify what you believe to be the origin of these ten poems. Naturally, a figurative origin is expected. (In other words, the origin would not be a feather-pen, a typewriter, or a word processor.) In composing this argument, identify the origin, and then employ support from the ten poems to advance your contention.

3. Whitman's *O Captain! My Captain!* is a response to the assassination of Abraham Lincoln. In a classification essay, classify various motives for assassinations. In other words, after researching the motives for different assassinations, classify these motives. Perhaps, for instance, John Lennon was assassinated by Mark David Chapman because Chapman believed Lennon to be a hypocrite. Then, perhaps, you would argue that one motive for assassination is hypocrisy. Other assassinations that might be examined include the assassination of Dr. Martin Luther King, Jr., Malcolm X, John F. Kennedy, or Lee Harvey Oswald. Identify potential motives for these assassinations, and classify them.

4. Like Abraham Lincoln, many leaders have affected their supporters, dissenters, and followers. What is interesting, though, is that like many leaders, Lincoln found a way to catapult himself to a position of leadership. In examining leadership, are there certain qualities (good or bad) that a leader must possess? Again, whether good or bad, leaders are likely to share many of the same qualities. Thus, research the qualities of leadership. You might begin with Abraham Lincoln, Napolean, Marcus Aurelias, Adolf Hitler, Mussolini, Pol Pot, Atilla the Hun, or Ganghis Kahn. In fact, there is even a book titled *Leadership Secrets of Atilla the Hun.* (You may wish to consult such books.) After researching various qualities of leadership, identify three or four qualities that, based on the leaders you have researched, every leader must possess.

---

*For an additional challenge, consider comparing and contrasting *Song of Myself* and an essay by Emerson titled *Nature*.

Emily Dickinson (1830–1886)

Born in Amherst, Massachusetts, and referred to as the Amherst Belle, Emily Dickinson published only 7 of her more than 1,700 poems while she was alive. Unlike Mark Twain, who hired salesmen to go door-to-door in hopes of selling his bundled books, Dickinson did not exert much effort in getting her works published. In fact, when her poetry was published, it was published without her consent. Interestingly, Dickinson was quite reclusive. Similar to Henry David Thoreau or J. D. Salinger, Dickinson stepped away from the public. But Dickinson chose to do so in her mid-twenties, choosing to remain at home where she might do housework and write poetry. About poetry, Dickinson once wrote: "If I feel physically as if the top of my head were taken off, I know that is poetry."

Dickinson's Poems

1. When reading Dickinson, note that even though it is a bit dry, she does have quite a sense of humor. Do not be afraid to chuckle while absorbing some of her observations.
2. Notice that Dickinson is writing about some of the larger phenomena associated with existence: the world, death, truth, and love.
3. Read her poems aloud. If you are not reading her poems aloud, then simply make sure to heed her punctuation marks; for instance, her use of the dash represents a significant pause.

This is my letter to the World

This is my letter to the World
That never wrote to Me—
The simple News that Nature told—
With tender Majesty

Her Message is committed
To Hands I cannot see
For love of Her—Sweet—countrymen—
Judge tenderly—of Me

Questions

1. Clearly the "World" would not write somebody a letter. Hence, when Dickinson writes, "This is my letter to the World / That never wrote to Me," what might she mean?
2. What "News" might "Nature" tell?
3. Dickinson writes: "Her Message is committed." What might "Her Message" be?
4. Do you see some type of distinction being made between "Her" and "Me"? Might this be some sort of competition? Is there an element of selfishness or egocentrism in this poem?

I heard a Fly buzz—when I died

I heard a Fly buzz—when I died—
The stillness in the Room
Was like the Stillness in the Air—
Between the Heaves of Storm—

The Eyes around—had wrung them dry—
And Breaths were gathering firm
For that last Onset—when the King
Be witnessed—in the Room—

I willed my Keepsakes—Signed away
What portion of me be
Assignable—and then it was
There interposed a Fly—

With Blue—uncertain stumbling Buzz—
Between the light—and me—
And then the Windows failed—and then
I could not see to see—

Questions

1. What is darkly comical about the first line of this poem?
2. When she writes, "For that last Onset—when the King / Be witnessed—in the Room," to whom might she be referring?
3. Dickinson writes: "Between the light—and me—." What might "the light" represent?
4. If the narrator is clearly on her way to the afterlife, what is fitting about her last earthly experience? Frankly, what type of person would write a poem that depicts a fly finding itself between a fading life and an ascension to the afterlife? What might this suggest about Dickinson's sense of humor?

Because I could not stop for Death

Because I could not stop for Death—
He kindly stopped for me—
The Carriage held but just Ourselves—
And Immortality.

We slowly drove—He knew no haste
And I had put away
My labor and my leisure too,
For His Civility—

We passed the School, where Children strove
At Recess—in the Ring—
We passed the Fields of Gazing Grain—
We passed the Setting Sun—

Or rather—He passed Us—
The Dews drew quivering and chill—
For only Gossamer, my Gown—
My Tippet—only Tulle—

We passed before a House that seemed
A Swelling of the Ground—
The Roof was scarcely visible—
The Cornice—in the Ground—

Since then—'tis Centuries—and yet
Feels shorter than the Day
I first surmised the Horses' Heads
Were toward Eternity—

Questions

1. Dickinson writes: "Because I could not stop for Death." This is intriguing for many reasons. Specifically, consider why the narrator could not stop for Death.
2. Once the narrator is in the carriage, are there two people (the narrator and Death), or are there three people (the narrator, Death, and Immortality)? Why?
3. If the narrator "put away / [her] labor and [her] leisure too, / For His Civility," why would she extend such courtesy to Death? Such courtesy seems especially disconcerting if one notes that in the first line, she clearly "could not stop for Death," yet she has now stopped for Death and done away with the mortal pleasures of "labor and leisure."
4. What do you make of the ending? What should we take from it? What do you think becomes of the narrator?

Tell all the Truth but tell it slant

Tell all the Truth but tell it slant—
Success in Circuit lies
Too bright for our infirm Delight
The Truth's superb surprise

As Lightening to the Children eased
With explanation kind
The Truth must dazzle gradually
Or every man be blind—

Questions

1. Dickinson writes: "Tell all the Truth but tell it slant." What might this mean?
2. When Dickinson writes "Success in Circuit," what might "Circuit" be?
3. What is the "superb surprise" of Truth?
4. Why do you think the "Truth must dazzle gradually"? And if it does not, then why would "every man be blind"?

That Love is all there is

> That Love is all there is,
> Is all we know of Love;
> It is enough, the freight should be
> Proportioned to the groove.

Questions

1. Is Dickinson suggesting that when we investigate our motivations for everything we do, in the end, the derivation of all things is love? If she is, in fact, attempting to communicate this, then what role does hate play in this pathology?
2. What is "the freight"? And why should it be "Proportioned to the groove"?

1. After reading Dickinson's *This is my letter to the World,* write *your* letter to the world. This might be a letter announcing your departure from the world or, perhaps, your arrival to it. In other words, maybe you are excited about the things you are about to accomplish, about the goals you are about to set, or the dreams you are about to realize. And maybe you wish to make an announcement of these things in your "letter to the world." Or, perhaps, you would like to look into the future. Hopefully, many years from now, after you have done much of what it is you intended to do, perhaps you should write your "letter to the world." What did you do? What did you learn? As noted in her poem, Dickinson writes: "Judge tenderly— of Me." In the end, should anybody "Judge tenderly—of [You]"?

Continued

2. It seems that both *I heard a Fly buzz—when I died* and *Because I could not stop for Death* revolve around a similar topic: death. Still, it seems reasonable to suggest that each is extending to its reader a different argument. Identify an argument in *I heard a Fly buzz—when I died.* Then, identify an argument in *Because I could not stop for Death.* Upon identifying both arguments, compare and contrast them within the context of the two poems.

3. After reading *Tell all the Truth but tell it slant* and noting the line, "The Truth must dazzle gradually," examine "truths" that have "dazzled." Examples might include "truths" about the Vietnam War, "truths" about corruption in the Los Angeles Police Department, or "truths" about O. J. Simpson, the N.R.A., Michael Moore, Osama bin Laden, or George W. Bush. Examine these "truths," and use support from them to show how they "dazzled."

4. In *That Love is all there is,* Dickinson seems to suggest that, perhaps, the derivation of all things is love. Take a stand, and show whether or not you agree that the derivation of all things is love. In taking this stand, examine five films to support your argument. Naturally, it would be unfair to examine five films specific to the love and romance genre, so do this: choose a romantic comedy, a drama, an action film, a science-fiction film, and an animated film. Thus, if following the aforementioned order, the five films might be these: *Two Weeks Notice, Empire of the Sun, The Rundown, Star Wars,* and *Finding Nemo.* Use support from each film to advance your argument.

Edwin Arlington Robinson (1869–1935)

Born in Maine and educated at Harvard, Edwin Arlington Robinson was often inspired to write after observing the tortured and disappointing lives of his family and friends. Regularly flirting with the American dream in a less than patriotic manner, Robinson's works have a tendency to shock people with their realism or pessimistic idealism. Still, even though he seemed to feel underappreciated for his literary contributions, it seems that he was living his dream, for in October 1893, he wrote to his friend Gledhill: "Writing has been my dream ever since I was old enough to lay a plan for an air castle."

Robinson's Poems

1. When reading these two poems, consider perceptions and, specifically, how we develop our perceptions of others.
2. Note the differences between "rhyming poetry" and poetry that does not rhyme. Some people argue that "rhyming poetry" is predictable, yet others argue that it has a certain musical, rhythmic quality. Thus, it may be important to ask yourself if such poetry can be written in such a way that it avoids predictability.
3. Observe the presence of dreams in both poems. In one poem, many people are dreaming about one man's life, and in another, one person is dreaming about the lives of many.

Richard Cory

Whenever Richard Cory went down town,
We people on the pavement looked at him:
He was a gentleman from sole to crown,
Clean favored, and imperially slim.

And he was always quietly arrayed,
And he was always human when he talked;
But still he fluttered pulses when he said,
"Good-morning," and he glittered when he walked.

And he was rich—yes, richer than a king—
And admirably schooled in every grace:
In fine, we thought that he was everything
To make us wish that we were in his place.

So on we worked, and waited for the light,
And went without meat, and cursed the bread;
And Richard Cory, one calm summer night,
Went home and put a bullet through his head.

Questions

1. Identify three arguments that are communicated in this poem. (These arguments do not need to be taken verbatim from the poem. Simply extract ideas from the poem, and create an argument representative of those ideas.)
2. What is unsettling about this poem? Is it simply that a rich man who had everything went home and killed himself? Or is there something more?
3. Identify three famous people (male or female) who were thought of as having "everything" and who, like Richard Cory, ended their lives. If, in the end, these people seem to have more than most, why would they kill themselves?

Miniver Cheevy

Miniver Cheevy, child of scorn,
    Grew lean when he assailed the seasons;
He wept that he was ever born,
    And he had reasons.

Miniver loved the days of old
    When swords were bright and steeds were
        prancing;
The vision of a warrior bold
    Would set him dancing.

Miniver sighed for what was not,
    And dreamed, and rested from his labors;
He dreamed of Thebes and Camelot,
    And Priam's neighbors.

Miniver mourned the ripe renown
    That made so many a name so fragrant;
He mourned Romance, now on the town,
    And Art, a vagrant.

Miniver loved the Medici,
    Albeit he had never seen one;
He would have sinned incessantly
    Could he have been one.

Miniver cursed the commonplace
    And eyed a khaki suit with loathing;
He missed the mediaeval grace
    Of iron clothing.

Miniver scorned the gold he sought,
    But sore annoyed was he without it;
Miniver thought, and thought, and thought,
    And thought about it.

Miniver Cheevy, born too late,
    Scratched his head and kept on thinking:
Miniver coughed, and called it fate,
    And kept on drinking.

Questions

1. This poem begins with "Miniver Cheevy, child of scorn." What does Robinson suggest by describing Cheevy as a "child of scorn"?
2. Based on the poem, what do you think Miniver Cheevy's age might be?
3. If "Miniver cursed the commonplace / And eyed a khaki suit with loathing," what might these two lines suggest? Might they suggest that he is a member of the commonplace and that he wears khaki suits? Or might these two lines suggest the opposite?
4. What type of profession might a person like Miniver Cheevy have?
5. There is something about human nature that compels us to seek what we currently do not have, yet condemn that which we are seeking. In *Miniver Cheevy,* "Miniver scorned the gold he sought, / But sore annoyed was he without it." Is this simply one of human nature's many foibles? Is it hypocrisy? Is it cognitive dissonance? And if things are so bad for Miniver Cheevy, why does he keep drinking? Why doesn't he simply follow the actions of Richard Cory?

1. Identify three arguments in *Richard Cory*. After doing so, identify three famous people (male or female) who were thought of as having "everything" and who, like Richard Cory, ended their lives. One person might be Marilyn Monroe. A more fitting example might be Kurt Cobain. Upon identifying three famous people, show how each person advances the three arguments that you have identified.

2. Examine *Richard Cory* and *Miniver Cheevy*. After doing so, compare and contrast the two. In comparing and contrasting the two poems, compare and contrast the characters, or compare and contrast the arguments that can be extracted from each poem.

3. Assign classifications to Richard Cory and Miniver Cheevy. Additionally, identify two more characters to classify. These characters do not, necessarily, have to come from a poem. For instance, one character might be Ahab, from Herman Melville's *Moby Dick*. Or, perhaps, you might identify Michael, played by Robert DeNiro, in *The Deer Hunter*. The goal is to find a way to classify various characters based on specific personality traits.

Paul Laurence Dunbar (1872–1906)

Paul Laurence Dunbar was born in Dayton, Ohio. Dunbar's mother, Matilda, was a former slave, and his father was an escaped slave who served in the 55th Massachusetts Infantry Regiment and the 5th Massachusetts Colored Cavalry Regiment during the Civil War. As the only African-American student in his class at Dayton Central High, Paul Laurence Dunbar had to overcome many hurdles. Still, he was a member of the debating society, editor of the school paper, and president of the school's literary society. Working as an elevator operator, it was at age twenty that Dunbar published his first book of poems. And while it was received well locally, Dunbar engaged in some self-promotion, including selling his book for a dollar to people who rode the elevator. In 1893, at age twenty-one, Dunbar met Frederick Douglass, and Douglass called Dunbar "the most promising young colored man in America." Dunbar continued to write, and he eventually attained national fame, but he developed tuberculosis and, by 1902, he had also become dependent on alcohol. In 1906, after producing a total of twelve books of poetry, four books of short stories, five novels, and a play, Paul Laurence Dunbar died in Dayton, Ohio, at the age of thirty-three.

Dunbar's Poems

1. While reading Dunbar's poems, note his choice to employ two distinct voices: the voice of standard English, and the voice of dialect.
2. In addition to writing poetry, Dunbar wrote songs. While differences abound between song lyrics and lines of poetry, there seems to be a song-like rhythm in Dunbar's poems. Listen for this rhythm as you, preferably, read his poems aloud.

We Wear the Mask

We wear the mask that grins and lies,
It hides our cheeks and shades our eyes,—
This debt we pay to human guile;
With torn and bleeding hearts we smile,
And mouth with myriad subtleties.

Why should the world be overwise,
In counting all our tears and sighs?
Nay, let them only see us, while
    We wear the mask.

We smile, but, O great Christ, our cries
To thee from tortured souls arise.
We sing, but oh the clay is vile
Beneath our feet, and long the mile;
But let the world dream otherwise,
    We wear the mask!

Questions

1. When considering a traditional mask, one's eyes are not covered. However, Dunbar writes: "It hides our cheeks and shades our eyes." How is it that a mask, whether literal or figurative, can shade one's eyes?
2. Dunbar writes: "This debt we pay to human guile." What is "human guile"? And why do we owe it a debt?
3. In his second stanza, Dunbar writes: "Nay, let them only see us, while / We wear the mask." What is it about allowing somebody to see us unmasked? Why might this be deemed unwise?
4. The last two lines of the poem are tricky. Dunbar writes: "But let the world dream otherwise, / We wear the mask!" Does Dunbar mean to suggest that we should let the world dream? Or does Dunbar mean to suggest that we should let the world dream otherwise? Clearly, the difference is monumental. What is this difference? And based on the poem, which meaning do you think Dunbar is attempting to advance?

When Dey 'Listed Colored Soldiers

DEY was talkin' in de cabin, dey was talkin' in de hall;
But I listened kin' o' keerless, not a-t'inkin' 'bout it all;
An' on Sunday, too, I noticed, dey was whisp' rin' mighty much
Stan'in' all erroun' de roadside w'en dey let us out o' chu'ch.
But I did n't t'ink erbout it 'twell de middle of de week,
An' my 'Lias come to see me, an' somehow he could n't speak.
Den I seed all in a minute whut he'd come to see me for;—
Dey had 'listed colo'ed sojers an' my 'Lias gwine to wah.

Oh, I hugged him, an' I kissed him, an' I baiged him not to go;
But he tol' me dat his conscience, hit was callin' to him so,
An' he could n't baih to lingah w'en he had a chanst to fight
For de freedom dey had gin him an' de glory of de right.
So he kissed me, an' he lef' me, w'en I'd p'omised to be true;
An' dey put a knapsack on him, an' a coat all colo'ed blue.
So I gin him pap's ol' Bible f'om de bottom of de draw',—
W'en dey 'listed colo'ed sojers an' my 'Lias went to wah.

But I t'ought of all de weary miles dat he would have to tramp,
An' I could n't be contented w'en dey tuk him to de camp.
W'y my hea't nigh broke wid grievin' 'twell I seed him on de street;
Den I felt lak I could go an' th'ow my body at his feet.
For his buttons was a-shinin', an' his face was shinin', too,
An' he looked so strong an' mighty in his coat o' sojer blue,
Dat I hollahed, "Step up, manny," dough my th'oat was so' an' raw,—
W'en dey 'listed colo'ed sojers an' my 'Lias went to wah.

Ol' Mis' cried w'en mastah lef' huh, young Miss mou'ned huh brothah Ned,
An' I did n't know dey feelin's is de ve'y wo'ds dey said
W'en I tol' 'em I was so'y. Dey had done gin up dey all;
But dey only seemed mo' proudah dat dey men had hyeahed de call.
Bofe my mastahs went in gray suits, an' I loved de Yankee blue,
But I t'ought dat I could sorrer for de losin' of 'em too;
But I could n't, for I did n't know de ha'f o' whut I saw,
'Twell dey 'listed colo'ed sojers an' my 'Lias went to wah.

Mastah Jack come home all sickly; he was broke for life, dey said;
An' dey lef' my po' young mastah some'r's on de roadside,—dead.
W'en de women cried an' mou'ned 'em, I could feel it thoo an' thoo,
For I had a loved un fightin' in de way o' dangah, too.
Den dey tol' me dey had laid him some'r's way down souf to res',
Wid de flag dat he had fit for shinin' daih across his breas'.
Well, I cried, but den I reckon dat 's whut Gawd had called him for,
W'en dey 'listed colo'ed sojers an' my 'Lias went to wah.

Questions

1. Who is "DEY"? In other words, to whom is Dunbar referring?
2. In the third stanza, Dunbar writes: "Den I felt lak I could go an' th'ow my body at his feet." Arguably, this could be the action of a male or female. Still, sometimes when something is written by a male, we simply assume that the narrator of the poem must be male as well. However, are there elements to this poem that suggest the narrator may be female?
3. Dunbar writes: "But I could n't, for I did n't know de ha'f o' whut I saw." What might this mean? What has the narrator seen?
4. In the last five lines of the poem, what realizations should the reader have? What has happened to 'Lias? And, now, what might happen to the narrator?

Sympathy

I KNOW what the caged bird feels, alas!
    When the sun is bright on the upland slopes;
When the wind stirs soft through the springing grass,
And the river flows like a stream of glass;
    When the first bird sings and the first bud opes,
And the faint perfume from its chalice steals—
I know what the caged bird feels!

I know why the caged bird beats his wing
    Till its blood is red on the cruel bars;
For he must fly back to his perch and cling
When he fain would be on the bough a-swing;
    And a pain still throbs in the old, old scars
And they pulse again with a keener sting—
I know why he beats his wing!

I know why the caged bird sings, ah me,
    When his wing is bruised and his bosom sore,—
When he beats his bars and he would be free;
It is not a carol of joy or glee,
    But a prayer that he sends from his heart's
        deep core,
But a plea, that upward to Heaven he flings—
I know why the caged bird sings!

Questions

1. Dunbar writes: "I KNOW what the caged bird feels, alas!" Then, he proceeds to reference "the sun," "the wind," and "the river." What might the purpose be of such a juxtaposition?
2. In the second stanza, Dunbar writes: "I know why the caged bird beats his wing / Till its blood is red on the cruel bars; / For he must fly back to his perch and cling." What might this suggest? Further, where might this bird's perch be?
3. Based on the poem, why does the caged bird sing?
4. Why might *Sympathy* be an ideal title for this poem?

1. Research famous people. These people might include politicians, musicians, actors, actresses, coaches, athletes, or serial killers. In performing your research, attempt to find discrepancies between the masks they wear in public and the lives they lead in private. One example, for instance, might be the mask worn by Bill Clinton. Such a mask seemed to communicate monogamy, yet when he removed the mask, the public was privy to seeing another side. Similarly, when a Catholic priest is accused of sodomizing an altar boy, it seems that a mask has been removed. It seems reasonable to suggest, as suggested by Dunbar in *We Wear the Mask,* that people do, indeed, wear masks. Nevertheless, it seems that some masks are more elusive than others. Thus, research public figures in an attempt to investigate the masks that some of these people wear. Then, develop a thesis statement that will guide your argument in a discourse on masks.

2. Classify the different masks that people wear. In order to advance your classifications, you will need to gather evidence. Do this by interviewing various people. (These people might consist of friends, relatives, or coworkers.) Make sure to get quotations from these people, and make sure that these quotations are specific to the "types" of masks that these people wear. In other words, make sure to gather quotations that help advance your classifications. Naturally, it would also seem reasonable to extract support from Dunbar's *We Wear the Mask.*

3. Identify two films that have one commonality: a mask. While there are myriad films that deal with this commonality, three very overt examples are *Mask,* starring Cher, *The Mask,* starring Jim Carrey, and *The Man in The Iron Mask,* starring Leonardo DiCaprio. But remember, one could also argue that masks—especially the type of mask to which Dunbar refers—are found in just about everything from Charlie Chaplin's *City Lights,* to Orson Welles' *Citizen Kane,* to Dustin Hoffman's *The Graduate,* to Tom Cruise's *Collateral.* Thus, once you have identified two films that share this commonality, compose a comparison and contrast essay. Clearly, it seems that the similarity would be that each film presents a character who wears a mask. Beyond that, there should still be other similarities. However, differences should abound as well.

4. Compose a comparison and contrast essay by examining Dunbar's *When Dey 'Listed Colored Soldiers* and the film *Glory.* Both address the presence of African-American soldiers in the Civil War, and both offer interesting arguments. Identify an argument presented by each text. Then, compare and contrast the arguments in an essay that draws upon both texts for its support. For additional credibility, and to further develop your essay, consider performing additional research on the presence of African-American soldiers in the Civil War.

5. In the film *Glory,* two of the African-American soldiers in the 54th Massachusetts Volunteer Regiment are Sergeant-Major John Rawlins, played by Morgan Freeman, and Trip, played by Denzel Washington. Choose one of these characters to compare and contrast with Carl Brashear, the main

character in *Men of Honor.* Brashear, played by Cuba Gooding, Jr., is an aspiring Navy diver, but he is suffering prejudices similar to the prejudices suffered by Rawlins and Trip in *Glory.* To further advance your comparison and contrast essay, consider researching the historic roles of African-Americans in the military, and consider drawing upon Dunbar's *When Dey 'Listed Colored Soldiers* for additional support.

6. After reading Dunbar's *Sympathy,* research famous "caged birds." These might include Martin Luther King, Jr., Malcolm X, and Nelson Mandella. However, because one of Maya Angelou's most famous works is *I Know Why the Caged Bird Sings,* it would seem reasonable to include her as well. And naturally, you should use Dunbar's *Sympathy.* Upon researching these famous "caged birds," take a stand that attempts to show specifically why these caged birds sing.

7. Read Maya Angelou's *I Know Why the Caged Bird Sings.* Upon doing so, compare and contrast it with Dunbar's *Sympathy.*

II.
19th Century Short Stories

It has been said that the short-story writer can do in twenty pages what a novelist can do in two-hundred. Whether or not this statement proves reasonable, what you will find are many differences when transitioning from the examination of poems to short stories. For instance, when tracing the events in a short story, it is common to find the following: equilibrium, loss of equilibrium, and the restoration of equilibrium (with new meaning). To illustrate this, note the way many films are written. *The Matrix,* for instance, begins with Neo living a relatively "normal" life until he learns that what he once considered reality is really just a series of computer codes. This, coupled with myriad attempts on his life, leads to a loss of equilibrium. Alas, Neo eventually learns that he is "The One," and equilibrium has been restored (with new meaning). While this example is not intended to trivialize the great short stories of the 19th century, it is intended to illustrate the key ingredients in story-telling, for these ingredients are often present in short-stories.

Also present in short stories is the use of implicit argumentation. (This might be referred to as a short-story's theme.) Similar to the poem that never actually has the line, "Slavery is unacceptable," a short story might house ten-thousand words, none of which reads: "Corporations are slowly turning humans into machines." And that is one of the wonders found in short-story writing. Through detail, dialogue, and controlled development, the short-story writer can plant seeds that may someday germinate, representing the impetus for the implicit argument the writer hoped to advance.

Herman Melville (1819–1891)

Herman Melville is probably best known for writing *Moby Dick,* which he finished when he was thirty-two years old. The grandson of two Revolutionary War heroes, Melville lived his early childhood in luxury. However, things eventually changed, and Melville grew into an adult who struggled to make a living as a writer, even though many people around him, like his brother, lived a very comfortable life through their work on Wall Street. Still, while many wondered why Melville continued to write, he eventually became recognized as not just a leading member in the American literary canon but the global canon as well. This, unfortunately, did not happen until after his death in 1891.

Bartleby, the Scrivener. A Story of Wall-street.

1. A "law copyist" is a person who copies documents. Nowadays, such exercises are usually reserved for photocopy machines. Note, however, that Melville does not only use the title "law copyist" but also "scrivener." "Scrivener" means "writer," and this might be interesting because Melville may be poking fun at not simply how dull and uneventful a law copyist's life is, but a writer's life as well.
2. Note the names of the characters in this story. Whose real name is given? Whose name is left unprovided?
3. Observe in Bartleby the power of passive resistance. Because he does not say "no," he is simply exerting a personal preference. Look for reasons that might show why his actions seem to compromise the structural integrity of his work environment.
4. *Bartleby the Scrivener*, published in 1852 in *Putnam's* magazine, did not find an enthusiastic readership in 1853 but is now considered one of the greatest short stories of the 19th century. In addition to its qualities of comedic disturbance, it is one of the first American stories of corporate discontent.

Bartleby, the Scrivener. A Story of Wall-street.

Herman Melville

I AM a rather elderly man. The nature of my avocations for the last thirty years has brought me into more than ordinary contact with what would seem an interesting and somewhat singular set of men, of whom as yet nothing that I know of has ever been written:—I mean the law-copyists or scriveners. I have known very many of them, professionally and privately, and if I pleased, could relate divers histories, at which good-natured gentlemen might smile, and sentimental souls might weep. But I waive the biographies of all other scriveners for a few passages in the life of Bartleby, who was a scrivener the strangest I ever saw or heard of. While of other law-copyists I might write the complete life of Bartleby, nothing of that sort can be done. I believe that no materials exist for a full and satisfactory biography of this man. It is an irreparable loss to literature. Bartleby was one of those beings of whom nothing is ascertainable, except from the original sources, and in his case those are very small. What my own astonished eyes saw of Bartleby, that is all I know of him, except, indeed, one vague report which will appear in the sequel.

Ere introducing the scrivener, as he first appeared to me, it is fit I make some mention of myself, my employees, my business, my chambers, and general surroundings; because some such description is indispensable to an adequate understanding of the chief character about to be presented.

Imprimis: I am a man who, from his youth upwards, has been filled with a profound conviction that the easiest way of life is the best. Hence, though I belong to a profession proverbially energetic and nervous, even to turbulence, at times, yet nothing of that sort have I ever suffered to invade my peace. I am one of those unambitious lawyers who never addresses a jury, or in any way draws down public applause; but in the cool tranquillity of a snug retreat, do a snug business among rich men's bonds and mortgages and title-deeds. All who know me consider me an eminently safe man. The late John Jacob Astor, a personage little given to poetic enthusiasm, had no hesitation in pronouncing my first grand point to be prudence; my next, method. I do not speak it in vanity, but simply record the fact, that I was not unemployed in my profession by the late John Jacob Astor; a name which, I admit, I love to repeat, for it hath a rounded and orbicular sound to it, and rings like unto bullion. I will freely add, that I was not insensible to the late John Jacob Astor's good opinion.

Some time prior to the period at which this little history begins, my avocations had been largely increased. The good old office, now extinct in the State of New York, of a Master in Chancery, had been conferred upon me. It was not a very arduous office, but very pleasantly remunerative. I seldom lose my temper; much more seldom indulge in dangerous indignation at wrongs and outrages; but I must be permitted to be rash here and declare, that I consider the sudden and violent abrogation of the office of Master of Chancery, by the new Constitution, as a—premature act; inasmuch as I had counted upon a life-lease of the profits, whereas I only received those of a few short years. But this is by the way.

My chambers were up stairs at No.—Wall-street. At one end they looked upon the white wall of the interior of a spacious sky-light shaft, penetrating the building from top to bottom. This view might have been considered rather tame than otherwise, deficient in what landscape painters call "life." But if so, the view from the other end of my chambers offered, at least, a contrast, if nothing more. In that direction my windows commanded an unobstructed view of a lofty brick wall, black by age and everlasting shade; which wall required no spy-glass to bring out its lurking beauties, but for the benefit of all near-sighted spectators, was pushed up to within ten feet of my window panes. Owing to the great height of the surrounding buildings, and my chambers being on the second floor, the interval between this wall and mine not a little resembled a huge square cistern.

At the period just preceding the advent of Bartleby, I had two persons as copyists in my employment, and a promising lad as an office-boy. First, Turkey; second, Nippers; third, Ginger Nut. These may seem names, the like of which are not usually found in the Directory. In truth they were nicknames, mutually conferred upon each other by my three clerks, and were deemed expressive of their respective persons or characters. Turkey was a short, pursy Englishman of about my own age, that is, somewhere not far from sixty. In the morning, one might say, his face was of a fine florid hue, but after twelve o'clock, meridian—his dinner hour—it blazed like a grate full of Christmas coals; and continued blazing—but, as it were, with a gradual wane—till 6 o'clock, P.M. or thereabouts, after which I saw no more of the proprietor of the face, which gaining its meridian with the sun, seemed to set with it, to rise, culminate, and decline the following day, with the like regularity and undiminished glory. There are many singular coincidences I have known in the course of my life, not the least among which was the fact, that exactly when Turkey displayed his fullest beams from his red and radiant countenance, just then, too, at that critical moment, began the daily period when I considered his business capacities as seriously disturbed for the remainder of the twenty-four hours. Not that he was absolutely idle, or averse to business then; far from it. The difficulty was, he was apt to be altogether too energetic. There was a strange, inflamed, flurried, flighty recklessness of activity about him. He would be incautious in dipping his pen into his inkstand. All his blots upon my documents, were dropped there after twelve o'clock, meridian. Indeed, not only would he be reckless and sadly given to making blots in the afternoon, but some days he went further, and was rather noisy. At such times, too, his face flamed with augmented blazonry, as if cannel coal had been heaped on anthracite. He made an unpleasant racket with his chair; spilled his sand-box; in mending his pens, impatiently split them all to pieces, and threw them on the floor in a sudden passion; stood up and leaned over his table, boxing his papers about in a most indecorous manner, very sad to behold in an elderly man like him. Nevertheless, as he was in many ways a most valuable person to me, and all the time before twelve o'clock, meridian, was the quickest, steadiest creature too, accomplishing a great deal of work in a style not easy to be matched—for these reasons, I was willing to overlook his eccentricities, though indeed, occasionally, I remonstrated with him. I did this very gently, however, because, though the civilest, nay, the blandest and most reverential of men in the morning, yet in the afternoon he was disposed, upon provocation, to be slightly rash with his tongue, in fact, insolent. Now, valuing his morning services as I did, and resolved not to lose them; yet, at the same time made uncomfortable by his inflamed ways after twelve o'clock; and being a man of peace, unwilling by my admonitions to call forth unseemly retorts from him; I took upon me, one Saturday noon (he was always worse on Saturdays), to hint to him, very kindly, that perhaps now that he was growing old, it might be well to abridge his labors; in short, he need not come to my chambers after twelve o'clock, but, dinner over, had best go home to his lodgings and rest himself till tea-time. But no; he insisted upon his afternoon devotions. His countenance became intolerably fervid, as he oratorically assured me—gesticulating with a long ruler at the other end of the room—that if his services in the morning were useful, how indispensible, then, in the afternoon?

"With submission, sir," said Turkey on this occasion, "I consider myself your right-hand man. In the morning I but marshal and deploy my columns; but in the afternoon I put myself at their head, and gallantly charge the foe, thus!"—and he made a violent thrust with the ruler.

"But the blots, Turkey," intimated I.

"True,—but, with submission, sir, behold these hairs! I am getting old. Surely, sir, a blot or two of a warm afternoon is not to be severely urged against gray hairs. Old age—even if it blot the page—is honorable. With submission, sir, we both are getting old."

This appeal to my fellow-feeling was hardly to be resisted. At all events, I saw that go he would not. So I made up my mind to let him stay, resolving, nevertheless, to see to it, that during the afternoon he had to do with my less important papers.

Nippers, the second on my list, was a whiskered, sallow, and, upon the whole, rather piratical-looking young man of about five and twenty. I always deemed him the victim of two evil powers—ambition and indigestion. The ambition was evinced by a certain impatience of the duties of a mere copyist, an unwarrantable usurpation of strictly professional affairs, such as the original drawing up of legal documents. The indigestion seemed betokened in an occasional nervous testiness and grinning irritability, causing the teeth to audibly grind together over mistakes committed in copying; unnecessary maledictions, hissed, rather than spoken, in the heat of business; and especially by a continual discontent with the height of the table where he worked. Though of a very ingenious mechanical turn, Nippers could never get this table to suit him. He put chips under it, blocks of various sorts, bits of pasteboard, and at last went so far as to attempt an exquisite adjustment by final pieces of folded blotting-paper. But no invention would answer. If, for the sake of easing his back, he brought the table lid at a sharp angle well up towards his chin, and wrote there like a man using the steep roof of a Dutch house for his desk:—then he declared that it stopped the circulation in his arms. If now he lowered the table to his waistbands, and stooped over it in writing, then there was a sore aching in his back. In short, the truth of the matter was, Nippers knew not what he wanted. Or, if he wanted any thing, it was to be rid of a scrivener's table altogether. Among the manifestations of his diseased ambition was a fondness he had for receiving visits from certain ambiguous-looking fellows in seedy coats, whom he called his clients. Indeed I was aware that not only was he, at times, considerable of a ward-politician, but he occasionally did a little business at the Justices' courts, and was not unknown on the steps of the Tombs. I have good reason to believe, however, that one individual who called upon him at my chambers, and who, with a grand air, he insisted was his client, was no other than a dun, and the alleged title-deed, a bill. But with all his failings, and the annoyances he caused me, Nippers, like his compatriot Turkey, was a very useful man to me; wrote a neat, swift hand; and, when he chose, was not deficient in a gentlemanly sort of deportment. Added to this, he always dressed in a gentlemanly sort of way; and so, incidentally, reflected credit upon my chambers. Whereas with respect to Turkey, I had much ado to keep him from being a reproach to me. His clothes were apt to look oily and smell of eating-houses. He wore his pantaloons very loose and baggy in summer. His coats were execrable; his hat not be to handled. But while the hat was a thing of indifference to me, inasmuch as his natural civility and deference, as a dependent Englishman, always led him to doff it the moment he entered the room, yet his coat was another matter. Concerning his coats, I reasoned with him; but with no effect. The truth was, I suppose, that a man with so small an income, could not afford to sport such a lustrous face and a lustrous coat at one and the same time. As Nippers once observed, Turkey's money went chiefly for red ink. One winter day I presented Turkey with a highly-respectable looking coat of my own, a padded gray coat, of a most comfortable warmth, and which buttoned straight up from the knee to the neck. I thought Turkey would appreciate the favor, and abate his rashness and obstreperousness of afternoons. But no. I verily believe that buttoning himself up in so downy and blanket-like a coat had a pernicious effect upon him; upon the same principle that too much oats are bad for horses. In fact, precisely as a rash, restive horse is said to feel his oats, so Turkey felt his coat. It made him insolent. He was a man whom prosperity harmed.

Though concerning the self-indulgent habits of Turkey I had my own private surmises, yet touching Nippers I was well persuaded that whatever might be his faults in other respects, he was, at least, a temperate young man. But indeed, nature herself seemed to have been his vintner, and at his birth charged him so thoroughly with an irritable, brandy-like disposition, that all subsequent potations were needless. When I consider how, amid the stillness of my chambers, Nippers would sometimes impatiently rise from his seat, and stooping over his table, spread his arms wide apart, seize the whole desk, and move it, and jerk it, with a grim, grinding motion on the floor, as if the table were a perverse voluntary agent, intent on thwarting and vexing him; I plainly perceive that for Nippers, brandy and water were altogether superfluous.

It was fortunate for me that, owing to its peculiar cause—indigestion—the irritability and consequent nervousness of Nippers, were mainly observable in the morning, while in the afternoon he was comparatively mild. So that Turkey's paroxysms only coming on about twelve o'clock, I never had to do with their eccentricities at one time. Their fits relieved each other like guards. When Nippers' was on, Turkey's was off; and vice versa. This was a good natural arrangement under the circumstances.

Ginger Nut, the third on my list, was a lad some twelve years old. His father was a carman, ambitious of seeing his son on the bench instead of a cart, before he died. So he sent him to my office as student at law, errand boy, and cleaner and sweeper, at the rate of one dollar a week. He had a little desk to himself, but he did not use it much. Upon inspection, the drawer exhibited a great array of the shells of various sorts of nuts. Indeed, to this quick-witted youth the whole noble science of the law was contained in a nut-shell. Not the least among the employments of Ginger Nut, as well as one which he discharged with the most alacrity, was his duty as cake and apple purveyor for Turkey and Nippers. Copying law papers being proverbially a dry, husky sort of business, my two scriveners were fain to moisten their mouths very often with Spitzenbergs to be had at the numerous stalls nigh the Custom House and Post Office. Also, they sent Ginger Nut very frequently for that peculiar cake—small, flat, round, and very spicy—after which he had been named by them. Of a cold morning when business was but dull, Turkey would gobble up scores of these cakes, as if they were mere wafers—indeed they sell them at the rate of six or eight for a penny—the scrape of his pen blending with the crunching of the crisp particles in his mouth. Of all the fiery afternoon blunders and flurried rashnesses of Turkey, was his once moistening a ginger-cake between his lips, and clapping it on to a mortgage for a seal. I came within an ace of dismissing him then. But he mollified me by making an oriental bow, and saying—"With submission, sir, it was generous of me to find you in stationery on my own account."

Now my original business—that of a conveyancer and title hunter, and drawer-up of recondite documents of all sorts—was considerably increased by receiving the master's office. There was now great work for scriveners. Not only must I push the clerks already with me, but I must have additional help. In answer to my advertisement, a motionless young man one morning, stood upon my office threshold, the door being open, for it was summer. I can see that figure now—pallidly neat, pitiably respectable, incurably forlorn! It was Bartleby.

After a few words touching his qualifications, I engaged him, glad to have among my corps of copyists a man of so singularly sedate an aspect, which I thought might operate beneficially upon the flighty temper of Turkey, and the fiery one of Nippers.

I should have stated before that ground glass folding-doors divided my premises into two parts, one of which was occupied by my scriveners, the other by myself. According to my humor I threw open these doors, or closed them. I resolved to assign Bartleby a corner by the folding-doors, but on my side of them, so as to have this quiet man within easy call, in case any trifling thing was to be done. I placed his desk close up to a small side-window in that part of the room, a window which originally had afforded a lateral view of certain grimy back-yards and bricks, but which, owing to subsequent erections, commanded at present no view at all, though it gave some light. Within three feet of the panes was a wall, and the light came down from far above, between two lofty buildings, as from a very small opening in a dome. Still further to a satisfactory arrangement, I procured a high green folding screen, which might entirely isolate Bartleby from my sight, though not remove him from my voice. And thus, in a manner, privacy and society were conjoined.

At first Bartleby did an extraordinary quantity of writing. As if long famishing for something to copy, he seemed to gorge himself on my documents. There was no pause for digestion. He ran a day and night line, copying by sun-light and by candle-light. I should have been quite delighted with his application, had be been cheerfully industrious. But he wrote on silently, palely, mechanically.

It is, of course, an indispensable part of a scrivener's business to verify the accuracy of his copy, word by word. Where there are two or more scriveners in an office, they assist each other in this examination, one reading from the copy, the other holding the original. It is a very dull, wearisome, and lethargic affair. I can readily imagine that to some sanguine temperaments it would be altogether intolerable. For example, I cannot credit that the mettlesome poet Byron would have contentedly sat down with Bartleby to examine a law document of, say five hundred pages, closely written in a crimpy hand.

Now and then, in the haste of business, it had been my habit to assist in comparing some brief document myself, calling Turkey or Nippers for this purpose. One object I had in placing Bartleby so handy to me behind the screen, was to avail myself of his services on such trivial occasions. It was on the third day, I think, of his being with me, and before any necessity had arisen for having his own writing examined, that, being much hurried to complete a small affair I had in hand, I abruptly called to Bartleby. In my haste and natural expectancy of instant compliance, I sat with my head bent over the original on my desk, and my right hand sideways, and somewhat nervously extended with the copy, so that immediately upon emerging from his retreat, Bartleby might snatch it and proceed to business without the least delay.

In this very attitude did I sit when I called to him, rapidly stating what it was I wanted him to do—namely, to examine a small paper with me. Imagine my surprise, nay, my consternation, when without moving from his privacy, Bartleby in a singularly mild, firm voice, replied, "I would prefer not to."

I sat awhile in perfect silence, rallying my stunned faculties. Immediately it occurred to me that my ears had deceived me, or Bartleby had entirely misunderstood my meaning. I repeated my request in the clearest tone I could assume. But in quite as clear a one came the previous reply, "I would prefer not to."

"Prefer not to," echoed I, rising in high excitement, and crossing the room with a stride. "What do you mean? Are you moon-struck? I want you to help me compare this sheet here—take it," and I thrust it towards him.

"I would prefer not to," said he.

I looked at him steadfastly. His face was leanly composed; his gray eye dimly calm. Not a wrinkle of agitation rippled him. Had there been the least uneasiness, anger, impatience or impertinence in his manner; in other words, had there been any thing ordinarily human about him, doubtless I should have violently dismissed him from the premises. But as it was, I should have as soon thought of turning my pale plaster-of-paris bust of Cicero out of doors. I stood gazing at him awhile, as he went on with his own writing, and then reseated myself at my desk. This is very strange, thought I. What had one best do? But my business hurried me. I concluded to forget the matter for the present, reserving it for my future leisure. So calling Nippers from the other room, the paper was speedily examined.

A few days after this, Bartleby concluded four lengthy documents, being quadruplicates of a week's testimony taken before me in my High Court of Chancery. It became necessary to examine them. It was an important suit, and great accuracy was imperative. Having all things arranged I called Turkey, Nippers and Ginger Nut from the next room, meaning to place the four copies in the hands of my four clerks, while I should read from the original. Accordingly Turkey, Nippers and Ginger Nut had taken their seats in a row, each with his document in hand, when I called to Bartleby to join this interesting group.

"Bartleby! Quick, I am waiting."

I heard a slow scrape of his chair legs on the uncarpeted floor, and soon he appeared standing at the entrance of his hermitage.

"What is wanted?" said he mildly.

"The copies, the copies," said I hurriedly. "We are going to examine them. There"—and I held towards him the fourth quadruplicate.

"I would prefer not to," he said, and gently disappeared behind the screen.

For a few moments I was turned into a pillar of salt, standing at the head of my seated column of clerks. Recovering myself, I advanced towards the screen, and demanded the reason for such extraordinary conduct.

"Why do you refuse?"

"I would prefer not to."

With any other man I should have flown outright into a dreadful passion, scorned all further words, and thrust him ignominiously from my presence. But there was something about Bartleby that not only strangely disarmed me, but in a wonderful manner touched and disconcerted me. I began to reason with him.

"These are your own copies we are about to examine. It is labor saving to you, because one examination will answer for your four papers. It is common usage. Every copyist is bound to help examine his copy. Is it not so? Will you not speak? Answer!"

"I prefer not to," he replied in a flute-like tone. It seemed to me that while I had been addressing him, he carefully revolved every statement that I made; fully comprehended the meaning; could not gainsay the irresistible conclusion; but, at the same time, some paramount consideration prevailed with him to reply as he did.

"You are decided, then, not to comply with my request—a request made according to common usage and common sense?"

He briefly gave me to understand that on that point my judgment was sound. Yes: his decision was irreversible.

It is not seldom the case that when a man is browbeaten in some unprecedented and violently unreasonable way, he begins to stagger in his own plainest faith. He begins, as it were, vaguely to surmise that, wonderful as it may be, all the justice and all the reason is on the other side. Accordingly, if any disinterested persons are present, he turns to them for some reinforcement for his own faltering mind.

"Turkey," said I, "what do you think of this? Am I not right?"

"With submission, sir," said Turkey, with his blandest tone, "I think that you are."

"Nippers," said I, "what do you think of it?"

"I think I should kick him out of the office."

(The reader of nice perceptions will here perceive that, it being morning, Turkey's answer is couched in polite and tranquil terms, but Nippers replies in ill-tempered ones. Or, to repeat a previous sentence, Nippers' ugly mood was on duty, and Turkey's off.)

"Ginger Nut," said I, willing to enlist the smallest suffrage in my behalf, "what do you think of it?"

"I think, sir, he's a little luny," replied Ginger Nut, with a grin.

"You hear what they say," said I, turning towards the screen, "come forth and do your duty."

But he vouchsafed no reply. I pondered a moment in sore perplexity. But once more business hurried me. I determined again to postpone the consideration of this dilemma to my future leisure. With a little trouble we made out to examine the papers without Bartleby, though at every page or two, Turkey deferentially dropped his opinion that this proceeding was quite out of the common; while Nippers, twitching in his chair with a dyspeptic nervousness, ground out between his set teeth occasional hissing maledictions against the stubborn oaf behind the screen. And for his (Nippers') part, this was the first and the last time he would do another man's business without pay.

Meanwhile Bartleby sat in his hermitage, oblivious to every thing but his own peculiar business there.

Some days passed, the scrivener being employed upon another lengthy work. His late remarkable conduct led me to regard his ways narrowly. I observed that he never went to dinner; indeed that he never went any where. As yet I had never of my personal knowledge known him to be outside of my office. He was a perpetual sentry in the corner. At about eleven o'clock though, in the morning, I noticed that Ginger Nut would advance toward the opening in Bartleby's screen, as if silently beckoned thither by a gesture invisible to me where I sat. The boy would then leave the office jingling a few pence, and reappear with a handful of ginger-nuts which he delivered in the hermitage, receiving two of the cakes for his trouble.

He lives, then, on ginger-nuts, thought I; never eats a dinner, properly speaking; he must be a vegetarian then; but no; he never eats even vegetables, he eats nothing but ginger-nuts. My mind then ran on in reveries concerning the probable effects upon the human constitution of living entirely on ginger-nuts. Ginger-nuts are so called because they contain ginger as one of their peculiar constituents, and the final flavoring one. Now what was ginger? A hot, spicy thing. Was Bartleby hot and spicy? Not at all. Ginger, then, had no effect upon Bartleby. Probably he preferred it should have none.

Nothing so aggravates an earnest person as a passive resistance. If the individual so resisted be of a not inhumane temper, and the resisting one perfectly harmless in his passivity; then, in the better moods of the former, he will endeavor charitably to construe to his imagination what proves impossible to be solved by his judgment. Even so, for the most part, I regarded Bartleby and his ways. Poor fellow! thought I, he means no mischief; it is plain he intends no insolence;

his aspect sufficiently evinces that his eccentricities are involuntary. He is useful to me. I can get along with him. If I turn him away, the chances are he will fall in with some less indulgent employer, and then he will be rudely treated, and perhaps driven forth miserably to starve. Yes. Here I can cheaply purchase a delicious self-approval. To befriend Bartleby; to humor him in his strange wilfulness, will cost me little or nothing, while I lay up in my soul what will eventually prove a sweet morsel for my conscience. But this mood was not invariable with me. The passiveness of Bartleby sometimes irritated me. I felt strangely goaded on to encounter him in new opposition, to elicit some angry spark from him answerable to my own. But indeed I might as well have essayed to strike fire with my knuckles against a bit of Windsor soap. But one afternoon the evil impulse in me mastered me, and the following little scene ensued:

"Bartleby," said I, "when those papers are all copied, I will compare them with you."

"I would prefer not to."

"How? Surely you do not mean to persist in that mulish vagary?"

No answer.

I threw open the folding-doors near by, and turning upon Turkey and Nippers, exclaimed in an excited manner—

"He says, a second time, he won't examine his papers. What do you think of it, Turkey?"*

"Think of it?" roared Turkey; "I think I'll just step behind his screen, and black his eyes for him!"

So saying, Turkey rose to his feet and threw his arms into a pugilistic position. He was hurrying away to make good his promise, when I detained him, alarmed at the effect of incautiously rousing Turkey's combativeness after dinner.

"Sit down, Turkey," said I, "and hear what Nippers has to say. What do you think of it, Nippers? Would I not be justified in immediately dismissing Bartleby?"

"Excuse me, that is for you to decide, sir. I think his conduct quite unusual, and indeed unjust, as regards Turkey and myself. But it may only be a passing whim."

---

*It was afternoon, be it remembered. Turkey sat glowing like a brass boiler, his bald head steaming, his hands reeling among his blotted papers.

"Ah," exclaimed I, "you have strangely changed your mind then—you speak very gently of him now."

"All beer," cried Turkey; "gentleness is effects of beer—Nippers and I dined together to-day. You see how gentle I am, sir. Shall I go and black his eyes?"

"You refer to Bartleby, I suppose. No, not to-day, Turkey," I replied; "pray, put up your fists."

I closed the doors, and again advanced towards Bartleby. I felt additional incentives tempting me to my fate. I burned to be rebelled against again. I remembered that Bartleby never left the office.

"Bartleby," said I, "Ginger Nut is away; just step round to the Post Office, won't you? (it was but a three minutes walk), and see if there is any thing for me."

"I would prefer not to."

"You will not?"

"I prefer not."

I staggered to my desk, and sat there in a deep study. My blind inveteracy returned. Was there any other thing in which I could procure myself to be ignominiously repulsed by this lean, penniless wight?—my hired clerk? What added thing is there, perfectly reasonable, that he will be sure to refuse to do?

"Bartleby!"

No answer.

"Bartleby," in a louder tone.

No answer.

"Bartleby," I roared.

Like a very ghost, agreeably to the laws of magical invocation, at the third summons, he appeared at the entrance of his hermitage.

"Go to the next room, and tell Nippers to come to me."

"I prefer not to," he respectfully and slowly said, and mildly disappeared.

"Very good, Bartleby," said I, in a quiet sort of serenely severe self-possessed tone, intimating the unalterable purpose of some terrible retribution very close at hand. At the moment I half intended something of the kind. But upon the whole, as it was drawing towards my dinner-hour, I thought it best to put on my hat and walk home for the day, suffering much from perplexity and distress of mind.

Shall I acknowledge it? The conclusion of this whole business was, that it soon became a fixed fact of my chambers, that a pale young scrivener, by the name of Bartleby, had a desk there; that he copied for me at the usual rate of four cents a folio (one hundred words); but he was permanently exempt from examining the work done by him, that duty being transferred to Turkey and Nippers, one of compliment doubtless to their superior acuteness; moreover, said Bartleby was never on any account to be dispatched on the most trivial errand of any sort; and that even if entreated to take upon him such a matter, it was generally understood that he would prefer not to—in other words, that he would refuse point-blank.

As days passed on, I became considerably reconciled to Bartleby. His steadiness, his freedom from all dissipation, his incessant industry (except when he chose to throw himself into a standing revery behind his screen), his great stillness, his unalterableness of demeanor under all circumstances, made him a valuable acquisition. One prime thing was this,—he was always there;—first in the morning, continually through the day, and the last at night. I had a singular confidence in his honesty. I felt my most precious papers perfectly safe in his hands. Sometimes to be sure I could not, for the very soul of me, avoid falling into sudden spasmodic passions with him. For it was exceeding difficult to bear in mind all the time those strange peculiarities, privileges, and unheard of exemptions, forming the tacit stipulations on Bartleby's part under which he remained in my office. Now and then, in the eagerness of dispatching pressing business, I would inadvertently summon Bartleby, in a short, rapid tone, to put his finger, say, on the incipient tie of a bit of red tape with which I was about compressing some papers. Of course, from behind the screen the usual answer, "I prefer not to," was sure to come; and then, how could a human creature with the common infirmities of our nature, refrain from bitterly exclaiming upon such perverseness—such unreasonableness. However, every added repulse of this sort which I received only tended to lessen the probability of my repeating the inadvertence.

Here it must be said, that according to the custom of most legal gentlemen occupying chambers in densely-populated law buildings, there were several keys to my door. One was kept by a woman residing in the attic, which person weekly scrubbed and daily swept and dusted my apartments. Another was kept by Turkey for convenience sake. The third I sometimes carried in my own pocket. The fourth I knew not who had.

Now, one Sunday morning I happened to go to Trinity Church, to hear a celebrated preacher, and finding myself rather early on the ground, I thought I would walk round to my chambers for a while. Luckily I had my key with me; but upon applying it to the lock, I found it resisted by something inserted from the inside. Quite surprised, I called out; when to my consternation a key was turned from within; and thrusting his lean visage at me, and holding the door ajar, the apparition of Bartleby appeared, in his shirt sleeves, and otherwise in a strangely tattered dishabille, saying quietly that he was sorry, but he was deeply engaged just then, and—preferred not admitting me at present. In a brief word or two, he moreover added, that perhaps I had better walk round the block two or three times, and by that time he would probably have concluded his affairs.

Now, the utterly unsurmised appearance of Bartleby, tenanting my law-chambers of a Sunday morning, with his cadaverously gentlemanly nonchalance, yet withal firm and self-possessed, had such a strange effect upon me, that incontinently I slunk away from my own door, and did as desired. But not without sundry twinges of impotent rebellion against the mild effrontery of this unaccountable scrivener. Indeed, it was his wonderful mildness chiefly, which not only disarmed me, but unmanned me, as it were. For I consider that one, for the time, is a sort of unmanned when he tranquilly permits his hired clerk to dictate to him, and order him away from his own premises. Furthermore, I was full of uneasiness as to what Bartleby could possibly be doing in my office in his shirt sleeves, and in an otherwise dismantled condition of a Sunday morning. Was any thing amiss going on? Nay, that was out of the question. It was not to be thought of for a moment that Bartleby was an immoral person. But what could he be doing there?—copying? Nay again, whatever might be his eccentricities, Bartleby was an eminently decorous person. He would be the last man to sit down to his desk in any state approaching to nudity. Besides, it was Sunday; and there was something about Bartleby that forbade the supposition that we would by any secular occupation violate the proprieties of the day.

Nevertheless, my mind was not pacified; and full of a restless curiosity, at last I returned to the door. Without hindrance I inserted my key, opened it, and entered. Bartleby was not to be seen. I looked round anxiously, peeped behind his screen; but it was very plain that he was gone. Upon more closely examining the place, I surmised that for an indefinite period Bartleby must have ate, dressed, and slept in my office, and that too without plate, mirror, or bed. The cushioned seat of a ricketty old sofa in one corner bore the faint impress of a lean, reclining form. Rolled away under his desk, I found a blanket; under the empty grate, a blacking box and brush; on a chair, a tin basin, with soap and a ragged towel; in a newspaper a few crumbs of ginger-nuts and a morsel of cheese. Yet, thought I, it is evident enough that Bartleby has been making his home here, keeping bachelor's hall all by himself. Immediately then the thought came sweeping across me, What miserable friendlessness and loneliness are here revealed! His poverty is great; but his solitude, how horrible! Think of it. Of a Sunday, Wall-street is deserted as Petra; and every night of every day it is an emptiness. This building too, which of week-days hums with industry and life, at nightfall echoes with sheer vacancy, and all through Sunday is forlorn. And here Bartleby makes his home; sole spectator of a solitude which he has seen all populous—a sort of innocent and transformed Marius brooding among the ruins of Carthage!

For the first time in my life a feeling of overpowering stinging melancholy seized me. Before, I had never experienced aught but a not-unpleasing sadness. The bond of a common humanity now drew me irresistibly to gloom. A fraternal melancholy! For both I and Bartleby were sons of Adam. I remembered the bright silks and sparkling faces I had seen that day, in gala trim, swan-like sailing down the Mississippi of Broadway; and I contrasted them with the pallid copyist, and thought to myself, Ah, happiness courts the light, so we deem the world is gay; but misery hides aloof, so we deem that misery there is none. These sad fancyings—chimeras, doubtless, of a sick and silly brain—led on to other and more special thoughts, concerning the eccentricities of Bartleby. Presentiments of strange discoveries hovered round me. The scrivener's pale form appeared to me laid out, among uncaring strangers, in its shivering winding sheet.

Suddenly I was attracted by Bartleby's closed desk, the key in open sight left in the lock.

I mean no mischief, seek the gratification of no heartless curiosity, thought I; besides, the desk is mine, and its contents too, so I will make bold to look within. Every thing was methodically arranged, the papers smoothly placed. The pigeon holes were deep, and removing the files of documents, I groped into their recesses. Presently I felt something there, and dragged it out. It was an old bandanna handkerchief, heavy and knotted. I opened it, and saw it was a savings' bank.

I now recalled all the quiet mysteries which I had noted in the man. I remembered that he never spoke but to answer; that though at intervals he had considerable time to himself, yet I had never seen him reading—no, not even a newspaper; that for long periods he would stand looking out, at his pale window behind the screen, upon the dead brick wall; I was quite sure he never visited any refectory or eating house; while his pale face clearly indicated that he never drank beer like Turkey, or tea and coffee even, like other men; that he never went any where in particular that I could learn; never went out for a walk, unless indeed that was the case at present; that he had declined telling who he was, or whence he came, or whether he had any relatives in the world; that though so thin and pale, he never complained of ill health. And more than all, I remembered a certain unconscious air of pallid—how shall I call it?—of pallid haughtiness, say, or rather an austere reserve about him, which had positively awed me into my tame compliance with his eccentricities, when I had feared to ask him to do the slightest incidental thing for me, even though I might know, from his long-continued motionlessness, that behind his screen he must be standing in one of those dead-wall reveries of his.

Revolving all these things, and coupling them with the recently discovered fact that he made my office his constant abiding place and home, and not forgetful of his morbid moodiness; revolving all these things, a prudential feeling began to steal over me. My first emotions had been those of pure melancholy and sincerest pity; but just in proportion as the forlornness of Bartleby grew and grew to my imagination, did that same melancholy merge into fear, that pity into repulsion. So true it is, and so terrible too, that up to a certain point the thought or sight of misery enlists our best affections; but, in certain spe-

cial cases, beyond that point it does not. They err who would assert that invariably this is owing to the inherent selfishness of the human heart. It rather proceeds from a certain hopelessness of remedying excessive and organic ill. To a sensitive being, pity is not seldom pain. And when at last it is perceived that such pity cannot lead to effectual succor, common sense bids the soul be rid of it. What I saw that morning persuaded me that the scrivener was the victim of innate and incurable disorder. I might give alms to his body; but his body did not pain him; it was his soul that suffered, and his soul I could not reach.

I did not accomplish the purpose of going to Trinity Church that morning. Somehow, the things I had seen disqualified me for the time from churchgoing. I walked homeward, thinking what I would do with Bartleby. Finally, I resolved upon this;—I would put certain calm questions to him the next morning, touching his history, and if he declined to answer then openly and reservedly (and I supposed he would prefer not), then to give him a twenty dollar bill over and above whatever I might owe him, and tell him his services were no longer required; but that if in any other way I could assist him, I would be happy to do so, especially if he desired to return to his native place, wherever that might be, I would willingly help to defray the expenses. Moreover, if, after reaching home, he found himself at any time in want of aid, a letter from him would be sure of a reply.

The next morning came.

"Bartleby," said I, gently calling to him behind his screen.

No reply.

"Bartleby," said I, in a still gentler tone, "come here; I am not going to ask you to do any thing you would prefer not to do—I simply wish to speak to you."

Upon this he noiselessly slid into view.

"Will you tell me, Bartleby, where you were born?"

"I would prefer not to."

"Will you tell me any thing about yourself?"

"I would prefer not to."

"But what reasonable objection can you have to speak to me? I feel friendly towards you."

He did not look at me while I spoke, but kept his glance fixed upon my bust of Cicero, which as I then sat, was directly behind me, some six inches above my head.

"What is your answer, Bartleby?" said I, after waiting a considerable time for a reply, during which his countenance remained immovable, only there was the faintest conceivable tremor of the white attenuated mouth.

"At present I prefer to give no answer," he said, and retired into his hermitage.

It was rather weak in me I confess, but his manner on this occasion nettled me. Not only did there seem to lurk in it a certain disdain, but his perverseness seemed ungrateful, considering the undeniable good usage and indulgence he had received from me.

Again I sat ruminating what I should do. Mortified as I was at his behavior, and resolved as I had been to dismiss him when I entered my office, nevertheless I strangely felt something superstitious knocking at my heart, and forbidding me to carry out my purpose, and denouncing me for a villain if I dared to breathe one bitter word against this forlornest of mankind. At last, familiarly drawing my chair behind his screen, I sat down and said: "Bartleby, never mind then about revealing your history; but let me entreat you, as a friend, to comply as far as may be with the usages of this office. Say now you will help to examine papers to-morrow or next day: in short, say now that in a day or two you will begin to be a little reasonable:—say so, Bartleby."

"At present I would prefer not to be a little reasonable," was his mildly cadaverous reply.

Just then the folding-doors opened, and Nippers approached. He seemed suffering from an unusually bad night's rest, induced by severer indigestion than common. He overheard those final words of Bartleby.

"Prefer not, eh?" gritted Nippers—"I'd prefer him, if I were you, sir," addressing me—"I'd prefer him; I'd give him preferences, the stubborn mule! What is it, sir, pray, that he prefers not to do now?"

Bartleby moved not a limb.

"Mr. Nippers," said I, "I'd prefer that you would withdraw for the present."

Somehow, of late I had got into the way of involuntarily using this word "prefer" upon all sorts of not exactly suitable occasions. And I trembled to think that my contact with the scrivener had already and seriously affected me in a mental way. And what further and deeper aberration might it not yet produce?

This apprehension had not been without efficacy in determining me to summary means.

As Nippers, looking very sour and sulky, was departing, Turkey blandly and deferentially approached.

"With submission, sir," said he, "yesterday I was thinking about Bartleby here, and I think that if he would but prefer to take a quart of good ale every day, it would do much towards mending him, and enabling him to assist in examining his papers."

"So you have got the word too," said I, slightly excited.

"With submission, what word, sir," asked Turkey, respectfully crowding himself into the contracted space behind the screen, and by so doing, making me jostle the scrivener. "What word, sir?"

"I would prefer to be left alone here," said Bartleby, as if offended at being mobbed in his privacy.

"That's the word, Turkey," said I—"that's it."

"Oh, prefer? oh yes—queer word. I never use it myself. But, sir, as I was saying, if he would but prefer—"

"Turkey," interrupted I, "you will please withdraw."

"Oh, certainly, sir, if you prefer that I should."

As he opened the folding-door to retire, Nippers at his desk caught a glimpse of me, and asked whether I would prefer to have a certain paper copied on blue paper or white. He did not in the least roguishly accent the word prefer. It was plain that it involuntarily rolled from his tongue. I thought to myself, surely I must get rid of a demented man, who already has in some degree turned the tongues, if not the heads of myself and clerks. But I thought it prudent not to break the dismission at once.

The next day I noticed that Bartleby did nothing but stand at his window in his dead-wall revery. Upon asking him why he did not write, he said that he had decided upon doing no more writing.

"Why, how now? what next?" exclaimed I, "do no more writing?"

"No more."

"And what is the reason?"

"Do you not see the reason for yourself," he indifferently replied.

I looked steadfastly at him, and perceived that his eyes looked dull and glazed. Instantly it occurred to me, that his unexampled diligence in copying by his dim window for the first few weeks of his stay with me might have temporarily impaired his vision.

I was touched. I said something in condolence with him. I hinted that of course he did wisely in abstaining from writing for a while; and urged him to embrace that opportunity of taking wholesome exercise in the open air. This, however, he did not do. A few days after this, my other clerks being absent, and being in a great hurry to dispatch certain letters by the mail, I thought that, having nothing else earthly to do, Bartleby would surely be less inflexible than usual, and carry these letters to the post-office. But he blankly declined. So, much to my inconvenience, I went myself.

Still added days went by. Whether Bartleby's eyes improved or not, I could not say. To all appearance, I thought they did. But when I asked him if they did, he vouchsafed no answer. At all events, he would do no copying. At last, in reply to my urgings, he informed me that he had permanently given up copying.

"What!" exclaimed I; "suppose your eyes should get entirely well—better than ever before—would you not copy then?"

"I have given up copying," he answered, and slid aside.

He remained as ever, a fixture in my chamber. Nay—if that were possible—he became still more of a fixture than before. What was to be done? He would do nothing in the office: why should he stay there? In plain fact, he had now become a millstone to me, not only useless as a necklace, but afflictive to bear. Yet I was sorry for him. I speak less than truth when I say that, on his own account, he occasioned me uneasiness. If he would but have named a single relative or friend, I would instantly have written, and urged their taking the poor fellow away to some convenient retreat. But he seemed alone, absolutely alone in the universe. A bit of wreck in the mid Atlantic. At length, necessities connected with my business tyrannized over all other considerations. Decently as I could, I told Bartleby that in six days' time he must unconditionally leave the office. I warned him to take measures, in the interval, for procuring some other abode. I offered to assist him in this endeavor, if he himself would but take the first step towards a removal. "And when you finally quit

me, Bartleby," added I, "I shall see that you go not away entirely unprovided. Six days from this hour, remember."

At the expiration of that period, I peeped behind the screen, and lo! Bartleby was there.

I buttoned up my coat, balanced myself; advanced slowly towards him, touched his shoulder, and said, "The time has come; you must quit this place; I am sorry for you; here is money; but you must go."

"I would prefer not," he replied, with his back still towards me.

"You must."

He remained silent.

Now I had an unbounded confidence in this man's common honesty. He had frequently restored to me sixpences and shillings carelessly dropped upon the floor, for I am apt to be very reckless in such shirt-button affairs. The proceeding then which followed will not be deemed extraordinary.

"Bartleby," said I, "I owe you twelve dollars on account; here are thirty-two; the odd twenty are yours.—Will you take it?" and I handed the bills towards him.

But he made no motion.

"I will leave them here then," putting them under a weight on the table. Then taking my hat and cane and going to the door I tranquilly turned and added—"After you have removed your things from these offices, Bartleby, you will of course lock the door—since every one is now gone for the day but you—and if you please, slip your key underneath the mat, so that I may have it in the morning. I shall not see you again; so good-bye to you. If hereafter in your new place of abode I can be of any service to you, do not fail to advise me by letter. Good-bye, Bartleby, and fare you well."

But he answered not a word; like the last column of some ruined temple, he remained standing mute and solitary in the middle of the otherwise deserted room.

As I walked home in a pensive mood, my vanity got the better of my pity. I could not but highly plume myself on my masterly management in getting rid of Bartleby. Masterly I call it, and such it must appear to any dispassionate thinker. The beauty of my procedure seemed to consist in its perfect quietness. There was no vulgar bullying, no bravado of any sort, no choleric hectoring, and striding to and fro across the apartment, jerking out vehement commands for Bartleby to bundle himself off with his beggarly traps. Nothing of the kind. Without loudly bidding Bartleby depart—as an inferior genius might have done—I assumed the ground that depart he must; and upon the assumption built all I had to say. The more I thought over my procedure, the more I was charmed with it. Nevertheless, next morning, upon awakening, I had my doubts—I had somehow slept off the fumes of vanity. One of the coolest and wisest hours a man has, is just after he awakes in the morning. My procedure seemed as sagacious as ever—but only in theory. How it would prove in practice—there was the rub. It was truly a beautiful thought to have assumed Bartleby's departure; but, after all, that assumption was simply my own, and none of Bartleby's. The great point was, not whether I had assumed that he would quit me, but whether he would prefer so to do. He was more a man of preferences than assumptions.

After breakfast, I walked down town, arguing the probabilities pro and con. One moment I thought it would prove a miserable failure, and Bartleby would be found all alive at my office as usual; the next moment it seemed certain that I should see his chair empty. And so I kept veering about. At the corner of Broadway and Canal-street, I saw quite an excited group of people standing in earnest conversation.

"I'll take odds he doesn't," said a voice as I passed.

"Doesn't go?—done!" said I, "put up your money."

I was instinctively putting my hand in my pocket to produce my own, when I remembered that this was an election day. The words I had overheard bore no reference to Bartleby, but to the success or non-success of some candidate for the mayoralty. In my intent frame of mind, I had, as it were, imagined that all Broadway shared in my excitement, and were debating the same question with me. I passed on, very thankful that the uproar of the street screened my momentary absent-mindedness.

As I had intended, I was earlier than usual at my office door. I stood listening for a moment. All was still. He must be gone. I tried the knob. The door was locked. Yes, my procedure had worked to a charm; he indeed must be vanished. Yet a certain melancholy mixed with this: I was almost sorry for my

brilliant success. I was fumbling under the door mat for the key, which Bartleby was to have left there for me, when accidentally my knee knocked against a panel, producing a summoning sound, and in response a voice came to me from within—"Not yet; I am occupied."

It was Bartleby.

I was thunderstruck. For an instant I stood like the man who, pipe in mouth, was killed one cloudless afternoon long ago in Virginia, by summer lightning; at his own warm open window he was killed, and remained leaning out there upon the dreamy afternoon, till some one touched him, when he fell.

"Not gone!" I murmured at last. But again obeying that wondrous ascendancy which the inscrutable scrivener had over me, and from which ascendency, for all my chafing, I could not completely escape, I slowly went down stairs and out into the street, and while walking round the block, considered what I should next do in this unheard-of perplexity. Turn the man out by an actual thrusting I could not; to drive him away by calling him hard names would not do; calling in the police was an unpleasant idea; and yet, permit him to enjoy his cadaverous triumph over me,—this too I could not think of. What was to be done? or, if nothing could be done, was there any thing further that I could assume in the matter? Yes, as before I had prospectively assumed that Bartleby would depart, so now I might retrospectively assume that departed he was. In the legitimate carrying out of this assumption, I might enter my office in a great hurry, and pretending not to see Bartleby at all, walk straight against him as if he were air. Such a proceeding would in a singular degree have the appearance of a home-thrust. It was hardly possible that Bartleby could withstand such an application of the doctrine of assumptions. But upon second thoughts the success of the plan seemed rather dubious. I resolved to argue the matter over with him again.

"Bartleby," said I, entering the office, with a quietly severe expression, "I am seriously displeased. I am pained, Bartleby. I had thought better of you. I had imagined you of such a gentlemanly organization, that in any delicate dilemma a slight hint would suffice—in short, an assumption. But it appears I am deceived. Why," I added, unaffectedly starting, "you have not even touched the money yet," pointing to it, just where I had left it the evening previous.

He answered nothing.

"Will you, or will you not, quit me?" I now demanded in a sudden passion, advancing close to him.

"I would prefer not to quit you," he replied, gently emphasizing the not.

"What earthly right have you to stay here? Do you pay any rent? Do you pay my taxes? Or is this property yours?"

He answered nothing.

"Are you ready to go on and write now? Are your eyes recovered? Could you copy a small paper for me this morning? or help examine a few lines? or step round to the post-office? In a word, will you do any thing at all, to give a coloring to your refusal to depart the premises?"

He silently retired into his hermitage.

I was now in such a state of nervous resentment that I thought it but prudent to check myself at present from further demonstrations. Bartleby and I were alone. I remembered the tragedy of the unfortunate Adams and the still more unfortunate Colt in the solitary office of the latter; and how poor Colt, being dreadfully incensed by Adams, and imprudently permitting himself to get wildly excited, was at unawares hurried into his fatal act—an act which certainly no man could possibly deplore more than the actor himself. Often it had occurred to me in my ponderings upon the subject, that had that altercation taken place in the public street, or at a private residence, it would not have terminated as it did. It was the circumstance of being alone in a solitary office, up stairs, of a building entirely unhallowed by humanizing domestic associations—an uncarpeted office, doubtless, of a dusty, haggard sort of appearance;—this it must have been, which greatly helped to enhance the irritable desperation of the hapless Colt.

But when this old Adam of resentment rose in me and tempted me concerning Bartleby, I grappled him and threw him. How? Why, simply by recalling the divine injunction: "A new commandment give I unto you, that ye love one another." Yes, this it was that saved me. Aside from higher considerations, charity often operates as a vastly wise and prudent principle—a great safeguard to its possessor. Men have committed murder for jealousy's sake, and anger's sake, and hatred's sake, and selfishness' sake, and spiritual pride's sake; but no man that ever I heard of, ever committed a diabolical murder for sweet charity's sake. Mere self-interest, then, if no better motive can be enlisted, should, especially with high-tempered men, prompt all beings to charity and philanthropy. At any rate, upon the occasion in question, I strove to drown my exasperated feelings towards the scrivener by benevolently construing his conduct. Poor fellow, poor fellow! thought I, he [don't] mean any thing; and besides, he has seen hard times, and ought to be indulged.

I endeavored also immediately to occupy myself, and at the same time to comfort my despondency. I tried to fancy that in the course of the morning, at such time as might prove agreeable to him, Bartleby, of his own free accord, would emerge from his hermitage, and take up some decided line of march in the direction of the door. But no. Half-past twelve o'clock came; Turkey began to glow in the face, overturn his inkstand, and become generally obstreperous; Nippers abated down into quietude and courtesy; Ginger Nut munched his noon apple; and Bartleby remained standing at his window in one of his profoundest dead-wall reveries. Will it be credited? Ought I to acknowledge it? That afternoon I left the office without saying one further word to him.

Some days now passed, during which, at leisure intervals I looked a little into "Edwards on the Will," and "Priestley on Necessity." Under the circumstances, those books induced a salutary feeling. Gradually I slid into the persuasion that these troubles of mine touching the scrivener, had been all predestinated from eternity, and Bartleby was billeted upon me for some mysterious purpose of an all-wise Providence, which it was not for a mere mortal like me to fathom. Yes, Bartleby, stay there behind your screen, thought I; I shall persecute you no more; you are harmless and noiseless as any of these old chairs; in short, I never feel so private as when I know you are here. At least I see it, I feel it; I penetrate to the predestinated purpose of my life. I am content. Others may have loftier parts to enact; but my mission in this world, Bartleby, is to furnish you with office-room for such period as you may see fit to remain.

I believe that this wise and blessed frame of mind would have continued with me, had it not been for the unsolicited and uncharitable remarks obtruded upon me by my professional friends who visited the rooms. But thus it often is, that the constant friction of illiberal minds wears out at last the best resolves of the more generous. Though to be sure, when I reflected upon it, it was not strange that people entering my office should be struck by the peculiar aspect of the unaccountable Bartleby, and so be tempted to throw out some sinister observations concerning him. Sometimes an attorney having business with me, and calling at my office, and finding no one but the scrivener there, would undertake to obtain some sort of precise information from him touching my whereabouts; but without heeding his idle talk, Bartleby would remain standing immovable in the middle of the room. So after contemplating him in that position for a time, the attorney would depart, no wiser than he came.

Also, when a Reference was going on, and the room full of lawyers and witnesses and business was driving fast; some deeply occupied legal gentleman present, seeing Bartleby wholly unemployed, would request him to run round to his (the legal gentleman's) office and fetch some papers for him. Thereupon, Bartleby would tranquilly decline, and yet remain idle as before. Then the lawyer would give a great stare, and turn to me. And what could I say? At last I was made aware that all through the circle of my professional acquaintance, a whisper of wonder was running round, having reference to the strange creature I kept at my office. This worried me very much. And as the idea came upon me of his possibly turning out a long-lived man, and keep occupying my chambers, and denying my authority; and perplexing my visitors; and scandalizing my professional reputation; and casting a general gloom over the premises; keeping soul and body together to the last upon his savings (for doubtless he spent but half a dime a day), and in the end perhaps outlive me, and claim possession of my office by right of his perpetual occupancy: as all these dark anticipations crowded upon me more and more, and my friends continually intruded their relentless remarks upon the apparition in my room; a great change was wrought in me. I resolved to gather all my faculties together, and for ever rid me of this intolerable incubus.

Ere revolving any complicated project, however, adapted to this end, I first simply suggested to Bartleby the propriety of his permanent departure. In a calm and serious tone, I commended the idea to his careful and mature consideration. But having taken three days to meditate upon it, he apprised me that his original determination remained the same; in short, that he still preferred to abide with me.

What shall I do? I now said to myself, buttoning up my coat to the last button. What shall I do? What ought I to do? What does conscience say I should do with this man, or rather ghost. Rid myself of him, I must; go, he shall. But how? You will not thrust him, the poor, pale, passive mortal,—you will not thrust such a helpless creature out of your door? You will not dishonor yourself by such cruelty? No, I will not, I cannot do that. Rather would I let him live and die here, and then mason up his remains in the wall. What then will you do? For all your coaxing, he will not budge. Bribes he leaves under your own paperweight on your table; in short, it is quite plain that he prefers to cling to you.

Then something severe, something unusual must be done. What! surely you will not have him collared by a constable, and commit his innocent pallor to the common jail? And upon what ground could you procure such a thing to be done?—a vagrant, is he? What! he a vagrant, a wanderer, who refuses to budge? It is because he will not be a vagrant, then, that you seek to count him as a vagrant. That is too absurd. No visible means of support: there I have him. Wrong again: for indubitably he does support himself, and that is the only unanswerable proof that any man can show of his possessing the means so to do. No more then. Since he will not quit me, I must quit him. I will change my offices; I will move elsewhere; and give him fair notice, that if I find him on my new premises I will then proceed against him as a common trespasser.

Acting accordingly, next day I thus addressed him: "I find these chambers too far from the City Hall; the air is unwholesome. In a word, I propose to remove my offices next week, and shall no longer require your services. I tell you this now, in order that you may seek another place."

He made no reply, and nothing more was said.

On the appointed day I engaged carts and men, proceeded to my chambers, and having but little furniture, every thing was removed in a few hours. Throughout, the scrivener remained standing behind the screen, which I directed to be removed the last thing. It was withdrawn; and being folded up like a huge folio, left him the motionless occupant of a naked room. I stood in the entry watching him a moment, while something from within me upbraided me.

I re-entered, with my hand in my pocket—and—and my heart in my mouth.

"Good-bye, Bartleby; I am going—good-bye, and God some way bless you; and take that," slipping something in his hand. But it dropped upon the floor, and then—strange to say—I tore myself from him whom I had so longed to be rid of.

Established in my new quarters, for a day or two I kept the door locked, and started at every footfall in the passages. When I returned to my rooms after any little absence, I would pause at the threshold for an instant, and attentively listen, ere applying my key. But these fears were needless. Bartleby never came nigh me.

I thought all was going well, when a perturbed looking stranger visited me, inquiring whether I was the person who had recently occupied rooms at No.—Wall-street.

Full of forebodings, I replied that I was.

"Then sir," said the stranger, who proved a lawyer, "you are responsible for the man you left there. He refuses to do any copying; he refuses to do any thing; he says he prefers not to; and he refuses to quit the premises."

"I am very sorry, sir," said I, with assumed tranquility, but an inward tremor, "but, really, the man you allude to is nothing to me—he is no relation or apprentice of mine, that you should hold me responsible for him."

"In mercy's name, who is he?"

"I certainly cannot inform you. I know nothing about him. Formerly I employed him as a copyist; but he has done nothing for me now for some time past."

"I shall settle him then—good morning, sir."

Several days passed, and I heard nothing more; and though I often felt a charitable prompting to call at the place and see poor Bartleby, yet a certain squeamishness of I know not what withheld me.

All is over with him, by this time, thought I at last, when through another week no further intelligence reached me. But coming to my room the day after, I found several persons waiting at my door in a high state of nervous excitement.

"That's the man—here he comes," cried the foremost one, whom I recognized as the lawyer who had previously called upon me alone.

"You must take him away, sir, at once," cried a portly person among them, advancing upon me, and whom I knew to be the landlord of No.—Wall-street. "These gentlemen, my tenants, cannot stand it any longer; Mr. B—" pointing to the lawyer, "has turned him out of his room, and he now persists in haunting the building generally, sitting upon the banisters of the stairs by day, and sleeping in the entry by night. Every body is concerned; clients are leaving the offices; some fears are entertained of a mob; something you must do, and that without delay."

Aghast at this torrent, I fell back before it, and would fain have locked myself in my new quarters. In vain I persisted that Bartleby was nothing to me—no more than to any one else. In vain:—I was the last person known to have any thing to do with him, and they held me to the terrible account. Fearful then of being exposed in the papers (as one person present obscurely threatened) I considered the matter, and at length said, that if the lawyer would give me a confidential interview with the scrivener, in his (the lawyer's) own room, I would that afternoon strive my best to rid them of the nuisance they complained of.

Going up stairs to my old haunt, there was Bartleby silently sitting upon the banister at the landing.

"What are you doing here, Bartleby?" said I.

"Sitting upon the banister," he mildly replied.

I motioned him into the lawyer's room, who then left us.

"Bartleby," said I, "are you aware that you are the cause of great tribulation to me, by persisting in occupying the entry after being dismissed from the office?"

No answer.

"Now one of two things must take place. Either you must do something, or something must be done to you. Now what sort of business would you like to engage in? Would you like to re-engage in copying for some one?"

"No; I would prefer not to make any change."

"Would you like a clerkship in a dry-goods store?"

"There is too much confinement about that. No, I would not like a clerkship; but I am not particular."

"Too much confinement," I cried, "why you keep yourself confined all the time!"

"I would prefer not to take a clerkship," he rejoined, as if to settle that little item at once.

"How would a bartender's business suit you? There is no trying of the eyesight in that."

"I would not like it at all; though, as I said before, I am not particular."

His unwonted wordiness inspirited me. I returned to the charge.

"Well then, would you like to travel through the country collecting bills for the merchants? That would improve your health."

"No, I would prefer to be doing something else."

"How then would going as a companion to Europe, to entertain some young gentleman with your conversation—how would that suit you?"

"Not at all. It does not strike me that there is any thing definite about that. I like to be stationary. But I am not particular."

"Stationary you shall be then," I cried, now losing all patience, and for the first time in all my exasperating connection with him fairly flying into a passion. "If you do not go away from these premises before night, I shall feel bound—indeed I am bound—to—to—to quit the premises myself!" I rather absurdly concluded, knowing not with what possible threat to try to frighten his immobility into compliance. Despairing of all further efforts, I was precipitately leaving him, when a final thought occurred to me—one which had not been wholly unindulged before.

"Bartleby," said I, in the kindest tone I could assume under such exciting circumstances, "will you go home with me now—not to my office, but my dwelling—and remain there till we can conclude upon some convenient arrangement for you at our leisure? Come, let us start now, right away."

"No: at present I would prefer not to make any change at all."

I answered nothing; but effectually dodging every one by the suddenness and rapidity of my flight, rushed from the building, ran up Wall-street towards Broadway, and jumping into the first omnibus was soon removed from pursuit. As soon as tranquility returned I distinctly perceived that I had now done all that I possibly could, both in respect to the demands of the landlord and his tenants, and with regard to my own desire and sense of duty, to benefit Bartleby, and shield him from rude persecution. I now strove to be entirely care-free and quiescent; and my conscience justified me in the attempt; though indeed it was not so successful as I could have wished. So fearful was I of being again hunted out by the incensed landlord and his exasperated tenants, that, surrendering my business to Nippers, for a few days I drove about the upper part of the town and through the suburbs, in my rockaway; crossed over to Jersey City and Hoboken, and paid fugitive visits to Manhattanville and Astoria. In fact I almost lived in my rockaway for the time.

When again I entered my office, lo, a note from the landlord lay upon the desk. I opened it with trembling hands. It informed me that the writer had sent to the police, and had Bartleby removed to the Tombs as a vagrant. Moreover, since I knew more about him than any one else, he wished me to appear at that place, and make a suitable statement of the facts. These tidings had a conflicting effect upon me. At first I was indignant; but at last almost approved. The landlord's energetic, summary disposition had led him to adopt a procedure which I do not think I would have decided upon myself; and yet as a last resort, under such peculiar circumstances, it seemed the only plan.

As I afterwards learned, the poor scrivener, when told that he must be conducted to the Tombs, offered not the slightest obstacle, but in his pale unmoving way, silently acquiesced.

Some of the compassionate and curious bystanders joined the party; and headed by one of the constables arm in arm with Bartleby, the silent procession filed its way through all the noise, and heat, and joy of the roaring thoroughfares at noon.

The same day I received the note I went to the Tombs, or to speak more properly, the Halls of Justice. Seeking the right officer, I stated the purpose of my call, and was informed that the individual I described was indeed within. I then assured the functionary that Bartleby was a perfectly honest man, and greatly to be compassionated, however unaccountably eccentric. I narrated all I knew, and closed by suggesting the idea of letting him remain in as indulgent confinement as possible till something less harsh might be done—though indeed I hardly knew what. At all events, if nothing else could be decided upon, the alms-house must receive him. I then begged to have an interview.

Being under no disgraceful charge, and quite serene and harmless in all his ways, they had permitted him freely to wander about the prison, and especially in the enclosed grass-platted yards thereof.

And so I found him there, standing all alone in the quietest of the yards, his face towards a high wall, while all around, from the narrow slits of the jail windows, I thought I saw peering out upon him the eyes of murderers and thieves.

"Bartleby!"

"I know you," he said, without looking round—"and I want nothing to say to you."

"It was not I that brought you here, Bartleby," said I, keenly pained at his implied suspicion. "And to you, this should not be so vile a place. Nothing reproachful attaches to you by being here. And see, it is not so sad a place as one might think. Look, there is the sky, and here is the grass."

"I know where I am," he replied, but would say nothing more, and so I left him.

As I entered the corridor again, a broad meat-like man, in an apron, accosted me, and jerking his thumb over his shoulder said—"Is that your friend?"

"Yes."

"Does he want to starve? If he does, let him live on the prison fare, that's all."

"Who are you?" asked I, not knowing what to make of such an unofficially speaking person in such a place.

"I am the grub-man. Such gentlemen as have friends here, hire me to provide them with something good to eat."

"Is this so?" said I, turning to the turnkey.

He said it was.

"Well then," said I, slipping some silver into the grub-man's hands (for so they called him). "I want you to give particular attention to my friend there; let him have the best dinner you can get. And you must be as polite to him as possible."

"Introduce me, will you?" said the grub-man, looking at me with an expression which seemed to say he was all impatienced for an opportunity to give a specimen of his breeding.

Thinking it would prove of benefit to the scrivener, I acquiesced; and asking the grub-man his name, went up with him to Bartleby.

"Bartleby, this is Mr. Cutlets; you will find him very useful to you."

"Your sarvant, sir, your sarvant," said the grub-man, making a low salutation behind his apron. "Hope you find it pleasant here, sir;—spacious grounds—cool apartments, sir—hope you'll stay with us some time—try to make it agreeable. May Mrs. Cutlets and I have the pleasure of your company to dinner, sir, in Mrs. Cutlets' private room?"

"I prefer not to dine to-day," said Bartleby, turning away. "It would disagree with me; I am unused to dinners." So saying he slowly moved to the other side of the enclosure, and took up a position fronting the dead-wall.

"How's this?" said the grub-man, addressing me with a stare of astonishment. "He's odd, aint he?"

"I think he is a little deranged," said I, sadly.

"Deranged? deranged is it? Well now, upon my word, I thought that friend of yourn was a gentleman forger; they are always pale and genteel-like, them forgers. I can't help pity 'em—can't help it, sir. Did you know Monroe Edwards?" he added touchingly, and paused. Then, laying his hand pityingly on my shoulder, sighed, "he died of consumption at Sing-Sing. So you weren't acquainted with Monroe?"

"No, I was never socially acquainted with any forgers. But I cannot stop longer. Look to my friend yonder. You will not lose by it. I will see you again."

Some few days after this, I again obtained admission to the Tombs, and went through the corridors in quest of Bartleby; but without finding him.

"I saw him coming from his cell not long ago," said a turnkey, "may be he's gone to loiter in the yards."

So I went in that direction.

"Are you looking for the silent man?" said another turnkey passing me. "Yonder he lies—sleeping in the yard there. 'Tis not twenty minutes since I saw him lie down."

The yard was entirely quiet. It was not accessible to the common prisoners. The surrounding walls, of amazing thickness, kept off all sounds behind them. The Egyptian character of the masonry weighed upon me with its gloom. But a soft imprisoned turf grew under foot. The heart of the eternal pyramids, it seemed, wherein, by some strange magic, through the clefts, grass-seed, dropped by birds, had sprung.

Strangely huddled at the base of the wall, his knees drawn up, and lying on his side, his head touching the cold stones, I saw the wasted Bartleby. But nothing stirred. I paused; then went close up to him; stooped over, and saw that his dim eyes were open; otherwise he seemed profoundly sleeping. Something prompted me to touch him. I felt his hand, when a tingling shiver ran up my arm and down my spine to my feet.

The round face of the grub-man peered upon me now. "His dinner is ready. Won't he dine to-day, either? Or does he live without dining?"

"Lives without dining," said I, and closed the eyes.

"Eh!—He's asleep, aint he?"

"With kings and counsellors," murmured I.

* * * * * * * *

There would seem little need for proceeding further in this history. Imagination will readily supply the meagre recital of poor Bartleby's interment. But ere parting with the reader, let me say, that if this little narrative has sufficiently interested him, to awaken curiosity as to who Bartleby was, and what manner of life he led prior to the present narrator's making his acquaintance, I can only reply, that in such curiosity I fully share, but am wholly unable to gratify it. Yet here I hardly know whether I should divulge one little item of rumor, which came to my ear a few months after the scrivener's decease. Upon what basis it rested, I could never ascertain; and hence, how true it is I cannot now tell. But inasmuch as this vague report has not been without a certain strange suggestive interest to me, however sad, it may prove the same with some others; and so I will briefly mention it. The report was this: that Bartleby had been a subordinate clerk in the Dead Letter Office at Washington, from which he had been suddenly removed by a change in the administration. When I think over this rumor, I cannot adequately express the emotions which seize me. Dead letters! does it not sound like dead men? Conceive a man by nature and misfortune prone to a pallid hopelessness, can any business seem more fitted to heighten it than that of continually handling these dead letters and assorting them for the flames? For by the cart-load they are annually burned. Sometimes from out the folded paper the pale clerk takes a ring:—the finger it was meant for, perhaps, moulders in the grave; a bank-note sent in swiftest charity:—he whom it would relieve, nor eats nor hungers any more; pardon for those who died despairing; hope for those who died unhoping; good tidings for those who died stifled by unrelieved calamities. On errands of life, these letters speed to death.

Ah Bartleby! Ah humanity!

Questions

1. Describe the narrator. What do we know about his appearance, age, beliefs, values, and pet peeves?
2. Prior to "the advent of Bartleby," the narrator employed two copyists and one office-boy. Their nicknames were Turkey, Nippers, and Ginger Nut. If Bartleby were to be assigned a nickname, what might it be?
3. When the narrator describes his relationship with Bartleby and, specifically, what happens when he attempts to relieve him of duty, what does this section convey regarding the narrator's countenance?
4. Describe Turkey, Nippers, and Ginger Nut. What do they look like? How do they dress? What are their ages? Identify any eccentricities they may have.
5. Melville offers some interesting couplings, for instance, "ambition and indigestion" or "privacy and society." What other interesting couplings does Melville offer? Furthermore, does he dovetail these words or simply couple them for effect?
6. After hearing Bartleby say, "I would prefer not to," the narrator tells the reader: "With any other man I should have flown outright into a dreadful passion, scorned all further words, and thrust him ignominiously from my presence. But there was something about Bartleby that not only strangely disarmed me, but in a wonderful manner touched and disconcerted me. I began to reason with him." What might it be about Bartleby that "strangely disarmed" the narrator? What might it be that "touched and disconcerted" him?

7. Melville writes: "'I prefer not to,' [Bartleby] replied in a flute-like tone." As the reader, what is your perception of Bartleby when his reply most resembles the tone of a flute? Would your perception differ if his reply resembled the tone of a trumpet or a tuba?

8. Identify what might be considered "Bartleby's eccentricities."

9. The narrator states: "[. . .] I slunk away from my own door, and did as desired. But not without sundry twinges of impotent rebellion against the mild effrontery of this unaccountable scrivener." Some would argue that Melville's language use is absolutely precise, for "slunk away" and "twinges of impotent rebellion" may just be the most applicable words for the narrator's reaction to Bartleby's unexpected presence in the narrator's law-chambers. Identify other examples of precise language use throughout the story.

10. The narrator states: "So true it is, and so terrible too, that up to a certain point the thought or sight of misery enlists our best affections; but, in certain special cases, beyond that point it does not." This quotation offers two very interesting observations. Offer examples supporting both.

11. The descriptions of Bartleby seem to change as the story progresses. For instance, while one of Bartleby's replies is described as delivered in "a flute-like tone," a reply delivered later in the story is described as "mildly cadaverous." Similarly, when Bartleby is first introduced, he is described as "pallidly neat, pitiably respectable, incurably forlorn." However, he is later described as "A bit of wreck in the mid Atlantic" and "the last column of some ruined temple." Does this suggest a legitimate change in Bartleby? Or might it simply suggest a change in the narrator's perception of Bartleby?

12. The narrator states this about Bartleby: "He was more of a man of preferences than assumptions." How might this be interpreted?

13. *Bartleby the Scrivener* ends with "Ah Bartleby! Ah humanity!" What reflection might Bartleby's story have upon humanity?

Research and Writing

1. Compare and contrast *Bartleby the Scrivener* and the film *Office Space.* Specifically, identify motivations for rebellion or mutiny within the workplace. After identifying similarities in motivations for the characters in both texts, extract differences from those similarities.

2. Extract three arguments from *Bartleby the Scrivener.* Find support from the story to show that each argument can, indeed, be extracted from the story. Then, take a stand on whether or not you agree with each of the arguments. In doing so, you might further promote your stance by citing examples from credible sources, sources you discovered after doing some research.

3. Identify the problems that are presented in *Bartleby the Scrivener.* After identifying these problems, offer a brief synopsis of how various characters attempt to solve these problems. Then, propose your own solutions to these problems. You might substantiate your solutions by citing examples from credible sources.

4. In *Bartleby the Scrivener,* Bartleby transforms into a haunting figure, something similar to the raven in Edgar Allan Poe's poem by the same name. Read *The Raven,* and then compare and contrast the raven to Bartleby.

Nathaniel Hawthorne (1804–1864)

To Nathaniel Hawthorne, Herman Melville once wrote: "I shall leave the world, I feel, with more satisfaction for having come to know you. Knowing you persuades me more than the Bible of our immortality." It can be said that Nathaniel Hawthorne, born on July 4, 1804, was influenced by Herman Melville and vice versa. Hawthorne, most famous for writing *The Scarlet Letter,* was raised in Salem, Massachusetts and, interestingly enough, was the descendent of a long line of Puritan ancestors. This included John Hawthorne, a presiding magistrate in the Salem witch trials. In Nathaniel Hawthorne's youth, he published a newspaper titled *The Spectator,* which included essays, poems, news, and advertisements. He was sixteen. And over the next forty-four years, he published copious short stories, sketches, novels, children's stories, and non-fiction pieces.

Young Goodman Brown

1. While reading *Young Goodman Brown,* ask yourself why Brown is taking the trip.
2. Note how the names of the characters contribute to the development of the story.
3. Consider the differences between a rite of passage and a rite of initiation.
4. Note the false dilemma which finds itself in the Puritans' persecution of Quakers and other non-believers.
5. In *Young Goodman Brown,* Hawthorne has an opportunity to reflect on his years in Salem. And while *Young Goodman Brown* is a short story and, hence, a work of fiction, some evidence of self-exploration is evident, especially since Salem is often considered the center of witchcraft frenzy, and especially since Hawthorne's lineage brings him face to face with the Salem witch trials.

Young Goodman Brown

Nathaniel Hawthorne

Young Goodman Brown came forth at sunset, into the street of Salem village, but put his head back, after crossing the threshold, to exchange a parting kiss with his young wife. And Faith, as the wife was aptly named, thrust her own pretty head into the street, letting the wind play with the pink ribbons of her cap, while she called to Goodman Brown.

"Dearest heart," whispered she, softly and rather sadly, when her lips were close to his ear, "pr'ythee, put off your journey until sunrise, and sleep in your own bed tonight. A lone woman is troubled with such dreams and such thoughts, that she's afeard of herself, sometimes. Pray, tarry with me this night, dear husband, of all nights in the year!"

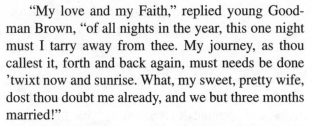

"My love and my Faith," replied young Goodman Brown, "of all nights in the year, this one night must I tarry away from thee. My journey, as thou callest it, forth and back again, must needs be done 'twixt now and sunrise. What, my sweet, pretty wife, dost thou doubt me already, and we but three months married!"

"Then God bless you!" said Faith, with the pink ribbons, "and may you find all well, when you come back."

"Amen!" cried Goodman Brown. "Say thy prayers, dear Faith, and go to bed at dusk, and no harm will come to thee."

So they parted; and the young man pursued his way, until, being about to turn the corner by the meeting-house, he looked back and saw the head of Faith still peeping after him, with a melancholy air, in spite of her pink ribbons.

"Poor little Faith!" thought he, for his heart smote him. "What a wretch am I, to leave her on such an errand! She talks of dreams, too. Methought, as she spoke, there was trouble in her face, as if a dream had warned her what work is to be done tonight. But, no, no! 'twould kill her to think it. Well; she's a blessed angel on earth; and after this one night, I'll cling to her skirts and follow her to Heaven."

With this excellent resolve for the future, Goodman Brown felt himself justified in making more haste on his present evil purpose. He had taken a dreary road, darkened by all the gloomiest trees of the forest, which barely stood aside to let the narrow path creep through, and closed immediately behind. It was all as lonely as could be; and there is this peculiarity in such a solitude, that the traveller knows not who may be concealed by the innumerable trunks and the thick boughs overhead; so that, with lonely footsteps, he may yet be passing through an unseen multitude.

"There may be a devilish Indian behind every tree," said Goodman Brown to himself; and he glanced fearfully behind him, as he added, "What if the devil himself should be at my very elbow!"

His head being turned back, he passed a crook of the road, and looking forward again, beheld the figure of a man, in grave and decent attire, seated at the foot of an old tree. He arose, at Goodman Brown's approach, and walked onward, side by side with him.

"You are late, Goodman Brown," said he. "The clock of the Old South was striking, as I came through Boston; and that is full fifteen minutes agone."

"Faith kept me back awhile," replied the young man, with a tremor in his voice, caused by the sudden appearance of his companion, though not wholly unexpected.

It was now deep dusk in the forest, and deepest in that part of it where these two were journeying. As nearly as could be discerned, the second traveller was about fifty years old, apparently in the same rank of life as Goodman Brown, and bearing a considerable resemblance to him, though perhaps more in expression than features. Still, they might have been taken for father and son. And yet, though the elder person was as simply clad as the younger, and as simple in manner too, he had an indescribable air of one who knew the world, and would not have felt abashed at the governor's dinner-table, or in King William's court, were it possible that his affairs should call him thither. But the only thing about him, that could be fixed upon as remarkable, was his staff, which bore the likeness of a great black snake, so curiously wrought, that it might almost be seen to twist and wriggle itself like a living serpent. This, of course, must have been an ocular deception, assisted by the uncertain light.

"Come, Goodman Brown!" cried his fellow-traveller, "this is a dull pace for the beginning of a journey. Take my staff, if you are so soon weary."

"Friend," said the other, exchanging his slow pace for a full stop, "having kept covenant by meeting thee here, it is my purpose now to return whence I came. I have scruples, touching the matter thou wot'st of."

"Sayest thou so?" replied he of the serpent, smiling apart. "Let us walk on, nevertheless, reasoning as we go, and if I convince thee not, thou shalt turn back. We are but a little way in the forest, yet."

"Too far, too far!" exclaimed the goodman, unconsciously resuming his walk. "My father never went into the woods on such an errand, nor his father before him. We have been a race of honest men and good Christians, since the days of the martyrs. And shall I be the first of the name of Brown, that ever took this path and kept—"

"Such company, thou wouldst say," observed the elder person, interrupting his pause. "Well said,

Goodman Brown! I have been as well acquainted with your family as with ever a one among the Puritans; and that's no trifle to say. I helped your grandfather, the constable, when he lashed the Quaker woman so smartly through the streets of Salem. And it was I that brought your father a pitch-pine knot, kindled at my own hearth, to set fire to an Indian village, in King Philip's War. They were my good friends, both; and many a pleasant walk have we had along this path, and returned merrily after midnight. I would fain be friends with you, for their sake."

"If it be as thou sayest," replied Goodman Brown, "I marvel they never spoke of these matters. Or, verily, I marvel not, seeing that the least rumor of the sort would have driven them from New England. We are a people of prayer, and good works to boot, and abide no such wickedness."

"Wickedness or not," said the traveller with the twisted staff, "have a very general acquaintance here in New England. The deacons of many a church have drunk the communion wine with me; the selectmen, of divers towns, make me their chairman; and a majority of the Great and General Court are firm supporters of my interest. The governor and I, too—but these are state-secrets."

"Can this be so!" cried Goodman Brown, with a stare of amazement at his undisturbed companion. "Howbeit, I have nothing to do with the governor and council; they have their own ways, and are no rule for a simple husbandman like me. But, were I to go on with thee, how should I meet the eye of that good old man, our minister, at Salem village? Oh, his voice would make me tremble, both Sabbath-day and lecture-day!"

Thus far, the elder traveller had listened with due gravity, but now burst into a fit of irrepressible mirth, shaking himself so violently that his snake-like staff actually seemed to wriggle in sympathy.

"Ha! ha! ha!" shouted he, again and again; then composing himself, "Well, go on, Goodman Brown, go on; but, prithee, don't kill me with laughing!"

"Well, then, to end the matter at once," said Goodman Brown, considerably nettled, "there is my wife, Faith. It would break her dear little heart; and I'd rather break my own!"

"Nay, if that be the case," answered the other, "e'en go thy ways, Goodman Brown. I would not,

for twenty old women like the one hobbling before us, that Faith should come to any harm."

As he spoke, he pointed his staff at a female figure on the path, in whom Goodman Brown recognized a very pious and exemplary dame, who had taught him his catechism in youth, and was still his moral and spiritual adviser, jointly with the minister and Deacon Gookin.

"A marvel, truly, that Goody Cloyse should be so far in the wilderness, at night-fall!" said he. "But, with your leave, friend, I shall take a cut through the woods, until we have left this Christian woman behind. Being a stranger to you, she might ask whom I was consorting with, and whither I was going."

"Be it so," said his fellow-traveller. "Betake you to the woods, and let me keep the path."

Accordingly, the young man turned aside, but took care to watch his companion, who advanced softly along the road, until he had come within a staff's length of the old dame. She, meanwhile, was making the best of her way, with singular speed for so aged a woman, and mumbling some indistinct words, a prayer, doubtless, as she went. The traveller put forth his staff, and touched her withered neck with what seemed the serpent's tail.

"The devil!" screamed the pious old lady.

"Then Goody Cloyse knows her old friend?" observed the traveller, confronting her, and leaning on his writhing stick.

"Ah, forsooth, and is it your worship, indeed?" cried the good dame. "Yea, truly is it, and in the very image of my old gossip, Goodman Brown, the grandfather of the silly fellow that now is. But, would your worship believe it? My broomstick hath strangely disappeared, stolen, as I suspect, by that unhanged witch, Goody Cory, and that, too, when I was all anointed with the juice of smallage and cinque-foil and wolf's-bane"—

"Mingled with fine wheat and the fat of a new-born babe," said the shape of old Goodman Brown. "Ah, your worship knows the recipe," cried the old lady, cackling aloud. "So, as I was saying, being all ready for the meeting, and no horse to ride on, I made up my mind to foot it; for they tell me, there is a nice young man to be taken into communion tonight. But now your good worship will lend me your arm, and we shall be there in a twinkling."

"That can hardly be," answered her friend. "I may not spare you my arm, Goody Cloyse, but here is my staff, if you will."

So saying, he threw it down at her feet, where, perhaps, it assumed life, being one of the rods which its owner had formerly lent to Egyptian Magi. Of this fact, however, Goodman Brown could not take cognizance. He had cast up his eyes in astonishment, and looking down again, beheld neither Goody Cloyse nor the serpentine staff, but his fellow-traveller alone, who waited for him as calmly as if nothing had happened.

"That old woman taught me my catechism!" said the young man; and there was a world of meaning in this simple comment.

They continued to walk onward, while the elder traveller exhorted his companion to make good speed and persevere in the path, discoursing so aptly, that his arguments seemed rather to spring up in the bosom of his auditor, than to be suggested by himself. As they went, he plucked a branch of maple, to serve for a walking-stick, and began to strip it of the twigs and little boughs, which were wet with evening dew. The moment his fingers touched them, they became strangely withered and dried up, as with a week's sunshine. Thus the pair proceeded, at a good free pace, until suddenly, in a gloomy hollow of the road, Goodman Brown sat himself down on the stump of a tree, and refused to go any farther.

"Friend," said he, stubbornly, "my mind is made up. Not another step will I budge on this errand. What if a wretched old woman does choose to go to the devil, when I thought she was going to Heaven! Is that any reason why I should quit my dear Faith, and go after her?"

"You will think better of this by-and-by," said his acquaintance, composedly. "Sit here and rest yourself awhile; and when you feel like moving again, there is my staff to help you along." Without more words, he threw his companion the maple stick, and was as speedily out of sight as if he had vanished into the deepening gloom. The young man sat a few moments by the road-side, applauding himself greatly, and thinking with how clear a conscience he should meet the minister, in his morning-walk, nor shrink from the eye of good old Deacon Gookin. And what calm sleep would be his, that very night, which was to have been spent so wickedly, but

purely and sweetly now, in the arms of Faith! Amidst these pleasant and praiseworthy meditations, Goodman Brown heard the tramp of horses along the road, and deemed it advisable to conceal himself within the verge of the forest, conscious of the guilty purpose that had brought him thither, though now so happily turned from it. On came the hoof-tramps and the voices of the riders, two grave old voices, conversing soberly as they drew near. These mingled sounds appeared to pass along the road, within a few yards of the young man's hiding-place; but owing, doubtless, to the depth of the gloom, at that particular spot, neither the travellers nor their steeds were visible. Though their figures brushed the small boughs by the way-side, it could not be seen that they intercepted, even for a moment, the faint gleam from the strip of bright sky, athwart which they must have passed. Goodman Brown alternately crouched and stood on tip-toe, pulling aside the branches, and thrusting forth his head as far as he durst, without discerning so much as a shadow. It vexed him the more, because he could have sworn, were such a thing possible, that he recognized the voices of the minister and Deacon Gookin, jogging along quietly, as they were wont to do, when bound to some ordination or ecclesiastical council. While yet within hearing, one of the riders stopped to pluck a switch. "Of the two, reverend Sir," said the voice like the deacon's, "I had rather miss an ordination-dinner than tonight's meeting. They tell me that some of our community are to be here from Falmouth and beyond, and others from Connecticut and Rhode Island; besides several of the Indian powwows, who, after their fashion, know almost as much deviltry as the best of us. Moreover, there is a goodly young woman to be taken into communion." "Mighty well, Deacon Gookin!" replied the solemn old tones of the minister. "Spur up, or we shall be late. Nothing can be done, you know, until I get on the ground." The hoofs clattered again, and the voices, talking so strangely in the empty air, passed on through the forest, where no church had ever been gathered, nor solitary Christian prayed. Whither, then, could these holy men be journeying, so deep into the heathen wilderness? Young Goodman Brown caught hold of a tree, for support, being ready to sink down on the ground, faint and overburthened with the heavy sickness of his heart. He looked up to the sky, doubting whether there really was a Heaven above him. Yet, there was the blue arch, and the stars brightening in it. "With Heaven above, and Faith below, I will yet stand firm against the devil!" cried Goodman Brown. While he still gazed upward, into the deep arch of the firmament, and had lifted his hands to pray, a cloud, though no wind was stirring, hurried across the zenith, and hid the brightening stars. The blue sky was still visible, except directly overhead, where this black mass of cloud was sweeping swiftly northward. Aloft in the air, as if from the depths of the cloud, came a confused and doubtful sound of voices. Once, the listener fancied that he could distinguish the accent of townspeople of his own, men and women, both pious and ungodly, many of whom he had met at the communion-table, and had seen others rioting at the tavern. The next moment, so indistinct were the sounds, he doubted whether he had heard aught but the murmur of the old forest, whispering without a wind. Then came a stronger swell of those familiar tones, heard daily in the sunshine, at Salem village, but never, until now, from a cloud of night. There was one voice, of a young woman, uttering lamentations, yet with an uncertain sorrow, and entreating for some favor, which, perhaps, it would grieve her to obtain. And all the unseen multitude, both saints and sinners, seemed to encourage her onward. "Faith!" shouted Goodman Brown, in a voice of agony and desperation; and the echoes of the forest mocked him, crying—"Faith! Faith!" as if bewildered wretches were seeking her, all through the wilderness. The cry of grief, rage, and terror, was yet piercing the night, when the unhappy husband held his breath for a response. There was a scream, drowned immediately in a louder murmur of voices, fading into far-off laughter, as the dark cloud swept away, leaving the clear and silent sky above Goodman Brown. But something fluttered lightly down through the air, and caught on the branch of a tree. The young man seized it, and beheld a pink ribbon. "My Faith is gone!" cried he, after one stupefied moment. "There is no good on earth; and sin is but a name. Come, devil! for to thee is this world given." And maddened with despair, so that he laughed loud and long, did Goodman Brown grasp his staff and set forth again, at such a rate, that he seemed to fly along the forest-path, rather than to walk or run. The road grew wilder and drearier, and more faintly traced, and vanished at length, leaving him in the heart of the dark wilderness, still rushing onward, with the instinct that guides mortal man to evil. The whole forest was peopled with frightful sounds; the creaking of the trees, the howling of wild beasts, and the yell of Indians; while, sometimes the wind tolled like a distant church-bell, and sometimes gave a broad roar around the traveller, as if all Nature were laughing him to scorn. But he was himself the chief horror of the scene, and shrank not from its other horrors. "Ha! ha! ha!" roared Goodman Brown, when the wind laughed at him. "Let us hear which will laugh loudest! Think not to frighten me with your deviltry! Come witch, come wizard, come Indian powwow, come devil himself! and here comes Goodman Brown. You may as well fear him as he fears you!" In truth, all through the haunted forest, there could be nothing more frightful than the figure of Goodman Brown. On he flew, among the black pines, brandishing his staff with frenzied gestures, now giving vent to an inspiration of horrid blasphemy, and now shouting forth such laughter, as set all the echoes of the forest laughing like demons around him. The fiend in his own shape is less hideous, than when he rages in the breast of man. Thus sped the demoniac on his course, until, quivering among the trees, he saw a red light before him, as when the felled trunks and branches of a clearing have been set on fire, and throw up their lurid blaze against the sky, at the hour of midnight. He paused, in a lull of the tempest that had driven him onward, and heard the swell of what seemed a hymn, rolling solemnly from a distance, with the weight of many voices. He knew the tune; it was a familiar one in the choir of the village meetinghouse. The verse died heavily away, and was lengthened by a chorus, not of human voices, but of all the sounds of the benighted wilderness, pealing in awful harmony together. Goodman Brown cried out; and his cry was lost to his own ear, by its unison with the cry of the desert. In the interval of silence, he stole forward, until the light glared full upon his eyes. At one extremity of an open space, hemmed in by the dark wall of the forest, arose a rock, bearing some rude, natural resemblance either to an altar or a pulpit, and surrounded by four blazing pines, their tops aflame, their stems untouched, like candles at an evening meeting. The mass of foliage, that had overgrown the summit of the rock, was all on fire, blazing high into the night, and fitfully illuminating the whole field. Each pendant twig and leafy festoon was in a blaze. As the red light arose and fell, a numerous congregation alternately shone forth, then disappeared in shadow, and again grew, as it were, out of the darkness, peopling the heart of the solitary woods at once. "A grave and dark-clad company!" quoth Goodman Brown. In truth, they were such. Among them, quivering to and fro, between gloom and splendor, appeared faces that would be seen, next day, at the council-board of the province, and others which, Sabbath after Sabbath, looked devoutly heavenward, and benignantly over the crowded pews, from the holiest pulpits in the land. Some affirm, that the lady of the governor was there. At least, there were high dames well known to her, and wives of honored husbands, and widows, a great multitude, and ancient maidens, all of excellent repute, and fair young girls, who trembled lest their mothers should espy them. Either the sudden gleams of light, flashing over the obscure field, bedazzled Goodman Brown, or he recognized a score of the church-members of Salem village, famous for their especial sanctity. Good old Deacon Gookin had arrived, and waited at the skirts of that venerable saint, his reverend pastor. But, irreverently consorting with these grave, reputable, and pious people, these elders of the church, these chaste dames and dewy virgins, there were men of dissolute lives and women of spotted fame, wretches given over to all mean and filthy vice, and suspected even of horrid crimes. It was strange to see, that the good shrank not from the wicked, nor were the sinners abashed by the saints. Scattered, also, among their palefaced enemies, were the Indian priests, or powwows, who had often scared their native forest with more hideous incantations than any known to English witchcraft. "But, where is Faith?" thought Goodman Brown; and, as hope came into his heart, he trembled. Another verse of the hymn arose, a slow and mournful strain, such as the pious love, but joined to words which expressed all that our nature can conceive of sin, and darkly hinted at far more. Unfathomable to mere mortals is the lore of fiends. Verse after verse was sung, and still the chorus of the desert swelled between, like the deepest tone of a mighty organ. And, with the final peal of that dreadful anthem, there came a sound, as if the roaring wind, the rushing streams, the howling beasts, and every other voice of the unconverted wilderness, were mingling and according with the voice of a guilty man, in homage to the prince of all.

The four blazing pines threw up a loftier flame, and obscurely discovered shapes and visages of horror on the smoke-wreaths, above the impious assembly. At the same moment, the fire on the rock shot redly forth, and formed a glowing arch above its base, where now appeared a figure. With reverence be it spoken, the apparition bore no slight similitude, both in garb and manner, to some grave divine of the New England churches. "Bring forth the converts!" cried a voice, that echoed through the field and rolled into the forest. At the word, Goodman Brown stepped forth from the shadow of the trees, and approached the congregation, with whom he felt a loathful brotherhood, by the sympathy of all that was wicked in his heart. He could have well nigh sworn, that the shape of his own dead father beckoned him to advance, looking downward from a smoke-wreath, while a woman, with dim features of despair, threw out her hand to warn him back. Was it his mother? But he had no power to retreat one step, nor to resist, even in thought, when the minister and good old Deacon Gookin seized his arms, and led him to the blazing rock. Thither came also the slender form of a veiled female, led between Goody Cloyse, that pious teacher of the catechism, and Martha Carrier, who had received the devil's promise to be queen of hell. A rampant hag was she! And there stood the proselytes, beneath the canopy of fire. "Welcome, my children," said the dark figure, "to the communion of your race! Ye have found, thus young, your nature and your destiny. My children, look behind you!" They turned; and flashing forth, as it were, in a sheet of flame, the fiend-worshippers were seen; the smile of welcome gleamed darkly on every visage. "There," resumed the sable form, "are all whom ye have reverenced from youth. Ye deemed them holier than yourselves, and shrank from your own sin, contrasting it with their lives of righteousness, and prayerful aspirations heavenward. Yet, here are they all, in my worshipping assembly! This night it shall be granted you to know their secret deeds; how hoary-bearded elders of the church have whispered wanton words to the young maids of their households; how many a woman, eager for widow's weeds, has given her husband a drink at bed-time, and let him sleep his last sleep in her bosom; how beardless youth have made haste to inherit their father's wealth; and how fair damsels—blush not, sweet ones—have dug little graves in the garden, and bidden me, the sole guest, to an infant's funeral. By the sympathy of your human hearts for sin, ye shall scent out all the places—whether in church, bed-chamber, street, field, or forest—where crime has been committed, and shall exult to behold the whole earth one stain of guilt, one mighty blood-spot. Far more than this! It shall be yours to penetrate, in every bosom, the deep mystery of sin, the fountain of all wicked arts, and which inexhaustibly supplies more evil impulses than human power—than my power at its utmost—can make manifest in deeds. And now, my children, look upon each other." They did so; and, by the blaze of the hell-kindled torches, the wretched man beheld his Faith, and the wife her husband, trembling before that unhallowed altar. "Lo! there ye stand, my children," said the figure, in a deep and solemn tone, almost sad, with its despairing awfulness, as if his once angelic nature could yet mourn for our miserable race. "Depending upon one another's hearts, ye had still hoped that virtue were not all a dream! Now are ye undeceived! Evil is the nature of mankind. Evil must be your only happiness. Welcome, again, my children, to the communion of your race!" "Welcome!" repeated the fiend-worshippers, in one cry of despair and triumph. And there they stood, the only pair, as it seemed, who were yet hesitating on the verge of wickedness, in this dark world. A basin was hollowed, naturally, in the rock. Did it contain water, reddened by the lurid light? or was it blood? or, perchance, a liquid flame? Herein did the Shape of Evil dip his hand, and prepare to lay the mark of baptism upon their foreheads, that they might be partakers of the mystery of sin, more conscious of the secret guilt of others, both in deed and thought, than they could now be of their own. The husband cast one look at his pale wife, and Faith at him. What polluted wretches would the next glance show them to each other, shuddering alike at what they disclosed and what they saw! "Faith! Faith!" cried the husband. "Look up to Heaven, and resist the Wicked One!" Whether Faith obeyed, he knew not. Hardly had he spoken, when he found himself amid calm night and solitude, listening to a roar of the wind, which died heavily away through the forest. He staggered against the rock, and felt it chill and damp, while a hanging twig, that had been all on fire, besprinkled his cheek with the coldest dew. The next morning, young Goodman Brown came slowly into the street of Salem village, staring around him like a bewildered man. The good old minister was taking a walk along the graveyard, to get an appetite for breakfast and meditate his sermon, and bestowed a blessing, as he passed, on Goodman Brown. He shrank from the venerable saint, as if to avoid an anathema. Old Deacon Gookin was at domestic worship, and the holy words of his prayer were heard through the open window. "What God doth the wizard pray to?" quoth Goodman Brown. Goody Cloyse, that excellent old Christian, stood in the early sunshine, at her own lattice, catechising a little girl, who had brought her a pint of morning's milk. Goodman Brown snatched away the child, as from the grasp of the fiend himself. Turning the corner by the meeting-house, he spied the head of Faith, with the pink ribbons, gazing anxiously forth, and bursting into such joy at sight of him, that she skipt along the street, and almost kissed her husband before the whole village. But Goodman Brown looked sternly and sadly into her face, and passed on without a greeting. Had Goodman Brown fallen asleep in the forest, and only dreamed a wild dream of a witch-meeting? Be it so, if you will. But, alas! it was a dream of evil omen for young Goodman Brown. A stern, a sad, a darkly meditative, a distrustful, if not a desperate man, did he become, from the night of that fearful dream. On the Sabbath-day, when the congregation were singing a holy psalm, he could not listen, because an anthem of sin rushed loudly upon his ear, and drowned all the blessed strain. When the minister spoke from the pulpit, with power and fervid eloquence, and with his hand on the open Bible, of the sacred truths of our religion, and of saint-like lives and triumphant deaths, and of future bliss or misery unutterable, then did Goodman Brown turn pale, dreading lest the roof should thunder down upon the gray blasphemer and his hearers. Often, awaking suddenly at midnight, he shrank from the bosom of Faith, and at morning or eventide, when the family knelt down at prayer, he scowled, and muttered to himself, and gazed sternly at his wife, and turned away. And when he had lived long, and was borne to his grave, a hoary corpse, followed by Faith, an aged woman, and children and grandchildren, a goodly procession, besides neighbors, not a few, they carved no hopeful verse upon his tombstone; for his dying hour was gloom.

Questions

1. In *Young Goodman Brown,* analyze the characters' names. How might they be relevant? What do their names contribute to what the story might be attempting to convey?
2. Hawthorne writes: "[Goodman Brown] had cast up his eyes in astonishment, and looking down again, beheld neither Goody Cloyse nor the serpentine staff, but his fellow-traveller alone, who waited for him as calmly as if nothing had happened." What may have happened to Goody Cloyse?
3. Often, Goodman Brown seems to make a reference to Faith. Is he referring to his wife, or is he referring to "belief"?
4. At one point, it seems like a baptism is being conducted. What is the purpose of a baptism? Further, what is the purpose of this baptism?
5. Have you ever had a dream that seemed so real that, at least for a little while, you were not able to dismiss it as just a dream? If so, how did you finally come to the realization that it was, in fact, a dream? Can such a methodology be employed in attempting to decipher whether or not Goodman Brown was dreaming? What exists in the story to suggest that he was dreaming?

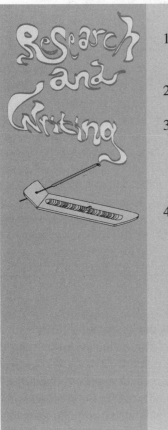

1. Examine *Young Goodman Brown,* Mark Twain's *The Mysterious Stranger,* and the film *The Devil's Advocate.* After doing so, compare and contrast the three in an essay.
2. Read "The Book of Job," which can be found in *The Old Testament.* Upon doing so, compare and contrast Job and Goodman Brown.
3. Arguably, one of the more mysterious players on the biblical stage is the Devil. Perform some research that might yield insight into the derivation of the Devil's mystery. Then, employ the fruits of this research when examining the presence of the Devil in *Young Goodman Brown* and the film *The Usual Suspects.*
4. In *Young Goodman Brown,* Hawthorne writes: "There [. . .] are all whom ye have reverenced from youth. Ye deemed them holier than yourselves, and shrank from your own sin, contrasting it with their lives of righteousness [. . .]." Essentially, Goodman Brown is being presented with the contradiction between people's perceived actions and their real actions. Some people might simply consider this an example of hypocrisy. Perform some research on famous hypocrites, and construct an argument around their hypocrisy. This might be a classification essay where you might classify various degrees of hypocrisy. Or, perhaps, this might be an essay that takes a stand, proposes a solution, offers a definition, or attempts to compare and contrast. Regardless, use *Young Goodman Brown* as your foundation for hypocrisy, research some famous hypocrites, and then construct your argument.

Continued

5. Examine a film titled *Memento*. After doing so, compare and contrast the dream-like qualities extant in *Memento* and *Young Goodman Brown*. Then, take a stand on whether or not the "dreams" are real. Make sure to support your stance by citing examples from both texts as well as examples gathered through additional research.

Washington Irving (1783–1859)

Washington Irving, also known as Dietrich Knickerbocker, Jonathan Oldstyle, and Geoffrey Crayon, was born in New York City in 1783. Named after George Washington, Irving was the youngest of eleven children. Before being deemed by many "the father of the American short story," he was a lawyer, a journalist, and a partner with his brothers in the family hardware business.

The Legend of Sleepy Hollow

1. When reading this, allow Irving to describe his Sleepy Hollow for you. In other words, if you have been privy to someone else's description of Sleepy Hollow, i.e., Tim Burton's film *Sleepy Hollow,* dismiss it. Realize that if we are attempting to locate authenticity, this is the story that inspired the others.
2. Make a conscious effort to read this story slowly, noting language precision, alliteration, and the poetic tone of Irving's prose.

The Legend of Sleepy Hollow

Washington Irving

Found among the papers of the late Dietrich Knickerbocker.

A pleasing land of drowsy head it was,
Of dreams that wave before the half-shut eye;
And of gay castles in the clouds that pass,
Forever flushing round a summer sky.
Castle of Indolence.

In the bosom of one of those spacious coves which indent the eastern shore of the Hudson, at that broad expansion of the river denominated by the ancient Dutch navigators the Tappan Zee, and where they always prudently shortened sail and implored the protection of St. Nicholas when they crossed, there lies a small market town or rural port, which by some is called Greensburgh, but which is more generally and properly known by the name of Tarry Town. This name was given, we are told, in former days, by the good housewives of the adjacent country, from the inveterate propensity of their husbands to linger about the village tavern on market days. Be that as it may, I do not vouch for the fact, but merely advert to it, for the sake of being precise and authentic. Not far from this village, perhaps about two miles, there is a little valley or rather lap of land among high hills, which is one of the quietest places in the whole world. A small brook glides through it, with just murmur enough to lull one to repose; and the occasional whistle of a quail or tapping of a woodpecker is almost the only sound that ever breaks in upon the uniform tranquility.

I recollect that, when a stripling, my first exploit in squirrel-shooting was in a grove of tall walnut-trees that shades one side of the valley. I had wandered into it at noontime, when all nature is peculiarly quiet, and was startled by the roar of my own gun, as it broke the Sabbath stillness around and was prolonged and reverberated by the angry echoes. If ever I should wish for a retreat whither I might steal from the world and its distractions, and dream quietly away the remnant of a troubled life, I know of none more promising than this little valley.

From the listless repose of the place, and the peculiar character of its inhabitants, who are descendants from the original Dutch settlers, this sequestered glen has long been known by the name of SLEEPY HOLLOW, and its rustic lads are called the Sleepy Hollow Boys throughout all the neighboring country. A drowsy, dreamy influence seems to hang over the land, and to pervade the very atmosphere. Some say that the place was bewitched by a High German doctor, during the early days of the settlement; others, that an old Indian chief, the prophet or wizard of his tribe, held his powwows there before the country was discovered by Master Hendrick Hudson. Certain it is, the place still continues under the sway of some witching power, that holds a spell over the minds of the good people, causing them to walk in a continual reverie. They are given to all kinds of marvelous beliefs; are subject to trances and visions, and frequently see strange sights, and hear music and voices in the air. The whole neighborhood abounds with local tales, haunted spots, and twilight superstitions; stars shoot and meteors glare oftener across the valley than in any other part of the country, and the nightmare, with her whole ninefold, seems to make it the favorite scene of her gambols.

The dominant spirit, however, that haunts this enchanted region, and seems to be commander-in-chief of all the powers of the air, is the apparition of a figure on horseback, without a head. It is said by some to be the ghost of a Hessian trooper, whose head had been carried away by a cannon-ball, in some nameless battle during the Revolutionary War, and who is ever and anon seen by the country folk hurrying along in the gloom of night, as if on the wings of the wind. His haunts are not confined to the valley, but extend at times to the adjacent roads, and especially to the vicinity of a church at no great distance. Indeed, certain of the most authentic historians of those parts, who have been careful in collecting and collating the floating facts concerning this spectre, allege that the body of the trooper having been buried in the churchyard, the ghost rides forth to the scene of battle in nightly quest of his head, and that the rushing speed with which he sometimes passes along the Hollow, like a midnight blast, is owing to his being belated, and in a hurry to get back to the churchyard before daybreak.

Such is the general purport of this legendary superstition, which has furnished materials for many a wild story in that region of shadows; and the spectre is known at all the country firesides, by the name of the Headless Horseman of Sleepy Hollow.

It is remarkable that the visionary propensity I have mentioned is not confined to the native inhabitants of the valley, but is unconsciously imbibed by every one who resides there for a time. However wide awake they may have been before they entered that sleepy region, they are sure, in a little time, to inhale the witching influence of the air, and begin to grow imaginative, to dream dreams, and see apparitions.

I mention this peaceful spot with all possible laud for it is in such little retired Dutch valleys, found here and there embosomed in the great State of New York, that population, manners, and customs remain fixed, while the great torrent of migration and improvement, which is making such incessant changes in other parts of this restless country, sweeps by them unobserved. They are like those little nooks of still water, which border a rapid stream, where we may see the straw and bubble riding quietly at anchor, or slowly revolving in their mimic harbor, undisturbed by the rush of the passing current. Though many years have elapsed since I trod the drowsy shades of Sleepy Hollow, yet I question whether I should not still find the same trees and the same families vegetating in its sheltered bosom.

In this by-place of nature there abode, in a remote period of American history, that is to say, some thirty years since, a worthy wight of the name of Ichabod Crane, who sojourned, or, as he expressed it, "tarried," in Sleepy Hollow, for the purpose of instructing the children of the vicinity. He was a native of Connecticut, a State which supplies the Union with pioneers for the mind as well as for the forest, and sends forth yearly its legions of frontier woodmen and country schoolmasters. The cognomen of Crane was not inapplicable to his person. He was tall, but exceedingly lank, with narrow shoulders, long arms and legs, hands that dangled a mile out of his sleeves, feet that might have served for shovels, and his whole frame most loosely hung together. His head was small, and flat at top, with huge ears, large green glassy eyes, and a long snipe nose, so that it looked like a weather-cock perched upon his spindle neck to tell which way the wind blew. To see him striding along the profile of a hill on a windy day, with his clothes bagging and fluttering about him, one might have mistaken him for the genius of famine descending upon the earth, or some scarecrow eloped from a cornfield.

His schoolhouse was a low building of one large room, rudely constructed of logs; the windows partly glazed, and partly patched with leaves of old copybooks. It was most ingeniously secured at vacant hours, by a withe twisted in the handle of the door, and stakes set against the window shutters; so that though a thief might get in with perfect ease, he would find some embarrassment in getting out—an idea most probably borrowed by the architect, Yost Van Houten, from the mystery of an eelpot. The schoolhouse stood in a rather lonely but pleasant situation, just at the foot of a woody hill, with a brook running close by, and a formidable birch-tree growing at one end of it. From hence the low murmur of his pupils' voices, conning over their lessons, might be heard in a drowsy summer's day, like the hum of a beehive; interrupted now and then by the authoritative voice of the master, in the tone of menace or command, or, peradventure, by the appalling sound

of the birch, as he urged some tardy loiterer along the flowery path of knowledge. Truth to say, he was a conscientious man, and ever bore in mind the golden maxim, "Spare the rod and spoil the child." Ichabod Crane's scholars certainly were not spoiled.

I would not have it imagined, however, that he was one of those cruel potentates of the school who joy in the smart of their subjects; on the contrary, he administered justice with discrimination rather than severity; taking the burden off the backs of the weak, and laying it on those of the strong. Your mere puny stripling, that winced at the least flourish of the rod, was passed by with indulgence; but the claims of justice were satisfied by inflicting a double portion on some little tough wrong headed, broad-skirted Dutch urchin, who sulked and swelled and grew dogged and sullen beneath the birch. All this he called "doing his duty by their parents"; and he never inflicted a chastisement without following it by the assurance, so consolatory to the smarting urchin, that "he would remember it and thank him for it the longest day he had to live."

When school hours were over, he was even the companion and playmate of the larger boys; and on holiday afternoons would convoy some of the smaller ones home, who happened to have pretty sisters, or good housewives for mothers, noted for the comforts of the cupboard. Indeed, it behooved him to keep on good terms with his pupils. The revenue arising from his school was small, and would have been scarcely sufficient to furnish him with daily bread, for he was a huge feeder, and, though lank, had the dilating powers of an anaconda; but to help out his maintenance, he was, according to country custom in those parts, boarded and lodged at the houses of the farmers whose children he instructed. With these he lived successively a week at a time, thus going the rounds of the neighborhood, with all his worldly effects tied up in a cotton handkerchief.

That all this might not be too onerous on the purses of his rustic patrons, who are apt to consider the costs of schooling a grievous burden, and schoolmasters as mere drones he had various ways of rendering himself both useful and agreeable. He assisted the farmers occasionally in the lighter labors of their farms, helped to make hay, mended the fences, took the horses to water, drove the cows from pasture, and cut wood for the winter fire. He laid aside, too, all the dominant dignity and absolute sway with which he lorded it in his little empire, the school, and became wonderfully gentle and ingratiating. He found favor in the eyes of the mothers by petting the children, particularly the youngest; and like the lion bold, which whilom so magnanimously the lamb did hold, he would sit with a child on one knee, and rock a cradle with his foot for whole hours together.

In addition to his other vocations, he was the singing-master of the neighborhood, and picked up many bright shillings by instructing the young folks in psalmody. It was a matter of no little vanity to him on Sundays, to take his station in front of the church gallery, with a band of chosen singers; where, in his own mind, he completely carried away the palm from the parson. Certain it is, his voice resounded far above all the rest of the congregation; and there are peculiar quavers still to be heard in that church, and which may even be heard half a mile off, quite to the opposite side of the mill-pond, on a still Sunday morning, which are said to be legitimately descended from the nose of Ichabod Crane. Thus, by divers little makeshifts, in that ingenious way which is commonly denominated "by hook and by crook," the worthy pedagogue got on tolerably enough, and was thought, by all who understood nothing of the labor of headwork, to have a wonderfully easy life of it.

The schoolmaster is generally a man of some importance in the female circle of a rural neighborhood; being considered a kind of idle, gentlemanlike personage, of vastly superior taste and accomplishments to the rough country swains, and, indeed, inferior in learning only to the parson. His appearance, therefore, is apt to occasion some little stir at the tea-table of a farmhouse, and the addition of a supernumerary dish of cakes or sweetmeats, or, peradventure, the parade of a silver teapot. Our man of letters, therefore, was peculiarly happy in the smiles of all the country damsels. How he would figure among them in the churchyard, between services on Sundays; gathering grapes for them from the wild vines that overran the surrounding trees; reciting for their amusement all the epitaphs on the tombstones; or sauntering, with a whole bevy of them, along the banks of the adjacent mill-pond; while the more bashful country bumpkins hung sheepishly back, envying his superior elegance and address.

From his half-itinerant life, also, he was a kind of traveling gazette, carrying the whole budget of local gossip from house to house, so that his appearance was always greeted with satisfaction. He was, moreover, esteemed by the women as a man of great erudition, for he had read several books quite through, and was a perfect master of Cotton Mather's "History of New England Witchcraft," in which, by the way, he most firmly and potently believed.

He was, in fact, an odd mixture of small shrewdness and simple credulity. His appetite for the marvelous, and his powers of digesting it, were equally extraordinary; and both had been increased by his residence in this spell-bound region. No tale was too gross or monstrous for his capacious swallow. It was often his delight, after his school was dismissed in the afternoon, to stretch himself on the rich bed of clover bordering the little brook that whimpered by his school-house, and there con over old Mather's direful tales, until the gathering dusk of evening made the printed page a mere mist before his eyes. Then, as he wended his way by swamp and stream and awful woodland, to the farmhouse where he happened to be quartered, every sound of nature, at that witching hour, fluttered his excited imagination—the moan of the whip-poor-will from the hillside, the boding cry of the tree toad, that harbinger of storm, the dreary hooting of the screech owl, to the sudden rustling in the thicket of birds frightened from their roost. The fireflies, too, which sparkled most vividly in the darkest places, now and then startled him, as one of uncommon brightness would stream across his path; and if, by chance, a huge blockhead of a beetle came winging his blundering flight against him, the poor varlet was ready to give up the ghost, with the idea that he was struck with a witch's token. His only resource on such occasions, either to drown thought or drive away evil spirits, was to sing psalm tunes and the good people of Sleepy Hollow, as they sat by their doors of an evening, were often filled with awe at hearing his nasal melody, "in linked sweetness long drawn out," floating from the distant hill, or along the dusky road.

Another of his sources of fearful pleasure was to pass long winter evenings with the old Dutch wives, as they sat spinning by the fire, with a row of apples roasting and spluttering along the hearth, and listen to their marvellous tales of ghosts and goblins, and haunted fields, and haunted brooks, and haunted bridges, and haunted houses, and particularly of the headless horseman, or Galloping Hessian of the Hollow, as they sometimes called him. He would delight them equally by his anecdotes of witchcraft, and of the direful omens and portentous sights and sounds in the air, which prevailed in the earlier times of Connecticut; and would frighten them woefully with speculations upon comets and shooting stars; and with the alarming fact that the world did absolutely turn round, and that they were half the time topsy-turvy!

But if there was a pleasure in all this, while snugly cuddling in the chimney corner of a chamber that was all of a ruddy glow from the crackling wood fire, and where, of course, no spectre dared to show its face, it was dearly purchased by the terrors of his subsequent walk homewards. What fearful shapes and shadows beset his path, amidst the dim and ghastly glare of a snowy night! With what wistful look did he eye every trembling ray of light streaming across the waste fields from some distant window! How often was he appalled by some shrub covered with snow, which, like a sheeted spectre, beset his very path! How often did he shrink with curdling awe at the sound of his own steps on the frosty crust beneath his feet; and dread to look over his shoulder, lest he should behold some uncouth being tramping close behind him! and how often was he thrown into complete dismay by some rushing blast, howling among the trees, in the idea that it was the Galloping Hessian on one of his nightly scourings!

All these, however, were mere terrors of the night, phantoms of the mind that walk in darkness; and though he had seen many spectres in his time, and been more than once beset by Satan in diverse shapes, in his lonely perambulations, yet daylight put an end to all these evils; and he would have passed a pleasant life of it, in despite of the Devil and all his works, if his path had not been crossed by a being that causes more perplexity to mortal man than ghosts, goblins, and the whole race of witches put together, and that was—a woman.

Among the musical disciples who assembled, one evening in each week, to receive his instructions in psalmody, was Katrina Van Tassel, the daughter and only child of a substantial Dutch farmer. She was a booming lass of fresh eighteen; plump as a partridge; ripe and melting and rosy-cheeked as one

of her father's peaches, and universally famed, not merely for her beauty, but her vast expectations. She was withal a little of a coquette, as might be perceived even in her dress, which was a mixture of ancient and modern fashions, as most suited to set of her charms. She wore the ornaments of pure yellow gold, which her great-great-grandmother had brought over from Saar dam; the tempting stomacher of the olden time, and withal a provokingly short petticoat, to display the prettiest foot and ankle in the country round.

Ichabod Crane had a soft and foolish heart towards the sex; and it is not to be wondered at, that so tempting a morsel soon found favor in his eyes, more especially after he had visited her in her paternal mansion. Old Baltus Van Tassel was a perfect picture of a thriving, contented, liberal-hearted farmer. He seldom, it is true, sent either his eyes or his thoughts beyond the boundaries of his own farm; but within those everything was snug, happy and well-conditioned. He was satisfied with his wealth, but not proud of it; and piqued himself upon the hearty abundance, rather than the style in which he lived. His stronghold was situated on the banks of the Hudson, in one of those green, sheltered, fertile nooks in which the Dutch farmers are so fond of nestling. A great elm tree spread its broad branches over it, at the foot of which bubbled up a spring of the softest and sweetest water, in a little well formed of a barrel; and then stole sparkling away through the grass, to a neighboring brook, that babbled along among alders and dwarf willows. Hard by the farmhouse was a vast barn, that might have served for a church; every window and crevice of which seemed bursting forth with the treasures of the farm; the flail was busily resounding within it from morning to night; swallows and martins skimmed twittering about the eaves; and rows of pigeons, some with one eye turned up, as if watching the weather, some with their heads under their wings or buried in their bosoms, and others swelling, and cooing, and bowing about their dames, were enjoying the sunshine on the roof. Sleek unwieldy porkers were grunting in the repose and abundance of their pens, from whence sallied forth, now and then, troops of sucking pigs, as if to snuff the air. A stately squadron of snowy geese were riding in an adjoining pond, convoying whole fleets of ducks; regiments of turkeys were gobbling through the farmyard, and Guinea fowls fretting about it, like ill-tempered housewives, with their peevish, discontented cry. Before the barn door strutted the gallant cock, that pattern of a husband, a warrior and a fine gentleman, clapping his burnished wings and crowing in the pride and gladness of his heart—sometimes tearing up the earth with his feet, and then generously calling his ever-hungry family of wives and children to enjoy the rich morsel which he had discovered.

The pedagogue's mouth watered as he looked upon this sumptuous promise of luxurious winter fare. In his devouring mind's eye, he pictured to himself every roasting-pig running about with a pudding in his belly, and an apple in his mouth; the pigeons were snugly put to bed in a comfortable pie, and tucked in with a coverlet of crust; the geese were swimming in their own gravy; and the ducks pairing cosily in dishes, like snug married couples, with a decent competency of onion sauce. In the porkers he saw carved out the future sleek side of bacon, and juicy relishing ham; not a turkey but he beheld daintily trussed up, with its gizzard under its wing, and, peradventure, a necklace of savory sausages; and even bright chanticleer himself lay sprawling on his back, in a side dish, with uplifted claws, as if craving that quarter which his chivalrous spirit disdained to ask while living.

As the enraptured Ichabod fancied all this, and as he rolled his great green eyes over the fat meadow lands, the rich fields of wheat, of rye, of buckwheat, and Indian corn, and the orchards burdened with ruddy fruit, which surrounded the warm tenement of Van Tassel, his heart yearned after the damsel who was to inherit these domains, and his imagination expanded with the idea, how they might be readily turned into cash, and the money invested in immense tracts of wild land, and shingle palaces in the wilderness. Nay, his busy fancy already realized his hopes, and presented to him the blooming Katrina, with a whole family of children, mounted on the top of a wagon loaded with household trumpery, with pots and kettles dangling beneath; and he beheld himself bestriding a pacing mare, with a colt at her heels, setting out for Kentucky, Tennessee—or the Lord knows where!

When he entered the house, the conquest of his heart was complete. It was one of those spacious farmhouses, with high-ridged but lowly sloping roofs, built in the style handed down from the first Dutch settlers; the low projecting eaves forming a piazza along the front, capable of being closed up in bad weather. Under this were hung flails, harness, various utensils of husbandry, and nets for fishing in the neighboring river. Benches were built along the sides for summer use; and a great spinning-wheel at one end, and a churn at the other, showed the various uses to which this important porch might be devoted. From this piazza the wondering Ichabod entered the hall, which formed the centre of the mansion, and the place of usual residence. Here rows of resplendent pewter, ranged on a long dresser, dazzled his eyes. In one corner stood a huge bag of wool, ready to be spun; in another, a quantity of linsey-woolsey just from the loom; ears of Indian corn, and strings of dried apples and peaches, hung in gay festoons along the walls, mingled with the gaud of red peppers; and a door left ajar gave him a peep into the best parlor, where the claw-footed chairs and dark mahogany tables shone like mirrors; andirons, with their accompanying shovel and tongs, glistened from their covert of asparagus tops; mock-oranges and conch-shells decorated the mantelpiece; strings of various-colored bird eggs were suspended above it; a great ostrich egg was hung from the centre of the room, and a corner cupboard, knowingly left open, displayed immense treasures of old silver and well-mended china.

From the moment Ichabod laid his eyes upon these regions of delight, the peace of his mind was at an end, and his only study was how to gain the affections of the peerless daughter of Van Tassel. In this enterprise, however, he had more real difficulties than generally fell to the lot of a knight-errant of yore, who seldom had anything but giants, enchanters, fiery dragons, and such like easily conquered adversaries, to contend with and had to make his way merely through gates of iron and brass, and walls of adamant to the castle keep, where the lady of his heart was confined; all which he achieved as easily as a man would carve his way to the centre of a Christmas pie; and then the lady gave him her hand as a matter of course. Ichabod, on the contrary, had to win his way to the heart of a country coquette, beset with a labyrinth of whims and caprices, which were forever presenting new difficulties and impediments; and he had to encounter a host of fearful adversaries of real flesh and blood, the numerous rustic admirers, who beset every portal to her heart, keeping a watchful and angry eye upon each other, but ready to fly out in the common cause against any new competitor.

Among these, the most formidable was a burly, roaring, roystering blade, of the name of Abraham, or, according to the Dutch abbreviation, Brom Van Brunt, the hero of the country round which rang with his feats of strength and hardihood. He was broad-shouldered and double-jointed, with short curly black hair, and a bluff but not unpleasant countenance, having a mingled air of fun and arrogance. From his Herculean frame and great powers of limb he had received the nickname of BROM BONES, by which he was universally known. He was famed for great knowledge and skill in horsemanship, being as dexterous on horseback as a Tartar. He was foremost at all races and cock fights; and, with the ascendancy which bodily strength always acquires in rustic life, was the umpire in all disputes, setting his hat on one side, and giving his decisions with an air and tone that admitted of no gainsay or appeal. He was always ready for either a fight or a frolic; but had more mischief than ill-will in his composition; and with all his overbearing roughness, there was a strong dash of waggish good humor at bottom. He had three or four boon companions, who regarded him as their model, and at the head of whom he scoured the country, attending every scene of feud or merriment for miles round. In cold weather he was distinguished by a fur cap, surmounted with a flaunting fox's tail; and when the folks at a country gathering described this well-known crest at a distance, whisking about among a squad of hard riders, they always stood by for a squall. Sometimes his crew would be heard dashing along past the farmhouses at midnight, with whoop and halloo, like a troop of Don Cossacks; and the old dames, startled out of their sleep, would listen for a moment till the hurry-scurry had clattered by, and then exclaim, "Ay, there goes Brom Bones and his gang!" The neighbors looked upon him with a mixture of awe, admiration, and good-will; and, when any madcap prank or rustic brawl occurred in the vicinity, always shook their heads, and warranted Brom Bones was at the bottom of it.

This rantipole hero had for some time singled out the blooming Katrina for the object of his un-couth gallantries, and though his amorous toyings were something like the gentle caresses and endearments of a bear, yet it was whispered that she did not altogether discourage his hopes. Certain it is, his advances were signals for rival candidates to retire, who felt no inclination to cross a lion in his amours; insomuch, that when his horse was seen tied to Van Tassel's paling, on a Sunday night, a sure sign that his master was courting, or, as it is termed, "sparking," within, all other suitors passed by in despair, and carried the war into other quarters.

Such was the formidable rival with whom Ichabod Crane had to contend, and, considering all things, a stouter man than he would have shrunk from the competition, and a wiser man would have despaired. He had, however, a happy mixture of pliability and perseverance in his nature; he was in form and spirit like a supple-jack-Äyielding, but tough; though he bent, he never broke; and though he bowed beneath the slightest pressure, yet, the moment it was away—jerk!—he was as erect, and carried his head as high as ever.

To have taken the field openly against his rival would have been madness; for he was not a man to be thwarted in his amours, any more than that stormy lover, Achilles. Ichabod, therefore, made his advances in a quiet and gently insinuating manner. Under cover of his character of singing-master, he made frequent visits at the farmhouse; not that he had anything to apprehend from the meddlesome interference of parents, which is so often a stumbling-block in the path of lovers. Balt Van Tassel was an easy indulgent soul; he loved his daughter better even than his pipe, and, like a reasonable man and an excellent father, let her have her way in everything. His notable little wife, too, had enough to do to attend to her housekeeping and manage her poultry; for, as she sagely observed, ducks and geese are foolish things, and must be looked after, but girls can take care of themselves. Thus, while the busy dame bustled about the house, or plied her spinning-wheel at one end of the piazza, honest Balt would sit smoking his evening pipe at the other, watching the achievements of a little wooden warrior, who, armed with a sword in each hand, was most valiantly fighting the wind on the pinnacle of the barn. In the mean time, Ichabod would carry on his suit with the daughter by the side of the spring under the great elm, or sauntering along in the twilight, that hour so favorable to the lover's eloquence.

I profess not to know how women's hearts are wooed and won. To me they have always been matters of riddle and admiration. Some seem to have but one vulnerable point, or door of access; while others have a thousand avenues, and may be captured in a thousand different ways. It is a great triumph of skill to gain the former, but a still greater proof of generalship to maintain possession of the latter, for man must battle for his fortress at every door and window. He who wins a thousand common hearts is therefore entitled to some renown; but he who keeps undisputed sway over the heart of a coquette is indeed a hero. Certain it is, this was not the case with the redoubtable Brom Bones; and from the moment Ichabod Crane made his advances, the interests of the former evidently declined: his horse was no longer seen tied to the palings on Sunday nights, and a deadly feud gradually arose between him and the preceptor of Sleepy Hollow.

Brom, who had a degree of rough chivalry in his nature, would fain have carried matters to open warfare and have settled their pretensions to the lady, according to the mode of those most concise and simple reasoners, the knights-errant of yore—by single combat; but Ichabod was too conscious of the superior might of his adversary to enter the lists against him; he had overheard a boast of Bones, that he would "double the schoolmaster up, and lay him on a shelf of his own schoolhouse"; and he was too wary to give him an opportunity. There was something extremely provoking, in this obstinately pacific system; it left Brom no alternative but to draw upon the funds of rustic waggery in his disposition, and to play off boorish practical jokes upon his rival. Ichabod became the object of whimsical persecution to Bones and his gang of rough riders. They harried his hitherto peaceful domains, smoked out his singing-school by stopping up the chimney, broke into the schoolhouse at night, in spite of its formidable fastenings of withe and window stakes, and turned everything topsy-turvy, so that the poor schoolmaster began to think all the witches in the country held their meetings there. But what was still more annoying, Brom took all Opportunities of turning him into ridicule in presence of his mistress, and had a scoundrel dog whom he taught to whine in the most ludicrous manner, and introduced as a rival of Ichabod's, to instruct her in psalmody.

In this way matters went on for some time, without producing any material effect on the relative situations of the contending powers. On a fine autumnal afternoon, Ichabod, in pensive mood, sat enthroned on the lofty stool from whence he usually watched all the concerns of his little literary realm. In his hand he swayed a ferule, that sceptre of despotic power; the birch of justice reposed on three nails behind the throne, a constant terror to evil doers, while on the desk before him might be seen sundry contraband articles and prohibited weapons, detected upon the persons of idle urchins, such as half-munched apples, popguns, whirligigs, fly-cages, and whole legions of rampant little paper game-cocks. Apparently there had been some appalling act of justice recently inflicted, for his scholars were all busily intent upon their books, or slyly whispering behind them with one eye kept upon the master; and a kind of buzzing stillness reigned throughout the schoolroom. It was suddenly interrupted by the appearance of a negro in tow-cloth jacket and trowsers, a round-crowned fragment of a hat, like the cap of Mercury, and mounted on the back of a ragged, wild, half-broken colt, which he managed with a rope by way of halter. He came clattering up to the school-door with an invitation to Ichabod to attend a merry-making or "quilting-frolic," to be held that evening at Mynheer Van Tassel's; and having, delivered his message with that air of importance and effort at fine language which a negro is apt to display on petty embassies of the kind, he dashed over the brook, and was seen scampering, away up the Hollow, full of the importance and hurry of his mission.

All was now bustle and hubbub in the late quiet schoolroom. The scholars were hurried through their lessons without stopping at trifles; those who were nimble skipped over half with impunity, and those who were tardy had a smart application now and then in the rear, to quicken their speed or help them over a tall word. Books were flung aside without being put away on the shelves, inkstands were overturned, benches thrown down, and the whole school was turned loose an hour before the usual time, bursting forth like a legion of young imps, yelping and racketing about the green in joy at their early emancipation.

The gallant Ichabod now spent at least an extra half hour at his toilet, brushing and furbishing up his best, and indeed only suit of rusty black, and arranging his locks by a bit of broken looking-glass that hung up in the schoolhouse. That he might make his appearance before his mistress in the true style of a cavalier, he borrowed a horse from the farmer with whom he was domiciliated, a choleric old Dutchman of the name of Hans Van Ripper, and, thus gallantly mounted, issued forth like a knight-errant in quest of adventures. But it is meet I should, in the true spirit of romantic story, give some account of the looks and equipments of my hero and his steed. The animal he bestrode was a broken-down plow-horse, that had outlived almost everything but its viciousness. He was gaunt and shagged, with a ewe neck, and a head like a hammer; his rusty mane and tail were tangled and knotted with burs; one eye had lost its pupil, and was glaring and spectral, but the other had the gleam of a genuine devil in it. Still he must have had fire and mettle in his day, if we may judge from the name he bore of Gunpowder. He had, in fact, been a favorite steed of his master's, the choleric Van Ripper, who was a furious rider, and had infused, very probably, some of his own spirit into the animal; for, old and broken-down as he looked, there was more of the lurking devil in him than in any young filly in the country.

Ichabod was a suitable figure for such a steed. He rode with short stirrups, which brought his knees nearly up to the pommel of the saddle; his sharp elbows stuck out like grasshoppers'; he carried his whip perpendicularly in his hand, like a sceptre, and as his horse jogged on, the motion of his arms was not unlike the flapping of a pair of wings. A small wool hat rested on the top of his nose, for so his scanty strip of forehead might be called, and the skirts of his black coat fluttered out almost to the horses tail.

It was, as I have said, a fine autumnal day; the sky was clear and serene, and nature wore that rich and golden livery which we always associate with the idea of abundance. The forests had put on their sober brown and yellow, while some trees of the tenderer kind had been nipped by the frosts into brilliant dyes of orange, purple, and scarlet. Streaming files of wild ducks began to make their appearance high in the air; the bark of the squirrel might be heard from the groves of beech and hickory-nuts, and the pensive whistle of the quail at intervals from the neighboring stubble field.

The small birds were taking their farewell banquets. In the fullness of their revelry, they fluttered, chirping and frolicking from bush to bush, and tree to tree, capricious from the very profusion and variety around them. There was the honest cockrobin, the favorite game of stripling sportsmen, with its loud querulous note; and the twittering blackbirds flying in sable clouds, and the golden-winged woodpecker with his crimson crest, his broad black gorget, and splendid plumage; and the cedar-bird, with its red-tipt wings and yellow-tipt tail and its little monteiro cap of feathers; and the blue jay, that noisy coxcomb, in his gay light blue coat and white underclothes, screaming and chattering, nodding and bobbing and bowing, and pretending to be on good terms with every songster of the grove.

As Ichabod jogged slowly on his way, his eye, ever open to every symptom of culinary abundance, ranged with delight over the treasures of jolly autumn. On all sides he beheld vast stores of apples: some hanging in oppressive opulence on the trees; some gathered into baskets and barrels for the market; others heaped up in rich piles for the cider-press. Farther on he beheld great fields of Indian corn, with its golden ears peeping from their leafy coverts, and holding out the promise of cakes and hasty-pudding; and the yellow pumpkins lying beneath them, turning up their fair round bellies to the sun, and giving ample prospects of the most luxurious of pies; and anon he passed the fragrant buckwheat fields breathing the odor of the beehive, and as he beheld them, soft anticipations stole over his mind of dainty slapjacks, well buttered, and garnished with honey or treacle, by the delicate little dimpled hand of Katrina Van Tassel.

Thus feeding his mind with many sweet thoughts and "sugared suppositions," he journeyed along the sides of a range of hills which look out upon some of the goodliest scenes of the mighty Hudson. The sun gradually wheeled his broad disk down in the west. The wide bosom of the Tappan Zee lay motionless and glassy, excepting that here and there a gentle undulation waved and prolonged the blue shallow of the distant mountain. A few amber clouds floated in the sky, without a breath of air to move them. The horizon was of a fine golden tint, changing gradually into a pure apple green, and from that into the deep blue of the mid-heaven. A slanting ray lingered on the woody crests of the precipices that overhung some parts of the river, giving greater depth to the dark gray and purple of their rocky sides. A sloop was loitering in the distance, dropping slowly down with the tide, her sail hanging uselessly against the mast; and as the reflection of the sky gleamed along the still water, it seemed as if the vessel was suspended in the air.

It was toward evening that Ichabod arrived at the castle of the Heer Van Tassel, which he found thronged with the pride and flower of the adjacent country Old farmers, a spare leathern-faced race, in homespun coats and breeches, blue stockings, huge shoes, and magnificent pewter buckles. Their brisk, withered little dames, in close crimped caps, long waisted short-gowns, homespun petticoats, with scissors and pin-cushions, and gay calico pockets hanging on the outside. Buxom lasses, almost as antiquated as their mothers, excepting where a straw hat, a fine ribbon, or perhaps a white frock, gave symptoms of city innovation. The sons, in short square-skirted coats, with rows of stupendous brass buttons, and their hair generally queued in the fashion of the times, especially if they could procure an eelskin for the purpose, it being esteemed throughout the country as a potent nourisher and strengthener of the hair.

Brom Bones, however, was the hero of the scene, having come to the gathering on his favorite steed Daredevil, a creature, like himself, full of mettle and mischief, and which no one but himself could manage. He was, in fact, noted for preferring vicious animals, given to all kinds of tricks which kept the rider in constant risk of his neck, for he held a tractable, wellbroken horse as unworthy of a lad of spirit.

Fain would I pause to dwell upon the world of charms that burst upon the enraptured gaze of my hero, as he entered the state parlor of Van Tassel's mansion. Not those of the bevy of buxom lasses, with their luxurious display of red and white; but the ample charms of a genuine Dutch country tea-table, in the sumptuous time of autumn. Such heaped up platters of cakes of various and almost indescribable kinds, known only to experienced Dutch house-

wives! There was the doughty doughnut, the tender olykoek, and the crisp and crumbling cruller; sweet cakes and short cakes, ginger cakes and honey cakes, and the whole family of cakes. And then there were apple pies, and peach pies, and pumpkin pies; besides slices of ham and smoked beef; and moreover delectable dishes of preserved plums, and peaches, and pears, and quinces; not to mention broiled shad and roasted chickens; together with bowls of milk and cream, all mingled higgledy-pigglely, pretty much as I have enumerated them, with the motherly teapot sending up its clouds of vapor from the midst—Heaven bless the mark! I want breath and time to discuss this banquet as it deserves, and am too eager to get on with my story. Happily, Ichabod Crane was not in so great a hurry as his historian, but did ample justice to every dainty.

He was a kind and thankful creature, whose heart dilated in proportion as his skin was filled with good cheer, and whose spirits rose with eating, as some men's do with drink. He could not help, too, rolling his large eyes round him as he ate, and chuckling with the possibility that he might one day be lord of all this scene of almost unimaginable luxury and splendor. Then, he thought, how soon he'd turn his back upon the old schoolhouse; snap his fingers in the face of Hans Van Ripper, and every other niggardly patron, and kick any itinerant pedagogue out of doors that should dare to call him comrade!

Old Baltus Van Tassel moved about among his guests with a face dilated with content and goodhumor, round and jolly as the harvest moon. His hospitable attentions were brief, but expressive, being confined to a shake of the hand, a slap on the shoulder, a loud laugh, and a pressing invitation to "fall to, and help themselves."

And now the sound of the music from the common room, or hall, summoned to the dance. The musician was an old gray-headed negro, who had been the itinerant orchestra of the neighborhood for more than half a century. His instrument was as old and battered as himself. The greater part of the time he scraped on two or three strings, accompanying every movement of the bow with a motion of the head; bowing almost to the ground, and stamping with his foot whenever a fresh couple were to start.

Ichabod prided himself upon his dancing as much as upon his vocal powers. Not a limb, not a fibre about him was idle; and to have seen his loosely hung frame in full motion, and clattering about the room, you would have thought St. Vitus himself, that blessed patron of the dance, was figuring before you in person. He was the admiration of all the negroes; who, having gathered, of all ages and sizes, from the farm and the neighborhood, stood forming a pyramid of shining black faces at every door and window; gazing with delight at the scene; rolling their white eye-balls, and showing grinning rows of ivory from ear to ear. How could the flogger of urchins be otherwise than animated and joyous? The lady of his heart was his partner in the dance, and smiling graciously in reply to all his amorous oglings; while Brom Bones, sorely smitten with love and jealousy, sat brooding by himself in one corner.

When the dance was at an end, Ichabod was attracted to a knot of the sager folks, who, with Old Van Tassel, sat smoking at one end of the piazza, gossiping over former times, and drawing out long stories about the war. This neighborhood, at the time of which I am speaking, was one of those highly favored places which abound with chronicle and great men. The British and American line had run near it during the war; it had, therefore, been the scene of marauding and infested with refugees, cow-boys, and all kinds of border chivalry. Just sufficient time had elapsed to enable each story-teller to dress up his tale with a little becoming fiction, and, in the indistinctness of his recollection, to make himself the hero of every exploit.

There was the story of Doffue Martling, a large blue-bearded Dutchman, who had nearly taken a British frigate with an old iron nine-pounder from a mud breastwork, only that his gun burst at the sixth discharge. And there was an old gentleman who shall be nameless, being too rich a mynheer to be lightly mentioned, who, in the battle of White Plains, being an excellent master of defence, parried a musket-ball with a small-sword, insomuch that he absolutely felt it whiz round the blade, and glance off at the hilt; in proof of which he was ready at any time to show the sword, with the hilt a little bent. There were several more that had been equally great in the field, not one of whom but was persuaded that he had a considerable hand in bringing the war to a happy termination.

But all these were nothing to the tales of ghosts and apparitions that succeeded. The neighborhood is rich in legendary treasures of the kind. Local tales and superstitions thrive best in these sheltered, long settled retreats; but are trampled under foot by the shifting throng that forms the population of most of our country places. Besides, there is no encouragement for ghosts in most of our villages, for they have scarcely had time to finish their first nap and turn themselves in their graves, before their surviving friends have travelled away from the neighborhood; so that when they turn out at night to walk their rounds, they have no acquaintance left to call upon. This is perhaps the reason why we so seldom hear of ghosts except in our long-established Dutch communities.

The immediate cause, however, of the prevalence of supernatural stories in these parts, was doubtless owing to the vicinity of Sleepy Hollow. There was a contagion in the very air that blew from that haunted region; it breathed forth an atmosphere of dreams and fancies infecting all the land. Several of the Sleepy Hollow people were present at Van Tassel's, and, as usual, were doling out their wild and wonderful legends. Many dismal tales were told about funeral trains, and mourning cries and wailings heard and seen about the great tree where the unfortunate Major Andre was taken, and which stood in the neighborhood. Some mention was made also of the woman in white, that haunted the dark glen at Raven Rock, and was often heard to shriek on winter nights before a storm, having perished there in the snow. The chief part of the stories, however, turned upon the favorite spectre of Sleepy Hollow, the Headless Horseman, who had been heard several times of late, patrolling the country; and, it was said, tethered his horse nightly among the graves in the churchyard.

The sequestered situation of this church seems always to have made it a favorite haunt of troubled spirits. It stands on a knoll, surrounded by locust, trees and lofty elms, from among which its decent, whitewashed walls shine modestly forth, like Christian purity beaming through the shades of retirement. A gentle slope descends from it to a silver sheet of water, bordered by high trees, between which, peeps may be caught at the blue hills of the Hudson. To look upon its grass-grown yard, where the sunbeams seem to sleep so quietly, one would think that there at least the dead might rest in peace. On one side of the church extends a wide woody dell, along which raves a large brook among broken rocks and trunks of fallen trees. Over a deep black part of the stream, not far from the church, was formerly thrown a wooden bridge; the road that led to it, and the bridge itself, were thickly shaded by overhanging trees, which cast a gloom about it, even in the daytime; but occasioned a fearful darkness at night. Such was one of the favorite haunts of the Headless Horseman, and the place where he was most frequently encountered. The tale was told of old Brouwer, a most heretical disbeliever in ghosts, how he met the Horseman returning from his foray into Sleepy Hollow, and was obliged to get up behind him; how they galloped over bush and brake, over hill and swamp, until they reached the bridge; when the Horseman suddenly turned into a skeleton, threw old Brouwer into the brook, and sprang away over the tree-tops with a clap of thunder.

This story was immediately matched by a thrice marvellous adventure of Brom Bones, who made light of the Galloping Hessian as an arrant jockey. He affirmed that on returning one night from the neighboring village of Sing Sing, he had been overtaken by this midnight trooper; that he had offered to race with him for a bowl of punch, and should have won it too, for Daredevil beat the goblin horse all hollow, but just as they came to the church bridge, the Hessian bolted, and vanished in a flash of fire.

All these tales, told in that drowsy undertone with which men talk in the dark, the countenances of the listeners only now and then receiving a casual gleam from the glare of a pipe, sank deep in the mind of Ichabod. He repaid them in kind with large extracts from his invaluable author, Cotton Mather, and added many marvellous events that had taken place in his native State of Connecticut, and fearful sights which he had seen in his nightly walks about Sleepy Hollow.

The revel now gradually broke up. The old farmers gathered together their families in their wagons, and were heard for some time rattling along the hollow roads, and over the distant hills. Some of the damsels mounted on pillions behind their favorite swains, and their light-hearted laughter, mingling with the clatter of hoofs, echoed along the silent woodlands, sounding fainter and fainter, until they gradually died away—and the late scene of noise and frolic was all silent and deserted. Ichabod only lin-

gered behind, according to the custom of country lovers, to have a tete-a-tete with the heiress; fully convinced that he was now on the high road to success. What passed at this interview I will not pretend to say, for in fact I do not know. Something, however, I fear me, must have gone wrong, for he certainly sallied forth, after no very great interval, with an air quite desolate and chapfallen. Oh, these women! these women! Could that girl have been playing off any of her coquettish tricks? Was her encouragement of the poor pedagogue all a mere sham to secure her conquest of his rival? Heaven only knows, not I! Let it suffice to say, Ichabod stole forth with the air of one who had been sacking a henroost, rather than a fair lady's heart. Without looking to the right or left to notice the scene of rural wealth, on which he had so often gloated, he went straight to the stable, and with several hearty cuffs and kicks roused his steed most uncourteously from the comfortable quarters in which he was soundly sleeping, dreaming of mountains of corn and oats, and whole valleys of timothy and clover.

It was the very witching time of night that Ichabod, heavy hearted and crest-fallen, pursued his travels homeward, along the sides of the lofty hills which rise above Tarry Town, and which he had traversed so cheerily in the afternoon. The hour was as dismal as himself. Far below him the Tappan Zee spread its dusky and indistinct waste of waters, with here and there the tall mast of a sloop, riding quietly at anchor under the land. In the dead hush of midnight, he could even hear the barking of the watchdog from the opposite shore of the Hudson; but it was so vague and faint as only to give an idea of his distance from this faithful companion of man. Now and then, too, the long-drawn crowing of a cock, accidentally awakened, would sound far, far off, from some farmhouse away among the hills—but it was like a dreaming sound in his ear. No signs of life occurred near him, but occasionally the melancholy chirp of a cricket, or perhaps the guttural twang of a bull-frog from a neighboring marsh, as if sleeping uncomfortably and turning suddenly in his bed.

All the stories of ghosts and goblins that he had heard in the afternoon now came crowding upon his recollection. The night grew darker and darker; the stars seemed to sink deeper in the sky, and driving clouds occasionally hid them from his sight. He had never felt so lonely and dismal. He was, moreover, approaching the very place where many of the scenes of the ghost stories had been laid. In the centre of the road stood an enormous tulip-tree, which towered like a giant above all the other trees of the neighborhood, and formed a kind of landmark. Its limbs were gnarled and fantastic, large enough to form trunks for ordinary trees, twisting down almost to the earth, and rising again into the air. It was connected with the tragical story of the unfortunate Andre, who had been taken prisoner hard by; and was universally known by the name of Major Andre's tree. The common people regarded it with a mixture of respect and superstition, partly out of sympathy for the fate of its ill-starred namesake, and partly from the tales of strange sights, and doleful lamentations, told concerning it.

As Ichabod approached this fearful tree, he began to whistle; he thought his whistle was answered; it was but a blast sweeping sharply through the dry branches. As he approached a little nearer, he thought he saw something white, hanging in the midst of the tree: he paused, and ceased whistling but, on looking more narrowly, perceived that it was a place where the tree had been scathed by lightning, and the white wood laid bare. Suddenly he heard a groan—his teeth chattered, and his knees smote against the saddle: it was but the rubbing of one huge bough upon another, as they were swayed about by the breeze. He passed the tree in safety, but new perils lay before him.

About two hundred yards from the tree, a small brook crossed the road, and ran into a marshy and thickly-wooded glen, known by the name of Wiley's Swamp. A few rough logs, laid side by side, served for a bridge over this stream. On that side of the road where the brook entered the wood, a group of oaks and chestnuts, matted thick with wild grape-vines, threw a cavernous gloom over it. To pass this bridge was the severest trial. It was at this identical spot that the unfortunate Andre was captured, and under the covert of those chestnuts and vines were the sturdy yeomen concealed who surprised him. This has ever since been considered a haunted stream, and fearful are the feelings of the school-boy who has to pass it alone after dark.

As he approached the stream, his heart began to thump; he summoned up, however, all his resolution,

gave his horse half a score of kicks in the ribs, and attempted to dash briskly across the bridge; but instead of starting forward, the perverse old animal made a lateral movement, and ran broadside against the fence. Ichabod, whose fears increased with the delay, jerked the reins on the other side, and kicked lustily with the contrary foot: it was all in vain; his steed started, it is true, but it was only to plunge to the opposite side of the road into a thicket of brambles and alder-bushes. The schoolmaster now bestowed both whip and heel upon the starveling ribs of old Gunpowder, who dashed forward, snuffling and snorting, but came to a stand just by the bridge, with a suddenness that had nearly sent his rider sprawling over his head. Just at this moment a plashy tramp by the side of the bridge caught the sensitive ear of Ichabod. In the dark shadow of the grove, on the margin of the brook, he beheld something huge, misshapen and towering. It stirred not, but seemed gathered up in the gloom, like some gigantic monster ready to spring upon the traveller.

The hair of the affrighted pedagogue rose upon his head with terror. What was to be done? To turn and fly was now too late; and besides, what chance was there of escaping ghost or goblin, if such it was, which could ride upon the wings of the wind? Summoning up, therefore, a show of courage, he demanded in stammering accents, "Who are you?" He received no reply. He repeated his demand in a still more agitated voice. Still there was no answer. Once more he cudgelled the sides of the inflexible Gunpowder, and, shutting his eyes, broke forth with involuntary fervor into a psalm tune. Just then the shadowy object of alarm put itself in motion, and with a scramble and a bound stood at once in the middle of the road. Though the night was dark and dismal, yet the form of the unknown might now in some degree be ascertained. He appeared to be a horseman of large dimensions, and mounted on a black horse of powerful frame. He made no offer of molestation or sociability, but kept aloof on one side of the road, jogging along on the blind side of old Gunpowder, who had now got over his fright and waywardness.

Ichabod, who had no relish for this strange midnight companion, and bethought himself of the adventure of Brom Bones with the Galloping Hessian, now quickened his steed in hopes of leaving him behind. The stranger, however, quickened his horse to an equal pace. Ichabod pulled up, and fell into a walk, thinking to lag behind—the other did the same. His heart began to sink within him; he endeavored to resume his psalm tune, but his parched tongue clove to the roof of his mouth, and he could not utter a stave. There was something in the moody and dogged silence of this pertinacious companion that was mysterious and appalling. It was soon fearfully accounted for. On mounting a rising ground, which brought the figure of his fellow-traveller in relief against the sky, gigantic in height, and muffled in a cloak, Ichabod was horror-struck on perceiving that he was headless! But his horror was still more increased on observing that the head, which should have rested on his shoulders, was carried before him on the pommel of his saddle! His terror rose to desperation; he rained a shower of kicks and blows upon Gunpowder, hoping by a sudden movement to give his companion the slip; but the spectre started full jump with him. Away, then, they dashed through thick and thin; stones flying and sparks flashing at every bound. Ichabod's flimsy garments fluttered in the air, as he stretched his long lank body away over his horse's head, in the eagerness of his flight.

They had now reached the road which turns off to Sleepy Hollow; but Gunpowder, who seemed possessed with a demon, instead of keeping up, made an opposite turn, and plunged headlong down hill to the left. This road leads through a sandy hollow shaded by trees for about a quarter of a mile, where it crosses the bridge famous in goblin story; and just beyond swells the green knoll on which stands the whitewashed church.

As yet the panic of the steed had given his unskillful rider an apparent advantage in the chase, but just as he had got half way through the hollow, the girths of the saddle gave way, and he felt it slipping from under him. He seized it by the pommel, and endeavored to hold it firm, but in vain; and had just time to save himself by clasping old Gunpowder round the neck, when the saddle fell to the earth, and he heard it trampled under foot by his pursuer. For a moment the terror of Hans Van Ripper's wrath passed across his mind—for it was his Sunday saddle; but this was no time for petty fears; the goblin was hard on his haunches; and (unskillful rider that he was!) he had much ado to maintain his seat; sometimes slipping on one side, sometimes on another, and sometimes jolted on the high ridge of his horse's backbone, with a violence that he verily feared would cleave him asunder.

An opening in the trees now cheered him with the hopes that the church bridge was at hand. The wavering reflection of a silver star in the bosom of the brook told him that he was not mistaken. He saw the walls of the church dimly glaring under the trees beyond. He recollected the place where Brom Bones' ghostly competitor had disappeard. "If I can but reach that bridge," thought Ichabod, "I am safe." Just then he heard the black steed panting and blowing close behind him; he even fancied that he felt his hot breath. Another convulsive kick in the ribs, and old Gunpowder sprang upon the bridge; he thundered over the resounding planks; he gained the opposite side; and now Ichabod cast a look behind to see if his pursuer should vanish, according to rule, in a flash of fire and brimstone. Just then he saw the goblin rising in his stirrups, and in the very act of hurling his head at him. Ichabod endeavored to dodge the horrible missile, but too late. It encountered his cranium with a tremendous crash—he was tumbled headlong into the dust, and Gunpowder, the black steed, and the goblin rider, passed by like a whirlwind.

The next morning the old horse was found without his saddle, and with the bridle under his feet, soberly cropping the grass at his master's gate. Ichabod did not make his appearance at breakfast; dinner-hour came, but no Ichabod. The boys assembled at the schoolhouse, and strolled idly about the banks of the brook; but no schoolmaster. Hans Van Ripper now began to feel some uneasiness about the fate of poor Ichabod, and his saddle. An inquiry was set on foot, and after diligent investigation they came upon his traces. In one part of the road leading to the church was found the saddle trampled in the dirt; the tracks of horses' hoofs deeply dented in the road, and evidently at furious speed, were traced to the bridge, beyond which, on the bank of a broad part of the brook, where the water ran deep and black, was found the head of the unfortunate Ichabod, and close beside it a shattered pumpkin.

The brook was searched, but the body of the schoolmaster was not to be discovered. Hans Van Ripper as executor of his estate, examined the bundle which contained all his worldly effects. They consisted of two shirts and a half; two stocks for the neck; a pair or two of worsted stockings; an old pair of corduroy small-clothes; a rusty razor; a book of psalm tunes full of dog's-ears; and a broken pitch-pipe. As to the books and furniture of the school-house, they belonged to the community, excepting Cotton Mather's History of Witchcraft, a New England Almanac, and book of dreams and fortune-telling; in which last was a sheet of foolscap much scribbled and blotted in several fruitless attempts to make a copy of verses in honor of the heiress of Van Tassel. These magic books and the poetic scrawl were forthwith consigned to the flames by Hans Van Ripper; who, from that time forward, determined to send his children no more to school; observing that he never knew any good come of this same reading and writing. Whatever money the schoolmaster possessed, and he had received his quarter's pay but a day or two before, he must have had about his person at the time of his disappearance.

The mysterious event caused much speculation at the church on the following Sunday. Knots of gazers and gossips were collected in the churchyard, at the bridge, and at the spot where the hat and pumpkin had been found. The stories of Brouwer, of Bones, and a whole budget of others were called to mind; and when they had diligently considered them all, and compared them with the symptoms of the present case, they shook their heads, and came to the conclusion that Ichabod had been carried off by the Galloping Hessian. As he was a bachelor, and in nobody's debt, nobody troubled his head any more about him; the school was removed to a different quarter of the Hollow, and another pedagogue reigned in his stead.

It is true, an old farmer, who had been down to New York on a visit several years after, and from whom this account of the ghostly adventure was received, brought home the intelligence that Ichabod Crane was still alive; that he had left the neighborhood partly through fear of the goblin and Hans Van Ripper, and partly in mortification at having been suddenly dismissed by the heiress; that he had changed his quarters to a distant part of the country; had kept school and studied law at the same time; had been admitted to the bar; turned politician; electioneered; written for the newspapers; and finally had been made a justice of the ten pound court. Brom Bones, too, who, shortly after his rival's disappearance conducted the blooming Katrina in triumph to the altar, was observed to look exceedingly knowing whenever the story of Ichabod was related, and always burst into a hearty laugh at the mention of the pumpkin; which led some to suspect that he knew more about the matter than he chose to tell.

The old country wives, however, who are the best judges of these matters, maintain to this day that Ichabod was spirited away by supernatural means; and it is a favorite story often told about the neighborhood round the winter evening fire. The bridge became more than ever an object of superstitious awe; and that may be the reason why the road has been altered of late years, so as to approach the church by the border of the mill-pond. The schoolhouse being deserted soon fell to decay, and was reported to be haunted by the ghost of the unfortunate pedagogue and the plough-boy, loitering homeward of a still summer evening, has often fancied his voice at a distance, chanting a melancholy psalm tune among the tranquil solitudes of Sleepy Hollow.

Questions

1. Describe Ichabod Crane. What does he look like? What are his interests? And what are some of his reasons for pursuing Katrina Van Tassel?
2. The Headless Horseman of Sleepy Hollow is described as the "commander-in-chief of all the powers of the air." What does this horseman look like? What are his motivations for riding through the night?

Continued

3. The narrator notes that Sleepy Hollow is a long-established Dutch community. Additionally, he states: "The immediate cause, however, of the prevalence of supernatural stories in these parts, was doubtless owing to the vicinity of Sleepy Hollow. There was a contagion in the very air that blew from that haunted region; it breathed forth an atmosphere of dreams and fancies infecting all the land." Sleepy Hollow seems like a mythical land infected with a minor case of reality. Picture Sleepy Hollow in your mind's eye. Why would the story of a headless horseman be more fitting in Sleepy Hollow as opposed to a more cosmopolitan setting?

4. What might some interpretations be regarding the relevance of the horses' names? Begin by interpreting the names "Gunpowder" and "Daredevil." Then, attempt to advance your interpretations by including the traits of each horse's rider.

5. Among Ichabod's things were "Cotton Mather's History of Witchcraft, a New England Almanac, and a book of dreams and fortune-telling." What might these books suggest about Ichabod?

6. In the beginning of the story, Ichabod is described as "being considered a kind of idle, gentlemanlike personage, of vastly superior taste and accomplishments to the rough country swains, and, indeed, inferior in learning only to the parson." This is fascinating, for this man who is "inferior in learning only to the parson" is reading Mather's *History of Witchcraft* and a book of dreams and fortune-telling. Does such a contradiction compromise the narrator's credibility? Might the narrator be unreliable?

7. At the end of this story, we are left with various hypotheses. What are these hypotheses, and with which one do you agree?

1. Examine the film *Sleepy Hollow.* After doing so, compare and contrast *Sleepy Hollow* with *The Legend of Sleepy Hollow.* Among the many things you might want to consider are setting, symbols, characters, and themes.

2. After reading *The Legend of Sleepy Hollow,* read Nathaniel Hawthorne's *Young Goodman Brown.* Upon doing so, compare and contrast *The Legend of Sleepy Hollow* and *Young Goodman Brown.*

3. Take a stand on one of many things: a) Did Brom Bones kill Ichabod Crane? b) Is Brom the Headless Horseman? c) Did Ichabod even die? Or did he simply move to New York? d) Is the narrator reliable?

4. Generally, a story will begin with equilibrium, and then it will lose equilibrium, and then equilibrium will be restored (with new meaning). Mark these stages in *The Legend of Sleepy Hollow.* Further, take a stand on whether equilibrium is restored (with new meaning).

5. While reading *The Legend of Sleepy Hollow,* some readers find themselves entranced by its dream-like qualities. Interestingly, Washington Irving flirts with dream-like qualities in *Rip Van Winkle,* another one of his more famous short stories. In a comparison and contrast essay, compare and contrast the dream-like qualities that find themselves in *The Legend of Sleepy Hollow* and *Rip Van Winkle.*

Samuel Clemens (1835-1910)

Most famous for writing *The Adventures of Huckleberry Finn* and *The Adventures of Tom Sawyer*, Samuel Langhorne Clemens enjoyed much success as a writer, lecturer, and humorist. Clemens, also known as Mark Twain (a term from his riverboat-piloting days that means "two fathoms deep" or "safe water"), was considered by some to be the "Lincoln of our literature." Among the greatest storytellers in American literary history, Clemens' range was Herculean, tackling everything from biblical idiosyncrasies and military madness to boyhood wonders and, arguably, his favorite foible: the human race.

The Private History of a Campaign That Failed

1. Realize that while this is "fiction," Samuel Clemens was a brief member of the Confederate militia.
2. Notice how Clemens is able to trivialize and mock the constructs of war by inviting the reader into his story world.

The Private History of a Campaign That Failed

Samuel Clemens

You have heard from a great many people who did something in the war, is it not fair and right that you listen a little moment to one who started out to do something in it but didn't? Thousands entered the war, got just a taste of it, and then stepped out again permanently. These, by their very numbers, are respectable and therefore entitled to a sort of voice, not a loud one, but a modest one, not a boastful one, but an apologetic one. They ought not be allowed much space among better people, people who did something. I grant that, but they ought at least be allowed to state why they didn't do anything and also to explain the process by which they didn't do anything.

Surely this kind of light must have some sort of value.

Out west there was a good deal of confusion in men's minds during the first months of the great trouble, a good deal of unsettledness, of leaning first this way then that, and then the other way. It was hard for us to get our bearings. I call to mind an example of this. I was piloting on the Mississippi when the news came that South Carolina had gone out of the Union on the 20th of December, 1860. My pilot mate was a New Yorker. He was strong for the Union; so was I. But he would not listen to me with any patience, my loyalty was smirched, to his eye, because my father had owned slaves. I said in palliation of this dark fact that I had heard my father say, some years before he died, that slavery was a great wrong and he would free the solitary Negro he then owned if he could think it right to give away the property of the family when he was so straitened in means. My mate retorted that a mere impulse was nothing, anyone could pretend to a good impulse, and went on decrying my Unionism and libelling my ancestry. A month later the secession atmosphere had considerably thickened on the Lower Mississippi and I became a rebel; so did he. We were together in New Orleans the 26th of January, when Louisiana went out of the Union. He did his fair share of the rebel shouting but was opposed to letting me do mine. He said I came of bad stock, of a father who had been willing to set slaves free. In the following summer he was piloting a Union gunboat and shouting for the Union again and I was in the Confederate army. I held his note for some borrowed money. He was one of the most upright men I ever knew but he repudiated that note without hesitation because I was a rebel and the son of a man who owned slaves.

In that summer of 1861 the first wash of the wave of war broke upon the shores of Missouri. Our state was invaded by the Union forces. They took possession of St. Louis, Jefferson Barracks, and some other points. The governor, Calib Jackson, issued his proclamation calling out fifty thousand militia to repel the invader.

I was visiting in the small town where my boyhood had been spent, Hannibal, Marion County. Several of us got together in a secret place by night and formed ourselves into a military company. One Tom Lyman, a young fellow of a good deal of spirit but of no military experience, was made captain; I was made second lieutenant. We had no first lieutenant, I do not know why, it was so long ago. There were fifteen of us. By the advice of an innocent connected with the organization we called ourselves the Marion Rangers. I do not remember that anyone found fault with the name. I did not, I thought it sounded quite well. The young fellow who proposed this title was perhaps a fair sample of the kind of stuff we were made of. He was young, ignorant, good natured, well meaning, trivial, full of romance, and given to reading chivalric novels and singing forlorn love ditties.

He had some pathetic little nickel plated aristocratic instincts and detested his name, which was Dunlap, detested it partly because it was nearly as common in that region as Smith but mainly because it had a plebian sound to his ears. So he tried to ennoble it by writing it in this way; d'Unlap. That contented his eye but left his ear unsatisfied, for people gave the new name the same old pronunciation, emphasis on the front end of it. He then did the bravest thing that can be imagined, a thing to make one shiver when one remembers how the world is given to resenting shams and affectations, he began to write his name so; d'Un'Lap. And he waited patiently through the long storm of mud that was flung at his work of art and he had his reward at last, for he lived to see that name accepted and the emphasis put where he wanted it put by people who had known him all his life, and to whom the tribe of Dunlaps had been as familiar as the rain and the sunshine for forty years. So sure of victory at last is the courage that can wait. He said he had found by consulting some ancient French chronicles that the name was rightly and originally written d'Un'Lap and said that if it were translated into English it would mean Peterson, Lap, Latin or Greek, he said, for stone or rock, same as the French Pierre, that is to say, Peter, d' of or from, un, a or one, hence d'Un'Lap, of or from a stone or a Peter, that is to say, one who is the son of a stone, the son of a Peter, Peterson. Our militia company were not learned and the explanation confused them, so they called him Peterson Dunlap. He proved useful to us in his way, he named our camps for us and generally struck a name that was "no slouch" as the boys said.

That is one sample of us. Another was Ed Stevens, son of the town jeweller, trim built, handsome, graceful, neat as a cat, bright, educated, but given over entirely to fun. There was nothing serious in life to him. As far as he was concerned, this military expedition of ours was simply a holiday. I should say about half of us looked upon it in much the same way, not consciously perhaps, but unconsciously. We did not think, we were not capable of it. As for myself, I was full of unreasoning joy to be done with turning out of bed at midnight and four in the morning, for a while grateful to have a change, new scenes, new occupations, a new interest. In my thoughts that was as far as I went. I did not go into the details, as a rule, one doesn't at twenty four.

Another sample was Smith, the blacksmith's apprentice. This vast donkey had some pluck, of a slow and sluggish nature, but a soft heart. At one time he would knock a horse down from some impropriety and at another he would get homesick and cry. However, he had one ultimate credit to his account which some of us hadn't. He stuck to the war and was killed in battle at last.

Joe Bowers, another sample, was a huge, good natured, flax headed lubber, lazy, sentimental, full of harmless brag, a grumbler by nature, [an experience and industrious ambitious and often quite picturesque liar], and yet not a successful one for he had no intelligent training but was allowed to come up just anyways. This life was serious enough to him, and seldom satisfactory. But he was a good fellow anyway and the boys all liked him. He was made orderly sergeant, Stevens was made corporal.

These samples will answer and they are quite fair ones. Well, this herd of cattle started for the war. What could you expect of them? They did as well as they knew how, but really, what was justly expected of them? Nothing I should say. And that is what they did.

We waited for a dark night, for caution and secrecy were necessary, then toward midnight we stole in couples and from various directions to the Griggith place beyond town. From that place we set out together on foot. Hannibal lies at the extreme south eastern corner of Marion County, on the Mississippi river. Our objective point was the hamlet of New London, ten miles away in Ralls County.

The first hour was all fun, all idle nonsense and laughter. But that could not be kept up. The steady drudging became like work, the play had somehow oozed out of it, the stillness of the woods and the sombreness of the night began to throw a depressing influence over the spirits of the boys and presently the talking died out and each person shut himself up in his own thoughts. During the last half of the second hour nobody said a word.

Now we approached a log farmhouse where, according to reports, there was a guard of five Union soldiers. Lyman called a halt, and there, in the deep gloom of the overhanging branches, he began to whisper a plan of assault upon the house, which made the gloom more depressing than it was before. We realized with a cold suddenness that here was no

jest—we were standing face to face with actual war. We were equal to the occasion. In our response there was no hesitation, no indecision. We said that if Lyman wanted to meddle with those soldiers he could go ahead and do it, but if he waited for us to follow him he would wait a long time.

Lyman urged, pleaded, tried to shame us into it, but it had no effect. Our course was plain in our minds, our minds were made up. We would flank the farmhouse, go out around. And that was what we did.

We struck into the woods and entered upon a rough time, stumbling over roots, getting tangled in vines and torn by briers. At last we reached an open place in a safe region and we sat down, blown and hot, to cool off and nurse our scratches and bruises. Lyman was annoyed but the rest of us were cheerful. We had flanked the farmhouse. We had made our first military movement and it was a success. We had nothing to fret about, we were feeling just the other way. Horseplay and laughing began again. The expedition had become a holiday frolic once more.

Then we had two more hours of dull trudging and ultimate silence and depression. Then about dawn, we straggled into New London, soiled, heel blistered, fagged with our little march, and all of us, except Stevens, in a sour and raspy humour and privately down on the war. We stacked our shabby old shotguns in Colonel Ralls's barn and then went in a body and breakfasted with that veteran of the Mexican war. Afterward he took us to a distant meadow, and there, in the shade of a tree, we listened to an old fashioned speech from him, full of gunpowder and glory, full of that adjective piling, mixed metaphor and windy declamation which was regarded as eloquence in that ancient time and region and then he swore on a bible to be faithful to the State of Missouri and drive all invaders from her soil no matter whence they may come or under what flag they might march. This mixed us considerably and we could not just make out what service we were involved in, but Colonel Ralls, the practised politician and phrase juggler, was not similarly in doubt. He knew quite clearly he had invested us in the cause of the Southern Confederacy. He closed the solemnities by belting around me the sword which his neighbour, Colonel brown, had worn at Buena Vista and Molino del Ray and he accompanied this act with another impressive blast.

Then we formed in line of battle and marched four hours to a shady and pleasant piece of woods on the border of a far reaching expanse of a flowery prairie. It was an enchanting region for war, our kind of war.

We pierced the forest about half a mile and took up a strong position with some low and rocky hills behind us, and a purling limpid creek in front. Straightaway half the command was in swimming and the other half fishing. The ass with the french name gave the position a romantic title but it was too long so the boys shortened and simplified it to Camp Ralls.

We occupied an old maple sugar camp whose half rotted troughs were still propped against the trees. A long corn crib served for sleeping quarters for the battalion. On our left, half a mile away, were Mason's farm and house, and he was a friend to the cause. Shortly after noon the farmers began to arrive from several different directions with mules and horses for our use, and these they lent us for as long as the war might last, which, they judged, might be about three months. The animals were of all sizes all colours and all breeds. They were mainly young and frisky and nobody in the command could stay on them long at a time, for we were town boys and ignorant of horsemanship. The creature that fell to my share was a very small mule, and yet so quick and active he could throw me off without difficulty and it did this whenever I got on. Then it would bray, stretching its neck out, laying its ears back and spreading its jaws till you could see down to its works. If I took it by the bridle and tried to lead it off the grounds it would sit down and brace back and no one could ever budge it. However, I was not entirely destitute of military resources and I did presently manage to spoil this game, for I had seen many a steamboat aground in my time and knew a trick or two which even a grounded mule would be obliged to respect. There was a well by the corn crib so I substituted thirty fathom of rope for the bridle and fetched him home with the windlass.

I will anticipate here sufficiently to say that we did learn to ride after some days' practice, but never well. We could not learn to like our animals. They were not choice ones and most of them had annoying peculiarities of one kind or another. Stevens's horse would carry him, when he was not noticing, under the huge excrescences on the trunks of oak trees, and wipe him out of the saddle this way. Stevens got several bad hurts. Sergeant Bowers's horse was very large and tall, slim with long legs, and looked like a railroad bridge. His size enabled him to reach all about, and as far as he wanted to go, so he was always biting Bowers's legs. On the march, in the sun, Bowers slept a good deal and as soon as the horse recognized he was asleep he would reach around and bite him on the leg. His legs were black and blue with bites. This was the only thing that could make him swear, [but this always did, whenever his horse bit him he swore, and of course,] Stevens, who laughed at everything, laughed at this and would get into such convulsions over it as to lose his balance and fall off his horse, and then Bowers, already irritated by the pain of the horse bite, would resent the laughter with hard language, and there would be a quarrel so that horse made no end of trouble and bad blood in the command.

However, I will get back to where I was, our first afternoon in the sugar camp. The sugar troughs came very handy as horse troughs and we had plenty of corn to fill them with. I ordered Sergeant Bowers to feed my mule, but he said that if I reckoned he went to war to be a dry nurse to a mule it wouldn't take me very long to find out my mistake. I believed that this was insubordination but I was full of uncertainties about everything military so I let the matter pass and went and ordered Smith, the blacksmith's apprentice, to feed the mule, but he merely gave me a large, cold, sarcastic grin, such as an ostensibly seven year old horse gives you when you lift up his lip and find he is fourteen, and turned his back on me. I then went to the captain and asked if it were not right and proper and military for me to have an orderly. He said it was, but as there was only one orderly in the corps, it was but right he himself should have Bowers on his staff. Bowers said he wouldn't serve on anyone's staff and if anybody thought he could make him, let him try. So, of course, the matter had to be dropped, there was no other way.

Next, nobody would cook. It was considered a degradation so we had no dinner. We lazed the rest of the pleasant afternoon away, some dozing under trees, some smoking cob pipes and talking sweethearts and war, others playing games. By late supper time all hands were famished and to meet the difficulty, all hands turned to an equal footing, and gathered wood, built fires, and cooked the evening meal. Afterward everything was smooth for a while then trouble broke out between the corporal and the sergeant, each claiming to rank the other. Nobody knew which was the higher office so Lyman had to settle the matter by making the rank of both officers equal. The commander of an ignorant crew like that has many troubles and vexations which probably do not occur in the regular army at all. However, with the song singing and yarn spinning around the campfire everything presently became serene again, and by and by we raked the corn down one level in one end of the crib and all went to bed on it, tying a horse to the door so he would neigh if anyone tried to get in. (It was always my impression that was always what the horse was there for and I know it was the impression of at least one other of the command, for we talked about it at the time and admired the military ingenuity of the device, but when I was out west three years ago, I was told by Mr. A. G. Fuqua, a member of our company, that the horse was his, that the tying him at the door was a mere matter of forgetfulness and that to attribute it to intelligent invention was to give him quite too much credit. In support of his position, he called my attention to the suggestive fact that the artifice was not employed again. I had not thought of that before.)

We had some horsemanship drill every forenoon, then, afternoons, we rode off here and there in squads a few miles and visited the farmer's girls and had a youthful good time and got an honest dinner or supper, and then home again to camp, happy and content.

For a time, life was idly delicious. It was perfect. There was no war to mar it. Then came some farmers with an alarm one day. They said it was rumoured that the enemy were advancing in our direction from over Hyde's prairie. The result was a sharp stir among us and general consternation. It was a rude awakening from our pleasant trance. The rumour was but a rumour, nothing definite about it, so in the confusion we did not know which way to retreat. Lyman was not for retreating at all in these uncertain circumstances but he found that if he tried to maintain that attitude he would fare badly, for the command were in no humour to put up with insubordination. So he yielded the point and called a council of

war, to consist of himself and three other officers, but the privates made such a fuss about being left out we had to allow them to remain, for they were already present and doing most of the talking too. The question was, which way to retreat; but all were so flurried that nobody even seemed to have even a guess to offer. Except Lyman. He explained in a few calm words, that inasmuch as the enemy were approaching from over Hyde's prairie our course was simple. All we had to do was not retreat toward him, another direction would suit our purposes perfectly. Everybody saw in a moment how true this was and how wise, so Lyman got a great many compliments. It was now decided that we should fall back on Mason's farm.

It was after dark by this time and as we could not know how soon the enemy might arrive, it did not seem best to try to take the horses and things with us, so we only took the guns and ammunition, and started at once. The route was very rough and hilly and rocky, and presently the night grew very black and rain began to fall, so we had a troublesome time of it, struggling and stumbling along in the dark and soon some person slipped and fell, and then the next person behind stumbled over him and fell, and so did the rest, one after the other, and then Bowers came along with the keg of powder in his arms, while the command were all mixed together, arms and legs on the muddy slope, and so he fell, of course, with the keg and this started the whole detachment down the hill in a body and they landed in a brook at the bottom in a pile and each that was undermost was pulling the hair, scratching and biting those that were on top of him and those that were being scratched and bitten scratching and biting the rest in their turn, and all saying they would die before they would ever go to war again if they ever got out of this brook this time and the invader might rot for all they cared, and the country along with him, and all such talk as that which was dismal to hear and take part in, in such smothered, low voices, and such a grisly dark place and so wet, and the enemy, maybe, coming along at any moment.

The keg of powder was lost, and the guns too; so the growling and complaining continued straight along while the brigade pawed around the pasty hill side and slopped around in the brook hunting for these things; consequently we lost considerable time at this, and then we heard a sound and held our breath and listened, and it seemed to be the enemy coming, though it could have been a cow, for it had a cough like a cow, but we did not wait but left a couple of guns behind and struck out for Mason's again as briskly as we could scramble along in the dark. But we got lost presently in among the rugged little ravines and wasted a deal of time finding the way again so it was after nine when we reached Mason's stile at last; and then before we could open our mouths to give the countersign several dogs came bounding over the fence with a great riot and noise, and each of them took a soldier by the slack of his trousers and began to back away with him. We could not shoot the dogs without endangering the persons they were attached to so we had to look on helpless at what was perhaps the most mortifying spectacle of the Civil War. There was light enough and to spare, for the Mason's had now run out on the porch with candles in their hands. The old man and his son came and undid the dogs without difficulty, all but Bowers's; but they couldn't undo his dog, they didn't know his combination, he was of the bull kind and seemed to be set with a Yale time-lock, but they got him loose at last with some scalding water, of which Bowers got his share and returned thanks. Peterson Dunlap afterwards made up a fine name for this engagement and also for the night march which preceded it but both have long ago faded out of my memory.

We now went into the house and they began to ask us a world of questions, whereby it presently came out that we did not know anything concerning who or what we were running from; so the old gentleman made himself very frank and said we were a curious breed of soldiers and guessed we could be depended on to end up the war in time.

"Marion Rangers! Good name, b'gosh," said he. And wanted to know why we hadn't had a picket guard at the place where the road entered the prairie, and why we hadn't sent out a scouting party to spy out the enemy and bring us an account of his strength, and so on, before jumping up and stampeding out of a strong position upon a mere vague rumour, and so on and so forth, till he made us all feel shabbier than the dogs had done, not so half enthusiastically welcome. So we went to bed shamed and low spirited, except Stevens. Soon Stevens began to

devise a garment for Bowers which could be made to automatically display his battle scars to the grateful or conceal them from the envious, according to his occasions, but Bowers was in no humour for this, so there was a fight and when it was over Stevens had some battle scars of his own to think about.

Then we got a little sleep. But after all we had gone through, our activities were not over for the night, for about two o'clock in the morning we heard a shout of warning from down the lane, accompanied by a chorus from all the dogs, and in a moment everybody was up and flying around to find out what the alarm was about. The alarmist was a horseman who gave notice that a detachment of Union soldiers was on its way from Hannibal with orders to capture and hang any bands like ours which it could find. Farmer Mason was in a flurry this time himself. He hurried us out of the house with all haste, and sent one of his negroes with us to show us where to hide ourselves and our telltale guns among the ravines half a mile away. It was raining heavily.

We struck down the lane, then across some rocky pasture land which offered good advantages for stumbling; consequently we were down in the mud most of the time, and every time a man went down he black guarded the war and everybody connected with it, and gave himself the master dose of all for being so foolish as to go into it. At last we reached the wooded mouth of a ravine, and there we huddled ourselves under the streaming trees and sent the negro back home. It was a dismal and heart breaking time. We were like to be drowned with the rain, deafened with the howling wind and the booming thunder, and blinded by the lightning. It was indeed a wild night. The drenching we were getting was misery enough, but a deeper misery still was the reflection that the halter might end us before we were a day older. A death of this shameful sort had not occurred to us as being among the possibilities of war. It took the romance all out of the campaign and turned our dreams of glory into a repulsive nightmare. As for doubting that so barbarous an order had been given, not one of us did that.

The long night wore itself out at last, and then the Negro came to us with the news that the alarm had manifestly been a false one and that breakfast would soon be ready. Straightaway we were light-hearted again and the world was bright and full of life, as full of hope and promise as ever; for we were young then. How long ago that was! Twenty four years.

The mongrel child of philology named the night's refuge Camp Devastation and no soul objected. The Masons gave us a Missouri country breakfast in Missourian abundance, and we needed it. Hot biscuits, hot wheat bread, prettily crossed in a lattice pattern on top, hot corn pone, fried chicken, bacon, coffee, eggs, milk, buttermilk etc. and the world may be confidently challenged to furnish the equal of such a breakfast, as it is cooked in the South.

We stayed several days at Mason's and after all these years the memory of the stillness and dullness and lifelessness of that slumberous farmhouse still oppresses my spirit as with a sense of the presence of death and mourning. There was nothing to do. Nothing to think about. There was no interest in life. The male part of the household were away in the fields all day, the women were busy and out of our sight. There was no sound but the plaintive wailing of a spinning wheel forever moaning out from some distant room, the most lonesome sound in nature, a sound steeped and sodden with homesickness and the emptiness of life. The family went to bed about dark every night and as we were not invited to intrude any new customs we naturally followed theirs. Those nights were a hundred years long to youths accustomed to being up till twelve. We lay awake and miserable till that hour of ovariotomy and grew old and decrepit waiting through the still eternities for the clock strikes. This was no place for town boys. So at last it was with something very like joy that we received word that the enemy were on our track again. With a new birth of the old warrior spirit, we sprang to our places in line of battle and fell back on Camp Ralls.

Captain Lyman had taken a hint from Mason's talk, and he now gave orders that our camp should be guarded from surprise by the posting of pickets. I was ordered to place a picket at the forks of the road in Hyde's prairie. Night shut down black and threatening. I told Sergeant Bowers to go out to that place and stay till midnight, and, just as I was expecting, he said he wouldn't do it. I tried to get others to go but all refused. Some excused themselves on account of the weather, but the rest were frank enough to say

they wouldn't go in any kind of weather. This kind of thing sounds odd now, and impossible, but there was no surprise in it at the time. On the contrary, it seemed a perfectly natural thing to do. There were scores of little camps scattered over Missouri where the same thing was happening. These camps were composed of young men who had been born and reared to a sturdy independence and who did not know what it meant to be ordered around by Tom, Dick, and Harry, who they had known familiarly all their lives in the village or the farm. It is quite within the probabilities that this same thing was happening all over the South. James Redpath recognized the justice of this assumption and furnished the following instance in support of it. During a short stay in East Tennessee he was in a citizen colonel's tent one day talking, when a big private appeared at the door and, without salute or other circumlocution, said to the colonel:

"Say, Jim, I'm a goin' home for a few days."

"What for?"

"Well, I hain't b'en there for a right smart while and I'd like to see how things is comin' on."

"How long are you gonna be gone?"

"Bout two weeks."

"Well, don't be gone longer than that and get back sooner if you can."

That was all, and the citizen officer resumed his conversation where the private had broken it off. This was in the first months of the war of course. The camps in our part of Missouri were under Brigadier-General Thomas H. Harris. He was a townsman of ours, a first rate fellow and well liked, but we had all familiarly known him as the soles and modest-salaried operator in the telegraph office, where he had to send about one dispatch a week in ordinary times and two when there was a rush of business. Consequently, when he appeared in our midst one day on the wing, and delivered a military command of some sort in a large military fashion, nobody was surprised at the response which he got from the assembled soldiery.

"Oh, now what'll you take to don't, Tom Harris?"

It was quite the natural thing. One might justly imagine that we were hopeless material for the war. And so we seemed in our ignorant state, but there were those among us who afterward learned the grim trade, learned to obey like machines, became valuable soldiers, fought all through the war, and came out at the end with excellent records. One of the very boys who refused to go out on picket duty that night and called me an ass for thinking he would expose himself to danger in such a foolhardy way, had become distinguished for intrepidity before he was a year older.

I did secure my picket that night, not by authority but by diplomacy. I got Bowers to go by agreeing to exchange ranks with him for the time being and go along and stand the watch with him as his subordinate. We stayed out there a couple of dreary hours in the pitchy darkness and the rain, with nothing to modify the dreariness but Bower's monotonous growling at the war and the weather, then we began to nod and presently found it next to impossible to stay in the saddle, so we gave up the tedious job and went back to the camp without interruption or objection from anybody and the enemy could have done the same, for there were no sentries. Everybody was asleep, at midnight there was nobody to send out another picket so none was sent. We never tried to establish a watch at night again, as far as I remember, but we generally kept a picket out in the daytime.

In that camp the whole command slept on the corn in the big corn crib and there was usually a general row before morning, for the place was full of rats and they would scramble over the boys' bodies and faces, annoying and irritating everybody, and now and then they would bite someone's toe, and the person who owned the toe would start up and magnify his English and begin to throw corn in the dark. The ears were half as heavy as bricks and when they struck they hurt. The persons struck would respond and inside of five minutes every man would be locked in a death grip with his neighbour. There was a grievous deal of blood shed in the corn crib but this was all that was spilt while I was in the war. No, that is not quite true. But for one circumstance it would have been all.

Our scares were frequent. Every few days rumours would come that the enemy were approaching. In these cases we always fell back on some other camp of ours; we never stayed where we were. But the rumours always turned out to be false, so at last we even began to grow indifferent to them. One night a negro was sent to our corn crib with the same old warning, the enemy was hovering in our neighbour-hood. We all said let him hover. We resolved to stay still and be comfortable. It was a fine warlike resolution, and no doubt we all felt the stir of it in our veins—for a moment. We had been having a very jolly time, that was full of horseplay and schoolboy hilarity, but that cooled down and presently the fast waning fire of forced jokes and forced laughs died out altogether and the company became silent. Silent and nervous. And soon uneasy—worried and apprehensive. We had said we would stay and we were committed. We could have been persuaded to go but there was nobody brave enough to suggest it. An almost noiseless movement began in the dark by a general but unvoiced impulse. When the movement was completed, each man knew that he was not the only person who had crept to the front wall and had his eye at a crack between the logs. No, we were all there, all there with our hearts in our throats and staring out towards the sugar-troughs where the forest footpath came through. It was late and there was a deep woodsy stillness everywhere. There was a veiled moonlight which was only just strong enough to enable us to mark the general shapes of objects. Presently a muffled sound caught our ears and we recognized the hoof-beats of a horse or horses. And right away, a figure appeared in the forest path; it could have been made of smoke, its mass had such little sharpness of outline. It was a man on horseback, and it seemed to me that there were others behind him. I got a hold of a gun in the dark, and pushed it through a crack between the logs, hardly knowing what I was doing, I was so dazed with fright. Somebody said "Fire!" I pulled the trigger, I seemed to see a hundred flashes and a hundred reports, then I saw the man fall down out of the saddle. My first feeling was of surprised gratification; my first impulse was an apprentice-sportsman's impulse to run and pick up his game. Somebody said, hardly audibly, "Good, we've got him. Wait for the rest!" But the rest did not come. There was not a sound, not the whisper of a leaf; just the perfect stillness, an uncanny kind of stillness which was all the more uncanny on account of the damp, earthy, late night smells now rising and pervading it. Then, wondering, we crept out stealthily and approached the man. When we got to him, the moon revealed him distinctly. He was laying on his back with his arms abroad, his mouth was open and his chest was heaving with long gasps, and his white shirt front was splashed with blood. The thought shot through me that I was a murderer, that I had killed a man, a man who had never done me any harm. That was the coldest sensation that ever went through my marrow. I was down by him in a moment, helplessly stroking his forehead, and I would have given anything then, my own life freely, to make him again what he had been five minutes before. And all the boys seemed to be feeling the same way; they hung over him, full of pitying interest, and tried all they could to help him, and said all sorts of regretful things. They had forgotten all about the enemy, they thought only of this one forlorn unit of the foe. Once my imagination persuaded me that the dying man gave me a reproachful look out of the shadow of his eyes, and it seemed to me that I could rather that he had stabbed me than he had done that. He muttered and mumbled like a dreamer in his sleep about his wife and his child, and, I thought with a new despair, "This thing that I have done does not end with him; it falls upon them too, and they never did me any harm, any more than he."

In a little while the man was dead. He was killed in war, killed in fair and legitimate war, killed in battles as you may say, and yet he was as sincerely mourned by the opposing force as if he had been their brother. The boys stood there a half-hour sorrowing over him and recalling the details of the tragedy, and wondering who he might be and if he was a spy, and saying if they had it to do over again, they would not hurt him unless he attacked them first. It soon turned out that mine was not the only shot fired; there were five others, a division of the guilt which was a great relief to me since it in some degree lightened and diminished the burden I was carrying. There were six shots fired at once but I was not in my right mind at the time, and my heated imagination had magnified my one shot into a volley.

The man was not in uniform and was not armed. He was a stranger in the country, that was all we ever found out about him. The thought of him got to preying on me every night, I could not get rid of it. I could not drive it away, the taking of that unoffending life seemed such a wanton thing. And it seemed an epitome of war, that all war must just be the killing of strangers against whom you feel no personal animosity, strangers who in other circumstances you would help if you found them in trouble, and who would help you if you needed it. My campaign was spoiled. It seemed to me that I was not rightly equipped for this awful business, that war was intended for men and I for a child's nurse. I resolved to retire from this avocation of sham soldiership while I could retain some remnant of my self-respect. These morbid thoughts clung to me against reason, for at the bottom I did not believe I had touched this man. The law of probabilities decreed me guiltless of his blood for in all my small experiences with guns, I had not hit anything I had tried to hit, and I knew I had done my best to hit him. Yet there was no solace in the thought. Against a diseased imagination, demonstration goes for nothing.

The rest of my war experience was of a piece with what I have already told of it. We kept monotonously falling back upon one camp or another and eating up the farmers and their families. They ought to have shot us; on the contrary they were as hospitably kind and courteous to us as if we had deserved it. In one of these camps we found Ab Grimes, an upper Mississippi pilot who afterwards became famous as a daredevil rebel spy, whose career bristled with desperate adventures. The loom and style of his comrades suggested that they had not come into the war to play and their deeds made good the conjecture later. They were fine horsemen and good revolver shots, but their favourite arm was the lasso. Each had one at his pommel, and could snatch a man out of his saddle with it, on a full gallop, at any reasonable distance.

In another camp, the chief was a fierce and profane old black-smith of sixty and he had furnished his twenty recruits with gigantic, home-made bowie-knives, to be swung with two hands like the machetes of the Isthmus. It was a grisly spectacle to see that earnest band practising their murderous cuts and slashes under the eye of that remorseless old fanatic.

The last camp which we fell back on was in a hollow near the village of Florida where I was born, in Monroe County. Here we were warned one day that a Union Colonel was sweeping down on us with a whole regiment at his heels. This looked decidedly serious. Our boys went apart and consulted; then we went back and told the other companies present that the war was a disappointment to us and we were going to disband. They were getting ready themselves to fall back on some place or another, and we were only waiting for General Tom Harris, who was expected to arrive at any moment, so they tried to persuade us to wait a little while but the majority of us said no, we were accustomed to falling back and didn't need any of Harris's help, we could get along perfectly without him and save time too. So, about half of our fifteen men, including myself, mounted, and left on the instant; the others yielded to persuasion, and stayed—stayed through the war.

An hour later we met General Harris on the road, with two or three people in his company, his staff probably, but we could not tell; none of them were in uniform; uniforms had not come into vogue among us yet. Harris ordered us back, but we told him there was a Union colonel coming with a whole regiment in his wake and it looked as if there was going to be a disturbance, so we had concluded to go home. He raged a little bit, but it was of no use, our minds were made up. We had done our share, killed one man, exterminated one army, such as it was; let him go and kill the rest and that would end the war. I did not see that brisk young general again until last year; he was wearing white hair and whiskers.

In time I came to learn that the Union colonel whose coming frightened me out of the war and crippled the Southern cause to that extent: General Grant. I came within a few hours of seeing him when he was as unknown as I was myself; at a time when anybody could have said, "Grant—Ulysses S Grant? I do not remember hearing the name before." It seems difficult to realize there was once a time when such a remark could be rationally made, but there was, I was within a few miles of the place and the occasion too, though proceeding in the other direction.

The thoughtful will not throw this war paper of mine lightly aside as being valueless. It has this value; it is not an unfair picture of what went on in many a militia camp in the first months of the rebellion, when the green recruits were without discipline, without the steadying and heartening influence of trained leaders, when all their circumstances were new and strange and charged with exaggerated terrors, and before the invaluable experience of actual collision in the field had turned them from rabbits into soldiers. If this side of the picture of that early day has not before been put into history, then history has been, to that degree incomplete, for it had and has its rightful place there. There was more Bull Run material scattered through the early camps of this country than exhibited itself at Bull Run. And yet, it learned its trade presently and helped to fight the great battles later. I could have become a soldier myself if I had waited. I had got part of it learned, I knew more about retreating than the man that invented retreating.

Questions

1. When the narrator and his fellow soldiers flank the farmhouse, what actually happens?
2. Twain often uses humor to advance his stories. Identify examples of this, and show how these examples advance the story.
3. How does the narrator get his mule to move?
4. In *The Catcher in the Rye,* Holden Caulfield is taking a class in Oral Expression, and even though the students are penalized for every digression, Holden's favorite speaker is a student who routinely digresses when attempting to deliver his speech. Similarly, while the narrator is attempting to simply tell the story of *The Private History of a Campaign That Failed,* he often digresses. One example of such a digression is found when the narrator tells of Sergeant Bowers' horse and then, after the narrator becomes conscious of this digression, he states: "However, I will get back to where I was, our first afternoon in the sugar camp." Do these digressions hinder or advance the story? How? Offer examples.
5. Note possible interpretations for the characters' names, i.e., Captain Lyman and James Redpath.

6. The narrator states: "It was quite the natural thing. One might justly imagine that we were hopeless material for the war. And so we seemed in our ignorant state, but there were those among us who afterward learned the grim trade, learned to obey like machines, became valuable soldiers, fought all through the war, and came out at the end with excellent records." Does this observation suggest a shift in tone? Or is the narrator's tone consistent with the tone he has maintained throughout the short story?

7. What arguments can be extracted from this story?

Research and Writing

1. Research famous draftdodgers and deserters. Compare and contrast their reasons for dodging the draft with the introductory paragraph of Twain's *The Private History of a Campaign That Failed.*

2. View Monty Python's *The Holy Grail.* Additionally, view another film titled *Top Secret.* Then, compare and contrast the antics of King Arthur's Men (in *The Holy Grail*) and *Top Secret* with the antics of the narrator and his men in *The Private History of a Campaign That Failed.*

3. In *The Private History of a Campaign That Failed,* the narrator attempts to explain the derivation of Dunbar's name. Identify some of your favorite names, and then research their derivations. After finding the supposed derivations of these names, construct an argument that revolves around intentional and unintentional meaning. For instance, if two people named their daughter Faith, it seems reasonable that some could immediately suggest that intentional meaning is suggested through that name. However, if their daughter were named Mary, perhaps the reference to the Virgin Mary (Jesus' mother) was unintentional. Construct your argument so that it examines meaning and intention.

4. In *The Private History of a Campaign That Failed,* the narrator describes Colonel Ralls as "the practised politician and phrase juggler." The context for this is Ralls' rallying around the protection of Missouri against all invaders. Perform some research with the intention of finding transcripts of speeches offered by U.S. presidents who have engaged in similar rallying and, arguably, "phrase juggling." You might begin by researching Presidents Roosevelt, Johnson, and Bush (father and son) regarding World War II, the Vietnam War, Desert Storm, and Operation Iraqi Freedom, respectively. In doing so, identify examples of "phrase juggling," and then show how such juggling can help advance an administration's agenda.

5. Read Mark Twain's *The War Prayer.* Then, compare and contrast it with *The Private History of a Campaign That Failed.* Additionally, you might research the ostensible motives for staging the Civil War. Why, arguably, did it occur? And what might Twain be poking fun at?

6. Read Dalton Trumbo's novel *Johnny Got His Gun.* Then, extract an argument from it, and examine that argument within the context of *The Private History of a Campaign That Failed.*

7. View *Apocalypse Now, Platoon,* and *The Deer Hunter.* Then examine each within the context of *The Private History of a Campaign That Failed.*

Ambrose Bierce (1842–1914)

Ambrose Bierce, also known as "Bitter Bierce," was the product of many negative experiences seeming to stem from an unhappy childhood and manifesting themselves in a life of perceived failure. Among these failures was a divorce from his wife in 1891 and the loss of his two sons—one was shot to death during a fight over a girl, and the other died of alcoholism. Eventually moving to Mexico and becoming the subject of myth and curiosity, Ambrose Bierce did leave some notable things behind. *The Devil's Dictionary,* for instance, has endured as one of the more humorous and cynical attempts to redefine terms whose meanings have not been fully explored. For example, Bierce's *Dictionary* defines *justice* as "A commodity which is a more or less adulterated condition the State sells to the citizen as a reward for his allegiance, taxes, and personal service." Ever the cynic, Bierce developed a following with *The Devil's Dictionary* and other important works like *Chickamauga, Tales of Soldiers and Civilians,* and *An Occurrence at Owl Creek Bridge.*

An Occurrence at Owl Creek Bridge

1. Bierce spent one year at a military academy in Kentucky and, later, was involved in many Civil War battles as a volunteer in the Union Army.
2. Notice the sentence variety employed by Bierce to heighten tension and suspense.

An Occurrence at Owl Creek Bridge

Ambrose Bierce

I

A man stood upon a railroad bridge in northern Alabama, looking down into the swift water twenty feet below. The man's hands were behind his back, the wrists bound with a cord. A rope closely encircled his neck. It was attached to a stout cross-timber above his head and the slack fell to the level of his knees. Some loose boards laid upon the sleepers supporting the metals of the railway supplied a footing for him and his executioners—two private soldiers of the Federal army, directed by a sergeant who in civil life may have been a deputy sheriff. At a short remove upon the same temporary platform was an officer in the uniform of his rank, armed. He was a captain. A sentinel at each end of the bridge stood with his rifle in the position known as "support," that is to say, vertical in front of the left shoulder, the hammer resting on the forearm thrown straight across the chest—a formal and unnatural position, enforcing an erect carriage of the body. It did not appear to be the duty of these two men to know what was occurring at the center of the bridge; they merely blockaded the two ends of the foot planking that traversed it. Beyond one of the sentinels nobody was in sight; the railroad ran straight away into a forest for a hundred yards, then, curving, was lost to view. Doubtless there was an outpost farther along. The other bank of the stream was open ground—a gentle acclivity topped with a stockade of vertical tree trunks, loopholed for rifles, with a single embrasure through which protruded the muzzle of a brass cannon commanding the bridge. Midway of the slope between the bridge and fort were the spectators—a single company of infantry in line, at "parade rest," the butts of the rifles on the ground, the barrels inclining slightly backward against the right shoulder, the hands crossed upon the stock. A lieutenant stood at the right of the line, the point of his sword upon the ground, his left hand resting upon his right. Excepting the group of four at the center of the bridge, not a man moved. The company faced the bridge, staring stonily, motionless. The sentinels, facing the banks of the stream, might have been statues to adorn the bridge. The captain stood with folded arms, silent, observing the work of his subordinates, but making no sign. Death is a dignitary who when he comes announced is to be received with formal manifestations of respect, even by those most familiar with him. In the code of military etiquette silence and fixity are forms of deference.

The man who was engaged in being hanged was apparently about thirty-five years of age. He was a civilian, if one might judge from his habit, which was that of a planter. His features were good—a straight nose, firm mouth, broad forehead, from which his long, dark hair was combed straight back, falling behind his ears to the collar of his well-fitting frock coat. He wore a mustache and pointed beard, but no whiskers; his eyes were large and dark gray, and had a kindly expression which one would hardly have expected in one whose neck was in the hemp. Evidently this was no vulgar assassin. The liberal military code makes provision for hanging many kinds of persons, and gentlemen are not excluded.

The preparations being complete, the two private soldiers stepped aside and each drew away the plank upon which he had been standing. The sergeant turned to the captain, saluted and placed himself immediately behind that officer, who in turn moved apart one pace. These movements left the condemned man and the sergeant standing on the two ends of the same plank, which spanned three of the cross-ties of the bridge. The end upon which the civilian stood almost, but not quite, reached a fourth. This plank had been held in place by the weight of the captain; it was now held by that of the sergeant. At a signal from the former the latter would step aside, the plank would tilt and the condemned man go down between two ties. The arrangement commended itself to his judgment as simple and effective. His face had not been covered nor his eyes bandaged. He looked a moment at his "unsteadfast footing," then let his gaze wander to the swirling water of the stream racing madly beneath his feet. A piece of dancing driftwood caught his attention and his eyes followed it down the current. How slowly it appeared to move. What a sluggish stream!

He closed his eyes in order to fix his last thoughts upon his wife and children. The water, touched to gold by the early sun, the brooding mists under the banks at some distance down the stream, the fort, the soldiers, the piece of drift—all had distracted him. And now he became conscious of a new disturbance. Striking through the thought of his dear ones was a sound which he could neither ignore nor understand, a sharp, distinct, metallic percussion like the stroke of a blacksmith's hammer upon the anvil; it had the same ringing quality. He wondered what it was, and whether immeasurably distant or near by—it seemed both. Its recurrence was regular, but as slow as the tolling of a death knell. He awaited each stroke with impatience and—he knew not why—apprehension. The intervals of silence grew progressively longer, the delays became maddening. With their greater infrequency the sounds increased in strength and sharpness. They hurt his ear like the thrust of a knife; he feared he would shriek. What he heard was the ticking of his watch.

He unclosed his eyes and saw again the water below him. "If I could free my hands," he thought, "I might throw off the noose and spring into the stream. By diving I could evade the bullets and, swimming vigorously, reach the bank, take to the woods and get away home. My home, thank God, is as yet outside their lines; my wife and little ones are still beyond the invader's farthest advance."

As these thoughts, which have here to be set down in words, were flashed into the doomed man's brain rather than evolved from it, the captain nodded to the sergeant. The sergeant stepped aside.

II

Peyton Farquhar was a well-to-do planter, of an old and highly respected Alabama family. Being a slave owner and like other slave owners, a politician, he was naturally an original secessionist and ardently devoted to the Southern cause. Circumstances of an imperious nature, which it is unnecessary to relate here, had prevented him from taking service with the gallant army that had fought the disastrous campaigns ending with the fall of Corinth, and he chafed under the inglorious restraint, longing for the release of his energies, the larger life of the soldier, the opportunity for distinction. That opportunity, he felt, would come, as it comes to all in war time. Meanwhile he did what he could. No service was too humble for him to perform in aid of the South, no adventure too perilous for him to undertake if consistent with the character of a civilian who was at heart a soldier, and who in good faith and without too much qualification assented to at least a part of the frankly villainous dictum that all is fair in love and war.

One evening while Farquhar and his wife were sitting on a rustic bench near the entrance to his grounds, a gray-clad soldier rode up to the gate and asked for a drink of water. Mrs. Farquhar was only too happy to serve him with her own white hands. While she was fetching the water her husband approached the dusty horseman and inquired eagerly for news from the front.

"The Yanks are repairing the railroads," said the man, "and are getting ready for another advance. They have reached the Owl Creek bridge, put it in order and built a stockade on the north bank. The commandant has issued an order, which is posted everywhere, declaring that any civilian caught interfering with the railroad, its bridges, tunnels or trains will be summarily hanged. I saw the order."

"How far is it to the Owl Creek bridge?" Farquhar asked.

"About thirty miles."

"Is there no force on this side of the creek?"

"Only a picket post half a mile out, on the railroad, and a single sentinel at this end of the bridge."

"Suppose a man—a civilian and student of hanging—should elude the picket post and perhaps get the better of the sentinel," said Farquhar, smiling, "what could he accomplish?"

The soldier reflected. "I was there a month ago," he replied. "I observed that the flood of last winter had lodged a great quantity of driftwood against the wooden pier at this end of the bridge. It is now dry and would burn like tow."

The lady had now brought the water, which the soldier drank. He thanked her ceremoniously, bowed to her husband and rode away. An hour later, after nightfall, he repassed the plantation, going northward in the direction from which he had come. He was a Federal scout.

III

As Peyton Farquhar fell straight downward through the bridge he lost consciousness and was as one already dead. From this state he was awakened—ages later, it seemed to him—by the pain of a sharp pressure upon his throat, followed by a sense of suffocation. Keen, poignant agonies seemed to shoot from his neck downward through every fiber of his body and limbs. These pains appeared to flash along well-defined lines of ramification and to beat with an inconceivably rapid periodicity. They seemed like streams of pulsating fire heating him to an intolerable temperature. As to his head, he was conscious of nothing but a feeling of fulness—of congestion. These sensations were unaccompanied by thought. The intellectual part of his nature was already effaced; he had power only to feel, and feeling was torment. He was conscious of motion. Encompassed in a luminous cloud, of which he was now merely the fiery heart, without material substance, he swung through unthinkable arcs of oscillation, like a vast pendulum. Then all at once, with terrible suddenness, the light about him shot upward with the noise of a loud splash; a frightful roaring was in his ears, and all was cold and dark. The power of thought was restored; he knew that the rope had broken and he had fallen into the stream. There was no additional strangulation; the noose about his neck was already suffocating him and kept the water from his lungs. To die of hanging at the bottom of a river!—the idea seemed to him ludicrous. He opened his eyes in the darkness and saw above him a gleam of light, but how distant, how inaccessible! He was still sinking, for the light became fainter and fainter until it was a mere glimmer. Then it began to grow and brighten, and he knew that he was rising toward the surface—knew it with reluctance, for he was now very comfortable. "To be hanged and drowned," he thought? "that is not so bad; but I do not wish to be shot. No; I will not be shot; that is not fair."

He was not conscious of an effort, but a sharp pain in his wrist apprised him that he was trying to free his hands. He gave the struggle his attention, as an idler might observe the feat of a juggler, without interest in the outcome. What splendid effort!—what magnificent, what superhuman strength! Ah, that was a fine endeavor! Bravo! The cord fell away; his arms parted and floated upward, the hands dimly seen on each side in the growing light. He watched them with a new interest as first one and then the other pounced upon the noose at his neck. They tore it away and thrust it fiercely aside, its undulations resembling those of a water snake. "Put it back, put it back!" He thought he shouted these words to his hands, for the undoing of the noose had been succeeded by the direst pang that he had yet experienced. His neck ached horribly; his brain was on fire; his heart, which had been fluttering faintly, gave a great leap, trying to force itself out at his mouth. His whole body was racked and wrenched with an insupportable anguish! But his disobedient hands gave no heed to the command. They beat the water vigorously with quick, downward strokes, forcing him to the surface. He felt his head emerge; his eyes were blinded by the sunlight; his chest expanded convulsively, and with a supreme and crowning agony his lungs engulfed a great draught of air, which instantly he expelled in a shriek!

He was now in full possession of his physical senses. They were, indeed, preternaturally keen and alert. Something in the awful disturbance of his organic system had so exalted and refined them that they made record of things never before perceived. He felt the ripples upon his face and heard their separate sounds as they struck. He looked at the forest on the bank of the stream, saw the individual trees, the leaves and the veining of each leaf—saw the very insects upon them: the locusts, the brilliant-bodied flies, the grey spiders stretching their webs from twig to twig. He noted the prismatic colors in all the dewdrops upon a million blades of grass. The humming of the gnats that danced above the eddies of the stream, the beating of the dragon flies' wings, the strokes of the water-spiders' legs, like oars which had lifted their boat—all these made audible music. A fish slid along beneath his eyes and he heard the rush of its body parting the water.

He had come to the surface facing down the stream; in a moment the visible world seemed to wheel slowly round, himself the pivotal point, and he saw the bridge, the fort, the soldiers upon the bridge, the captain, the sergeant, the two privates, his executioners. They were in silhouette against the blue sky. They shouted and gesticulated, pointing at him. The captain had drawn his pistol, but did not fire; the others were unarmed. Their movements were grotesque and horrible, their forms gigantic.

Suddenly he heard a sharp report and something struck the water smartly within a few inches of his head, spattering his face with spray. He heard a second report, and saw one of the sentinels with his rifle at his shoulder, a light cloud of blue smoke rising from the muzzle. The man in the water saw the eye of the man on the bridge gazing into his own through the sights of the rifle. He observed that it was a grey eye and remembered having read that grey eyes were keenest, and that all famous marksmen had them. Nevertheless, this one had missed.

A counter-swirl had caught Farquhar and turned him half round; he was again looking into the forest on the bank opposite the fort. The sound of a clear, high voice in a monotonous singsong now rang out behind him and came across the water with a distinctness that pierced and subdued all other sounds, even the beating of the ripples in his ears. Although no soldier, he had frequented camps enough to know the dread significance of that deliberate, drawling, aspirated chant; the lieutenant on shore was taking a part in the morning's work. How coldly and pitilessly—with what an even, calm intonation, presaging, and enforcing tranquility in the men—with what accurately measured intervals fell those cruel words:

"Attention, company! . . . Shoulder arms! . . . Ready! . . . Aim! . . . Fire!"

Farquhar dived—dived as deeply as he could. The water roared in his ears like the voice of Niagara, yet he heard the dulled thunder of the volley and, rising again toward the surface, met shining bits of metal, singularly flattened, oscillating slowly downward. Some of them touched him on the face and hands, then fell away, continuing their descent. One lodged between his collar and neck; it was uncomfortably warm and he snatched it out.

As he rose to the surface, gasping for breath, he saw that he had been a long time under water; he was perceptibly farther down stream nearer to safety. The soldiers had almost finished reloading; the metal ramrods flashed all at once in the sunshine as they were drawn from the barrels, turned in the air, and thrust into their sockets. The two sentinels fired again, independently and ineffectually.

The hunted man saw all this over his shoulder; he was now swimming vigorously with the current. His brain was as energetic as his arms and legs; he thought with the rapidity of lightning.

"The officer," he reasoned, "will not make that martinet's error a second time. It is as easy to dodge a volley as a single shot. He has probably already given the command to fire at will. God help me, I cannot dodge them all!"

An appalling splash within two yards of him was followed by a loud, rushing sound, diminuendo, which seemed to travel back through the air to the fort and died in an explosion which stirred the very river to its deeps!

A rising sheet of water curved over him, fell down upon him, blinded him, strangled him! The cannon had taken a hand in the game. As he shook his head free from the commotion of the smitten water he heard the deflected shot humming through the air ahead, and in an instant it was cracking and smashing the branches in the forest beyond.

"They will not do that again," he thought; "the next time they will use a charge of grape. I must keep my eye upon the gun; the smoke will apprise me— the report arrives too late; it lags behind the missile. That is a good gun."

Suddenly he felt himself whirled round and round—spinning like a top. The water, the banks, the forests, the now distant bridge, fort and men—all were commingled and blurred. Objects were represented by their colors only; circular horizontal streaks of color—that was all he saw. He had been caught in a vortex and was being whirled on with a velocity of advance and gyration that made him giddy and sick. In a few moments he was flung upon the gravel at the foot of the left bank of the stream—the southern bank—and behind a projecting point which concealed him from his enemies. The sudden arrest of his

motion, the abrasion of one of his hands on the gravel, restored him, and he wept with delight. He dug his fingers into the sand, threw it over himself in handfuls and audibly blessed it. It looked like diamonds, rubies, emeralds; he could think of nothing beautiful which it did not resemble. The trees upon the bank were giant garden plants; he noted a definite order in their arrangement, inhaled the fragrance of their blooms. A strange, roseate light shone through the spaces among their trunks and the wind made in their branches the music of Aeolian harps. He had no wish to perfect his escape—was content to remain in that enchanting spot until retaken.

A whiz and rattle of grapeshot among the branches high above his head roused him from his dream. The baffled cannoneer had fired him a random farewell. He sprang to his feet, rushed up the sloping bank, and plunged into the forest.

All that day he traveled, laying his course by the rounding sun. The forest seemed interminable; nowhere did he discover a break in it, not even a woodman's road. He had not known that he lived in so wild a region. There was something uncanny in the revelation.

By nightfall he was fatigued, footsore, famishing. The thought of his wife and children urged him on. At last he found a road which led him in what he knew to be the right direction. It was as wide and straight as a city street, yet it seemed untraveled. No fields bordered it, no dwelling anywhere. Not so much as the barking of a dog suggested human habitation. The black bodies of the trees formed a straight wall on both sides, terminating on the horizon in a point, like a diagram in a lesson in perspective. Overhead, as he looked up through this rift in the wood, shone great garden stars looking unfamiliar and grouped in strange constellations. He was sure they were arranged in some order which had a secret and malign significance. The wood on either side was full of singular noises, among which— once, twice, and again—he distinctly heard whispers in an unknown tongue.

His neck was in pain and lifting his hand to it found it horribly swollen. He knew that it had a circle of black where the rope had bruised it. His eyes felt congested; he could no longer close them. His tongue was swollen with thirst; he relieved its fever by thrusting it forward from between his teeth into the cold air. How softly the turf had carpeted the untraveled avenue—he could no longer feel the road-way beneath his feet!

Doubtless, despite his suffering, he had fallen asleep while walking, for now he sees another scene—perhaps he has merely recovered from a delirium. He stands at the gate of his own home. All is as he left it, and all bright and beautiful in the morning sunshine. He must have traveled the entire night. As he pushes open the gate and passes up the wide white walk, he sees a flutter of female garments; his wife, looking fresh and cool and sweet, steps down from the veranda to meet him. At the bottom of the steps she stands waiting, with a smile of ineffable joy, an attitude of matchless grace and dignity. Ah, how beautiful she is! He springs forward with extended arms. As he is about to clasp her he feels a stunning blow upon the back of the neck; a blinding white light blazes all about him with a sound like the shock of a cannon—then all is darkness and silence!

Peyton Farquhar was dead; his body, with a broken neck, swung gently from side to side beneath the timbers of the Owl Creek bridge.

Questions

1. Naturally, if someone is to be hanged, suspense may find itself in the air. In addition to the looming execution, what contributes to the suspenseful feeling that Ambrose Bierce creates? Identify specific examples from the story.
2. When reading this story for the first time, is it evident that Peyton Farquhar was imagining his escape and eventual reunion with his wife? Does Bierce offer any clues to his readers?
3. What is known of Peyton Farquhar? What might we infer?
4. Why is Farquhar being hanged?
5. Is anything to be suggested by this story's title? In other words, sometimes a title sheds light on the author's intentions; this can be seen in Jonathan Swift's *A Modest Proposal,* where Swift is proposing that people consider eating the babies of Ireland. Similarly, Bierce titles his piece *An Occurrence at Owl Creek Bridge.* Just as little is "modest" about Swift's proposal, is there more than an "occurrence" at Owl Creek Bridge?

1. While Peyton Farquhar is awaiting death, he enjoys a delirium. Similar deliriums are experienced by William Wallace (as he is awaiting death in the film *Braveheart*) and Maximus (as he is awaiting death in the film *Gladiator*). How do these deliriums advance each story? Further, what would be lost if each was without said delirium?
2. While hangings are, essentially, a thing of the past in the U.S.A., capital punishment is still legal in many states. Specifically, electrocution, lethal injection, and the gas chamber can be employed to dispatch those convicted of a crime that warrants the death penalty. Perform some research, and then take a stand on whether or not capital punishment and, specifically, the death penalty, should be supported. Further, if you support the death penalty, specify which modus operandi should be employed. Should, for instance, hangings be reintroduced? Or, as is still legal in some countries, should death by firing squad be an option?

3. Much of *An Occurrence at Owl Creek Bridge* consists of a supposed get-away. Still, there is more. Some references in the story might suggest that Peyton Farquhar was innocent. For whatever reason, however, he has been sentenced to death. Something very similar occurs to Richard Kimble in the film *The Fugitive*. Compare and contrast *The Fugitive* with *An Occurrence at Owl Creek Bridge*. Among what you choose to compare and contrast might be the arguments offered by each text, the situational similarities, and the plight of each text's main character.

Kate Chopin (1850–1904)

Kate Chopin was born Kate O'Flaherty in St. Louis, Missouri. As the third of five children, she was raised primarily by her mother, grandmother, and great-grandmother who were, interestingly, all widows and all educated, independent, single women. Then, at the age of twenty, Kate O'Flaherty married Oscar Chopin and, in an eight-year period, gave birth to five boys and two girls. Unfortunately, four years later Oscar Chopin died of swamp fever, leaving Kate Chopin with his general store, a plantation, and seven children to support. Realizing after one year that running a general store and a plantation would not work for her, Kate Chopin decided to begin writing. She had immediate success with *The Awakening,* and she became a well-known writer, having over one hundred stories, essays, and sketches published. Among them was *The Story of an Hour,* published in *Vogue* magazine in 1894. Even though it is brief, *The Story of an Hour* was rediscovered during the 1960s and the rise of the feminist movement, perhaps due to Chopin's portrayal of women's roles in marriage and feminine identity.

The Story of an Hour

1. Note that this story is written in the passive voice, and note what might be achieved by constructing the story in this manner.
2. While reading this story, observe the contrast between motion and stillness in the language that Chopin employs.
3. Note images that are associated with things being opened or closed, and note how such images might advance the story.
4. Note appearances and disappearances within this story. Some of these may be physical while others may be emotional.

The Story of an Hour

Kate Chopin

Knowing that Mrs. Mallard was afflicted with a heart trouble, great care was taken to break to her as gently as possible the news of her husband's death.

It was her sister Josephine who told her, in broken sentences; veiled hints that revealed in half concealing. Her husband's friend Richards was there, too, near her. It was he who had been in the newspaper office when intelligence of the railroad disaster was received, with Brently Mallard's name leading the list of "killed." He had only taken the time to assure himself of its truth by a second telegram, and had hastened to forestall any less careful, less tender friend in bearing the sad message.

She did not hear the story as many women have heard the same, with a paralyzed inability to accept its significance. She wept at once, with sudden, wild abandonment, in her sister's arms. When the storm of grief had spent itself she went away to her room alone. She would have no one follow her.

There stood, facing the open window, a comfortable, roomy armchair. Into this she sank, pressed down by a physical exhaustion that haunted her body and seemed to reach into her soul.

She could see in the open square before her house the tops of trees that were all aquiver with the new spring life. The delicious breath of rain was in the air. In the street below a peddler was crying his wares. The notes of a distant song which some one was singing reached her faintly, and countless sparrows were twittering in the eaves.

There were patches of blue sky showing here and there through the clouds that had met and piled one above the other in the west facing her window.

She sat with her head thrown back upon the cushion of the chair, quite motionless, except when a sob came up into her throat and shook her, as a child who has cried itself to sleep continues to sob in its dreams.

She was young, with a fair, calm face, whose lines bespoke repression and even a certain strength. But now there was a dull stare in her eyes, whose gaze was fixed away off yonder on one of those patches of blue sky. It was not a glance of reflection, but rather indicated a suspension of intelligent thought.

There was something coming to her and she was waiting for it, fearfully. What was it? She did not know; it was too subtle and elusive to name. But she felt it, creeping out of the sky, reaching toward her through the sounds, the scents, the color that filled the air.

Now her bosom rose and fell tumultuously. She was beginning to recognize this thing that was approaching to possess her, and she was striving to beat it back with her will—as powerless as her two white slender hands would have been.

When she abandoned herself a little whispered word escaped her slightly parted lips. She said it over and over under her breath: "free, free, free!" The vacant stare and the look of terror that had followed it went from her eyes. They stayed keen and bright. Her pulses beat fast, and the coursing blood warmed and relaxed every inch of her body.

She did not stop to ask if it were or were not a monstrous joy that held her. A clear and exalted perception enabled her to dismiss the suggestion as trivial.

She knew that she would weep again when she saw the kind, tender hands folded in death; the face that had never looked save with love upon her, fixed and gray and dead. But she saw beyond that bitter moment a long procession of years to come that would belong to her absolutely. And she opened and spread her arms out to them in welcome.

There would be no one to live for during those coming years; she would live for herself. There would be no powerful will bending hers in that blind persistence with which men and women believe they have a right to impose a private will upon a fellow-creature. A kind intention or a cruel intention made the act seem no less a crime as she looked upon it in that brief moment of illumination.

And yet she had loved him—sometimes. Often she had not. What did it matter! What could love, the unsolved mystery, count for in face of this possession of self-assertion which she suddenly recognized as the strongest impulse of her being!

"Free! Body and soul free!" she kept whispering.

Josephine was kneeling before the closed door with her lips to the keyhole, imploring for admission. "Louise, open the door! I beg, open the door— you will make yourself ill. What are you doing Louise? For heaven's sake open the door."

"Go away. I am not making myself ill." No; she was drinking in a very elixir of life through that open window.

Her fancy was running riot along those days ahead of her. Spring days, and summer days, and all sorts of days that would be her own. She breathed a quick prayer that life might be long. It was only yesterday she had thought with a shudder that life might be long.

She arose at length and opened the door to her sister's importunities. There was a feverish triumph in her eyes, and she carried herself unwittingly like a goddess of Victory. She clasped her sister's waist, and together they descended the stairs. Richards stood waiting for them at the bottom.

Some one was opening the front door with a latchkey. It was Brently Mallard who entered, a little travel-stained, composedly carrying his grip-sack and umbrella. He had been far from the scene of the accident, and did not even know there had been one. He stood amazed at Josephine's piercing cry; at Richards' quick motion to screen him from the view of his wife.

But Richards was too late.

When the doctors came they said she had died of heart disease—of joy that kills.

Questions

1. Why might Louise be described as the "goddess of Victory"?
2. The story ends with this: "When the doctors came they said she had died of heart disease—of joy that kills." What might this mean?
3. Identify the internal and external conflicts within *The Story of an Hour*.

1. Read Plato's *Allegory of the Cave*. After doing so, identify Louise's "cave" in *The Story of an Hour*. Then, identify two other literary characters' caves. (It is possible to draw from various stories; for instance, one could identify the caves of Bartleby, Goodman Brown, or Ichabod Crane.) After identifying these caves, explain what these characters might do to become conscious of their caves and what they might do to eventually exit them.
2. Ralph Waldo Emerson, the famous essayist and poet, was once asked why he did not address slavery in his writings. In response, he explained that almost all of what he wrote dealt with slavery. However, to rid his interrogator of her befuddled look, he explained that he is currently working on freeing people from "mental slavery." In *The Story of an Hour*, Louise seems to be enduring some type of mental enslavement. At last, however, she exclaims that she is "free, free, free!" Within the context of mental enslavement, extract an argument from *The Story of an Hour*. Then, compare and contrast it with an argument from Ralph Waldo Emerson's *Self-reliance*.

Louisa May Alcott (1832–1888)

Born in Germantown, Pennsylvania, and raised in Boston and Concord, Massachusetts, Louisa May Alcott was influenced at an early age by transcendentalism (a philosophy of nature that holds that everything is an approximation to an ideal standard or type). Not only was her father a noted transcendentalist, but she had access to Ralph Waldo Emerson's personal library of classics and philosophy. As if this were not enough exposure to the literary world, her botany instructor was Henry David Thoreau. While *Little Women* was the publication that put Alcott on the map, her publications ran the gamut from novels, to short stories, to poems, often shining a spotlight on temperance, education, and women's suffrage.

The Brothers

1. In 1862, Alcott went to Washington, D.C. to serve as a nurse to soldiers wounded in the American Civil War.
2. Notice how Alcott constructs the notion of masculinity in this story.
3. Observe the relationship between racial sacrifice and citizenship.

The Brothers

Louisa May Alcott

Doctor Franck came in as I sat sewing up the rents in an old shirt, that Tom might go tidily to his grave. New shirts were needed for the living, and there was no wife or mother to "dress him handsome when he went to meet the Lord," as one woman said, describing the fine funeral she had pinched herself to give her son.

"Miss Dane, I'm in a quandary," began the Doctor, with that expression of countenance which says as plainly as words, "I want to ask a favor, but I wish you'd save me the trouble."

"Can I help you out of it?"

"Faith! I don't like to propose it. But you certainly can, if you please."

"Then give it a name, I beg."

"You see a Reb has just been brought in crazy with typhoid; a bad case every way; a drunken, rascally little captain somebody took the trouble to capture, but whom nobody wants to take the trouble to cure. The wards are full, the ladies worked to death, and willing to be for our own boys, but rather slow to risk their lives for a Reb. Now you've had the fever, you like queer patients, your mate will see to your ward for a while, and I will find you a good attendant. The fellow won't last long, I fancy; but he can't die without some sort of care, you know. I've put him in the fourth story of the west wing, away from the rest. It is airy, quiet, and comfortable there. I'm on that ward, and will do my best for you in every way. Now, then, will you go?"

"Of course I will, out of perversity, if not common charity; for some of these people think that because I'm an abolitionist I am also a heathen, and I should rather like to show them, that, though I cannot quite love my enemies, I am willing to take care of them."

"Very good; I thought you'd go; and speaking of abolition reminds me that you can have a contraband for servant, if you like. It is that fine mulatto fellow who was found burying his Rebel master after the fight, and, being badly cut over the head, our boys brought him along. Will you have him?"

"By all means—for I'll stand to my guns on that point, as on the other; these black boys are far more faithful and handy than some of the white scamps given me to serve, instead of being served by. But is this man well enough?"

"Yes, for that sort of work, and I think you'll like him. He must have been a handsome fellow before he got his face slashed; not much darker than myself; his master's son, I dare say, and the white blood makes him rather high and haughty about some things. He was in a bad way when he came in, but vowed he'd die in the street rather than turn in with the black fellows below; so I put him up in the west wing, to be out of the way, and he's seen to the captain all the morning. When can you go up?"

"As soon as Tom is laid out, Skinner moved, Haywood washed, Marble dressed, Charley rubbed, Downs taken up, Upham laid down, and the whole forty fed."

We both laughed, though the Doctor was on his way to the dead-house and I held a shroud on my lap. But in a hospital one learns that cheerfulness is one's salvation; for, in an atmosphere of suffering and death, heaviness of heart would soon paralyze usefulness of hand, if the blessed gift of smiles had been denied us.

In an hour I took possession of my new charge, finding a dissipated-looking boy of nineteen or twenty raving in the solitary little room, with no one near him but the contraband in the room adjoining. Feeling decidedly more interest in the black man than in the white, yet remembering the Doctor's hint of his being "high and haughty," I glanced furtively

at him as I scattered chloride of lime about the room to purify the air, and settled matters to suit myself. I had seen many contrabands, but never one so attractive as this. All colored men are called "boys," even if their heads are white; this boy was five-and-twenty at least, strong-limbed and manly, and had the look of one who never had been cowed by abuse or worn with oppressive labor. He sat on his bed doing nothing; no book, no pipe, no pen or paper anywhere appeared, yet anything less indolent or listless than his attitude and expression I never saw. Erect he sat with a hand on either knee, and eyes fixed on the bare wall opposite, so rapt in some absorbing thought as to be unconscious of my presence, though the door stood wide open and my movements were by no means noiseless. His face was half averted, but I instantly approved the Doctor's taste, for the profile which I saw possessed all the attributes of comeliness belonging to his mixed race. He was more quadroon than mulatto, with Saxon features, Spanish complexion darkened by exposure, color in lips and cheek, waving hair, and an eye full of the passionate melancholy which in such men always seems to utter a mute protest against the broken law that doomed them at their birth. What could he be thinking of? The sick boy cursed and raved, I rustled to and fro, steps passed the door, bells rang, and the steady rumble of army-wagons came up from the street, still he never stirred. I had seen colored people in what they call "the black sulks," when, for days, they neither smiled nor spoke, and scarcely ate. But this was something more than that; for the man was not dully brooding over some small grievance—he seemed to see an all-absorbing fact or fancy recorded on the wall, which was a blank to me. I wondered if it were some deep wrong or sorrow, kept alive by memory and impotent regret; if he mourned for the dead master to whom he had been faithful to the end; or if the liberty now his were robbed of half its sweetness by the knowledge that some one near and dear to him still languished in the hell from which he had escaped. My heart quite warmed to him at that idea; I wanted to know and comfort him; and, following the impulse of the moment, I went in and touched him on the shoulder.

In an instant the man vanished and the slave appeared. Freedom was too new a boon to have wrought its blessed changes yet, and as he started up, with his hand at his temple and an obsequious "Yes, Ma'am," any romance that had gathered round him fled away, leaving the saddest of all sad facts in living guise before me. Not only did the manhood seem to die out of him, but the comeliness that first attracted me; for, as he turned, I saw the ghastly wound that had laid open cheek and forehead. Being partly healed, it was no longer bandaged, but held together with strips of that transparent plaster which I never see without a shiver and swift recollections of scenes with which it is associated in my mind. Part of his black hair had been shorn away, and one eye was nearly closed; pain so distorted, and the cruel sabrecut so marred that portion of his face, that, when I saw it, I felt as if a fine medal had been suddenly reversed, showing me a far more striking type of human suffering and wrong than Michelangelo's bronze prisoner. By one of those inexplicable processes that often teach us how little we understand ourselves, my purpose was suddenly changed, and though I went in to offer comfort as a friend, I merely gave an order as a mistress.

"Will you open these windows? This man needs more air."

He obeyed at once, and, as he slowly urged up the unruly sash, the handsome profile was again turned toward me, and again I was possessed by my first impression so strongly that I involuntarily said—

"Thank you, Sir."

Perhaps it was fancy, but I thought that in the look of mingled surprise and something like reproach which be gave me there was also a trace of grateful pleasure. But he said, in that tone of spiritless humility these poor souls learn so soon—

"I ain't a white man, Ma'am, I'm a contraband."

"Yes, I know it; but a contraband is a free man, and I heartily congratulate you."

He liked that; his face shone, he squared his shoulders, lifted his head, and looked me full in the eye with a brisk—

"Thank ye, Ma'am; anything more to do fer yer?"

"Doctor Franck thought you would help me with this man, as there are many patients and few nurses or attendants. Have you had the fever?"

"No, Ma'am."

"They should have thought of that when they put him here; wounds and fevers should not be together. I'll try to get you moved."

He laughed a sudden laugh—if he had been a white man, I should have called it scornful; as he was a few shades darker than myself, I suppose it must be considered an insolent, or at least an unmannerly one.

"It don't matter, Ma'am. I'd rather be up here with the fever than down with those niggers; and there ain't no other place fer me."

Poor fellow! that was true. No ward in all the hospital would take him in to lie side by side with the most miserable white wreck there. Like the bat in Aesop's fable, he belonged to neither race; and the pride of one, the helplessness of the other, kept him hovering alone in the twilight a great sin has brought to overshadow the whole land.

"You shall stay, then; for I would far rather have you than any lazy Jack. But are you well and strong enough?"

"I guess I'll do, Ma'am."

He spoke with a passive sort of acquiescence—as if it did not much matter, if he were not able, and no one would particularly rejoice, if he were.

"Yes, I think you will. By what name shall I call you?"

"Bob, Ma'am."

Every woman has her pet whim; one of mine was to teach the men self-respect by treating them respectfully. Tom, Dick, and Harry would pass, when lads rejoiced in those familiar abbreviations; but to address men often old enough to be my father in that style did not suit my old-fashioned ideas of propriety. This "Bob" would never do; I should have found it as easy to call the chaplain "Gus" as my tragical-looking contraband by a title so strongly associated with the tail of a kite.

"What is your other name?" I asked. "I like to call my attendants by their last names rather than by their first."

"I've got no other, Ma'am; we have our masters' names, or do without. Mine's dead, and I won't have anything of his about me."

"Well, I'll call you Robert, then, and you may fill this pitcher for me, if you will be so kind."

He went; but, through all the tame, obedience years of servitude had taught him, I could see that the proud spirit his father gave him was not yet subdued, for the look and gesture with which he repudiated his master's name were a more effective declaration of independence than any Fourth-of-July orator could have prepared.

We spent a curious week together. Robert seldom left his room, except upon my errands; and I was a prisoner all day, often all night, by the bedside of the Rebel. The fever burned itself rapidly away, for there seemed little vitality to feed it in the feeble frame of this old young man, whose life had been none of the most righteous, judging from the revelations made by his unconscious lips; since more than once Robert authoritatively silenced him, when my gentler bushings were of no avail, and blasphemous wanderings or ribald camp-songs made my cheeks burn and Robert's face assume an aspect of disgust. The captain was a gentleman in the world's eye, but the contraband was the gentleman in mine—I was a fanatic, and that accounts for such depravity of taste, I hope. I never asked Robert of himself, feeling that somewhere there was a spot still too sore to bear the lightest touch; but, from his language, manner, and intelligence, I inferred that his color had procured for him the few advantages within the reach of a quick-witted, kindly treated slave. Silent, grave, and thoughtful, but most serviceable, was my contraband; glad of the books I brought him, faithful in the performance of the duties I assigned to him, grateful for the friendliness I could not but feel and show toward him. Often I longed to ask what purpose was so visibly altering his aspect with such daily deepening gloom. But I never dared, and no one else had either time or desire to pry into the past of this specimen of one branch of the chivalrous "F.F.Vs."

On the seventh night, Dr. Franck suggested that it would be well for some one, besides the general watchman of the ward, to be with the captain, as it might be his last. Although the greater part of the two preceding nights had been spent there, of course I offered to remain—for there is a strange fascination in these scenes, which renders one careless of fatigue and unconscious of fear until the crisis is passed.

"Give him water as long as he can drink, and if he drops into a natural sleep, it may save him. I'll look in at midnight, when some change will probably take place. Nothing but sleep or a miracle will keep him now. Good night."

Away went the Doctor; and, devouring a whole mouthful of grapes, I lowered the lamp, wet the captain's head, and sat down on a hard stool to begin my watch. The captain lay with his hot, haggard face turned toward me, filling the air with his poisonous breath, and feebly muttering, with lips and tongue so parched that the sanest speech would have been difficult to understand. Robert was stretched on his bed in the inner room, the door of which stood ajar, that a fresh draught from his open window might carry the fever-fumes away through mine. I could just see a long, dark figure, with the lighter outline of a face, and, having little else to do just then, I fell to thinking of this curious contraband, who evidently prized his freedom highly, yet seemed in no haste to enjoy it. Doctor Franck had offered to send him on to safer quarters, but he had said, "No, thank yer, Sir, not yet," and then had gone away to fall into one of those black moods of his, which began to disturb me, because I had no power to lighten them. As I sat listening to the clocks from the steeples all about us, I amused myself with planning Robert's future, as I often did my own, and had dealt out to him a generous hand of trumps wherewith to play this game of life which hitherto had gone so cruelly against him, when a harsh, choked voice called—

"Lucy!"

It was the captain, and some new terror seemed to have gifted him with momentary strength.

"Yes, here's Lucy," I answered, hoping that by following the fancy I might quiet him—for his face was damp with the clammy moisture, and his frame shaken with the nervous tremor that so often precedes death. His dull eye fixed upon me, dilating with a bewildered look of incredulity and wrath, till he broke out fiercely—

"That's a lie! she's dead—and so's Bob, damn him!"

Finding speech a failure, I began to sing the quiet tune that had often soothed delirium like this; but hardly had the line,

"See gentle patience smile on pain,"

passed my lips, when he clutched me by the wrist, whispering like one in mortal fear—

"Hush! she used to sing that way to Bob, but she never would to me. I swore I'd whip the Devil out of her, and I did; but you know before she cut her throat she said she'd haunt me, and there she is!"

He pointed behind me with an aspect of such pale dismay, that I involuntarily glanced over my shoulder and started as if I had seen a veritable ghost; for, peering from the gloom of that inner room, I saw a shadowy face, with dark hair all about it, and a glimpse of scarlet at the throat. An instant showed me that it was only Robert leaning from his bed's-foot, wrapped in a gray army-blanket, with his red shirt just visible above it, and his long hair disordered by sleep. But what a strange expression was on his face! The unmarred side was toward me, fixed and motionless as when I first observed it—less absorbed now, but more intent. His eye glittered, his lips were apart like one who listened with every sense, and his whole aspect reminded me of a hound to which some wind had brought the scent of unsuspected prey.

"Do you know him, Robert? Does he mean you?"

"Lord, no, Ma'am; they all own half a dozen Bobs: but hearin' my name woke me; that's all."

He spoke quite naturally, and lay down again, while I returned to my charge, thinking that this paroxysm was probably his last. But by another hour I perceived a hopeful change, for the tremor had subsided, the cold dew was gone, his breathing was more regular, and Sleep, the healer, had descended to save or take him gently away. Doctor Franck looked in at midnight, bade me keep all cool and quiet, and not fail to administer a certain draught as soon as the captain woke. Very much relieved, I laid my head on my arms, uncomfortably folded on the little table, and fancied I was about to perform one of the feats which practice renders possible—"sleeping with one eye open," as we say: a half-and-half doze, for all senses sleep but that of hearing; the faintest murmur, sigh, or motion will break it, and give one back one's wits much brightened by the permission to "stand at ease." On this night, the experiment was a failure, for previous vigils, confinement, and much care had rendered naps a dangerous indulgence. Having roused half a dozen times in an hour to find all quiet, I dropped my heavy head on my arms, and, drowsily

resolving to look up again in fifteen minutes, fell fast asleep.

The striking of a deep-voiced clock woke me with a start. "That is one," thought I, but, to my dismay, two more strokes followed; and in remorseful haste I sprang up to see what harm my long oblivion had done. A strong hand put me back into my seat, and held me there. It was Robert. The instant my eye met his my heart began to beat, and all along my nerves tingled that electric flash which foretells a danger that we cannot see. He was very pale, his mouth grim, and both eyes full of sombre fire—for even the wounded one was open now, all the more sinister for the deep scar above and below. But his touch was steady, his voice quiet, as he said—

"Sit still, Ma'am; I won't hurt yer, nor even scare yer, if I can help it, but yer waked too soon."

"Let me go, Robert—the captain is stirring—I must give him something."

"No, Ma'am, yer can't stir an inch. Look here!"

Holding me with one hand, with the other he took up the glass in which I had left the draught, and showed me it was empty.

"Has he taken it?" I asked, more and more bewildered.

"I flung it out o' winder, Ma'am; he'll have to do without."

"But why, Robert? why did you do it?"

"Because I hate him!"

Impossible to doubt the truth of that; his whole face showed it, as he spoke through his set teeth, and launched a fiery glance at the unconscious captain. I could only hold my breath and stare blankly at him, wondering what mad act was coming next. I suppose I shook and turned white, as women have a foolish habit of doing when sudden danger daunts them; for Robert released my arm, sat down upon the bedside just in front of me, and said, with the ominous quietude that made me cold to see and hear—

"Don't yer be frightened, Ma'am: don't try to run away, fer the door's locked an' the key in my pocket; don't yer cry out, fer yer'd have to scream a long while, with my hand on yer mouth, before yer was heard. Be still, an' I'll tell yer what I'm goin' to do."

"Lord help us! he has taken the fever in some sudden, violent way, and is out of his head. I must humor him till some one comes"; in pursuance of which swift determination, I tried to say, quite composedly—

"I will be still and hear you; but open the window. Why did you shut it?"

"I'm sorry I can't do it, Ma'am; but yer'd jump out, or call, if I did, an' I'm not ready yet. I shut it to make yer sleep, an' heat would do it quicker'n anything else I could do."

The captain moved, and feebly muttered, "Water!" Instinctively I rose to give it to him, but the heavy hand came down upon my shoulder, and in the same decided tone Robert said—

"The water went with the physic; let him call."

"Do let me go to him! he'll die without care!"

"I mean he shall—don't yer interfere, if yer please, Ma'am."

In spite of his quiet tone and respectful manner, I saw murder in his eyes, and turned faint with fear; yet the fear excited me, and, hardly knowing what I did, I seized the hands that had seized me, crying—

"No, no, you shall not kill him! it is base to hurt a helpless man. Why do you hate him? He is not your master?"

"He's my brother."

I felt that answer from head to foot, and seemed to fathom what was coming, with a prescience vague, but unmistakable. One appeal was left to me, and I made it.

"Robert, tell me what it means? Do not commit a crime and make me accessory to it—There is a better way of righting wrong than by violence—let me help you find it."

My voice trembled as I spoke, and I heard the frightened flutter of my heart; so did he, and if any little act of mine had ever won affection or respect from him, the memory of it served me then. He looked down, and seemed to put some question to himself; whatever it was, the answer was in my favor, for when his eyes rose again, they were gloomy, but not desperate.

"I will tell you, Ma'am; but mind, this makes no difference; the boy is mine. I'll give the Lord a chance to take him fust; if He don't, I shall."

"Oh, no! remember, he is your brother."

An unwise speech; I felt it as it passed my lips, for a black frown gathered on Robert's face, and his strong hands closed with an ugly sort of grip. But he did not touch the poor soul gasping there before him, and seemed content to let the slow suffocation of that stifling room end his frail life.

"I'm not like to forget that, Ma'am, when I've been thinkin' of it all this week. I knew him when they fetched him in, an' would 'a' done it long 'fore this, but I wanted to ask where Lucy was; he knows—he told to-night—an' now he's done for."

"Who is Lucy?" I asked hurriedly, intent on keeping his mind busy with any thought but murder.

With one of the swift transitions of a mixed temperament like this, at my question Robert's deep eyes filled, the clenched hands were spread before his face, and all I heard were the broken words—

"My wife—he took her—"

In that instant every thought of fear was swallowed up in burning indignation for the wrong, and a perfect passion of pity for the desperate man so tempted to avenge an injury for which there seemed no redress but this. He was no longer slave or contraband, no drop of black blood marred him in my sight, but an infinite compassion yearned to save, to help, to comfort him. Words seemed so powerless I offered none, only put my hand on his poor head, wounded, homeless, bowed down with grief for which I had no cure, and softly smoothed the long neglected hair, pitifully wondering the while where was the wife who must have loved this tenderhearted man so well.

The captain moaned again, and faintly whispered, "Air!" but I never stirred. God forgive me! Just then I hated him as only a woman thinking of a sister woman's wrong could hate. Robert looked up; his eyes were dry again, his mouth grim. I saw that, said, "Tell me more," and he did—for sympathy is a gift the poorest may give, the proudest stoop to receive.

"Yer see, Ma'am, his father—I might say ours, if I warn't ashamed of both of 'em—his father died two years ago, an' left us all to Marster Ned—that's him here, eighteen then. He always hated me, I looked so like old Marster: he don't—only the light skin an' hair. Old Marster was kind to all of us, me 'specially, an' bought Lucy off the next plantation down there in South Car'lina, when he found I liked her. I married her, all I could, Ma'am; it warn't much, but we was true to one another till Marster

Ned come home a year after an' made hell fer both of us. He sent my old mother to be used up in his rice swamp in Georgy; he found me with my pretty Lucy, an' though young Miss cried, an' I prayed to him on my knees, an' Lucy run away, he wouldn't have no mercy; he brought her back, an'—took her, Ma'am."

"Oh! what did you do?" I cried, hot with helpless pain and passion.

How the man's outraged heart sent the blood flaming up into his face and deepened the tones of his impetuous voice, as he stretched his arm across the bed, saying, with a terribly expressive gesture—

"I half murdered him, an' to-night I'll finish."

"Yes, yes—but go on now; what came next?"

He gave me a look that showed no white man could have felt a deeper degradation in remembering and confessing these last acts of brotherly oppression.

"They whipped me till I couldn't stand, an' then they sold me further South. Yer thought I was a white man once—look here!"

With a sudden wrench he tore the shirt from neck to waist, and on his strong brown shoulders showed me furrows deeply ploughed, wounds which, though healed, were ghastlier to me than any in that house. I could not speak to him, and, with the pathetic dignity a great grief lends the humblest sufferer, he ended his brief tragedy by simply saying—

"That's all. Ma'am. I've never seen her since, an' now I never shall in this world—maybe not in t' other."

"But, Robert, why think her dead? The captain was wandering when he said those sad things; perhaps he will retract them when he is sane. Don't despair; don't give up yet."

"No, Ma'am, I guess he's right; she was too proud to bear that long. It's like her to kill herself. I told her to, if there was no other way; an' she always minded me, Lucy did. My poor girl! Oh, it warn't right! No, by God, it warn't!"

As the memory of this bitter wrong, this double bereavement, burned in his sore heart, the devil that lurks in every strong man's blood leaped up; he put his hand upon his brother's throat, and, watching the white face before him, muttered low between his teeth—

"I'm lettin' him go too easy; there's no pain in this; we a'n't even yet. I wish he knew me. Marster Ned! it's Bob; where's Lucy?"

From the captain's lips there came a long faint sigh, and nothing but a flutter of the eyelids showed that he still lived. A strange stillness filled the room as the elder brother held the younger's life suspended in his hand, while wavering between a dim hope and a deadly hate. In the whirl of thoughts that went on in my brain, only one was clear enough to act upon. I must prevent murder, if I could—but how? What could I do up there alone, locked in with a dying man and a lunatic?—for any mind yielded utterly to any unrighteous impulse is mad while the impulse rules it. Strength I had not, nor much courage, neither time nor wit for stratagem, and chance only could bring me help before it was too late. But one weapon I possessed—a tongue—often a woman's best defence: and sympathy, stronger than fear, gave me power to use it. What I said Heaven only knows, but surely Heaven helped me; words burned on my lips, tears streamed from my eyes, and some good angel prompted me to use the one name that had power to arrest my hearer's hand and touch his heart. For at that moment I heartily believed that Lucy lived, and this earnest faith roused in him a like belief.

He listened with the lowering look of one in whom brute instinct was sovereign for the time—a look that makes the noblest countenance base. He was but a man—a poor, untaught, outcast, outraged man. Life had few joys for him; the world offered him no honors, no success, no home, no love. What future would this crime mar? and why should he deny himself that sweet, yet bitter morsel called revenge? How many white men, with all New England's freedom, culture, Christianity, would not have felt as he felt then? Should I have reproached him for a human anguish, a human longing for redress, all now left him from the ruin of his few poor hopes? Who had taught him that self-control, self-sacrifice, are attributes that make men masters of the earth and lift them nearer heaven? Should I have urged the beauty of forgiveness, the duty of devout submission? He had no religion, for he was no saintly "Uncle Tom," and Slavery's black shadow seemed to darken all the world to him and shut out God. Should I have warned him of penalties, of judgments, and the potency of law? What did he know of justice, or the mercy that should temper that stern virtue, when every law, human and divine, had been broken on his hearthstone? Should I have tried to touch him by appeals to filial duty, to brotherly love? How had his appeals been answered? What memories had father and brother stored up in his heart to plead for either now? No—all these influences, these associations, would have proved worse than useless, had I been calm enough to try them. I was not; but instinct, subtler than reason, showed me the one safe clue by which to lead this troubled soul from the labyrinth in which it groped and nearly fell. When I paused, breathless, Robert turned to me, asking, as if human assurances could strengthen his faith in Divine Omnipotence—

"Do you believe, if I let Marster Ned live, the Lord will give me back my Lucy?"

"As surely as there is a Lord, you will find her here or in the beautiful hereafter, where there is no black or white, no master and no slave."

He took his hand from his brother's throat, lifted his eyes from my face to the wintry sky beyond, as if searching for that blessed country, happier even than the happy North. Alas, it was the darkest hour before the dawn!—there was no star above, no light below but the pale glimmer of the lamp that showed the brother who had made him desolate. Like a blind man who believes there is a sun, yet cannot see it, he shook his head, let his arms drop nervously upon his knees, and sat there dumbly asking that question which many a soul whose faith is firmer fixed than his has asked in hours less dark than this—

"Where is God?" I saw the tide had turned, and strenuously tried to keep this rudderless lifeboat from slipping back into the whirlpool wherein it had been so nearly lost.

"I have listened to you, Robert; now hear me, and heed what I say, because my heart is full of pity for you, full of hope for your future, and a desire to help you now. I want you to go away from here, from the temptation of this place, and the sad thoughts that haunt it. You have conquered yourself once, and I honor you for it, because, the harder the battle, the more glorious the victory; but it is safer to put a greater distance between you and this man. I will write you letters, give you money, and send you to good old Massachusetts to begin your new life a freeman—yes, and a happy man; for when the captain is himself again, I will learn where Lucy is, and move heaven and earth to find and give her back to you. Will you do this, Robert?"

Slowly, very slowly, the answer came; for the purpose of a week, perhaps a year, was hard to relinquish in an hour.

"Yes, Ma'am, I will."

"Good! Now you are the man I thought you, and I'll work for you with all my heart. You need sleep, my poor fellow; go, and try to forget. The captain is still alive, and as yet you are spared the sin. No, don't look there; I'll care for him. Come, Robert, for Lucy's sake."

Thank Heaven for the immortality of love! for when all other means of salvation failed, a spark of this vital fire softened the man's iron will until a woman's hand could bend it. He let me take from him the key, let me draw him gently away and lead him to the solitude which now was the most healing balm I could bestow. Once in his little room, he fell down on his bed and lay there as if spent with the sharpest conflict of his life. I slipped the bolt across his door, and unlocked my own, flung up the window, steadied myself with a breath of air, then rushed to Doctor Franck. He came; and till dawn we worked together, saving one brother's life, and taking earnest thought how best to secure the other's liberty. When the sun came up as blithely as if it shone only upon happy homes, the Doctor went to Robert. For an hour I heard the murmur of their voices; once I caught the sound of heavy sobs, and for a time a reverent hush, as if in the silence that good man were ministering to soul as well as sense. When he departed he took Robert with him, pausing to tell me he should get him off as soon as possible, but not before we met again.

Nothing more was seen of them all day; another surgeon came to see the captain, and another attendant came to fill the empty place. I tried to rest, but could not, with the thought of poor Lucy tugging at my heart, and was soon back at my post again, anxiously hoping that my contraband had not been too hastily spirited away. Just as night fell there came a tap, and opening, I saw Robert literally "clothed and in his right mind." The Doctor had replaced the ragged suit with tidy garments, and no trace of that tempestuous night remained but deeper lines upon the forehead, and the docile look of a repentant child. He did not cross the threshold, did not offer me his hand—only took off his cap, saying, with a traitorous falter in his voice—

"God bless you, Ma'am! I'm goin'."

I put out both my hands, and held his fast.

"Good-bye, Robert! Keep up good heart, and when I come home to Massachusetts we'll meet in a happier place than this. Are you quite ready, quite comfortable for your journey?"

"Yes, Ma'am, Yes; the Doctor's fixed everything; I'm goin' with a friend of his; my papers are all right, an' I'm as happy as I can be till I find—"

He stopped there; then went on, with a glance into the room—

"I'm glad I didn't do it, an' I thank yer, Ma'am, fer hinderin' me—thank yer hearty; but I'm afraid I hate him jest the same."

Of course he did; and so did I; for these faulty hearts of ours cannot turn perfect in a night, but need frost and fire, wind and rain, to ripen and make them ready for the great harvest-home. Wishing to divert his mind, I put my poor mite into his hand, and, remembering the magic of a certain little book, I gave him mine, on whose dark cover whitely shone the Virgin Mother and the Child, the grand history of whose life the book contained. The money went into Robert's pocket with a grateful murmur, the book into his bosom with a long look and a tremulous—

"I never saw my baby, Ma'am."

I broke down then; and though my eyes were too dim to see, I felt the touch of lips upon my hands, heard the sound of departing feet, and knew my contraband was gone.

When one feels an intense dislike, the less one says about the subject of it the better; therefore I shall merely record that the captain lived—in time was exchanged; and that, whoever the other party was, I am convinced the Government got the best of the bargain. But long before this occurred, I had fulfilled my promise to Robert; for as soon as my patient recovered strength of memory enough to make his answer trustworthy, I asked, without any circumlocution—

"Captain Fairfax, where is Lucy?"

And too feeble to be angry, surprised, or insincere, he straightway answered—

"Dead, Miss Dane."

"And she killed herself, when you sold Bob?"

"How the Devil did you know that?" he muttered, with an expression half-remorseful, half-amazed; but I was satisfied, and said no more.

Of course, this went to Robert, waiting far away there in a lonely home—waiting, working, hoping for his Lucy. It almost broke my heart to do it; but delay was weak, deceit was wicked; so I sent the heavy tidings. And very soon the answer came—only three lines; but I felt that the sustaining power of the man's life was gone.

"I thought I'd never see her any more; I'm glad to know she's out of trouble. I thank yer, Ma'am; an' if they let us, I'll fight fer yer till I'm killed. Which I hope will be 'fore long."

Six months later he had his wish, and kept his word.

Every one knows the story of the attack on Fort Wagner; but we should not tire yet of recalling how our Fifty-Fourth, spent with three sleepless nights, a day's fast, and a march under the July sun, stormed the fort as night fell, facing death in many shapes, following their brave leaders through a fiery rain of shot and shell, fighting valiantly for "God and Governor Andrew,"—how the regiment that went into action seven hundred strong came out having had nearly half its number captured, killed, or wounded, leaving their young commander to be buried, like a chief of earlier times, with his body-guard around him, faithful to the death. Surely, the insult turns to honor, and the wide grave needs no monument but the heroism that consecrates it in our sight; surely, the hearts that held him nearest see through their tears a noble victory in the seeming sad defeat; and surely, God's benediction was bestowed, when this loyal soul answered, as Death called the roll, "Lord, here I am, with the brothers Thou hast given me!"

The future must show how well that fight was fought; for though Fort Wagner still defies us, public prejudice is down; and through the cannon smoke of that black night the manhood of the colored race shines before many eyes that would not see, rings in many ears that would not hear, wins many hearts that would not hitherto believe.

When the news came that we were needed, there was none so glad as I to leave teaching contrabands, the new work I had taken up, and go to nurse "our boys," as my dusky flock so proudly called the wounded of the Fifty-Fourth. Feeling more satisfaction, as I assumed my big apron and turned up my cuffs, than if dressing for the President's levee, I fell to work on board the hospital-ship in Hilton-Head harbor. The scene was most familiar, and yet strange; for only dark faces looked up at me from the pallets so thickly laid along the floor, and I missed the sharp accent of my Yankee boys in the slower, softer voices calling cheerily to one another, or answering my questions with a stout, "We'll never give it up, Ma'am, till the last Reb's dead," or, "If our people's free, we can afford to die."

Passing from bed to bed, intent on making one pair of hands do the work of three, at least, I gradually washed, fed, and bandaged my way down the long line of sable heroes, and coming to the very last, found that he was my contraband. So old, so worn, so deathly weak and wan, I never should have known him but for the deep scar on his cheek. That side lay uppermost, and caught my eye at once; but even then I doubted, such an awful change had come upon him, when, turning to the ticket just above his head, I saw the name, "Robert Dane." That both assured and touched me, for, remembering that he had no name, I knew that he had taken mine. I longed for him to speak to me, to tell how he had fared since I lost sight of him, and let me perform some little service for him in return for many he had done for me; but he seemed asleep; and as I stood re-living that strange night again, a bright lad, who lay next to him softly waving an old fan across both beds, looked up and said—

"I guess you know him, Ma'am?"

"You are right. Do you?"

"As much as any one was able to, Ma'am."

"Why do you say 'was,' as if the man were dead and gone?"

"I s'pose because I know he'll have to go. He's got a bad jab in the breast, an' is bleedin' inside, the Doctor says. He don't suffer any, only gets weaker 'n' weaker every minute. I've been fannin' him this long while, an' he's talked a little; but he don't know me now, so he's most gone, I guess."

There was so much sorrow and affection in the boy's face, that I remembered something, and asked, with redoubled interest—

"Are you the one that brought him off? I was told about a boy who nearly lost his life in saving that of his mate."

I dare say the young fellow blushed, as any modest lad might have done; I could not see it, but I heard the chuckle of satisfaction that escaped him, as he glanced from his shattered arm and bandaged side to the pale figure opposite.

"Lord, Ma'am, that's nothin'; we boys always stan' by one another, an' I warn't goin' to leave him to be tormented any more by them cussed Rebs. He's been a slave once, though he don't look half so much like it as me, an' was born in Boston."

He did not; for the speaker was as black as the ace of spades—being a sturdy specimen, the knave of clubs would perhaps be a fitter representative—but the dark freeman looked at the white slave with the pitiful, yet puzzled expression I have so often seen on the faces of our wisest men, when this tangled question of Slavery presents itself, asking to be cut or patiently undone.

"Tell me what you know of this man; for, even if he were awake, he is too weak to talk."

"I never saw him till I joined the regiment, an' no one 'peared to have got much out of him. He was a shut-up sort of feller, an' didn't seem to care for anything but gettin' at the Rebs. Some say he was the fust man of us that enlisted; I know he fretted till we were off, an' when we pitched into old Wagner, he fought like the Devil."

"Were you with him when he was wounded? How was it?"

"Yes, Ma'am. There was somethin' queer about it; for he 'peared to know the chap that killed him, an' the chap knew him. I don't dare to ask, but I rather guess one owned the other some time—for, when they clinched, the chap sung out, 'Bob!' an' Dane, 'Marster Ned!' Then they went at it."

I sat down suddenly, for the old anger and compassion struggled in my heart, and I both longed and feared to hear what was to follow.

"You see, when the Colonel—Lord keep an' send him back to us!—it a'n't certain yet, you know, Ma'am, though it's two days ago we lost him—well, when the Colonel shouted, 'Rush on, boys, rush on!' Dane tore away as if he was goin' to take the fort alone; I was next him, an' kept close as we went through the ditch an' up the wall. Hi! warn't that a rusher!" and the boy flung up his well arm with a whoop, as if the mere memory of that stirring moment came over him in a gust of irrepressible excitement.

"Were you afraid?" I said—asking the question women often put, and receiving the answer they seldom fail to get.

"No, Ma'am!"—emphasis on the "Ma'am,"—"I never thought of anything but the damn Rebs, that scalp, slash, an' cut our ears off, when they git us. I was bound to let daylight into one of 'em at least, an' I did. Hope he liked it!"

"It is evident that you did, and I don't blame you in the least. Now go on about Robert, for I should be at work."

"He was one of the fust up; I was just behind, an' though the whole thing happened in a minute. I remember how it was, for all I was yellin' an' knockin' round like mad. Just where we were, some sort of an officer was wavin' his sword an' cheerin' on his men; Dane saw him by a big flash that come by; he flung away his gun, give a leap, an' went at that feller as if he was Jeff, Beauregard, an' Lee, all in one. I scrabbled after as quick as I could, but was only up in time to see him git the sword straight through him an' drop into the ditch. You needn't ask what I did next, Ma'am, for I don't quite know myself; all I'm clear about is, that I managed somehow to pitch that Reb into the fort as dead as Moses, git hold of Dane, an' bring him off. Poor old feller! We said we went in to live or die; he said he went in to die, an' he's done it."

I had been intently watching the excited speaker; but as he regretfully added those last words I turned again, and Robert's eyes met mine—those melancholy eyes, so full of an intelligence that proved he had heard, remembered, and reflected with that preternatural power which often outlives all other faculties. He knew me, yet gave no greeting; was glad to see a woman's face, yet had no smile wherewith to welcome it; felt that he was dying, yet uttered no farewell. He was too far across the river to return or linger now; departing thought, strength, breath, were spent in one grateful look, one murmur of submission to the last pang he could ever feel. His lips moved, and, bending to them, a whisper chilled my cheek, as it shaped the broken words—

"I would have done it—but it's better so—I'm satisfied."

Ah! well he might be—for, as he turned his face from the shadow of the life that was, the sunshine of the life to be touched it with a beautiful content, and in the drawing of a breath my contraband found wife and home, eternal liberty and God.

Questions

1. Alcott writes: "He was more quadroon than mulatto, with Saxon features, Spanish complexion darkened by exposure, color in lips and cheek, waving hair, and an eye full of the passionate melancholy which in such men always seems to utter a mute protest against the broken law that doomed them at their birth." What might it mean when a reference is made to the "broken law that doomed them at their birth"?
2. When Alcott writes, "In an instant the man vanished and the slave appeared," what might this mean?
3. Robert says: "I half murdered him [. . .] ." What does that mean?
4. Alcott writes: "When one feels an intense dislike, the less one says about the subject of it the better [. . .] ." Do you agree?

5. Originally, why was Robert in the hospital with his brother?
6. Does it seem contrived or conceivable that Robert and his brother meet on the battlefield?
7. As the story progresses, it becomes clear that Robert is without a full name. However, at the story's end, he does seem to have a full name. Whose name does he adopt? What does this suggest about his new identity?

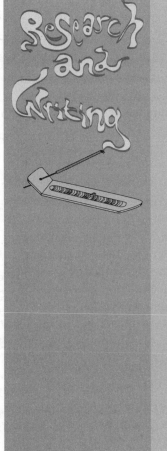

1. The term "passing" was sometimes applied to African-Americans who could pass for a color other than black. This is addressed in Nella Larsen's novel *Passing.* Is it addressed in *The Brothers?* Identify where it is addressed in *The Brothers,* and then note what the benefits and the consequences are to "passing." Compare and contrast these benefits and consequences with those presented in Nella Larsen's *Passing.*
2. Slavery still exists in the world today. Research this, and include in your research indentured servitude, sex slavery, and "legalized slavery." Construct an argument that revolves around slavery, and, in doing so, make reference to *The Brothers.*
3. In *The Brothers,* Robert is fighting for the 54th. While little is mentioned of the 54th in *The Brothers,* a film titled *Glory* bases its story on the African-American soldiers who composed the 54th Massachusetts Volunteer Regiment. Construct an argument that revolves around *The Brothers* and *Glory.* Also, consider doing some independent research, and consider examining Paul Lawrence Dunbar's *When Dey 'Listed Colored Soldiers.*
4. Throughout *The Brothers,* there are many religious references. In fact, it could be argued that Miss Dane keeps Robert from killing his brother by relying on religious references. While religion might be considered ubiquitous, it seems reasonable to suggest that when Africans were brought to America and labeled "slaves," they were without an allegiance to Christianity. However, over time many of these "slaves" became Christians. Research the role of Christianity in slaves' lives. If slaves were considered "chattel," and if they were not, by many, even considered human, how and why was Christianity promoted?

Edgar Allan Poe (1809–1849)

Sometimes likened to the Stephen King of the 19th century, Edgar Allan Poe is credited with starting the "dark tradition" in American Literature. Unfortunately, unlike King, Poe did not enjoy much fame and recognition for his contributions to the literary world. This may be what contributed to his depression, eventual alcoholism, and death, which occurred as he lay face down in the streets of Baltimore, Maryland. But as a former resident of Baltimore, it is no coincidence that Baltimore's football team, the Ravens, has the same name as one of Poe's most famous works.

The Pit and the Pendulum

1. The setting for this story is Toledo, Spain where the Spanish Inquisition had placed its central command for the past three centuries. This is where, historically, courtroom trials centering around the religious persecution of Jews, Muslims, and alleged heretics were conducted until 1808, the year in which Napolean Bonaparte attacked and captured Toledo.
2. For heightened effect, read this story slowly, by candlelight or flashlight, in a large, dark room.

The Pit and the Pendulum

Edgar Allan Poe

Impia tortorum longos hic turba furores

Sanguinis innocui, non satiata, aluit.

Sospite nunc patria, fracto nunc funeris antro,

Mors ubi dira fuit vita salusque patent.

(Quatrain composed for the gates of a market to he erected upon the site of the Jacobin Club House at Paris.)

I WAS sick—sick unto death with that long agony; and when they at length unbound me, and I was permitted to sit, I felt that my senses were leaving me. The sentence—the dread sentence of death—was the last of distinct accentuation which reached my ears. After that, the sound of the inquisitorial voices seemed merged in one dreamy indeterminate hum. It conveyed to my soul the idea of revolution—perhaps from its association in fancy with the burr of a mill wheel. This only for a brief period; for presently I heard no more. Yet, for a while, I saw; but with how terrible an exaggeration! I saw the lips of the black-robed judges. They appeared to me white—whiter than the sheet upon which I trace these words—and thin even to grotesqueness; thin with the intensity of their expression of firmness—of immoveable resolution—of stern contempt of human torture. I saw that the decrees of what to me was Fate, were still issuing from those lips. I saw them writhe with a deadly locution. I saw them fashion the syllables of my name; and I shuddered because no sound succeeded. I saw, too, for a few moments of delirious horror, the soft and nearly imperceptible waving of the sable draperies which enwrapped the walls of the apartment. And then my vision fell upon the seven tall candles upon the table. At first they wore the aspect of charity, and seemed white and slender angels who would save me; but then, all at once, there came a most deadly nausea over my spirit, and I felt every fibre in my frame thrill as if I had touched the wire of a galvanic battery, while the angel forms became meaningless spectres, with heads of flame, and I saw that from them there would be no help. And then there stole into my fancy, like a rich musical note, the thought of what sweet rest there must be in the grave. The thought came gently and stealthily, and it seemed long before it attained full appreciation; but just as my spirit came at length properly to feel and entertain it, the figures of the judges vanished, as if magically, from before me; the tall candles sank into nothingness; their flames went out utterly; the blackness of darkness supervened; all sensations appeared swallowed up in a mad rushing descent as of the soul into Hades. Then silence, and stillness, night were the universe.

I had swooned; but still will not say that all of consciousness was lost. What of it there remained I will not attempt to define, or even to describe; yet all was not lost. In the deepest slumber—no! In delirium—no! In a swoon—no! In death—no! even in the grave all is not lost. Else there is no immortality for man. Arousing from the most profound of slumbers, we break the gossamer web of some dream. Yet in a second afterward, (so frail may that web have been) we remember not that we have dreamed. In the return to life from the swoon there are two stages; first, that of the sense of mental or spiritual; secondly, that of the sense of physical, existence. It seems probable that if, upon reaching the second stage, we could recall the impressions of the first, we should find these impressions eloquent in memories of the gulf beyond. And that gulf is—what? How at least shall we distinguish its shadows from those of the tomb? But if the impressions of what I have termed the first stage, are not, at will, recalled, yet, after long interval, do they not come unbidden, while we marvel whence they come? He who has never swooned, is not he who finds strange palaces and wildly familiar faces in coals that glow; is not he who beholds floating in mid-air the sad visions that the many may not view; is not he who ponders over the perfume of some novel flower—is not he whose brain grows bewildered with the meaning of some musical cadence which has never before arrested his attention.

Amid frequent and thoughtful endeavors to remember; amid earnest struggles to regather some token of the state of seeming nothingness into which my soul had lapsed, there have been moments when I have dreamed of success; there have been brief, very brief periods when I have conjured up remembrances which the lucid reason of a later epoch assures me could have had reference only to that condition of seeming unconsciousness. These shadows of memory tell, indistinctly, of tall figures that lifted and bore me in silence down—down—still down— till a hideous dizziness oppressed me at the mere idea of the interminableness of the descent. They tell also of a vague horror at my heart, on account of that heart's unnatural stillness. Then comes a sense of sudden motionlessness throughout all things; as if those who bore me (a ghastly train!) had outrun, in their descent, the limits of the limitless, and paused from the wearisomeness of their toil. After this I call to mind flatness and dampness; and then all is madness—the madness of a memory which busies itself among forbidden things.

Very suddenly there came back to my soul motion and sound—the tumultuous motion of the heart, and, in my ears, the sound of its beating. Then a pause in which all is blank. Then again sound, and motion, and touch—a tingling sensation pervading my frame. Then the mere consciousness of existence, without thought—a condition which lasted long. Then, very suddenly, thought, and shuddering terror, and earnest endeavor to comprehend my true state. Then a strong desire to lapse into insensibility. Then a rushing revival of soul and a successful effort to move. And now a full memory of the trial, of the judges, of the sable draperies, of the sentence, of the sickness, of the swoon. Then entire forgetfulness of all that followed; of all that a later day and much earnestness of endeavor have enabled me vaguely to recall.

So far, I had not opened my eyes. I felt that I lay upon my back, unbound. I reached out my hand, and it fell heavily upon something damp and hard. There I suffered it to remain for many minutes, while I strove to imagine where and what I could be. I longed, yet dared not to employ my vision. I dreaded the first glance at objects around me. It was not that I feared to look upon things horrible, but that I grew aghast lest there should be nothing to see. At length, with a wild desperation at heart, I quickly unclosed my eyes. My worst thoughts, then, were confirmed. The blackness of eternal night encompassed me. I struggled for breath. The intensity of the darkness seemed to oppress and stifle me. The atmosphere was intolerably close. I still lay quietly, and made effort to exercise my reason. I brought to mind the inquisitorial proceedings, and attempted from that point to deduce my real condition. The sentence had passed; and it appeared to me that a very long interval of time had since elapsed. Yet not for a moment did I suppose myself actually dead. Such a supposition, notwithstanding what we read in fiction, is altogether inconsistent with real existence;—but where and in what state was I? The condemned to death, I knew, perished usually at the autos-da-fe, and one of these had been held on the very night of the day of my trial. Had I been remanded to my dungeon, to await the next sacrifice, which would not take place for many months? This I at once saw could not be. Victims had been in immediate demand. Moreover, my dungeon, as well as all the condemned cells at Toledo, had stone floors, and light was not altogether excluded.

A fearful idea now suddenly drove the blood in torrents upon my heart, and for a brief period, I once more relapsed into insensibility. Upon recovering, I at once started to my feet, trembling convulsively in every fibre. I thrust my arms wildly above and around me in all directions. I felt nothing; yet dreaded to move a step, lest I should be impeded by the walls of a tomb. Perspiration burst from every pore, and stood in cold big beads upon my forehead. The agony of suspense grew at length intolerable, and I cautiously moved forward, with my arms extended, and my eyes straining from their sockets, in the hope of catching some faint ray of light. I proceeded for many paces; but still all was blackness and vacancy. I breathed more freely. It seemed evident that mine was not, at least, the most hideous of fates.

And now, as I still continued to step cautiously onward, there came thronging upon my recollection a thousand vague rumors of the horrors of Toledo. Of the dungeons there had been strange things narrated—fables I had always deemed them—but yet strange, and too ghastly to repeat, save in a whisper. Was I left to perish of starvation in this subterranean world of darkness; or what fate, perhaps even more fearful, awaited me? That the result would be death, and a death of more than customary bitterness, I knew too well the character of my judges to doubt. The mode and the hour were all that occupied or distracted me.

My outstretched hands at length encountered some solid obstruction. It was a wall, seemingly of stone masonry—very smooth, slimy, and cold. I followed it up; stepping with all the careful distrust with which certain antique narratives had inspired me. This process, however, afforded me no means of ascertaining the dimensions of my dungeon; as I might make its circuit, and return to the point whence I set out, without being aware of the fact; so

perfectly uniform seemed the wall. I therefore sought the knife which had been in my pocket, when led into the inquisitorial chamber; but it was gone; my clothes had been exchanged for a wrapper of coarse serge. I had thought of forcing the blade in some minute crevice of the masonry, so as to identify my point of departure. The difficulty, nevertheless, was but trivial; although, in the disorder of my fancy, it seemed at first insuperable. I tore a part of the hem from the robe and placed the fragment at full length, and at right angles to the wall. In groping my way around the prison, I could not fail to encounter this rag upon completing the circuit. So, at least I thought: but I had not counted upon the extent of the dungeon, or upon my own weakness. The ground was moist and slippery. I staggered onward for some time, when I stumbled and fell. My excessive fatigue induced me to remain prostrate; and sleep soon overtook me as I lay.

Upon awaking, and stretching forth an arm, I found beside me a loaf and a pitcher with water. I was too much exhausted to reflect upon this circumstance, but ate and drank with avidity. Shortly afterward, I resumed my tour around the prison, and with much toil came at last upon the fragment of the serge. Up to the period when I fell I had counted fifty-two paces, and upon resuming my walk, I had counted forty-eight more;—when I arrived at the rag. There were in all, then, a hundred paces; and, admitting two paces to the yard, I presumed the dungeon to be fifty yards in circuit. I had met, however, with many angles in the wall, and thus I could form no guess at the shape of the vault; for vault I could not help supposing it to be.

I had little object—certainly no hope these researches; but a vague curiosity prompted me to continue them. Quitting the wall, I resolved to cross the area of the enclosure. At first I proceeded with extreme caution, for the floor, although seemingly of solid material, was treacherous with slime. At length, however, I took courage, and did not hesitate to step firmly; endeavoring to cross in as direct a line as possible. I had advanced some ten or twelve paces in this manner, when the remnant of the torn hem of my robe became entangled between my legs. I stepped on it, and fell violently on my face.

In the confusion attending my fall, I did not immediately apprehend a somewhat startling circumstance, which yet, in a few seconds afterward, and while I still lay prostrate, arrested my attention. It was this—my chin rested upon the floor of the prison, but my lips and the upper portion of my head, although seemingly at a less elevation than the chin, touched nothing. At the same time my forehead seemed bathed in a clammy vapor, and the peculiar smell of decayed fungus arose to my nostrils. I put forward my arm, and shuddered to find that I had fallen at the very brink of a circular pit, whose extent, of course, I had no means of ascertaining at the moment. Groping about the masonry just below the margin, I succeeded in dislodging a small fragment, and let it fall into the abyss. For many seconds I hearkened to its reverberations as it dashed against the sides of the chasm in its descent; at length there was a sullen plunge into water, succeeded by loud echoes. At the same moment there came a sound resembling the quick opening, and as rapid closing of a door overhead, while a faint gleam of light flashed suddenly through the gloom, and as suddenly faded away.

I saw clearly the doom which had been prepared for me, and congratulated myself upon the timely accident by which I had escaped. Another step before my fall, and the world had seen me no more. And the death just avoided, was of that very character which I had regarded as fabulous and frivolous in the tales respecting the Inquisition. To the victims of its tyranny, there was the choice of death with its direst physical agonies, or death with its most hideous moral horrors. I had been reserved for the latter. By long suffering my nerves had been unstrung, until I trembled at the sound of my own voice, and had become in every respect a fitting subject for the species of torture which awaited me.

Shaking in every limb, I groped my way back to the wall; resolving there to perish rather than risk the terrors of the wells, of which my imagination now pictured many in various positions about the dungeon. In other conditions of mind I might have had courage to end my misery at once by a plunge into one of these abysses; but now I was the veriest of cowards. Neither could I forget what I had read of these pits—that the sudden extinction of life formed no part of their most horrible plan.

Agitation of spirit kept me awake for many long hours; but at length I again slumbered. Upon arous-

ing, I found by my side, as before, a loaf and a pitcher of water. A burning thirst consumed me, and I emptied the vessel at a draught. It must have been drugged; for scarcely had I drunk, before I became irresistibly drowsy. A deep sleep fell upon me—a sleep like that of death. How long it lasted of course, I know not; but when, once again, I unclosed my eyes, the objects around me were visible. By a wild sulphurous lustre, the origin of which I could not at first determine, I was enabled to see the extent and aspect of the prison.

In its size I had been greatly mistaken. The whole circuit of its walls did not exceed twenty-five yards. For some minutes this fact occasioned me a world of vain trouble; vain indeed! for what could be of less importance, under the terrible circumstances which environed me, then the mere dimensions of my dungeon? But my soul took a wild interest in trifles, and I busied myself in endeavors to account for the error I had committed in my measurement. The truth at length flashed upon me. In my first attempt at exploration I had counted fifty-two paces, up to the period when I fell; I must then have been within a pace or two of the fragment of serge; in fact, I had nearly performed the circuit of the vault. I then slept, and upon awaking, I must have returned upon my steps—thus supposing the circuit nearly double what it actually was. My confusion of mind prevented me from observing that I began my tour with the wall to the left, and ended it with the wall to the right.

I had been deceived, too, in respect to the shape of the enclosure. In feeling my way I had found many angles, and thus deduced an idea of great irregularity; so potent is the effect of total darkness upon one arousing from lethargy or sleep! The angles were simply those of a few slight depressions, or niches, at odd intervals. The general shape of the prison was square. What I had taken for masonry seemed now to be iron, or some other metal, in huge plates, whose sutures or joints occasioned the depression. The entire surface of this metallic enclosure was rudely daubed in all the hideous and repulsive devices to which the charnel superstition of the monks has given rise. The figures of fiends in aspects of menace, with skeleton forms, and other more really fearful images, overspread and disfigured the walls. I observed that the outlines of these monstrosities were sufficiently distinct, but that the colors seemed faded and blurred, as if from the effects of a damp atmosphere. I now noticed the floor, too, which was of stone. In the centre yawned the circular pit from whose jaws I had escaped; but it was the only one in the dungeon.

All this I saw indistinctly and by much effort: for my personal condition had been greatly changed during slumber. I now lay upon my back, and at full length, on a species of low framework of wood. To this I was securely bound by a long strap resembling a surcingle. It passed in many convolutions about my limbs and body, leaving at liberty only my head, and my left arm to such extent that I could, by dint of much exertion, supply myself with food from an earthen dish which lay by my side on the floor. I saw, to my horror, that the pitcher had been removed. I say to my horror; for I was consumed with intolerable thirst. This thirst it appeared to be the design of my persecutors to stimulate: for the food in the dish was meat pungently seasoned.

Looking upward, I surveyed the ceiling of my prison. It was some thirty or forty feet overhead, and constructed much as the side walls. In one of its panels a very singular figure riveted my whole attention. It was the painted figure of Time as he is commonly represented, save that, in lieu of a scythe, he held what, at a casual glance, I supposed to be the pictured image of a huge pendulum such as we see on antique clocks. There was something, however, in the appearance of this machine which caused me to regard it more attentively. While I gazed directly upward at it (for its position was immediately over my own) I fancied that I saw it in motion. In an instant afterward the fancy was confirmed. Its sweep was brief, and of course slow. I watched it for some minutes, somewhat in fear, but more in wonder. Wearied at length with observing its dull movement, I turned my eyes upon the other objects in the cell.

A slight noise attracted my notice, and, looking to the floor, I saw several enormous rats traversing it. They had issued from the well, which lay just within view to my right. Even then, while I gazed, they came up in troops, hurriedly, with ravenous eyes, allured by the scent of the meat. From this it required much effort and attention to scare them away.

It might have been half an hour, perhaps even an hour, (for I could take but imperfect note of time) before I again cast my eyes upward. What I then saw confounded and amazed me. The sweep of the pendulum had increased in extent by nearly a yard. As a natural consequence, its velocity was also much greater. But what mainly disturbed me was the idea that had perceptibly descended. I now observed—with what horror it is needless to say—that its nether extremity was formed of a crescent of glittering steel, about a foot in length from horn to horn; the horns upward, and the under edge evidently as keen as that of a razor. Like a razor also, it seemed massy and heavy, tapering from the edge into a solid and broad structure above. It was appended to a weighty rod of brass, and the whole hissed as it swung through the air.

I could no longer doubt the doom prepared for me by monkish ingenuity in torture. My cognizance of the pit had become known to the inquisitorial agents—the pit whose horrors had been destined for so bold a recusant as myself—the pit, typical of hell, and regarded by rumor as the Ultima Thule of all their punishments. The plunge into this pit I had avoided by the merest of accidents, I knew that surprise, or entrapment into torment, formed an important portion of all the grotesquerie of these dungeon deaths. Having failed to fall, it was no part of the demon plan to hurl me into the abyss; and thus (there being no alternative) a different and a milder destruction awaited me. Milder! I half smiled in my agony as I thought of such application of such a term.

What boots it to tell of the long, long hours of horror more than mortal, during which I counted the rushing vibrations of the steel! Inch by inch—line by line—with a descent only appreciable at intervals that seemed ages—down and still down it came! Days passed—it might have been that many days passed—ere it swept so closely over me as to fan me with its acrid breath. The odor of the sharp steel forced itself into my nostrils. I prayed—I wearied heaven with my prayer for its more speedy descent. I grew frantically mad, and struggled to force myself upward against the sweep of the fearful scimitar. And then I fell suddenly calm, and lay smiling at the glittering death, as a child at some rare bauble.

There was another interval of utter insensibility; it was brief; for, upon again lapsing into life there had been no perceptible descent in the pendulum. But it might have been long; for I knew there were demons who took note of my swoon, and who could have arrested the vibration at pleasure. Upon my recovery, too, I felt very—oh, inexpressibly sick and weak, as if through long inanition. Even amid the agonies of that period, the human nature craved food. With painful effort I outstretched my left arm as far as my bonds permitted, and took possession of the small remnant which had been spared me by the rats. As I put a portion of it within my lips, there rushed to my mind a half formed thought of joy—of hope. Yet what business had I with hope? It was, as I say, a half formed thought—man has many such which are never completed. I felt that it was of joy—of hope; but felt also that it had perished in its formation. In vain I struggled to perfect—to regain it. Long suffering had nearly annihilated all my ordinary powers of mind. I was an imbecile—an idiot.

The vibration of the pendulum was at right angles to my length. I saw that the crescent was designed to cross the region of the heart. It would fray the serge of my robe—it would return and repeat its operations—again—and again. Notwithstanding terrifically wide sweep (some thirty feet or more) and the hissing vigor of its descent, sufficient to sunder these very walls of iron, still the fraying of my robe would be all that, for several minutes, it would accomplish. And at this thought I paused. I dared not go farther than this reflection. I dwelt upon it with a pertinacity of attention—as if, in so dwelling, I could arrest here the descent of the steel. I forced myself to ponder upon the sound of the crescent as it should pass across the garment—upon the peculiar thrilling sensation which the friction of cloth produces on the nerves. I pondered upon all this frivolity until my teeth were on edge.

Down—steadily down it crept. I took a frenzied pleasure in contrasting its downward with its lateral velocity. To the right—to the left—far and wide—with the shriek of a damned spirit; to my heart with the stealthy pace of the tiger! I alternately laughed and howled as the one or the other idea grew predominant.

Down—certainly, relentlessly down! It vibrated within three inches of my bosom! I struggled violently, furiously, to free my left arm. This was free only from the elbow to the hand. I could reach the latter, from the platter beside me, to my mouth, with great effort, but no farther. Could I have broken the fastenings above the elbow, I would have seized and attempted to arrest the pendulum. I might as well have attempted to arrest an avalanche!

Down—still unceasingly—still inevitably down! I gasped and struggled at each vibration. I shrunk convulsively at its every sweep. My eyes followed its outward or upward whirls with the eagerness of the most unmeaning despair; they closed themselves spasmodically at the descent, although death would have been a relief, oh! how unspeakable! Still I quivered in every nerve to think how slight a sinking of the machinery would precipitate that keen, glistening axe upon my bosom. It was hope that prompted the nerve to quiver—the frame to shrink. It was hope—the hope that triumphs on the rack—that whispers to the death-condemned even in the dungeons of the Inquisition.

I saw that some ten or twelve vibrations would bring the steel in actual contact with my robe, and with this observation there suddenly came over my spirit all the keen, collected calmness of despair. For the first time during many hours—or perhaps days—I thought. It now occurred to me that the bandage, or surcingle, which enveloped me, was unique. I was tied by no separate cord. The first stroke of the razorlike crescent athwart any portion of the band, would so detach it that it might be unwound from my person by means of my left hand. But how fearful, in that case, the proximity of the steel! The result of the slightest struggle how deadly! Was it likely, moreover, that the minions of the torturer had not foreseen and provided for this possibility! Was it probable that the bandage crossed my bosom in the track of the pendulum? Dreading to find my faint, and, as it seemed, in last hope frustrated, I so far elevated my head as to obtain a distinct view of my breast. The surcingle enveloped my limbs and body close in all directions—save in the path of the destroying crescent.

Scarcely had I dropped my head back into its original position, when there flashed upon my mind what I cannot better describe than as the unformed half of that idea of deliverance to which I have previously alluded, and of which a moiety only floated indeterminately through my brain when I raised food to my burning lips. The whole thought was now present—feeble, scarcely sane, scarcely definite,—but still entire. I proceeded at once, with the nervous energy of despair, to attempt its execution.

For many hours the immediate vicinity of the low framework upon which I lay, had been literally swarming with rats. They were wild, bold, ravenous; their red eyes glaring upon me as if they waited but for motionlessness on my part to make me their prey. "To what food," I thought, "have they been accustomed in the well?"

They had devoured, in spite of all my efforts to prevent them, all but a small remnant of the contents of the dish. I had fallen into an habitual see-saw, or wave of the hand about the platter: and, at length, the unconscious uniformity of the movement deprived it of effect. In their voracity the vermin frequently fastened their sharp fangs in my fingers. With the particles of the oily and spicy viand which now remained, I thoroughly rubbed the bandage wherever I could reach it; then, raising my hand from the floor, I lay breathlessly still.

At first the ravenous animals were startled and terrified at the change—at the cessation of movement. They shrank alarmedly back; many sought the well. But this was only for a moment. I had not counted in vain upon their voracity. Observing that I remained without motion, one or two of the boldest leaped upon the frame-work, and smelt at the surcingle. This seemed the signal for a general rush. Forth from the well they hurried in fresh troops. They clung to the wood—they overran it, and leaped in hundreds upon my person. The measured movement of the pendulum disturbed them not at all. Avoiding its strokes they busied themselves with the anointed bandage. They pressed—they swarmed upon me in ever accumulating heaps. They writhed upon my throat; their cold lips sought my own; I was half stifled by their thronging pressure; disgust, for which the world has no name, swelled my bosom, and chilled, with a heavy clamminess, my heart. Yet one minute, and I felt that the struggle would be over. Plainly I perceived the loosening of the bandage. I knew that in more than one place it must be already severed. With a more than human resolution I lay still.

Nor had I erred in my calculations—nor had I endured in vain. I at length felt that I was free. The surcingle hung in ribands from my body. But the stroke of the pendulum already pressed upon my bosom. It had divided the serge of the robe. It had cut through the linen beneath. Twice again it swung, and a sharp sense of pain shot through every nerve. But the moment of escape had arrived. At a wave of my hand my deliverers hurried tumultuously away. With a steady movement—cautious, sidelong, shrinking, and slow—I slid from the embrace of the bandage and beyond the reach of the scimitar. For the moment, at least, I was free.

Free!—and in the grasp of the Inquisition! I had scarcely stepped from my wooden bed of horror upon the stone floor of the prison, when the motion of the hellish machine ceased and I beheld it drawn up, by some invisible force, through the ceiling. This was a lesson which I took desperately to heart. My every motion was undoubtedly watched. Free!—I had but escaped death in one form of agony, to be delivered unto worse than death in some other. With that thought I rolled my eyes nervously around on the barriers of iron that hemmed me in. Something unusual—some change which, at first, I could not appreciate distinctly—it was obvious, had taken place in the apartment. For many minutes of a dreamy and trembling abstraction, I busied myself in vain, unconnected conjecture. During this period, I became aware, for the first time, of the origin of the sulphurous light which illumined the cell. It proceeded from a fissure, about half an inch in width, extending entirely around the prison at the base of the walls, which thus appeared, and were, completely separated from the floor. I endeavored, but of course in vain, to look through the aperture.

As I arose from the attempt, the mystery of the alteration in the chamber broke at once upon my understanding. I have observed that, although the outlines of the figures upon the walls were sufficiently distinct, yet the colors seemed blurred and indefinite. These colors had now assumed, and were momentarily assuming, a startling and most intense brilliancy, that gave to the spectral and fiendish portraitures an aspect that might have thrilled even firmer nerves than my own. Demon eyes, of a wild and ghastly vivacity, glared upon me in a thousand directions, where none had been visible before, and gleamed with the lurid lustre of a fire that I could not force my imagination to regard as unreal.

Unreal!—Even while I breathed there came to my nostrils the breath of the vapour of heated iron! A suffocating odour pervaded the prison! A deeper glow settled each moment in the eyes that glared at my agonies! A richer tint of crimson diffused itself over the pictured horrors of blood. I panted! I gasped for breath! There could be no doubt of the design of my tormentors—oh! most unrelenting! oh! most demoniac of men! I shrank from the glowing metal to the centre of the cell. Amid the thought of the fiery destruction that impended, the idea of the coolness of the well came over my soul like balm. I rushed to its deadly brink. I threw my straining vision below. The glare from the enkindled roof illumined its inmost recesses. Yet, for a wild moment, did my spirit refuse to comprehend the meaning of what I saw. At length it forced—it wrestled its way into my soul—it burned itself in upon my shuddering reason.—Oh! for a voice to speak!—oh! horror!—oh! any horror but this! With a shriek, I rushed from the margin, and buried my face in my hands—weeping bitterly.

The heat rapidly increased, and once again I looked up, shuddering as with a fit of the ague. There had been a second change in the cell—and now the change was obviously in the form. As before, it was in vain that I, at first, endeavoured to appreciate or understand what was taking place. But not long was I left in doubt. The Inquisitorial vengeance had been hurried by my two-fold escape, and there was to be no more dallying with the King of Terrors. The room had been square. I saw that two of its iron angles were now acute—two, consequently, obtuse. The fearful difference quickly increased with a low rumbling or moaning sound. In an instant the apartment had shifted its form into that of a lozenge. But the alteration stopped not here—I neither hoped nor desired it to stop. I could have clasped the red walls to my bosom as a garment of eternal peace. "Death," I said, "any death but that of the pit!" Fool! might I have not known that into the pit it was the object of the burning iron to urge me? Could I resist its glow? or, if even that, could I withstand its pressure? And now, flatter and flatter grew the lozenge, with a rapidity that left me no time for contemplation. Its centre, and of course, its greatest width, came just over the yawning gulf. I shrank back—but the closing walls pressed me resistlessly onward. At length for my seared and writhing body there was no longer an inch of foothold on the firm floor of the prison. I struggled no more, but the agony of my soul found vent in one loud, long, and final scream of despair. I felt that I tottered upon the brink—I averted my eyes—

There was a discordant hum of human voices! There was a loud blast as of many trumpets! There was a harsh grating as of a thousand thunders! The fiery walls rushed back! An outstretched arm caught my own as I fell, fainting, into the abyss. It was that of General Lasalle. The French army had entered Toledo. The Inquisition was in the hands of its enemies.

Questions

1. "Lasalle" means "the room" in French. What is the relevance of this in *The Pit and the Pendulum?*
2. While it appears that General Lasalle saved the narrator, can his survival be attributed to anything else?
3. The narrator begins the story with "I WAS sick [. . .]." If we are to assume that this sickness is one of a mental nature, should we find the narrator's story reliable? In other words, what exists in the story to suggest that it is either believable or, alas, unbelievable?
4. What is the narrator's gender?

1. Among Poe's short stories, *The Pit and the Pendulum* is interesting, for its main character employs hope. Arguably, it is his hope for survival that keeps him from perishing. Examine the presence of hope in other short stories by Poe. While the examples may not be as explicit as those in *The Pit and the Pendulum,* use these examples to construct an argument regarding the presence of hope in Poe's short stories.

2. *The Pit and the Pendulum* centers around a man condemned to death. This is similar to Ambrose Bierce's *An Occurrence at Owl Creek Bridge.* Identify various arguments in these two stories, and then compare and contrast them with the hopes of gaining insight into the individual psyche of the condemned.

3. Examine the presence of symbols in the works of Edgar Allan Poe. In *The Pit and the Pendulum,* for instance, symbols might consist of lips, rats, a clock, and a pit. In *The Tell-Tale Heart,* one symbol might be the old man's eye. Identify various symbols in Poe's works, showing what they symbolize and how they help advance his stories.

4. Research the evolution of torture. Attempt to identify various motivations for the tools, mechanisms, and techniques of which many have been unfortunate recipients. Attempt to trace this evolution to the 21st century, constructing an argument that addresses the value of torture.

III.
19th Century American Essays

Essays are supposed to be non-fiction, but that does not mean they are devoid of metaphor and simile, alliteration and allusion, and the many things that make poetry and short-story writing so enjoyable. Essays often include these elements, but they also rely heavily on various appeals, such as logical appeals, emotional appeals, and ethical appeals. Also, unlike short stories or poems, essays are often less reliant on implicit arguments. In other words, essays often attempt to advance an explicitly-stated argument, referred to by some as a thesis statement, and referred to by others (those well-versed in formal argumentation) as a claim. Further, it is common to find one of three claims in an essay: a claim of fact (this is a statement attempting to demonstrate that something is, indeed, factual or true), a claim of policy (this is a statement attempting to show that something should be done), or a claim of value (this is a statement attempting to show that something is right or wrong). Sometimes, as is the case with essayists like Ralph Waldo Emerson or Henry David Thoreau, their arguments attempt to amalgamate all three claims. Such argumentative orgies can be delightful or discombobulating, depending on the reader's reception of the writer's ideas.

Something else that essayists often deem integral to their essay's development is an attempt at refuting the opposition. Naturally, an argument should have at least two sides and, thus, opposition should exist. In attempting to refute the opposition, the discerning reader will often see how the essayist has employed the following three steps: (Step 1) Address the opposition. (Step 2) Identify with the opposition. (Step 3) Refute the opposition.

When the aforementioned steps are implemented effectively, it should become evident that the essayist may, in fact, be more familiar with her opposition's contention than she is with her own.

And remember, if the essayist truly wishes to persuade her readers, she should not simply "preach to the choir," for the "choir" already supports her argument. Instead, she must address her opposition. And she must attempt to identify with her opposition's objections. And then, somehow, she must provide new information that somehow acts as a counterargument in hopes of getting the opposition to reconsider its contention.

Finally, in essays it is common to find what William Golding, in his essay *Thinking as a Hobby*, referred to as Grade One, Grade Two, and Grade Three Thinking. In essence, Grade-One Thinkers offer solutions. Grade-Two Thinkers detect contradictions. And Grade-Three Thinkers feel as opposed to think. Indeed, there is value to an essay that focuses on any of the three Grades of Thinking. In the end, however, it seems that emotional appeals can only bring the reader so far. It also seems that after plethoric contradictions have been detected, the engaged reader will demand more. Fortunately, this is where the Grade-One Thinker should make an appearance, offering solutions to the problems that have already been introduced and established. Look for these three grades of thinking, observing how the implementation of each one tends to take the essayist's argument in a different direction.

William Apess (1798–1839)

William Apess is known as the author of one of the earliest published writings by a Native American. The autobiographical work, *A Son of the Forest,* details his early life as the descendant of Pequot Indians and alcoholic grandparents, who severely beat him until he was sold as an indentured laborer at four or five years of age to his master who, fortunately, allowed him to attend school for six years. While this constituted his entire formal education, he eventually became an author, a Methodist minister, and a political activist. Little is known of Apess, but one thing seems certain: given the subjects of his discourse, he believed in bringing attention to social and political inequality, speaking out against racial prejudice, and the rights of minorities.

An Indian Looking-Glass for the White Man

1. Much credence is given to the power of the spoken word in native cultures. Consider reading parts of this essay aloud in hopes of hearing it as Apess may have intended.
2. Apess' ideas may not be considered novel today. But in 1833, when this essay was printed, consider the war that Apess was beginning to wage. Specifically, observe how he uses the Bible to support his argument. Consider the notion of a "savage" making an argument for equality by citing John, St. Peter, and Jesus Christ.

An Indian Looking-Glass for the White Man

William Apess

Having a desire to place a few things before my fellow creatures who are traveling with me to the grave, and to that God who is the maker and preserver both of the white man and the Indian, whose abilities are the same and who are to be judged by one God, who will show no favor to outward appearances but will judge righteousness. Now I ask if degradation has not been heaped long enough upon the Indians? And if so, can there not be a compromise? Is it right to hold and promote prejudices? If not, why not put them all away? I mean here, among those who are civilized. It may be that many are ignorant of the situation of many of my brethren within the limits of New England. Let me for a few moments turn your attention to the reservations in the different states of New England, and, with but few exceptions, we shall find them as follows: the most mean, abject, miserable race of beings in the world—a complete place of prodigality and prostitution.

Another reason is because those men who are Agents, many of them are unfaithful and care not whether the Indians live or die; they are much imposed upon by their neighbors, who have no principles. They would think it no crime to go upon Indian lands and cut and carry off their most valuable timber, or anything else they chose; and I doubt not but they think it clear gain. Another reason is because they have no education to take care of themselves; if they had, I would risk them to take care of their own property.

Now I will ask if the Indians are not called the most ingenious people among us. And are they not said to be men of talents? And I would ask: Could there be a more efficient way to distress and murder them by inches than the way they have taken? And there is no people in the world but who may be destroyed in the same way. Now, if these people are what they are held up in our view to be, I would take the liberty to ask why they are not brought forward and pains taken to educate them, to give them all a common education, and those of the brightest and first-rate talents put forward and held up to office. Perhaps some unholy, unprincipled men would cry out, "The skin was not good enough, but stop, friends—I am not talking about the skin but about principles. I would ask if there cannot be as good feelings and principles under a red skin as there can be under a white. And let me ask: Is it not on the account of a bad principle that we who are red children have had to suffer so much as we have? And let me ask: Did not this bad principle proceed from the whites or their forefathers? And I would ask: Is it worthwhile to nourish it any longer? If not, then let us have a change, although some men no doubt will spout their corrupt principles against it, that are in the halls of legislation and elsewhere. But I presume this kind of talk will seem surprising and horrible. I do not see why it should so long as they (the whites) say that they think as much of us as they do of themselves."

This I have heard repeatedly, from the most respectable gentlemen and ladies—and having heard so much precept, I should now wish to see the example. And I would ask who has a better right to look for these things than the naturalist himself—the candid man would say none.

I know that many say that they are willing, perhaps the majority of the people, that we should enjoy our rights and privileges as they do. If so, I would ask, Why are not we protected in our persons and property throughout the Union? Is is not because there reigns in the breast of many who are leaders a most unrighteous, unbecoming, and impure black principle, and as corrupt and unholy as it can be—while these very same unfeeling, self-esteemed characters pretend to take the skin as a pretext to keep us from our unalienable and lawful rights? I would ask you if you would like to be disfranchised from all your rights, merely because your skin is white, and for no other crime. I'll venture to say, these very characters who hold the skin to be such a barrier in the way would be the first to cry out, "Injustice! awful injustice!"

But, reader, I acknowledge that this is a confused world, and I am not seeking for office, but merely placing before you the black inconsistency that you place before me—which is ten times blacker than any skin that you will find in the universe. And now let me exhort you to do away that principle, as it appears ten times worse in the sight of God and candid men than skins of color—more disgraceful than all the skins that Jehovah ever made. If black or red skins or any other skin of color is disgraceful to God, it appears that he has disgraced himself a great deal—for he has made fifteen colored people to one white and placed them here upon this earth.

Now let me ask you, white man, if it is a disgrace to eat, drink, and sleep with the image of God, or sit, or walk and talk with them. Or have you the folly to think that the white man, being one in fifteen or sixteen, are the only beloved images of God? Assemble all nations together in your imagination, and then let the whites be seated among them, and then let us look for the whites, and I doubt not it would be hard finding them; for to the rest of the nations, they are still but a handful. Now suppose these skins were put together, and each skin had its national crimes written upon it—which skin do you think would have the greatest? I will ask one question more. Can you charge the Indians with robbing a nation almost of their whole continent, and murdering their women and children, and then depriving the remainder of their lawful rights, that nature and God require them to have? And to cap the climax, rob another nation to till their grounds and welter out their days under the lash with hunger and fatigue under the scorching rays of a burning sun? I should look at all the skins, and I know that when I cast my eye upon that white skin, and if I saw those crimes written upon it, I should enter my protest against it immediately and cleave to that which is more honorable. And I can tell you that I am satisfied with the manner of my creation, fully—whether other are or not.

But we will strive to penetrate more fully in to the conduct of those who profess to have pure principles and who tell us to follow Jesus Christ and imitate him and have his Spirit. Let us see if they come anywhere near him and his ancient disciples. The first thing we are to look at are his precepts, of which we will mention a few. "Thou shalt love the Lord thy God with all thy heart, with all thy soul, with all thy mind, and with all thy strength. The second is like unto it. Thou shalt love thy neighbor as thyself. On these two precepts hang all the law and the prophets"

(Matthew 22.37, 38, 39, 40). "By this shall all men know that they are my disciples, if ye have love one to another" (John 13.35). Our Lord left his special command with his followers, that they should love one another.

Again, John in his Epistles says, "He who loveth God loveth his brother also" (1 John 4.21). "Let us not love in word but in deed" (1 John 3.18). "Let your love be without dissimulation. See that ye love one another with a pure heart fervently" (1 Peter 1.22). "If any man say, I love God, and hateth his brother, he is a liar" (1 John 4.20). "Whosoever hateth his brother is a murderer, and no murderer hath eternal life abiding in him" (1 John 3.15). The first thing that takes our attention is the saying of Jesus, "Thou shalt love," etc. The first question I would ask my brethren in the ministry, as well as that of the membership: What is love, or its effects? Now, if they who teach are not essentially affected with pure love, the love of God, how can they teach as they ought? Again, the holy teachers of old said, "Now if any man have not the spirit of Christ, he is none of his" (Romans 8.9). Now, my brethren in the ministry, let me ask you a few sincere questions. Did you ever hear or read of Christ teaching his disciples that they ought to despise one because his skin was different from theirs? Jesus Christ being a Jew, and those of his Apostles certainly were not whites—and did not he who completed the plan of salvation complete it for the whites as well as for the Jews, and others? And were not the whites the most degraded people on the earth at that time? And none were more so, for they sacrificed their children to dumb idols! And did not St. Paul labor more abundantly for building up a Christian nation among you than any of the Apostles? And you know as well as I that you are not indebted to a principle beneath a white skin for your religious services but to a colored one.

What then is the matter now? Is not religion the same now under a colored skin as it ever was? If so, I would ask, why is not a man of color respected? You may say, as many say, we have white men enough. But was this the spirit of Christ and his Apostles? If it had been, there would not have been one white preacher in the world—for Jesus Christ never would have imparted his grace or word to them, for he could forever have withheld it from them. But we find that Jesus Christ and his Apostles never looked at the outward appearances. Jesus in particular looked at the hearts, and his Apostles through him, being discerners of the spirit, looked at their fruit without any regard to the skin, color, or nation; as St. Paul himself speaks, "Where there it neither Greek nor Jew, circumcision nor uncircumcision, Barbarian nor Scythian, bond nor free—but Christ is all, and in all" (Collossians 3.11). If you can find a spirit like Jesus Christ and his Apostles prevailing now in any of the white congregations, I should like to know it. I ask: Is it not the case that everybody that is not white is treated with contempt and counted as barbarians? And I ask if the word of God justifies the white man in so doing. When the prophets prophesied, of whom did they speak? When they spoke of heathens, was it not the whites and others who were counted Gentiles? And I ask if all nations with the exception of the Jews were not counted heathens. And according to the writings of some, it could not mean the Indians, for they are counted Jews. And now I would ask: Why is all this distinction made among these Christian societies? I would ask: What is all this ado about missionary societies, if it be not to Christianize those who are not Christians? And what is it for? To degrade them worse, to bring them into society where they must welter out their days in disgrace merely because their skin is of a different complexion. What folly it is to try to make the state of human society worse than it is. How astonished some may be at this—but let me ask: Is it not so? Let me refer to the churches only. And, my brethren, is there any agreement? Do brethren and sisters love one another? Do they not rather hate one another? Outward forms and ceremonies, the lusts of the flesh, the lusts of the eye, and pride of life is of more value to many professors than the love of God shed abroad in their hearts, or an attachment to his altar, to his ordinances, or to his children. But you may ask: Who are the children of God? Perhaps you may say, none but white. If so, the word of the Lord is not true.

I will refer you to St. Peter's precepts (Acts 10): "God is no respecter of persons," etc. Now if this is the case, my white brother, what better are you than God? And if no better, why do you, who profess his Gospel and to have his spirit, act so contrary to it? Let me ask why the men of a different skin are so despised. Why are not they educated and placed in your

pulpits? I ask if his services well performed are not as good as if a white man performed them. I ask if a marriage or a funeral ceremony or the ordinance of the Lord's house would not be as acceptable in the sight of God as though he was white. And if so, why is it not to you? I ask again: Why is it not as acceptable to have men to exercise their office in one place as well as in another? Perhaps you will say that if we admit you to all of these privileges you will want more. I expect that I can guess what that is—Why, say you, there would be intermarriages. How that would be I am not able to say—and if it should be, it would be nothing strange or new to me; for I can assure you that I know a great many that have intermarried, both of the whites and the Indians—and many are their sons and daughters and people, too, of the first respectability. And I could point to some in the famous city of Boston and elsewhere. You may look now at the disgraceful act in the statute law passed by the legislature of Massachusetts, and behold the fifty-pound fine levied upon any clergyman or justice of the peace that dare to encourage the laws of God and nature by a legitimate union in holy wedlock between the Indians and whites. I would ask how this looks to your lawmakers. I would ask if this corresponds with your sayings—that you think as much of the Indians as you do of the whites. I do not wonder that you blush, many of you, while you read; for many have broken the ill-fated laws made by man to hedge up the laws of God and nature. I would ask if they who have made the law have not broken it—but there is no other state in New England that has this law but Massachusetts; and I think, as many of you do not, that you have done yourselves no credit.

But as I am not looking for a wife, having one of the finest cast, as you no doubt would understand while you read her experience and travail of soul in the way to heaven, you will see that it is not my object. And if I had none, I should not want anyone to take my right from me and choose a wife for me; for I think that I or any of my brethren have a right to choose a wife for themselves as well as the whites—and as the whites have taken the liberty to choose my brethren, the Indians, hundreds and thousands of them, as partners in life, I believe the Indians have as much right to choose their partners among the whites if they wish. I would ask you if you can see anything inconsistent in your conduct and talk about the Indians. And if you do, I hope you will try to become more consistent. Now, if the Lord Jesus Christ, who is counted by all to be a Jew—and it is well known that the Jews are a colored people, especially those living in the East, where Christ was born—and if he should appear among us, would he not be shut out of doors by many, very quickly? And by those too who profess religion?

By what you read, you may learn how deep your principles are. I should say they were skin-deep. I should not wonder if some of the most selfish and ignorant would spout a charge of their principles now and then at me. But I would ask: How are you to love your neighbors as yourself? Is it to cheat them? Is it to wrong them in anything? Now, to cheat them out of any of their rights is robbery. And I ask: Can you deny that you are not robbing the Indians daily, and many others? But at last you may think I am what is called a hard and uncharitable man. But not so. I believe there are many who would not hesitate to advo-cate our cause; and those too who are men of fame and respectability—as well as ladies of honor and virtue. There is a Webster, an Everett, and a Wirt, and many others who are distinguished characters—besides a host of my fellow citizens, who advocate our cause daily. And how I congratulate such noble spirits—how they are to be prized and valued; for they are well calculated to promote the happiness of mankind. They well know that man was made for society, and not for hissing-stocks and outcasts. And when such a principle as this lies within the hearts of men, how much it is like its God—and how it honors its Maker—and how it imitates the feelings of the Good Samaritan, that had his wounds bound up, who had been among thieves and robbers.

Do not get tired, ye noble-hearted—only think how many poor Indians want their wounds done up daily; the Lord will reward you, and pray you stop not till this tree of distinction shall be leveled to the earth, and the mantle of prejudice torn from every American heart—then shall peace pervade the Union.

Questions

1. Apess writes: "Now I ask if degradation has not been heaped long enough upon the Indians?" What is the degradation that he is referring to?

2. Apess writes: "But, reader, I acknowledge that this is a confused world, and I am not seeking for office, but merely placing before you the black inconsistency that you place before me—which is ten times blacker than any skin that you will find in the universe." Is Apess relying on more than one meaning of "black"? Further, when he argues that "the black inconsistency that you place before [him] [. . .] is ten times blacker [. . .]," what might he mean? How can something be "ten times blacker"?

3. This essay is titled *An Indian's Looking-Glass for the White Man*. Why might this title be appropriate?

4. Apess writes: "And you know as well as I that you are not indebted to a principle beneath a white skin for your religious services but to a colored one." What might this mean? How does this help advance Apess' argument?

5. Apess engages in some deductive reasoning to eventually conclude that "[. . .] the word of the Lord is not true." What is this reasoning? Further, does it seem reasonable?

6. Toward the end of his essay, Apess writes: "By what you read, you may learn how deep your principles are. I should say they were skin-deep." Here, is Apess attacking the reader?

7. Apess refers to a "tree of distinction" when writing: "[. . .] and pray you stop not till this tree of distinction shall be leveled to the earth [. . .]." What is this "tree of distinction"?

1. Apess writes: "Perhaps some unholy, unprincipled men would cry out, 'The skin was not good enough'; but stop, friends—I am not talking about the skin but about the principles." After researching historic accounts of racist behavior, make a comparison to contemporary accounts of racist behavior. For instance, you might research racism in 19th century America and compare it to racism in 21st century Africa. After doing so, examine the role of principles in racism, specifically the difference between principled and unprincipled men attempting to advance a racist agenda.

2. Apess writes: "If black or red skins or any other skin of color is disgraceful to God, it appears that he has disgraced himself a great deal—for he has made fifteen colored people to one white and placed them here upon this earth." If, after reading this, you believe that Apess may be challenging God (or simply challenging his adherents), read Jonathan Edwards' *Sinners in the Hands of an Angry God.* Then, compare and contrast the two, taking a stand that either supports or refutes their contentions.

3. Throughout his essay, Apess alludes to what many historians would deem "manifest destiny." Perform some research with the intention of defining manifest destiny and finding historical examples of it. After doing so, identify the functions of manifest destiny, i.e., societal, cultural, religious, financial.

4. Apess writes: "Now, if the Lord Jesus Christ, who is counted by all to be a Jew—and it is well known that the Jews are a colored people, especially those living in the East, where Christ was born—and if he should appear among us, would he not be shut out of doors by many, very quickly? And by those too who profess religion?" Within this quotation is the suggestion that Jesus Christ was not white. Interestingly, however, many of the images of Christ that have been popularized by various churches reveal a white Jesus. Perform some research on the images of Jesus Christ, and see if you can find some examples of a brown or black Jesus. Then, construct an argument around the possible motivations for creating a white Jesus as opposed to a Jesus of another color.

5. In the state of California, "Indian Casinos" have become a concern for many. Some believe that Native American Indians have been given tax breaks and other "breaks" that are unreasonable. Others, however, believe that the Native American Indians deserve "a leg up," in other words, reparations for the suffering they underwent. Such reparations are sometimes supported for African-Americans (because of slavery) and Japanese-Americans (because of their forced internment during World War II). However, are these reparations justified? Further, when do they end? In other words, when do we say "enough is enough"? After researching this, take a stand on whether or not reparations should be offered under certain circumstances; assuming you agree that reparations should be offered, for how long should they last?

Ralph Waldo Emerson (1803–1882)

Born in Boston, Massachusetts, Ralph Waldo Emerson seemed destined to become a minister like his father and grandfather. Shortly after graduating from Harvard College, he became a pastor at Boston's Second Church. After two years, however, he decided that he could no longer serve communion in good conscience. Thus, he became a writer and a lecturer. Though once labeled by Herman Melville as a "big-nosed buffoon," Emerson wrote with a certain éclat, arguing passionately that "envy is ignorance" and "imitation is suicide." At Emerson's grave, nine days after his passing, Walt Whitman stated: "A just man, poised on himself, all-loving, all-inclosing, and sane and clear as the sun."

The Poet

1. Emerson spends much of his essay arguing for poetry. Specifically, he wants a poet to reflect the American experience, just as Shakespeare has reflected the British experience and Dante has reflected the Italian experience.
2. Eleven years after this essay was published, America was given Walt Whitman's *Leaves of Grass,* which many consider an answer to Emerson's call for an American poet.
3. Emerson alludes to the poet as the creator of the universe. Assuming he is not suggesting that the poet is God, consider how such an allusion might be interpreted.

The Poet
from Essays: Second Series (1844)

Ralph Waldo Emerson

A moody child and wildly wise
Pursued the game with joyful eyes,
Which chose, like meteors, their way,
And rived the dark with private ray:
They overleapt the horizon's edge,
Searched with Apollo's privilege;
Through man, and woman, and sea, and star,
Saw the dance of nature forward far;

Through worlds, and races, and terms, and
   times,
Saw musical order, and pairing rhymes.

Olympian bards who sung
Divine ideas below,
Which always find us young,
And always keep us so.

Those who are esteemed umpires of taste, are often persons knowledge of admired pictures or sculptures, and have an inclination for whatever is elegant; but if you inquire whether they are beautiful souls, and whether their own acts are like fair pictures, you learn that they are selfish and sensual. Their cultivation is local, as if you should rub a log of dry wood in one spot to produce fire, all the rest remaining cold. Their knowledge of the fine arts is some study of rules and particulars, or some limited judgment of color or form, which is exercised for amusement or for show. It is a proof of the shallowness of the doctrine of beauty, as it lies in the minds of our amateurs, that men seem to have lost the perception of the instant dependence of form upon soul. There is no doctrine of forms in our philosophy. We were put into our bodies, as fire is put into a pan, to be carried about; but there is no accurate adjustment between the spirit and the organ, much less is the latter the germination of the former. So in regard to other forms, the intellectual men do not believe in any essential dependence of the material world on thought and volition. Theologians think it a pretty air-castle to talk of the spiritual meaning of a ship or a cloud, of a city or a contract, but they prefer to come again to the solid ground of historical evidence; and even the poets are contented with a civil and conformed manner of living, and to write poems from the fancy, at a safe distance from their own experience. But the highest minds of the world have never ceased to explore the double meaning, or, shall I say, the quadruple, or the centuple, or much more manifold meaning, of every sensuous fact: Orpheus, Empedocles, Heraclitus, Plato, Plutarch, Dante, Swedenborg, and the masters of sculpture, picture, and poetry. For we are not pans and barrows, nor even porters of the fire and torch-bearers, but children of the fire, made of it, and only the same divinity transmuted, and at two or three removes, when we know least about it. And this hidden truth, that the fountains whence all this river of Time, and its creatures, floweth, are intrinsically ideal and beautiful, draws us to the consideration of the nature and functions of the Poet, or the man of Beauty, to the means and materials he uses, and to the general aspect of the art in the present time.

The breadth of the problem is great, for the poet is representative. He stands among partial men for the complete man, and apprises us not of his wealth, but of the common-wealth. The young man reveres men of genius, because, to speak truly, they are more himself than he is. They receive of the soul as he also receives, but they more. Nature enhances her beauty, to the eye of loving men, from their belief that the poet is beholding her shows at the same time. He is isolated among his contemporaries, by truth and by his art, but with this consolation in his pursuits, that they will draw all men sooner or later. For all men live by truth, and stand in need of expression. In love, in art, in avarice, in politics, in labor, in games, we study to utter our painful secret. The man is only half himself, the other half is his expression.

Notwithstanding this necessity to be published, adequate expression is rare. I know not how it is that we need an interpreter; but the great majority of men seem to be minors, who have not yet come into possession of their own, or mutes, who cannot report the conversation they have had with nature. There is no man who does not anticipate a supersensual utility in the sun, and stars, earth, and water. These stand and wait to render him a peculiar service. But there is some obstruction, or some excess of phlegm in our constitution, which does not suffer them to yield the due effect. Too feeble fall the impressions of nature on us to make us artists. Every touch should thrill. Every man should be so much an artist, that he could report in conversation what had befallen him. Yet, in our experience, the rays or appulses have sufficient force to arrive at the senses, but not enough to reach the quick, and compel the reproduction of themselves in speech. The poet is the person in whom these powers are in balance, the man without impediment, who sees and handles that which others dream of, traverses the whole scale of experience, and is representative of man, in virtue of being the largest power to receive and to impart.

For the Universe has three children, born at one time, which reappear, under different names, in every system of thought, whether they be called cause, operation, and effect; or, more poetically, Jove, Pluto, Neptune; or, theologically, the Father, the Spirit, and the Son; but which we will call here, the Knower, the Doer, and the Sayer. These stand respectively for the love of truth, for the love of good, and for the love of beauty. These three are equal.

Each is that which he is essentially, so that he cannot be surmounted or analyzed, and each of these three has the power of the others latent in him, and his own patent.

The poet is the sayer, the namer, and represents beauty. He is a sovereign, and stands on the centre. For the world is not painted, or adorned, but is from the beginning beautiful; and God has not made some beautiful things, but Beauty is the creator of the universe. Therefore the poet is not any permissive potentate, but is emperor in his own right. Criticism is infested with a cant of materialism, which assumes that manual skill and activity is the first merit of all men, and disparages such as say and do not, overlooking the fact, that some men, namely, poets, are natural sayers, sent into the world to the end of expression, and confounds them with those whose province is action, but who quit it to imitate the sayers. But Homer's words are as costly and admirable to Homer, as Agamemnon's victories are to Agamemnon. The poet does not wait for the hero or the sage, but, as they act and think primarily, so he writes primarily what will and must be spoken, reckoning the others, though primaries also, yet, in respect to him, secondaries and servants; as sitters or models in the studio of a painter, or as assistants who bring building materials to an architect.

For poetry was all written before time was, and whenever we are so finely organized that we can penetrate into that region where the air is music, we hear those primal warblings, and attempt to write them down, but we lose ever and anon a word, or a verse, and substitute something of our own, and thus miswrite the poem. The men of more delicate ear write down these cadences more faithfully, and these transcripts, though imperfect, become the songs of the nations. For nature is as truly beautiful as it is good, or as it is reasonable, and must as much appear, as it must be done, or be known. Words and deeds are quite indifferent modes of the divine energy. Words are also actions, and actions are a kind of words.

The sign and credentials of the poet are, that he announces that which no man foretold. He is the true and only doctor; he knows and tells; he is the only teller of news, for he was present and privy to the appearance which he describes. He is a beholder of ideas, and an utterer of the necessary and causal. For we do not speak now of men of poetical talents, or of industry and skill in metre, but of the true poet. I took part in a conversation the other day, concerning a recent writer of lyrics, a man of subtle mind, whose head appeared to be a music-box of delicate tunes and rhythms, and whose skill, and command of language, we could not sufficiently praise. But when the question arose, whether he was not only a lyrist, but a poet, we were obliged to confess that he is plainly a contemporary, not an eternal man. He does not stand out of our low limitations, like a Chimborazo under the line, running up from the torrid base through all the climates of the globe, with belts of the herbage of every latitude on its high and mottled sides; but this genius is the landscape-garden of a modern house, adorned with fountains and statues, with well-bred men and women standing and sitting in the walks and terraces. We hear, through all the varied music, the ground-tone of conventional life. Our poets are men of talents who sing, and not the children of music. The argument is secondary, the finish of the verses is primary.

For it is not metres, but a metre-making argument, that makes a poem,—a thought so passionate and alive, that, like the spirit of a plant or an animal, it has an architecture of its own, and adorns nature with a new thing. The thought and the form are equal in the order of time, but in the order of genesis the thought is prior to the form. The poet has a new thought: he has a whole new experience to unfold; he will tell us how it was with him, and all men will be the richer in his fortune. For, the experience of each new age requires a new confession, and the world seems always waiting for its poet. I remember, when I was young, how much I was moved one morning by tidings that genius had appeared in a youth who sat near me at table. He had left his work, and gone rambling none knew whither, and had written hundreds of lines, but could not tell whether that which was in him was therein told: he could tell nothing but that all was changed,—man, beast, heaven, earth, and sea. How gladly we listened! how credulous! Society seemed to be compromised. We sat in the aurora of a sunrise which was to put out all the stars. Boston seemed to be at twice the distance it had the night before, or was much farther than that. Rome,—

what was Rome? Plutarch and Shakspeare were in the yellow leaf, and Homer no more should be heard of. It is much to know that poetry has been written this very day, under this very roof, by your side. What! that wonderful spirit has not expired! These stony moments are still sparkling and animated! I had fancied that the oracles were all silent, and nature had spent her fires, and behold! All night, from every pore, these fine auroras have been streaming. Every one has some interest in the advent of the poet, and no one knows how much it may concern him. We know that the secret of the world is profound, but who or what shall be our interpreter, we know not. A mountain ramble, a new style of face, a new person, may put the key into our hands. Of course, the value of genius to us is in the veracity of its report. Talent may frolic and juggle; genius realizes and adds. Mankind, in good earnest, have availed so far in understanding themselves and their work, that the foremost watchman on the peak announces his news. It is the truest word ever spoken, and the phrase will be the fittest, most musical, and the unerring voice of the world for that time.

All that we call sacred history attests that the birth of a poet is the principal event in chronology. Man, never so often deceived, still watches for the arrival of a brother who can hold him steady to a truth, until he has made it his own. With what joy I begin to read a poem, which I confide in as an inspiration! And now my chains are to be broken; I shall mount above these clouds and opaque airs in which I live,—opaque, though they seem transparent,—and from the heaven of truth I shall see and comprehend my relations. That will reconcile me to life, and renovate nature, to see trifles animated by a tendency, and to know what I am doing. Life will no more be a noise; now I shall see men and women, and know the signs by which they may be discerned from fools and satans. This day shall be better than my birthday: then I became an animal: now I am invited into the science of the real. Such is the hope, but the fruition is postponed. Oftener it falls, that this winged man, who will carry me into the heaven, whirls me into the clouds, then leaps and frisks about with me from cloud to cloud, still affirming that he is bound heavenward; and I, being myself a novice, am slow in perceiving that he does not know the way into the heavens, and is merely bent that I should ad-mire his skill to rise, like a fowl or a flying fish, a little way from the ground or the water; but the all-piercing, all-feeding, and ocular air of heaven, that man shall never inhabit. I tumble down again soon into my old nooks, and lead the life of exaggerations as before, and have lost my faith in the possibility of any guide who can lead me thither where I would be.

But leaving these victims of vanity, let us, with new hope, observe how nature, by worthier impulses, has ensured the poet's fidelity to his office of announcement and affirming, namely, by the beauty of things, which becomes a new, and higher beauty, when expressed. Nature offers all her creatures to him as a picture-language. Being used as a type, a second wonderful value appears in the object, far better than its old value, as the carpenter's stretched cord, if you hold your ear close enough, is musical in the breeze. "Things more excellent than every image," says Jamblichus, "are expressed through images." Things admit of being used as symbols, because nature is a symbol, in the whole, and in every part. Every line we can draw in the sand, has expression; and there is no body without its spirit or genius. All form is an effect of character; all condition, of the quality of the life; all harmony, of health; (and, for this reason, a perception of beauty should be sympathetic, or proper only to the good.) The beautiful rests on the foundations of the necessary. The soul makes the body, as the wise Spenser teaches:—

"So every spirit, as it is most pure,
And hath in it the more of heavenly light,
So it the fairer body doth procure
To habit in, and it more fairly dight,
With cheerful grace and amiable sight.
For, of the soul, the body form doth take,
For soul is form, and doth the body make."

Here we find ourselves, suddenly, not in a critical speculation, but in a holy place, and should go very warily and reverently. We stand before the secret of the world, there where Being passes into Appearance, and Unity into Variety.

The Universe is the externisation of the soul. Wherever the life is, that bursts into appearance around it. Our science is sensual, and therefore superficial. The earth, and the heavenly bodies, physics, and chemistry, we sensually treat, as if they were self-existent; but these are the retinue of that Being we have. "The mighty heaven," said Proclus, "exhibits, in its transfigurations, clear images of the splendor of intellectual perceptions; being moved in conjunction with the unapparent periods of intellectual natures." Therefore, science always goes abreast with the just elevation of the man, keeping step with religion and metaphysics; or, the state of science is an index of our self-knowledge. Since everything in nature answers to a moral power, if any phenomenon remains brute and dark, it is that the corresponding faculty in the observer is not yet active.

No wonder, then, if these waters be so deep, that we hover over them with a religious regard. The beauty of the fable proves the importance of the sense; to the poet, and to all others; or, if you please, every man is so far a poet as to be susceptible of these enchantments of nature: for all men have the thoughts whereof the universe is the celebration. I find that the fascination resides in the symbol. Who loves nature? Who does not? Is it only poets, and men of leisure and cultivation, who live with her? No; but also hunters, farmers, grooms, and butchers, though they express their affection in their choice of life, and not in their choice of words. The writer wonders what the coachman or the hunter values in riding, in horses, and dogs. It is not superficial qualities. When you talk with him, he holds these at as slight a rate as you. His worship is sympathetic; he has no definitions, but he is commanded in nature, by the living power which he feels to be there present. No imitation, or playing of these things, would content him; he loves the earnest of the northwind, of rain, of stone, and wood, and iron. A beauty not explicable, is dearer than a beauty which we can see to the end of. It is nature the symbol, nature certifying the supernatural, body overflowed by life, which he worships, with coarse, but sincere rites.

The inwardness, and mystery, of this attachment, drives men of every class to the use of emblems. The schools of poets, and philosophers, are not more intoxicated with their symbols, than the populace with theirs. In our political parties, compute the power of badges and emblems. See the great ball which they roll from Baltimore to Bunker hill! In the political processions, Lowell goes in a loom, and Lynn in a shoe, and Salem in a ship. Witness the cider-barrel, the log-cabin, the hickory-stick, the palmetto, and all the cognizances of party. See the power of national emblems. Some stars, lilies, leopards, a crescent, a lion, an eagle, or other figure, which came into credit God knows how, on an old rag of bunting, blowing in the wind, on a fort, at the ends of the earth, shall make the blood tingle under the rudest, or the most conventional exterior. The people fancy they hate poetry, and they are all poets and mystics!

Beyond this universality of the symbolic language, we are apprised of the divineness of this superior use of things, whereby the world is a temple, whose walls are covered with emblems, pictures, and commandments of the Deity, in this, that there is no fact in nature which does not carry the whole sense of nature; and the distinctions which we make in events, and in affairs, of low and high, honest and base, disappear when nature is used as a symbol. Thought makes every thing fit for use. The vocabulary of an omniscient man would embrace words and images excluded from polite conversation. What would be base, or even obscene, to the obscene, becomes illustrious, spoken in a new connexion of thought. The piety of the Hebrew prophets purges their grossness. The circumcision is an example of the power of poetry to raise the low and offensive. Small and mean things serve as well as great symbols. The meaner the type by which a law is expressed, the more pungent it is, and the more lasting in the memories of men: just as we choose the smallest box, or case, in which any needful utensil can be carried. Bare lists of words are found suggestive, to an imaginative and excited mind; as it is related of Lord Chatham, that he was accustomed to read in Bailey's Dictionary, when he was preparing to speak in Parliament. The poorest experience is rich enough for all the purposes of expressing thought. Why covet a knowledge of new facts? Day and night, house and garden, a few books, a few actions, serve us as well as would all trades and all spectacles. We are far from having exhausted the significance of the few symbols we use. We can come to use them yet with a terrible simplicity. It does not need that a poem should be long. Every word was once a poem. Every new relation is a new word. Also, we use defects and deformities to a sacred purpose, so expressing our sense that the evils of the world are such only to the evil eye. In the old mythology, mythologists observe, defects are ascribed to divine natures, as lameness to Vulcan, blindness to Cupid, and the like, to signify exuberances.

For, as it is dislocation and detachment from the life of God, that makes things ugly, the poet, who re-attaches things to nature and the Whole,—re-attaching even artificial things, and violations of nature, to nature, by a deeper insight,—disposes very easily of the most disagreeable facts. Readers of poetry see the factory-village, and the railway, and fancy that the poetry of the landscape is broken up by these; for these works of art are not yet consecrated in their reading; but the poet sees them fall within the great Order not less than the beehive, or the spider's geometrical web. Nature adopts them very fast into her vital circles, and the gliding train of cars she loves like her own. Besides, in a centred mind, it signifies nothing how many mechanical inventions you exhibit. Though you add millions, and never so surprising, the fact of mechanics has not gained a grain's weight. The spiritual fact remains unalterable, by many or by few particulars; as no mountain is of any appreciable height to break the curve of the sphere. A shrewd country-boy goes to the city for the first time, and the complacent citizen is not satisfied with his little wonder. It is not that he does not see all the fine houses, and know that he never saw such before, but he disposes of them as easily as the poet finds place for the railway. The chief value of the new fact, is to enhance the great and constant fact of Life, which can dwarf any and every circumstance, and to which the belt of wampum, and the commerce of America, are alike.

The world being thus put under the mind for verb and noun, the poet is he who can articulate it. For, though life is great, and fascinates, and absorbs,—and though all men are intelligent of the symbols through which it is named,—yet they cannot originally use them. We are symbols, and inhabit symbols; workman, work, and tools, words and things, birth and death, all are emblems; but we sympathize with the symbols, and, being infatuated with the economical uses of things, we do not know that they are thoughts. The poet, by an ulterior intellectual perception, gives them a power which makes their old use forgotten, and puts eyes, and a tongue, into every dumb and inanimate object. He perceives the independence of the thought on the symbol, the stability of the thought, the accidency and fugacity of the symbol. As the eyes of Lynceus were said to see through the earth, so the poet turns the world to glass, and shows us all things in their right series and procession. For, through that better perception, he stands one step nearer to things, and sees the flowing or metamorphosis; perceives that thought is multiform; that within the form of every creature is a force impelling it to ascend into a higher form; and, following with his eyes the life, uses the forms which express that life, and so his speech flows with the flowing of nature. All the facts of the animal economy, sex, nutriment, gestation, birth, growth, are symbols of the passage of the world into the soul of man, to suffer there a change, and reappear a new and higher fact. He uses forms according to the life, and not according to the form. This is true science. The poet alone knows astronomy, chemistry, vegetation, and animation, for he does not stop at these facts, but employs them as signs. He knows why the plain, or meadow of space, was strewn with these flowers we call suns, and moons, and stars; why the great deep is adorned with animals, with men, and gods; for, in every word he speaks he rides on them as the horses of thought.

By virtue of this science the poet is the Namer, or Language-maker, naming things sometimes after their appearance, sometimes after their essence, and giving to every one its own name and not another's, thereby rejoicing the intellect, which delights in detachment or boundary. The poets made all the words, and therefore language is the archives of history, and, if we must say it, a sort of tomb of the muses. For, though the origin of most of our words is forgotten, each word was at first a stroke of genius, and obtained currency, because for the moment it symbolized the world to the first speaker and to the hearer. The etymologist finds the deadest word to have been once a brilliant picture. Language is fossil poetry. As the limestone of the continent consists of infinite masses of the shells of animalcules, so language is made up of images, or tropes, which now, in their secondary use, have long ceased to remind us of their poetic origin. But the poet names the thing because he sees it, or comes one step nearer to it than any other. This expression, or naming, is not art, but a second nature, grown out of the first, as a leaf out of a tree. What we call nature, is a certain self-regulated motion, or change; and nature does all things by her own hands, and does not leave another to baptise her, but baptises herself; and this through the metamorphosis again. I remember that a certain poet described it to me thus:

Genius is the activity which repairs the decays of things, whether wholly or partly of a material and finite kind. Nature, through all her kingdoms, insures herself. Nobody cares for planting the poor fungus: so she shakes down from the gills of one agaric countless spores, any one of which, being preserved, transmits new billions of spores to-morrow or next day. The new agaric of this hour has a chance which the old one had not. This atom of seed is thrown into a new place, not subject to the accidents which destroyed its parent two rods off. She makes a man; and having brought him to ripe age, she will no longer run the risk of losing this wonder at a blow, but she detaches from him a new self, that the kind may be safe from accidents to which the individual is exposed. So when the soul of the poet has come to ripeness of thought, she detaches and sends away from it its poems or songs,—a fearless, sleepless, deathless progeny, which is not exposed to the accidents of the weary kingdom of time: a fearless, vivacious offspring, clad with wings (such was the virtue of the soul out of which they came), which carry them fast and far, and infix them irrecoverably into the hearts of men. These wings are the beauty of the poet's soul. The songs, thus flying immortal from their mortal parent, are pursued by clamorous flights of censures, which swarm in far greater numbers, and threaten to devour them; but these last are not winged. At the end of a very short leap they fall plump down, and rot, having received from the souls out of which they came no beautiful wings. But the melodies of the poet ascend, and leap, and pierce into the deeps of infinite time.

So far the bard taught me, using his freer speech. But nature has a higher end, in the production of new individuals, than security, namely, ascension, or, the passage of the soul into higher forms. I knew, in my younger days, the sculptor who made the statue of the youth which stands in the public garden. He was, as I remember, unable to tell directly, what made him happy, or unhappy, but by wonderful indirections he could tell. He rose one day, according to his habit, before the dawn, and saw the morning break, grand as the eternity out of which it came, and, for many days after, he strove to express this tranquillity, and, lo! his chisel had fashioned out of marble the form of a beautiful youth, Phosphorus, whose aspect is such, that, it is said, all persons who look on it become silent. The poet also resigns himself to his mood, and that thought which agitated him is expressed, but alter idem, in a manner totally new. The expression is organic, or, the new type which things themselves take when liberated. As, in the sun, objects paint their images on the retina of the eye, so they, sharing the aspiration of the whole universe, tend to paint a far more delicate copy of their essence in his mind. Like the metamorphosis of things into higher organic forms, is their change into melodies. Over everything stands its daemon, or soul, and, as the form of the thing is reflected by the eye, so the soul of the thing is reflected by a melody. The sea, the mountain-ridge, Niagara, and every flower-bed, pre-exist, or super-exist, in pre-cantations, which sail like odors in the air, and when any man goes by with an ear sufficiently fine, he overhears them, and endeavors to write down the notes, without diluting or depraving them. And herein is the legitimation of criticism, in the mind's faith, that the poems are a corrupt version of some text in nature, with which they ought to be made to tally. A rhyme in one of our sonnets should not be less pleasing than the iterated nodes of a sea-shell, or the resembling difference of a group of flowers. The pairing of the birds is an idyl, not tedious as our idyls are; a tempest is a rough ode, without falsehood or rant: a summer, with its harvest sown, reaped, and stored, is an epic song, subordinating how many admirably executed parts. Why should not the symmetry and truth that modulate these, glide into our spirits, and we participate the invention of nature?

This insight, which expresses itself by what is called Imagination, is a very high sort of seeing, which does not come by study, but by the intellect being where and what it sees, by sharing the path, or circuit of things through forms, and so making them translucid to others. The path of things is silent. Will they suffer a speaker to go with them? A spy they will not suffer; a lover, a poet, is the transcendency of their own nature,—him they will suffer. The condition of true naming, on the poet's part, is his resigning himself to the divine aura which breathes through forms, and accompanying that.

It is a secret which every intellectual man quickly learns, that, beyond the energy of his possessed and conscious intellect, he is capable of a new energy (as of an intellect doubled on itself), by abandonment to the nature of things; that, beside his privacy of power as an individual man, there is a great public power, on which he can draw, by unlocking, at all risks, his human doors, and suffering the ethereal tides to roll and circulate through him: then he is caught up into the life of the Universe, his speech is thunder, his thought is law, and his words are universally intelligible as the plants and animals. The poet knows that he speaks adequately, then, only when he speaks somewhat wildly, or, "with the flower of the mind;" not with the intellect, used as an organ, but with the intellect released from all service, and suffered to take its direction from its celestial life; or, as the ancients were wont to express themselves, not with intellect alone, but with the intellect inebriated by nectar. As the traveller who has lost his way, throws his reins on his horse's neck, and trusts to the instinct of the animal to find his road, so must we do with the divine animal who carries us through this world. For if in any manner we can stimulate this instinct, new passages are opened for us into nature, the mind flows into and through things hardest and highest, and the metamorphosis is possible.

This is the reason why bards love wine, mead, narcotics, coffee, tea, opium, the fumes of sandalwood and tobacco, or whatever other species of animal exhilaration. All men avail themselves of such means as they can, to add this extraordinary power to their normal powers; and to this end they prize conversation, music, pictures, sculpture, dancing, theatres, travelling, war, mobs, fires, gaming, politics, or love, or science, or animal intoxication, which are several coarser or finer quasi-mechanical substitutes for the true nectar, which is the ravishment of the intellect by coming nearer to the fact. These are auxiliaries to the centrifugal tendency of a man, to his passage out into free space, and they help him to escape the custody of that body in which he is pent up, and of that jail-yard of individual relations in which he is enclosed. Hence a great number of such as were professionally expressors of Beauty, as painters, poets, musicians, and actors, have been more than oth-

ers wont to lead a life of pleasure and indulgence; all but the few who received the true nectar; and, as it was a spurious mode of attaining freedom, as it was an emancipation not into the heavens, but into the freedom of baser places, they were punished for that advantage they won, by a dissipation and deterioration. But never can any advantage be taken of nature by a trick. The spirit of the world, the great calm presence of the creator, comes not forth to the sorceries of opium or of wine. The sublime vision comes to the pure and simple soul in a clean and chaste body. That is not an inspiration which we owe to narcotics, but some counterfeit excitement and fury. Milton says, that the lyric poet may drink wine and live generously, but the epic poet, he who shall sing of the gods, and their descent unto men, must drink water out of a wooden bowl. For poetry is not 'Devil's wine,' but God's wine. It is with this as it is with toys. We fill the hands and nurseries of our children with all manner of dolls, drums, and horses, withdrawing their eyes from the plain face and sufficing objects of nature, the sun, and moon, the animals, the water, and stones, which should be their toys. So the poet's habit of living should be set on a key so low and plain, that the common influences should delight him. His cheerfulness should be the gift of the sunlight; the air should suffice for his inspiration, and he should be tipsy with water. That spirit which suffices quiet hearts, which seems to come forth to such from every dry knoll of sere grass, from every pine-stump, and half-imbedded stone, on which the dull March sun shines, comes forth to the poor and hungry, and such as are of simple taste. If thou fill thy brain with Boston and New York, with fashion and covetousness, and wilt stimulate thy jaded senses with wine and French coffee, thou shalt find no radiance of wisdom in the lonely waste of the pinewoods.

If the imagination intoxicates the poet, it is not inactive in other men. The metamorphosis excites in the beholder an emotion of joy. The use of symbols has a certain power of emancipation and exhilaration for all men. We seem to be touched by a wand, which makes us dance and run about happily, like children. We are like persons who come out of a cave or cellar into the open air. This is the effect on us of tropes, fables, oracles, and all poetic forms. Poets are thus liberating gods. Men have really got a new sense, and found within their world, another world, or nest of worlds; for, the metamorphosis once seen, we divine that it does not stop. I will not now consider how much this makes the charm of algebra and the mathematics, which also have their tropes, but it is felt in every definition; as, when Aristotle defines space to be an immovable vessel, in which things are contained;—or, when Plato defines a line to be a flowing point; or, figure to be a bound of solid; and many the like. What a joyful sense of freedom we have, when Vitruvius announces the old opinion of artists, that no architect can build any house well, who does not know something of anatomy. When Socrates, in Charmides, tells us that the soul is cured of its maladies by certain incantations, and that these incantations are beautiful reasons, from which temperance is generated in souls; when Plato calls the world an animal; and Timaeus affirms that the plants also are animals; or affirms a man to be a heavenly tree, growing with his root, which is his head, upward; and, as George Chapman, following him, writes,—

"So in our tree of man, whose nervie root
     Springs in his top;"

when Orpheus speaks of hoariness as "that white flower which marks extreme old age;" when Proclus calls the universe the statue of the intellect; when Chaucer, in his praise of 'Gentilesse,' compares good blood in mean condition to fire, which, though carried to the darkest house betwixt this and the mount of Caucasus, will yet hold its natural office, and burn as bright as if twenty thousand men did it behold; when John saw, in the apocalypse, the ruin of the world through evil, and the stars fall from heaven, as the figtree casteth her untimely fruit; when Aesop reports the whole catalogue of common daily relations through the masquerade of birds and beasts;—we take the cheerful hint of the immortality of our essence, and its versatile habit and escapes, as when the gypsies say, "it is in vain to hang them, they cannot die."

The poets are thus liberating gods. The ancient British bards had for the title of their order, "Those who are free throughout the world." They are free, and they make free. An imaginative book renders us much more service at first, by stimulating us through its tropes, than afterward, when we arrive at the precise sense of the author. I think nothing is of any value in books, excepting the transcendental and ex-

traordinary. If a man is inflamed and carried away by his thought, to that degree that he forgets the authors and the public, and heeds only this one dream, which holds him like an insanity, let me read his paper, and you may have all the arguments and histories and criticism. All the value which attaches to Pythagoras, Paracelsus, Cornelius Agrippa, Cardan, Kepler, Swedenborg, Schelling, Oken, or any other who introduces questionable facts into his cosmogony, as angels, devils, magic, astrology, palmistry, mesmerism, and so on, is the certificate we have of departure from routine, and that here is a new witness. That also is the best success in conversation, the magic of liberty, which puts the world, like a ball, in our hands. How cheap even the liberty then seems; how mean to study, when an emotion communicates to the intellect the power to sap and upheave nature: how great the perspective! Nations, times, systems, enter and disappear, like threads in tapestry of large figure and many colors; dream delivers us to dream, and, while the drunkenness lasts, we will sell our bed, our philosophy, our religion, in our opulence.

There is good reason why we should prize this liberation. The fate of the poor shepherd, who, blinded and lost in the snow-storm, perishes in a drift within a few feet of his cottage door, is an emblem of the state of man. On the brink of the waters of life and truth, we are miserably dying. The inaccessibleness of every thought but that we are in, is wonderful. What if you come near to it,—you are as remote, when you are nearest, as when you are farthest. Every thought is also a prison; every heaven is also a prison. Therefore we love the poet, the inventor, who in any form, whether in an ode, or in an action, or in looks and behavior, has yielded us a new thought. He unlocks our chains, and admits us to a new scene.

This emancipation is dear to all men, and the power to impart it, as it must come from greater depth and scope of thought, is a measure of intellect. Therefore all books of the imagination endure, all which ascend to that truth, that the writer sees nature beneath him, and uses it as his exponent. Every verse or sentence, possessing this virtue, will take care of its own immortality. The religions of the world are the ejaculations of a few imaginative men.

But the quality of the imagination is to flow, and not to freeze. The poet did not stop at the color, or the form, but read their meaning; neither may he rest in this meaning, but he makes the same objects exponents of his new thought. Here is the difference betwixt the poet and the mystic, that the last nails a symbol to one sense, which was a true sense for a moment, but soon becomes old and false. For all symbols are fluxional; all language is vehicular and transitive, and is good, as ferries and horses are, for conveyance, not as farms and houses are, for homestead. Mysticism consists in the mistake of an accidental and individual symbol for an universal one. The morning-redness happens to be the favorite meteor to the eyes of Jacob Behmen, and comes to stand to him for truth and faith; and he believes should stand for the same realities to every reader. But the first reader prefers as naturally the symbol of a mother and child, or a gardener and his bulb, or a jeweller polishing a gem. Either of these, or of a myriad more, are equally good to the person to whom they are significant. Only they must be held lightly, and be very willingly translated into the equivalent terms which others use. And the mystic must be steadily told,—All that you say is just as true without the tedious use of that symbol as with it. Let us have a little algebra, instead of this trite rhetoric,—universal signs, instead of these village symbols,—and we shall both be gainers. The history of hierarchies seems to show, that all religious error consisted in making the symbol too stark and solid, and, at last, nothing but an excess of the organ of language.

Swedenborg, of all men in the recent ages, stands eminently for the translator of nature into thought. I do not know the man in history to whom things stood so uniformly for words. Before him the metamorphosis continually plays. Everything on which his eye rests, obeys the impulses of moral nature. The figs become grapes whilst he eats them. When some of his angels affirmed a truth, the laurel twig which they held blossomed in their hands. The noise which, at a distance, appeared like gnashing and thumping, on coming nearer was found to be the voice of disputants. The men, in one of his visions, seen in heavenly light, appeared like dragons, and seemed in darkness: but, to each other, they appeared as men, and, when the light from heaven shone into their cabin, they complained of the darkness, and were compelled to shut the window that they might see.

There was this perception in him, which makes the poet or seer, an object of awe and terror, namely, that the same man, or society of men, may wear one aspect to themselves and their companions, and a different aspect to higher intelligences. Certain priests, whom he describes as conversing very learnedly together, appeared to the children, who were at some distance, like dead horses: and many the like misappearances. And instantly the mind inquires, whether these fishes under the bridge, yonder oxen in the pasture, those dogs in the yard, are immutably fishes, oxen, and dogs, or only so appear to me, and perchance to themselves appear upright men; and whether I appear as a man to all eyes. The Bramins and Pythagoras propounded the same question, and if any poet has witnessed the transformation, he doubtless found it in harmony with various experiences. We have all seen changes as considerable in wheat and caterpillars. He is the poet, and shall draw us with love and terror, who sees, through the flowing vest, the firm nature, and can declare it.

I look in vain for the poet whom I describe. We do not, with sufficient plainness, or sufficient profoundness, address ourselves to life, nor dare we chaunt our own times and social circumstance. If we filled the day with bravery, we should not shrink from celebrating it. Time and nature yield us many gifts, but not yet the timely man, the new religion, the reconciler, whom all things await. Dante's praise is, that he dared to write his autobiography in colossal cipher, or into universality. We have yet had no genius in America, with tyrannous eye, which knew the value of our incomparable materials, and saw, in the barbarism and materialism of the times, another carnival of the same gods whose picture he so much admires in Homer; then in the middle age; then in Calvinism. Banks and tariffs, the newspaper and caucus, methodism and unitarianism, are flat and dull to dull people, but rest on the same foundations of wonder as the town of Troy, and the temple of Delphos, and are as swiftly passing away. Our logrolling, our stumps and their politics, our fisheries, our Negroes, and Indians, our boasts, and our repudiations, the wrath of rogues, and the pusillanimity of honest men, the northern trade, the southern planting, the western clearing, Oregon, and Texas, are yet unsung. Yet America is a poem in our eyes; its ample geography dazzles the imagination, and it will not wait long for metres. If I have not found that excellent combination of gifts in my countrymen which I seek, neither could I aid myself to fix the idea of the poet by reading now and then in Chalmers's collection of five centuries of English poets. These are wits, more than poets, though there have been poets among them. But when we adhere to the ideal of the poet, we have our difficulties even with Milton and Homer. Milton is too literary, and Homer too literal and historical.

But I am not wise enough for a national criticism, and must use the old largeness a little longer, to discharge my errand from the muse to the poet concerning his art.

Art is the path of the creator to his work. The paths, or methods, are ideal and eternal, though few men ever see them, not the artist himself for years, or for a lifetime, unless he come into the conditions. The painter, the sculptor, the composer, the epic rhapsodist, the orator, all partake one desire, namely, to express themselves symmetrically and abundantly, not dwarfishly and fragmentarily. They found or put themselves in certain conditions, as, the painter and sculptor before some impressive human figures; the orator, into the assembly of the people; and the others, in such scenes as each has found exciting to his intellect; and each presently feels the new desire. He hears a voice, he sees a beckoning. Then he is apprised, with wonder, what herds of dæmons hem him in. He can no more rest; he says, with the old painter, "By God, it is in me, and must go forth of me." He pursues a beauty, half seen, which flies before him. The poet pours out verses in every solitude. Most of the things he says are conventional, no doubt; but by and by he says something which is original and beautiful. That charms him. He would say nothing else but such things. In our way of talking, we say, 'That is yours, this is mine;' but the poet knows well that it is not his; that it is as strange and beautiful to him as to you; he would fain hear the like eloquence at length. Once having tasted this immortal ichor, he cannot have enough of it, and, as an admirable creative power exists in these intellections, it is of the last importance that these things get spoken. What a little of all we know is said! What drops of all the sea of our science are baled up! and

by what accident it is that these are exposed, when so many secrets sleep in nature! Hence the necessity of speech and song; hence these throbs and heart-beatings in the orator, at the door of the assembly, to the end, namely, that thought may be ejaculated as Logos, or Word.

Doubt not, O poet, but persist. Say, 'It is in me, and shall out.' Stand there, baulked and dumb, stuttering and stammering, hissed and hooted, stand and strive, until, at last, rage draw out of thee that dream-power which every night shows thee is thine own; a power transcending all limit and privacy, and by virtue of which a man is the conductor of the whole river of electricity. Nothing walks, or creeps, or grows, or exists, which must not in turn arise and walk before him as exponent of his meaning. Comes he to that power, his genius is no longer exhaustible. All the creatures, by pairs and by tribes, pour into his mind as into a Noah's ark, to come forth again to people a new world. This is like the stock of air for our respiration, or for the combustion of our fire-place, not a measure of gallons, but the entire atmosphere if wanted. And therefore the rich poets, as Homer, Chaucer, Shakspeare, and Raphael, have obviously no limits to their works, except the limits of their lifetime, and resemble a mirror carried through the street, ready to render an image of every created thing.

O poet! a new nobility is conferred in groves and pastures, and not in castles, or by the sword-blade, any longer. The conditions are hard, but equal. Thou shalt leave the world, and know the muse only. Thou shalt not know any longer the times, customs, graces, politics, or opinions of men, but shalt take all from the muse. For the time of towns is tolled from the world by funereal chimes, but in nature the universal hours are counted by succeeding tribes of animals and plants, and by growth of joy on joy. God wills also that thou abdicate a manifold and duplex life, and that thou be content that others speak for thee. Others shall be thy gentlemen, and shall represent all courtesy and worldly life for thee; others shall do the great and resounding actions also. Thou shalt lie close hid with nature, and canst not be afforded to the Capitol or the Exchange. The world is full of renunciations and apprenticeships, and this is thine: thou must pass for a fool and a churl for a long season. This is the screen and sheath in which Pan has protected his well-beloved flower, and thou shalt be known only to thine own, and they shall console thee with tenderest love. And thou shalt not be able to rehearse the names of thy friends in thy verse, for an old shame before the holy ideal. And this is the reward: that the ideal shall be real to thee, and the impressions of the actual world shall fall like summer rain, copious, but not troublesome, to thy invulnerable essence. Thou shalt have the whole land for thy park and manor, the sea for thy bath and navigation, without tax and without envy; the woods and the rivers thou shalt own; and thou shalt possess that wherein others are only tenants and boarders. Thou true land-lord! sea-lord! air-lord! Wherever snow falls, or water flows, or birds fly, wherever day and night meet in twilight, wherever the blue heaven is hung by clouds, or sown with stars, wherever are forms with transparent boundaries, wherever are outlets into celestial space, wherever is danger, and awe, and love, there is Beauty, plenteous as rain, shed for thee, and though thou shouldest walk the world over, thou shalt not be able to find a condition inopportune or ignoble.

Questions

1. Emerson writes: "Their knowledge of the fine arts is some study of rules and particulars, or some limited judgment of color or form, which is exercised for amusement or for show." What is Emerson suggesting about the stereotypical person's purpose for pursuing an education in the arts? Why might Emerson believe that such a purpose is a problem?

2. Emerson argues that "[. . .] there is some obstruction, or some excess of phlegm in our constitution, which does not suffer them to yield the due effect. Too feeble fall the impressions of nature on us to make us artists." First of all, what is this "excess of phlegm in our constitution"? Second, what might Emerson mean when writing, "Too feeble fall the impressions of nature on us to make us artists"?

3. Emerson writes: "Words are also actions, and actions are a kind of words." What might this mean? How does this quotation help advance Emerson's essay?

4. Emerson writes: "Our poets are men of talents who sing, and not the children of music." How might this be interpreted?

5. Emerson writes: "Life will no more be a noise; now I shall see men and women, and know the signs by which they may be discerned from fools and satans." What might Emerson mean when he refers to Life as "a noise"? And how is it that he might refer to men and women as "fools and satans"? Is he condemning people, or is he simply attempting to advance an argument?

6. Emerson writes: "The vocabulary of the omniscient man would embrace words and images excluded from polite conversation." Here, what might Emerson be attempting to communicate?

7. Emerson writes about stimulants and their effects on attaining "the sublime vision." He, in fact, writes: "All men avail themselves of such means as they can, to add this extraordinary power to their normal powers [. . .]." Examine this passage. Is Emerson encouraging the use of such stimulants?

8. Emerson refers to America as a poem. If America were a poem, what elements would find themselves in such poetry?

1. Compare and contrast *The Poet* to the film *Dead Poet's Society.* Specifically, compare and contrast Emerson's perception of poetry and its purposes with John Keating's. Then, after doing this, identify specific lines from various poems that help advance both Emerson's and Keating's perceptions and purposes of poetry.

2. Emerson writes: "For the Universe has three children, born at one time, which reappear, under different names, in every system of thought, whether they be called cause, operation, and effect; or, more poetically, Jove, Pluto, Neptune; or, theologically, the Father, the Spirit, and the Son; but which we will call here, the Knower, the Doer, and the Sayer. These stand respectively for the love of truth, for the love of good, and for the love of beauty." Here, Emerson has engaged in a type of classification. After performing some research, classify a system of thought through "cause, operation, and effect." Or, classify a system of thought through "the love of truth, the love of good, and the love of beauty." In a classification essay, show how these classifications find themselves in the examples you have unearthed through your research.

3. Emerson writes: "The poet does not wait for the hero or the sage, but, as they act and think primarily, so he writes primarily what will and must be spoken [. . .]." What Emerson writes of a poet's actions is similar to what is expected of a whistleblower. After researching whistleblowers, which might include viewing films such as *Serpico, Brubaker, Silkwood, Erin Brokovich,* or *The Insider,* compare the actions of a whistleblower to the actions of a poet (based on Emerson's quotation). Then, take a stand that expresses the value, or lack thereof, of blowing the whistle. Specifically, take a stand on how valuable it is (or is not) to have people in our global society who "[write] primarily what will and must be spoken."

4. Emerson writes: "Every word was once a poem." Identify five words in *The Oxford English Dictionary,* and after thoroughly examining each word's etymology and multiple definitions, show how each word was once a poem.

5. Emerson writes: "The sublime vision comes to the pure and simple soul in a clean and chaste body." However, he has also argued that "[. . .] bards love wine, mead, narcotics [. . .]." Arguably, many contemporary bards may consist of not only our writers but our song writers, musicians, and actors. Steven Tyler, of Aerosmith, for instance, wrote what some may consider his best song lyrics while under the influence of cocaine. Charles Bukowski, an author of over forty books, used to glamorize his drunkeness and, specifically, how he used red wine to help aid him in the writing process. After researching various writers and the role of chemical stimulants in their lives, take a stand on Emerson's quotation: "The sublime vision comes to the pure and simple soul in a clean and chaste body." If you find quotations from writers suggesting that their most sublime visions came from their drug-induced states (check Jim Morrison, Bob Marley, Hunter S. Thompson, and Edgar Allan Poe), such quotations might be used to refute Emerson's quotation. Naturally, you should also be able to find people who represent the converse. After examining the fruits of your research, take a stand.

Harriet Jacobs (1813–1897)

Harriet Jacobs was born a slave in Edenton, North Carolina, and for the next thirty-five years, she endured physical and sexual abuse, botched escape attempts, the pursuits of slave catchers, and the promises of emancipation. Then, in 1853, Jacobs was emancipated by her legal owner, Cornelia Willis. At this point, Jacobs had been working for the Anti-Slavery Office in Rochester, New York, where she became friends with many abolitionists. It is around this time that Jacobs began writing *Incidents in the Life of a Slave Girl*. And while critics argue over whether it should be regarded as truth or fiction, *Incidents in the Life of a Slave Girl* gives testimony to the strength of the human spirit and to the power of one woman's voice.

XLI. Free at Last

1. *XLI. Free at Last* is the final chapter of *Incidents in the Life of a Slave Girl*.
2. This chapter's title, *Free at Last,* is elusive. The passage of the Fugitive Slave Law in 1850 means that the narrator is not really free.

XLI. Free at Last

Harriet Jacobs

MRS. BRUCE, and every member of her family, were exceedingly kind to me. I was thankful for the blessings of my lot, yet I could not always wear a cheerful countenance. I was doing harm to no one; on the contrary, I was doing all the good I could in my small way; yet I could never go out to breathe God's free air without trepidation at my heart. This seemed hard; and I could not think it was a right state of things in any civilized country.

From time to time I received news from my good old grandmother. She could not write; but she employed others to write for her. The following is an extract from one of her last letters:—

"Dear Daughter: I cannot hope to see you again on earth; but I pray to God to unite us above, where pain will no more rack this feeble body of mine; where sorrow and parting from my children will be no more. God has promised these things if we are faithful unto the end. My age and feeble health deprive me of going to church now; but God is with me here at home. Thank your brother for his kindness. Give much love to him, and tell him to remember the Creator in the days of his youth, and strive to meet me in the Father's kingdom. Love to Ellen and Benjamin. Don't neglect him. Tell him for me, to be a good boy. Strive, my child, to train them for God's children. May he protect and provide for you, is the prayer of your loving old mother."

These letters both cheered and saddened me. I was always glad to have tidings from the kind, faithful old friend of my unhappy youth; but her messages of love made my heart yearn to see her before she died, and I mourned over the fact that it was impossible. Some months after I returned from my flight to New England, I received a letter from her, in which she wrote, "Dr. Flint is dead. He has left a distressed family. Poor old man! I hope he made his peace with God."

I remembered how he had defrauded my grandmother of the hard earnings she had loaned; how he had tried to cheat her out of the freedom her mistress had promised her, and how he had persecuted her children; and I thought to myself that she was a better Christian than I was, if she could entirely forgive him. I cannot say, with truth, that the news of my old master's death softened my feelings towards him. There are wrongs which even the grave does not bury. The man was odious to me while he lived, and his memory is odious now.

His departure from this world did not diminish my danger. He had threatened my grandmother that his heirs should hold me in slavery after he was gone; that I never should be free so long as a child of his survived. As for Mrs. Flint, I had seen her in deeper afflictions than I supposed the loss of her husband would be, for she had buried several children; yet I never saw any signs of softening in her heart. The doctor had died in embarrassed circumstances, and had little to will to his heirs, except such property as he was unable to grasp. I was well aware what I had to expect from the family of Flints; and my fears were confirmed by a letter from the south, warning me to be on my guard, because Mrs. Flint openly declared that her daughter could not afford to lose so valuable a slave as I was.

I kept close watch of the newspapers for arrivals; but one Saturday night, being much occupied, I forgot to examine the Evening Express as usual. I went down into the parlor for it, early in the morning, and found the boy about to kindle a fire with it. I took it from him and examined the list of arrivals. Reader, if you have never been a slave, you cannot imagine the acute sensation of suffering at my heart, when I read the names of Mr. and Mrs. Dodge, at a hotel in Courtland Street. It was a third-rate hotel, and that circumstance convinced me of the truth of what I had heard, that they were short of funds and had need of my value, as they valued me; and that was by dollars and cents. I hastened with the paper to Mrs. Bruce. Her heart and hand were always open to every one in distress, and she always warmly sympathized with mine. It was impossible to tell how near the enemy was. He might have passed and repassed the house while we were sleeping. He might at that moment be waiting to pounce upon me if I ventured out of doors. I had never seen the husband of my young mistress, and therefore I could not distinguish him from any other stranger. A carriage was hastily ordered; and, closely veiled, I followed Mrs. Bruce, taking the baby again with me into exile. After various turnings and crossings and returnings, the carriage stopped at the house of one of Mrs. Bruce's friends, where I was kindly received. Mrs. Bruce returned immediately, to instruct the domestics what to say if any one came to inquire for me.

It was lucky for me that the evening paper was not burned up before I had a chance to examine the list of arrivals. It was not long after Mrs. Bruce's return to her house, before several people came to inquire for me. One inquired for me, another asked for my daughter Ellen, and another said he had a letter from my grandmother, which he was requested to deliver in person.

They were told, "She has lived here, but she has left."

"How long ago?"

"I don't know, sir."

"Do you know where she went?"

"I do not, sir." And the door was closed.

This Mr. Dodge, who claimed me as his property, was originally a Yankee pedler in the south; then he became a merchant, and finally a slaveholder. He managed to get introduced into what was called the first society, and married Miss Emily Flint. A quarrel arose between him and her brother, and the brother cowhided him. This led to a family feud, and he proposed to remove to Virginia. Dr. Flint left him no property, and his own means had become circumscribed, while a wife and children depended upon him for support. Under these circumstances, it was very natural that he should make an effort to put me into his pocket.

I had a colored friend, a man from my native place, in whom I had the most implicit confidence. I sent for him, and told him that Mr. and Mrs. Dodge had arrived in New York. I proposed that he should call upon them to make inquiries about his friends at the south, with whom Dr. Flint's family were well acquainted. He thought there was no impropriety in his doing so, and he consented. He went to the hotel, and knocked at the door of Mr. Dodge's room, which was opened by the gentleman himself, who gruffly inquired, "What brought you here? How came you to know I was in the city?"

"Your arrival was published in the evening papers, sir; and I called to ask Mrs. Dodge about my friends at home. I didn't suppose it would give any offence."

"Where's that negro girl, that belongs to my wife?"

"What girl, sir?"

"You know well enough. I mean Linda, that ran away from Dr. Flint's plantation, some years ago. I dare say you've seen her, and know where she is."

"Yes, sir, I've seen her, and know where she is. She is out of your reach, sir."

"Tell me where she is, or bring her to me, and I will give her a chance to buy her freedom."

"I don't think it would be of any use, sir. I have heard her say she would go to the ends of the earth, rather than pay any man or woman for her freedom, because she thinks she has a right to it. Besides, she couldn't do it, if she would, for she has spent her earnings to educate her children."

This made Mr. Dodge very angry, and some high words passed between them. My friend was afraid to come where I was; but in the course of the day I received a note from him. I supposed they had not come from the south, in the winter, for a pleasure excursion; and now the nature of their business was very plain.

Mrs. Bruce came to me and entreated me to leave the city the next morning. She said her house was watched, and it was possible that some clew to me might be obtained. I refused to take her advice. She pleaded with an earnest tenderness, that ought to have moved me; but I was in a bitter, disheartened mood. I was weary of flying from pillar to post. I had been chased during half my life, and it seemed as if the chase was never to end. There I sat, in that great city, guiltless of crime, yet not daring to worship God in any of the churches. I heard the bells ringing for afternoon service, and, with contemptuous sarcasm, I said, "Will the preachers take for their text, 'Proclaim liberty to the captive, and the opening of prison doors to them that are bound'? or will they preach from the text, 'Do unto others as ye would they should do unto you'?" Oppressed Poles and Hungarians could find a safe refuge in that city; John Mitchell was free to proclaim in the City Hall his desire for "a plantation well stocked with slaves;" but there I sat, an oppressed American, not daring to show my face. God forgive the black and bitter thoughts I indulged on that Sabbath day! The Scripture says, "Oppression makes even a wise man mad;" and I was not wise.

I had been told that Mr. Dodge said his wife had never signed away her right to my children, and if he could not get me, he would take them. This it was, more than any thing else, that roused such a tempest in my soul. Benjamin was with his uncle William in California, but my innocent young daughter had come to spend a vacation with me. I thought of what I had suffered in slavery at her age, and my heart was like a tiger's when a hunter tries to seize her young.

Dear Mrs. Bruce! I seem to see the expression of her face, as she turned away discouraged by my obstinate mood. Finding her expostulations unavailing, she sent Ellen to entreat me. When ten o'clock in the evening arrived and Ellen had not returned, this watchful and unwearied friend became anxious. She came to us in a carriage, bringing a well-filled trunk for my journey—trusting that by this time I would listen to reason. I yielded to her, as I ought to have done before.

The next day, baby and I set out in a heavy snow storm, bound for New England again. I received letters from the City of Iniquity, addressed to me under an assumed name. In a few days one came from Mrs. Bruce, informing me that my new master was still searching for me, and that she intended to put an end to this persecution by buying my freedom. I felt grateful for the kindness that prompted this offer, but the idea was not so pleasant to me as might have been expected. The more my mind had become enlightened, the more difficult it was for me to consider myself an article of property; and to pay money to those who had so grievously oppressed me seemed like taking from my sufferings the glory of triumph. I wrote to Mrs. Bruce, thanking her, but saying that being sold from one owner to another seemed too much like slavery; that such a great obligation could not be easily cancelled; and that I preferred to go to my brother in California.

Without my knowledge, Mrs. Bruce employed a gentleman in New York to enter into negotiations with Mr. Dodge. He proposed to pay three hundred dollars down, if Mr. Dodge would sell me, and enter into obligations to relinquish all claim to me or my children forever after. He who called himself my master said he scorned so small an offer for such a valuable servant. The gentleman replied, "You can do as you choose, sir. If you reject this offer you will never get any thing; for the woman has friends who will convey her and her children out of the country."

Mr. Dodge concluded that "half a loaf was better than no bread," and he agreed to the proffered terms. By the next mail I received this brief letter from Mrs. Bruce: "I am rejoiced to tell you that the money for your freedom has been paid to Mr. Dodge. Come home to-morrow. I long to see you and my sweet babe."

My brain reeled as I read these lines. A gentleman near me said, "It's true; I have seen the bill of sale." "The bill of sale!" Those words struck me like a blow. So I was sold at last! A human being sold in the free city of New York! The bill of sale is on record, and future generations will learn from it that women were articles of traffic in New York, late in the nineteenth century of the Christian religion. It may hereafter prove a useful document to antiquaries, who are seeking to measure the progress of civilization in the United States. I well know the value of that bit of paper; but much as I love freedom, I do not like to look upon it. I am deeply grateful to the generous friend who procured it, but I despise the miscreant who demanded payment for what never rightfully belonged to him or his.

I had objected to having my freedom bought, yet I must confess that when it was done I felt as if a heavy load had been lifted from my weary shoulders. When I rode home in the cars I was no longer afraid to unveil my face and look at people as they passed. I should have been glad to have met Daniel Dodge himself; to have had him seen me and known me, that he might have mourned over the untoward cir-cumstances which compelled him to sell me for three hundred dollars.

When I reached home, the arms of my benefactress were thrown round me, and our tears mingled. As soon as she could speak, she said, "O Linda, I'm so glad it's all over! You wrote to me as if you thought you were going to be transferred from one owner to another. But I did not buy you for your services. I should have done just the same, if you had been going to sail for California to-morrow. I should, at least, have the satisfaction of knowing that you left me a free woman."

My heart was exceedingly full. I remembered how my poor father had tried to buy me, when I was a small child, and how he had been disappointed. I hoped his spirit was rejoicing over me now. I remembered how my good old grandmother had laid up her earnings to purchase me in later years, and how often her plans had been frustrated. How that faithful, loving old heart would leap for joy, if she could look on me and my children now that we were free! My relatives had been foiled in all their efforts, but God had raised me up a friend among strangers, who had bestowed on me the precious, long-desired boon. Friend! It is a common word, often lightly used. Like other good and beautiful things, it may be tarnished by careless handling; but when I speak of Mrs. Bruce as my friend, the word is sacred.

My grandmother lived to rejoice in my freedom; but not long after, a letter came with a black seal. She had gone "where the wicked cease from troubling, and the weary are at rest."

Time passed on, and a paper came to me from the south, containing an obituary notice of my uncle Phillip. It was the only case I ever knew of such an honor conferred upon a colored person. It was written by one of his friends, and contained these words: "Now that death has laid him low, they call him a good man and a useful citizen; but what are eulogies to the black man, when the world has faded from his vision? It does not require man's praise to obtain rest in God's kingdom." So they called a colored man a citizen! Strange words to be uttered in that region!

Reader, my story ends with freedom; not in the usual way, with marriage. I and my children are now free! We are as free from the power of slaveholders as are the white people of the north; and though that, according to my ideas, is not saying a great deal, it is a vast improvement in my condition. The dream of my life is not yet realized. I do not sit with my children in a home of my own. I still long for a hearthstone of my own, however humble. I wish it for my children's sake far more than for my own. But God so orders circumstances as to keep me with my friend Mrs. Bruce. Love, duty, gratitude, also bind me to her side. It is a privilege to serve her who pities my oppressed people, and who has bestowed the inestimable boon of freedom on me and my children.

It has been painful to me, in many ways, to recall the dreary years I passed in bondage. I would gladly forget them if I could. Yet the retrospection is not altogether without solace; for with those gloomy recollections come tender memories of my good old grandmother, like light, fleecy clouds floating over a dark and troubled sea.

Questions

1. Jacobs writes: "I had objected to having my freedom bought [. . .]." If Jacobs longed for her freedom, why does she object to having it bought?
2. In *Free at Last,* what is the role of religion?
3. Jacobs seems to be offering many arguments. What are some of these arguments?

1. Jacobs writes: "The more my mind had become enlightened, the more difficult it was for me to consider myself an article of property [. . .]." This may be similar to the notion that "ignorance is bliss." Research different methods for keeping people unenlightened. You might begin by researching "book burning," "book banning," and laws prohibiting certain people's educational pursuits. Attempt to construct an argument that examines the relationship between education (or lack thereof) and the ability to oppress people. In constructing your argument, you may wish to research Germany's Nazi Party and Cambodia's Kumher Rouge.
2. Jacobs writes of her grandmother, stating that "[. . .] she was a better Christian than I was, if she could entirely forgive [Dr. Flint]." Examine the roles of religion in the life of a slave. What might some of the motivations be for introducing slaves to Christianity? If many slaves were not allowed to read, if many slaves had their Achilles Tendons cut to keep them from running, if, essentially, everything was stripped from them, why were many allowed to develop their faith in Christianity? What roles did Christianity play in the life of a slave?

Continued

3. When Jacobs learns that she is officially free, she states: "My brain reeled as I read these lines. A gentleman near me said, 'It's true; I have seen the bill of sale.' 'The bill of sale!' Those words struck me like a blow. So I was *sold* at last! A human being *sold* in the free city of New York! The bill of sale is on record, and future generations will learn from it that women were articles of traffic in New York, late in the nineteenth century of the Christian religion. It may hereafter prove a useful document to antiquaries, who are seeking to measure the progress of civilization in the United States." Arguably, in the United States of America, people of the 21st century have concluded that slavery is wrong. However, only two centuries ago, slavery was considered perfectly acceptable by many Americans. To what do we owe this societal transformation? What caused this shift from what was once deemed "right" to what is now deemed "wrong"? Once you have identified what caused this shift, note whether or not similar things have yet to occur in nations that still support slavery. In other words, if what happened in America eventually happens in nations that currently support slavery, will we someday live in a world where slavery no longer exists?

4. Jacobs writes of Dr. Flint: "He had threatened my grandmother that his heirs should hold me in slavery after he was gone; that I never should be free so long as a child of his survived." Arguably, Dr. Flint is simply employing the power of fear as a means to controlling his "property." Examine the relationship between fear and control. While both are illusions, it seems that fear was used not only to control slaves but that it is used in many segments of society as well. For instance, some may argue that parents employ fear to control their children, that the government employs fear to control its citizens, and that the media employ fear to control its listeners / viewers. In the last example, the media (radio, film, print, and Internet), seem to employ fear in order to control what people consume. Attempt to construct an argument that examines the relationship between fear and control.

5. Compare and contrast Jacobs' *Free at Last* with Martin Luther King, Jr.'s *I Have a Dream*. Examine the relationship between perception and reality within the context of "freedom."

Henry David Thoreau (1817-1862)

Famous for living in a crude hut on the shores of Walden Pond and for spending a night in jail for refusing to pay a poll tax in protest over the U.S. invasion of Mexico, this Harvard graduate might be what some would consider a transcendental radical. As a student and friend of Ralph Waldo Emerson, it is clear that an Emersonian influence pervades his work. However, Thoreau quickly developed his own voice, telling his readers in *Civil Disobedience* to, if necessary, "break the law." Such pointed language, though, was interpreted differently by different people, which is demonstrated by Mohandas Gandhi's adoption of Thoreau's passive resistance as a tactic against the British.

Life Without Principle

1. Use this essay as a mirror to observe your life. According to Thoreau's arguments, are you living a life without principle?
2. While reading this essay, ask yourself what your purpose is for working. Does your purpose jibe with Thoreau's?

Life Without Principle

Henry David Thoreau

AT A LYCEUM, not long since, I felt that the lecturer had chosen a theme too foreign to himself, and so failed to interest me as much as he might have done. He described things not in or near to his heart, but toward his extremities and superficies. There was, in this sense, no truly central or centralizing thought in the lecture. I would have had him deal with his privatest experience, as the poet does. The greatest compliment that was ever paid me was when one asked me what I thought, and attended to my answer. I am surprised, as well as delighted, when this happens, it is such a rare use he would make of me, as if he were acquainted with the tool. Commonly, if men want anything of me, it is only to know how many acres I make of their land—since I am a surveyor—or, at most, what trivial news I have burdened myself with. They never will go to law for my meat; they prefer the shell. A man once came a considerable distance to ask me to lecture on Slavery; but on conversing with him, I found that he and his clique expected seven eighths of the lecture to be theirs, and only one eighth mine; so I declined. I take it for granted, when I am invited to lecture anywhere—for I have had a little experience in that business—that there is a desire to hear what I think on some subject, though I may be the greatest fool in the country—and not that I should say pleasant things merely, or such as the audience will assent to; and I resolve, accordingly, that I will give them a strong dose of myself. They have sent for me, and engaged to pay for me, and I am determined that they shall have me, though I bore them beyond all precedent.

So now I would say something similar to you, my readers. Since you are my readers, and I have not been much of a traveller, I will not talk about people a thousand miles off, but come as near home as I can. As the time is short, I will leave out all the flattery, and retain all the criticism.

Let us consider the way in which we spend our lives.

This world is a place of business. What an infinite bustle! I am awaked almost every night by the panting of the locomotive. It interrupts my dreams. There is no sabbath. It would be glorious to see mankind at leisure for once. It is nothing but work, work, work. I cannot easily buy a blank-book to write thoughts in; they are commonly ruled for dollars and cents. An Irishman, seeing me making a minute in the fields, took it for granted that I was calculating my wages. If a man was tossed out of a window when an infant, and so made a cripple for life, or seared out of his wits by the Indians, it is regretted chiefly because he was thus incapacitated for business! I think that there is nothing, not even crime, more opposed to poetry, to philosophy, ay, to life itself, than this incessant business.

There is a coarse and boisterous money-making fellow in the outskirts of our town, who is going to build a bank-wall under the hill along the edge of his meadow. The powers have put this into his head to keep him out of mischief, and he wishes me to spend three weeks digging there with him. The result will be that he will perhaps get some more money to board, and leave for his heirs to spend foolishly. If I do this, most will commend me as an industrious and hard-working man; but if I choose to devote myself to certain labors which yield more real profit, though but little money, they may be inclined to look on me as an idler. Nevertheless, as I do not need the police of meaningless labor to regulate me, and do not see anything absolutely praiseworthy in this fellow's undertaking any more than in many an enterprise of our own or foreign governments, however amusing it may be to him or them, I prefer to finish my education at a different school.

If a man walk in the woods for love of them half of each day, he is in danger of being regarded as a loafer; but if he spends his whole day as a speculator, shearing off those woods and making earth bald before her time, he is esteemed an industrious and enterprising citizen. As if a town had no interest in its forests but to cut them down!

Most men would feel insulted if it were proposed to employ them in throwing stones over a wall, and then in throwing them back, merely that they might earn their wages. But many are no more worthily employed now. For instance: just after sunrise, one summer morning, I noticed one of my neighbors walking beside his team, which was slowly drawing a heavy hewn stone swung under the axle, surrounded by an atmosphere of industry—his day's work begun—his brow commenced to sweat—a reproach to all sluggards and idlers—pausing abreast the shoulders of his oxen, and half turning round with a flourish of his merciful whip, while they gained their length on him. And I thought, Such is the labor which the American Congress exists to protect—honest, manly toil—honest as the day is long—that makes his bread taste sweet, and keeps society sweet—which all men respect and have consecrated; one of the sacred band, doing the needful but irksome drudgery. Indeed, I felt a slight reproach, because I observed this from a window, and was not abroad and stirring about a similar business. The day went by, and at evening I passed the yard of another neighbor, who keeps many servants, and spends much money foolishly, while he adds nothing to the common stock, and there I saw the stone of the morning lying beside a whimsical structure intended to adorn this Lord Timothy Dexter's premises, and the dignity forthwith departed from the teamster's labor, in my eyes. In my opinion, the sun was made to light worthier toil than this. I may add that his employer has since run off, in debt to a good part of the town, and, after passing through Chancery, has settled somewhere else, there to become once more a patron of the arts.

The ways by which you may get money almost without exception lead downward. To have done anything by which you earned money merely is to have been truly idle or worse. If the laborer gets no more than the wages which his employer pays him, he is cheated, he cheats himself. If you would get money as a writer or lecturer, you must be popular, which is to go down perpendicularly. Those services which the community will most readily pay for, it is most disagreeable to render. You are paid for being something less than a man. The State does not commonly reward a genius any more wisely. Even the poet laureate would rather not have to celebrate the accidents of royalty. He must be bribed with a pipe of wine; and perhaps another poet is called away from his muse to gauge that very pipe. As for my own business, even that kind of surveying which I could do with most satisfaction my employers do not want. They would prefer that I should do my work coarsely and not too well, ay, not well enough. When I observe that there are different ways of surveying, my employer commonly asks which will give him the most land, not which is most correct. I once invented a rule for measuring cord-wood, and tried to introduce it in Boston; but the measurer there told me that the sellers did not wish to have their wood measured correctly—that he was already too accurate for them, and therefore they commonly got their wood measured in Charlestown before crossing the bridge. The aim of the laborer should be, not to get his living, to get "a good job," but to perform well a certain work; and, even in a pecuniary sense, it would be economy for a town to pay its laborers so well that they would not feel that they were working for low ends, as for a livelihood merely, but for scientific, or even moral ends. Do not hire a man who does your work for money, but him who does it for love of it.

It is remarkable that there are few men so well employed, so much to their minds, but that a little money or fame would commonly buy them off from their present pursuit. I see advertisements for active young men, as if activity were the whole of a young man's capital. Yet I have been surprised when one has with confidence proposed to me, a grown man, to embark in some enterprise of his, as if I had absolutely nothing to do, my life having been a complete failure hitherto. What a doubtful compliment this to pay me! As if he had met me half-way across the ocean beating up against the wind, but bound nowhere, and proposed to me to go along with him! If I did, what do you think the underwriters would say? No, no! I am not without employment at this stage of the voyage. To tell the truth, I saw an advertisement for able-bodied seamen, when I was a boy, sauntering in my native port, and as soon as I came of age I embarked.

The community has no bribe that will tempt a wise man. You may raise money enough to tunnel a mountain, but you cannot raise money enough to hire a man who is minding his own business. An efficient and valuable man does what he can, whether the community pay him for it or not. The inefficient offer their inefficiency to the highest bidder, and are forever expecting to be put into office. One would suppose that they were rarely disappointed.

Perhaps I am more than usually jealous with respect to my freedom. I feel that my connection with and obligation to society are still very slight and transient. Those slight labors which afford me a livelihood, and by which it is allowed that I am to some extent serviceable to my contemporaries, are as yet commonly a pleasure to me, and I am not often reminded that they are a necessity. So far I am successful. But I foresee that if my wants should be much increased, the labor required to supply them would become a drudgery. If I should sell both my

forenoons and afternoons to society, as most appear to do, I am sure that for me there would be nothing left worth living for. I trust that I shall never thus sell my birthright for a mess of pottage. I wish to suggest that a man may be very industrious, and yet not spend his time well. There is no more fatal blunderer than he who consumes the greater part of his life getting his living. All great enterprises are self-supporting. The poet, for instance, must sustain his body by his poetry, as a steam planing-mill feeds its boilers with the shavings it makes. You must get your living by loving. But as it is said of the merchants that ninety-seven in a hundred fail, so the life of men generally, tried by this standard, is a failure, and bankruptcy may be surely prophesied. Merely to come into the world the heir of a fortune is not to be born, but to be still-born, rather. To be supported by the charity of friends, or a government pension—provided you continue to breathe—by whatever fine synonyms you describe these relations, is to go into the almshouse. On Sundays the poor debtor goes to church to take an account of stock, and finds, of course, that his outgoes have been greater than his income. In the Catholic Church, especially, they go into chancery, make a clean confession, give up all, and think to start again. Thus men will lie on their backs, talking about the fall of man, and never make an effort to get up.

As for the comparative demand which men make on life, it is an important difference between two, that the one is satisfied with a level success, that his marks can all be hit by point-blank shots, but the other, however low and unsuccessful his life may be, constantly elevates his aim, though at a very slight angle to the horizon. I should much rather be the last man—though, as the Orientals say, "Greatness doth not approach him who is forever looking down; and all those who are looking high are growing poor."

It is remarkable that there is little or nothing to be remembered written on the subject of getting a living; how to make getting a living not merely holiest and honorable, but altogether inviting and glorious; for if getting a living is not so, then living is not. One would think, from looking at literature, that this question had never disturbed a solitary individual's musings. Is it that men are too much disgusted with their experience to speak of it? The lesson of value which money teaches, which the Author of the Universe has taken so much pains to teach us, we are inclined to skip altogether. As for the means of living, it is wonderful how indifferent men of all classes are about it, even reformers, so called—whether they inherit, or earn, or steal it. I think that Society has done nothing for us in this respect, or at least has undone what she has done. Cold and hunger seem more friendly to my nature than those methods which men have adopted and advise to ward them off.

The title wise is, for the most part, falsely applied. How can one be a wise man, if he does not know any better how to live than other men?—if he is only more cunning and intellectually subtle? Does Wisdom work in a tread-mill? or does she teach how to succeed by her example? Is there any such thing as wisdom not applied to life? Is she merely the miller who grinds the finest logic? It is pertinent to ask if Plato got his living in a better way or more successfully than his contemporaries—or did he succumb to the difficulties of life like other men? Did he seem to prevail over some of them merely by indifference, or by assuming grand airs? or find it easier to live, because his aunt remembered him in her will? The ways in which most men get their living, that is, live, are mere makeshifts, and a shirking of the real business of life—chiefly because they do not know, but partly because they do not mean, any better.

The rush to California, for instance, and the attitude, not merely of merchants, but of philosophers and prophets, so called, in relation to it, reflect the greatest disgrace on mankind. That so many are ready to live by luck, and so get the means of commanding the labor of others less lucky, without contributing any value to society! And that is called enterprise! I know of no more startling development of the immorality of trade, and all the common modes of getting a living. The philosophy and poetry and religion of such a mankind are not worth the dust of a puffball. The hog that gets his living by rooting, stirring up the soil so, would be ashamed of such company. If I could command the wealth of all the worlds by lifting my finger, I would not pay such a price for it. Even Mahomet knew that God did not make this world in jest. It makes God to be a moneyed gentleman who scatters a handful of pennies in order to see mankind scramble for them. The world's raffle! A subsistence in the domains of Nature a thing to be raffled for! What a comment, what a satire, on our institutions! The conclusion will be, that mankind will hang itself upon a tree. And have all the precepts in all the Bibles taught men only this? and is the last and most admirable invention of the human race only an improved muck-rake? Is this the ground on which Orientals and Occidentals meet? Did God direct us so to get our living, digging where we never planted—and He would, perchance, reward us with lumps of gold?

God gave the righteous man a certificate entitling him to food and raiment, but the unrighteous man found a facsimile of the same in God's coffers, and appropriated it, and obtained food and raiment like the former. It is one of the most extensive systems of counterfeiting that the world has seen. I did not know that mankind was suffering for want of old. I have seen a little of it. I know that it is very malleable, but not so malleable as wit. A grain of gold gild a great surface, but not so much as a grain of wisdom.

The gold-digger in the ravines of the mountains is as much a gambler as his fellow in the saloons of San Francisco. What difference does it make whether you shake dirt or shake dice? If you win, society is the loser. The gold-digger is the enemy of the honest laborer, whatever checks and compensations there may be. It is not enough to tell me that you worked hard to get your gold. So does the Devil work hard. The way of transgressors may be hard in many respects. The humblest observer who goes to the mines sees and says that gold-digging is of the character of a lottery; the gold thus obtained is not the same thing with the wages of honest toil. But, practically, he forgets what he has seen, for he has seen only the fact, not the principle, and goes into trade there, that is, buys a ticket in what commonly proves another lottery, where the fact is not so obvious.

After reading Howitt's account of the Australian gold-diggings one evening, I had in my mind's eye, all night, the numerous valleys, with their streams, all cut up with foul pits, from ten to one hundred feet deep, and half a dozen feet across, as close as they can be dug, and partly filled with water—the locality to which men furiously rush to probe for their fortunes—uncertain where they shall break ground—not knowing but the gold is under their camp itself—

sometimes digging one hundred and sixty feet before they strike the vein, or then missing it by a foot—turned into demons, and regardless of each others' rights, in their thirst for riches—whole valleys, for thirty miles, suddenly honeycombed by the pits of the miners, so that even hundreds are drowned in them—standing in water, and covered with mud and clay, they work night and day, dying of exposure and disease. Having read this, and partly forgotten it, I was thinking, accidentally, of my own unsatisfactory life, doing as others do; and with that vision of the diggings still before me, I asked myself why I might not be washing some gold daily, though it were only the finest particles—why I might not sink a shaft down to the gold within me, and work that mine. There is a Ballarat, a Bendigo for you—what though it were a sulky-gully? At any rate, I might pursue some path, however solitary and narrow and crooked, in which I could walk with love and reverence. Wherever a man separates from the multitude, and goes his own way in this mood, there indeed is a fork in the road, though ordinary travellers may see only a gap in the paling. His solitary path across lots will turn out the higher way of the two.

Men rush to California and Australia as if the true gold were to be found in that direction; but that is to go to the very opposite extreme to where it lies. They go prospecting farther and farther away from the true lead, and are most unfortunate when they think themselves most successful. Is not our native soil auriferous? Does not a stream from the golden mountains flow through our native valley? and has not this for more than geologic ages been bringing down the shining particles and forming the nuggets for us? Yet, strange to tell, if a digger steal away, prospecting for this true gold, into the unexplored solitudes around us, there is no danger that any will dog his steps, and endeavor to supplant him. He may claim and undermine the whole valley even, both the cultivated and the uncultivated portions, his whole life long in peace, for no one will ever dispute his claim. They will not mind his cradles or his toms. He is not confined to a claim twelve feet square, as at Ballarat, but may mine anywhere, and wash the whole wide world in his tom.

Howitt says of the man who found the great nugget which weighed twenty-eight pounds, at the Bendigo diggings in Australia: "He soon began to drink; got a horse, and rode all about, generally at full gallop, and, when he met people, called out to inquire if they knew who he was, and then kindly informed them that he was 'the bloody wretch that had found the nugget.' At last he rode full speed against a tree, and nearly knocked his brains out." I think, however, there was no danger of that, for he had already knocked his brains out against the nugget. Howitt adds, "He is a hopelessly ruined man." But he is a type of the class. They are all fast men. Hear some of the names of the places where they dig: "Jackass Flat"—"Sheep's-Head Gully"—"Murderer's Bar," etc. Is there no satire in these names? Let them carry their ill-gotten wealth where they will, I am thinking it will still be "Jackass Flat," if not "Murderer's Bar," where they live.

The last resource of our energy has been the robbing of graveyards on the Isthmus of Darien, an enterprise which appears to be but in its infancy; for, according to late accounts, an act has passed its second reading in the legislature of New Granada, regulating this kind of mining; and a correspondent of the "Tribune" writes: "In the dry season, when the weather will permit of the country being properly prospected, no doubt other rich guacas [that is, graveyards] will be found." To emigrants he says: "do not come before December; take the Isthmus route in preference to the Boca del Toro one; bring no useless baggage, and do not cumber yourself with a tent; but a good pair of blankets will be necessary; a pick, shovel, and axe of good material will be almost all that is required": advice which might have been taken from the "Burker's Guide." And he concludes with this line in Italics and small capitals: "If you are doing well at home, STAY THERE," which may fairly be interpreted to mean, "If you are getting a good living by robbing graveyards at home, stay there."

But why go to California for a text? She is the child of New England, bred at her own school and church. It is remarkable that among all the preachers there are so few moral teachers. The prophets are employed in excusing the ways of men. Most reverend seniors, the illuminati of the age, tell me, with a gracious, reminiscent smile, betwixt an aspiration and a shudder, not to be too tender about these things—to lump all that, that is, make a lump of gold of it. The highest advice I have heard on these subjects was grovelling. The burden of it was—It is not worth your while to undertake to reform the world in this particular. Do not ask how your bread is buttered; it will make you sick, if you do—and the like. A man had better starve at once than lose his innocence in the process of getting his bread. If within the sophisticated man there is not an unsophisticated one, then he is but one of the devil's angels. As we grow old, we live more coarsely, we relax a little in our disciplines, and, to some extent, cease to obey our finest instincts. But we should be fastidious to the extreme of sanity, disregarding the gibes of those who are more unfortunate than ourselves.

In our science and philosophy, even, there is commonly no true and absolute account of things. The spirit of sect and bigotry has planted its hoof amid the stars. You have only to discuss the problem, whether the stars are inhabited or not, in order to discover it. Why must we daub the heavens as well as the earth? It was an unfortunate discovery that Dr. Kane was a Mason, and that Sir John Franklin was another. But it was a more cruel suggestion that possibly that was the reason why the former went in search of the latter. There is not a popular magazine in this country that would dare to print a child's thought on important subjects without comment. It must be submitted to the D.D.'s. I would it were the chickadee-dees.

You come from attending the funeral of mankind to attend to a natural phenomenon. A little thought is sexton to all the world. I hardly know an intellectual man, even, who is so broad and truly liberal that you can think aloud in his society. Most with whom you endeavor to talk soon come to a stand against some institution in which they appear to hold stock—that is, some particular, not universal, way of viewing things. They will continually thrust their own low roof, with its narrow skylight, between you and the sky, when it is the unobstructed heavens you would view. Get out of the way with your cobwebs; wash your windows, I say! In some lyceums they tell me that they have voted to exclude the subject of religion. But how do I know what their religion is, and when I am near to or far from it? I have walked into such an arena and done my best to make a clean breast of what religion I have experienced, and the audience never suspected what I was about. The lecture was as harmless as moonshine to them.

Whereas, if I had read to them the biography of the greatest scamps in history, they might have thought that I had written the lives of the deacons of their church. Ordinarily, the inquiry is, Where did you come from? or, Where are you going? That was a more pertinent question which I overheard one of my auditors put to another one—"What does he lecture for?" It made me quake in my shoes.

To speak impartially, the best men that I know are not serene, a world in themselves. For the most part, they dwell in forms, and flatter and study effect only more finely than the rest. We select granite for the underpinning of our houses and barns; we build fences of stone; but we do not ourselves rest on an underpinning of granitic truth, the lowest primitive rock. Our sills are rotten. What stuff is the man made of who is not coexistent in our thought with the purest and subtilest truth? I often accuse my finest acquaintances of an immense frivolity; for, while there are manners and compliments we do not meet, we do not teach one another the lessons of honesty and sincerity that the brutes do, or of steadiness and solidity that the rocks do. The fault is commonly mutual, however; for we do not habitually demand any more of each other.

That excitement about Kossuth, consider how characteristic, but superficial, it was!—only another kind of politics or dancing. Men were making speeches to him all over the country, but each expressed only the thought, or the want of thought, of the multitude. No man stood on truth. They were merely banded together, as usual one leaning on another, and all together on nothing; as the Hindus made the world rest on an elephant, the elephant on a tortoise, and the tortoise on a serpent, and had nothing to put under the serpent. For all fruit of that stir we have the Kossuth hat.

Just so hollow and ineffectual, for the most part, is our ordinary conversation. Surface meets surface. When our life ceases to be inward and private, conversation degenerates into mere gossip. We rarely meet a man who can tell us any news which he has not read in a newspaper, or been told by his neighbor; and, for the most part, the only difference between us and our fellow is that he has seen the newspaper, or been out to tea, and we have not. In proportion as our inward life fails, we go more constantly and desperately to the post-office. You may depend on it, that the poor fellow who walks away with the greatest number of letters, proud of his extensive correspondence, has not heard from himself this long while.

I do not know but it is too much to read one newspaper a week. I have tried it recently, and for so long it seems to me that I have not dwelt in my native region. The sun, the clouds, the snow, the trees say not so much to me. You cannot serve two masters. It requires more than a day's devotion to know and to possess the wealth of a day.

We may well be ashamed to tell what things we have read or heard in our day. I did not know why my news should be so trivial—considering what one's dreams and expectations are, why the developments should be so paltry. The news we hear, for the most part, is not news to our genius. It is the stalest repetition. You are often tempted to ask why such stress is laid on a particular experience which you have had—that, after twenty-five years, you should meet Hobbins, Registrar of Deeds, again on the sidewalk. Have you not budged an inch, then? Such is the daily news. Its facts appear to float in the atmosphere, insignificant as the sporules of fungi, and impinge on some neglected thallus, or surface of our minds, which affords a basis for them, and hence a parasitic growth. We should wash ourselves clean of such news. Of what consequence, though our planet explode, if there is no character involved in the explosion? In health we have not the least curiosity about such events. We do not live for idle amusement. I would not run round a corner to see the world blow up.

All summer, and far into the autumn, perchance, you unconsciously went by the newspapers and the news, and now you find it was because the morning and the evening were full of news to you. Your walks were full of incidents. You attended, not to the affairs of Europe, but to your own affairs in Massachusetts fields. If you chance to live and move and have your being in that thin stratum in which the events that make the news transpire—thinner than the paper on which it is printed—then these things will fill the world for you; but if you soar above or dive below that plane, you cannot remember nor be reminded of them. Really to see the sun rise or go down every day, so to relate ourselves to a universal fact, would preserve us sane forever. Nations! What are nations? Tartars, and Huns, and Chinamen! Like insects, they swarm. The historian strives in vain to make them memorable. It is for want of a man that there are so many men. It is individuals that populate the world. Any man thinking may say with the Spirit of Lodin— "I look down from my height on nations, And they become ashes before me;—Calm is my dwelling in the clouds; Pleasant are the great fields of my rest."

Pray, let us live without being drawn by dogs, Esquimaux-fashion, tearing over hill and dale, and biting each other's ears.

Not without a slight shudder at the danger, I often perceive how near I had come to admitting into my mind the details of some trivial affair—the news of the street; and I am astonished to observe how willing men are to lumber their minds with such rubbish—to permit idle rumors and incidents of the most insignificant kind to intrude on ground which should be sacred to thought. Shall the mind be a public arena, where the affairs of the street and the gossip of the tea-table chiefly are discussed? Or shall it be a quarter of heaven itself—an hypaethral temple, consecrated to the service of the gods? I find it so difficult to dispose of the few facts which to me are significant, that I hesitate to burden my attention with those which are insignificant, which only a divine mind could illustrate. Such is, for the most part, the news in newspapers and conversation. It is important to preserve the mind's chastity in this respect. Think of admitting the details of a single case of the criminal court into our thoughts, to stalk profanely through their very sanctum sanctorum for an hour, ay, for many hours! to make a very bar-room of the mind's inmost apartment, as if for so long the dust of the street had occupied us—the very street itself, with all its travel, its bustle, and filth, had passed through our thoughts' shrine! Would it not be an intellectual and moral suicide? When I have been compelled to sit spectator and auditor in a court-room for some hours, and have seen my neighbors, who were not compelled, stealing in from time to time, and tiptoeing about with washed hands and faces, it has appeared to my mind's eye, that, when they took off their hats, their ears suddenly expanded into vast hoppers for sound, between which even their narrow heads were crowded. Like the vanes of windmills, they caught the broad but shallow stream of sound, which, after a few titillating gyrations in their coggy brains, passed out the other side. I wondered if, when they got home, they were as careful to wash their ears as before their hands and faces. It has seemed to me, at such a time, that the auditors and the witnesses, the jury and the counsel, the judge and the criminal at the bar—if I may presume him guilty before he is convicted—were all equally criminal, and a thunderbolt might be expected to descend and consume them all together.

By all kinds of traps and signboards, threatening the extreme penalty of the divine law, exclude such trespassers from the only ground which can be sacred to you. It is so hard to forget what it is worse than useless to remember! If I am to be a thoroughfare, I prefer that it be of the mountain brooks, the Parnassian streams, and not the town sewers. There is inspiration, that gossip which comes to the ear of the attentive mind from the courts of heaven. There is the profane and stale revelation of the bar-room and the police court. The same ear is fitted to receive both communications. Only the character of the hearer determines to which it shall be open, and to which closed. I believe that the mind can be permanently profaned by the habit of attending to trivial things, so that all our thoughts shall be tinged with triviality. Our very intellect shall be macadamized, as it were—its foundation broken into fragments for the wheels of travel to roll over; and if you would know what will make the most durable pavement, surpassing rolled stones, spruce blocks, and asphaltum, you have only to look into some of our minds which have been subjected to this treatment so long.

If we have thus desecrated ourselves—as who has not?—the remedy will be by wariness and devotion to reconsecrate ourselves, and make once more a fane of the mind. We should treat our minds, that is, ourselves, as innocent and ingenuous children, whose guardians we are, and be careful what objects and what subjects we thrust on their attention. Read not the Times. Read the Eternities. Conventionalities are at length as had as impurities. Even the facts of science may dust the mind by their dryness, unless they are in a sense effaced each morning, or rather rendered fertile by the dews of fresh and living truth. Knowledge does not come to us by details, but in flashes of light from heaven. Yes, every thought that passes through the mind helps to wear and tear it, and to deepen the ruts, which, as in the streets of

Pompeii, evince how much it has been used. How many things there are concerning which we might well deliberate whether we had better know them—had better let their peddling-carts be driven, even at the slowest trot or walk, over that bride of glorious span by which we trust to pass at last from the farthest brink of time to the nearest shore of eternity! Have we no culture, no refinement—but skill only to live coarsely and serve the Devil?—to acquire a little worldly wealth, or fame, or liberty, and make a false show with it, as if we were all husk and shell, with no tender and living kernel to us? Shall our institutions be like those chestnut burs which contain abortive nuts, perfect only to prick the fingers?

America is said to be the arena on which the battle of freedom is to be fought; but surely it cannot be freedom in a merely political sense that is meant. Even if we grant that the American has freed himself from a political tyrant, he is still the slave of an economical and moral tyrant. Now that the republic—the respublica—has been settled, it is time to look after the res-privata—the private state—to see, as the Roman senate charged its consuls, "ne quid res-PRIVATA detrimenti caperet," that the private state receive no detriment.

Do we call this the land of the free? What is it to be free from King George and continue the slaves of King Prejudice? What is it to be born free and not to live free? What is the value of any political freedom, but as a means to moral freedom? Is it a freedom to be slaves, or a freedom to be free, of which we boast? We are a nation of politicians, concerned about the outmost defences only of freedom. It is our children's children who may perchance be really free. We tax ourselves unjustly. There is a part of us which is not represented. It is taxation without representation. We quarter troops, we quarter fools and cattle of all sorts upon ourselves. We quarter our gross bodies on our poor souls, till the former eat up all the latter's substance.

With respect to a true culture and manhood, we are essentially provincial still, not metropolitan—mere Jonathans. We are provincial, because we do not find at home our standards; because we do not worship truth, but the reflection of truth; because we are warped and narrowed by an exclusive devotion to trade and commerce and manufactures and agriculture and the like, which are but means, and not the end.

So is the English Parliament provincial. Mere country bumpkins, they betray themselves, when any more important question arises for them to settle, the Irish question, for instance—the English question why did I not say? Their natures are subdued to what they work in. Their "good breeding" respects only secondary objects. The finest manners in the world are awkwardness and fatuity when contrasted with a finer intelligence. They appear but as the fashions of past days—mere courtliness, knee-buckles and small-clothes, out of date. It is the vice, but not the excellence of manners, that they are continually being deserted by the character; they are cast-off-clothes or shells, claiming the respect which belonged to the living creature. You are presented with the shells instead of the meat, and it is no excuse generally, that, in the case of some fishes, the shells are of more worth than the meat. The man who thrusts his manners upon me does as if he were to insist on introducing me to his cabinet of curiosities, when I wished to see himself. It was not in this sense that the poet Decker called Christ "the first true gentleman that ever breathed." I repeat that in this sense the most splendid court in Christendom is provincial, having authority to consult about Transalpine interests only, and not the affairs of Rome. A praetor or proconsul would suffice to settle the questions which absorb the attention of the English Parliament and the American Congress.

Government and legislation! these I thought were respectable professions. We have heard of heaven-born Numas, Lycurguses, and Solons, in the history of the world, whose names at least may stand for ideal legislators; but think of legislating to regulate the breeding of slaves, or the exportation of tobacco! What have divine legislators to do with the exportation or the importation of tobacco? what humane ones with the breeding of slaves? Suppose you were to submit the question to any son of God—and has He no children in the Nineteenth Century? is it a family which is extinct?—in what condition would you get it again? What shall a State like Virginia say for itself at the last day, in which these have been the principal, the staple productions? What ground is there for patriotism in such a State? I derive my facts from statistical tables which the States themselves have published.

A commerce that whitens every sea in quest of nuts and raisins, and makes slaves of its sailors for this purpose! I saw, the other day, a vessel which had been wrecked, and many lives lost, and her cargo of rags, juniper berries, and bitter almonds were strewn along the shore. It seemed hardly worth the while to tempt the dangers of the sea between Leghorn and New York for the sake of a cargo of juniper berries and bitter almonds. America sending to the Old World for her bitters! Is not the sea-brine, is not shipwreck, bitter enough to make the cup of life go down here? Yet such, to a great extent, is our boasted commerce; and there are those who style themselves statesmen and philosophers who are so blind as to think that progress and civilization depend on precisely this kind of interchange and activity—the activity of flies about a molasses—hogshead. Very well, observes one, if men were oysters. And very well, answer I, if men were mosquitoes.

Lieutenant Herndon, whom our government sent to explore the Amazon, and, it is said, to extend the area of slavery, observed that there was wanting there "an industrious and active population, who know what the comforts of life are, and who have artificial wants to draw out the great resources of the country." But what are the "artificial wants" to be encouraged? Not the love of luxuries, like the tobacco and slaves of, I believe, his native Virginia, nor the ice and granite and other material wealth of our native New England; nor are "the great resources of a country" that fertility or barrenness of soil which produces these. The chief want, in every State that I have been into, was a high and earnest purpose in its inhabitants. This alone draws out "the great resources" of Nature, and at last taxes her beyond her resources; for man naturally dies out of her. When we want culture more than potatoes, and illumination more than sugar-plums, then the great resources of a world are taxed and drawn out, and the result, or staple production, is, not slaves, nor operatives, but men—those rare fruits called heroes, saints, poets, philosophers, and redeemers.

In short, as a snow-drift is formed where there is a lull in the wind, so, one would say, where there is a lull of truth, an institution springs up. But the truth blows right on over it, nevertheless, and at length blows it down.

What is called politics is comparatively something so superficial and inhuman, that practically I have never fairly recognized that it concerns me at all. The newspapers, I perceive, devote some of their columns specially to politics or government without charge; and this, one would say, is all that saves it; but as I love literature and to some extent the truth also, I never read those columns at any rate. I do not wish to blunt my sense of right so much. I have not got to answer for having read a single President's Message. A strange age of the world this, when empires, kingdoms, and republics come a-begging to a private man's door, and utter their complaints at his elbow! I cannot take up a newspaper but I find that some wretched government or other, hard pushed and on its last legs, is interceding with me, the reader, to vote for it—more importunate than an Italian beggar; and if I have a mind to look at its certificate, made, perchance, by some benevolent merchant's clerk, or the skipper that brought it over, for it cannot speak a word of English itself, I shall probably read of the eruption of some Vesuvius, or the overflowing of some Po, true or forged, which brought it into this condition. I do not hesitate, in such a case, to suggest work, or the almshouse; or why not keep its castle in silence, as I do commonly? The poor President, what with preserving his popularity and doing his duty, is completely bewildered. The newspapers are the ruling power. Any other government is reduced to a few marines at Fort Independence. If a man neglects to read the Daily Times, government will go down on its knees to him, for this is the only treason in these days.

Those things which now most engage the attention of men, as politics and the daily routine, are, it is true, vital functions of human society, but should be unconsciously performed, like the corresponding functions of the physical body. They are infrahuman, a kind of vegetation. I sometimes awake to a half-consciousness of them going on about me, as a man may become conscious of some of the processes of digestion in a morbid state, and so have the dyspepsia, as it is called. It is as if a thinker submitted himself to be rasped by the great gizzard of creation. Politics is, as it were, the gizzard of society, full of grit and gravel, and the two political parties are its two opposite halves—sometimes split into quarters, it may be, which grind on each other. Not only individuals, but states, have thus a confirmed dyspepsia, which expresses itself, you can imagine by what sort of eloquence. Thus our life is not altogether a forgetting, but also, alas! to a great extent, a remembering, of that which we should never have been conscious of, certainly not in our waking hours. Why should we not meet, not always as dyspeptics, to tell our had dreams, but sometimes as eupeptics, to congratulate each other on the ever-glorious morning? I do not make an exorbitant demand, surely.

Questions

1. Even if you have never read Thoreau before, many of his works house quotations that speak to his personality and his method for doing things. For instance, when he writes, "As the time is short, I will leave out all the flattery, and retain all the criticism," what does this suggest about him?

2. When Thoreau writes, "This world is a place of business," is he using "business" to mean more than one thing?

3. Thoreau writes: "The ways by which you may get money almost without exception lead downward." How might this be interpreted? Can you find any examples to help support or refute this quotation?

4. Thoreau writes: "When I observe that there are different ways of surveying, my employer commonly asks which will give him the most land, not which is most correct." Are you ever guilty of this? Do you ever choose to do what's easiest or of most benefit to you as opposed to what is right?

5. Thoreau suggests that people should be hired for their love of the job when he writes: "Do not hire a man who does your work for money, but him who does it for love of it." Is this reasonable? For instance, can this quotation be applied to jobs that entail flipping hamburgers on a grill or picking vegetables in a field? In other words, is "loving the job" a luxury or a necessity?

6. When Thoreau writes, "The inefficient offer their inefficiency to the highest bidder, and are forever expecting to be put into office," is he taking a jab at a certain group?

7. Sometimes people say, "I wish I were born rich!" Thoreau, however, writes: "Merely to come into the world the heir of a fortune is not to be born, but to be still-born, rather." Why would Thoreau make such a declaration? What might he be attempting to communicate?

8. Thoreau pokes fun at religion and apathy when he writes: "Thus men will lie on their backs, talking about the fall of man, and never make an effort to get up." How does this quotation, delivered within the context of the Catholic Church and the act of confession, help advance Thoreau's essay?

9. Thoreau quotes "the Orientals" as saying: "Greatness doth not approach him who is forever looking down; and all those who are looking high are growing poor." What might this quotation mean?

10. Thoreau writes: "The lesson of value which money teaches, which the Author of the Universe has taken so much pains to teach us, we are inclined to skip altogether." What is the lesson of value? And who is "the Author of the Universe"?

11. Thoreau seems to find more value in possessing wit as opposed to possessing gold. This is evident when he writes: "I did not know that mankind were suffering for want of gold. I have seen a little of it. I know that it is very malleable, but not so malleable as wit. A grain of gold will gild a great surface, but not so much as a grain of wisdom." Do you agree? Why?

12. Thoreau writes: "Get out of the way with your cobwebs, wash your windows, I say!" Based on this, what might Thoreau want his readers to do?

13. Is Thoreau articulating things representative of a reasonable man or a cynic? For instance, he writes: "We rarely meet a man who can tell us any news which he has not read in a newspaper, or been told by his neighbor; and, for the most part, the only difference between us and our fellow is, that he has seen the newspaper, or been out to tea, and we have not." Frankly, Thoreau seems to view people as sheep. Does this view seem reasonable? What might people do to combat this "sheepishness"?

14. Thoreau writes: "We do not live for idle amusement. I would not run round a corner to see the world blow up." At whom is Thoreau poking fun?

15. Thoreau often has fun with language. One example is when he writes: "Read not the Times. Read the Eternities." What might he mean here?

16. Thoreau ends his essay with this: "I do not make an exorbitant demand, surely." Given what Thoreau has argued, why might this be appropriate?

1. Thoreau writes: "Most men would feel insulted, if it were proposed to employ them in throwing stones over a wall, and then in throwing them back, merely that they might earn their wages. But many are no more worthily employed now." This quotation is interesting, for it questions the notion of being "worthily employed." Although it seems that many are employed simply because they must earn money, others seem to seek employment that not only earns them money but a certain satisfaction or sense of worth as well. Interview various people and the jobs they hold. Then, construct an argument that explores whether or not their jobs are allowing them to lead what Thoreau might deem a "life without principle."

2. For many people, the American Dream comprises more than life, liberty, and the pursuit of happiness. (As a matter of fact, "life, liberty, and the pursuit of happiness" were originally "life, liberty, and the pursuit of property.") Regardless, many people associate the American Dream with the accumulation of wealth. However, Thoreau writes: "To have done anything by which you earned money *merely* is to have been truly idle or worse. If the laborer gets no more than the wages which his employer pays him, he is cheated, he cheats himself." What is it that Thoreau thinks people should seek in addition to money? What does he think people should get from their labor? After researching famous workaholics and famous philanthropists, compare and contrast the fruits of their labor within the context of *Life Without Principle.*

3. Similar to Oliver Stone or Michael Moore, Henry David Thoreau seems to make many arguments against Corporate America. This is evident when Thoreau writes: "What difference does it make, whether you shake dirt or shake dice? If you win, society is the loser. The gold-digger is the enemy of the honest laborer, whatever checks and compensations there may be. It is not enough to tell me that you worked hard to get your gold. So does the Devil work hard." Take this quotation, coupled with anything else deemed relevant from *Life Without Principle,* and compare and contrast it with Oliver Stone's *JFK* and Michael Moore's *Roger and Me* and *Farenheit 9 / 11.* In comparing and contrasting these works, you may wish to identify the main arguments of each and, by employing additional sources, take a stand for or against these arguments.

4. Thoreau references miners who toil endlessly for gold: "[. . .] standing in water, and covered with mud and clay, they work night and day, dying of exposure and disease." Today's miners are still mining gold, but they are also mining coal and diamonds. Specifically, the diamond mines of Africa are notorious for promoting slave labor that causes the "dying of exposure and disease." Research the diamond mines of Africa, and then research the value placed on diamonds in the United States of America. After doing so, construct an argument that takes a stand on the diamond industry, for just as "diamonds are forever," so is death.

Continued

5. Thoreau writes: "No man stood on truth. They were merely banded to-gether, as usual, one leaning on another, and all together on nothing [. . .]." What this quotation suggests is very similar to what many quotations in *Self-reliance,* by Ralph Waldo Emerson, suggests. In a comparison and contrast essay, compare and contrast *Life Without Principle* and *Self-reliance.* In doing so, you should do some biographical research on Thoreau and Emerson. Then, note the similarities and differences between these two essays and the men who wrote them.

6. Thoreau seems to take a stand against "the news in newspapers and con-versation" in favor of preserving "the mind's chastity," which might be done by spending more time taking solitary walks, observing nature, and "attending to your own affairs." Note the pros and cons of embracing a more introspective, egocentric, self-reliant, isolationistic perspective on life as opposed to expressing a legitimate concern in the affairs of the world around you. In doing so, you may wish to further examine *Life Without Principle* and Thoreau's *Walden.* Also, you may wish to examine Emerson's *Self-reliance* and *Nature* as well as the works of Lao Tzu and Chuang Tsu (the founders of Taoism).

7. It has been said that "one's input determines one's output." Similarly, Thoreau writes: "I believe that the mind can be permanently profaned by the habit of attending to trivial things, so that all our thoughts shall be tinged with triviality. Our very intellect shall be macadamized [. . .]." The "macadamization" of the intellect is a reference to John McAdam, a Scot-tish engineer who pioneered paving roads with asphalt. Thus, Thoreau is suggesting that if one develops the habit of attending to trivial things, it is analogous to paving the intellect with asphalt. Clearly, the context in which this suggestion is made seems to consist, primarily, of one's em-ployment, but the context may also consist of daily conversation and folly. Further, if Thoreau were alive today, might he address television and the notion that, according to *The Los Angeles Times,* the television is on six to eight hours per day in the average North American household? Might this exposure to "trivial things" lead to "macadamization"? After performing some research, attempt to support or refute Thoreau's contention.

8. Thoreau writes: "[. . .] we do not worship truth, but the reflection of truth [. . .]." Even though Thoreau has not overtly addressed reliance on physi-cal beauty, based on what he has written in *Life Without Principle,* how might he react to the current trend toward attaining physical perfection that might be achieved through breast augmentations, tummy tucks, penile enhancements, and Botox injections? Further, how might he react to the airbrushing and other manipulations that occur on many covers of "beauty" magazines? After performing some research, take a stand on the current trend toward attaining physical perfection, and employ quotations from Thoreau's *Life Without Principle* to help advance your stance.

Section II

Academic Writing

Easy Reference

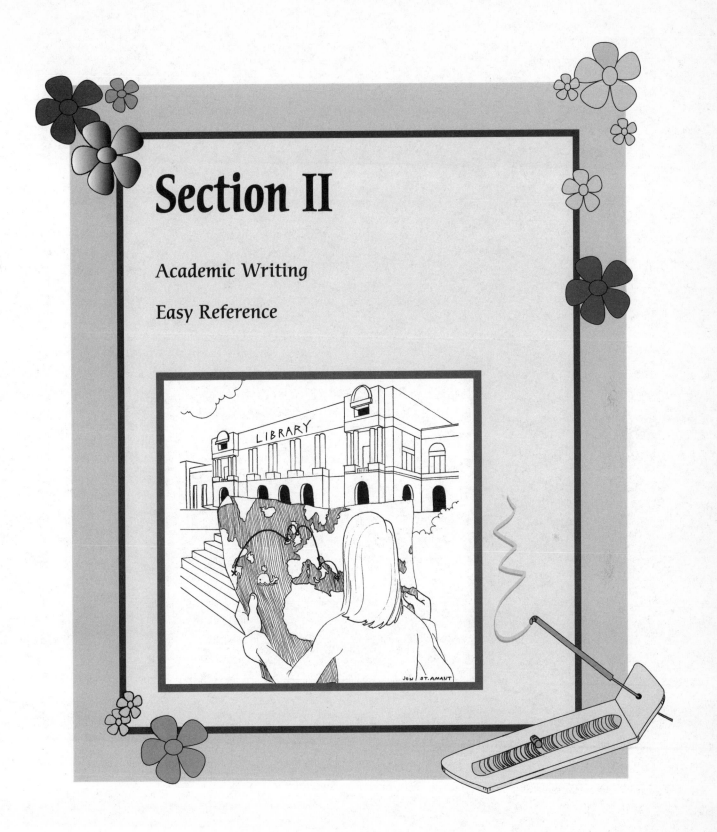

Academic Writing

Let's begin by addressing some fundamentals of academic writing. In addressing these fundamentals, let's address the evolution of the academic paper, starting with the paragraph. First, while you have probably been writing paragraphs for many years, please note that the academic paragraph often adheres to a formal structure, and this structure houses five components:

❀ **Topic Sentence**
❀ **Point**
❀ **Example**
❀ **Commentary**
❀ **Concluding Sentence**

The **Topic Sentence** represents what the writer intends to "prove" to her reader. Here is an example of a topic sentence: "The death penalty should remain legal in California for many reasons." Naturally, this would be the topic sentence (the first sentence) of a paragraph designed to "prove" that the death penalty should remain legal in California. (Note that "prove" is placed in quotation marks, for even though the writer intends to "prove" that the death penalty should remain legal in California, it is something that cannot be proven. It can be well-supported and well-argued, but it cannot be proven.) Still, if the prompt is "Take a stand on whether or not the death penalty should remain legal in California," one way to develop a strong topic sentence is to ask, "What do I want to prove?" In doing so, you might write the following: "I want to prove that the death penalty should remain legal in California for many reasons." Then, simply remove "I want to prove that." (This is important, for as a writer, you do not want to bring attention to yourself. In other words, even though each argument you write will be based on your opinion, when you use "I," it shines a spotlight on you, and it prompts the reader to question your religious beliefs, political affiliation, sexual orientation, etc.)

The **Point** is an assertion. Consider, for instance, the aforementioned **Topic Sentence:** "The death penalty should remain legal in California for many reasons." Directly following the **Topic Sentence** is the first **Point.** In this case, it might read: "First, the death penalty is a crime deterrent." Now, it is essential that every **Point** be coupled with an **Example.**

The **Example** supports each **Point.** Thus, if the **Point** were, "First, the death penalty is a crime deterrent," then the **Example** might be, "For example, in an article titled 'Victim's family: Jury sent a message in dragging death case,' Mary Verrett said this shortly after Bill King was sentenced to death: 'They sent a message throughout the world that hate crime must stop, and if you do not believe that, see what happened to Bill King. So it's a deterrent to even younger children that you're going to pay for your decisions [. . .]'" (Zewe, Candiotti). Here, the **Example** is a quotation. While it is possible to advance your **Point** without employing a quotation, quotations are often the most credible way to advance your **Point** and to shift the burden of proof. Remember, unless you are an expert in the field upon which you are writing, it is important to shift the burden of proof so that your entire argument is not teetering on your personal examples. This is one of the many reasons to use secondary sources whenever you need to employ an **Example.**

After each **Example,** it is important to have at least one sentence of **Commentary.** This is essential, for it is irresponsible for writers to assume that their readers have made the requisite connection between the **Point** and the **Example.** Further, if there is any chance that the reader did not find the relevance between the **Point** and the **Example** within the context of the **Topic Sentence,** then that is simply one more reason to employ **Commentary.** In its simplest form, **Commentary** links the **Example** to the **Point,** and the **Point** to the **Topic Sentence.** Let's take the aforementioned **Topic Sentence, Point,** and **Example:**

Topic Sentence: The death penalty should remain legal in California for many reasons.
Point: First, the death penalty is a crime deterrent.
Example: For example, in an article titled "Victim's family: Jury sent a message in dragging death case," Mary Verrett said this shortly after Bill King was sentenced to death: "They sent a message throughout the world that hate crime must stop, and if you do not believe that, see what happened to Bill King. So it's a deterrent to even younger children that you're going to pay for your decisions [. . .]."

Now, after reading the **Topic Sentence, Point,** and **Example,** it should become evident that something is needed to explain the relevance of the **Example** to the **Point,** and the relevance of the **Point** to the **Topic Sentence.** Specifically, what is needed is **Commentary.** Thus, two sentences of **Commentary** might read:

Commentary: Clearly, Verrett believes that people have been sent a powerful message as a result of Bill King's death sentence. Such a message should help deter crime, and it further reinforces why the death penalty should remain legal in California.

Now, in a well-developed paragraph, there should be at least two **Points, Examples,** and **Commentaries.** Of course, once the paragraph has been adequately developed, it is important to employ a **Concluding Sentence.**

The **Concluding Sentence** should not simply regurgitate what was already argued in the paragraph. Instead, it should attempt to show relevance between the issue and "the real world." This can be done by reading everything that precedes the **Concluding Sentence** and asking the following question: "Why should anybody care about this?" Also, while the **Concluding Sentence** may restate the **Topic Sentence,** it should make an attempt to offer new information and, again, a new perspective from which to look at the argument. One example of a **Concluding Sentence** for a paragraph on the death penalty might be this: "A murderer is a thief, for he has stolen something; unfortunately, if what he has stolen cannot be replaced, then the citizens of California should have the right to steal something from the murderer, even if it is his own life."

Before moving on to the essay, let's take a look at a completed paragraph that uses the **Topic Sentence, Point, Example, Commentary,** and **Concluding Sentence.**

This paragraph (similar to the aforementioned examples) will respond to the following prompt: Take a stand on whether or not the death penalty should remain legal in California.

Alex Brunner

Professor Sas

English IA

20 December 2004

California Dreamin'

The death penalty should remain legal in California for many reasons. First, the death

penalty is a crime deterrent. For example, in an article titled "Victim's family: Jury sent a message

in dragging death case," Mary Verrett said this shortly after Bill King was sentenced to death:

"They sent a message throughout the world that hate crime must stop, and if you do not believe

that, see what happened to Bill King. So it's a deterrent to even younger children that you're going

to pay for your decisions [. . .]" (www.cnn.com). Clearly, Verrett believes that people have been

sent a powerful message as a result of Bill King's death sentence. Such a message should help

deter crime, and it further reinforces why the death penalty should remain legal in California.

Another reason why the death penalty should remain legal can be found when examining

recidivism, the notion that if a person murders once, he will do it again. This is supported by an

article titled "Former death row inmate may again face death penalty charge filed after 25 years":

> [Darryl] Kemp has been out of custody for only eight of the 49 years since he
>
> turned 18. [. . .] Kemp was convicted of murder by strangulation and several
>
> rapes in 1960 and sent to death row. His sentence was commuted to life when the
>
> death penalty was declared unconstitutional in the mid-1970s. He was paroled
>
> less than four months before [he killed Armida Wiltsey near the Lafayette
>
> Reservoir in California]. (www.prodeathpenalty.com)

Here, Darryl Kemp's murder of Armida Wiltsey could have been prevented had he been sentenced to death. While all convicted murderers may not possess recidivistic tendencies, and while some can be rehabilitated, it seems clear that Armida Wiltsey would not have been murdered by Darryl Kemp had he simply been put to death after his first murder conviction. A final reason for supporting the death penalty in California is a sense of retribution not only for the victim's family members but for society as well. According to Robert Macy, District Attorney of Oklahoma City, "In 1991, a young mother was rendered helpless and made to watch as her baby was executed. The mother was then mutilated and killed. The killer should not lie in some prison with three meals a day, clean sheets, cable TV, family visits and endless appeals. For justice to prevail, some killers just need to die" (http://deathpenaltyinfo.msu.). Macy's contention should be embraced, for it does not seem fair that in exchange for taking two lives, the murderer can spend the rest of his life enjoying the comforts that many law-abiding, tax-paying citizens hope to attain. Clearly, if people are expected to support the justice system, then justice must be exacted; such retribution, especially after brutally killing a baby and its mother, cannot be found in rewarding the killer with the perks of penal lore. A murderer is a thief, for he has stolen something; unfortunately, if what he has stolen cannot be replaced, then the citizens of California should have the right to steal something from the murderer, even if it is his own life.

Works Cited

"A just society requires the death penalty for the taking of a life."

    <http://deathpenaltyinfo.msu.edu/c/about/arguments/argument2a.htm>.

Candiotti, Susan and Charles Zewe. "Victim's family: Jury sent a message in dragging death

    case." <http://www.cnn.com/US/9902/25/dragging.death.04/>.

"Former death row inmate may again face death penalty charge filed after 25 years." 3 Oct. 2003.

    <http://www.prodeathpenalty.com/repeat_murder.htm>.

The aforementioned paragraph is written according to the Point / Example / Commentary structure. As a matter of fact, those examining the paragraph's organizational strategy should note the way in which it is constructed:

Topic Sentence: The Death Penalty should remain legal in California for many reasons.
Point 1: Crime deterrent.
Example 1: Bill King's death sentence.
Commentary: Explain the Example and its relationship to the Point and Topic Sentence.
Point 2: Recidivism.
Example 1: Darryl Kemp's parole.
Commentary: Explain the Example and its relationship to the Point and Topic Sentence.
Point 3: Retribution.
Example 1: Robert Macy, District Attorney of Oklahoma City.
Commentary: Explain the Example and its relationship to the Point and Topic Sentence.
Concluding Sentence: A murderer is a thief, for he has stolen something; unfortunately, if what he has stolen cannot be replaced, then the citizens of California should have the right to steal something from the murderer, even if it is his own life.

This is an example of the five components (Topic Sentence, Point, Example, Commentary, and Concluding Sentence) in a **well-developed paragraph.** In an essay, the main difference is that such a paragraph is referred to as a Body Paragraph, and instead of ending with a Concluding Sentence, it will often end with a Transition. Before applying this structure to an essay, however, see how it works for you in a **well-developed paragraph.**

    Begin by **Pre-Writing** (Journalist's Six, Listing, Brainstorming, or Sprinting). Then, compose an outline in order to promote **Organization.** Finally, compose your first draft, which should represent the **Development** of the ideas found in your outline.

PRE-WRITING

Choose a pre-writing exercise (Journalist's Six, Listing, Brainstorming, or Sprinting), and begin developing a response to the prompt you've chosen to address.

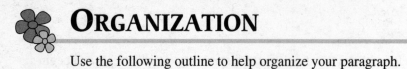

ORGANIZATION

Use the following outline to help organize your paragraph.

Well-developed Paragraph

Topic Sentence:

_____

_____

Point 1:

_____

_____

Example 1:

_____

_____

Commentary:

_____

_____

Point 2:

_____

_____

Example 1:

_____

_____

Commentary:

_____

_____

Point 3:

_____

_____

Example 1:

_____

_____

Commentary:

_____

_____

Point 4:

_____

_____

Example 1:

_____

_____

Commentary:

_____

_____

Concluding Sentence:

_____

_____

DEVELOPMENT

Use these pages to construct your first draft.

In This Section

In transitioning from the well-developed paragraph to the essay, it is important to note that the well-developed paragraph (as illustrated in the aforementioned model) can now be used as a Body Paragraph in an essay. Essays often house Introductions, Body Paragraphs, and Conclusions. While there is generally one Introduction and one Conclusion, the number of Body Paragraphs is reliant upon many factors. For instance, how many Body Paragraphs will be required to adequately advance the essay's thesis statement? How many sources are required? What are the expectations regarding the essay's length? Once these questions are answered, one might begin pre-writing or constructing an outline, and then it may be time to begin composing the first draft. And then, after writing, re-writing, and proofreading, the essay may be ready for its formal submission.

Clearly, it has been shown that a Body Paragraph houses certain components. And in adhering to the Topic Sentence / Point / Example / Commentary structure, questions regarding how to organize a Body Paragraph are, essentially, answered. But students often wonder, "How should the Introduction or the Conclusion be organized?" The answer to this question is not intended to seem ambiguous. However, there are copious organizational strategies for the Introduction and the Conclusion. What does seem essential, though, is that the Introduction contain a well-articulated thesis statement. Further, the Conclusion should contain a re-statement of the thesis. But realize this: just as the Conclusion should not consist of regurgitated ideas from the Body Paragraphs, the Introduction should not spoil the essay by introducing all that will be addressed. In other words, if seen from the perspective of a restaurateur, the Introduction might be the appetizer, and the Conclusion might be the dessert. Nonetheless, in realizing that different people possess different learning styles, an "Easy Reference" is found at the end of this chapter. In this section, students will also find hints on composing Introductions and Conclusions.

Since many people learn through modeling, three student essays and one essay written by a professional writer have been included in this chapter. Read these essays, read the Conversations with Writers, and read the Play-by-play. In doing so, more light should be shed on the construction of Introductions, Body Paragraphs, and Conclusions.

What follows is a completed student essay, written by Dominique Valencia, in response to this prompt:

Thoreau writes: "Most men would feel insulted, if it were proposed to employ them in throwing stones over a wall, and then in throwing them back, merely that they might earn their wages. But many are no more worthily employed now." This quotation is interesting, for it questions the notion of being "worthily employed." Although it seems that many are employed simply because they must earn money, others seem to seek employment that not only earns them money but a certain satisfaction or sense of worth as well. Interview various people and the jobs they hold. Then, construct an argument that explores whether or not their jobs are allowing them to lead what Thoreau might deem a "Life Without Principle."

Dominique Valencia

Professor Ivanovic

English 1A

23 December 2004

"If you pick up a starving dog and make him prosperous, he will not bite you. That is the principle difference between a dog and a man."

—Mark Twain

The Power of the Penny over Principle

Amidst societal rubble, a decomposing sense of humanism rots, with the fleshly desires materialism brings. The world no longer resounds each morning with the dawning of the sun bursting through the atmosphere, for now the sun must battle through the clouds in a smoldering layer of soot, better referred to as smog—the excrement of industry. As the air thickens, tickling the throat of corporate America and suffocating the lungs of the *not so privileged,* so does thicken the skin of the working class. It is utter necessity. Henry David Thoreau once wrote in his inspired essay, "Life Without Principle": "Have we no culture, no refinement—but skill only to live coarsely and serve the Devil?—to acquire a little worldly wealth, or fame, or liberty, and make a false show with it, as if we were all husk and shell, with no tender and living kernel to us? Shall our institutions be like those chestnut-burs which contain abortive nuts, perfect only to prick the fingers?" (www.walden.org). As in the rapidly industrializing day in which Thoreau writes, so is the homogenization of industry at present. There is no shelter from the corporate tempest

which sweeps over the nation, the world, overturning man to sweat and toil in order to gain

monetary sustenance, often forgoing all sense of self in the process, all remnant of personal

principle. It is evident that the lives led by many workers are drudged with such tainted societal

ideology, condoning the abandonment of personal principle, if all for the vain sake of getting a

share of that "good ole' piece o' pie." Given the testimonies of two working class individuals,

Kimberly Winderman and Ronald "Reagan" Pratt, two clients of Ilene Philipson, Ph.D, "Brenda"

and "Ingrid," and analysis by Philipson, as well as testimonies straight from corporate America, it

can be seen precisely how difficult it is to maintain personal principle in a universe which so

freely sacrifices the orbiting of virtue and, instead, remains loyal to the passing of pennies.

Kimberly Winderman has been an independently contracting, graphic designer for two

years, and considers herself lucky to have a job designing sans a bachelor's degree. However,

her principles have been jeopardized by her work due to the lack of artistic freedom awarded her

by her company, despite the profuse talent she displays on the job, which is recognized by not

only her workmates but also her higher ups. Winderman says, "What hinders me are the limits

placed on me as a graphic designer. You are always creating for someone else. [. . .] I've found

myself designing packaging for dolls [. . .]. It's nothing I'd frame and be proud of." The

underlying sacrifices made by Winderman and other artists alike become evident in this all-too-

common exploitation process, where art is used as a monetary commodity instead of for

personal pleasure. As if this were not enough of a social travesty, Winderman also must be

marked with the vile stench of notoriety that might be related to her by merely working for a

company. Winderman says, "Everything that comes out of a studio is representation of who the

workers of the studio are. [. . .] David and Goliath play on stereotypes. If I worked there,

people would think I was immature. [. . .] You work for that studio, and you have the studio branded on your forehead." It is clear in this statement that Winderman must tolerate being

marred with a corporate label, and defy personal principle, just to make a decent living. The

stresses of maintaining individual economic homeostasis are also apparent when Winderman

introduces the standards by which Europeans live. Winderman says, "Germany gets six weeks'

paid vacation. Here, we don't have time to have hobbies. People think that watching

The Sopranos is a suitable hobby. [. . .] People's perceptions of hobbies don't develop until their

40s. [. . .] Our society's working system sucks the life out of you." It is evident that the studio

that Winderman works for not only overworks her, but that also, she may be leading a life that

she does not necessarily approve of herself, doing so because this industrialized society requires

that individuals live to work, instead of live, then work. By working excessively, it is obvious

that another area will be neglected, this area more commonly than not being personal principle.

Winderman also suggests that her work seems to demand too much out of an artist, depleting her

of dignity and pride. Winderman says, "Who wants to make art for money? Someone is

dictating what you create. Artists don't take orders. It doesn't make sense. Unless you can

come up with a brilliant idea, and someone likes it [can an artist be truly free to do what they

wish]." It is obvious that principles are easily put on the backburner in order to make ends meet,

once again dictated by a penny-pushing society. In a society where capitalism reigns supreme,

morality waves on the sidelines waiting patiently for its chance to show worth in the big game, a

worth that should not have ever become so widely overlooked. Another person who has been

stripped of principle subconsciously in American society is Ronald "Reagan" Pratt, Greyhound

Senior Dog for almost 30 years.

Unlike Winderman, Pratt seems to be inconsistent with his feelings toward his chosen

profession. Upon being interviewed on day one, Pratt was insistent that he loves his job, and

would not want to be anywhere else. The next day, after work, Pratt says the opposite. "I'm like

George from Seinfeld. I have no dignity. [. . .] I changed my mind; I hate my job. [. . .] Just call

me George. I'm gonna shave my hair. [Lowly] I'm gonna go outside and smoke. That's what

George would do." In likening himself to a fictional television character, it is not difficult to see

how easily it is for the working class to flip-flop on their attitude toward their jobs. Americans

seem to do this in order to rationalize the career choices they have made in their lives, quelling the

demands placed on them by our "industrious" society. Pratt also displays an underlying hostility

toward work when he is asked the question, first proposed by Thoreau's "Life Without Principle,"

"If you were proposed to throw rocks over a wall, just so that you could throw them back, would

you take the job?" Pratt replied, "I'd do my best to find the most efficient way to do the job so

that one day I could be the person who gets to tell people to throw rocks over the wall." This

answer suggests that Americans have an easier time doing a job that they feel, perhaps one day,

could be their own, rather than taking enjoyment out of work for the purpose of just that:

personal enjoyment in doing a job well. This corruption of thought is caused by the capitalistic

nature that treads upon the moral core of society. Pratt seems also to, in accordance, liken his

pleasures to work, which denotes an evasion of dealing with the realities at hand. Pratt says,

"Even if you have sex seven days a week, you're gonna want a rest." Here, Pratt reveals that he is

overworked and compares the act of intercourse with work. There is an issue when the working

class cannot distinguish the line between work and play. When Pratt tells of the incentives that

are produced by his job, it is apparent what the driving force of society is. Pratt says, "My

rewards are my paycheck." Once again it can be seen that principles are routinely thrown out the

window if dollars and cents are in the equation. Comparatively, two patients of Ilene Philipson,

Ph.D., deal with the same detriments and delusions, due to the exchanging of work for principle.

Society has become so shallow that the exchange process, principle for work, is done almost

solely in the subconscious mind of the working. Brenda's desire to work had become almost addictive, to the point where it was impossible for her to even imagine a life where she was not

indebted to a company. Philipson states:

> Brenda's attachment to the firm was not merely an emotional or economical one;
>
> it was also remarkably sensual. She described the smell (a mélange of expensive
>
> cologne, leather, and gourmet coffee), the feel (of leather chairs, thick carpets),
>
> and the sounds (KDFC, the local classical music station, playing in the
>
> background). As in any marriage, Brenda's wedlock spoke to a variety of
>
> psychological needs and longings that were satisfied nowhere else in her life.
>
> Without her job, Brenda indeed believed her life was over. (18, 19)

This "necessity" for work makes it clear how easily the working class of society has slipped into a

sort of working coma, with each passing day, falling into a more unfathomable depth. Believing

that one's life could possibly be over without a job to occupy time is merely a delusion, and an

utter lack of personal principle. Concordantly, Philipson's client, Ingrid, denied self for work,

placing herself in a constant state of emotional, psychological, and moral jeopardy. Ingrid states:

> It's like nothing else, going public and being at a company like this [. . .] We set
>
> the pace; we're making history [. . .] I love the people I work with [. . .] So many
>
> of us have been through it all and we still respect each other and work well
>
> together [. . .] I know you think it's crazy I work so much, but it's not like I'm
>
> sitting in front of a computer all day. A lot of it's talking to really smart people
>
> about what we're going to do. I don't think some *relationship* [with contempt] or
>
> a bunch of rug rats are exactly going to make me feel that good, at the top of my
>
> game, you know? (Philipson 18)

Ingrid portrays an individual who has for too long restrained personal principle, and allowed the

standards set forth by society to dictate her entire existence. But Ingrid neglects not only herself, but all life. Philipson adds that for the sake of work and monetary gain, Ingrid works 110 hours a

week, killing her tropical fish out of negligence in the process. But it is all worthwhile for Ingrid,

who states: "Here I was at 28 making over $100,000 a year and they think I'm great! I can do no

wrong. I'm hot!" (Philipson 20). The mass ego produced by overworking depletes man of all

principle. It is evident that Ingrid's life consists of all work and no real life, no real time to think

for herself, thus being easily controlled by the corporate life as a marionette on strings, being

teetered from whim to whim. Philipson addresses that man is ruled by current social standard,

and thus ruled by mass materialism. Philipson states: "It is a common belief that Americans

work longer hours because we are consumerists, a voracious people who see work as a means to

garnering possessions. Our materialistic culture inflames our desires for more, bigger, designer-

labeled, luxurious, brand-named stuff. We'll do whatever it takes to be able to consume what we

want" (11). This unquenchable desire for the material most obviously supports the argument that

there is no principle in the chaos that industry brings. And what worsens the situation is that with

the more "stuff" man "creates," the more polluting garbage we heap upon the surface of the globe.

Soon trash will outnumber man, all a result of man's incessant denial of principle, and the

worshipping of the material. As desire deteriorates all sense of humanly principle, so does the

deterioration of the ecosystem persist.

The decomposition of the biological world is largely impacted by the corporations who rape

the natural world in order to make a buck. It was clear in the 1989 Exxon oil spill in Valdez,

Alaska, just how many principles were thwarted by the ill-attitude of Exxon president, Lee

Raymond. The Wall Street Journal issue of December 1, 1999, states: "Amid the restructuring,

the Exxon Valdez ran aground in 1989. Lee Raymond, who was Exxon president at the time, was

dispatched to oversee the clean up and the immense fallout. He was so faceless that he once

walked into an office in Alaska to file a claim, posing as a Valdez resident, so he could assess the claims process" (Bing 112). This incredulous display exhibits the lengths to which corporations

will go to preserve their companies' well-being at the expense of anyone other than themselves.

The obvious repercussions this spill had on the environment seemed to pose no bearing on

Raymond's principles. On the banks of the Maumee River, natural resources are being used to

provide corporations with environmental fuel to keep their companies afloat. The Economic

Development of Defiance County states:

> Defiance County is the place to do business. Automotive, technology, and
>
> logistics companies seeking a new location are drawn to Defiance County's
>
> Enterprise Industrial Park, a 700-acre park zoned for manufacturing, which
>
> provides industrial and commercial businesses with dual rail, highway access to
>
> U.S. Route 24 and water resources from the Maumee River, the largest tributary
>
> of Lake Erie. Three million gallons per day of excess water capacity are
>
> available for industrial use throughout the City of Defiance. (Forbes 76)

It is apparent in the county's name, "Defiance," and in the heavy commercialization of the county,

that the ecosystem is not questioned over the "bustling" economy. Once again, money is a god

that reigns supreme over principle. Further, the Northwest Ohio Regional Economic

Development hopes to compete in the vastly industrializing world. The association states:

"(NORED) has become a dominant global player, efficiently working together as a powerful

alliance to facilitate economic development projects in the region" (Forbes 75). It is evident in

this statement that the goal is to create businesses which make money, as the life in the densely-

forested Ohio is destroyed for the sake of manufacturing material goods. Principle is abandoned

for fleeting wealth again when the University of Toledo likens their mechanical creations to

something naturally created. An advertisement from the University of Toledo states: "As a

partner in research and an intellectual resource, we empower the region's business and industry to excel in an ever-increasing competitive landscape" (<u>Forbes</u> 74). Here, the University of Toledo

implies that the development of industry is just as natural as *The Creation,* referring to the

commercialization of a naturally-forested terrain, as a "competitive landscape." It can be seen

further, in the statements made by leading corporation owners, the similarly disillusioning

attitudes that empower the denial of human principle.

    From the manufacturers of candy bars to the providers of "wholesome family amusement,"

the one, solitary goal is to make money. When the founder of Mars Incorporated, Forrest Mars,

jokes about his high principles, it is clear what the wealthy truly feel about their overall morality.

Forrest states: "I'm a religious man. I pray for Milky Way. I pray for Snickers" (Bing 106).

Although probably intended as a quip aimed at his audience, the underlying truth of the statement

contends with his own principles. Whether or not the heads of huge corporations have any

principles at all is questionable. The cut-throat, capitalistic nature of society today is learned by

none other than the money-hungry heads of corporations who push their employees to the limit

for the benefit of the company, and ultimately themselves. Jeffrey Katzenburg demands of Disney

chairperson, Michael Eisner, less than 36 hours after the death of Disney #2, Frank Wells: "Either

I get Frank's job as president, or I'm going to leave the company" (Bing 112). Attitudes such as

these mould the model on which society bases its own standards of competition, trampling any

personal principles as a result of the socially-accepted way of doing things. It is something that

the major corporations have conditioned in man from the launching of the industrial age. Stanley

Bing's, <u>Throwing the Elephant: Zen and the Art of Managing Up</u>, warns against such corruption.

Bing states: "Work is suffering. The ability to boss other people around destroys much of human

decency [. . .]" (7). And this destruction of humanism and decency is not difficult to realize by

the previous statements of Forrest and Katzenberg. It is clear how easily conformed man's

principles have become with the advancing of an industrial society. Founder of Wal-Mart, Sam

Walton, had to up his standards in order to compete with one of the bigger corporations, K-Mart.

Walton states: "We are a flea attacking an elephant" (Bing 151). Walton was able to come up as

the little guy and battle it out with K-mart, all in the name of the "Benjamins."

If money equals prosperity in this day in age, it is not surprising that workers overwork and

compromise their original principles. It is also not surprising that man bites the hand that feeds

him in order to retain monetary wealth, and add more to the heap of goods that soon proves

insufficient, and becomes mere waste. The idea that man will never be satisfied with the material

pleasures the world has to offer is not a new revelation by any means. However, it is difficult to

combat the conformities that the corporate world challenges our principles with, when the

corporations of the world are the ones technically feeding our fancies. The key might be found in

depriving our desires of materialism, from time to time, in order to put into perspective just how

addicted man is to the material realm. Only then will man be able to find true identity,

fulfillment, and enjoyment, in work and play alike, thus finding the peace that loyalties to self and

principle bring.

Valencia 10

Works Cited

Bing, Stanley. Throwing the Elephant: Zen and the Art of Managing Up. New York:

HarperCollins Publishers, 2002.

"Building a High-Tech, High-Performance Economy in Northwest Ohio." Forbes, March

29, 2004: 73-77.

Philipson, Ph.D., Ilene. Married to the Job: Why We Live to Work and What We Can Do

About It. New York: The Free Press, 2002.

Pratt, Ronald "Reagan." Personal interview. 15 Dec. 2004.

Thoreau, Henry David. "Life Without Principle." 22 December 2004.

<http://www.walden.org/Institute/thoreau/writings/essays/Life_without_Principle.htm>.

Winderman, Kimberly. Personal interview. 15 Dec. 2004.

Conversations with Writers

The following conversation is with Dominique Valencia, author of "The Power of the Penny over Principle."

Describe your writing process:

My writing process has normally been fueled by procrastination and the pressure of a deadline. I do not suggest this method, however, and it is a questionable element of my writing process. In all honesty, procrastination has been the driving force of some of my best work, but this only suggests to me that if more thought and reflection are expelled into a given work, then the outcome has much more potential. My early morning writing (after a full night's rest) seems to be fresh, alive, and focused, whereas writing on an empty tank of gas seems to work against my work's overall flavor. Outlines, including methods of brainstorming and sprinting, are a regular part of my idea development, helping shape the core of my academic writing.

Did you employ a strategy when developing your introductory paragraph?

Usually when writing anything academic, I write my introduction and conclusions both after I have already constructed the body of my essay. This aids in focusing the body of the text, which traditionally is the most important element of academic writing. I attempt, when writing my introduction, however, to hook my audience, in most cases, my professor, giving him / her information that I suspect may be new or of interest. Giving reference to the broader ideas of books, periodical articles, or well-known historical events has also helped me in building an interesting introduction.

How did you construct your thesis statement?

According to the text that you may be evaluating, the thesis statement may be formed. I have found it opportune to choose a thesis statement that will adequately support every argument that I will use in my essay. The thesis statement must tell the reader exactly what arguments you will be supporting, and from what text or texts.

Did you perform research first? Or did you write, and then research, write, and then research?

I find that outlining what I wish to research not only helps me focus on what I want to communicate to the reader, but also helps to later form a stronger essay. My method goes as follows: Outline what will be researched, Research what will be later communicated in the essay, Outine what will I write, then First Draft, Research, and Second Draft, alternating as necessary.

How long did it take you to write this paper?

It took, give or take, three hours to construct the body of the paper. However, the time spent on the essay's reflection, research, and digestion, may have taken anywhere from five to ten hours of thought, and thought put into practice (research time).

How many times did you read or view the texts that were being examined?

I read "Life Without Principle," by Henry David Thoreau, once in full, but then skimmed through the parts of the text, which I felt would be extremely profitable to my essay. It helped to highlight parts of the text that I found interesting, significant, and might guide the development of my essay.

Did you employ a strategy when developing your conclusion?

Like my introductory paragraph, my conclusion is written at the end of the essay. Concordantly, leaving my reader with insightful, interesting, and fulfilling information is an integral element of my concluding thoughts.

Have you always considered yourself to be a good writer?

Normally receiving above average marks in English, I am led to believe that my writing is, more than likely, better than satisfactory. Realizing that there is always room for improvement, even in the midst of my being able to follow instructions well, I have always strived to not merely have good writing, but be a great writer. Yes, I believe that I am a writer. Categorizing myself as a "good writer," however, is entirely dependent on the opinion of my audience.

What is your advice to the aspiring academic writers of today?

What I feel has set me apart from my fellow writers is the fact that I am entirely myself in all that I write. Being yourself when writing, however, using your favorite authors to guide your writing, is a superb way to showcase your own unique writing style. If you feel that you do not necessarily possess one, emulate your favorite writers. This will bring out your own interpretation of the works of already esteemed and established writers, causing your writing to possess an enlightening verve that could not come from anyone other than yourself. Above all, READ! READ! READ!!! This will automatically program your brain to know what to do when you are stumped by the strange sentence structure that the mind can so easily spawn.

Play-by-play

JON ST. AMANT

Dominique begins her paper with a quotation by Mark Twain that seems to set the mood for the looming discourse. It is witty, and it is indicative of the contention she expects to advance. And note this: because many students do not begin their papers with a quotation, doing so will set yours apart from the rest. It may very well act as an "attention getter," one of those things that prompts your reader to place her right index finger to her temple and mutter, intriguingly, "hmmmm." With this the stage has been set, and if the writer is the director, then Dominique is putting her players in position.

In Dominique's first paragraph, notice how she develops her stance on the notion of being "worthily employed." She begins by enveloping the reader in a metaphorical wonderland, choosing to use "societal rubble" and "humanism rots." And she soon finds herself referring to smog as "the excrement of industry." As a discerning reader, you may ask yourself, "Is the employment of metaphor necessary in an academic essay?" Frankly, it is not. However, there are, ostensibly, millions of ways to skin this proverbial cat, and Dominique has chosen to advance hers in this manner. What the reader should note, though, is that as soon as her introduction becomes a bit lofty and in need of grounding, she appropriately inserts the following quotation: "Have we no culture, no refinement—but skill only to live coarsely and serve the Devil?—to acquire a little worldly wealth, or fame, or liberty, and make a false show with it, as if we were all husk and shell, with no tender and living kernel to us? Shall our institutions be like those chestnut-burs which contain abortive nuts, perfect only to prick the fingers?" Here, Thoreau's quotation simply advances Dominique's contention, for not only is Thoreau arguing along the same lines, but he is employing metaphor to advance his contention as well. Additionally, ask yourself where Dominique's introduction would go if she hadn't chosen to employ the quotation by Thoreau. Chances are strong that you can see the grounding effect of a quotation from a credible source. If Dominique were to continue without the quotation, her language might seem more indicative of a snake-oil salesman or one pedaling applesauce as opposed to a serious academic writer engaged in an examination of worthy employment in the United States of America. And remember, when we are theorizing or hypothesizing, it is important (assuming we are not experts on the subject) to shift the burden of proof. In this case, Dominique has shifted the burden of proof and given it, dutifully, to Henry David Thoreau.

Something else in Dominique's introduction should be spotlighted. Notice how her introduction might compare visually to an upside-down triangle. In other words, it begins with broad, sweeping generalizations, and it slowly reaches its point. In this case, Dominique reaches her point by writing the following:

> As in the rapidly industrializing day in which Thoreau writes, so is the homogenization of industry at present. There is no shelter from the corporate tempest which sweeps over the nation, the world, overturning man to sweat and toil in order to gain monetary sustenance, often forgoing all sense of self in the process, all remnants of personal principle. It is evident that the lives led by many workers are drudged with such tainted societal ideology, condoning the abandonment of personal principle, if all for the vain sake of getting a share of that "good ol' piece a' pie." Given the testimonies of two working class individuals, Kimberly Winderman and Ronald "Reagan" Pratt, two clients of Ilene Philipson, Ph.D, "Brenda" and "Ingrid," and analysis by Philipson, as well as testimonies straight from corporate America, it can be seen precisely how difficult it is to maintain personal principle in a universe which so freely sacrifices the orbiting of virtue and, instead, remains loyal to the passing of pennies.

Remember, when constructing an argument and taking a stand, it is important to do so with tact. Such tact is analogous to cooking a frog. If, carnivorous reader, you have never cooked a frog, note the following steps: Do not simply toss the frog into a pot of boiling water. (The frog will hop out!) Instead, place it in a pot of lukewarm water. (The frog should sit comfortably, looking from side to side.) Then, slowly turn up the heat. (Do this slowly!) And before the frog realizes it, he's cooked.

While the aforementioned example may have been "amphibiously incorrect," please realize that a good writer must understand this theory. If Dominique were to simply toss the reader into a pot of boiling water by writing something like, "It is clear that people are leading their lives without principle," we might not have confidence in her as a writer and, more importantly, we might find her inappropriately aggressive. Notice how, instead, she follows the triangular lines that slowly narrow as the introduction progresses. She tactfully asserts that industry has been homogenized, that man often forgoes "all sense of self in the process," and that the abandonment of personal principle is being condoned. And at this point, she finally commits to her thesis statement which, essentially, is this: "It can be seen precisely how difficult it is to maintain personal principle in a universe which so freely sacrifices the orbiting of virtue and, instead, remains loyal to the passing of pennies." Remember, dear reader, this is Dominique's thesis statement and, arguably, the most important sentence in her entire essay. If it has been compromised, then the structural integrity of her argument will be compromised as well. (In other words, the thesis statement's relationship to an argument is similar to the relationship between a ship and its rudder. Without a viable rudder, a ship is paralyzed. Similarly, an argument will find itself directionless without a viable thesis statement.)

As we move to Dominique's body paragraphs, notice how even though her command of the English language is impressive, she attempts to control it. This is often achieved through conscious adherence to structure. (Professional writers, for instance, may write instinctively, but their instinctive writing is often the product of many years of conscious adherence to structure. And so it is with you.) Dominique adheres to the Topic Sentence, Point / Example / Commentary structure. This structure enables her to ply her wares and display her literary latitude while remaining focused on the task at hand. For example, notice how she blends freedom and restraint when she offers the following Point / Example / Commentary in her second paragraph:

> However, her principles have been jeopardized by her work due to the lack of artistic freedom awarded her by her company, despite the profuse talent she displays on the job, which is recognized by not only her workmates but also her higher ups. Winderman says, 'What hinders me are the limits placed on me as a graphic designer. You are always creating for someone else. [. . .] I've found myself designing packaging for dolls [. . .]. It's nothing I'd frame and be proud of.' The underlying sacrifices made by Winderman and other artists alike become evident in this all-too-common exploitation process, where art is used as a monetary commodity instead of for personal pleasure.

Here, Dominique displays the freedom to write what she wants while exercising the restraint required to keep from digressing and engaging in something tangential. She offers one Point, one Example, and one sentence of Commentary. And then, though it is not obvious that she is adhering to a formal structure, she introduces her second Point / Example / Commentary:

> As if this were not enough of a social travesty, Winderman also must be marked with the vile stench of notoriety that might be related to her by merely working for a company. Winderman says, 'Everything that comes out of a studio is representation of who the workers of the studio are. [. . .] David and Goliath play on stereotypes. If I worked there, people would think I was immature. [. . .] You work for that studio, and you have the studio branded on your forehead.' It is clear in this statement that Winderman must tolerate being marred with a corporate label, and defy personal principle, just to make a decent living.

Again, Dominique introduces one Point. Then, she employs one Example. And then she explains the relevance of the Example to the Point in her sentence of Commentary. Remember that even though control is an illusion, restraint is not. Such restraint, or focus, can be attained by adhering to the Topic Sentence, Point / Example / Commentary structure. And notice, that after continuing to develop her argument, Dominique employs a Transition before beginning her next paragraph. (Budding academic writers often share the fantasy of shedding all clothes and possessions to run naked through a literary wilderness, abandoning the fundamentals that have been stressed by structuralists and their aspirants. Please realize, however, that there is tremendous value to formal constructs like the Topic Sentence and the Transition. Such sentences provide the reader with necessary direction.)

Upon reaching Dominique's conclusion, it becomes evident that she has adequately advanced her thesis statement. Still, she does restate her thesis statement in her conclusion. But note that she doesn't merely regurgitate what the reader has been asked to consume. Instead, she offers Commentary on the entire paper. She offers some new ideas while continuing to remain focused on the argument. And she even attempts to identify with her opposition when she writes: "The idea that man will never be satisfied with the material pleasures the world has to offer is not a new revelation by any means." Appropriately, however, she pursues this with an attempt at refuting the opposition: "However, it is difficult to combat the conformities that the corporate world challenges our humanly principles with, when the corporations of the world are the ones technically feeding our fancies." And then, instead of closing, she offers the following solution: "The key might be found in depriving our desires of materialism, from time to time, in order to put into perspective just how addicted man is to the material realm. Only then will man be able to find true identity, fulfillment, and enjoyment, in work and play alike, thus finding the peace that loyalties to self and principle bring." Dominique's conclusion is fitting, for it is a fine end to an excellent examination of Thoreau's "Life Without Principle."

PRE-WRITING

Choose a pre-writing exercise (Journalist's Six, Listing, Brainstorming, or Sprinting), and begin developing a response to the prompt you've chosen to address.

ORGANIZATION

Use the following outline to help organize your paragraph.

Paragraph I: Introduction

_____

_____

_____

_____

_____

_____

_____

_____

_____

_____

Paragraph II: Body Paragraph

Topic Sentence:

_____

_____

Point 1:

_____

_____

Example 1:

_____

_____

Commentary:

_____

_____

Point 2:

_____

_____

Example 1:

_____

_____

Commentary:

_____

_____

Point 3:

_____

_____

Example 1:

_____

_____

Commentary:

_____

_____

Point 4:

_____

_____

Example 1:

_____

_____

Commentary:

_____

_____

Transition:

_____

_____

Paragraph III: Body Paragraph

Topic Sentence:

_____

_____

Point 1:

_____

_____

Example 1:

_____

_____

Commentary:

_____

_____

Point 2:

_____

_____

Example 1:

_____

_____

Commentary:

_____

_____

Point 3:

_____

_____

Example 1:

_____

_____

Commentary:

_____

_____

Point 4:

_____

_____

Example 1:

_____

_____

Commentary:

_____

_____

Transition:

_____

_____

Paragraph IV: Body Paragraph

Topic Sentence:

_____

_____

Point 1:

_____

_____

Example 1:

_____

_____

Commentary:

_____

_____

 414

Point 2:

_____

_____

Example 1:

_____

_____

Commentary:

_____

_____

Point 3:

_____

_____

Example 1:

_____

_____

Commentary:

_____

_____

Point 4:

_____

_____

Example 1:

_____

_____

Commentary:

_____

_____

Transition:

_____

_____

Paragraph V: Body Paragraph

Topic Sentence:

_____

_____

Point 1:

_____

_____

Example 1:

_____

_____

Commentary:

_____

_____

Point 2:

_____

_____

 416

Example 1:

_____

_____

Commentary:

_____

_____

Point 3:

_____

_____

Example 1:

_____

_____

Commentary:

_____

_____

Point 4:

_____

_____

Example 1:

_____

_____

Commentary:

_____

_____

Transition:

_____

_____

Paragraph VI: Body Paragraph

Topic Sentence:

_____

_____

Point 1:

_____

_____

Example 1:

_____

_____

Commentary:

_____

_____

Point 2:

_____

_____

Example 1:

_____

_____

 **418**

Commentary:

_____

_____

Point 3:

_____

_____

Example 1:

_____

_____

Commentary:

_____

_____

Point 4:

_____

_____

Example 1:

_____

_____

Commentary:

_____

_____

Transition:

_____

_____

Paragraph VII: Conclusion

_____

_____

_____

_____

_____

_____

_____

_____

_____

_____

DEVELOPMENT

Use these pages to construct your first draft.

Name _____ Date _____

In This Section

In the next essay, Jordan Saiz was asked to construct an argument in response to the following prompt:

> Research famous people. These people might include politicians, musicians, actors, actresses, coaches, athletes, or serial killers. In performing your research, attempt to find discrepancies between the masks they wear in public and the lives they lead in private. One example, for instance, might be the mask worn by Bill Clinton. Such a mask seemed to communicate monogamy, yet when he removed the mask, the public was privy to seeing another side. Similarly, when a Catholic priest is accused of sodomizing an altar boy, it seems that a mask has been removed. It seems reasonable to suggest, as suggested by Dunbar in "We Wear the Mask," that people do, indeed, wear masks. Nevertheless, it seems that some masks are more elusive than others. Thus, research some public figures in an attempt to investigate the masks that some of these people wear. Then, develop a thesis statement that will guide your argument in a discourse on masks.

Notice how Jordan develops his argument. Specifically, notice how with every body paragraph, Jordan further advances his thesis statement.

Jordan Saiz

Professor Ipkiss

English 1A

18 December 2004

Casual Agents

A definition of the word "mask" is false face. Untrue face. Secretive face. Deceptive face.

A broad range of people wear masks every day, becoming casual agents, beings interested in relationships purely for personal advantages. Sometimes faces are easily interchangeable and other times, they are violently different. Paul Dunbar, "the most promising young colored man in America," wrote a poem titled, "We Wear the Mask," eloquently depicting the process of hiding our true selves in a tortured manner. The discrepancies between people's public and private lives, paralleling Dunbar's description, are not always easily seen, yet ever-present, producing double-lives throughout the population, particularly exhibited in four seemingly "normal" celebrity figures.

The first example, Fritz Haarmann, is probably the most extreme, embodying severely brutal potential. Living in Hannover, Germany in the twenties, Haarmann was known as a public homosexual and a meat and clothing dealer. As it turned out, Haarmann was selling the meat and clothing from young boys he had raped and killed by way of gnawing through their throats, nearly severing their heads. The means he used to attract these boys willingly signifies the outermost mask he wore. Alexander Gilbert, an educated man in the ways of true crime and the psychology of serial killers, states:

> In almost every scenario, the victim was met at the train station and offered
>
> accommodation or work; or apprehended on the pretence that his abductor was a
>
> police officer. This guise was used so often that on one occasion, after a youth
>
> welfare worker had asked the guard as to whether Haarmann was employed in
>
> the same capacity, the station official replied, 'No, he's a detective.'
>
> (www.crimelibrary.com)

This shows the level of deliberate deception and careful precision he incorporated into his everyday life. To get to this position he had to first have the respectability to accompany it. For this he moved his residence, continued his clothing sales, and learned about the police system. Gilbert states: "[he earned his money through] his newfound role as a police informer. Haarmann double-crossed everybody and became a 'custodian of the law and an information office for all criminal matters' Amazingly, the clothes that Haarmann passed around Hannover earned him the reputation as a benefactor of the homeless" (www.crimelibrary.com). Of course, he stole the clothes and made alliances where needed to develop standing in the public, providing him a route lack of petty questioning when going about his "business." And his final mask is the one he wore to hide himself from himself. Giving himself the psychological runaround, he knew of his problem, and seemed to fight against it, but also seemed to involuntarily be drawn about in his deeds, able only to watch them happen. Evident in an interview, he states: "I never intended to kill those youths. Some of the boys had come before. I wanted to protect them from myself because I knew what would happen if I had my way with them" (Vronsky 147). Under examination, Haarmann's characters seem to be layered, slightly overlapping each other, fairly seamlessly. While he was labeled mentally unstable, his actions show a control of himself that is orderly and admirable. That, mixed with the last quotation, gives him the air of a man like anyone, only slightly confused, almost pity worthy, instead of the "Hannover vampire" as he was called before he was executed for brutalizing, sodomizing, and gutting an accounted-for twenty-six boys.

The next example is the beloved Robert Reed, also layered in his deceptions, although generally harmless. Reed, a.k.a. Mike Brady, is best known for his role-model persona in the situation-comedy, The Brady Bunch. His first layer is more or less a wall, a barrier preventing outsiders into his personal life. This included close friends and co-workers. Sherwood Schwartz, creator and producer of The Brady Bunch states: "I've dealt with all sorts of performers and temperaments over the years, but he is the hardest nut I've ever had to crack. Somehow I can't get around him. He is very guarded" (Nachman). Robert Reed, although possessing celebrity status, represents a lot of the general population who may be more introverted, preferring to keep their work and personal life separate. Furthering his disinterest in publicity, Reed lived in Pasadena, assuring his anonymity among fellow Americans. He was quoted as saying, "I love the business, but isn't it nice to get away from it? Maybe one of my neighbors knows I'm an actor, but otherwise I'm just somebody that lives there and we discuss our roses" (Nachman). For a classically trained actor, the man seems very bland. But his mask becomes visible in the fact that he was gay, contracted HIV, and died of colon lymphoma, a complication of the virus. Robert Huerta, described as a close friend of Reed's, claims: "Because of his career, and despite his sexual preference, I believe it was very hard for him to acknowledge that he was gay" (Nachman). But, despite internal conflicts, Reed managed his lives simultaneously with few people ever knowing about more than one of his layers. He was a fairly boring, fairly average American, representative of most people, wearing a mask that many have worn. Another mask-wearing, extremely introverted, and seemingly conservative man is Robert Hanssen.

The all-American, church-going, gun-collecting, sex-taping Robert Hanssen joined the Federal Bureau of Investigation during the Cold War, hoping to live out his lifelong dream of being a spy. What he found was droll work, poor living with very little pay, and a cult-obsessed wife who bore children that he just did not seem to know what to do with. Adrian Havill, in an article on Hanssen, writes about the obvious ease of the justification of betrayal available to agents in the New York office: "Hanssen's boss, Thomas Sheer, was concerned. He told Washington that a beginning agent in his office made less than a New York City trash collector. 'His men were vulnerable,' he said. 'If the Russians made a good offer there would be agents who couldn't resist the money'" (www.crimelibrary.com). This was very true of Hanssen, already flirting with the idea of becoming a master of the spy game. As he slipped deeper and deeper into the betrayal of his country and employer, he became more and more wealthy. The only thing in his defense was the use of most of the money:

> There is a greater-good theory that partly explains Hanssen. Although he was
>
> betraying his country, he was using the money from the Russians to put his six

children through approved—and expensive—private schools. His children were

good students, and he believed they might in the future be part of a holy war that

would remerge God and country, whose leaders would then ban abortion,

divorce, and other evils of the world that he and Opus Dei opposed. (Havill)

It is interesting, however, that through his brilliance, he did not see through the mask of Opus Dei,

an extremist cult; he must have been too busy confessing his numerous sins of espionage and

perversion. While his wife knew somewhat of his work with the Soviets, she knew nothing of his

exploitation of their intimate moments with his long-time friend Jack Hoschouer. Havill states:

Despite Hanssen's conservatism, he and Hoschouer, buddies since high school in

Chicago, had done some kinky things together. Hanssen had once taken nude

photos of his wife Bonnie and mailed them without her knowledge to Hoschouer

when he was in the Army and stationed in Vietnam. Years later, he topped that by

hiding a miniature video camera in his bedroom where he photographed himself

making love to Bonnie. Hoschouer and Hanssen later watched the homemade

sex film together in the family den. (www.crimelibrary.com)

What is odd is that Hanssen seems to emotionally have more in common with the serial killer

than the television star with his cold expressions, lack of guilt, and general "if I can, I will"

attitude. But according to his hero, Kim Philby, "To betray, you must first belong. I never

belonged" (Havill); this fits his relationship with his job, his marriage, and general self, and it

represents an integral layer in the masks he wore. The next example, also enamored with what

most might call perversion, is Bob Crane, the illustrious star of Hogan's Heroes.

In accordance with biographies, Crane was every bit the suave, clever, lady-killer he

portrayed on television, only much more amplified. In quoting the book, Auto Focus, by Robert

Graysmith, light is shed on the secret interests of the actor: "I recalled how Crane taped sex sessions with women and immediately watched them afterwards. One woman commented that this excited him more than the act" (364). It seemed that Crane was absolutely addicted to sex and never went anywhere without a sufficient amount of cameras and film. It also appears that Crane's wife wrote him a blank check upon marriage, having full knowledge of his "hobby." She stated: "We had an open marriage. I told him I never wanted him to miss anything in life because of me. Bob was consumed by his hobby of photography and would videotape any and all sexual encounters he could get his partners to agree to" (Graysmith 368). She loved him fully, and never dated or re-married after he was murdered. But among those donning masks, it seems that one man's perversion is another man's Sunday afternoon at the country club. Graysmith states: "Patti not only condoned her husband's unusual sexual habits and many escapades, but occasionally viewed videos of his conquests" (368). Apparently this sort of thing became normal in their relationship. This is the kind of family that helps to put food on our nation's psychologists' tables.

Everything seems to come down to personal preferences and general ideals. It is safe to assume that most masks worn are used to hide something that might be heralded as socially unacceptable. This is the negative, conservative, jealous way of putting it. Masks are freedom. Putting on a mask allows a person to live out their desires, whether it is a secluded, private life, the consumption of human flesh, or the desires that may otherwise disallow a person from continuing in their viewable life. The people that master the mask can take on another and another and so on, successfully. This allows them to use their human nature to its full potential. It is unfortunate that this game pays top dollar to Hollywood actors and nothing to the people who have mastered it by practicing it every day.

Saiz 7

Works Cited

Gilbert, Alexander. "Court TV's Crime Library." 17 Dec. 2004

    <http://www.crimelibrary.com/serial_killers/history/haarman/index_1.html>.

Graysmith, Robert. Auto Focus. New York: Berkley Books, 2002.

Havill, Adrian. Court TV's Crime Library. 17 Dec. 2004.

    <http://www.crimelibrary.com/terrorists_spies/spies/hanssen/1.html>.

Nachman, Laura. "Brady Residence—Second Home to the Brady Bunch." 17 Dec. 2004

    <http://www.bradyresidence.com/articlesreed.htm>.

Vronsky, Peter. Serial Killers: The Method and Madness of Monsters. New York: Berkley

    Books, 2004.

Conversations with Writers

The following conversation is with Jordan Saiz, author of "Casual Agents."

Describe your writing process:

Unfortunately, I can't really imagine my writing process being very helpful to many, but I have no problem with it. My general writing process seems to be a lack thereof. I usually write everything in one go, but not without many distractions. To write a whole paper it could take me forty-five minutes to an hour unheeded. But there are so many other things that catch my attention, so the process can last up to five hours depending on the distraction. Other than that, my process involves looking at the prompt and writing with little thought before, or during, really. It just seems to come out right.

Did you employ a strategy when developing your introductory paragraph?

I did not consciously employ a strategy as I tend to view an introduction as an elongated prompt. Once I understand the prompt, I suppose I re-write it in a way pertaining to my choice of argument. To be honest, as I write this, and re-read my essay, I have no idea what was going on in my head at the time. The only recollection of the night I wrote this, besides the satisfaction of finishing the paper, were the few odd distractions I had: VH1, a visiting friend, and so on.

How did you construct your thesis statement?

I do seem to have a system for constructing thesis statements. Although, I'm not sure how it is pertinent to an accepted method of thesis writing. Somewhat childishly, I usually focus on a couple words, generally "big" or "intelligent" words, and try to incorporate all of them, and then have a game at trying to write the longest sentence possible without creating a run-on. I suppose this is to fit the complexity of the essay fully into one statement.

Did you perform research first? Or did you write, and then research, write, and then research?

I went in the morning to Borders and found as many book sources as I could. And then I gathered the rest online. And commenced writing. I did not know which quotes I would use. I simply gathered a few over the minimum to pick and choose from.

How long did it take you to write this paper?

It took me about an hour and a half of actual writing, but this took place from around 1–4 P.M., and then 9 P.M.–12 A.M.

How many times did you need to read or view the texts that were being examined?

To my recollection, I needed to read the examined texts once or twice.

Did you employ a strategy when developing your conclusion?

No. I'm usually very tired and ready to quit by that point. I try to restate my essay in a satirical way, also bringing in one or two side subjects not necessarily mentioned in the body paragraphs.

Have you always considered yourself a good writer?

Actually, yes. I have always been a bit prideful about that.

What is your advice to the aspiring academic writers of today?

Read as many books as possible. Try to develop your own style, I suppose. To be honest, I'm just repeating things I have heard. Outside of essays for class, I hardly write anything. I do believe in learning as much as possible though, and that's always helpful when covering broad ranges of topics.

Play-by-play

JON ST.AMANT

Jordan titles his paper "Casual Agents," and then he proceeds to define "mask." And if the seas of interest remain calm, he does seem to stir things up with his use of fragments in the introduction: "Untrue face. Secretive face. Deceptive face." This is done for effect, and if it succeeded with you, dear reader, then you probably visualized faces in your mind's eye, appearing and then disappearing, a cinematic heartbeat. Jordan soon returns to conventional sentence construction as he introduces Paul Laurence Dunbar and his poem, "We Wear the Mask." And then, with little fanfare, Jordan offers the reader his thesis statement: "The discrepancies between people's public and private lives, paralleling Dunbar's description, are not always easily seen, yet ever-present, producing double-lives throughout the population, particularly exhibited in four seemingly 'normal' celebrity figures." Jordan's thesis statement is well-constructed, for it adequately conveys what he will attempt to "prove" in his examination of four celebrity figures. Naturally, because this is an argument, little will be proven. Realize, however, that even though it may be impossible to prove an argument "right" or "wrong," it is possible to suggest that an argument is viable, or that it is worthy of further contemplation, or that it really should be embraced by those considering its many sides. Jordan succeeds in taking a successful step with the reader toward his argument's viability, worth, or eventual embrace by writing responsibly. Note, for instance, how he has worded his thesis statement. The first part of his thesis reads: "The discrepancies between people's public and private lives, paralleling Dunbar's description [. . .] ." Why, might you ask, is this responsible? Jordan includes Dunbar in his thesis. Jordan, in fact, attributes a parallel between his observation and Dunbar's description. This not only helps promote focus in Jordan's examination, but it lends credence to Jordan's argument, for he invites Dunbar to share the burden of proof. Also, as Jordan continues, note how he suggests to the reader, "Look! Sometimes these discrepancies are not easy to see, but they are present! Follow me in this examination of double-lives. I'll show you four!" Jordan does communicate this, but he does it diplomatically. And if, like many readers, you find his voice credible and responsible, then you will probably look upon paragraph two with great interest.

In paragraph two, Jordan begins with the following topic sentence: "The first example, Fritz Haarmann, is probably the most extreme, embodying severely brutal potential." Assuming, dear reader, that you acknowledge how "the topic sentence is to a paragraph as a thesis statement is to an essay," then you see the importance of Jordan's topic sentence. Simply examine the rest of his paragraph, and you will see that what Jordan has employed exists chiefly for the advancement of his topic sentence. And since his topic sentence is merely an extension of his thesis statement, the essay's ideas coagulate nicely.

One deviation, however, from the prescribed structure (Topic Sentence, Point / Example / Commentary) can be found after Jordan's Topic Sentence. Instead of proceeding to his first Point, Jordan chooses to offer the following two sentences: "Living in Hannover, Germany in the 1920s, Haarmann was known as a public homosexual and a meat and clothing dealer. As it turned out, Haarmann was selling the meat and clothing from young boys he had raped and killed by way of gnawing through their throats, nearly severing their heads." Jordan's decision to deviate seems well-calculated, for these two sentences provide justifiable context for his examination of the mask Fritz Haarmann wore. And appropriately, after providing said context, Jordan articulates his first Point: "The means he used to attract these boys willingly signifies the outermost mask he wore." Jordan then couples this Point with the following Example / Commentary:

> Alexander Gilbert, an educated man in the ways of true crime and the psychology of serial killers, states: 'In almost every scenario, the victim was met at the train station and offered accommodation or work; or apprehended on the pretence that his abductor was a police officer. This guise was used so often that on one occasion, after a youth welfare worker had asked the guard as to whether Haarmann was employed in the same capacity, the station official replied, 'No, he's a detective' (Gilbert). This shows the level of deliberate deception and careful precision he incorporates into his everyday life. To get to this position he had to first have the respectability to accompany it.

Jordan adequately introduces his quotation, and then he explains the relevance of the quotation to his Point. Jordan continues pledging adherence to this structure until his argument crescendos in his sixth paragraph.

Jordan's sixth paragraph is his conclusion. In it, he essentially unleashes Commentary upon the reader, making sure to unveil one very startling observation: "Masks are freedom." This is a pleasant inversion, for many associate masks with hiding, but clearly Jordan sees things differently. Such Commentary, especially when coupled with reasonable support, can be poignant and provocative. Jordan, in fact, continues to push the envelope when observing that Hollywood actors get paid extraordinarily well for wearing their masks, suggesting that the society choosing to condemn hypocrisy is the same society that condones it.

PRE-WRITING

Choose a pre-writing exercise (Journalist's Six, Listing, Brainstorming, or Sprinting), and begin developing a response to the prompt you've chosen to address.

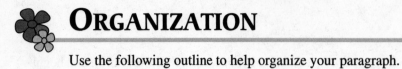

ORGANIZATION

Use the following outline to help organize your paragraph.

Paragraph I: Introduction

_____

_____

_____

_____

_____

_____

_____

_____

_____

Paragraph II: Body Paragraph

Topic Sentence:

_____

_____

Point 1:

_____

_____

440

Example 1:

_____

_____

Commentary:

_____

_____

Point 2:

_____

_____

Example 1:

_____

_____

Commentary:

_____

_____

Point 3:

_____

_____

Example 1:

_____

_____

Commentary:

_____

_____

Point 4:

_____

_____

Example 1:

_____

_____

Commentary:

_____

_____

Transition:

_____

_____

Paragraph III: Body Paragraph

Topic Sentence:

_____

_____

Point 1:

_____

_____

Example 1:

_____

_____

 442

Commentary:

_____

_____

Point 2:

_____

_____

Example 1:

_____

_____

Commentary:

_____

_____

Point 3:

_____

_____

Example 1:

_____

_____

Commentary:

_____

_____

Point 4:

_____

_____

Example 1:

_____

_____

Commentary:

_____

_____

Transition:

_____

_____

Paragraph IV: Body Paragraph

Topic Sentence:

_____

_____

Point 1:

_____

_____

Example 1:

_____

_____

Commentary:

_____

_____

Point 2:

_____

_____

Example 1:

_____

_____

Commentary:

_____

_____

Point 3:

_____

_____

Example 1:

_____

_____

Commentary:

_____

_____

Point 4:

_____

_____

Example 1:

_____

_____

Commentary:

_____

_____

Transition:

_____

_____

Paragraph V: Body Paragraph

Topic Sentence:

_____

_____

Point 1:

_____

_____

Example 1:

_____

_____

Commentary:

_____

_____

Point 2:

_____

_____

Example 1:

_____

_____

Commentary:

_____

_____

Point 3:

_____

_____

Example 1:

_____

_____

Commentary:

_____

_____

Point 4:

_____

_____

Example 1:

_____

_____

Commentary:

_____

_____

Transition:

_____

_____

Paragraph VI: Body Paragraph

Topic Sentence:

_____

_____

_____

Point 1:

_____

_____

Example 1:

_____

_____

Commentary:

_____

_____

Point 2:

_____

_____

Example 1:

_____

_____

 **448**

Commentary:

_____

_____

Point 3:

_____

_____

Example 1:

_____

_____

Commentary:

_____

_____

Point 4:

_____

_____

Example 1:

_____

_____

Commentary:

_____

_____

Transition:

_____

_____

Paragraph VII: Conclusion

_____

_____

_____

_____

_____

_____

_____

_____

_____

_____

🌸 DEVELOPMENT

Use these pages to construct your first draft.

Name _____ Date _____

In This Section

The following student essay, submitted by Monea Longoria, is worthy of examination because it is a Comparison and Contrast essay and, hence, adheres to a slightly different organizational strategy than the others. While essays written within other rhetorical modes, i.e., Taking a Stand, Proposing a Solution, Classification, Cause-effect, can house two, three, four (or more) sets of Point / Example / Commentary in their body paragraphs, the Comparison and Contrast essay must rely on sets of two. In other words, each body paragraph should house two, four, or six sets of Point / Example / Commentary. This is done to adequately represent both subjects under examination. For instance, in the following essay, Monea compares and contrasts Herman Melville's "Bartleby the Scrivener" and the film *Office Space*. In doing so, she chooses to employ Point / Example / Commentary four times in each body paragraph. This is an important realization, for if the writer of a Comparison and Contrast essay employs an odd number of Point / Example / Commentary in each body paragraph, one of the two subjects will find itself inadequately represented.

In reading Monea's essay, notice how she organizes it, and notice how transitional words are integral to jelling her ideas. Without well-placed transitional words, her argument will lack the requisite cohesion.

Monea composed her essay in response to the following prompt:

Compare and contrast Herman Melville's "Bartleby the Scrivener" and the film *Office Space*. Specifically, identify motivations for rebellion or mutiny within the workplace. After identifying similarities in motivations for the characters in both texts, extract differences from those similarities.

Longoria 1

Monea Longoria

Professor Krishnan

English 1A

31 December 2004

Nothing Like a Little Satisfaction

A job is defined as a regular position for which a person is paid to perform specified duties.

This daily task can have a profound effect on one's life. For instance, if a person does not receive

Longoria 2

internal satisfaction from their job or simply does not like it, it can be significantly detrimental to their mental well-being. Furthermore, job dissatisfaction can lead to various motivations to rebel in the workplace. Specifically, these motivations for rebellion within the workplace are present in two tales of office discontent: the short story, "Bartleby the Scrivener," and the film, Office Space. In fact, based on these two tales, it is possible to identify motivations for rebellion or mutiny within the workplace as well as identify similarities and extract differences from these similarities.

First, the two main characters' motives for rebellion seem to mutually stem from their lifeless and bleak atmospheres. In "Bartleby the Scrivener," for instance, the narrator describes a very drab and unnatural work atmosphere. In fact, he states: "At one end [of the office] they looked upon the white wall of the interior of a spacious skylight shaft, penetrating the building from top to bottom. This view might have been considered rather tame than otherwise, deficient in what landscape painters call 'life'" (Melville). In this simple description, the narrator creates a lifeless scene that stresses the feelings of isolation and sterility. This lifeless, bleak atmosphere helps establish Bartleby's cheerless and uninterested manner toward his work. Similarly, in the film, Office Space, Peter's motives for rebellion are due to his dislike of his dreary work atmosphere. In the film, Peter decides to take it upon himself to better his environment; he does this by unscrewing a wall in his cubicle, which reveals a window exposing a natural landscape. To enlighten this, according to a monthly publication, Monitor on Psychology, the author explains why rebellion in the workplace may exist. In fact, the author states, "[. . .] employees who work in cubicles, for example, are subject to more noise and may be more stressed" (Daw). It becomes clear that unnatural atmospheres such as cubicles, add to work-related stress and, consequently, work-related rebellion. Another example of the bleak atmosphere Bartleby endures is evident from a lucid description by the narrator. Here, the narrator states: "[. . .] The view from the other end of my chambers offered, at least, a contrast, if nothing more. In that direction my windows

commanded an unobstructed view of a lofty brick wall, black by age and everlasting shade"

(Melville). The description of the office is incredibly bleak: on one side, the windows open onto

a light shaft, and on the other, the windows look out onto a brick wall. Evidently, this uninspiring

atmosphere is one that can invoke such feelings as isolation, seclusion, and boredom; apparently,

Bartleby acquired these feelings from his work environment, evident from his many refusals to

cooperate with his boss's requests. Lastly, the notion that Peter is adversely affected by his work

atmosphere is further supported through his own telling description about his job. Peter states:

"We weren't meant to spend [life] this way. Human beings weren't meant to sit in little cubicles,

staring at computer screens all day [. . .]" (Office Space). Here, it is evident that Peter's job

setting has annoyed and bored him, for he displays these feelings when he ignores his work

obligations, shows up late to work, does not follow the dress code, and arrives to work as he

pleases. In each instance, Peter is attempting to escape his workplace, which suggests that he is

not only tired of his job's setting, but he also dislikes his job. While the aforementioned compares

motivations derived from the work atmosphere, the next comparison deals with motivations of

Bartleby and Peter that have stemmed from their unhappiness with their monotonous career tasks.

Each character's motives for rebellion are also clear when noting their unhappiness with their

work's duties. In "Bartleby the Scrivener," the narrator lucidly depicts Bartleby's demeanor while

he does his work. The narrator states: "He ran a day and night line, copying by sun-light and by

candle-light. I should have been quite delighted with his application, had been cheerfully

industrious. But he wrote on silently, palely, mechanically" (Melville). Here, it becomes evident

that Bartleby's relentless application of his work duties led to his dislike for them. Clearly, when a

person rigorously applies himself or herself to a tedious and monotonous task, this task can become

disliked. Likewise, in Office Space, Peter clarifies his dislike for his dull and unvarying work tasks.

In fact, he states: "Yeah, I just stare at my desk, but it looks like I'm working. I do that for probably another hour after lunch too. I'd probably say in a given week, I probably do about fifteen minutes of real, actual work" (Office Space). Peter's blatant remark clearly clarifies his feelings about his work duties. Arguably, when people have an apathetic attitude and deliberately disregard their work duties, it implies that they detest their job. A second example of Bartleby's dislike for his job becomes apparent when he nonchalantly refuses to do one of his required tasks. In fact, when the narrator excitingly questions Bartleby's lack of cooperation, Bartleby dispassionately replies, "I prefer not to" (Melville). It is evident that this indifferent statement of Bartleby's is indicative of work-related stress; furthermore, this stress was triggered from feeling overwhelmed by tedious work he dislikes. In support of this, according to www.employer-employee.com, "Employees under stress are insubordinate because they are overwhelmed. An employee may be under stress due to factors occurring in the workplace or in their personal life. Whatever the reason for their stress, they reach a point where they simply cannot function anymore. So, they tell their supervisor 'no,' they cannot do anymore work or tasks." Likewise, this stress is also apparent in Peter's motivation for rebellion when he candidly tells his boss that he does not have a report that is due. As a matter of fact, after his boss has asked Peter if he has his reports, Peter replies, "No! Not right now, Lumbergh! I'm kinda busy" (Office Space). Based on this, one can surmise that not only has Peter disregarded his work, but he also has disrespected his superior. Evidently, when people deliberately show little care for their work and little care for their superiors, it indicates that they don't care anymore because they have become overly frustrated with their work tasks. In addition to Bartleby and Peter's unhappiness with their work tasks, their discontent also stems from the lack of stimulation they obtain from their jobs.

The final motivation for rebellion displayed by Bartleby and Peter is evident through the little motivation they receive from their job. This is first evident when the narrator explains

Bartleby's wearisome position. The narrator states: "I can readily imagine that to some sanguine temperaments it would be altogether intolerable. For example, I cannot credit that the mettlesome poet Byron would have contentedly sat down with Bartleby to examine a law document of, say five hundred pages, closely written in a crimpy hand" (Melville). Based on this, one can surmise that not only did Bartleby's occupation offer him little, if any, motivation, but also that the job of legal copyists is blinding, cramping, uncreative work, and it clearly would not amuse someone as creative and adventurous as the poet Byron. In addition, this passage clearly suggests that a creative person could not survive such work, and it further supports the notion that Bartleby received little motivation from it. Similarly, this lack of motivation is also present in Peter's work conditions. Actually, this becomes apparent in a lucid remark by Peter when he states: "It's a problem of motivation, alright? Now, if I work my ass off and Initech ships a few extra units, I don't see another dime. So where's the motivation?" (Office Space). With this clear statement, it becomes evident that Peter obviously realizes his unfortunate position. In addition, motivation is defined as being an action, thought, person, or other influence that inspires. With this understanding, it is clear that Peter did not attain inspiration from his job. An additional example of the lack of motivation Bartleby received from his job is apparent in a telling description by the narrator. The narrator states: "It is, of course, an indispensable part of a scrivener's business to verify the accuracy of his copy, word by word. [. . .] It is a very dull, wearisome, and lethargic affair" (Melville). Here, it becomes evident that Bartleby's occupation is, indeed, a mind-numbing one. Arguably, when one repetitively engages in mind-numbing activities, it is reasonable to infer that this would lead to a feeling of mental and physical indolence. Furthermore, in support of these statements, motivation is the solitary inspiration that drives people. To enlighten this perception, according to Susan M. Johnston's The Career Adventure, "Motivations are the forces that move you to form goals and strive to achieve them. [. . .]

Motivations are 'fire' or fuel that drives you forward" (7). Conversely, this motivation is not evident in a comment Peter made to his friends. Peter stated: "I gotta get outa here, I think I'm gonna lose it" (Office Space). Debatably, when Peter delivers a rather desperate statement, one that reflects the desire to escape his setting, it suggests that he is lacking the stimulation and interest needed to stay motivated. Cleary, both characters, Bartleby and Peter, lacked this integral motivation needed to stay interested with their work. Moreover, in addition to comparing motivations in these two tales, it is also possible to identify similarities and extract differences in those similarities.

Unfortunately, Bartleby and Peter's bosses both seem to contribute to their stress; however, each boss's personality is quite different. First, this becomes apparent when Bartleby's boss describes his supportive, supervisory nature. The narrator states: "The beauty of my procedure seemed to consist in its perfect quietness. There was no vulgar bullying, no bravado of any sort, no choleric hectoring and striding to and fro across the apartment, jerking out vehement commands for Bartleby to bundle himself off with his beggarly traps. Nothing of the kind" (Melville). Here, the narrator describes his supervisory nature as a kind, gentle, and approachable one. However, it is apparent that Bartleby did not interpret this of his boss's nature, for Bartleby was not receptive to his boss's attempts at conversation. On the contrary, Peter's boss takes a different, unsupportive, supervisory role. This is evident when Peter has a feeling that his boss is going to ask him to work on the weekend. In fact, his boss states: "I'm gonna need you to go ahead and come in [Saturday]. So if you could be here around nine, that would be great. Oh, oh, yeah I forgot. I'm gonna also need you to come in Sunday, too" (Office Space). Here, when Peter's boss asks him to come in on the weekend, after Peter has worked a full week, it implies that his boss is obviously not concerned with his well-being. Obviously, when one works relentlessly and does not have time to rest, it can be very damaging to one's mental and physical health. Consequently, Bartleby's boss felt the opposite. This is evident when Bartleby has stated

that he will "do no more writing" (Melville), and consequently, his boss makes a suggestion to

Bartleby. The narrator states: "I hinted that of course he did wisely in abstaining from writing for

a while and urged him to embrace that opportunity of taking wholesome exercise in the open air"

(Melville). Here, his boss suggests that Bartleby get some much-needed rest. With this

suggestion, it becomes clear that Bartleby's boss is genuinely concerned with Bartleby's well-

being. Furthermore, the notion that Peter's boss is an inconsiderate boss is further cemented

when Peter's bosses are discussing lay-offs and how they plan on not personally telling the

employees. In fact, one of the bosses states, "We always like to avoid confrontation whenever

possible" (Office Space). This statement clearly depicts the lack of compassion that Peter's

supervisors have for their employees. Noticeably, when Peter's bosses brusquely disregard their

employees' feelings, it suggests that they are uninterested and unsupportive employers. As well

as this similarity and difference, it is possible to identify additional similarities and differences in

the story, "Bartleby the Scrivener" and the film, Office Space.

Conclusively, the final similarity apparent in "Bartleby the Scrivener" and Office Space, is

that both workers refuse to finish their work duties; however, their behaviors are unmistakably

different. This is first evident when the narrator describes Bartleby's hermitage. The narrator

states: "I now recalled all the quiet mysteries which I had noted in the man. I remembered that

he never spoke but to answer; [. . .] that he never went anywhere in particular that I could learn;

never went out for a walk, [. . .] that he had declined telling who he was, or whence he came

[. . .]" (Melville). Based on this, one could surmise that Bartleby has chosen this solitary and

reclusive lifestyle. Debatably, when people deliberately eschew conversation and the outside

world, it suggests that they do not desire the friendship of others and, instead, wish for isolation;

hence, they become miserable and depressed. Contrary to Bartleby, Peter likes to escape his workplace and find retreat elsewhere. In an effort to relieve himself of his mind-numbing workplace, Peter recruits the help of his friends. Here, Peter states: "Wanna go to Chotchkie's, get some coffee? [. . .] I gotta get out of here. [. . .]" (Office Space). Peter's statement is an obvious declaration of desperation; however, unlike Bartleby, Peter chooses to take haven outside the workplace. In addition, unlike Bartleby, Peter is not reclusive; he chooses to enlist his friends for his escape. Bartleby, on the other hand, seems to have no friends and appears as if he does not want any. This is apparent in an expressive description by the narrator:

> Yet, thought I, it is evident enough that Bartleby has been making his home here
> [. . .]. Immediately then the thought came sweeping across me, what miserable
> friendlessness and loneliness are here revealed! His poverty is great; but his
> solitude, how horrible! [. . .] Of a Sunday, Wall-street is deserted as Petra; and every
> night of every day it is emptiness. This building too, which of week-days hums with
> industry and life, at nightfall echoes with sheer vacancy, and all through Sunday is
> forlorn. And here Bartleby makes his home; sole spectator of a solitude which he
> has seen all populous [. . .]. (Melville)

This statement strengthens the impression that Bartleby is a reclusive, solitary soul, for it is apparent that Bartleby did not seek support from the outside world. Additionally, it appears that Bartleby retires to his hermitage to forgo his monotonous and droning work. On the other hand, Peter opts to flee his stressful workplace and find tranquility elsewhere. This is evident when one day, Peter decides not to go to work; instead, he takes refuge in going fishing with friends. In actuality, according to www.allsands.com/Health, Peter's action displays a good stress-coping skill, for they recommend to "Take a break from the stressful situation and return refreshed. [. . .] It can be a short break, a rejuvenating sleep or a longer break like going away on vacation." Distinct from Bartleby, Peter opts to alleviate himself from his stress, instead of dwelling on it.

This coping mechanism may be what saved Peter, and on the contrary, Bartleby's lack of coping skills may be what led him to his unfortunate, untimely fate. Furthermore, it is apparent that there is an unmistakable, underlying theme constant in these motivations, similarities, and differences; it appears that Bartleby and Peter simply did not know what they wanted in their career and, thus, did not receive satisfaction from their jobs.

  With these two tales, it is evident that job satisfaction is essential to one's well-being. Certainly, everyone wants to obtain satisfaction out of his or her job. After all, we spend so much time at work, and there's nothing like having to drag yourself into work, day in and day out, if it is giving you little meaning. Evidently, both Bartleby and Peter were unhappy in their careers and unsure of what paths to take and, therefore, unsure of what they really wanted from life. Alas, Bartleby and Peter did not take the time to find out what could truly satisfy them. Perhaps if they attempted to do this, it could have proved to benefit them significantly. Maybe we should all take the time to discover what our true dreams are. After all, if we don't know what our dreams are, or what truly satisfies us, then what do we really have?

Works Cited

"Coping Skills for Stress." Web Sand, Inc. 2002. Page Wise, Inc,. Dec. 2004.

    <http://www.allsands.com/Health>.

Daw, Jennifer. "Road rage, Air rage and now 'Desk Rage'." Monitor on Psychology Jun. 2001.

Johnston, Susan. The Career Adventure. 3rd ed. Upper Saddle River: Jeffery W. Johnston,

    2002.

Melville, Herman. "Bartleby the Scrivener." Putnam's Monthly. A Magazine of Literature,

    Science, and Art. II.XI. Nov. 1853:546-557, II.XII Dec.1853: 609-615. Bartleby.com. 20

    Dec. 2004. <http://www.bartleby.com>.

Office Space. Dir. Mike Judge. Perf. Ron Livingston, Gary Cole, Jennifer Aniston, David

    Herman, and Steven Root. Twentieth Century Fox, 1999.

Vikesland, Gary. "Mutiny at Work." Employer-Employee. Sep. 2003. 29 Dec. 2004.

    <http://www.employer-employee.com>.

Conversations with Writers

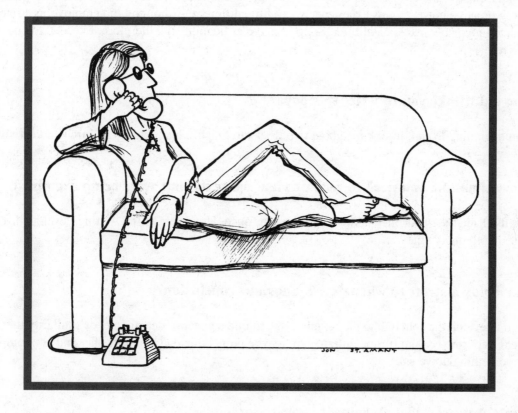

The following conversation is with Monea Longoria, author of "Nothing Like a Little Satisfaction."

Describe your writing process:

I usually prefer to be as prepared as possible before I begin the process, specifically, examining the texts, identifying my argument / arguments, and researching. I find this helps with the flow of ideas, thoughts, and areas that I plan on discussing in the paper. The pre-writing comes next; I prefer to use the "listing" method. Then, the general process begins.

Did you employ a strategy when developing your introductory paragraph?

I generally like to look at the entire project as a whole. From there, I like to find a parallel idea, theme, or similarity that the paper can explain, verify, or enlighten.

How did you construct your thesis statement?

I based my thesis off of the professor's prompt.

Did you perform research first? Or did you write, and then research, write, and then research?

I usually like to conduct research first, have quotations and sources out of the way before I start the writing process; however, this experience was a little different. Although I did employ this strategy, I realized my paper needed additional support and clarification and, therefore, I needed to conduct more research.

How long did it take you to write this paper?

From beginning to end, it took me about two weeks to finish. This includes research and revising.

How many times did you need to read or view the texts that were being examined?

Initially, I read the text once and viewed the film once. However, as the writing developed, I reviewed both many times.

Did you employ a strategy when developing your conclusion?

When I develop the concluding paragraph, I like to find a general idea, theme, or similarity that the paper has portrayed, and further enlighten it, maybe propel the idea a little further and / or compare it to something universal.

Have you always considered yourself a good writer?

No. (I remain skeptical.)

What is your advice to the aspiring academic writers of today?

My advice for aspiring writers is to be as thorough as possible. When examining your topic, explore every aspect of it; approach it from as many angles as possible. From there, it will be easier to develop a comprehensive argument, therefore, making it easier and more convincing for the reader. Lastly, when revising and editing, I find it particularly useful to read the paper aloud. I find that I miss a lot when I simply read it in my head.

Play-by-play

JON ST. AMANT

In reading Monea's essay, examine her thesis statement: "In fact, pertaining to these two tales, it is possible to identify motivations for rebellion or mutiny within the workplace as well as identify similarities and extract differences from these similarities." Here, Monea has done a fine job of capturing the prompt's expectations in a clear, concise thesis statement. Additionally, she noted that she will "identify similarities and extract differences from these similarities." This is important, for some people spend countless hours attempting to fabricate differences between two subjects when, as Monea has observed, differences can simply be extracted from the two subject's apparent similarities.

Monea's second paragraph begins with the following topic sentence: "First, the two main characters' motives for rebellion seem to mutually stem from their lifeless and bleak atmospheres." What will follow, then, is an examination of these similarities. And if, dear reader, you examine Monea's organizational strategy meticulously, you will see four sets of Point / Example / Commentary. Her first set is given to examining "Bartleby the Scrivener." Her second set is given to examining *Office Space*. She then further develops her examination of "Bartleby the Scrivener." And then, appropriately, she cross-references it with *Office Space*. In doing this, Monea makes it look easy. But please observe how she negotiates this terrain. Her primary weapon is the use of transitional language.

Notice, for instance, how she begins each Point:

Point 1: In "Bartleby the Scrivener," for instance . . .
Point 2: Similarly, in the film *Office Space* . . .
Point 3: Another example of the bleak atmosphere Bartleby endures . . .
Point 4: Lastly, the notion that Peter is adversely affected by . . .

In employing this transitional language, Monea keeps her reader focused on both subjects. Additionally, her transitional language promotes flow and cohesion. As a simple test, cross out her transitional language in an attempt to see how her paragraph reads without it. The result is a nebulous mass.

What also should not go overlooked is Monea's use of secondary sources. Not only does she include quotations from "Bartleby the Scrivener" and *Office Space* but from other sources as well. In paragraph two, for instance, she quotes the *Monitor on Psychology*. In paragraph three, she quotes www.employer-employee.com. In paragraph four, she quotes *The Career Adventure*. This is testimony to Monea's sagacity, for her examination of "Bartleby the Scrivener" and *Office Space* becomes more credible when "expert opinions" are added to her own.

After constructing five body paragraphs, Monea finds herself writing her essay's seventh paragraph: the conclusion. In examining her conclusion, notice that she uses it to continue developing her essay. She offers Commentary on the ideas presented in her essay, and then she offers a potential solution when she writes: "Alas, Bartleby and Peter did not take the time to find out what could truly satisfy them. Perhaps if they attempted to do this, it could have proved to benefit them significantly." This is refreshing, for much of the essay has been spent belaboring problems, so it is nice to reach a solution. Monea, however, does not stop there but, instead, attempts to transcend Bartleby and Peter by making her solution relevant to the reader as well. She writes: "Maybe we should all take the time to discover what our true dreams are. After all, if we don't know what our dreams are, or what truly satisfies us, then what do we really have?" This is well done, for she has attempted to make her argument societally relevant. She has attempted to transcend "Bartleby the Scrivener" and *Office Space*. And in ending with a question, she acts as a provocateur, prompting the reader to contemplate his or her own condition.

PRE-WRITING

Choose a pre-writing exercise (Journalist's Six, Listing, Brainstorming, or Sprinting), and begin developing a response to the prompt you've chosen to address.

ORGANIZATION

Use the following outline to help organize your paragraph.

Paragraph I: Introduction

_____

_____

_____

_____

_____

_____

_____

_____

_____

Paragraph II: Body Paragraph

Topic Sentence:

_____

_____

Point 1:

_____

_____

Example 1:

_____

_____

Commentary:

_____

_____

Point 2:

_____

_____

Example 1:

_____

_____

Commentary:

_____

_____

Point 3:

_____

_____

Example 1:

_____

_____

Commentary:

_____

_____

Point 4:

_____

_____

Example 1:

_____

_____

Commentary:

_____

_____

Transition:

_____

_____

Paragraph III: Body Paragraph

Topic Sentence:

_____

_____

Point 1:

_____

_____

Example 1:

_____

_____

 472

Commentary:

_____

_____

Point 2:

_____

_____

Example 1:

_____

_____

Commentary:

_____

_____

Point 3:

_____

_____

Example 1:

_____

_____

Commentary:

_____

_____

Point 4:

_____

_____

Example 1:

_____

_____

Commentary:

_____

_____

Transition:

_____

_____

Paragraph IV: Body Paragraph

Topic Sentence:

_____

_____

Point 1:

_____

_____

Example 1:

_____

_____

Commentary:

_____

_____

 474

Point 2:

_____

_____

Example 1:

_____

_____

Commentary:

_____

_____

Point 3:

_____

_____

Example 1:

_____

_____

Commentary:

_____

_____

Point 4:

_____

_____

Example 1:

_____

_____

Commentary:

_____

_____

Transition:

_____

_____

Paragraph V: Body Paragraph

Topic Sentence:

_____

_____

Point 1:

_____

_____

Example 1:

_____

_____

Commentary:

_____

_____

Point 2:

_____

_____

Example 1:

_____

_____

Commentary:

_____

_____

Point 3:

_____

_____

Example 1:

_____

_____

Commentary:

_____

_____

Point 4:

_____

_____

Example 1:

_____

_____

Commentary:

_____

_____

Transition:

_____

_____

Paragraph VI: Body Paragraph

Topic Sentence:

_____

_____

Point 1:

_____

_____

Example 1:

_____

_____

Commentary:

_____

_____

Point 2:

_____

_____

Example 1:

_____

_____

 478

Commentary:

_____

_____

Point 3:

_____

_____

Example 1:

_____

_____

Commentary:

_____

_____

Point 4:

_____

_____

Example 1:

_____

_____

Commentary:

_____

_____

Transition:

_____

_____

Paragraph VII: Conclusion

_____

_____

_____

_____

_____

_____

_____

_____

_____

_____

DEVELOPMENT

Use these pages to construct your first draft.

Name _____   Date _____

In This Section

Unlike the three preceding essays, this essay is written by a professional writer. In this essay, Jim Thomas has examined libidinal desire and domestic economy in *Pamela: Or, Virtue Rewarded* and *Clarissa: Or the History of a Young Lady,* two books by Samuel Richardson.

While many students are not endeavoring to become professional writers, some students are genuinely interested in taking their writing to the next level. In the spirit of doing so, such students may begin reading the Op / Ed pages in *The Los Angeles Times, The New York Times,* or *The Wall Street Journal.* Further, such students may begin reading essays in *The New Yorker* or in *The Chronicle of Higher Education.* Interestingly, however, what many will find is a similarity between the structure prescribed in this text and the structure adhered to by many professional writers. This is no coincidence. The Point / Example / Commentary organizational strategy is simply a representation of academic writing's fundamentals. To quote Jim Rohn, "There are no new fundamentals. You have to be wary of the man who says, 'We're manufacturing antiques.'" In other words, fundamentals are like antiques, and it is difficult to create new ones. Thus, when reading Jim Thomas' essay on *Pamela* and *Clarissa,* observe his use of Point / Example / Commentary. Even though many have probably not read *Pamela* and *Clarissa,* simply realize that an examination of this essay is essential to realizing how creatively one might use Point / Example / Commentary. Note how Thomas may not necessarily employ these fundamentals in order (as done in the preceding student essays), but note how he employs them nonetheless.

Thomas 1

"The End of the Institution":
Libidinal Desire and Domestic Economy in Richardson's
Pamela and *Clarissa*
by
Jim Thomas

The closest one gets to the erotic in <u>Pamela</u> occurs when Mr. B ("The Pretended She")

enters Pamela's bed disguised as the drunken Nan. He clasps her around the waist and kisses her "with a frightful vehemence." But the expected violence never occurs. Instead, as Pamela

documents, "His voice broke upon me like a clap of thunder. Now, Pamela, said he, is the

dreadful Time of Reckoning come, that I have threatened" (176). This verbal assault proves to be

a mere staging of Mr. B's power over the girl designed to intimidate her into compliance with his

desires. The most vehement instigation of violence comes, not from Mr. B's arousal, but from the

rallying of Mrs. Jewkes: "What you do, Sir, do; don't stand dilly-dallying. She cannot exclaim

worse than she has done. And she'll be quieter when she knows the worst" (176). The

conspicuous lack of violent action on the part of Mr. B reveals the extent to which male sexuality

(as opposed to rape) is dependent upon intimidation and / or reciprocity but it also reveals the

limitations of language in depicting male sexuality, the objectification of which appears, in this

case, to be negotiated only through the feminine. Sex (or rather, the "trace" of sex) in

Richardson's novels is nearly always depicted as repulsive and female even in cases of rape. My

project here is to evaluate some of the implications of this ambiguous gendering of sexuality in

Pamela and Clarissa, and to suggest that this reflects a larger tendency on the part of patriarchy to

marginalize all eroticism outside of a purely pronatalist dispensation.

The libidinous sexuality of both Lovelace and Mr. B is depicted as aberrational from the

beginning, what Ian Watt has called a conflict in Pamela "between the sexual instinct and the

moral code" (138). Lovelace's reputation, although it breeds intrigue, is for the most part

condemned by both his family and public opinion, and Mr. B's flirtation with Pamela is

something he does in spite of his true, aristocratic nobility. In fact, it is largely Pamela's

recognition of his own best interests that returns him to normalcy, transforming his lust for

transgressive sexuality into the desire for legitimate heirs and an orderly estate.

The most surprising thing about these texts isn't that Richardson is squeamish about his

presentation of sex but that his villains are constantly surrounded by an entourage of sadistic women who are characterized as far more vicious than the men themselves. When Lovelace has

second thoughts about the rape, he is ridiculed by Mrs. Sinclair and the other prostitutes. When

Mr. B turns his assault into a mere scare tactic, Mrs. Jewkes encourages him to get on with it.

What are we to make of this female predilection for violence? According to statistics compiled

by J.M. Beattie, women in the period from 1660 to 1800 committed approximately one criminal

offense for every three committed by men, and were far less likely to participate in violent crimes,

particularly those involving a direct confrontation with a victim (238). While this statistic is far

too broad to account for individual behavior, it does suggest that we need to look beyond the

lifestyles of the average18th century woman to account for Richardson's misogynistic linking of

rape with the female gender.

One possible approach to this dilemma is to follow Monique Wittig in separating the

objective phenomenon of sex in its various manifestations from that which animates it: desire.

"'Sex' is always already female, and there is only one sex, the feminine. To be male is not to be

'sexed'; to be 'sexed' is always a way of becoming particular and relative, and males within this

system participate in the form of the universal person" (Butler 113). The "universal person"

might best be seen as veiled by language, capable of acting in a non-discursive space which

allows him both anonymity and the unlimited power to define his own desire.

Most of Lovelace's and Mr. B's strategies are enacted by their female coteries. Lovelace's

conviction that "there have been more girls ruined, at least prepared for ruin, by their own sex

[. . .] than *directly* by the attempts and delusions of men" (Clarissa 865) is supported by his own

experience as well as a number of passages in the novel. Indeed, Mrs. Sinclair, Dorcas, and Sally

appear to be more anxious for Clarissa's deflowering than Lovelace:

>Mrs. Sinclair and the nymphs are all of opinion that I am now so much a
>
>favourite [. . .] that I may do what I will, and plead violence of passion; which,

they will have it, makes violence of action pardonable with their sex [. . .] and

they will all offer their helping hands [. . .] They remind me that the situation of

their house is such, that no noises can be heard out of it; and ridicule me for

making it necessary for a lady to be undressed. It was not always so with me,

poor old man! Sally told me; saucily slinging her handkerchief in my face. (702)

The "nymphs" offer him a soundproof room, an alibi, and their "helping hands." But this isn't

meant to strike the reader as merely comical. As the blank despondency and subsequent death of

Clarissa are supposed to make clear, abduction and rape are a serious business.

Immediately preceding this passage we read a letter that Clarissa has written describing

her latest encounter with Lovelace. Unlike the bawdy, largely comical encounters that Pamela

has with Mr. B, the one-on-one scenes between Clarissa and Lovelace are more serious. He is

unable to maintain his jocularity when he is alone with her, and we sense that he suffers pangs

of guilt: "He endeavored as once before, to conceal his emotion [. . .] But why [. . .] should

these men [. . .] think themselves above giving these proofs of a feeling heart?" (Clarissa 699).

Clarissa follows these reflections with a Petrarchian sonnet which reads, "Compassion proper

to mankind appears [. . .] to weep is our prerogative [. . .] Who can all sense of others' ills

escape / Is but a brute at best in human shape" (ibid.). Richardson's juxtaposition of this

"high," tragic register with the generically "low," comic register used in the account of the

prostitutes' banter is surely suggestive. Sally's telling remark, "It was not always so with me,

poor old man," suggests that she was initiated into the world of sexuality through rape as well,

but not only does it fail to destroy her as immediately as it does Clarissa, but she helps plot the

ruin of others as well. Poverty and promiscuity are associated with the "base" sexuality of the

prostitute, while emotional sensitivity, classical learning, and female virtue are united in the tragic figure of Clarissa. These characteristics are largely exclusive; ladies have no lust, and prostitutes feel no compassion. Men, caught someplace in between, may cross this boundary at will anonymously.

The feminine presence surrounding the rape is so pervasive that it diverts all language from the actual event. Clarissa's own account suggests that she is so horrified and repulsed by the women who are present during the rape that she is only half-conscious that she has been assaulted by a man. This absence of signification, the "hole at the center of the novel" where the rape occurs, has led Judith Wilt to doubt that it occurred at all (Eagleton 61). Terry Castle, although she doesn't deny the rape, recognizes the degree to which it depends upon its linguistic construction, describing it as only "the final arbitrary turn in [Lovelace's] great argument" (114): "I was so senseless that I dare not aver that the horrid creatures of the house were personally aiding and abetting: but some visionary remembrances I have of female figures flitting, as I may say, before my sight; the wretched woman's particularly" (Clarissa 1011). A related awareness of displacement is even remarked by Lovelace who complains that he has been robbed of his pleasure by the contrivance of a feminine "mediatress" who drugs Clarissa. "But have not I the worst of it; since her insensibility has made me but a thief to my own joys?" (Clarissa 887).

I would not suggest that Richardson intends this as a denial of rape or male violence; that would seem to miss the point. Rather, I want to suggest that there is something missing in Richardson's linguistic register which continues to veil male hegemony even in an account which is surely intended to descry violent acts against women. The written account of a rape trial in the year 1759 suggests a similar gap. Elizabeth Hewer, testifying against a soldier who had attacked her near Farnham, England is quoted as saying that he threw her to the ground and "lay with me, and entered his _____ into my _____." This is followed by an editorial addendum which states:

"'This witness fully proved every minute circumstance necessary in the sense of the law, to constitute a rape,' which 'for the sake of common decency' [I] was 'obliged to conceal from the public'" (Beattie 125). There is, of course, nothing surprising in the demand for the minute particulars in a case to justify conviction. What is curious here is the notion of "common decency" which requires the absence of these particulars in the written account. It's not at all difficult to envision what the editor has omitted. Do either Richardson or this editor somehow render their accounts impotent by leaving gaps in them? Or is this unsignifiable space being preserved for the "universal" productions of male desire which seek to preserve the physical "fact" of sex for the domestic economy?

The disadvantage of "becoming particular and relative," of becoming the objectification and locus of another's desire, is that it denies the right to self-definition (the impossibility of being a compassionate prostitute, for example). Universality, on the other hand, grants the power of unbounded interpretation. In a remarkable moment of self-deconstruction, Lovelace describes himself as hermaphroditic and, therefore, capable of reading women's innermost thoughts: "But I was originally a bashful whelp [. . .] yet I know the sex so well! But that indeed is the reason that I know it so well [. . .] a bashful man has a good deal of the soul of a woman; and so, like Tiresias, can tell what they think and what they drive at, as well as themselves" (Clarissa 441). We, of course, recognize that Lovelace cannot, in fact, read Clarissa's mind, but this is irrelevant in a world where the power of interpretation has the authority of the real. In Lacanian terms, the question that begs to be asked here has nothing to do with what Lovelace knows about Clarissa. It is, instead, a prior, methodological question: "How is [her] 'being' instituted and allocated through the signifying practices of the paternal economy?" (Butler 43).

In Lovelace's case, this question is doubly revealing. It both uncovers the fallacy which founds Lovelace's private vision as well as undermines the signifying economy of which he is a part. Lovelace's interpretation of Clarissa's innermost thoughts are purely fictional. Perhaps the

most obvious and self-revelatory of these "knowledges" is the Popian claim that "All women are

rakes in their hearts." Far from being a rake, Clarissa is the victim of a rake; her dilemma (and

this is where the abstractions of signification reveal their power) is that she must die in order to

disprove him. It isn't simply that women are what men want in this economy, but that women

become whatever men want: sex object, servant, or bearer of progeny.

In a macabre twist, Pamela's "virtue rewarded" becomes in Clarissa a "history [. . .]

particularly showing the distresses that may attend the *misconduct both of parents and children,*

in relation to marriage" (Clarissa, title page; my emphasis). According to the title page, Clarissa

becomes the victim of her own misconduct. The precise nature of her error, however, is difficult

to determine. Aside from a few self-deprecating remarks, the most substantial accusation is that

Clarissa has presumed to trust herself with a man, an act tantamount to giving Lovelace absolute

sovereignty over her. In effect, she becomes his fantasy:

> Let me perish, Belford, if I would not forgo the brightest diadem in the world for
>
> the pleasure of seeing a twin Lovelace at each charming breast, drawing from it
>
> his first sustenance; the pious task continued for one month, and no more!
>
> I now, methinks, behold this most charming of women in this sweet office,
>
> pressing with her fine fingers the generous flood into the purple mouths of each
>
> eager hunter by turns: her conscience eye now dropped on one, now on the other,
>
> with a sigh of maternal tenderness; and then raised up to my own delighted eye, full
>
> of wishes, for the sake of the pretty varlets, and for her own sake, that I would deign
>
> to legitimate; that I would condescend to put on the nuptial fetters. (Clarissa 706)

The precise object of Lovelace's desire here is difficult to identify. He is clearly fascinated with

the biological functioning of Clarissa's body as well as with her expressions of "maternal tenderness." He also reflects upon the possibility of his own reduplication ("twin Lovelaces").

But these features all focus themselves in his intoxication with Clarissa's fear of illegitimacy:

that he might not "deign" to legitimate the children. The vision of maternity here is less a locus

for Lovelace's fascination with his progeny, or even his reproductive capability, than it is an

aesthetic rendering of power. Clarissa's physical features play an important part in Lovelace's

fantasy, but more important is the protean fantasy itself.

Even in death Clarissa remains the object of this fixation. Writing from Knightsbridge late

in the novel, Lovelace declares, "Living or dying, she is mine—and only mine. Have I not earned

her dearly?" (Clarissa 1358). And later,

> I think it absolutely right that my ever-dear and beloved lady should be opened
>
> and embalmed [. . .] Everything that can be done to preserve *the charmer* from
>
> decay shall also be done. And when she will descend to her original dust, or
>
> cannot be kept longer, I will have her laid in my family vault [. . .] But her heart
>
> [. . .] I will have. I will keep it in Spirits. It shall never be out of my sight.
>
> (Clarissa 1384; my emphasis).

As might be expected, Lovelace believes that his right to possess Clarissa includes the right to

possess and interpret her writings. "I will take her papers [. . .] as no one can do her memory

justice equal to myself [. . .] Although her will may in some respects cross mine, yet I expect to be

observed. I will be the interpreter of hers" (Clarissa 1385). In a novel that consists wholly of

letters, such a move is surely conscious on Richardson's part. In the most fundamental way, what

Clarissa writes and the way these writings are interpreted become what Clarissa is. In a self-

conscious parody of Dryden, Lovelace quotes, "The cause of Love can never be assigned; / 'Tis in

no face;—but in the Lover's Mind" (Clarissa 146).

This same relationship between the male right to possession and interpretation plays a

significant role in Pamela as well. What becomes clear after a reading of the second novel is that

Lovelace simply takes to an extreme notions of female possession already exercised by Mr. B.

A comparison of both men's fascination with natality makes this clear:

> He was pleased to take the notice of my dress, and spanning my Waste with his
>
> hands, said, What a sweet Shape is here! It would make one regret to lose it; and
>
> yet, my beloved Pamela, I shall think of nothing but that loss wanting to complete
>
> my happiness! [. . .] Such an innocent wish, my Dearest, may be permitted me,
>
> because it is the End of the Institution. (Pamela 132)

Pamela's only asset, her virtue, is represented here as capital which needs to be "invested."

Progeny, the "End of the Institution," is the return on this investment. The need for legitimate

progeny is a kind of growth which is both physical and economic, the loss of "that shape" which,

along with Pamela's neck and "bosom," has always acted as a synecdoche, for her sexuality is

now transformed into Mr. B's progenitive capability: the power to perpetuate his name and his

fortune in time. Once sex (the libidinal desire of Mr. B) becomes honor (the desire for production

of legitimate heirs), it becomes both "universal" and more closely regulated. Pamela's journal

leaves only a "pregnant" gap on her wedding night even though the journal is putatively for the

exclusive reading of Mr. B. Sex within marriage is subsumed under the heading of legitimacy

and signifies as a function of male property. Female sexuality outside of marriage signifies only

as ruin, the mutation of virtue.

Pamela regards her marriage as a complete transformation of both herself and her world.

"Oh, my prison is become my palace," she exclaims (Pamela 293). This metamorphosis,

however, involves a fundamental loss of self which she regards as normative: "I shall think myself more and more his Servant" (<u>Pamela</u> 257). As we might expect, Pamela is under as rigorous an observation after her marriage as she is before it. The fact of its being voluntary (or, in her case, expedient) is less a proof of her newfound domestic authority (as Nancy Armstrong suggests) as it is evidence that she has become subject to a new set of regulatory fictions which leave her no room for selfhood: "It is almost a hard thing to lie under the Weight of such deep obligations on one side; and such a Sense of one's own Unworthiness of the other!—*O! What a Godlike power* is that of doing good!—I envy the Rich and the Great for nothing else!" (<u>Pamela</u> 264; italics mine). Pamela becomes hypersensitive to even the most subtle of Mr. B's requests. "It concerns me [. . .] lest he should have [. . .] the least Shadow of a Doubt, that I am not, Mind and Person, entirely his (<u>Pamela</u> 287). Whatever remains of her self-initiative is controlled by right of property. Just as in the case of Lovelace and Clarissa, the right to control the circulation and interpretation of Pamela's letters (all of her creative production) is considered a fundamental aspect of this ownership.

With no self-identity except as a part of Mr. B's productive machine, disobedience is tantamount to self-destruction. This explains the logic behind Pamela's codification of "the rules I am to observe" after her marriage:

> 33. That a Wife should not desire to convince her husband for contradiction's
>
>   sake; but for his own. As both will find their account in this, if one does
>
>   [. . .] .
>
> 37. That a Wife should [. . .] draw a kind of veil over her husband's faults.
>
> 38. That such as she could not conceal, she should extenuate. (<u>Pamela</u> 371)

The most conspicuous thing about these rules is the fact that they promote Mr. B's anonymity allowing him to function, as it were, "behind" the real. Miss Godfrey becomes a useful case in point. In a tellingly euphemistic phrase, Mr. B explains that as regards the history of Miss

Godfrey, "the Truth is as much preserved as possible" (<u>Pamela</u> 396). Whatever is not "preserved"

fails to signify as reality: the humanity of the prostitute, the "maleness" of male rape, and the

fundamental selfhood of the wife.

Ian Watt has suggested that Richardson was only partially aware of the implications of his

portrayal of the "social situation of women" in his novels (Watt 154-55). I believe that this is

largely true. Even so, Richardson deserves a great deal of credit for the accuracy with which he

transcribed the dilemma of gender encoded in the assumptions of his time. Many of his gender

reversals are intended as more than comic relief. Picturing Mr. B in the guise of a female servant

and Lovelace as hermaphroditic are highly critical depictions which would have signaled in them

a kind of social suicide.

The enlightenment conception of the fop may be the last nominally acceptable manifestation

of transvestitism until well into the 19th century. Drawing a contrast between the largely

heterosexual phenomenon of cross dressing in the renaissance, as opposed to that of the 1700s,

Alan Bray writes:

> The transvestitism of the eighteenth-century molly house was [. . .] about
>
> homosexuality; it was not intended to deceive and, as the molly house
>
> themselves, was wisely kept as unobtrusive as possible. Effeminacy and
>
> transvestitism with specifically homosexual connotations were a crucial part of
>
> what gave the molly houses their identity. (Garber 131)

It's not necessary to conclude from this that Richardson intended to depict Mr. B. or Lovelace as

homosexual in order to make sense of his feminization of their characters. Rather, Richardson

appears to be making use of the connotations of effeminacy to suggest that the behavior of the

rake is unmanly despite its obsession with heterosexual sex. In the above, the term "molly"

designated both male homosexuals as well as female prostitutes (Moll Flanders, for example, was named after her profession), suggesting that any exercise of sexuality outside of the domestic

economy had to be categorized within its terms.

Inasmuch as illicit sexualities may be said to exist in this period, they are considered

mercenary, suggesting that rakes, like prostitutes, sell their cultural legitimacy for a marginalized

"life of pleasure." As Marjorie Garber has pointed out, even the word "effeminacy appears to

derive [. . .] from the notion of men excessively devoted to women [. . .]," suggesting "that

effeminacy is generated by sexual voluptuousness directed toward women, not toward men.

Historically, then, 'effeminacy' is misogynistic as well as homophobic [. . .] . Once again, what is

being protected here is a notion of manhood or manliness as a social norm" (Garber 139). Using

Lovelace's fantasy of the weaning "twin Lovelaces" as an example, Richardson surely intended to

suggest that Lovelace's fascination with his own exercise of power was ultimately self-

destructive, a prophecy that proves true in that Clarissa, unlike Pamela, uses all of her maternal

instincts to "court death." Mr. B, who returns to normalcy, is "rewarded" with "a numerous and

hopeful progeny" (Pamela 409).

Works Cited

Armstrong, Nancy. Desire and Domestic Fiction. Oxford: Oxford University Press, 1987.

Beattie, J.M. Crime and the Courts in England 1660-1800. New Jersey: Princeton University

Press, 1986.

Butler, Judith. Gender Trouble: Feminism and the Subversion of Identity. New York:

Routledge, Chapman and Hall, Inc., 1990.

Castle, Terry. Clarissa's Ciphers: Meaning and Disruption in Richardson's *Clarissa*. Ithaca:

Cornell University Press, 1982.

Eagleton, Terry. The Rape of Clarissa: Writing, Sexuality, and the Class Struggle in Samuel

Richardson. Minneapolis: University of Minnesota Press, 1982.

Garber, Marjorie. Vested Interests: Cross Dressing and Cultural Anxiety. New York: Harper /

Collins Publishers, 1993.

Richardson, Samuel. Clarissa: Or the History of a Young Lady. London: Penguin Books, Inc.,

1985.

Richardson, Samuel. Pamela: Or, Virtue Rewarded. Boston: Houghton, Mifflin Co., 1971.

Trumback, Randolph. "Erotic Fantasy and Male Libertinism in Enlightenment England."

The Invention of Pornography: Obscenity and the Origins of Modernity, 1500-1800. Ed.

Lynn Hunt. New York: Zone Books, 1993.

Watt, Ian. The Rise of the Novel. Berkeley: University of California Press, 1957.

Conversations with Writers

The following conversation is with Jim Thomas, author of "'The End of the Institution': Libidinal Desire and Domestic Economy in Richardson's *Pamela* and *Clarissa*."

Describe your writing process:

I always compose on a computer since I can type faster than I write, and I sometimes find that actually putting pen to paper sets up a barrier between what I'm thinking and how I express these thoughts. Typing is more spontaneous and natural to me. Most of the time I have the texts that I wish to discuss next to me on the desk, and I simply work my way through them, discussing key details that interest me and paying relatively little attention to the organization of these ideas at first. It isn't that organization and structure aren't important as much as that I would prefer this organization to be consistent with the internal logic of my ideas rather than imposed from the outside. If I do use an outline it is almost always very rudimentary, more like a list of topics that I will cover than a detailed listing of points, sub-points, and support. Once my ideas are typed up I revise and reorganize my thoughts, usually working on the same draft. This also gives me the opportunity to anticipate objections to my ideas and to follow up on ideas that seem to need further attention. I find that I can work like this for five or six hours at a time without breaks except perhaps to get a cup of coffee. I then set my writing aside for at least one day before I revise it once again. I often find that this gives me the distance I need to really see my writing afresh, and I often find that the changes I make during this final revision are things that make a significant improvement to the readability of the original drafts.

Did you employ a strategy when developing your introductory paragraph?

I don't plan my introductions, although I am conscious of the fact that my reader needs whatever preliminary information is necessary to comprehend the argument of the paper. I prefer to be as efficient as possible in my introductions. The whole idea is to transition the reader from a complete lack of information to the heart of the argument. I don't assume that I'm going to win my reader's sympathy until I get to the specifics in the body paragraphs, and I've always considered emotional appeals and anecdotal introductions as digressive.

How did you construct your thesis statement?

My thesis statements are always the product of writing and revision, and the final version of the thesis may be quite different from the first draft. I have a general idea of what I want to argue, so I get this down in a single sentence, but I almost always have a significantly more focused, more defensible thesis by the time I'm done. The close readings in the body paragraphs force me to make adjustments to the topic sentences in my paragraphs, and these, in turn, inevitably force me to change the thesis to guarantee a close fit between the argument of the paper as a whole and what I think I'm demonstrating in the body paragraphs. These adjustments are just part of the process of writing and are much easier now that I'm composing on a computer as opposed to a typewriter.

Did you perform research first? Or did you write, and then research, write, and then research?

Since all of the writing I do is literary analysis, my writing begins with a close reading of the texts I am considering. I keep a running list of page numbers, citing passages that I think might be of use in an essay. These might include common categories of analysis such as gender issues, religion, epistemology and so forth, but they also include symbols that I see operating in the text, idiosyncrasies in the style, major concerns of the author, anything that seems to stand out and call for analysis. Oftentimes it is those aspects of a text that are least transparent on a first reading that prove to be most useful. I think most careful readers can spot these focal points almost by instinct, but they usually need to be revisited to be fully worked out. By the time I've finished reading the text the first or second time, I have at least a handful of listings that strike me as possible focal points for an essay. I sometimes think of approaches to these texts as I'm reading, so I also jot down notes to remind myself of these later. I might, for example, see a developing contrast between two characters or a developing theme. If I'm particularly attuned to the text, I feel like I can almost anticipate how the text might build on a developing theme as I read. Finding the next relevant passage then seems almost like an inevitability than a surprise. Often a theme or concept that is only vaguely alluded to early in the text becomes impossible to ignore as the author shapes it over time, and authors tend to dwell on things that are significant. Authorial intention isn't really the point; the emphasis could be a result of subconscious or social factors at work in the author as well as a more conscious didactic purpose. The reason I think my process works for me is that it really focuses my attention on specific issues and channels my thinking about the text from the beginning. Once I've finished the text I go back over the passages that I've listed in each category for review and evaluation. I don't free write, brainstorm, or create elaborate outlines for my papers even though I often encourage my students to do these things because my analytical technique is painstaking enough that these are usually superfluous. I think I've simply internalized these processes so that they have become part of the way I think when doing analysis.

How long did it take you to write this paper?

This paper took an absurd amount of time to write, mainly because Richardson's *Clarissa* is the longest novel in the English language. I think it fills six volumes in the Oxford edition. I think I originally took it on as a challenge rather than with any view toward writing about it. By the time I was finished reading, I had probably 100 pages of typed notes. Because this was a scholarly essay, I was also working through the relevant critical essays and several important books on the novels, and I had to be sure that I read this material thoroughly so as not to be called to task for omitting important arguments or failing to acknowledge intellectual debts. Writing about an eighteenth-century novel also meant that I couldn't be sure that I understood how some of the gender issues in the novel would have been understood in Richardson's time, so I had to research these things as well. A scholar who was more specialized than I was at the time might have already had this background. If I had to guess, I would say that this essay was a six-month project with about forty hours dedicated to the composition and revision of the essay.

How many times did you need to read or view the texts that were being examined?

I only read *Clarissa* through once and *Pamela* two or three times, but I reviewed the passages that I had taken notes on many more times. Oftentimes I would isolate a key passage and simply dedicate a day to thinking and writing about that passage.

Did you employ a strategy when developing your conclusion?

I don't have a set strategy for conclusions, but I always try to draw implications from my argument at the end of a paper. I may allude to the thesis in an indirect way to begin, but the task of the conclusion is to give the reader further applications for the arguments made in the essay or to propose what a next step in thinking about the novel, poem, or author might be.

Have you always considered yourself a good writer?

I've always had some ability with language. When I was in high school I wrote speeches for the speech team, and I always had a natural inclination to write. I think I originally wanted to major in business when a college student, but once I began taking literature classes there was really no turning back. I've always found writing gratifying, more like an intellectual game than work.

What is your advice to the aspiring academic writers of today?

I've never been particularly good at providing words of wisdom, but I think it would be easy to underestimate the amount of work involved in earning a graduate degree and, more difficult still, of getting a job. I would recommend academia to anyone who truly loves it and finds writing and research as gratifying as I do. Looking back, the biggest threats to my academic work were always the temptation to take time off to earn some money or to buy a better car or something like that. At times I succumbed to these pressures and lost a lot of precious time, but at my most productive I learned to live with public transportation, cheap housing, and an inexpensive social life, and thus had more resources to devote to my work.

Play-by-play

JON ST.AMANT

From the beginning, observe how creatively Jim Thomas employs Point / Example / Commentary. He begins with what might be labeled his first Point. Then, he offers his first Example. And then, cleverly, he offers a brief sentence of Commentary. Then, he blends his next Point with an Example. This is followed by one sentence of Commentary. After this sentence, he blends his next Point with an Example. And then he follows this with two sentences of Commentary. Finally, he ends his introductory paragraph with his Thesis Statement. What should be noted, then, is how he has employed organizational variety and economy in choosing to combine his Point and his Example. Of course, in the preceding student essays, each Point, Example, and Commentary represented its own sentence. To clarify what Thomas has done, observe the following diagram of his first paragraph:

Point: The closest one gets to the erotic in *Pamela* occurs when Mr. B ("The Pretended She") enters Pamela's bed disguised as the drunken Nan.

Example: He clasps her around the waist and kisses her "with a frightful vehemence."

Commentary: But the expected violence never occurs.

Point / Example: Instead, as Pamela documents, "his voice broke upon me like a clap of thunder. Now, Pamela, said he, is the dreadful Time of Reckoning come, that I have threatened" (176).

Commentary: This verbal assault proves to be a mere staging of Mr. B's power over the girl designed to intimidate her into compliance with his desires.

Point / Example: The most vehement instigation of violence comes, not from Mr. B's arousal, but from the rallying of Mrs. Jewkes: "What you do, Sir, do; don't stand dilly-dallying. She cannot exclaim worse than she has done. And she'll be quieter when she knows the worst" (176).

Commentary: The conspicuous lack of violent action on the part of Mr. B reveals the extent to which male sexuality (as opposed to rape) is dependent upon intimidation and / or reciprocity but it also reveals the limitations of language in depicting male sexuality, the objectification of which appears, in this case, to be negotiated only through the feminine.

Commentary: Sex (or rather, the "trace" of sex) in Richardson's novels is nearly always depicted as repulsive and female even in cases of rape.

Thesis Statement: My project here is to evaluate some of the implications of this ambiguous gendering of sexuality in *Pamela* and *Clarissa,* and to suggest that this reflects a larger tendency on the part of patriarchy to marginalize all eroticism outside of a purely pronatalist dispensation.

Take a moment to consider this. While many view the writing process as some sort of mystery multiplied times the depths of infinity, others can see that, just as two plus two equals four (chaos theorists aside) Point / Example / Commentary is a logical application for advancing an argument. And while it may not be easy, it *is* quite simple: a Point is necessary to articulate what will be asserted. An Example is necessary to support the assertion. Finally, Commentary must be employed to explain the relevance of the Example to the Point.

   Next, what must be noted is Thomas' diction. A distinguishing characteristic between professional essays and student essays, diction (word choice) often demonstrates its versatility and its latitude in essays composed by more accomplished writers. For example, some may not even comprehend Thomas' thesis statement, for they do not know how to define the following words: *ambiguous, gendering, marginalize, eroticism, pronatalist, dispensation.* Before rattling Pandora, however, please note this for clarification: using precise diction involves choosing the "right" word for the occasion. In other words, if you have a polysyllabic word (a word with multiple syllables) to use in place of a word that will definitely suffice, you may choose the monosyllabic word instead. Further, if the monosyllabic word is more appropriate or precise, then use it. An exaggerated example would be choosing what to say in response to, "How was that burrito?" You could say, "Good." Or you could say, "Super-cala-fragalistic-expealidocious." Remember, if the goal is to communicate effectively, choose the most precise word. Anything else might seem unnecessarily precocious. That stated, there is tremendous value in possessing a well-developed vocabulary, and this should be evident when examining Thomas' diction. As we read his second paragraph, for instance, we see *libidinous, aberrational, normalcy,* and *transgressive.* Given the context in which these words are used, it seems that Thomas' objective was attained, for these words do not seem to demonstrate his desire to be ostentatious or pedantic but, rather, his desire to communicate effectively and efficiently, using the precise words for the occasion. And please note that possessing a well-developed vocabulary is not enough. One must be able to use these words appropriately when advancing an argument. A good rule, thus, may be this: When in doubt, leave it out. (If uncertainty plagues your academic prose, remedy this ailment by attacking the text. Do not make the mistake of allowing others to transform your argument simply because you used ambiguous or inappropriate language.)

Now, observe Thomas' strategy in his third paragraph. Here, Thomas still employs Point / Example / Commentary, but it is done creatively. Note the following diagram of his paragraph:

Topic Sentence: The most surprising thing about these texts isn't that Richardson is squeamish about his presentation of sex but that his villains are constantly surrounded by an entourage of sadistic women who are characterized as far more vicious than the men themselves.

Example: When Lovelace has second thoughts about the rape, he is ridiculed by Mrs. Sinclair and the other prostitutes.

Example: When Mr. B turns his assault into a mere scare tactic, Mrs. Jewkes encourages him to get on with it.

Commentary / Point: What are we to make of this female predilection for violence?

Example: According to statistics compiled by J.M. Beattie, women in the period from 1660 to 1800 committed approximately one criminal offense for every three committed by men, and were far less likely to participate in violent crimes, particularly those involving a direct confrontation with a victim (238).

Commentary: While this statistic is far too broad to account for individual behavior, it does suggest that we need to look beyond the lifestyles of the average 18th century woman to account for Richardson's misogynistic linking of rape with the female gender.

In examining Thomas' paragraph, note how he begins with a Topic Sentence, which lets the reader know what he will attempt to prove. Then, notice how he skips his first Point. (But ask yourself if he skipped his first Point, or if his *implied* Point is clear because of his Topic Sentence.) Then, notice his Example. It does not include a quotation but, instead, a direct reference to the text. This serves as his Example, and since it seems self-evident, he skips Commentary in lieu of employing another Example. Then, he asks the following question: "What are we to make of this female predilection for violence?" Generally, asking questions in an essay is tricky. Some writers, for instance, will ask a question and then proceed to answer it. What Thomas has done, however, is ask a multi-functional question. Not only does it connect a "female predilection for violence" to his two Examples, but it also introduces his *next* Example. In other words, the question Thomas has asked serves as both his Commentary and his Point. This leads to a paraphrased Example and, alas, the Commentary that should follow.

Take the time to diagram Thomas' additional paragraphs, noting how creatively one can use Point / Example / Commentary. Further, note how each of Thomas' body paragraphs further advances his thesis: "This ambiguous gendering of sexuality in *Pamela* and *Clarissa* reflects a larger tendency on the part of patriarchy to marginalize all eroticism outside of a purely pronatalist dispensation." Chances are strong that a careful examination of Thomas' essay will prompt the reader to reach the following conclusion: Not only has he adequately supported his argument but he has effectively embraced the role of provocateur as well. Through assertions like, "Drawing a contrast between the largely heterosexual phenomenon of cross dressing in the renaissance," and conclusions like, "Female sexuality outside of marriage signifies only as ruin, the mutation of virtue," Thomas succeeds in employing provocative language that embraces the Churchillian mantra, "If you're not stepping on toes, you're not moving." Thomas' trenchant eye for literary and societal criticism finds itself in a bottled voice that, once uncorked, floods his essay with the right mix of original thought coupled with support from secondary sources.

PRE-WRITING

Choose a pre-writing exercise (Journalist's Six, Listing, Brainstorming, or Sprinting), and begin developing a response to the prompt you've chosen to address.

ORGANIZATION

Use the following outline to help organize your paragraph. (This outline does not incorporate Point / Example / Commentary in a manner representative of the three preceding outlines. In an effort to emulate the professional essayist, employ Point / Example / Commentary creatively, blending your Point / Example and / or your Commentary and its ensuing Point.) Notice that with exception to the Topic Sentence and Transition, the placement of each component in the following Body Paragraphs has been left to your discretion.

Paragraph I: Introduction

_____

_____

_____

_____

_____

_____

_____

_____

_____

_____

Paragraph II: Body Paragraph

Topic Sentence:

_____

_____

_____ :

_____ :

_____ :

_____ :

_____ :

_____ :

_____ :

_____:

_____

_____

_____:

_____

_____

_____:

_____

_____

_____:

_____

_____

Transition:

_____

_____

Paragraph III: Body Paragraph

Topic Sentence:

_____

_____

_____:

_____

_____

_____:

_____

_____

_____:

_____

_____

_____:

_____

_____

_____:

_____

_____

_____:

_____

_____

_____:

_____

_____

_____:

_____

_____

_____:

_____

_____

_____:

_____

_____

_____:

_____

_____

Transition:

_____

_____

Paragraph IV: Body Paragraph

Topic Sentence:

_____

_____

_____:

_____

_____

_____:

_____

_____

 510

Name _____ Date _____

_____:

_____

_____

_____:

_____

_____

_____:

_____

_____

_____:

_____

_____

_____:

_____

_____

_____:

_____

_____

_____:

_____

_____

_____:

_____

_____

_____:

_____

_____

Transition:

_____

_____

Paragraph V: Body Paragraph

Topic Sentence:

_____

_____

_____:

_____

_____

_____:

_____

_____

_____:

_____

_____

_____:

_____

_____

_____:

_____

_____

_____:

_____

_____

_____:

_____

_____

_____:

_____

_____

_____:

_____

_____

_____:

_____

_____

_____:

_____

_____

Transition:

_____

_____

Paragraph VI: Body Paragraph

Topic Sentence:

_____

_____

_____:

_____

_____

_____:

_____

_____

_____:

_____

_____

_____:

_____

_____

_____:

_____

_____

_____:

_____

_____

_____:

_____

_____

_____:

_____

_____

_____:

_____

_____

_____:

_____

_____

_____:

_____

_____

Transition:

_____

_____

Paragraph VII: Conclusion

_____

_____

_____

_____

_____

_____

_____

_____

_____

_____

Name _____ Date _____

DEVELOPMENT

Use these pages to construct your first draft.

_____

_____

_____

_____

_____

_____

_____

_____

_____

_____

_____

_____

_____

_____

_____

_____

_____

_____

_____

Name _____ Date _____

519

Easy Reference

I. Rhetorical Modes

Various rhetorical modes exist in essay writing. Some of these include Definition, Comparison / Contrast, Causal Analysis / Cause-effect, Taking a Stand, and Proposing a Solution. While some essay prompts should be addressed in one rhetorical mode, others invite the writer to amalgamate several. In other words, one might "compare and contrast" two types of presidential character and then "take a stand" on the type of presidential character most beneficial to the people of a given country. Another prompt might invite the writer to "define" *racism,* show how it is a problem, and then "propose a solution." What follows, then, is simply a short description of various rhetorical modes; additionally, tips are offered to help writers use such modes with greater ease.

Definition

Definition often gives form and substance to a person, place, thing, or idea. It may include shape, size, weight, color, and odor. Definition also refers to manner, frequency, time, location, and absence of a quality. Often, Definition essays follow two methods:

1. Implement a series of clear details which can be seen, heard, smelled, tasted, felt, counted, or verified. Do this from various perspectives.
2. Offer an extended illustration or example. In other words, compose a story about an incident in which the subject shows its qualities and characteristics.

When composing a Definition essay, observe the following:

1. Avoid a circular definition.
   Weak: "A circle is a round shape."
   Strong: "A circle is a shape on a flat surface where all edges are the same distance from the center."
2. Avoid definitions that complicate rather than simplify.
   Weak: "A clandestine trip is a surreptitious one."
   Strong: "A clandestine trip is one taken secretly."
3. Avoid using examples rather than defining qualities.
   Weak: "A bad celebrity is Jerry Springer."
   Strong: "A bad celebrity accomplishes very little, gets paid for questionable accomplishments, and has far too much influence for his work; Dennis Rodman is a good example of this."

Comparison and Contrast

One of the most well-used modes of illustration, exemplification, analysis, or basic explanation in academic writing is Comparison and Contrast. Comparison and Contrast attempts to show the similarities and differences between two objects. There must, however, be some kind of existing similarity between the two objects, or the idea of comparison is a waste of time. For example, comparing and contrasting a loaf of bread to a rock would be silly. The whole idea challenges reason, logic, and necessity. Similarly, if one were to argue that "Hemingway was a better writer than Fitzgerald," or that "Tim Allen is a funnier comedian than Jerry Seinfeld," problems exist. Primarily, both comparisons address the human idea of preference. Such comparisons may be interesting but not fruitful.

A more appropriate Comparison and Contrast essay might examine the following: "A part-time job is easier for a first-year college student than a full-time job." Instead of relying on preference, this argument might address ease and time. Similarly, one could compose a Comparison and Contrast essay that examines the following: "English and German share many traits, but English is simpler; though in its simplicity, it can be confusing." This comparison attempts to clarify something about both languages, it asserts an idea, and it suggests that even that idea is not ironclad.

Comparison and Contrast essays often adhere to one of two formats:

1. SOD / STD (Subject-one-details / Subject-two-details)
   I. Introduction (reason for comparison, main idea, thesis statement)
   II. Subject One
       A. Detail One
       B. Detail Two
       C. Detail Three
   III. Subject One
       A. Detail Four
       B. Detail Five
       C. Detail Six
   IV. Transition (prepare your reader for Subject Two)
   V. Subject Two
       A. Detail One
       B. Detail Two
       C. Detail Three

     VI. Subject Two
        A. Detail Four
        B. Detail Five
        C. Detail Six
     VII. Conclusion
2. DIP (Details-in-parallel)
     I. Introduction (reason for comparison, main idea, thesis statement)
     II. Detail One
        A. Subject One
        B. Subject Two
     III. Detail Two
        A. Subject One
        B. Subject Two
     IV. Detail Three
        A. Subject One
        B. Subject Two
     V. Detail Four
        A. Subject One
        B. Subject Two
     VI. Detail Five
        A. Subject One
        B. Subject Two
     VII. Conclusion

In examining both formats, realize that the DIP format is more cohesive, for both subjects are compared and contrasted in each paragraph. The SOD / STD format, on the other hand, seems a bit fragmented (it's as if two paragraphs are being glued together via one transition). Please note that the DIP format, while producing a more cohesive argument, relies on numerous transitions. Be conscious of employing such transitions when shifting from Subject One to Subject Two.

Causal Analysis / Cause-effect

Causal Analysis / Cause-effect is the expository form of writing which attempts to show the variables or things that affected something or made something occur; Causal Analysis / Cause-effect is also the expository form of writing which attempts to show the variables or things that resulted from an event. When composing a Causal Analysis / Cause-effect essay, please note the following:

1. Effect is usually easier to write about, for it is often easier to detect contradictions in another person's explanation of causes.
2. One person's cause may be another person's effect.
3. Causal Analysis / Cause-effect can often be developed with pictures, graphs, and diagrams.

Ideally, the Causal Analysis / Cause-effect essay will begin with the cause and then focus on the effect.

Taking a Stand

Taking a Stand essays require a writer to identify a stance regarding an issue or problem. This, however, should not be done until the writer has performed the following:

1. Investigation
   a. Search for evidence.
   b. Hunt for any data that will answer the key question about the issue or problem.
   c. The evidence must be both relevant and sufficient.
2. Interpretation
   a. Decide what the evidence means.
3. Judgment
   a. Reach a conclusion about the issue.
   b. The conclusion must meet the test of logic.

After performing these activities, it should be time to identify a stance and begin composing a Taking a Stand essay.

Proposing a Solution

When composing a Proposing a Solution essay, show that a problem exists. For instance, if writing on affirmative action, show that a problem currently exists regarding affirmative action. In doing so, consider referring to sit-ins at UCLA and protests at UC Berkeley to help establish the existing problem. Then, because the assignment is to propose a solution, offer a solution (or many solutions) to the problem that has already been identified. Thus, when writing this type of essay, do the following in this order:

1. Show that a problem exists.
2. Propose at least one solution.

Remember not to rely on warrants (shared assumptions) in order to advance your argument. In other words, make sure that a problem has been adequately established. If the "problem" relies too heavily on shared assumptions, and if the reader does not share these assumptions with the writer, then the solution will be groundless.

II. Thesis Statements

A well-articulated thesis statement lets the reader know what the writer intends to prove. For example, if the reader wants to prove that animal experimentation should be supported, or that marijuana should be legalized as a medicinal drug, the thesis statements should read like this:

> Animal experimentation should be supported.
> Marijuana should be legalized as a medicinal drug.

Note that a thesis statement must be argumentative. The thesis statement, "Huck Finn spends a lot of time in the Mississippi Valley," would not be acceptable, for few would oppose such a claim, especially since the Mississippi Valley is the setting for *The Adventures of Huckleberry Finn.*

Arguably, the thesis statement is the most important statement in an essay, for it is the statement around which all of the other statements are born. In other words, without a thesis statement, an academic essay has little purpose.

Take the following terms and construct a thesis statement for each:

Talk shows

_____

_____

Parking

_____

_____

Films

_____

_____

Rap music

_____

_____

Playboy magazine

_____

_____

NOTE: One strategy for composing thesis statements is to begin with "I want to prove that . . . " and then cross out "I want to prove that," but keep the rest. For example, regarding *Playboy* magazine, one can write the following: I want to prove that *Playboy* magazine degrades women for the purpose of entertaining men. Now, simply remove "I want to prove that," and the following thesis statement is the result: *Playboy* magazine degrades women for the purpose of entertaining men.

III. Introductions

Once you have clearly identified your thesis statement, it is time to begin constructing your introductory paragraph. Here are some strategies for constructing an introductory paragraph in response to the following prompt: Address an issue or problem about which you feel passionate.

Once you have picked an issue, it's time to do some pre-writing with hopes of not only composing an introduction but discovering ideas that will advance the rest of the essay. The following five introductory paragraphs differ subtly, but each one is responding to this issue: Should circuses with animals be supported?

Each strategy can be embellished upon, or you might even choose to employ several of these strategies within the same introductory paragraph. The following five models were composed with the purpose of demonstrating each strategy.

1. Journalist's Six (Who? What? Where? When? Why? How? Answer these questions, and then amalgamate the answers in the development of an introductory paragraph.)

    In the United States, many circuses use animals to attract large audiences. Audience members often pay to see elephants standing on one leg, bears riding bicycles, or tigers jumping through rings of fire. Unfortunately, what many do not know is that the tigers usually live and travel in small cages, the bears rarely have the chain around their neck removed, and the elephants often die prematurely of disease and the stress of confinement. Therefore, unless animal-free, circuses should not be supported.

2. Emotional Appeal (Emotional appeals are used to identify with an audience's emotions.)

    After wearing handcuffs for a prolonged period, what usually happens is this: the handcuffs tear into the skin. Then, after the blood has clotted and scabs have developed, the handcuffs cut into the scabs, eventually causing scars. Then, as one's wrists thrash about, the scars are re-opened, and the whole process begins again. However, rarely does this happen with humans, and if it does happen, chances are strong that the person wearing the handcuffs was accused or convicted of a crime. Circus animals, though, are accustomed to being treated as criminals. Elephants, tigers, and lions are rarely separated from their chains, and when they are, they're often on the receiving end of whips and electric prods. This is unfair, and if circus audiences were aware of such treatment, it is possible that they wouldn't support it. Thus, unless circus animals are treated better, or unless animal-free, circuses should not be supported.

3. Logical Appeal (Logical Appeals are factual, including dates, statistics, and the results of research by credible researchers.)

    According to Henry Ringling North in his book *The Circus Kings,* "Bears may have their noses broken while being trained or have their paws burned to force them to stand on their hind legs." While this is interesting, note what was written in the *Hudson News* on August 8, 1986 after a reporter traveled with the Ringling Bros. Circus: "The sound of a trainer's club repeatedly striking a chimpanzee, as well as the chimpanzee's screams, could be heard outside the arena building." Both quotations paint a disturbing picture of circus life, especially for the animals. Because animals such as bears and chimpanzees are abused by circus trainers, and because there is evidence suggesting that other circus animals are abused as well, it is important to further examine this issue. Assuming this examination shows that circus animals are physically abused, the following solution should be considered: unless animal-free, circuses should not be supported.

4. Ethical Appeal (Ethical appeals are used to identify with an audience's moral code. When employing such a strategy, questions might be asked to help advance the paragraph.)

    Is it wrong to physically abuse animals? If, for instance, a bear were beaten into submission, or if an elephant spent most of its life chained to the bars of its cage, should such actions be deemed right or wrong? Assuming animals have rights, such actions are definitely wrong. According to People for the Ethical Treatment of Animals, "Animal rights means that animals deserve a certain kind of consideration—consideration of what is in their own best interests, regardless of whether they are cute, useful to humans, or an endangered species [. . .] ." Based on this definition of animal rights, it is reasonable to consider that there is something wrong about the way animals are treated at circuses. It's quite possible that being beaten, whipped, and tortured is not in an animal's "own best interest." Therefore, unless animal-free, circuses should not be supported.

5. Recipe (This strategy requires the writer to define the issue, delineate its parts, and organize them like one would in a recipe.)

Take three tigers, two bears, and one elephant. Then take six cages, fifteen chains (for the animals' legs and heads), an electric prod, a whip, and some food. Then shock, whip, chain, starve, and cage the tigers, bears, and elephant. This should be done in order for the animals to know what will happen when they refuse to jump through rings of fire, ride bikes, or stand on one leg. After doing this, and after noting their eagerness to perform various types of tricks, simply cage the animals, chain them to the bars of the cage, and give them a taste of food (but not too much or they may become satisfied and not perform in the second show). Unfortunately, the aforementioned recipe is often used by circus trainers, and it should not be condoned. Of course, until people stop going to circuses, this treatment will continue. Thus, unless animal-free, circuses should not be supported.

Regarding introductory paragraphs, there are many ways to skin this proverbial cat. Simply attempt to provide your reader with some context for the looming argument and, in doing so, you may be able to apply one of the aforementioned strategies.

IV. Conclusions

The last paragraph of your essay should be the conclusion. (For examples of different conclusions, consult this book's student essays.) Among the many things a conclusion should accomplish are the following:

❀ It should include a restatement of your thesis statement.
❀ It should advance your argument; however, adding new information to your essay via the conclusion is tricky. Make sure the new information is pertinent to your thesis statement and, hence, your argument.
❀ It should attempt to transcend the context of your argument. In other words, if your essay is based on the analysis of two poems, show how your argument is not just specific to the two poems. Try to show how your argument has societal relevance. One way to do this is to ask: "Why should people consider my argument important? Why might it be relevant to their lives?"
❀ It should make your reader ponder the ideas presented in your essay. This can be accomplished by ending your essay with a final, poignant statement. (If you cannot create a relatively brilliant statement on your own, consider ending with a quotation relevant to your argument.)

Your conclusion should not house the following:

❀ It should not mirror your introduction. If you have composed a short-essay (five-ten pages), do not simply write in your conclusion what you wrote in your introduction. This is ludicrous, for it sends an implied message to your reader: "Just in case you have a lousy memory, I will repeat all that was written six paragraphs ago." Please note, however, that in a longer essay, a summary may be warranted.
❀ It should not overtly address the assignment (i.e., "This assignment was a lot of fun.")

❀ It should not apologize for your carelessness (i.e., "I'm sorry about the spelling errors, but I was in a hurry!")

❀ It should not complain about the assignment's difficulty (i.e., "Boy, this assignment was hard.")

❀ It should not end with inappropriate cuteness (i.e., "That's it, hope reading it was fun!")

When considering whether or not your essay is complete, ask yourself this question: "Must I add anything else for the reader to adequately comprehend my essay and my intentions?" If your answer is "No," then you've completed the first step. Then, eye the last sentence of your essay, and ask this question: "Does the reader absolutely need this sentence to adequately comprehend my essay?" If you answer is "Yes," then you're fine. However, if your answer is "No," then delete the sentence, eye the "new last sentence," and ask the question again.

V. Research

In order to compose a well-developed essay replete with credible examples and evidence, research is often required. In today's age of the Internet, research is less about spending time in the periodical section of the library and more about going online and being as efficient as possible. This should not suggest, however, that looking through scholarly journals and magazines to find suitable quotations is antiquated. This approach is still favored by many. Thus, in the end, the choice is yours.

Getting Started and Finding Relevant Sources

Many colleges have something called an "Article Database." This can often be accessed via the Internet or computers at the college's library, and it is a useful source for obtaining information on a myriad of topics. Once in a school's Article Database, there are usually a variety of choices that have been made available to the budding researcher.

When to Incorporate Outside Sources and How to Incorporate Them

Try to avoid including too many sources in your essay. If the reader sees a constant stream of quotations from outside sources, then the authenticity of the writer's argument is lost. Too many quotations from outside sources can make the essay an examination of literary analysis instead of an essay that has a central argument.

The Works Cited Page

It is important to properly document outside sources. The format to follow when documenting sources is known as the MLA Style of Bibliographic Citation. MLA stands for Modern Language Association, and it is an Arts and Letters association that sets the guidelines for citing outside sources and documenting them on the Works Cited page. Composing a Works Cited page is one of the more laborious tasks that a writer must confront when it comes to writing any research paper.

First of all, "Works Cited" should be located one inch from the top of your Works Cited page. Further, your last name and the essay's respective page number are to be included on this page as well. Make sure to double space, and make sure that each work descends alphabetically. In other words, after "Works Cited," the first source should appear on the page, in alphabetical order, according to the author's last name. Use the *first word* of the title if the author is unknown (note, however, that the articles "a," "an" and "the" at the beginning of a title are not considered *first words*). Also, every line after the first line of a source must be tabbed one-half inch. Then, when the next source is listed, it should align with the left margin, and it should begin with the author's last name. The following is a list of some of the more common sources that typically get used when writing a paper that employs outside sources, such as books, articles from magazines and journals, works in anthologies, poems, and Internet sources.

Books

1. **A book by a single author** is simple to document. Two errors, however, are very common. First, do not underline the period after the book's title. Second, make sure to end the entire source citation with a period (in other words, if your source citation ends with the year of publication or copyright, make sure to end it with a period).

   Last name of author, First name. Name of book. City of publication: publisher, copyright
      year.

   ### Example

   Kingston, Maxine. The Woman Warrior: Memoirs of a Girlhood among Ghosts. New York:

      Knopf, 1976.

2. **A book by two or three authors** is sometimes confusing because writers do not know which author to list first when listing them. Essentially, documentation is the same for this type of book except that two authors (or three) must be listed in alphabetical order. Notice that only the first author's name is in reverse order.

   Last name of first author, First name of author and First and Last name of second author.
      Name of book. City of publication: publisher, copyright year.

   ### Example

   Sexton, James and Peggy Tran. The Whole Enchilada. Des Moines: Kensing, 1986.

3. **A book by more than three authors** is practically identical to the first two sources except that all of the authors do not get listed. The writer only needs to list one of the writers' names, preferably the author's last name that comes first, according to alphabetical order.

   Last name of author, First name of author, et al., eds. Name of book. City of publication:
      publisher, copyright year.

   ### Example

   Yushi, Van, et al., eds. The Great Nation of Japan. San Francisco: Smith and Barney, 1999.

4. **Two or more works by the same author** is similar to the above documentation, with some minor exceptions. Essentially, all of the information is the same except that the second book is put into quotation marks.

Last name of author, First name of author. <u>Name of book</u>. City of publication: publisher, copyright year. "Name of second book." City of publication: publisher, copyright year.

Example

Gillian, Jill. <u>The Great Smile</u>. New York: Mt. Olympus, 2001. "Out of the Darkness." New York: Mt. Olympus, 2000.

5. **An Edited book** is very simple to document. The only difference is that there is an abbreviation after the author's first name, which stands for "editor."

Last name of author, First name of author, ed. <u>Name of book</u>. City of publication: publisher, copyright year.

Example

Porticalus, Gus, ed. <u>Every Word is Greek</u>. Chicago: Dancing Zorbas, 2002.

6. **A book with a volume number** is simple to document. Make sure, however, to include the Volume number.

Last name of author, First name of author. <u>Name of book</u>. Vol. #. City of publication: publisher, copyright year.

Example

Fields, Susan. <u>It All Comes Down to Me</u>. Vol. 25. Austin: Harrier Press, 1980.

7. **A short story, poem, or play in a collection of the author's works** is similar to the documentation of an article from a magazine or journal.

Last name of poet, First name of poet. "Title of Poem." <u>Name of the book that the short story, poem, or play came from</u>. City of publication: publisher, copyright year. Pages where piece is located in book (i.e., 23-26.)

Example

Guffman, Phil. "Ode to My Cat." <u>Great Poetry of Cats</u>. St. Petersburg: Herald Publishing Company, 1999. 23-25.

8. **A short story or poem in an anthology** is different than the above documentation because it is a collection of works from various authors.

Last name of author who wrote short story or poem, First name of author. "Title of poem or short story." <u>Name of anthology</u>. Ed. Name of author or authors who wrote anthology (first name first then last name). City of publication: publisher, copyright year. Pages where short story or poem is located in anthology.

Example

Houston, Lance. "Coffee at Star Café." <u>The Little Book of Thoughts: A Book of Relaxing Poetry</u>. Ed. Nancy Yates. Philadelphia: Utopia Press, 2002. 22-23.

9. **A play in an anthology** is very similar to a short story or a poem from an anthology. The difference is that instead of quotation marks, the name of the play gets underlined.

Last name of author who wrote play, First name of author. Title of play. Name of anthology. Ed. Name of author or authors who wrote anthology (first name first then last name). City of publication: publisher, copyright year. Pages where play is located in anthology.

Example

McGuire, Jason. Once in a Night's Wind. Modern Poetry of France. Ed. Frances Russ and

Erica Jennings. Eureka: Huntz Publishing Compnay, 2003. 22.

10. **An article in an anthology** is very similar to a short story and a poem.

Last name of author who wrote article, First name of author. "Title of article." Name of anthology. Ed. Name of author or authors who wrote anthology (first name first then last name). City of publication: publisher, copyright year. Pages where article is located in anthology.

Example

Sebastian, Joseph. "Are We Making Things Better Over There?" War Time. Ed. Ben Hughes

and Kelly Stenson. San Francisco: Gettysburg, 2002. 68-72.

11. **Using more than one selection from an anthology** can be confusing to document. The anthology gets cited separately, and each individual selection gets listed separately, with the author and title of the selection, the anthology editor's last name, and the selection's respective page numbers.

Last name of author who wrote the selection, First name of author. "Title of selection." Editor(s) of anthology. Pages that selection is located on.

Last name(s) of author(s) who wrote anthology, first name(s), eds. Name of anthology. #ed. City of publication: Publisher, copyright year.

Last name of author who wrote second selection, First name of author. "Title of selection." Editor(s). Pages that selection is located on.

Example

Mencinidas, Andrew. "Yet Another One." Tim Rodriguez. 109-15.

Nunez, Hugo and Todd Ornalles. eds. Coming to the New World. 12ed. Chicago: Quintus

Press, 2004.

Stevenson, Anthony. "Over the Atlantic." Tim Rodriguez. 146-59.

12. **A translation** is very simple to document.

Last name of author who wrote the selection, First name of author. Title. Trans. First name of translator and last name of translator. City of publication: Publisher, copyright year.

Example

Bravo, Olivia. A Very Cold Summer in Venice. Trans. Doug Descenz. Boston: Great Falls,

2004.

13. **An article in a journal with continuous pagination throughout an annual volume** is complicated at first glance.

Last name of author who wrote article, First name of author. "Title of article." Name of journal. volume # (year): pages article is located on in journal.

Example

Adams, Samantha. "How the West was Won." Great Tales of Early America. vol. 12 (1986):

39-45.

14. **An article with separate pagination in each issue** is slightly different than the above documentation.

Last name of author who wrote article, First name of author. "Title of article." Name of journal. volume and issue number (year): pages article is located on in journal.

Example

Wetland, Rainy. "Moving too Fast." The Great Art of Teaching. 12.3 (1996): 78-84.

15. **An article in a magazine** can be confusing because sometimes articles begin on one page and then continue ten to twenty pages later. This is very similar to reading a newspaper and at the end of a paragraph it reads, "continued on A-22."

Last name of author who wrote article, First name of author. "Title of article." Name of magazine. date month. Year: page number.

Example

Kendall, Kathryn. "Escaping the Abyss." Timeless. 12 Feb. 1999: 23-24.

16. **An article in a magazine that appears on pages that are not consecutive** is slightly different from the above documentation. For example, an article that begins on page twenty and continues on page forty-eight can be documented by putting the plus sign after the page number that the article starts on in the magazine, thus indicating non-consecutive pagination.

Last name of author who wrote article, First name of author. "Title of article." Name of magazine. date month. Year: page+.

Example

Huffy, George. "Riding on Today's Roads." Epic. 12 Feb. 2000: 37+.

17. **An article in a daily newspaper** is documented almost exactly like an article in a magazine.

Last name of author who wrote article, First name of author. "Title of article." Name of newspaper. date month. Year: page(s).

Example

Errickson, Mike. "Taking Back the Office." <u>Suncoast Times</u>. 25 Jan. 1996: A1+.

18. **An article in a reference work** is a simple type of documentation that typically gets used for information that is taken from encyclopedias.

"Title of article." <u>Name of Encyclopedia</u>. number ed. Year.

Example

"Early Ireland." <u>New Encyclopedia</u>. 4th ed. 2000.

19. **A scholarly project or information database on the Internet** is relatively simple to document. The first two details that get listed are the name of the project or information and the editor of the project.

<u>Name of project or information</u>. Ed. Name of Editor. Date of electronic publication.
     University where site was accessed. Date month year <website>.

Example

<u>The Utopian Project</u>. Ed. Bert Gustefson. 3-19-01. University of Riverbank. 12 Nov. 2004

     <www.Utopians.riverbend.edu>.

20. **A book on the Internet is** one of the more popular sources to use because full texts are becoming accessible on the Internet.

Last name of author, First name of author. <u>Name of book</u>. City of publication: copyright year.
     Date site was accessed month year <website>.

Example

Lachey, Priscilla. <u>Unlocking the Door to Greatness</u>. Anchorage: 1978. 21 Apr. 2004

     <www.greatbooks.com>.

21. **An article in a scholarly journal on the Internet** is something that many students have access to when they are surfing the net for information regarding articles that pertain to literature.

Last name of author who wrote article, First name of author. "Name of article." <u>Name of</u>
     <u>scholarly journal</u> volume.issue (year): number of pages. Date site was accessed month year
     <website>.

Example

Rutegar, Rusty. "Playing with Purpose." <u>Sports Journal of American Football</u>. 12.2 (2001):

     p3. 26 Aug. 2003 <www.sportsjournal.amer.football.com>.

22. **A newspaper article or magazine article found on the Internet** is consistent with the rules of online documentation.

Last name of author who wrote article, First name of author. "Name of article." <u>Name of</u>
     <u>source</u> date of publication month year. Date site was accessed month year <website>.

Example

Vicci, Pedro. "The Game has not Changed." <u>Latin American Timely</u>. 15 Feb. 1989. 24 June

2003 <www.latintimely.vicci.game.com>.

23. **An article from an online database** is what many students use today.

Last name of author who wrote article, First name of author. "Name of article." <u>Title of</u> <u>source</u> volume.issue (year): pages article is located on. Name of database. Name of institution where database was accessed. Date month year.

Example

Jacobs, Olivia. "Willy's Madness." <u>New York Monitor of Drama</u>. 23.3 (2002): 23-28.

E-journal. California State University, Woodward. 7 Apr. 2004.

24. **A film or cassette** is difficult to document. The name of the film gets underlined. Then, the director or directors of the film are listed, followed by the type of source (either videocassette or film).

<u>Name of Film</u>. Dir. Videocassette or film. Name of company that produced film, copyright year.

Example

<u>A Worn Path</u>. Dir. John Reid and Claudia Velasco. Videocassette. Harcourt, 1994.

VI. Grammar

When writing an argument, it is important to avoid distracting your reader through haphazard comma, semicolon, and colon placement. Hence, what follows is a series of antidotes for ailing prose.

Commas

Here are some of the most commonly fractured comma rules:

1. Use a comma before a coordinating conjunction joining independent clauses. The seven coordinating conjunctions are *for, and, nor, but, or, yet, so*. These seven create an acronym: FANBOYS. An independent clause is a complete thought, one housing a subject and a verb. Here is an example: *We ate*. When joining two independent clauses via one of the FANBOYS, a comma must precede it. Here are two examples:

We ate, and they danced.
Dave studied German for seven years, but he still couldn't speak it fluently.

2. Use a comma after an introductory word group. Here are three examples:

    When Bob went jogging, he forgot to wear his shoes.
    Impressed with the film, Tom recommended it to others.
    *After considering the ramifications of legalizing active euthanasia, the doctors at St. Luke's
        Hospital chose against its legalization.*

3. Use a comma between items in a series, including the last two items in a series. Here are two ex-
    amples:

    *Many oppose affirmative action programs because they promote reverse discrimination, special
        treatment, and ill-will.*
    *Animal experimentation is essential because it saves human lives, provides the pharmaceutical
        industry with important data, and curbs the population of stray animals in society.*

4. Use commas between coordinate adjectives. If you have two or more adjectives modifying a
    noun, a comma must separate each adjective. Here are two examples:

    He was an old, ornery man.
    When people with creative, right-hemispheric attributes enter English classes, they often excel.

Semicolons

Use semicolons between independent clauses. Here are four examples:

Many love to read traditional arguments; however, others prefer satire.
Sheep are in need of someone to follow; thus, shepherds will always be in demand.
*Cases of road rage are steadily increasing in California; conversely, cases of voluntary roadside
    assistance by motorists are declining.*
*The Prohibition benefited some and hurt others; it was, however, quite profitable for some bootleg-
    gers, like the Kennedys.*

Here are some examples of how *not* to use the semicolon:

When inmates complain of prison overcrowding; taxpayers have trouble listening.
One great example of passive euthanasia; an elderly person suffering.
The stock market is doing well; thus, helping small investors prepare for retirement.
*Public schools are overcrowded in California; as a result, making it difficult for teachers to teach
    and students to learn.*

Colons

Use a colon after an independent clause to emphasize the words that follow it. Here are five examples:

Joe should be allowed to pass for three reasons: he is a hard worker, he has attended every class, and he has a good attitude.
Joe should not be allowed to pass for one reason: he is failing the class.
Day traders focus on one thing: market fluctuations.
These four people will survive: Dr. Dane, Mrs. Dane, Bobby Dane, and Mr. Newton.
After learning these grammar rules, one thing is certain: you will not trouble your professors with misplaced colons, semicolons, and commas.

Here are examples of how *not* to use the colon:

Some examples of euthanasia are: passive and active.
There are different types of affirmative action such as: class-based and race-based.
Sheila went to the store and bought: carrots, celery, potatoes, and a pumpkin.

Dashes

Use dashes to offer additional information in a sentence; usually, this additional information will be highlighted or emphasized as a result of the dash. When typing a dash, realize that a dash consists of two hyphens.

In "Just As Fierce," Katherine Dunn states: "In the rare case where a woman is seen as genuinely responsible, she is branded a monster—an 'unnatural' woman."
In "Femininity," Susan Brownmiller states: "Large numbers of women—those with small children, those left high and dry after a mid-life divorce—need financial support."

Ellipses

Use the ellipsis to indicate that you have omitted something from a quoted passage.
    Here is the original passage taken from D.H. Lawrence's *Sketches of Etruscan Places and Other Italian Essays:*

He did not reply, but obstinately looked as though he would be venomous if he could. He peered at the passport—though I doubt if he could make head or tail of it—asked where we were going, peered at B.'s passport, half excused himself in a whining, disgusting sort of fashion, and disappeared into the nigh. A real lout.

Here is the passage *with* the ellipses:

D.H. Lawrence writes: "He did not reply, but obstinately looked as though he would be venomous if he could. He peered at the passport [. . .] peered at B.'s passport, half excused himself in a whining, disgusting sort of fashion [. . .] ."

Here is the passage *with* the ellipses *and* parenthetical referencing:

D.H. Lawrence writes: "He did not reply, but obstinately looked as though he would be venomous if he could. He peered at the passport [. . .] peered at B.'s passport, half excused himself in a whining, disgusting sort of fashion [. . .]" (28).

Here is the passage with *an* ellipsis which does not connect one section of Lawrence's passage to another:

D.H. Lawrence writes: "He did not reply, but obstinately looked as though he would be venomous if he could. He peered at the passport—though I doubt if he could make head or tail of it—asked where we were going, peered at B.'s passport [. . .]" (28).

Brackets

Use brackets to insert explanatory material within quotations.
Here is an example from John G. Neihardt's *Black Elk Speaks:*

Then he painted High Horse solid white all over, and after that he painted black stripes all over the white and put black rings around High Horse's eyes. High Horse looked terrible.

Unfortunately, we do not know who "he" is. By using brackets, however, we can insert the necessary explanatory material:

Then [Red Deer] painted High Horse solid white all over, and after that [Red Deer] painted black stripes all over the white and put black rings around High Horse's eyes. High Horse looked terrible.

Another reason to use brackets is to insert the word *sic,* which means "so." It tells the readers that the mistake which appears in the quotation was the mistake of the person quoted, or it was the mistake of the person originally formulating the quotation; regardless, it shows the mistake was not yours. Here is an example:

F. Scott Fitzgerld was fond of dressing his characters in vivid colors.

"Fitzgerald" is improperly spelled; simply adding [*sic*] addresses and helps ameliorate this problem:

F. Scott Fitgerld [sic] was fond of dressing his characters in vivid colors.

VII. Vocabulary Development

Among the two compact disks included with this book is the Money Words™ vocabulary-building program. What should be obvious, especially after reading the student essays and the essay written by the professional writer, is that a developed vocabulary is essential. Not only should

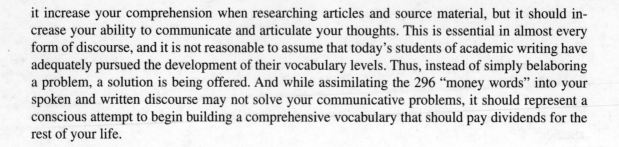

it increase your comprehension when researching articles and source material, but it should increase your ability to communicate and articulate your thoughts. This is essential in almost every form of discourse, and it is not reasonable to assume that today's students of academic writing have adequately pursued the development of their vocabulary levels. Thus, instead of simply belaboring a problem, a solution is being offered. And while assimilating the 296 "money words" into your spoken and written discourse may not solve your communicative problems, it should represent a conscious attempt to begin building a comprehensive vocabulary that should pay dividends for the rest of your life.

Section III

Money Words™

Quizzes

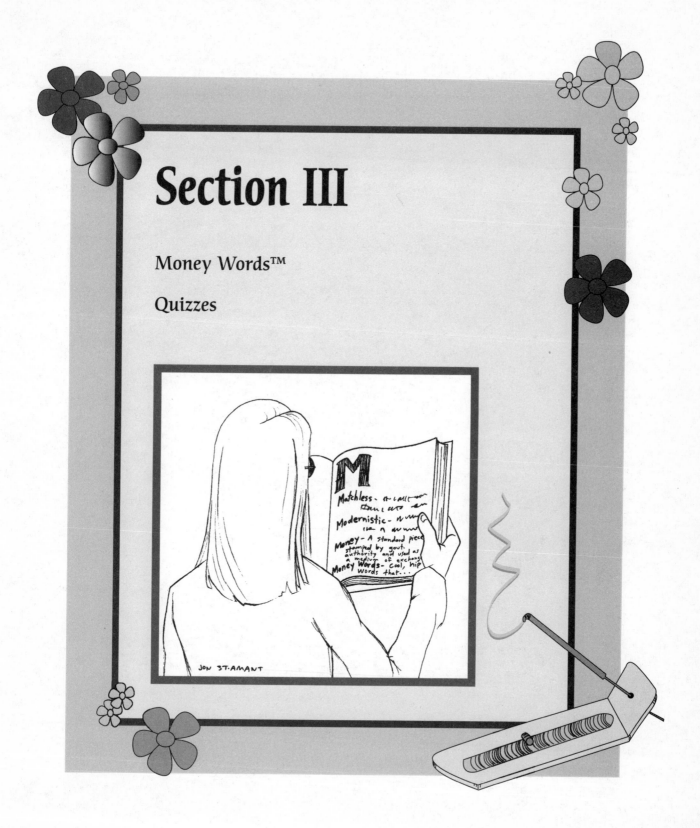

JON ST.AMANT

Money Words™

The following words are introduced in this program:

1. **Poignant:** keenly distressing to the feelings; keen or strong in mental appeal; affecting or moving the emotions.

   SYNONYMS: **penetrating, moving, heartfelt, piquant, sharp.**
   ANTONYMS: **mild, temperate, moderate, clement, bland.**

2. **Discombobulating:** confusing or disconcerting; upsetting; frustrating.

   SYNONYMS: **discomposing, perplexing, bewildering, abashing, discomfiting.**
   ANTONYMS: **placid, serene, unruffled, collected, self-possessed.**

3. **Epiphany:** a sudden intuitive perception; an insight into the reality or essential meaning of something, usually initiated by some simple, homely, or commonplace occurrence or experience.

   SYNONYMS: **conception, notion, revelation, awakening, transcendence.**
   NEAR ANTONYMS: **disillusionment, disenchantment, mental indolence, cognitive apathy, paralysis.**

4. **Unparalleled:** not paralleled; unprecedented.

   SYNONYMS: **matchless, peerless, inimitable, unrivaled, unsurpassed.**
   ANTONYMS: **comparable, typical, equivalent, derivative, commonplace.**

5. **Eschew:** to abstain or keep away from; to avoid.

   SYNONYMS: **circumvent, boycott, forgo, shun, evade.**
   ANTONYMS: **employ, invite, actuate, exploit, implement.**

6. **Ruminate:** to chew the cud; to meditate or muse; to ponder.

   SYNONYMS: **deliberate, contemplate, meditate, ponder, cogitate.**
   NEAR ANTONYMS: **deduce, conjecture, suppose, presume, speculate.**

7. **Expunge:** to strike or blot out; to erase; to wipe out or destroy.

   SYNONYMS: **obliterate, efface, abrogate, countermand, rescind.**
   ANTONYMS: **retain, safeguard, maintain, uphold, espouse.**

8. **Omnipotent:** almighty or infinite in power; having very great or unlimited authority or power.

   SYNONYMS: **supreme, sizeable, infinite, sovereign, puissant.**
   ANTONYMS: **powerless, immobilized, toothless, indolent, lethargic.**

9. **Lucid:** easily understood; completely intelligible or comprehensible; characterized by clear perception or understanding.

   SYNONYMS: **evident, sound, comprehensible, limpid, pellucid.**
   ANTONYMS: **nebulous, obscure, irrational, dubious, veiled.**

10. **Conscious:** aware of one's own existence, sensations, thoughts, surroundings; fully aware of or sensitive to something.

    SYNONYMS: **percipient, cognizant, aware, mindful, sentient.**
    ANTONYMS: **oblivious, unaware, unsuspecting, unknowing, benumbed.**

11. **Infer:** to derive by reasoning; to conclude or judge from premises or evidence.

    SYNONYMS: **deduce, reason, speculate, surmise, gather.**
    ANTONYMS: **intuit, assume, presuppose, presume, opine.**

12. **Assiduous:** constant; constant in application or effort; working diligently at a task; persevering.

    SYNONYMS: **continuous, tireless, persistent, studious, diligent.**
    ANTONYMS: **inconstant, capricious, vacillating, mercurial, apathetic.**

13. **Antiquated:** resembling or adhering to the past; old-fashioned; no longer used.

    SYNONYMS: **obsolescent, archaic, bygone, dowdy, passé.**
    ANTONYMS: **contemporary, modernistic, timely, newfangled, modish.**

14. **Ambiguous:** open to or having several possible meanings or interpretations; of doubtful or uncertain nature; difficult to comprehend, distinguish, or classify.

    SYNONYMS: **equivocal, cryptic, enigmatic, obscure, nebulous.**
    ANTONYMS: **perspicuous, categorical, unequivocal, intelligible, lucid.**

15. **Altruistic:** unselfishly concerned for or devoted to the welfare of others.

    SYNONYMS: **benevolent, philanthropic, charitable, humanitarian, benign.**
    ANTONYMS: **egoistic, self-centered, self-absorbed, self-obsessed, egocentric.**

16. **Malleable:** capable of being extended or shaped by hammering or by pressure from rollers; adaptable.

    SYNONYMS: **impressionable, tractable, pliable, ductile, supple.**
    ANTONYMS: **intractable, refractory, headstrong, recalcitrant, ungovernable.**

17. **Defeatist:** a person who surrenders easily.

    SYNONYMS: **doomsayer, killjoy, misanthrope, pessimist, fussbudget.**
    ANTONYMS: **optimist, idealist, Pangloss, Pollyanna, enthusiast.**

18. **Bombastic:** high-sounding, high-flown, or inflated—especially in relation to speech and writing.

    SYNONYMS: **pompous, grandiloquent, pretentious, turgid, highfalutin.**
    ANTONYMS: **humble, meek, unassuming, forbearing, modest.**

    The following three words are introduced in the audio program when defining *bombastic:*

    replete: filled with.
    polysyllabic: consisting of four or more syllables.
    satiating: satisfying.

19. **Incongruous:** not harmonious in character; lacking harmony of parts; inconsistent.

    SYNONYMS: **discordant, incompatible, inharmonious, discrepant, contradictory.**
    ANTONYMS: **consonant, consistent, invariable, unfailing, harmonious.**

20. **Lackadaisical:** without interest, vigor, or determination; lazy.

    SYNONYMS: **languid, spiritless, apathetic, enervated, phlegmatic.**
    ANTONYMS: **vivacious, spirited, brisk, ardent, animated.**

21. **Sagacious:** having or showing acute mental discernment and keen practical sense.

    SYNONYMS: **discerning, wise, judicious, perspicacious, acute.**
    ANTONYMS: **ignorant, nescient, benighted, primitive, unenlightened.**

22. **Ephemeral:** lasting a very short time; short-lived; lasting but one day.

    SYNONYMS: **fleeting, evanescent, transient, momentary, fugitive.**
    ANTONYMS: **invariable, changeless, immutable, permanent, constant.**

23. **Prodigious:** extraordinary in size, amount, extent, degree, or force.

    SYNONYMS: **immense, stupendous, Herculean, astounding, voluminous.**
    ANTONYMS: **bantam, petite, inconsequential, petty, infinitesimal.**

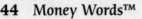

24. **Prodigal:** wastefully or recklessly extravagant.

   SYNONYMS: **lavish, profligate, licentious, improvident, thriftless.**
   ANTONYMS: **provident, economical, cautious, prudent, frugal.**

25. **Copious:** large in quantity or number; having or yielding an abundant supply.

   SYNONYMS: **abundant, bountiful, ample, profuse, plethoric.**
   ANTONYMS: **sparse, scarce, meager, exiguous, skimpy.**

26. **Absolve:** to free from guilt or blame; to set free or release.

   SYNONYMS: **exculpate, acquit, exonerate, liberate, remit.**
   ANTONYMS: **censure, denounce, denunciate, castigate, rebuke.**

27. **Verbose:** characterized by the use of many or too many words; wordy.

   SYNONYMS: **chatty, loquacious, wordy, effusive, garrulous.**
   ANTONYMS: **laconic, pithy, terse, succinct, concise.**

❀ Quiz 1

1. _____ means "keenly distressing to the feelings; keen or strong in mental appeal; affecting

   or moving the emotions.

   Three synonyms include: _____, _____, _____.

   Three antonyms include: _____, _____, _____.

   For extra credit, identify two more synonyms: _____, _____.

   For extra credit, identify two more antonyms: _____, _____.

2. _____ means "confusing or disconcerting; upsetting; frustrating."

   Three synonyms include: _____, _____, _____.

   Three antonyms include: _____, _____, _____.

   For extra credit, identify two more synonyms: _____, _____.

   For extra credit, identify two more antonyms: _____, _____.

3. _____ means "a sudden intuitive perception; an insight into the reality or essential meaning

   of something, usually initiated by some simple, homely, or commonplace occurrence or experience."

   Three synonyms include: _____, _____, _____.

   Three antonyms include: _____, _____, _____.

   For extra credit, identify two more synonyms: _____, _____.

   For extra credit, identify two more antonyms: _____, _____.

*In order to promote fair grading and uniformity, all of the words must come from the Money Words™

vocabulary-development program.

**In the space below, compose a complete sentence for words 1, 2, and 3.

1. _____

_____

_____

2. _____

_____

_____

3. _____

_____

_____

❀ QUIZ 2

1. _____ means "not paralleled; unprecedented."

   Three synonyms include: _____, _____, _____.

   Three antonyms include: _____, _____, _____.

   For extra credit, identify two more synonyms: _____, _____.

   For extra credit, identify two more antonyms: _____, _____.

2. _____ means "to abstain or keep away from; to avoid."

   Three synonyms include: _____, _____, _____.

   Three antonyms include: _____, _____, _____.

   For extra credit, identify two more synonyms: _____, _____.

   For extra credit, identify two more antonyms: _____, _____.

3. _____ means "to chew the cud; to meditate or muse; to ponder."

   Three synonyms include: _____, _____, _____.

   Three antonyms include: _____, _____, _____.

   For extra credit, identify two more synonyms: _____, _____.

   For extra credit, identify two more antonyms: _____, _____.

   *In order to promote fair grading and uniformity, all of the words must come from the Money Words™

   vocabulary-development program.

**In the space below, compose a complete sentence for words 1, 2, and 3.

1. _____

   _____

   _____

2. _____

   _____

   _____

3. _____

   _____

   _____

🌸 QUIZ 3

1. _____ means "to strike or blot out; to erase; to wipe out or destroy."

   Three synonyms include: _____, _____, _____.

   Three antonyms include: _____, _____, _____.

   For extra credit, identify two more synonyms: _____, _____.

   For extra credit, identify two more antonyms: _____, _____.

2. _____ means "almighty or infinite in power; having very great or unlimited authority

   or power."

   Three synonyms include: _____, _____, _____.

   Three antonyms include: _____, _____, _____.

   For extra credit, identify two more synonyms: _____, _____.

   For extra credit, identify two more antonyms: _____, _____.

3. _____ means "easily understood; completely intelligible or comprehensible; characterized

   by clear perception or understanding."

   Three synonyms include: _____, _____, _____.

   Three antonyms include: _____, _____, _____.

   For extra credit, identify two more synonyms: _____, _____.

   For extra credit, identify two more antonyms: _____, _____.

   *In order to promote fair grading and uniformity, all of the words must come from the Money Words™

   vocabulary-development program.

**In the space below, compose a complete sentence for words 1, 2, and 3.

1. _____

_____

_____

2. _____

_____

_____

3. _____

_____

_____

 550

🌺 QUIZ 4

1. _____ means "aware of one's existence, sensations, thoughts, surroundings; fully aware of or sensitive to something."

    Three synonyms include: _____, _____, _____.

    Three antonyms include: _____, _____, _____.

    For extra credit, identify two more synonyms: _____, _____.

    For extra credit, identify two more antonyms: _____, _____.

2. _____ means "to derive by reasoning; to conclude or judge from premises or evidence."

    Three synonyms include: _____, _____, _____.

    Three antonyms include: _____, _____, _____.

    For extra credit, identify two more synonyms: _____, _____.

    For extra credit, identify two more antonyms: _____, _____.

3. _____ means "constant; constant in application or effort; working diligently at a task; persevering."

    Three synonyms include: _____, _____, _____.

    Three antonyms include: _____, _____, _____.

    For extra credit, identify two more synonyms: _____, _____.

    For extra credit, identify two more antonyms: _____, _____.

    *In order to promote fair grading and uniformity, all of the words must come from the Money Words™ vocabulary-development program.

**In the space below, compose a complete sentence for words 1, 2, and 3.

1. _____

_____

_____

2. _____

_____

_____

3. _____

_____

_____

QUIZ 5

1. _____ means "resembling or adhering to the past; old-fashioned; no longer used."

   Three synonyms include: _____, _____, _____.

   Three antonyms include: _____, _____, _____.

   For extra credit, identify two more synonyms: _____, _____.

   For extra credit, identify two more antonyms: _____, _____.

2. _____ means "open to or having several possible meanings or interpretations; of doubtful or

   uncertain nature; difficult to comprehend, distinguish, or classify."

   Three synonyms include: _____, _____, _____.

   Three antonyms include: _____, _____, _____.

   For extra credit, identify two more synonyms: _____, _____.

   For extra credit, identify two more antonyms: _____, _____.

3. _____ means "unselfishly concerned for or devoted to the welfare of others."

   Three synonyms include: _____, _____, _____.

   Three antonyms include: _____, _____, _____.

   For extra credit, identify two more synonyms: _____, _____.

   For extra credit, identify two more antonyms: _____, _____.

*In order to promote fair grading and uniformity, all of the words must come from the Money Words™

vocabulary-development program.

**In the space below, compose a complete sentence for words 1, 2, and 3.

1. _____

_____

_____

2. _____

_____

_____

3. _____

_____

_____

🌸 QUIZ 6

1. _____ means "capable of being extended or shaped by hammering or by pressure from

    rollers; adaptable."

    Three synonyms include: _____, _____, _____.

    Three antonyms include: _____, _____, _____.

    For extra credit, identify two more synonyms: _____, _____.

    For extra credit, identify two more antonyms: _____, _____.

2. _____ means "a person who surrenders easily."

    Three synonyms include: _____, _____, _____.

    Three antonyms include: _____, _____, _____.

    For extra credit, identify two more synonyms: _____, _____.

    For extra credit, identify two more antonyms: _____, _____.

3. _____ means "high-sounding, high-flown, or inflated—especially in relation to speech and

    writing."

    Three synonyms include: _____, _____, _____.

    Three antonyms include: _____, _____, _____.

    For extra credit, identify two more synonyms: _____, _____.

    For extra credit, identify two more antonyms: _____, _____.

    *In order to promote fair grading and uniformity, all of the words must come from the Money Words™

    vocabulary-development program.

**In the space below, compose a complete sentence for words 1, 2, and 3.

1. _____

   _____

   _____

2. _____

   _____

   _____

3. _____

   _____

   _____

❀ QUIZ 7

1. _____ means "not harmonious in character; lacking harmony of parts; inconsistent."

   Three synonyms include: _____, _____, _____.

   Three antonyms include: _____, _____, _____.

   For extra credit, identify two more synonyms: _____, _____.

   For extra credit, identify two more antonyms: _____, _____.

2. _____ means "without interest, vigor, or determination; lazy."

   Three synonyms include: _____, _____, _____.

   Three antonyms include: _____, _____, _____.

   For extra credit, identify two more synonyms: _____, _____.

   For extra credit, identify two more antonyms: _____, _____.

3. _____ means "having or showing acute mental discernment and keen practical sense."

   Three synonyms include: _____, _____, _____.

   Three antonyms include: _____, _____, _____.

   For extra credit, identify two more synonyms: _____, _____.

   For extra credit, identify two more antonyms: _____, _____.

*In order to promote fair grading and uniformity, all of the words must come from the Money Words™

vocabulary-development program.

**In the space below, compose a complete sentence for words 1, 2, and 3.

1. _____

_____

_____

2. _____

_____

_____

3. _____

_____

_____

🌸 QUIZ 8

1. _____ means "lasting a very short time; short-lived; lasting but one day."

   Three synonyms include: _____, _____, _____.

   Three antonyms include: _____, _____, _____.

   For extra credit, identify two more synonyms: _____, _____.

   For extra credit, identify two more antonyms: _____, _____.

2. _____ means "extraordinary in size, amount, extent, degree, or force."

   Three synonyms include: _____, _____, _____.

   Three antonyms include: _____, _____, _____.

   For extra credit, identify two more synonyms: _____, _____.

   For extra credit, identify two more antonyms: _____, _____.

3. _____ means "wastefully or recklessly extravagant."

   Three synonyms include: _____, _____, _____.

   Three antonyms include: _____, _____, _____.

   For extra credit, identify two more synonyms: _____, _____.

   For extra credit, identify two more antonyms: _____, _____.

*In order to promote fair grading and uniformity, all of the words must come from the Money Words™

vocabulary-development program.

**In the space below, compose a complete sentence for words 1, 2, and 3.

1. _____

_____

_____

2. _____

_____

_____

3. _____

_____

_____

🌸 QUIZ 9

1. _____ means "large in quantity or number; having or yielding an abundant supply."

   Three synonyms include: _____, _____, _____.

   Three antonyms include: _____, _____, _____.

   For extra credit, identify two more synonyms: _____, _____.

   For extra credit, identify two more antonyms: _____, _____.

2. _____ means "to free from guilt or blame; to set free or release."

   Three synonyms include: _____, _____, _____.

   Three antonyms include: _____, _____, _____.

   For extra credit, identify two more synonyms: _____, _____.

   For extra credit, identify two more antonyms: _____, _____.

3. _____ means "characterized by the use of many or too many words; wordy."

   Three synonyms include: _____, _____, _____.

   Three antonyms include: _____, _____, _____.

   For extra credit, identify two more synonyms: _____, _____.

   For extra credit, identify two more antonyms: _____, _____.

*In order to promote fair grading and uniformity, all of the words must come from the Money Words™

vocabulary-development program.

**In the space below, compose a complete sentence for words 1, 2, and 3.

1. _____

_____

_____

2. _____

_____

_____

3. _____

_____

_____

Afterword

By Professor Matthew Judd

You have reached the journey's end. Where does that leave you? At the end of most trips, we can reflect back on the successes and failures of our journey. What did we most enjoy? What will we skip next time? What did we miss that will be first on the list the next time we are here?

But because this has been a trip through literature and learning, you are far less limited in your reflections. As you traveled the pages of this book, you have grown. You are now more well read, more critical in your thinking, and more skilled in your ability to craft essays. These are all major accomplishments, and yet all of them can be improved with further adventures through the pages of this book and its support CDs. Have you found a genre, time period, or author that you have enjoyed? Now is the time to explore that new interest further. That exploration can begin in the pages of this book that haven't yet been assigned to you. Yet aside from the broad range of works included, hopefully this text will inspire you to seek the work of your new-found favorites and explore all that they have to offer.

Has your life changed yet as a result of this book? It will. The great beauty of literature is that it forever changes the way we look at ourselves and the world around us. As Plato said, "The unexamined life is not worth living." Studying literature teaches us to examine lives—those of the characters and our own. If we embrace what we have learned, we are never able to look at the world in the same way again. The critical eye that you have developed while reading the literature of these pages will focus intently on the moments and relationships of your own life, bringing changes in perspective, understanding, and new direction.

As you begin new journeys, I encourage you to revisit the journey you have taken with this book. It is a valuable reference, as well as an excellent guide. For the journeys you have left in school, the writing sections and MLA guide will always prove valuable. This volume is a tremendous source of quotations and ideas to help you create thoughtful papers for many disciplines. Throughout the journeys of your life, this book may prove equally useful as you shatter your own myths, deal with your own tragedies, face your own epic struggles, and live the poetry of your life. You will be able to reflect on the great works you have found here and realize that it is the journey itself that is the most rewarding experience. Have a nice trip!

Matthew Judd

Index